Foundations of American Education

Peter Hlebowitsh
University of Iowa

KENDALL/HUNT PUBLISHING COMPANY
4050 Westmark Drive   Dubuque, Iowa 52002

Cover images provided by Shutter Stock

For Margaret

Falling in our lives as rain falls, steady and nurturing

Our first gift

For Paul
Number voyager
Our voice of reason and truth

For Nadia
Singing the songs of life
Our painting of joy and love

For Nikolai
The son of bread
Our protector

And, of course, for Erica

Contents

PART ONE   The Teacher and the School   1

Chapter 1   The American School Tradition   3

The School as a Normative Environment   3
The Unified System and the Comprehensive School   7
Decentralized Governance   8
Nationalizing Influences   11
Teaching in a Comprehensive and Unified System   15
    Teaching for Individual-Personal Growth   15
    Teaching for Socio-Civic Growth   17
    Teaching for Academic-Intellectual Growth   19
    Teaching for Vocational Growth   21
Summary   22
References   23
Key Questions   24
Research Exercises   25

Chapter 2   The Teacher and the Classroom   27

Classroom Life   28
Planned and Emergent Decisions   30
Levels of Classroom Performance   32
    Level I: Imitative-Maintenance   33
    Level II: Mediative   33
    Level III: Creative-Generative   34
Sources for Professional Decision-Making   34
    The Nature of the Learner   35
    The Values and Aims of Society   37
    Subject Matter   37
What Is an Effective Teacher?   39
Testing and Classroom Control   41
    Teaching-to-the-Test   41
    Classroom Control   43
Summary   47
References   47
Key Questions   48
Research Exercises   49

Chapter 3   Teachers and the School Curriculum   51

Defining the School Curriculum   51
The Explicit Curriculum   53
   Objectives, Goals, and Aims   53
   Curriculum Standards   54
   Instructional Methods   56
   Evaluating the School Experience   62
The Latent Curriculum   63
The Null Curriculum   65
Summary   66
References   66
Key Questions   67
Research Exercises   69

Chapter 4   The Emergence of a Profession   71

Who Educates the Masses?   71
The Status of the Teaching Profession   75
Teacher Education and Teacher Licensure   82
NCLB and Highly Qualified Teachers   86
Professional Teacher Organizations   88
   The National Association Education   88
   The American Federation of Teachers   91
Summary   92
References   93
Key Questions   95
Research Exercises   97

Chapter 5   The Philosophy of Teaching   99

Teaching in the Conservative Tradition   100
   Perennialism   100
   Essentialism   102
Teaching in the Progressive Tradition   105
   Experimentalism   105
   Romantic Naturalism   107
   Social Efficiency   109
Education in the Radical Tradition   113
   Social Reconstructionism   113
   Postmodernism   116
Summary   118
References   119
Key Questions   120
Research Exercises   121

Chapter 6   The Laws and Ethics of Teaching   123

Professional Ethics   123
    Legal Ethics and the Idea of "Conduct Unbecoming"   123
    Classroom Issues   125
Teacher Liability   129
Freedoms of Expression   131
    Teachers' Academic Freedom   131
    Teachers' Personal Views   133
    Student Expression   134
    Written Expression   135
    Symbolic Speech   136
Teacher Tenure and Teacher Dismissal   138
Search and Seizure   140
Summary   142
References   143
Key Questions   144
Research Exercises   145

PART TWO   The History of the American School Experience   147

Chapter 7   The Early Development of the Public School   149

Colonial Schooling and the Idea of Local Control   150
    School Life   152
    Regional Differences   155
The Movement Toward a Secular Mandate   157
Bringing the School to the People   158
    Education in the New Nation   159
    The Struggle for the American Public School   161
    Horace Mann and the Rise of State Authority   165
    The Cause of Teacher Education   166
The Upward and Outward Extension of Schooling   168
Summary   169
References   170
Key Questions   171
Research Exercises   173

Chapter 8   Defining the School Experience at the Turn of the Twentieth Century   175

The Ascendancy of the Traditional Liberal Arts   175
    The Doctrine of Mental Discipline   175
    The Committee Reports and the Identification of the Curriculum   177
The Child-Centered Counterreaction   181
    The Doctrine of Original Goodness   181
    Early European Influences on Classroom Practice   182

American Child Centeredness   187
    The Americanization of Johann Pestalozzi   187
    The Child Study Movement   188
    The Progressive Criticism of Child Centeredness   190
Summary   191
References   192
Key Questions   193
Research Exercises   195

Chapter 9   Defining the School Experience into the Twentieth Century   197

Progressivism and the Cause of Social Reform   197
    Dewey and the Educative Process   197
    Lester Ward and the Founding Progressive Principle of Environmentalism   198
Progressive Ideas in Action   199
    Booker T. Washington, W. E. B. Du Bois, and the Black American Struggle for Schooling   199
    Jane Addams and the Settlement House Movement   203
    The Conception of Subject Matter as Activity   204
    The Cardinal Principles Report of 1918   208
    The American Kindergarten   209
Summary   213
References   214
Key Questions   215
Research Exercises   217

PART THREE   The School and Society   219

Chapter 10   The Structure of American Education   221

Grade- and School-Level Orientations   221
School Governance   224
Funding Public Education   227
Church and State   236
    The Establishment and Free Exercise Clauses   237
    School Prayer   240
    Religious Holidays and Religious Symbols   242
    The Teaching of Creationism   244
    State Aid to Religious Schools   247
Summary   250
References   250
Key Questions   253
Research Exercises   255

Chapter 11   The Condition of American Education   257

Understanding School Achievement   258
The National Assessment of Educational Progress   259
    The Reading Report Card   260
    The Mathematics Report Card · 266
International Comparisons   272
    Cross-National Outcomes   272
School Dropouts   277
Technology and Schooling   285
Summary   286
References   287
Key Questions   289
Research Exercises   291

Chapter 12   School Equity   293

Curriculum Tracking   293
    Ability Grouping and Tracking   293
    Why Is Tracking Used in the School?   295
    Inequities in Tracking   296
    Responses to Criticisms of Tracking   298
    Alternatives to Tracking   299
School Desegregation   300
    Legal and Legislative Influences   300
    The Effects of Desegregation   308
Gender and Schooling   310
    Gender Bias   310
    Gender Segregated Classrooms   313
    School-Based Differences   314
Poverty in the Home   319
Summary   327
References   328
Key Questions   330
Research Exercises   331

Chapter 13   The Culture and the Language of Schooling   333

Cultural Diversity and Commonality   333
The Culture of Schooling   335
    Sources of a Common Culture   335
    Melting Pot Versus Salad Bowl   339
Multicultural Education   339
Culture and Critical Theory   341
The Language of Schooling   344
    Bilingual Education   344
    Types of Bilingual Education   347
    Continued Resistance   350

Summary   350
References   350
Key Questions   352
Research Exercises   353

Chapter 14   School Reform and the Shifting Sociopolitical Context Since Mid-Century   355

Education During the Cold War and Space Race Crisis: The 1950s   355
Humanizing the Schools in a Period of Social Protest: The 1960s   358
Back to Basics and Educational Retrenchment: The 1970s   360
Academic Excellence in a Period of Technological and Economic
   Mobilization: The 1980s   362
Extending Academic Excellence through National Educational Goals and
   Standards: The 1990s   363
The New Century: No Child Left Behind and the Drive for Accountability   365
   Testing for Proficiency   *365*
   The Construct of Proficiency   *369*
   Consequences for the Classroom and the School   *370*
Summary   371
References   371
Key Questions   373
Research Exercises   375

Chapter 15   The Idea of School Choice   377

Public School Choice Programs   377
   Intradistrict and Interdistrict Choice   *378*
   Charter Schools   *380*
   Magnet Schools   *382*
Privatization, Vouchers, and the Debate Over School Choice   382
   The Milwaukee Parental Choice Program (MPCP)   *385*
Home Schooling   387
Summary   388
References   389
Key Questions   391
Research Exercises   393

Index   395

PART 1

The Teacher and the School

And you, America
Cast you the real reckoning for your present?
The lights and shadows of your future, good *or* evil?
To girlhood, boyhood look, the teacher and the school.
Walt Whitman

CHAPTER 1

The American School Tradition

The American public school has always carried a heavy burden of responsibility. Its mandate has historically underscored the importance of offering learning experiences that contribute to not only the academic-intellectual growth of students, but also to their personal, social, and vocational development. The American public expects nothing less from the school and, if anything, expects quite a bit more. Today, for instance, publicly-financed schools are expected to socialize the rising generation of youth in the principles of democracy; to instill in youth the skills of competence needed to advance the interests of business and industry; to play a direct role in the psychological, social, intellectual, and physical betterment of each individual child; to affect the development of good character and the embrace of enlightened values in youth; to have some hand in curbing various societal ills; and to even provide the intellectual capital needed for the defense of the nation.

The argument that popular schooling exists to serve society has a long history. In Plato's *Republic*, for instance, the very essence of a good society implied a set of educational policies and practice that could give life to the highest ideals of the society. To Plato, societies did not get created by whim or accident, but by a deliberate and conscious socialization process that occurred at the level of the community. In the early history of the United States, the core of Plato's idea was maintained and applied to the popularization of the common public school (Cremin, 1965). American intellectuals such as Thomas Jefferson promoted the universalization of public schooling as an essential condition for an enlightened and vital citizenry. To Jefferson's mind, there could be no democracy unless each upcoming generation had the intellectual dexterity and ethical convictions needed to operate and preserve such a complex social arrangement. He believed that such a mission could only be carried out through the agency of mass public schooling. This line of thought continued into the nineteenth century with the work of Horace Mann, who used his position of Superintendent of Schools in Massachusetts to make common schooling mandatory up through the elementary grades (Butts, 1989), as well as with the work of Lester Ward (1883) and John Dewey (1916), who both held that schools were essential to building the dispositions, skills, and general insights needed to conduct a democratic community. Dewey (1916), in fact, observed that the role of the school was to provide an enlarging experience that went beyond the less encompassing nature of education in the home, church, and community.

THE SCHOOL AS A NORMATIVE ENVIRONMENT

The school is a special environment. It has a special mandate that it is expected to fulfill with deliberative focus. Dewey (1916) described the school as "a purified medium of action" that intentionally filtered out miseducative forces and supported educative ones. He observed that, "the business of the school environment is to eliminate, as far as possible, the unworthy features of the existing environment from influence upon mental habitities. It establishes a purified medium of action. Selection not only aims at simplifying but at weeding out what is undesirable" (p. 20). Thus, the school, by its very design, is a place that is deliberately and consciously conceived to fulfill an educational function linked to a public agenda. It is a purified medium with a carefully calculated mandate.

The nature of the school's mandate is mostly normative, meaning that it is largely comprised of the essential things that the state expects all children to learn. We know, for instance, that all schools need to teach children to be literate and that we cannot rely on any institution but the school to complete such a task. Thus, teaching the skill of reading is normative to the school. If the school does not teach it, it may not be learned. Along these same lines, schools might seek to teach school children something about core democratic values and attitudes, about diversity concerns, or even about what it might mean to lead an ethical and principled life. Similarly, schools might seek to inculcate a common foundation of knowledge in school children in order to help build a common culture, realizing again that such opportunities cannot be left exclusively to families, places of worship, or neighborhoods. So, all the things we say schools must do, irrespective of local demands, are the things we view as the normative agenda of the school.

The idea of the normative naturally goes hand in hand with a commitment to compulsory schooling. Most of the states in the nation have had compulsory schooling laws in place since the mid-nineteenth century, although enforcement of such laws in the early years was spotty and the actual capacity of the school to administratively handle the whole school-age population was wanting (Tyack, 1978). By the turn of the twentieth century, however, a broad swath of elementary schools took in growing numbers of children. The enrollment trajectory of the school was promising, as local school systems grew in their sophistication over how to teach and retain school children.

Early advocacy for compulsory schooling was not only driven by a desire to promote the possibilities for general enlightenment, but also by doubts about the role of the family in the education of its own progeny. The school, in fact, was often rationalized as a child saving agency, as a place that could protect children from the limitations and prejudices of their own home environments. Many supporters of public schooling felt that families were neither interested nor capable of offering the kind of education needed for the widest benefit of society. Understanding that the family was not always a benevolent institution, advocates of public schooling understood that the best hope for a broad and enlarging educational experience resided in a place called school.

So what was it about the school, historically speaking, that made it so important? The first and most obvious answer is associated with the idea of citizenship and nationalism. In a democracy marked by varied religious, ethnic, political, and even regional differences, some center of gravity had to be found to create what we might call an American citizen: someone whose identity transcends the parochial nature of the home or community. As Dewey (1916) noted "it is the office of the school environment to balance the various elements in the social environment, and to see to it that each individual gets an opportunity to escape from the limitations of the social group in which he was born, and to come into living contact with a broader environment" (p. 20). Such an expanded notion of schooling meant that there were specific skill sets, character traits, values, and even political outlooks that needed to be brought into the experience of children so that they could identify with the broadest causes of the nation-state.

But the rationale for public schooling went beyond matters related to democracy and civism. Supporters of the public school had other key goals in mind. Many believed, for instance, that the institutionalization of the school would produce economic advantages to the society, bring vocational and psychological benefits to the individual, and generally intellectualize and civilize the population. The general result of such expectations was that the school assumed an increasingly comprehensive program of goals, so much so that many began to see the idea of education as synonymous with the act of schooling. As Tyack (1978) put it, "the common query, 'Why aren't you in school?' signified that attendance in school had become the normal career of the young" (p. 64).

Obviously, the institutionalization of the school required the centralization of school authority. In the United States, this responsibility eventually fell to the states. But the growth of the school also depended on the development of a complex organizational network of professional educators and school administrators who could abide by some common notion on how to proceed with the public education of all youth. Naturally, quite a bit of debate prevailed over how to balance a sense of the common good against sympathy or even tolerance for ethnic, religious, and even political differences. Notable difficulties occurred, for instance, over what it meant to offer a nonsectarian education (Delafatorre, 2004) and even what it meant to offer a common cultural experience in a multicultural society (Schlesinger, 1998). The shameful history of segregated schools in the country testified to even deeper problems with the management of diversity concerns along the color line (Irons, 2004).

In the end, however, the historic ascent of the school represented the solidification of the normative agenda in the school lives of children. It meant that, minimally, more children would get the chance to learn how to read, to use mathematics, and to embrace the central values of democratic living than would otherwise be the case. To be sure, all youth did not derive these benefits, but as time passed more did than did not. And to the extent that the enrollment and graduation numbers increased, the chances of advancing a more enlightened society increased as well.

The historical data on enrollment rates in the American public schools demonstrate the incremental realization of the school's normative agenda in the lives of schoolchildren, and thus underscore two significant achievements. The first has to do with the upward extension of the school, meaning the extent to which the school not only kept children enrolled but also kept them enrolled for longer periods of time. Thus one finds, for instance, that from 1850 to 1991, the percentage of children between the ages of 5 to 19 who actually attended public schools rose from about 47% to over 93% (see Figure 1.1), and that, even more significantly, the number of students who graduated from high school climbed from less than 5% in 1890 to close to 80% in 1992 (see Figure 1.2). Clearly, the opportunity to learn what the school was teaching had expanded its reach and its longevity across the whole of the

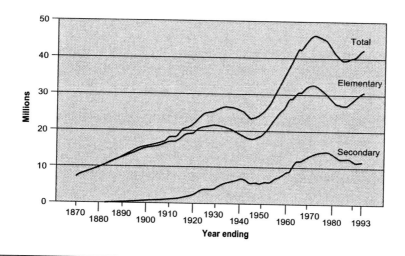

FIGURE 1.1 Enrollment of Public Elementary and Secondary Schools, by Level: 1869–70 to 1992–93. Taken from: NCES (1993) 120 Years of American Education: A Statistical Portrait (Washington, DC: Department of Education) p. 26.

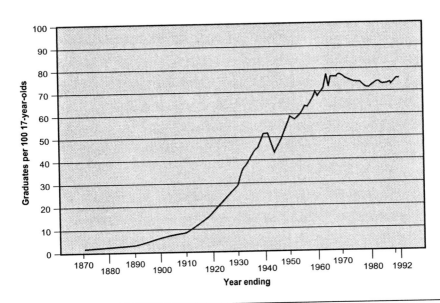

Figure 1.2 Number of Public and Private School Graduates per 100 17-Year-Olds: 1869–70 to 1992–93. Taken from: NCES (1993) 120 Years of American Education: A Statistical Portrait (Washington, DC: Department of Education) p. 31.

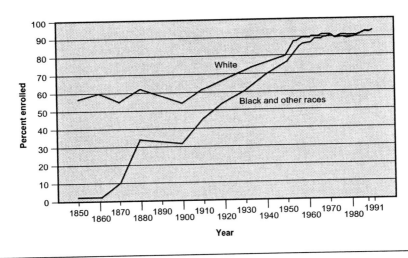

Figure 1.3 Percent of 5–19-Year-Olds Enrolled in School, by Race: 1850 to 1991. Taken from: NCES (1993) 120 Years of American Education: A Statistical Portrait (Washington, DC: Department of Education) p. 6.

school-age population. The other important feature to note in the historical record has to do with the outward extension of the school, meaning the extent to which the school reached out to historically underserved populations. For instance, improvements in the historical enrollment and graduation rates of marginalized groups, such as African-Americans, signified an important accomplishment (see Figure 1.3). Where the public education of African-American children was essentially denied in the nineteenth century, it grew precipitously in the twentieth century and eventually reached parity with the white population, at least in terms of secondary school enrollment. The same trend was witnessed on the scale of gender and income. The school's reach clearly expanded into historically-marginalized populations. Thus, we could say that, by the turn of the twentieth century, the universalization of the elementary school was close to becoming a completed project, as the universalization of the secondary school emerged as the new century's target—one that still eludes realization today.

THE UNIFIED SYSTEM AND THE COMPREHENSIVE SCHOOL

Another key principle in the American schooling tradition has to do with the notion that all youth should be educated in one unified setting, as opposed to separate academic and vocational schools. Such a principle is moved by a democratic rationale, by a belief in using the school as an instrument of democracy, where all youth could be taught together under one roof, without regard to their class status. Because of its inclusive nature, a unified school setting has to be sure that everyone enrolled is offered something educationally worthwhile. This means that the curriculum must show sensitivity to individual differences and to different career outlooks.

The standard organizational arrangement for most secondary schools in a unified system of schooling is known as the comprehensive high school. The curriculum of the comprehensive high school endeavors to provide an education in common learnings, to offer elective and exploratory courses for individual improvement, and to support strong specialized programs for both academic and vocational learning (Tanner and Tanner, 1995). Its purpose is to educate all youth widely in one setting, making use of common learning experiences for the development of common insight and balancing that with the support of differentiated learning experiences for the development of individual talents and interests.

One should note that such a school arrangement is not likely to be found in other advanced nations. In fact, the school tradition outside of the United States, especially at the secondary school level, is typically organized as a dual or bipartite system in which schoolchildren are enrolled in separate schools according to separate career purposes. Children entering into pre-adolescence in such societies, for instance, will often be identified and divided into "curriculum tracks" or "curriculum streams" (as they are sometimes known in Europe), and sent off to separate schools designated by academic and terminal-vocational categories. Thus, for a small percentage of the college-bound youth, schooling is provided in a college preparatory high school, while for the remaining majority, vocational schools, technical schools, and assorted job training schools are the reality. Although many American schools practice some version of internal "curriculum tracking," the idea of separate schools for different life destinies and different career-based skills has not been part of the American school tradition.

The notion of constructing the school experience comprehensively has long been supported not only by educators, but by parents as well. Goodlad's study of the American school system in the early 1980's found that parents and teachers—although believing that academic-intellectual goals were most important in the education of youth—held that the school also had an obligation to provide comprehensive educational experiences dealing with various personal, socio–civic, and vocational concerns. As Goodlad (1984) stated, "when it comes to education, it appears that most parents want their children to have it all" (p. 39).

But if schoolchildren are going to "have it all" in their public education, teachers have to find a way to support the many-sided purposes of the comprehensive learning agenda. For elementary school teachers this is a natural agenda. The teaching expectation placed on the elementary school teacher is removed from the pressures of college preparation and its inherent association with specialized knowledge. Although some elementary school teachers might feel the pressure of teaching the basic skills (and nothing but the basic skills), in most cases, lessons taught in elementary school are not strictly academic. Because elementary education teachers are usually with the same group of students all day, they teach a wide range of subject areas that can be brought together and dealt with in any number of ways. Linking ideas to social concerns, setting up experiences that account for individual differences, allowing individual talents and interests to find some expression in the classroom, and encouraging the development of a core or common experience in democracy are all matters that are part of the elementary school teacher's day. High school teachers, on the other hand, whose training and experience are often linked to a specific discipline of study (mathematics, English, history, and so forth) inherit certain limitations in this regard. Their contribution to the comprehensive school agenda is sometimes compromised by the specific obligations they have to teach their specialized subject area. This, of course, is a problem that can find some relief in the manner in which the school curriculum is organized. Depending on how the curriculum is arranged, some high school teachers are expected to seek interdisciplinary linkages, to connect their classroom to community outreach efforts, and to find ways to encourage individual talents and interests. But because of the specializing influences on the high school teacher, the school has to be vigilant about arranging the curriculum in a way that captures the comprehensive schooling mandate.

DECENTRALIZED GOVERNANCE

As indicated, the basic governance structure of the American school system is decentralized, with most of the power wielded at the state level. The American system has never embraced the kind of centralized system preferred in many other advanced nations, such as one might find in various European and Asian nations. Centralized systems typically vest national authority in the administration of the public schools. In Japan, for instance, a national ministry prescribes the curriculum, sets national standards, and mandates various school-based requirements. It also approves textbooks, assumes responsibility for the content and the administration of the public examinations, and otherwise supervises the school districts (Frasz and Kato, 1999). A decentralized public school system eschews the national management of schooling. One cannot find the use of national standards, national exams, national curricula, national textbooks, or any national supervision of schooling in the United States, although as will be discussed, some nationalizing influences are present.

Thus, we can say that the so-called American school system is actually fifty school systems (one for each state), all of which regulate themselves in significantly different ways. The differences can manifest in the requirements for high school graduation, in the conditions for teacher licensure, in the rules for textbook adoptions, in the amount of state money dedicated to the education of each pupil, and in the nature of the content standards used in the curriculum.

Such differences in state regulations and in the general latitude that the states give to local sources of school management obviously affect what happens in classrooms. In the State of Iowa, for instance, statewide content standards are shunned and only minimal direction is given on high school graduation requirements. But in more regulatory states, such as Texas, statewide content standards and graduation requirements are taken quite seriously, as are even more invasive rules, such as controlling what books can be used in classrooms. The orientation of the State of Iowa to its local schools is largely permissive. Iowa prefers to defer to the judgment of local school authorities in various matters related to the conduct of the school, including the use of content standards and the issuance of graduation requirements. But in many other states, the preference is to regulate local school authorities from the state house.

What a state imposes on its local school districts varies in ways that significantly affect what gets taught in the classroom, and even in some cases, how it gets taught. A number of states, for example, have implemented limits on class size; some have stipulated the number of credits that need to be achieved in each academic subject for high school graduation; others have even mandated advanced course offerings (NCES, 2002). Over 20 states have laws ordering the use of exit exams as a requirement for graduation. Approximately eight states require students to pass an end-of-year exam before they can be promoted to the next grade, starting as early as third grade. Even seemingly straightforward institutional matters, such as the length of the school day or school year, can also differ across the states. Most states abide by a 180-day school year, but there is some range, as Hawaii mandates 184 days in a school year, while North Dakota mandates only 173 days. A few states have no statewide policy on the length of the school year at all (NCES, 2002a).

Most states retain course area requirements for high school graduation. The states usually stipulate an exposure requirement to a list of four or five core subject areas (commonly language arts, social studies, mathematics, and science) for graduation (see Table 1.1). These are typically expressed as Carnegie unit requirements. The Carnegie unit is a metric used to represent a 120-hour instructional obligation of time to a subject area over the course of an academic year. Thus, one Carnegie unit usually means that a subject area will be taught regularly—say, 40 minutes per day, over the period of about a 35-week academic year. The required exposure to subject matter requirements in high school is divergent across the states (NCES, 2002) and even over time, as states generally seem to be increasing the number of required units. And the Carnegie unit requirement often go beyond the core academic areas. Various states, for instance, support Carnegie unit requirements in health (28 states), physical education (33 states), foreign language (10 states), and the arts (27 states). Most of these Carnegie unit requirements are modest in number, ranging between one-half to two credit units. Overall, however, the total number of Carnegie units required for graduation ranges from a total of one and a half credits (in Iowa) to 24 credits in several other states.

Family access to different types of public schools is also a factor that varies from state to state. Many states have adopted policies that allow students and their families to select a public school beyond the one zoned for their residence. Some permit school choice across school districts, which is known as interdistrict choice, and others offer only choice within the student's home district, which is known as intradistrict choice. Some states have particular school choice policies for students who are attending low performing schools; several states permit dual enrollment between different schools. In about 17 states, intradistrict choice is, in fact, a mandatory policy imposed on school districts (NCES, 2002). One also finds dramatically different regulations across the states on the management of charter schools and the education of "home-schooled" children.

Not surprisingly, the financing of the public schools at the state level also differs considerably, with some states relying heavily on state sources of revenue, as others draw mostly from local sources. Hawaii receives almost full funding at the state level. Because public education in Hawaii is organized, in effect, as one large statewide school system, the per-pupil expenditure within the state varies very little. States, however, that allow for the influence of local monies on school expenditures are likely to see differences in per-pupil spending amounts, as each locality varies in its capacity to produce tax revenue for the schools. Thus, where local funding and local control prevail in a state, one can expect to find funding inequities within the states—some of which, as we will discover later in the book, are quite startling.

Public education is a state right in the United States and is a diametric opposite of the uniformly national systems of schooling popular in many other advanced nations. The nature of statewide operations in the life of the school obviously depends on how heavy-handed the state becomes in supervising its local districts. Thus, we find a decentralized system of schooling that differs from state to state in policy, prevailing practices, and financial investment.

TABLE 1.1   State Course Requirements for High School Graduation, 2004

State	Math	Science	English	Social Studies	Arts	Total Credits
Alabama	4	4	2	4	0.5	24
Alaska	2	2	4	3	0	21
Arizona	2	2	4	2.5	1	20
Arkansas	4	3	4	3	0.5	21
California	2	2	3	3	1	13
Colorado	LD	LD	LD	LD	LD	LD
Connecticut	3	2	4	3	1	20
Delaware	3	3	4	3	0	22
District of Columbia	3	3	4	3.5	1	23.5
Florida[1]	3	3	4	3	1	24 or 18
Georgia	4	3	4	3	0	22
Hawaii	3	3	4	4	0	22
Idaho[2]	4	4	9	5	2	42
Illinois	2	1	3	2	1	10.25
Indiana[2]	4	4	8	4	0	24
Iowa	LD	LD	LD	1.5	LD	1.5 and LD
Kansas	2	2	4	3	0	21
Kentucky	3	3	4	3	1	22
Louisiana	3	3	4	3	0	23
Maine	2	2	4	2	1	16
Maryland	3	3	4	3	1	21
Massachusetts	LD	LD	LD	LD	LD	LD
Michigan	LD	LD	LD	0.5	LD	0.5 and LD
Minnesota	3	3	4	3.5	1	21.5
Mississippi	3	3	4	3	1	20
Missouri	2	2	3	2	1	22
Montana	2	2	4	2	1	20
Nebraska	LD	LD	LD	LD	LD	LD
Nevada	3	2	4	2	1	22.5
New Hampshire	2	2	4	2.5	0.5	19.75
New Jersey	3	3	4	3	1	22
New Mexico	3	2	4	3	0	23
New York	2	2	4	4	0	12
North Carolina	3	LD	4	LD	LD	20
North Dakota	LD	LD	LD	LD	LD	LD
Ohio	3	3	4	3	LD	21
Oklahoma	3	3	4	3	2	23
Oregon	2	2	3	3	1	22
Pennsylvania	LD	LD	LD	LD	LD	LD
Rhode Island	2	2	4	2	0	16

State	Math	Science	English	Social Studies	Arts	Total Credits
South Carolina	4	3	4	3	0	24
South Dakota	2	2	4	3	0.5	20
Tennessee	3	3	4	3	0	20
Texas	3	3	4	3.5	1	24
Utah	2	2	3	2.5	0	24
Vermont[3]	0–5	0–5	4	3	1	12
Virginia	3	3	4	3	1	22
Washington	2	2	3	2.5	1	19
West Virginia	3	3	4	4	0	24
Wisconsin	2	2	4	3	0	13
Wyoming	3	3	4	3	LD	13 and LD

[1] Florida offers three programs: 4-year, 24-credit; 3-year, 18-credit; or 3-year 18-credit career-prep.

[2] Credits in Idaho and Indiana refer to semester credits rather than Carnegie credits.

[3] Students are required to complete 5 credits between Mathematics and Science.

NOTE: LD=Local decision. Credits are measured in Carnegie credits. A single Carnegie credit is assigned to an academic course consisting of two semesters. A total for the United States was not reported by the source organization.

SOURCE: Table 8 from Cavell, L., Blank, R. F., Toye, C., and Williams, A. (2005). *Key State Education Policies on PK-12 Education: 2004.* Washington, DC: Council of Chief State School Officers.

Nationalizing Influences

Given all the differences described above, is it even possible to reliably generalize about the American schools? In light of the vast regulatory variance that exists between the states, can any claim be made for a common American school experience? Is there not an expectation for the public school to have an agenda that goes beyond it moorings in the fifty states? Clearly, a national dimension has to come into play in the organization and management of the American school if we are to believe that it has a wider obligation rooted in the sustenance of our constitutional democracy. And the historical reality is that, despite decentralization, the public school has indeed capitulated to some nationalizing influences and goals.

The federal government has been especially adroit at finding ways to influence school policy at the state level. Knowing its limited role in the school curriculum, the federal government has often attached strings to its funding appropriations in order to influence the nature of the curriculum used in the schools and the kind of teaching that goes on. The most recent example is the federal legislation represented in the well-known No Child Left Behind Act (NCLB). Under the conditions of NCLB, the federal government has been able to influence the nature of the classroom indirectly by forcing states to use an accountability system that issues penalties against schools failing to meet publicly articulated proficiency standards. The effect has given the federal government considerable command and control over the school curriculum because the accountability system used in each state very much influences what gets taught in the schools. One national survey indicated that about 25 percent of both superintendents and principals reported that NCLB had generated "a lot of change" in the policy and practice of their schools, and another 50 percent indicated that "some change" had occurred (Public Agenda, 2003).

The states, of course, have the right to reject the federal legislation, but that would mean relinquishing federal funding altogether, which poses not only a financial burden on the states but a political one as well. One needs to remember that the federal government, especially as it has been represented in the work of the Department of Education, is often adept at using its national stature in the media to sway public opinion on matters relevant to the public schools. The federal Secretary of Education is a cabinet-level appointment that carries the weight and prestige of the Office of the Presidency. Thus, states are often politically compelled to follow federal urgings because of the effectiveness of federal persuasion on public opinion.

Other kinds of nationalizing influences prevail in the schools as well. The popularity of certain commercial exams and textbooks certainly point to some national identity. The most widely used tests and textbooks in America represent, in some key subject areas, a qualified national curriculum for the schools. Similarly, almost all of the states in the nation have now adopted statewide content standards, which are often drawn from common sources, and thus have the effect, especially in the high schools, of standardizing what gets taught.

We could also begin to find some national sense of schooling by looking at the fundamental purposes and goals embraced by the public schools. If we look closely at the history of the public school experience in the United States, we can find at least four macro goals that have captured the essence of a public school education. These goals have no official sanction in government but they do represent a historical, if not traditional, sense of what public schools are committed to doing. They include broadly defined goals related to:

1.   individual-personal growth;
2.   socio-civic growth;
3.   intellectual-academic growth; and,
4.   career-based or vocational growth.

In combination, the four goals represent a comprehensive framework for the design of the school experience.

We return to the broad conception of schooling articulated in the beginning of this chapter to understand this American school tradition. Individual-personal goals in the school encompass a range of concerns pertaining to the emotional and physical well-being of students, the pursuit of their interests and aptitudes, their sense of aesthetic or existential understanding, and ultimately, their constructions of self-identity. Socio-civic goals speak directly to interpersonal relations, which include dealings with different cultures, opposing viewpoints, the skills of compromise and negotiation, and the values of compassion and concern for others. Socio-civic also involves issues of citizenship, such as democratic participation and the workings of government, while also seeking to raise consciousness for global understanding, universal human rights, and the appreciation of cultural differences. The socio-civic side of public education also serves the interests of moral and character education by stressing moral integrity, an understanding of truth, and critical interpretations of good and evil. Academic-intellectual goals in the school involve establishing the basics for literacy and numeracy. In the early grades, this means mastery of the fundamental processes or what we might view as the basic skills of reading, writing, and arithmetical operations. Thinking skills, problem solving skills, inquiry skills, and the accumulation and application of general as well as specialized knowledge also have their place among academic intellectual goals. Finally, the school promotes vocational goals that affect career outlooks and career choices, that inculcate habits and attitudes of craftsmanship, and that encourage a positive attitude toward work. The full and complete range of goals, taken from Goodlad's work (1984), is expressed in the following outline.

Goals for Schooling in the United States

A. **Individual-Personal**
  1. *Emotional and Physical Well-Being*
     1-1 Develop the willingness to receive emotional impressions and to expand one's affective sensitivity.
     1-2 Develop the competence and skills for continuous adjustment and emotional stability, including coping with social change.
     1-3 Develop a knowledge of one's own body and adopt health practices that support and sustain it, including avoiding the consumption of harmful or addictive substances.
     1-4 Learn to use leisure time effectively.
     1-5 Develop physical fitness and recreational skills.
     1-6 Develop the ability to engage in constructive self-criticism.
  2. *Creativity and Aesthetic Expression*
     2-1 Develop the ability to deal with problems in original ways.
     2-2 Develop the ability to be tolerant of new ideas.
     2-3 Develop the ability to be flexible and to consider different points of view.
     2-4 Develop the ability to experience and enjoy different forms of creative expression.
     2-5 Develop the ability to evaluate various forms of aesthetic expression.
     2-6 Develop the willingness and ability to communicate through creative work in an active way.
     2-7 Seek to contribute to cultural and social life through one's artistic, vocational, and avocational interests.
  3. *Self-Realization*
     3-1 Learn to search for meaning in one's activities and develop a philosophy of life.
     3-2 Develop the self-confidence necessary for knowing and confronting one's self.
     3-3 Learn to assess realistically and live with one's limitations and strengths.
     3-4 Recognize that one's self-concept is developed in interaction with other people.
     3-5 Develop skill in making decisions with purposes.
     3-6 Learn to plan and organize the environment in order to realize one's goals.
     3-7 Develop willingness to accept responsibility for one's own decisions and their consequences.
     3-8 Develop skill in selecting some personal life-long learning goals and the means to attain them.

B. **Socio-Civic**
  4. *Interpersonal Understandings*
     4-1 Develop knowledge of opposing value systems and their influence on the individual and society.
     4-2 Develop an understanding of how members of a family function under different family patterns as well as within one's own family.
     4-3 Develop skill in communicating effectively in groups.
     4-4 Develop the ability to identify with and advance the goals and concerns of others.
     4-5 Learn to form productive and satisfying relations with others based on respect, trust, cooperation, consideration, and caring.
     4-6 Develop a concern for humanity and an understanding of international relations.
     4-7 Develop an understanding and appreciation of cultures different from one's own.

5. *Citizenship Participation*

   5-1   Develop historical perspective.

   5-2   Develop knowledge of the basic workings of the government.

   5-3   Develop a willingness to participate in the political life of the nation and the community.

   5-4   Develop a commitment to the values of liberty, government by consent of the governed, representational government, and one's responsibility for the welfare of all.

   5-5   Develop an understanding of the interrelationships among complex organizations and agencies in a modern society and learn to act in accordance with it.

   5-6   Exercise the democratic right to dissent in accordance with personal conscience.

   5-7   Develop economic and consumer skills necessary for making informed choices that enhance one's quality of life.

   5-8   Develop an understanding of the basic interdependence of the biological and physical resources of the environment.

   5-9   Develop the ability to act in light of this understanding of interdependence.

6. *Enculturation*

   6-1   Develop insight into the values and characteristics, including language of the civilization of which one is a member.

   6-2   Develop an awareness and understanding of one's cultural heritage and become familiar with the achievement of the past that have inspired and influenced humanity.

   6-3   Develop understanding of the manner in which traditions from the past are operative today and influence the direction and values of society.

   6-4   Understand and adopt the norms, values, and traditions of the groups of which one is a member.

   6-5   Learn how to apply the basic principles and concepts of the fine arts and humanities to the appreciation of the aesthetic contributions of other cultures.

7. *Moral and Ethical Character*

   7-1   Develop the judgment to evaluate events and phenomena as good or evil.

   7-2   Develop a commitment to truth and values.

   7-3   Learn to utilize values in making choices.

   7-4   Develop moral integrity.

   7-5   Develop an understanding of the necessity for moral conduct.

C. Academic-Intellectual

8. *Mastery of Basic Skills and Fundamental Processes*

   8-1   Learn to read, write, and handle basic arithmetical operations.

   8-2   Learn to acquire ideas through reading and listening.

   8-3   Learn to communicate ideas through writing and speaking.

   8-4   Learn to utilize mathematical concepts.

   8-5   Develop the ability to utilize available sources of information.

9. *Intellectual Development*

   9-1   Develop the ability to think rationally, including problem-solving skills, application of principles of logic, and skill in using different modes of inquiry.

   9-2   Develop the ability to use and evaluate knowledge, i.e., critical and independent thinking that enables one to make judgments and decisions in a wide variety of life roles—citizen, consumer, and worker—as well as in intellectual activities.

   9-3   Accumulate a general fund of knowledge, including information and concepts in mathematics, literature, natural science, and social science.

9-4 Develop positive attitudes toward intellectual activities, including curiosity and a desire for further learning.

9-5 Develop an understanding of change in society.

D. Vocational

10. Career Education-Vocational Education

10-1 Learn how to select an occupation that will be personally satisfying and suitable to one's skills and interests.

10-2 Learn to make decisions based on an awareness and knowledge of career options.

10-3 Develop salable skills and specialized knowledge that will prepare one to become economically independent.

10-4 Develop habits and attitudes, such as pride in good workmanship, that will make one a productive participant in economic life.

10-5 Develop positive attitudes toward work, including acceptance of the necessity of making a living and an appreciation of the social values and dignity of work.

These goals, in general terms, outline the comprehensive mandate for public education in America.

TEACHING IN A COMPREHENSIVE AND UNIFIED SYSTEM

As mentioned, four major objectives outline the terms of a comprehensive school experience. These are not formulated as exclusive objectives. In fact, they are complimentary and often overlap in the school experience. The four objectives, however, do set out an explicit charge to teachers, reminding them of their wide ranging teaching duties. How then might these four major objectives be organized in the classroom?

Teaching for Individual-Personal Growth

The individual-personal aspects of the school experience should emphasize the development of individual responsibility, seek to cultivate individual talents and skills, aim to assist youth in their emotional, cognitive and physical development, and generally serve the objectives of self-understanding and self-expression.

One feature of individual-personal goals goes directly to the question of individual interest and individual aptitude. To put it simply, schools are expected to help develop the aptitudes and interests of individual students. Students showing a high aptitude in, say, mathematics, art, music, writing, or athletics should have access to some outlet in the school that affords them the opportunity to continue to develop their skill. Conversely, those with limited aptitudes or with particular disabilities should receive remedial assistance. The school, besides considering options within the classroom, might also point to provisions in the macrocurriculum (such as advanced placement courses, various enrichment opportunities, remedial assistance or experiences external to the school) that support individual talents and address individual weaknesses. The same rules apply to student interests. Most schools make some effort to represent individual interests in the design of their curriculum. In most elementary schools, individualization is the responsibility of a teacher who tries to find some way to deal with individual concerns within a self-contained classroom, although it is not unusual to find pullout programs for remedial education or for the education of gifted and talented children. At the middle and high school levels, however, individualization usually takes shape through systematically designed course work that might get promoted as elective study, advanced placement, or remedial education. Classroom teachers, of course, continue to do their part as well.

Instructional concerns related to individual-personal growth also have a lot to do with individual well-being, such as maintaining emotional stability, coping with change, taking good care of one's health, engaging in fulfilling leisure time activities, and maintaining an honest and constructive self-image. This means that teachers might direct some attention to introspective issues, to habits of individual responsibility, to constructive uses of leisure time, and ultimately, to finding balance and perspective in life.

The guiding principle here is that attending to the unique needs of children is what the individual-personal phase of the curriculum is generally about. This could include making adjustments in instruction, which might include pacing differences and differences in the structure of the teaching strategy (as influenced by, say, developmental processes). But, as indicated, the individual-personal phase of the curriculum is more ambitious than that. It is also directly tied into the exploration of personal abilities and individual interests, and into the development of the emotional and physical well-being of each child.

In the classroom, individualization can be accomplished through individual and group projects, and through various extra-classroom activities. All this means is that certain students will have the opportunity to participate in certain projects on their own (or in small groups) for the purpose of pursuing a question or an interest that they personally find worthwhile. The teacher, of course, has to spark this initiative by providing options for extended exploratory education. Students might spontaneously suggest ideas for a project, but most projects should be deliberately designed in the classroom as opportunities to pursue issues raised in the classroom and as opportunities to develop new interests.

A teacher could, for example, list ways to extend and further develop interests related to the classroom. To the mathematics educator, this might mean getting students involved in a math club or in other extra-classroom initiatives focusing on numeracy. In high school, extra-classroom activities or even classroom-based activities—such as a school-wide group dedicated to polling student views on various social issues, or a consumer advocacy group interested in discerning the best local buys for various items typically purchased by students, or a computer group interested in exploring fractals—could all be possibilities for cultivating student interest in mathematics. For students showing a particular aptitude and keen interest in advanced mathematics, the teacher's role is usually limited, but curriculum options for elective study or study outside the school should be available.

The teacher can reserve some time each day for the pursuit of an individualized program of studies related to a student's own interests. During this period, small groups might meet to work on their projects, some individuals might go to the library to conduct research, other students might sit with their favorite books for a quiet reading session, and yet others might pursue an interest in an area like computers. The teacher could also use this time to arrange for special instruction outside the classroom. A child with particular gifts in the visual arts, for instance, might arrange to work with the art teacher for a period. Similarly, a child with an aptitude for writing, music, or mathematics could find opportunities in meetings with accomplished experts.

It should be stressed, however, that a classroom period devoted to individual interests does not translate into a laissez-faire "do-your-own-thing" classroom climate. The teacher must be an active participant in each student's work and should have a fundamental sense of what each student intends to do during these sessions. To accomplish this, the teacher might ask that all projects be approved before being pursued in class and establish a list of generic activities that all students could follow during the so-called individual period. In an elementary school, for example, each individual period might allow for a reasonable number of children to read or research in the library (or another quiet area), to read the local newspaper or children magazines, to work in the computer lab or on classroom computers, or to work on approved ongoing projects.

All teachers should realize that the role of individualizing the curriculum is not designed simply for students to pursue preexisting interests, which is undoubtedly important, but also to widen and explore new interests. Thus, educators should try to keep an inventory of what each student is doing in the individualized phase of the curriculum. It is probably not in the student's best interests to devote all of his or her time to one area of pursuit during the course of an academic year. For example, a student who only works on the computer or who only reads to himself all of the time needs to be encouraged, if not required, to widen his areas of participation.

Finally, teachers must consider the mental, emotional, and physical well-being of each individual, which raises the possibilities for treating concerns related to self-realization, aesthetic understanding, and even spiritual growth. Although there are clear prohibitions on any actions a teacher might take to establish a religious point of view in the classroom, religion, per se, is not banned from school. Thus, on an individual basis, there is room to explore religious or spiritual convictions, and to examine in more general terms what stirs students and gives their life purpose and meaning. Specifically, students might pursue these interests through expressions in music, art, poetry, dance, sport, and forms of recreation. Activities that encourage varied modes of expression, that spark the imagination and sense of wonder, that give life purpose and place it in perspective, or that help us define or see how we understand virtues such as love, trust, honesty, and courage—all have a place here. To high school English teachers, and perhaps to elementary school teachers, these instructional concerns are more customary than in other more specialized classrooms. But these are not matters that should be limited to such places.

Teaching for Socio-Civic Growth

Public schools have long been viewed as fundamental agencies in the social development of children. Most public schools, after all, try to advance the highest ideals of the society in their policies and in their practices. In recent years, however, this aspect of the school curriculum has been dealt with dismally in the practice of teaching. Often the mission of socio-civic learning has been relegated to extra-classroom experiences and to the belief that socio-civic issues are served naturally in the ebb and flow of school life (e.g., team sports, classroom and cafeteria conversations).

In a democracy, the public schools should provide experiences that embody civic virtues like social responsibility, cooperation, tolerance, and equity, preferably in a social context that is characteristic of the society's population. The schools should support experiences that promote the development of interpersonal relations, that speak to the roles and responsibilities of democratic citizenship, that enculturate the student population into a common heritage and that teach students to develop a critical moral perspective on their conduct.

It is probably fair to say that most schools have undervalued these ideals and practices. In high school, socio-civic education is often seen as belonging to the disciplines of social studies and history, or to extra-classroom activities like student government. In lower schools, it is believed to be served by social interactions and by some component in social studies curriculum. Few schools, however, devote an actual block of time to citizenship education. Still, in most cases, the public school continues to represent the best hope for providing an experience in democratic living.

How does one begin to operationalize socio-civic learning throughout the grades? What might the curriculum look like in either an elementary, middle, or secondary school, and how might it be operationalized in a school long accustomed to departmentalized subject area requirements? Depending on the organizational structure of the school curriculum, elementary teachers can carry out socio-civic traditions of learning in any numbers of ways. The first step might be to specify a time in the classroom schedule to deal specifically with socio-civic issues in the school and community. During these common learning sessions, for instance, children in first grade could be taught a unit on the people who provide important services to their homes, neighborhood, or town. In third grade, the session can be used to prepare a formal presentation of a news hour that deals with vital social concerns in the school and community. In the higher elementary grades, students might develop a monthly classroom newsletter, invite guests from the community to discuss local issues, prepare interview questions for authorities in the community or survey questions for fellow students, engage in letter-writing campaigns to public officials, or prepare a series of occasional reports on important social issues.

Each of these initiatives is difficult to contain in traditional subject areas, although, depending on the project, vital subject area skills in reading, language arts, social studies, and science are developed. Thus, teaching events can also be organized along lines of inquiry that raise socio-civic questions in separate subject areas. The science-related line of inquiry in elementary school, for instance, might result in a series of units dealing with environmental concerns, with health and nutrition issues, or with issues of technology. The social studies line might deal systematically with current events, with upcoming election-year voter decisions, or with a direct treatment of the Constitution and the Bill of Rights. The mathematical line might lead to the creation of a classroom or school store, a treatment of consumer issues, or an economic analysis of the sports industry. Language arts might focus on maintaining an ongoing correspondence with a wide range of pen pals from across the country or the world, or the analysis of the language used in advertising, political campaigning, or newspaper writing. In short, we can see how socio-civic objectives, at least in the elementary school, could color subject area treatments in the curriculum.

Socio-civic learning, of course, does not always call for large group meetings. Some of its mandate can be fulfilled with a series of smaller groups that devote themselves to the analysis of various civic issues. For example, a four- to seven-member team could do mathematical analyses of how much water is wasted in a typical household in the community (showing through extrapolation cumulative effects). Or another team could work on an artistic depiction of the cultures represented in the school. Yet another team could study a social problem such as the care of the aged in the society that might move its members to engage in actions that assist the local senior citizen community.

The community-based facet of common learning is also quite important. Local problems should, of course, be studied in the classroom through reading, library work, and discussions with peers, but where possible, they should also be viewed through the lens of a volunteer service organization. Middle and high school students might get involved in a study of the quality of life for young children in their community. The students might then report their findings and views to local politicians and media sources, as well as offer their services to local recreational agencies or to organizations that care for children in need (e.g., battered children, homeless children). Students in elementary schools, with the guidance and assistance of parents and teachers, might participate in local recycling projects, local food drives, local civic events, and other activities that assist people in need and improve the civic life of the community. In addition to fulfilling the service duties associated with these projects, the students will also be studying the social problems that underscore the projects.

Socio-civic learning can find its place in virtually any classroom. Many schools, especially middle schools, are now designing the curriculum in a way that encourages cross disciplinary teaching, including team teaching arrangements and block time allocations expressly dedicated to the study of socio-personal issues and problems. And in high school, as will be described later, in some traditional academic disciplines, socio-civic goals are finding new visibility.

Teaching for Academic-Intellectual Growth

Academic-intellectual concerns in the curriculum are most often associated with college entrance demands in middle school and high school, and with basic intellectual competencies in elementary schools. Academic priorities are also usually related to the development of thinking skills, which includes skills of inquiry, logic and evaluation, skills of literacy and numeracy, and knowledge in the traditional disciplines. Historically, the academic function of the curriculum has valued specialized knowledge and has been organized along strict subject-centered lines. In the high school, this has led to a traditional menu of coursework covering a discipline-centered knowledge base.

In the elementary school, similar content categories have been in place, as students jump from mathematics lessons to science lessons to reading lessons and so on. At all levels, academic concerns have dominated the curriculum. Academic learning in the elementary school has usually meant education in the so-called basic skills. This has often resulted in teaching that has emphasized skill-drill routines and various rote and recitation exercises. Believing that inculcation of the basic skills is the preparation for later academic work in the disciplines, many elementary school teachers have been keen to develop these skills in focused isolation. Thus, this emphasis on the basic skills has been a mainstay in the elementary school classroom.

The idea of teaching the basic skills in relation to larger instructional ends, as means toward ends instead of as ends in and of themselves, is attracting more proponents in the classroom. The reality is that the basic skills (or fundamental processes, as they are also known), have no full and complete residency in any one particular subject area; rather the skills of reading, writing, and numeracy are needed in virtually all academic subject areas. The prevalence of the self-contained classroom in the elementary school means that academic learning need not be subject-specific. A teacher can think of teaching reading not only as a discrete skill (say, during reading instruction) but as a skill that finds application in the teaching of science, mathematics, and social studies. Similarly, the teaching of mathematical skills and skills related to effective communication (writing, speaking, debating, and artistic communication) has wide-ranging possibilities in all subject areas. As a result, in the elementary school, there is a natural blending of academic goals with individual-personal goals and socio-civic goals.

This is not to say that there are no subject-specific knowledge requirements for elementary school teachers. They exist in science and social studies, and as basic skills in reading, language arts, and mathematics. But the pressure to convey a specialized body of knowledge to the learner is weak in the elementary school. Consequently, the teacher has a certain latitude to think about securing connections between academic goals and socio-civic ones: to build bridges across certain content areas, to design special supplemental units, to re-sequence certain materials in the text, or to even consider offering a set of independent materials as supplemental to the textbook.

At the high school level, the instructional equation is quite different. The academic tradition in the secondary school has essentially two roles: 1) one that deals expressly with specialized knowledge in pre-college education, and 2) one that has a place in interdisciplinary settings dedicated to socio-civic objectives. In the high school, for instance, there is a clear and pressing need for youth to be given the opportunity to enroll in specialized courses, especially in courses that serve the interests of students intent on pursuing a college education.

A specializing pressure can also be felt from the tendency to build graduation requirements around an accumulation of credits in a certain range of traditional subject areas. Such a tendency goes all the way back to the turn of the 20th century, when established learning doctrine at the time upheld the view that certain subjects had intrinsic qualities to strengthen the intellectual potency of the mind. Such a view, known as the doctrine of mental discipline, was wedded to a concept of curriculum that equated learning with knowledge acquisition in an essential body of prescribed subject matter (Kliebard, 1986). The idea was that learning proceeded through an interaction with certain studies believed to be uniquely endowed with the powers to exercise the mind. The biases inherent in the doctrine of mental discipline prejudiced certain studies over others, with the effect of giving low priority to the modern social sciences, interdisciplinary subject areas, vocational education, physical education, aesthetics, and other "non-academic" pursuits. The elevation of certain subjects to the status of being intellective placed all other studies in an anti-intellectual position, which itself perpetuated a narrow view of what is viewed as worthy in the school curriculum.

Over the years, the doctrine of mental discipline has been largely defrocked in the literature, but its subject-centered legacy has lingered in the schools. Because post-secondary schools set their admissions criteria according to traditional subject areas, high schools have had trouble breaking away from them. Moreover, the preparation of the high school teachers continues to be aligned with specialized training in one particular discipline, which also reinforces the subject-centered lines. As mentioned, some of this makes good sense; after all, one feature of the academic curriculum in high school does need to provide highly specialized courses. This typically means that science will be broached through the standard specializations (biology, chemistry, and physics); mathematics through algebra, geometry, and trigonometry; social studies through civics and history; and English through the standard fare of grammar, composition, and classical literature. College entrance requirements and state-mandated objectives typically influence the character of these specialized offerings.

The academic curriculum in high school could allow for linkages to interdisciplinary and socio-civic concerns. Obviously, a broad field, such as social studies, has multiple claims on subject disciplines and on the realization of socio-civic goals. But educators from science, math, and English also direct their efforts toward the goal of making interdisciplinary connections in the socio-civic arena. In science education, for instance, the last decade witnessed the growth of a movement, known as Science-Technology and Society (STS), which used issue-centered themes that touch on critical social topics. Sanctioned by the National Science Teachers Association (1982) and sponsored by the National Science Foundation, STS has sought to transcend the discipline-centered lines of traditional science and to deal with points of argument that cut across a broad range of environmental, industrial, technological, social, and political problems. It unabashedly claimed to prepare youth for constructive citizenship roles. English educators have also gotten in on the action, mobilizing their energies to deal with the relation of their discipline to democratizing practices in the school. The teaching standards supported by the National Council of Teachers of English (1996), for example, include references made to the teaching of language in the context of cultural diversity, to the teaching of literature as it relates to improving understanding of society and to the encouragement of problem-focused research inquiries on various socio-personal issues and interests. Mathematics educators have acknowledged a similar position, going as far as to argue that mathematics can be used to teach children about the cause of social justice. Topics to study could include the government budget, the meaning of a national debt, the economics of sweatshops, the unequal distribution of wealth, or the long-term effects of a proposal such as the privatization of Social Security (Gutstein and Peterson, 2005). Understanding issues such as environmental protection, nuclear energy, defense spending, space exploration, and taxation requires high achievement in mathematics (National Council of Teachers of Mathematics, 1989). Thus, the academic merges, in some sectors of the curriculum, with the socio-civic.

Along these lines, we could begin to see certain formations in the curriculum encouraging the commingling of academic and socio-civic goals. "Academic" goals in social studies might result in a course on the problems of democracy. In science, a course dedicated to exploring environmental or health problems might be offered. In mathematics, a series of courses that deal with understanding sociological phenomena through quantitative means could be planned. And in English, the possibilities of linking the examination of literature to the social conditions of humankind are virtually endless.

Teaching for Vocational Growth

Part of the conventional wisdom about public schooling speaks to its importance in equipping youth with the skills, competencies, and attitudes needed to perform successfully in labor markets. At the college or university level, "vocational" programs exist for the preparation of accountants, educators, engineers, economists, social workers, musicians, and physicists. In secondary schools, vocational programs exist in relation to employment in the agricultural, health, trade, and industrial sectors. Such programs have long been situated in comprehensive school settings, although one can also sometimes find them in separate technical schools, usually rationalized as magnet schools.

Vocational education is a phenomenon that applies mostly to middle school and high school settings. Middle schools have traditionally offered courses in the prevocational arts in an attempt to offer youth an opportunity to learn something about vocational life-skills. These are typically viewed as exploratory courses that give preadolescents an early exposure to either consumer education courses or general labor preparation courses. The possibilities could also include home economics courses, any courses related to food and nutrition, family and social relationships, personal development, or even beginning courses in prevocational development, such as drafting, basic motor mechanics, and carpentry.

In the secondary school, however, a good share of the vocational education program becomes more specialized and more closely associated with the education of youth not destined for higher education. Vocational education in the American high school is usually organized along three different orientations: occupational labor market preparation, general market preparation, and family and consumer education (NCES, 2000). Each orientation speaks for itself, as occupational preparation takes on a specificity particular to occupations or sets of occupations (including agriculture, business, marketing, health care, protective services, trade and industry, food service and hospitality, child care, and education), while general labor preparation consists of courses that teach general employment skills, such as uses of technology and keyboarding. Family and consumer science is naturally more of a general education offering, intended to prepare students for their roles as family members and consumers.

A wide range of critics has questioned the placement of vocational education in the comprehensive school design. Conservatives generally argue that vocational programs are anti-intellectual, too costly, and without much value in the actual job market. They also claim that opportunities to enjoy a rigorous academic education are lost on students who participate heavily in vocational education programs. Other critics argue that vocational education is too specialized and too slow to respond to changes in the technological and occupational conditions of the marketplace. As a result, they criticize vocational education for restricting student career opportunities. Vocational education students, they claim, may become solely trained as, say, welders and nothing else, which gives them little flexibility in the job market, and consequently, more restricted options for social and economic advancement. In this manner, vocational education, which is largely populated by students from lower socio-economic sectors of the society, is seen as a mechanism that perpetuates the socio-economic status quo. Participation rates in vocation education indeed demonstrate relatively high levels of enrollment of students who attend high poverty schools, but they also show high levels of enrollment from males, students with disabilities, low academic achievers, and graduates from rural schools (NCES, 2000).

But the economic consequences of vocational education demonstrate some positive economic effects for those pursuing occupational courses. Seven years after graduation from high school, for example, students earned about 2 percent more for each extra high school occupational course they took (NCES, 2000). These economic benefits continued into postsecondary vocational education, which also produced a positive yield on earnings for the vast majority of participants, depending on how much course work was completed. The past practice of denying students in vocational programs access to rigorous academic programs seems to be easing. During the 1990s, for instance, high school students in occupational programs took more academic courses than in the past, with the effect of narrowing the academic credit gap between those who are in occupational programs and those who took little or no vocational education. The widest consequence of this change could be seen in the postsecondary transition rates for vocational students, which have increased dramatically. National trend data show that higher proportions of students in occupational programs are now enrolling in some form of postsecondary education or training than in the past, although the vocational education students still have relatively low participation rates in four-year colleges and universities (NCES, 2000).

The vocational macro-feature of the comprehensive school is the least pervasive feature in the practice of the school. Although most classroom teachers would likely agree that they have some influence in shaping the attitudes of students toward work by helping to teach children to be responsible, to meet deadlines, and to have some pride in their workmanship, these are nevertheless relatively subtle features of the planned school experience. In middle school, however, one could often find a more obvious exposure to a vocational orientation in the course work. Usually the school will at least identify exploratory courses that deal with family or consumer issues or even with the development of some prevocational skill. And in high school, vocational education becomes largely a matter of occupational preparation for those not planning to attend a four-year college.

SUMMARY

The American national school system is structurally decentralized and empowered at the state level, allowing state jurisdictions to have the final say on how local school districts should be supervised. This makes it difficult to generalize about the nature of schooling in the United States. Historically speaking, however, the schools across the fifty states have abided by a loose set of principles and goals. Among them is a general commitment to a unified system of schooling that houses all students, irrespective of their post-secondary plans, in one common facility. Such a unified arrangement is not typical in the school systems of advanced nations. American schools have also embraced a de facto set of national goals that have had the support of parents and school leaders. These goals are part of a comprehensive school design that aims to equip all American youth with the general skills, competencies, knowledge, attitudes, values, and outlooks that they need to conduct intelligent, fulfilling, and empowering lives as individuals, as workers, and as citizens. Education for academic and intellectual growth has an undeniably significant place on such an agenda, but objectives more intimately attached to personal, civic, and vocational learning also have their place. And school teachers, aware of the comprehensive program of goals, continue to look for ways to give life to this comprehensive program, both in the classroom and in the structural design of the curriculum.

REFERENCES

Butts, R. F. (1989). *The civic mission of educational reform.* Stanford, CA: Hoover Institute Press.

Conant, J. B. (1959). *The American high school today.* New York: McGraw-Hill.

Cremin, L. A. (1965). *The genius of American education.* New York: Vintage Books.

Delefatorre, J. (2004). *The fourth R.* Yale University Press.

Dewey, J. (1916). *Democracy and education.* New York: Macmillan.

Frasz, C., & Kato, K. (1999). The educational structure of the Japanese school system. In H. W. Stevenson, R. Nerison-Low, & S.-Y. Lee (eds.), *Contemporary research in the United States, Germany, and Japan on four educational issues: Standards in education, the role of school in adolescents' lives, individual differences among students, and teachers' lives.* Washington, DC: Department of Education.

Goodlad, J. I. (1984). *A place called school.* New York: McGraw-Hill.

Gutstein, E., and Peterson, B. (2005). *Rethinking mathematics.* Milwaukee, WI: Rethinking Schools.

Irons, P. (2004). *Jim Crow's children.* New York, NY: Penguin Books.

Kliebard, H. M. (1986). *The struggle for the American curriculum.* New York: Routledge and Kegan Paul.

National Center for Education Statistics. (1993). *120 years of American education: A statistical portrait.* Washington, DC: Department of Education.

National Center for Education Statistics. (2000). *Vocational education in the United States: Toward the year 2000.* Washington, DC: Department of Education.

National Center for Education Statistics. (2002). *Overview and inventory of state education reforms: 1990–2000.* Washington, DC: Department of Education.

National Center for Education Statistics. (2002a). *Digest of education statistics.* Washington, DC: Department of Education.

National Council of Teachers of English and the International Reading Association. (1996). *Standards for the English language arts.* Washington, DC: NCTE.

National Council of Teachers of Mathematics. (1989). *Curriculum and evaluation standards for school mathematics.* Reston, VA: NCTM.

National Science Teachers Association. (1982). *Science technology and society.* Washington, DC: United States Government Printing Office.

Public Agenda. (2003). *Rolling up their sleeves: Superintendents and principals talk about what's needed to fix public schools.* New York: NY: Public Agenda.

Rickover, H. G. (1959). *Education and freedom.* New York: E. P. Dutton and Co.

Schlesinger, A. (1998). *The disuniting of America.* New York, NY: W. W. Norton and Co.

Sizer, T. R. (1984). *Horace's compromise.* Boston: Houghton-Mifflin Co.

Tanner, D., & Tanner, L. N. (1995). *Curriculum development, 3rd ed.* New York: Macmillan Co.

Tyack, D. (1978). Ways of seeing: An essay on the history of compulsory schooling. In Donald Warren, *History, education, and public policy.* Berkeley, CA: McCutchan Publishing Company.

Ward, L. (1883). *Dynamic sociology.* New York: Appleton.

KEY QUESTIONS

1. What is the normative agenda of the school? Who decides what is normative?

2. How can the public schools be regulated at the state level and still abide by some sense of national goals?

3. What is the American unified system of schooling and how does it differ from a dual or bipartite system? What is the rationale for a unified system?

4. In 1959, Rickover criticized the American comprehensive high school for promoting a *soft* and anti-intellectual education: "In the American comprehensive high school, he stated, the pupils find a display of courses resembling the variegated dishes in a cafeteria. No wonder he often gorges himself on sweets instead of taking solid meat that must be chewed" (p. 143). What do you think of Rickover's metaphor? Is this a criticism that bears any resemblance to the experience you might have had in a comprehensive high school?

5. James B. Conant's view of the comprehensive school was linked to democracy. In the *American High School Today* (1959), he wrote: "I think it is safe to say that the comprehensive high school is characteristic of our society and further that it has come into being because of our economic history and our devotion to the ideals of equality of opportunity and equality of status" (p. 8). What do you think about these observations? Is the unified school arrangement vital to our democracy?

6. In 1984, Theodore Sizer acknowledged his antipathy toward the American comprehensive high school in his widely read *Horace's Compromise*. "High schools cannot be comprehensive and should to try to be comprehensive," he declared. "Helping students to use their minds is a large enough assignment." What is Sizer's message? Do you agree that by being comprehensive, the high school takes on too much and is therefore likely to compromise on the education of the mind, what we might see as the intellectual-academic goals of the school curriculum?

7. What are the four main objectives in a school committed to offering youth a comprehensive education? Explain their purposes.

8. What are the main differences between the way that the elementary school and the high school might deal with individual needs in the curriculum?

9. What are some classroom possibilities for an elementary school teacher wanting to reflect the individual needs and interests of her students?

10. From your own experience as a student or as a student teacher, can you identify how socio-civic skills were taught in your school? Was there a common core of studies dedicated to the socio-civic curriculum?

11. If you were asked to redesign the high school or elementary school you attended, what might you do to better fulfill the comprehensive school agenda?

12. Think of a conceptual outline for an elementary school unit or a secondary school course dedicated to using mathematical skills for promoting socio-civic understanding.

13. Why are specialized courses much less necessary in elementary and middle schools than in high schools?

14. Participation in vocational education programs at the high school level decreases as graduates' socioeconomic status, academic ability, and high school grades increases (NCES, 2000, p. xxii). Do you see this as a problem? Why or why not?

15. What have been the main criticisms against vocational education in a comprehensive high school?

16. Some reformers believe that vocational education is better placed at the post-secondary level, leaving the high school to focus on the other three major objectives in the curriculum. What do you think of such a reform? *Are* there general limitations or general strengths to the idea?

RESEARCH EXERCISES

1. Examine state by state differences in school policy and schooling funding. You could find good data on state regulatory differences in the National Center for Educational Statistics website (nces.ed.gov). Which are the most regulatory and least regulatory states in your view? Which ones have the highest and lowest cost-adjusted per-pupil expenditures? Which states have the highest and lowest average achievement scores in reading and math? Can you find any relationship between the factors of regulation, expenditure, and/or achievement?

2. Examine how the school system of the United States compares to schools of other advanced nations. Select one other nation and focus on how it differs from the United States by finding data on achievement, means of institutional regulation, classroom dynamics, teacher preparedness, educational expenditure, and so forth. Target one or two areas of significant difference. A good place to start this inquiry is on the National Center for Educational Statistics website (nces.ed.gov), the national ministry of education sites for other nations, the OECD's Programme for International Student Assessment (pisa.oecd.org), and Unesco (unesco.org).

CHAPTER 2

The Teacher and the Classroom

As John Dewey once observed, we are all born to be teachers as we are not born to be engineers or sculptors. His point was that teaching is preeminently a social act, one that attaches itself to life situations and to people. Thus, to be human is, in many ways, to be a teacher. The very sustenance of society depends on its capacity to learn from itself and to encourage a sense of social mutuality and social progress.

Today much of the teaching/learning process has been formalized in an institution we call school. Scholars of schooling have not hesitated to use dramatic language to characterize the high purpose of the school. One could find references to the school as the main building block of democracy, as the great leveler of inequalities, as the chief agency for social improvement, and as the one public experience deliberately designed to give youth a cosmopolitan understanding of the world. Teachers, of course, become the main workers in the fulfillment of the public school agenda. Close to fifty million public school children in America can attest to this fact.

But education is not always a matter of schooling. Families, churches, and various special interest groups also carry educating agendas. In all cases, teachers, albeit of a different sort, are needed to get the job done. Thus, we find the skills of an educator manifesting obviously in the role of parent, spouse, sibling, citizen, worker, friend, and colleague. The native capacity for teaching exists, to varying degrees, in all of us. It is part of our humanity.

Professional school teaching, however, especially in the context of public schools, occupies a unique mandate. It is, without exaggerating, allied with arguably one of the most important tasks facing our society: the enlightenment of an immature generation of youth for informed participation in society. Although various people have some role to play in this task, professional teachers are intentionally placed in the role of realizing this mandate. We expect them to teach our children how to read, how to be numerate, how to be good citizens, and so forth. We also expect teachers to be role models for ethical and moral behavior, wise counselors, fair-minded authorities, gatekeepers of knowledge, and ultimately professionals whose judgments in the school are always justified by some consideration of the learner in the context of the highest purposes of the society.

The very virtue of the teaching profession, in fact, resides in these actions. Other professions, of course, have their own claim on virtue. Doctors save lives and attend to our health and physical well-being. Lawyers act in the interests of justice and rule of law. Engineers help build our infrastructure. But all of these professionals have necessarily had teachers in their lives—often public school teachers—who helped to move them toward the development of their particular professional skills and their life skills as citizens and family members. The dignity in the calling of a teacher is reflected in its commitment to social service, in its dedication to the long-term project of educating the upcoming generation in a way that will ensure a better future and make life better for those who are yet to be born.

CLASSROOM LIFE

The teacher is always the final arbiter of what occurs in the classroom. As a result, teachers face considerable pressure from forces external to the classroom seeking to influence their judgments. Pressures to raise test scores, to be responsive to state or local standards, to follow the latest pedagogic fad, and to honor parental and community wishes all push up against the classroom door. Whether these pressures find their way into the classroom and actually affect the school experience depends on the teacher who, in the final analysis, decides what gets taught and how it gets taught. Naturally, teachers cannot do whatever they please. They are required to be attentive to district and state policy, to execute professionally defensible judgments and to follow a curriculum that will protect the equal opportunity to learn. But teachers are not simple functionaries whose job is to follow an instructional script or someone else's instructional orders. We expect them to exercise intelligence and creativity in the classroom and to regulate their actions through a professional rationale. As Dewey (1904) once observed, teachers "should be given to understand that they are not only permitted to act on their own initiative, but that they are expected to do so, and that their ability to take on a situation for themselves would be more important in judging them than their following any particular set method or scheme." Needless to say, the freedom to think according to a professional rationale is fundamental to the development of educational environments for the nation's schoolchildren.

Over the years, schoolteachers have been criticized—sometimes appropriately—for their failure to bring innovation and instructional variance to the classroom. Teachers have been frequently faulted for using a stale and uniform methodology. This, however, is not a completely fair appraisal. Considerable variance, both within and between public schools, exists in the teaching styles and teaching approaches of school teachers, something that most of us have probably witnessed in our own experiences as students. Understanding the complexity of the situation in which they are placed, most teachers exercise varied educational strategies in the classroom, often basing their decisions on the context and character of the school, the community, and the student population.

We know, in fact, that the act of teaching varies according to situational conditions. Generally speaking, a high school teacher of mathematics will engage in teaching approaches that vary, often considerably, from a teacher of, say, social studies or science. Math teachers, for instance, spend more time working with individual students than social studies teachers (Henke, Chen, & Goldman, 1999), while science teachers are more apt to integrate projects, experiments, and exploratory investigations in their classrooms (National Center for Education Statistics, 1997, p. 64). Similarly, teachers in elementary schools engage in classroom actions that vary from the secondary school teacher. Children in elementary school classrooms, much more so than their secondary school counterparts, work individually on projects, spend time on small group instruction, and collectively discuss work done in small groups (Henke, Chen, & Goldman, 1999). But the situational context goes even deeper. Instructional decisions will also be influenced by variables related to family status, income, and ethnicity, as well as individual factors related to disability, aptitude, and maturation. Teachers rarely treat students in exactly the same ways because there is no universal line of best fit between a particular approach toward teaching and the considerable scatter plot of differences represented in the demography of the student population. Teachers bear the professional responsibility of acknowledging the individuality brought to the classroom by students and of making appropriate instructional adjustments, understanding that no particular approach toward teaching is necessarily suitable for all students.

To begin to understand the nuances of classroom life, one must acknowledge the social dynamics and cultural calculus resident in classrooms. Take, for instance, the nature of the social arrangement in a typical classroom. The teacher, in most instances, is locked into set periods of interaction with groups of students in what amounts to be relatively small physical spaces. The entire group (students and teachers alike) is enjoined in what Jackson called a daily grind of activity that the teacher, in the end, must organize, implement and supervise. Jackson (1968) describes the classroom as an unparalleled social arrangement our society:

> Buses and movie theaters may be more crowded than classrooms, but people rarely stay in such densely populated settings for extended periods of time and while there, they usually are not expected to concentrate on work or to interact with each other. Even factory workers are not clustered as close together as students *in* a standard classroom. Indeed, imagine what would happen if a factory the size of a typical elementary school contained three or four hundred adult workers. In all likelihood the unions would not allow it. Only in schools do thirty or more people spend several hours each day literally side by side. Once we leave the classroom we seldom again are required to have contact with so many people for so long a time (p. 8).

Together in one space for the long haul of an academic year, teachers and students have no choice but to create a community of understanding in the classroom. Not surprisingly, such a necessity ultimately leads to the framing of classroom rules and regulations. Anyone who has ever taught school understands how vulnerable the classroom is to being undermined. One student can easily scuttle a teacher's best laid plans. And to get anything accomplished, the entire classroom has to exercise considerable cooperation and individual restraint. This might explain why teachers often find the reality of exercising control and authority in the classroom to be among the most difficult features of their job. Failure to control a classroom is still the most commonly cited reason for the dismissal of teachers. Without control, the teacher cannot secure the teaching agenda and cannot get to the matter of using the student's strengths, weaknesses, and interests for educational gain. Thus, finding a way to exercise authority and direction in the classroom without resorting to iron fist methods (while still ensuring some responsiveness to individual differences) is a complex and ongoing challenge for the teacher. The most interesting aspect of this challenge is that each classroom reveals a dynamic that requires different strategies for different sites. As indicated, generic strategies have little standing in the real classroom lives of teachers.

The proximity and the frequency of social interactions in the classroom also give the teacher a unique place in the lives of children. The teacher accumulates an enormous amount of contact time with students, sometimes even more than the students' parents, and hence has an impressive visibility in the student's life. The authoritative stature of teachers in the lives of students, especially very young children, is usually so powerfully linked to school that many students have trouble seeing their teachers in any other light. Younger students often express surprise when they see their teachers out of a school context, when they witness them, say, shopping for groceries or gassing up their car. Such actions, in the eyes of the students, must be too mundane for someone as important as a school teacher.

The point is that teaching simply cannot be reduced to the act of preparing and executing explicitly rationalized lessons and other instructional events. Teachers are the principal actors on the social stage of the school, which means that there is an expectation that in everything they do, teachers must aim at an educational benefit. This is another way of saying that a teacher is always teaching in the classroom, not just when they are executing formal lessons. Because of a role-model expectation, the community's eyes are on the teacher even outside of school hours and off school grounds. This is the case because teaching messages accompany virtually everything the teacher does. These messages exist in the rectitude of the teacher's own behaviors (both inside and outside of the classroom), in the manner in which teachers respond to student questions and concerns, and in the general interactive pattern between teachers and students (the tone of a teacher's voice, the style of his or her body language, the language used and favored in the classroom, the forms of affection, if any, conveyed, and so forth). These implicit ways of teaching are the processes that we associate with what is often referred to as the latent curriculum, an idea we will discuss in the next chapter. Implicit teaching lives in the thousands of interactions that occur between teachers and students each school day.

The nature of classroom life should also reflect an outreach to individual differences. A teacher who uses only a frontal expository method of whole group teaching fails to take good account of classroom dynamics. Variance is the key to good teaching. The deeper the reservoir of instructional insight, the greater the possibilities of finding an adequate instructional approach suited to different individuals and different purposes. In this sense, variety is not simply the spice of the instructional side of the curriculum, it is the very essence of it. Pratt (1994) made the same point when he asserted that only "variety can absorb variety," meaning that the action of the classroom depends on the presence of strategies varied enough to deal with the variety of purposes in the system.

PLANNED AND EMERGENT DECISIONS

To completely understand the nature of teacher judgment in the classroom, it is useful to make an analytical separation between decisions that are planned and decisions that are emergent in the classroom. We could do this effectively by making a distinction between the idea of instruction and the idea of pedagogy.

Instruction refers to a planned course of learning experiences, designed and justified by the teacher, which aims to fulfill the purposes of the school curriculum. A teacher's decision to use methodology x in order to fulfill a set of central purposes or objectives is principally an instructional decision. If, for instance, various socio-personal skills were viewed as important targets for a history course, an instructional response that favored methodologies suited to such targets (such as cooperative learning techniques, inquiry-based activities, and other methods that value interactive engagements) would logically follow. Any deliberate rationalization for the application of a particular teaching strategy, such as the design of a lesson plan, is a planned event that qualifies as instruction.

Pedagogy, on the other hand, is what actually happens when teachers begin to teach, when they begin to interact with students and conduct or implement the planned instructional experience. It is what we might view as the emergent or expressive side of teaching. We witness pedagogy in the spontaneous and situationally-bound behaviors of teachers. We see it, for instance, in the nuances of a teacher's questioning techniques, in the manner in which feedback is offered to students, in the modeling of certain behaviors, in the nature of the conversations had between the teacher and the students, and in the general way that social behaviors are handled in the classroom. Pedagogy is the very behavior that leads teachers to embrace what Eisner (1998) calls expressive goals or expressive outcomes in the curriculum. These are the goals and activities that rise-up from the experience itself. Expressive goals represent situational or emergent decisions in the curriculum that, unlike instruction, are generally not preplanned and are mostly impossible to anticipate.

Let's think about the planned side or instructional side of the classroom first. The planning feature of the classroom has to account for a wide range of activities. Lessons have to be designed, independent activities have to be assigned, various problems, ranging from the social dynamics of interaction in the classroom to the nature of student aptitude and student weaknesses, have to be understood and integrated into the working routines of the classroom. Instruction has to be planned because teachers have some obligation to teach the content expected to be taught in the curriculum and to cultivate the sets of skills, values, and appreciations that the school embraces. If, for instance, the school mandate includes teaching children how to read, or how to solve mathematical equations, or how to strengthen their critical thinking and persuasive writing skills, then the school curriculum has an obligation to ensure that all children gain an equal opportunity to learn these skills. Thus, it is clear that, although teachers plan and implement instructional events in the classroom, they must accept some direction from the curriculum and plan accordingly. Such planning implies that the school has a coherent mandate and that the teacher is reflective about what happens in the classroom and does not simply approach each school day in an impulsive manner.

As mentioned, the decision to use one type of methodology over another is an example of an instructional decision. This is a decision that belongs exclusively to the teacher. It is a large component of what teachers get paid to do. The planned instructional features of the classroom experience represent decisions teachers make to actualize the objectives of the curriculum (the content, skills, and values that need to be taught). Teachers do this by designing lessons or a series of lesson plans, as well as by planning extension activities, independent assignments, and other related activities.

Good teachers also have a strong sense of the emergent condition in the classroom and are able to think and act on their feet in accordance with the objectives of the curriculum and the best interests of the learner. These are largely pedagogical judgments. It is important to note that, in the end, the implementation of the curriculum (its very life in the classroom) is a pedagogical matter. This means that the action of teaching is largely an emergent phenomenon, which underscores the fact that answers to questions about how to proceed in a classroom cannot be found in manuals or universal declarations about what constitutes good teaching (particular lesson designs, or some invariant models of so-called effective teaching). The answers are in the emergent judgments of the teacher, who is naturally obligated to follow some instructional plan but who also understands that the "right" decision in a classroom depends on weighing factors related to the nature of the child, to available resources, to the defined purposes in the curriculum, to available evaluative evidence, and to a raft of other variables residing in the educational situation. Schwab (1983) described the situation:

> There are thousands of ingenious ways in which commands on what and how to teach can, will and must be modified or circumvented in the actual moments of teaching... Moments of choice of what to do, how to do it, and whom and at what pace, arise hundreds of times a school day and arise differently every day and with every group of students. No command or instruction can be so formulated as to control that kind of artistic judgment and behavior, with its demand for frequent, instant choices of ways to meet an ever varying situation (p. 245).

Doyle (1990) reinforced Schwab's point by showing how teaching is marked by overlapping levels of multidimensionality, simultaneity, unpredictability, and immediacy, which leave the teachers with ample on-the-spot decisions. Just think of all the factors that come together at once in an elementary school classroom. Walk into an elementary school classroom and you might see some students working in different ability groups, while others are working individually or in small groups. Yet other students might be temporarily out of the classroom, perhaps receiving ESL instruction or gifted and talented instruction. When they return, some way will have to be found to ensure that they know what they missed and what assignments might need to get completed. The teacher, for her part, will likely be involved with a student or a set of students, while keeping a vigilant eye on the whole classroom and noting whether the students outside of her immediate proximity are engaged and pursuing their independent work assignments.

If the teacher begins to teach, say, a reading group, she must also be sure that everyone else in engaged in thoughtful pursuits, while also handling the possibility that disciplinary problems might arise, that students will need to be excused to go the bathroom, that some students might be confused by something in their assignments, or might otherwise be distracted and off task. All of this has the potential of happening all at once. Jackson (1968) reports that teachers have something like a thousand interactions with students each day. Many of these occur virtually simultaneously and demand an immediate response. Those of us who have taught school know what it is like to feel the effects of having intervened and dealt with literally hundreds of situations with children in the span of one day. It is exhausting work.

Teachers also understand that everything that is worth doing in a school does not have to emerge from a plan. Eisner (1998) articulated the idea of expressive goals to describe events in the classroom that have no explicit or manifest plan or objective. The reference to the term *goal* is slightly confusing here because of the convention of equating the idea of a goal with a preplanned event. What we have to try to imagine is a teacher embracing new and unanticipated goals as they materialize in the heat of classroom action, usually in response to some situational nuance. Decisions to take a student, or more generally an entire classroom, in an unforeseen teaching direction can be influenced by a teacher's intuition, by a desire to remedy an emergent problem, or by an effort to attend to interest levels. The intention of expressive goals is to inject something valuable in the experience that was not part of the preplanned sequence of instructional events.

Expressive goals are important to the classroom because they give the school experience important flexibility while also honoring the professional judgment of the teacher. They are the main ways that teachers can honestly respond to the particularities of the classroom situation. To have expressive goals is to have a classroom whose teachers are on the lookout for what others have referred to as a teachable moment: a point in time that surfaces in the classroom and presents itself as worthy of continued discussion and examination. Expressive goals can also manifest as efforts to individualize the school experience for children—as efforts, in other words, rationalized by an understanding of individual needs and interests (as they express themselves in the life of the classroom). The pedagogy of the teacher is very much shaped by expressive goals, by decisions to venture from routine, or from some other preplanned event, in order to pursue something that is viewed as educative.

LEVELS OF CLASSROOM PERFORMANCE

Teaching can be analytically categorized into three main levels of classroom performance (Tanner & Tanner, 1995). Level I, known as imitative-maintenance, is the most simplistic. It is marked by routine and adoptive practices. Activities could be scripted by teacher manuals, delimited by closed instructional systems, or otherwise dumbed down by a regard to "teach to the test." The notion that learning is based on emergent conditions is not part of the instructional calculation. Level II, known as mediative, registers at a higher professional scale because it represents a movement away from simple maintenance and adoption, and a movement toward refinements or adjustments based on some awareness of the unique features of the classroom. Level II, in essence, is an acknowledgment that teaching is not solely a pre-fashioned affair that leaves the teacher with little more to do than follow someone else's instructional plan. Finally, Level III, generative-creative, stands as the highest ideal of professionalism because it defines teaching as a problem-solving process that requires the teacher to make judgments based on the widest school purposes and the evaluation of learning needs.

These three levels are not designed as developmental levels for teachers. No professional growth theory points to the conclusion that teachers must start at Level I, and with experience, move to Level III. All teaching professionals, novices and veterans alike, should be working at Level III, but various factors related to school policy and experience will obviously have some hand in determining how successful a teacher might be in working at this level.

Level I: Imitative-Maintenance

Teachers who work at this level usually see the classroom in pure management terms. Reliant on routine activities that keep children busy, Level I teachers readily use pre-made commercial materials in the interests of keeping good classroom order. Because of the concern for smooth operations, the classroom experience is largely reduced to lower-level exercises and lower skill development. The idea of problem-focused inquiry or idea-centered learning poses a methodological concern to this teacher because it requires some assessment of the classroom condition and some imaginative planning that goes on outside the lines of the textbook or workbook.

Teachers operating at Level I are quasi-technicians, whose main function in the classroom is to carry out the instructional directions of a prescribed system of learning. The dominance of competency-based instruction, mastery learning, teacher proof materials, and programmed instruction all testifies to a Level I condition. Such instructional systems tend to reduce the teacher's role in the classroom to its most rudimentary and routine elements. The main duties of the teacher in such a context usually revolve around clerical acts, mostly handing out worksheets and exams in proper sequence, documenting the results, and keeping the children on task. Under these conditions, the teacher, as one could tell, has a limited instructional and pedagogical role.

Level I teachers are also more prone to teach-to-the-test than teachers working at a higher level of professional development. Any teacher inclined to engage in the most blatant form of teaching-to-the-test, such as taking past exam items and teaching directly to the items, is operating at Level I. The use of reflective intelligence in the classroom to make adjustments in teaching based on interactions in the curriculum and on emerging knowledge of the learner is lost at Level I. Classroom assessment for the purpose of diagnosing of learner weaknesses (with the presumption of making instructional corrections) essentially does not exist.

Level II: Mediative

Level II represents some professional awareness of the situational context of the classroom. As a result, it is a considerable jump up from Level I. Teachers at the mediative level only make partial use of their classroom awareness, limiting their decisions to certain refinements and adaptations. Thus, one could find, among Level II teachers, some of the very instructional strategies supported by Level I teachers, but their strategies will likely be offered with some adaptations, in a way that shows some understanding of the situational context. A reliance on a competency-based method of learning, for instance, could still exist, but with some refinements. Teachers at Level II might note its effects in the classroom and make adjustments, such as skipping certain sections of the curriculum, adding supplementary materials here and there, or deciding to use another instructional approach together with the competency-based approach. Thus, one cannot expect any grand innovations in the curriculum from the teacher at Level II, but certain modest changes, justified by some consideration of the learner, will likely occur.

Many teachers working at the mediative level are held down by poor curriculum design. This is especially the case if a school district and certain superordinates in a teacher's professional life require the use of a closed and instructionally prescriptive curriculum. Thus, labored with a curriculum that constricts judgment, teachers could only, at their best, make some alterations or perhaps find the time to offer some alternative instructional approaches. Pressures to teach-to-the-test, to use certain textbooks, and to engage in instructional techniques favored by in-service training programs could have the same effect.

Level III: Creative-Generative

Level III represents the highest standard of professional actualization. At Level III, teaching is moved by the widest educational purposes of the school, not simply those that have priority on standardized tests or that are conveniently encapsulated in competency-based learning systems. Hence, classroom activity has a wide ranging quality to it, finding itself concerned not only with academic and intellectual skills, but also socio-civic attitudes, individual interests and talents, an array of thinking, communication, and inquiry skills, constructive attitudes toward learning, and so forth. Activities in the classroom are problem-focused and idea-centered, and are planned and operated through the creative judgment of the teacher, whose thinking is always inspired by some regard for the nature of the learner, the values of the society, and the knowledge embodied in the subject matter. The curriculum is organized in any number of ways but often reflects interconnections between ideas and between disciplines, and shows good articulation between grades or age levels.

The Level III teacher is fundamentally a diagnostician, who reflects on the classroom in ways that draw from a wealth of instructional and assessment strategies. The idea of assessment is especially important because it demonstrates that attention is being paid to whether instructional strategies are resulting in the kinds of effects desired. If they are not, the teacher (using experience, theory, and research) will make changes that will ultimately be retested in the experience of the classroom. Thus, the teacher at Level III must be a consumer of research and must have the authority to exercise independent judgment in selecting materials and methods. Teaching-to-the-test does not register here because no test could possibly privilege everything that the teacher would seek in the education of the learner. A generative-creative teacher very much relies on expressive goals because of the demand to diagnose classroom problems and convert them into problem solutions.

All of this underscores the dynamicity and complexity of the classroom situation, and the difficulties one encounters in trying to capture its essence with generalities. But, in acknowledging the dynamicity of the classroom, one must also come to terms with a general ground of commonality that constitutes what we might call professional knowledge. All teacher decision-making has to be enlivened by what one knows about learners, by how one sees the role of the school in the society, and by the capacity to organize knowledge and experience in a manner that serves the education of all youngsters. There is no one single way to behave when it comes to teaching, but there is a principled sense of what it means to be an educator and what it means to make professionally-justifiable decisions.

SOURCES FOR PROFESSIONAL DECISION-MAKING

What do teachers need to know to make professionally-defensible decisions? The progressive educational literature provides a clear signal by highlighting the importance of three key sources: 1) the nature of the learner, 2) the values and aims of the society, and 3) the world of knowledge represented in organized subject matter (Tanner & Tanner, 1995). These three factors, when taken together, represent a working framework for teacher judgment. Combined, the factors force the educator to weight their decisions in light of the learners' interests and developmental needs, in the spirit of democratic values and skills and in regard to some sense of what is worthy knowledge.

The Nature of the Learner

Accounting for the nature of the learner essentially means holding the teacher responsible for making some effort to respond to the interests and living conditions of students as well as to the literature on how students learn. The net effect should be a classroom that has some meaningful placement in the students' lives, that deals with age-appropriate issues and problems, and that identifies individual strengths and weaknesses.

Most of us, in fact, would think it wise for an educator to try to gain the learner's vantage point on educational matters, to try to see the world as the students themselves might see or experience it, and to attempt to otherwise connect the life of the school to the life of the learner. Moreover, knowledge of learners could help us decide the best time to teach a particular set of skills and the best way to sequence and organize instruction. It could give us insight on readiness and pacing and provide us with the instructional advantage of knowing individual strengths and weaknesses. Understanding the nature of the learner also reminds us of a vital instructional principle, which is that no two individuals develop in exactly the same way, and that intellectual capacity (as well as social, emotional, and physical maturity) are unevenly distributed across the student population and are all set to different biological clocks.

Such an understanding requires practical action. Teachers, for instance, might take an interest inventory of their students' interests and explore student community life with the aim of identifying prevailing group problems and needs. This is not just a matter of reflecting what children like to do, but trying to capture the broadest dimensions of a student's life (interests, problems, issues) in the curriculum. Such judgments not only help the teacher decide what should be taught, but they also provide important information on how certain skills, knowledge, and values should be taught.

Where group problems might arise, the effort to account for the nature of the learner might call for an investigative strategy. If middle school students, for instance, are found to be experimenting with cigarettes at some disconcerting rate, the teacher might look to the learner to try to find some insight. She might find that certain advertising gimmicks are preying on preadolescent social pressures, that peer pressures are exerting a strong pull, that the children who are smoking have parents who smoke, and that no fundamental conception exists among the students about the facts of lung cancer. These locally derived insights could then color the instructional strategy in the area of teaching about the dangers of smoking, or in the more general area of health care. A curriculum plan might include objectives dedicated to learning about the facts of lung cancer, and learning about the tactics of Madison Avenue advertisers. Instructional strategies might stress peer pressure scenarios that provide students working handles of action and group projects that involve the participation of parents (smokers and nonsmokers alike).

Sometimes the investigative effort might be driven by certain professional priorities regarding the teaching of particular skills. Thus, the teacher of reading might want to know what children are reading, if anything, at home, how often they are reading outside of school, and where they are reading. Insight into these questions could very much shape instructional tactics that aim to instill children with a love for reading. It might also offer the teacher some insight into what should be read in class.

Hence, examining circulation rates at the school library, taking reading interest inventories from children, asking parents to provide information on home reading behaviors, and noting the genre of reading interest among certain children all become potential sources for better responsiveness to the learner in reading instruction.

Responsiveness to the learner also means that teachers might scan the psychological literature to find insight on the developmental processes in teaching school children. Different-aged learners operate at qualitatively different levels of thinking and are under different social and biological pressures. The psychological literature in these areas might have solid implications for the construction of motivation in the classroom, and for the development of lesson plans and learning objectives. Where a particular learning problem might arise in an individual, the effort to account for the nature of the learner might reveal a disability or a remediable deficiency.

The effort to respond to the nature of the learner brings the teacher face to face with the literature on developmental processes, the nature of human intelligence, and the character of cognitive and affective processes in learning. In recent years, for instance, researchers have offered new conceptions about intelligence and learning that assist the teacher's chances of educating the whole child. Howard Gardner's work on multiple intelligences (1983) has allowed teachers and administrators to expand their notions of intelligence to include actions and processes not typically recognized in traditional versions of intelligence. These include a range of intelligences that account for linguistic, musical, logical-mathematical, spatial, bodily kinesthetic, interpersonal, and intrapersonal competence. The effect of Gardner's work puts a broad scope of intelligence on an equal ground, which in turn points to the need for schools to attend to all of the abilities implied by these multiple intelligences, as opposed to the linguistic and mathematical traditions that are typically stressed in the schools. Intelligence viewed in such a manner should be considered part of what we associate as belonging to the nature of the learner. Similarly, Benjamin Bloom's work on cognitive and affective processes (Bloom, 1956; Krathwohl, Bloom, & Masia, 1964), which provides teachers with working taxonomies that can be used to bring out a wider range of cognitive and affective variation in the classroom, and Piaget's (1950) work on developmental processes, provide insight that allows a teacher to make the case for certain teaching strategies as they might be justified for certain learners.

Accounting for the learner also means being conscious of meeting a hierarchy of basic needs. Maslow (1962) described the hierarchy, arguing that the most fundamental needs were physiological ones (i.e., sleep and food), followed by a succession of needs that included safety, love and acceptance, self-esteem, and self-actualization. This was Maslow's way of saying that children who come to school tired or hungry will not likely be able to learn. Maslow's work underscored the rationale for the Congressional authorization of the National School Lunch Act, which provides free or reduced breakfast and lunch to needy children. The linkage between the need for proper physical nutrition and the cognitive and social development of young children has of course been established for many years. The implications of Maslow's work, however, go deeper than meeting physiological requirement because of the value that he placed on needs related to safety, love and affection, and self-esteem. Children who attend school where safety is an issue or who have to deal with some form of dislocation in the home (i.e., an impending divorce between parents or a family illness), or who live in homes where love and acceptance might be in short supply, will have their schooling compromised. Similarly, a child who is roundly rejected or ridiculed by his peers, for whatever reasons, will not be positioned to succeed in school. Thus, the teacher has a role to play in regulating these factors.

The Values and Aims of Society

The source described as the values and aims of society provides direction on judgments related to the kinds of knowledge, skills, and values that students should be taught in school. It also influences the process of teaching by reminding the teacher that schooling is fundamentally moved by a social democratic theory and by some expression of hope for the kind of society we aim to have.

The source of society points to the need to teach certain values and certain kinds of skills in the actual life of the classroom. These values and skills transcend subject matter lines. For example, all teachers, regardless of what they are teaching, should have some consciousness of democratic processes and values in their teaching. These values might include objectives related to, say, group cooperation. With such a concern in mind, the classroom teacher might try to get children to learn how to consider the consequences of their action in the lives of others, to learn to demonstrate critical tolerance for divergent viewpoints, to act with a faith in the worth of all individuals, and to offer help, when one can, to those who are most needy. Accounting for the values of society might lead to certain cognitive actions, such as teaching children to seek relevant information and alternative viewpoints, to support open and honest communication, to be able to obtain information from appropriate and various sources, to distinguish fact from opinion (reliable information from unreliable) and to detect logical errors, unstated assumptions, and unsupported statements. These actions are laden with democratic overtones. They are important for the education of all children in all places and thus represent an important source for teacher decision-making.

The source of society also takes us into questions about what is taught. As indicated, teachers do not have free rein over what they are supposed to teach, but they do have a certain instructional leeway that allows them to make certain linkages with ideas, problems, and issues that might be relevant to promoting a better understanding of society. Thus, the standard line of discipline-centered skills and knowledge in, say, a math, science, or history course can be taught in a context responsive to community or societal concerns. Quantitative reasoning, for instance, could become, at least partly, a method of social analysis; scientific knowledge, depending on its nature, could become understood in terms that show its application in the life experience.

All teachers cannot be active teachers of civics or social studies or even of democracy for that matter. But all teachers are required to conduct their classrooms in a manner attuned to the values and aims of our democracy. This means that all teachers, whether teaching kindergarten or in an advanced Calculus course, must think about the development of a wide range of skills and values. These might include the development of positive values toward self, social skills that encourage social responsibility and social cooperation, thinking skills that engage the intelligence and produce analytical and discerning minds, inquiry skills that promote making independent judgments based on the best available evidence, and communication skills that recognize the importance of clear and persuasive forms of writing and speaking. Just how these things will be taught, and the extent of their placement in the classroom, is a decision we leave to the teacher.

Subject Matter

The question of subject matter also has an undeniably significant place in the professional judgment of teachers. The responsiveness of the teacher to the source of subject matter is rooted in an educational demand to convey a world of knowledge to students—to bring useful ideas, concepts, generalizations, definitions, and facts to the school experience. Students, after all, need to be taught something, and selectively choosing just what knowledge to teach in the school is a profoundly important consideration for educators. For instance, the decision to include certain content or subject matter in the curriculum is one that is moved by the notion that some subject matter is more worthy and more important than other subject matter. In other words, when we say that x is worthy of the time and energy dedicated to studying it, we are also saying that we value x because we believe that our school children will be served by knowing it. Because the world of knowledge is so vast, each inclusion of content in the curriculum will likely displace something else, making it all that much more important that our selections are careful. Thus, the question of what content or what knowledge is most worthwhile in the experience of the school has been an enduring one for educators.

Subject matter decisions in the curriculum are also important from the standpoint of empowering students with useful and empowering knowledge. What we know has much to do with how we behave and with how successful we become at directing and controlling our own life destinies. Knowledge, in fact, is only knowledge to the extent that it induces intelligent action and results in an informed sense of meaning in the world—an evolving perspective on how best to go forward in life. To know is to be given an empowered capacity to do. The source of subject matter in the curriculum also represents a key principle in building a common culture for a society. To have a common culture, one needs a common language, common values, and a common cultural vocabulary. On this last matter, the subject matter of the curriculum makes an especially profound contribution. Our common vocabulary is forged by what we commonly learn in school. Hirsch (1987) refers to this body of knowledge as cultural literacy. The purpose behind cultural literacy is to facilitate a common discourse of social exchange and social understanding; it is a way to build units of community and social mutuality with shared bases of knowledge. Thus, the selection of content in the school curriculum is partly influenced by a normative project that defines and cultivates a national sense of literacy, or as Hirsch phrased it, "something every American should know."

Such a normative project reminds us that important cultural considerations are at work. The decision to teach English high school classes through literature drawn mostly from the Western canon reflects an overt enfranchisement of one set of writings over another and even the concomitant privileging of one cultural perspective over another. Can we say then that if we give Shakespeare a prominent place in the English curriculum that we are sending a message to school children about the important of white, male, European voices? It is something to think about. The school curriculum, especially the content of the curriculum, carries cultural weight. But part of the normative enterprise of the school is to transmit cultural knowledge, and given our nation's Western heritage, Shakespeare has an indisputable place at the nation's cultural table. The question becomes: How important is it to the school to invite a diverse audience of writers into the English classroom? To what extent, for instance, is the school prepared to see the teaching of English as a phenomenon that expresses cultural priorities? How important is it to screen or select the readings used in high school English class by noting and accounting for the gender, skin color, cultural background, and even social class status of the authors?

The role of subject matter as a source of teacher decision-making is slightly different from the others because of the visible authority of the state in the domain of content. The content of the curriculum is a normative concern. States and school districts often take an active hand in setting forth content requirements in the school. This means that often the teacher's main duty in relation to subject matter is to integrate it into the instructional design of the classroom in a way that reflects sensitivity to the other two sources. For example, in high school mathematics, a teacher will likely have very little liberty with the content of the curriculum. But, the teacher will still be expected to exercise considerable creativity and instructional judgment in teaching the appropriate mathematical content, in a way that is instructionally sound and attendant to other purposes accompanying the curriculum. And it goes without saying that the teacher is also expected to be thoroughly versed with the subject matter being taught.

WHAT IS AN EFFECTIVE TEACHER?

Historically speaking, the determination of effectiveness has been closely tied to purely instructional behaviors, to the "how" of teaching, and to the management of established techniques or methodologies. When focused solely on these kinds of instructional manipulations, the teacher's main concern is fixed on the mechanics of the lesson and its implementation. The result is that a teacher's sense of worth becomes associated with an ability to engage certain instructional manipulations. But good teaching requires insight beyond instructional methodology. Questions pertaining to the responsiveness of instruction to varied objectives or to some judgment of the fundamental educative character of the learning experience call for answers that goes beyond instructional methods.

The nature of the so-called teacher effectiveness literature illustrates this point. For many years now, researchers have been touting the importance of the principle of *time on task* in the classroom. It is, at its most superficial level, an unremarkable idea that espouses the need for teachers to keep learners engaged in classroom activities. Obviously engagement is a requisite condition for learning, but when such a principle stands at the forefront of how one views good teaching, potential problems can occur. To put it simply, all forms of engagement are not necessarily educative. Because the *time on task* dictum does nothing to highlight or underscore the qualitative character of the task, it is of limited value. Thus, a teacher might achieve high grades from supervisors in keeping children on task, but if the task itself is not educationally worthwhile, or if the task has no good linkage to key purposes in the school curriculum, the issue of student engagement is moot.

Another manifestation of the same problem emerges from the teacher effects research, which is research that has identified and promoted the value of certain universally "effective" instructional practices. Research findings indicate (to name a few generalizations) that effective teachers have high expectations for performance, that they convey enthusiasm in their teaching, and that they are vigilant about monitoring student work. When the term "effective" is used in this context, one needs to be able to show the criteria by which such a term is being operationally defined. The term "effective" is theoretically neutral. One could be "effective" at, say, thievery or murder. In the context of the effective teaching literature, the use of the term "effective" is tied into how well certain practices raise standardized test scores. The problem is that what one might do to raise test scores may not always lead to enlightened teaching. For instance, one teacher effectiveness researcher stated that "effective" teachers of disadvantaged pupils 1) ask "low level" questions; 2) tend not "to amplify, discuss or use pupil answers"; 3) "do not encourage pupil-initiated questions"; and 4) "give little feedback on pupil questions" (Medley, 1979). Another teacher effectiveness researcher stated that "effective" teachers of basic skills "ask questions at a low cognitive level so that students can produce many correct responses" (Rosenshine, 1978). A preoccupation with asking low-level questions might raise test scores on some basic skills exam (and is therefore judged to be effective teaching), but it comes at the expense of a vital and dynamic cognitive experience. To advise teachers against providing substantive feedback, or to encourage them to ask questions at a low cognitive level, all in the name of effectiveness, signifies the extent of the problem.

In-service training programs have sometimes shown a similar preoccupation with instructional technique. The Hunter (1980) approach is perhaps best known. Hunter's program, often referred to as the "Seven-Step Lesson" or the "Elements of Effective Instruction," was one of the most enduring features on the educational landscape during the 1980s and 1990s. The Hunter approach lists various structural elements of a lesson (anticipatory set, statement of objectives, careful monitoring for understanding, guided and independent practice, and a sense of closure) as the foundation for effective pedagogy. It dominated teacher in-service programs throughout American schools, affecting the thinking and behavior of thousands of teachers. Some school districts even went so far as to adopt the Hunter model as their choice for assessing teacher performance and staked it into promotion and salary decisions.

As one instructional method, the Hunter model is certainly worthy. On the other hand, if used as an exclusive instructional method, the Hunter model runs the risk of saying that a good teacher is someone who follows the step-by-step lesson design, irrespective of the nature of the objectives or purpose driving the curriculum. In such a way, the instructional elements of the lesson become the ends of a teacher's performance rather than the vital means toward securing an educative learning environment.

Interestingly, federal legislation, embodied in the No Child Left Behind Act, has recently carved out its own position on the nature of effective teaching, preferring to call it scientifically-based teaching. According to guidelines set down in NCLB, the education of public school children is best served by compelling school districts and individual schools to use scientifically-based programs and practices. The No Child Left Behind (NCLB) Act mentions the term scientifically-based research (SBR) over one hundred times. SBR, in fact, is viewed as one of the key principles for the reform of low achieving schools. NCLB requires state and local education agencies to use SBR to bring improvements to low-achieving schools targeted for assistance. It also calls for a general commitment to school reforms that seek to "identify and implement professional development, instructional strategies, and methods of instruction that are based on scientifically-based research and that have proven effective in addressing the specific instructional issues that caused the school to be identified for school improvement" (NCLB Act, 2002, Title I, Part A, Section 1116 [4] [B] [ii]). The law also specifically authorizes funds "to provide assistance to State educational agencies and local educational agencies in establishing reading programs for students in kindergarten through grade 3 that are based on scientific reading research, to ensure that every student can read at grade level or above no later than the end of grade 3" (NCLB Act, 2002, 20 U.S.C.§ 6361). One can see that the tools of the effective teacher under these federal mandates must be scientifically-rationalized.

As a result, the federal government is interested in generating a body of instructional programs and practices that will presumably be portable to the classroom and give at least some evidence-based direction to educators on how best to teach their charges. Consequently, instructional practice is now increasingly being subjected to experimental studies that use randomized samples of the population and control groups. The use of this methodology, viewed as the gold standard of research, is seen as the key to increasing our understanding of teaching and learning in the school setting.

Such a research approach is confident that it can identify the best materials, curricula, and teaching strategies for all children, using aggregate average effects. But, as indicated, teaching always inherits a local condition; it occurs in a particular dynamic that may or may not be in alignment with what the averages tell us. SBR averages, in most cases, would likely be built on achievement measures, rather than a more nuanced framework that accounts for both cognitive and non-cognitive effects. The danger in identifying best teaching practices is believing that one practice is always good for all children, in all places, at all times.

How then can we begin to frame effectiveness in the classroom? Most people, when asked this question, would probably answer that although it is hard to say what makes an effective teacher, they know it when they see it. And when they see it and try to describe it, the portrayal will likely have two main features. First, teacher effectiveness certainly must speak to outcome expectations in the classroom, meaning that there is no denying the fact that teachers must produce results indicating that students have learned (among many other things) how to read, how to do mathematics, how to write well, how to be good citizens, and so forth. This is the aspect of effectiveness that most schools understand because of the visibility of testing instruments in this process. Evidence of success (outcomes) must also be found in relation to *all* school purposes, including those not typically tested. If schools expect students to be critical thinkers, to be capable of using a wide range of communication skills, to be good at studying and taking notes, to be competent inquirers and cooperative individuals who can work effectively in groups, then the teacher's skills should be evaluated against these wider features as well. When was the last time a judgment of, say, an elementary school teacher's "effectiveness" at least partly accounted for whether her students loved to learn or loved to read recreationally? Effectiveness must be accountable to a comprehensive construction of cognitive and non-cognitive effects or outcomes.

The second dimension to determining teacher effectiveness has to do with process concerns; that is, whether the decisions made by the teacher are professionally defensible, demonstrate receptivity to the nature of the learner and the values of society, and in the end, produce a learning experience that is attuned to the moving purposes of the school. If measured outcomes on a fairly limited range of tests (i.e., reading and mathematics achievement) are the only factors that calculate in the teacher effectiveness equation, then anyone who teaches to the test is going to be viewed as a great teacher. We expect good teachers to not only positively affect key outcomes, but to do it in a way that speaks to a vital and dynamic learning experience. We should expect to see in their teaching evidence of responsiveness to the nature of the learner, to the values of society, and to some critical transmission of subject matter.

TESTING AND CLASSROOM CONTROL

The classroom, as suggested, is a vastly dynamic place. Still, some problems and issues seem to prevail in virtually all classrooms. For teachers, understanding the place and proper usage of the test in the teaching situation, and dealing with the ongoing and complex problem of maintaining classroom control are two especially important issues.

Teaching-to-the-Test

Since the early parts of the 1980s, standardized testing in public education has gained undiminished popularity and authority in the school curriculum. In fact, the penchant for measurement has shaped virtually all facets of the school. In many schools, decisions affecting grade promotion, admission into gifted and talented programs, assignment into special education programs and various curriculum tracks and even, in some cases, graduation from high school, are based primarily, if not entirely, on the results obtained from standardized tests. In some schools, such tests have stood as the key criterion for assessing a teacher's performance in the classroom and for judging the overall educational value of a school. Even recent federal legislation in education, as articulated in No Child Left Behind, demands that schools meet various test proficiency scores and threatens sanctions against any schools that fail.

In all of the situations described above, the standardized test is granted a "high stakes" status in the curriculum (Madaus, 1999). A test becomes known as a high stakes exam when it is used in a way that has a pronounced effect on the school destinies of children and on the professional destinies of teachers and administrators. In a high stakes testing environment, educators are persuaded or otherwise compelled into thinking that the best way to improve education (or at least to demonstrate improvement) is to raise standardized scores. This inevitably leads to a form of teaching that tries to conform to the test.

The mandate to teach-to-the-test emerges in the life of a classroom in various ways. School principals and district-level administrators are often key personnel in promoting the influence of high stakes testing. School administrators are usually keen on showing visible signs of improvement in their schools, and nothing meets this demand better than favorable school-wide results on norm-referenced standardized examinations. With the public image of the school at stake, administrators sometimes exercise pressure to ensure favorable examination outcomes. If one considers the fact that real estate agencies have not hesitated to tout local test scores as a selling point for homes in a particular neighborhood, one gets a picture of how serious the public stakes could get. Under these conditions, the very evaluation of a teacher could be and often is reduced to student performance outcomes on high stakes tests. In other words, a good teacher is viewed as someone who demonstrates high student performance outcomes on standardized exams. But support for teaching-to-the-test can also emerge from the teachers themselves, who reasonably observe that if student destinies are being dictated by examination results, then educators, like it or not, must do their utmost to boost these all-important scores. Other factors include school policies that have the effect of elevating the importance of a particular standardized test. For instance, the increasing popularity of grade retention policies that only allow students to be promoted to the next grade if they perform at or above some minimal score on a standardized exam, has given the standardized exam a prominent place in the curriculum. Grade retention obviously has a dramatic effect on a school youngster's life and aggregate grade promotion rates have considerable public relations currency. The stakes are indeed high when such policies are in place, compelling teachers to think first and foremost about how to teach in ways that lift standardized exam scores.

Naturally, a serious problem emerges under these circumstances. The test, which is supposed to be designed in a way that is responsive to the wider purposes of the school curriculum instead takes on a life of its own. Schoolteachers, concerned about test scores, become fixed on the exam. As a consequence, the exam, depending on the intensity of high stakes pressure, becomes, quite literally, the whole of the school curriculum experience.

Some commentators have no problem with the act of teaching-to-the-test, stating that whatever works to raise scores should be embraced as a viable instructional strategy. But there are critics who contend that teaching-to-the-test not only invalidates the test, but creates a training atmosphere that concentrates mostly on teaching the skills most amenable to quantification. Such critics also complain that when too great a faith is placed in the fallible mechanism of standardized testing, the place or priority of anything not systematically tested becomes marginalized and pushed to the very boundary of the school experience. The teacher, for instance, who aims to cultivate certain healthy values and attitudes toward learning or who is dedicated to teaching children the values of respect, integrity, and honesty, or who wants to highlight the importance of higher-order thinking skills, will find that such concerns typically have little or no place on the standardized school examination. Knowing this, the teacher in a high stakes testing climate will have little incentive to teach such things, fearing such initiatives as time lost to the all-consuming need to raise test scores. What we privilege on the test is often the clearest sign of what we instructionally privilege in the classroom. This is evermore the case where the test takes on a high stakes status.

The problem is not simply what gets taught; it is also a matter of how it gets taught. In one study, the self-reported commitment of elementary school teachers to various instructional strategies was compared against their commitment to openly teaching to a state-mandated test. Among elementary teachers of reading, the teachers most openly committed to teaching-to-the-test were also those most overtly reliant on the teacher's manual. Among elementary math teachers, those reporting a high commitment to teaching-to-the-test also reported a high commitment to skill-drill exercises, student memorization tactics, and using the teacher's manual (Hlebowitsh, 1992). The correlations in the study pointed to the possibility that the teachers who were most inclined to teach directly to the exam were also those most broadly committed to instructional strategies that were low-level and mechanical in orientation. This is another way of saying that where teaching-to-the-test occurs, one is likely to find less instructional innovation and certainly less of the independence of thought that we expect from a generative-creative teacher, than in settings where teaching-to-the-test is not occurring.

Teaching-to-the-test also raises ethical questions. In some forms, it is little more than cheating, especially if teachers use actual test items on the exam and teach to them directly. One teacher was fired and ten others disciplined after officials with the Los Angeles Unified School District accused them of copying the actual items from an achievement exam and tailoring their instruction to the items (Hoff, 9 January 2000). This has become a problem of growing proportions, an issue we will consider again in chapter five. Other ethical concerns have to do with the fact that when student-school fortunes are so visibly linked to test scores, as they are with test-linked grade promotion policies and test-linked curriculum placement policies, the students most likely to experience a taught-to-the-test curriculum will be disproportionately represented by low-income, limited English, and minority student group populations.

Classroom Control

If one asks experienced teachers and principals to identify the greatest problem facing a young teacher in the classroom, they will almost always point to classroom discipline and classroom control. The failure of a classroom teacher to maintain classroom discipline is very serious business. It can be, and sometimes is, viewed as grounds for the dismissal of a teacher. The bottom line is that teachers have a professional obligation to engage students in purposeful and meaningful activities that aim to fulfill the educational agenda of the school. This is a task that cannot be accomplished if a classroom is troubled by disruption or disorder.

Most parents express positive views about the level of discipline found in the public schools. A national study found that 93 percent of parents with children in elementary school agreed or strongly agreed that their child's teacher maintained good discipline in the classroom. At the middle school level, the number drops to 87 percent and rises again in the high school to 91 percent (National Center for Education Statistics, 1997). Teachers, it seems, have control, as they must, of their classrooms. Little learning could occur if they did not.

To many people, the term control has negative connotations because it is often associated with acts of coercion and authoritarianism. The truth, however, is that elements of control are essential to every social arrangement and that, one way or another, they will prevail in every context of learning. Even the idea of freedom requires controls, lest anarchy or chaos result. Because the school is a deliberately designed and consciously conceived environment that aims to fulfill certain goals, it can only have a sense of itself by supporting certain objectives, expectations, and controls. The question, then, is not whether there will be control but what its nature shall be.

Most teachers understand the idea of imposing external controls in the classroom. They must set rules, enforce them, consider reward and punishment strategies, establish expectations and routines, and make independent authoritative decisions about what gets included into and excluded from the purview of the classroom experience. There is no getting away from some of these decisions.

Professional educators also understand the importance of vesting control in the learning engagement, in opting to teach their students responsibility and behavior management by placing them in a classroom where they can learn to *be in* control of their environment rather than *under* the control of their environment. Dewey (1916) observed, that "internal control through identity of interest and understanding is the business of education" (p. 39–40). In this sense, classroom discipline relies primarily (although not exclusively) on learning activities and social engagements for control, and not on the exercise of threat, coercion, punishment, and other forms of authoritarianism (Dewey, 1938). The teacher does not keep order as much as create order through engagement in the learning experiences of the school. Thus, where there are failings in classroom discipline there will usually be failings in quality of the learning activities of the classroom. Problems with discipline often amount to problems with teaching.

The role that motivation plays in contributing to classroom control is a case in point. Some teachers believe motivation is best secured by using the looming threat of punishment. Avoidance of punishment thus becomes the main motivating force in the classroom. Others might view motivation as a simple inducement strategy designed to make learning as palatable as possible. Such teachers might, as a result, resort to various reward mechanisms and finding instructional ways to make learning as much fun as possible. In each of the two orientations mentioned above, motivation is moved mostly by external conditions.

Yet another view of motivation distances itself from the idea that educators should always be looking to create or compel interest and instead proposes the idea that motivation is inherent to the nature of the classroom experience. The difference is fundamental. In one case, the interest is appended to the experience and is, to paraphrase Dewey (1902, p. 29), held in contrast to an alternate experience, such as receiving a scolding, being held up to ridicule, staying after school, or receiving low marks. In the other case, interest is umbilically tied, again to paraphrase Dewey, to the consciousness of the child, to his own doings, thinkings and struggles (Dewey, 1902, p. 29). From this perspective, motivation is about making an effort to construct learning experiences intrinsically appealing to youth. Interest is of the experience, not external to it.

This is sometimes known as intrinsic motivation. When students are moved by an intrinsic motivation, they engage in activity for its own sake, motivated not by a dangling carrot but by a genuine self-interest. Csikszentmihalyi (1990) has described the idea of intrinsic motivation as "flow," as a condition of being lost and immersed in the enjoyment of the activity. Finding flow in the classroom is no easy matter. Teachers who are responsive to the nature of the learner, who give students opportunities to make choices and to set some of their own learning goals, and who offer idea-oriented and problem-focused opportunities to learn, have a better chance of finding it than others.

Much of classroom control, especially as it manifests in classroom management practices, has been under the influence of a behavioristic psychology that touts the power of external controls. Behaviorism established itself as a distinct school of human psychology in the early part of the twentieth century. Early spokespersons for behaviorism, such as John Watson, believed that they had developed the key to analyzing, interpreting, predicting, and controlling behavior. Watson was convinced that animal behavior held the key to understanding human behavior and stressed the need for experimentation in the area of animal learning.

Given the focus on animal behavior, behaviorism eventually hit upon the idea of the conditioned response. To behaviorists, a response is conditioned when it attaches itself or is associated with a stimulus. The Russian psychologist Pavlov, proved that hungry dogs could be conditioned to salivate at the sound of a bell instead of the sight of food. To early behaviorists, such as Watson, this work with animal learning pointed to the centrality of the stimulus-response bond in human learning. The vast complexity of human behavior could now be studied along its most rudimentary lines, its stimulus/response bonds, and learning could now be powerfully viewed in relation to the influence of the environment. Children could be taught to learn through reinforcement and punishment strategies.

Today behaviorism is still the driving psychology behind many classroom management strategies. This is because it provides a ready handle on the management of behaviors (or misbehaviors) through a technique known as behavior modification. The process of behavior modification focuses on the consequences of student behavior for the purpose of modifying or correcting poor behavior and maintaining good behavior. Generally speaking, all behavior is believed to be influenced by external controls, often manifesting as either rewards or punishments. To behave properly, children need to be under the control of their environment, understanding the environmental consequences of desirable and undesirable behavior.

B. F. Skinner (1968), behaviorism's most celebrated advocate, observed that the act of teaching "is simply the arrangement of contingencies of reinforcement" (p. 33), meaning that virtually every aspect of the classroom, from cognitive learning to behavior, could be reduced to a grid of operational objectives that could be conditioned into learners. The equation for success was straightforward: behavior that is positively reinforced will continue to be vital, while behavior that is negatively reinforced or punished will become extinct.

Punishment is, of course, an oft-used option when a teacher seeks to control behavior. Behaviorism teaches us that the introduction of an aversive event will make it less likely that the behavior will reoccur. Most teachers see this as a helpful principle, while also acknowledging that teaching is not always well served by punishment tactics. In fact, to argue for the role of punishment in the classroom immediately raises questions about its form and about the latent effects it might have on students. The use of educational activities as punishments (i.e., homework, writing assignments) has to be noted for the kinds of latent messages they send. The teacher, for instance, who might consider a punishment that requires a child to write an essay on why his behavior was not acceptable, might have a working rationale for the punishment that includes a desire for the child to think through his behavior, to acknowledge his wrong, and to presumably suffer the strain of writing. But because this punishment is associated with the act of writing, it could easily be seen as counterproductive, even miseducative, to an educator interested in teaching children to appreciate the communicative powers of good writing.

The effects of punishment also have to be noted as they might apply particularly to a student, accounting for factors related to disability, family-home life, and individual character. Determining an appropriate punishment will have everything to do with previous problems the child might have had in class, with a detailed understanding of the incident, with a sense of student's background, and with any other mitigating factors related to the individual child. Depending on its nature, punishment could arouse resentment and a lack of trust in the classroom, or perhaps adversarial relations between the teacher and the students. It could also reduce or undermine opportunities to develop a sense of responsibility and cooperation. All of this is not enough to dismiss the idea of punishment out of hand, but it certainly complicates it.

Professional educators use punishment judiciously. Generally speaking, they issue a fair warning before punishing and convey the punishment with a tone that communicates concern and disappointment, and perhaps even surprise, rather than anger and hostility. Professional teachers think about whether the punishment "fits the crime" and understand the importance of explaining the punishment to the student. They keep a watchful eye on the student response to punishment, noting any hostile or otherwise unhealthy tendencies, and try to anticipate any latent negative effects.

Another response in a teacher's management repertoire is the tactic of omission training. In classrooms and schools, this is otherwise known as "time out." The rationale behind omission training is that the removal of the student from pleasant and meaningful social environment will be motivation to change future behaviors. This strategy has overtones of punishment to it, especially if the act of removal results in humiliation or embarrassment to the student.

But the removal of the opportunity to be positively rewarded is different from punishment. In most cases, it is less likely to generate many of the unwanted side effects associated with punishment. Most importantly, it hinges on the proposition that the student is being removed from an attractive and engaging learning experience. It is a negative experience only if the student is being removed from something worthwhile. Thus, the cornerstone to classroom control and classroom discipline, under these conditions, is the development of attractive and relevant learning experiences. This is, in fact, the basic premise to many school discipline techniques. Even the traditional idea of school suspension is based on the belief that one is being suspended from a worthy and important experience. If being suspended from school turns out to be a holiday away from a repressive and stultifying experience, it could hardly be seen as an effective disciplining strategy.

Teachers also use positive reinforcement to manage behavior. In the classroom environment, the use of verbal praise and verbal encouragement are among the more obvious forms. All children, of course, need to be recognized and praised for their accomplishments. Some teachers believe this so strongly that they routinely employ praising reinforcements in the classroom in very large frequencies. But a teacher who praises students very often and who praises uncritically can do a disservice to students. For instance, if teachers offer effusive praise for the smallest accomplishments, even with so-called low achieving children, their actions could result in humiliating a child, especially if it is an accomplishment that other students have already mastered with some ease. Similarly, rewarding or praising students for what they are already doing without external reinforcement could be viewed as unwise because it might tend to attenuate intrinsic motivational drives. In other words, if students have internalized certain constructive routines and behaviors, they need not be continuously praised for these actions. Naturally, such behaviors should not always be completely taken for granted either, so there is a balance here.

All classrooms likely have a small handful of students whose behavioral problems in the classroom are severe enough to warrant special attention. In fact, youth who exhibit persistent behavioral problems in school usually, in due time, find their way to the school psychologist. Their problems, if severe enough, might result in special curricular attention, although federal legislation during the past few decades has promoted the mainstreaming of special populations of students in the interests of keeping them in "regular" education. These students, who typically make up approximately 10 percent of a class, might simply be confused and frustrated in their personal lives; they might be from families whose lives have little consistency and even less love; and they might suffer from any number of emotional or neurological disorders. These are the students whose behavior often threatens to undermine the educational process of others. Such students usually force teachers to make concessions to external reinforcement strategies, because the thing that makes these particular students so frustrating is their inability to develop internal self-control and self-responsibility.

Teachers work in emergent situations, with students who have distinctively different personalities, varied home and family backgrounds, and different levels of ability, interest, effort and maturity. It is difficult, if not impossible, to find a universally accepted procedure for classroom management or classroom control. There is simply no substitute for the exercise of teacher intelligence, as teachers contemplate the design and implementation of activities intrinsically engaging and controlling, and the appropriate use of reinforcement strategies in an emergent setting.

SUMMARY

Teaching is a complex undertaking set in a complex social arrangement that requires both planned and emergent judgments. The ideal of the professional in the classroom is of someone who is in active engagement with the best evidence on teaching and learning, who diagnoses classroom problems and tests working solutions, and who is ultimately responsive to a vision of teaching that accounts for the nature of the learner, the values of the society, and the integration of worthy subject matter or knowledge. In the classroom, this professional perspective is sometimes compromised by factors external to the school. The tradition of high stakes testing, for instance, has put unhealthy pressure on the teacher to teach-to-the-test. Efforts to define effective teaching in mechanistic and instructionally generic ways and to see classroom management as primarily a matter of managing external controls has had a similar compromising effect.

REFERENCES

Bloom, B. S. (1956). *Taxonomy of educational objectives: Cognitive domain.* New York: David McKay Co.

Czikszentmihalyi, M. (1990). *Flow: The psychology of optimal experience.* New York: Harper and Row.

Dewey, J. (1902). *Child and the curriculum/School and the society.* Chicago: University of Chicago Press.

Dewey, J. (1904). The relation of theory to practice in education. In the Society for the Study of Education 3rd Yearbook, Part 1. *The relation of theory to practice in the education of teachers.* Bloomington, IL: Public School Publishing.

Dewey, J. (1916). *Democracy and education.* New York: Macmillan Co.

Dewey, J. (1938). *Experience and education.* New York: Macmillan Co.

Doyle, W. (1990). *Classroom Knowledge as a Foundation of Teaching. Teachers College Record* 91(3): 347–360.

Eisner, E. (1998). *The educational imagination.* New York: Macmillan Co.

Gardner, H. (1983). *Frames of mind: The theory of multiple intelligences.* New York: Basic Books.

Henke, R. R., Chen, X., & Goldman, G. (1999). What happens in the classroom? Instructional practices in elementary and secondary schools: 1994-1995. *Education Quarterly* 1(2):7–13.

Hirsch, E. D. (1987). *Cultural literacy: What every American needs to know.* Boston: Houghton Mifflin.

Hlebowitsh, P. S. (1992). Time on TAAS. *Texas Researcher* 3, 81–89.

Hoff, D. J. (9 January, 2000). LA teachers caught cheating. *Education Week.*

Hunter, M. (1980). *Teach more—faster.* El Segundo, CA: TIP Publications.

Jackson, P. (1968). *Life in Classrooms.* New York: Holt Rinehart and Winston.

Krathwohl, D. L., Bloom, B. S., & Masia, B. B. (1964). *Taxonomy of educational objectives: Affective domain.* New York, David McKay Co.

Madaus, G. F. (1999). The influence of testing on the curriculum. In *Issues in curriculum: 98th yearbook of the National Society for the Study of Education.* Chicago: University of Chicago Press.

Maslow, A. H. (1962). *Toward a psychology of being.* New York: Von Nostrand Reinhold.

Medley, D. (1979). The effectiveness of teachers. In P. L. Peterson and H. L. Walberg (eds.) *Research on teaching: Concept, findings and implications.* Berkeley, CA: McCutchen.

National Center for Education Statistics. (1997). *America's teachers: Profile of a profession, 1993–1994.* Washington, DC: Department of Education.

NCLB Act, 2002, Title I, Part A, Section 1116 [4] [B] [ii].

Piaget, J. (1950). *The psychology of intelligence.* London: Routledge and Paul.

Pratt, D. (1994). *Curriculum planning.* New York: Harcourt Brace.

Rosenshine, B. (1978). Time, content and direct instruction. In P. L. Peterson and H. L. Walberg (eds). *Research on teaching: Concept, findings and implications.* Berkeley, CA: McCutchen.

Schwab J. J. (1983). *The practical 4: Something for curriculum professors to do.* Curriculum Inquiry 13(Fall):239-256.

Skinner, B. F. (1968). *The technology of teaching.* New York: Appleton, Century, and Crofts.

Tanner, D., & Tanner, L. (1995). *Curriculum development.* New York: Macmillan Co.

KEY QUESTIONS

1. Describe the ways that teaching is both a planned and an emergent activity.
2. Observe a teacher for a set period of time, noting the number and the nature of interactions with students. What do these observations have to say about a teacher's classroom life?
3. Do you believe that there is one best way to teach? If so, describe it. Do you believe that there is one principled way to teach? If so, describe it. What is the difference between a best method way of teaching and a principled way of teaching?
4. Examine a curriculum program, curriculum unit, or textbook adopted in a school and determine the extent that it allows a teacher to operate at the highest level of professional awareness *(Level III: Generative-Creative).* What factors in the curriculum open up or close down the opportunities?
5. George Madaus (1999), a well-known specialist in testing, concluded that "the more any qualitative social indicator is used for social decision-making, the more likely it will be used to distort and corrupt the socials processes it is intended to monitor" (p. 79). What do you think he means by this? How does this apply to education and schooling?
6. Define high stakes testing. Provide examples from your own experience.
7. Describe a classroom scenario in which a teacher makes use of expressive goals.
8. What factors inside and outside of school contribute to the formation of high stakes testing in the schools? How do principals, parents, politicians, colleges, and even real estate agents factor into the problem?
9. How is control fundamental to freedom?
10. What is the distinction between external and internal control? What are the teaching implications of such a distinction?
11. Is praise always a good thing? What factors should be considered when using praise in the classroom?
12. What are the theoretical problems associated with the effective teaching literature?

RESEARCH EXERCISES

1. Investigate the portrayal of teachers in the major national media outlets, including national news journals and newspapers, over the past several decades. What conclusions can you draw?

2. Research the NCLB literature on scientifically-based teaching and try to describe what it might mean to be, say, a scientifically-based teacher of reading? Are you convinced that a teacher who employs a scientifically-based methodology will be more effective in the classroom, as you define effective, than one who does not use a scientifically-based teaching strategy? Survey teachers, parents, and school administrators on the topic and discuss commonalities and differences in the views.

3. Observe professional teachers at work and judge their classroom performance in relation to one of the three levels of professional development (Level I: Imitative-Maintenance, Level II: Mediative, and Level III: Generative-Creative). Detail the things that the teachers do (or do not do) to support your conclusions.

4. Examine a school reform initiative by subjecting it to an analysis using the three sources for professional decision making (the learner, the society, and the subject matter). For instance, how might you evaluate whole language reading instruction, the Great Books Curriculum in English education, the idea of middle school, or any locally-derived reform initiative, using the three factors? Visit a classroom and evaluate the nature of the school experience using the same three factors.

CHAPTER 3

Teachers and the School Curriculum

Teachers are the main implementers of the school curriculum. They are the engines that drive the school experience. Their judgments in the classroom matter the most, largely because they are in living interaction with school children. As Eisner (1998) noted, "one could only have a curriculum after it is experienced by a child" (p. 26). Thus, understanding the nature of the school curriculum is essential to understanding successful classroom practices. The school curriculum does, after all, provide vital direction to the teacher by framing the school's purposes, the content taught, and the manner in which the learning experience is evaluated. There are dangers here too because the school curriculum can sometimes get in the way of good teacher judgment by attempting to dictate instruction to the teacher or by otherwise imposing unreasonable burdens on the teacher's discretionary space. The question we face in this chapter asks how the school curriculum should be positioned and balanced in the professional lives of school teachers.

DEFINING THE SCHOOL CURRICULUM

The Latin derivative of the term curriculum is *currere*, which is associated with the idea of running a racecourse. The reader might find this to be an odd derivative. How, for instance, can we begin to see a connection between our current usage of curriculum and the idea of a racecourse? But if we think about a racecourse as a metaphor for the school curriculum, we could find the derivative helpful in describing what the school is like today. Using the metaphor, we could imagine students running on a planned course, completing the requirements of the race and receiving some certificate of participation—one that might include some judgment of or even reward for distinguished or meritorious participation. Along the way, professionally-trained personnel assist the participants with the development of the skills needed to perform on the course, coaching and prodding their students to meet its demands, sometimes with success and sometimes not. Those personally staked in the race, including parents and members of the community, make their own observations and in most cases do their best to assist as well. The race, after all, is an ongoing one, with very clear effects in the life destinies of the participants. The metaphor is, of course, imprecise. It puts too much emphasis on the idea of competing and fails to apprehend one of the more fundamental processes of schooling, which is to learn how to cooperate and work together and build common associations around common problems, common knowledge, and common values.

This might explain why, in present-day parlance, we have retained the use of the term "course" in the school setting, while dropping the reference to a race. When talking about schooling, in at least post-elementary school settings, most students still refer to taking a "course" or enrolling in a "course" with a teacher—running through it, as it were, according to the rules and regulations set down by the teacher and other school leaders. When one thinks about the school curriculum, one is immediately brought to the question of what course (or course of action) best embodies the societal (or institutional) agenda to enlighten and inform the upcoming generation of youth. What knowledge is most worthwhile for all youth? What behaviors are most desirable? What forms of experience produce the kinds of effects wanted in the education of youth? How does one know whether such effects were secured? The school curriculum becomes, for lack of a better descriptor, the course for society's youth—the public educational experience needed to build the kind of society we desire.

When we begin to think about the curriculum in more procedural terms, other ways to define the curriculum come into play. One of the more popular ones equates the curriculum with the subject matter of schooling. The result is that the curriculum is viewed as a kind of registry for what is taught, often organized along content lines that rarely stray too far from the subject matter boundaries found in the traditional academic disciplines. Our expectations from the curriculum under these terms are modest, chiefly reduced to ensuring an exposure to content knowledge in English, mathematics, science, history, the foreign languages, and so forth. Such a view has its greatest following in high school settings, where specialized academic subjects still reign, but it could also be found in elementary schools, which continue to organize instruction, even in self-contained classrooms, by discipline-centered content areas. We improve the curriculum, under theses circumstances, by simply changing what gets taught.

The bias inherent in the characterization of curriculum as subject matter is underscored by the fact that we often use the term "curriculum" in relation to the term "instruction," implying at least some analytical separation between what is taught (the curriculum) and how it is taught (instruction). The distinction, however, does not hold up very well because, as most teachers know, any determination about how to teach has to be done in relation to what gets taught.

Fortunately, professional efforts to give meaning to the curriculum commonly speak to broader issues than content, and depending on the perspective, call attention to a process that we could begin to identify as curriculum design or curriculum development. Eisner (1998), for instance, observed that "the curriculum of a school or a course or a classroom can be conceived of as a series of planned events intended to have educational consequences for one or more students" (p 31).

Eisner's view of the curriculum carries many of the conventional components of design: a planning component, a regard for an educational effect, an effort to see learning in the totality of the school experience, and an implied understanding that different students might require different experiences. Hilda Taba (1962) was even more specific in speaking directly to the point of design, stating that "all curricula, no matter what their particular design, are composed of certain elements" (p. 10). "A curriculum," she continued, "usually contains a statement of aims and of specific objectives; it indicates some selection and organization of content; it either implies or manifests patterns of learning and teaching....Finally it includes a program of evaluation of the outcomes" (Taba, 1962, p. 10). Taba's definition reflects a procedural view of the curriculum that has had resiliency in the field of curriculum studies for many years. Ralph Tyler (1949) was the first to advise curricularists to see their work moving along the continuum that Taba described—from the formation of purposes (aims and objectives), to the organization of experiences based on the purposes, to the eventual evaluation of effects attributable to the experiences.

In the end, we can say that the school curriculum is, even in the face of the differences in outlook expressed above, a blueprint for school operations. It makes a point of identifying purposes and content so that teachers can better frame their instructional planning, and of ensuring that some mechanism is in place to judge whether such purposes have been attained.

The Explicit Curriculum

The reference to the explicit curriculum should be fairly obvious. It simply refers to the planned condition of the school—the full range of explicitly rationalized decisions, including, say, the expression of the school's purposes, the detailing of various instructional objections and content standards, the actual design of lesson plans, the use of particular readings and materials, the ways that students are evaluated, and even the intended plans for homework and follow-up activities.

Objectives, Goals, and Aims

The use of objectives, goals, and aims used in the school curriculum is a time-worn practice. Few teachers can conceive of designing lessons and otherwise framing experiences in their classroom without resorting to some construction of objectives or goals. This high regard for objectives makes good sense because to understand the curriculum, one must examine its intentions. The school curriculum exists by some formulation of intention or by some vision of an ideal to be accomplished. If we say the curriculum is deliberately conceived, we mean that it is conceived in the expectation of fulfilling a particular mandate or purpose. The curriculum, in this sense, is always purposeful, always full of a sense of what is desirable in the experience of school children.

We can begin to better understand the nature of objectives, goals, and aims in the school curriculum by using the analogy of a target to characterize the relationship (Zais, 1976). An aim, one could say, represents a target set far in the field. Educators might be able to see the distant target but because it is not distinct in its particulars, they will likely have to overcome difficult odds to strike it directly. Here we are talking about the very kind of broad statements that might make their way into, say, a school's mission statement. If we speak of broad socio-civic or broad intellectual aims, for instance, we understand that such aims are, by their sweeping nature, next to impossible to strike directly. Therefore, the natural reaction is to try to find a way to bring the target in, to make it more distinguishable to the eye in order to inspire some judgment on the instrumentation one might use to hit it. The movement in the direction of specificity is a movement in the direction of articulating goals and objectives as well as in the direction of defining purposes closer to the living experience of the teacher and the student. Sometimes educators might want to bring the target in all the way, setting it close so that, tactically speaking, the target cannot be missed. These nearby targets are plainly visible and knowable, sitting ducks, as it were, for educators seeking their attainment, and are analogous to what we might traditionally view as instructional objectives in the curriculum. Objectives obviously become key to the work of classroom teachers, who use them to frame instructional events, but their degree of specificity in the classroom is determined by teacher judgment.

The metaphor of a target demonstrates some important differences between aims, goals, and objectives. Generally speaking, an aim is orienting or perspectival. It marks out a general commitment or purpose for the whole school, but it is insufficient in guiding decisions in the classroom. Objectives (and even goals), in contrast, have a more tactical flavor. They are much more specific in outlining what should be done, but they still have their origin in a statement of aims. Objectives draw their sense of the particular from the general. A school, for example, might support the aim of developing critical thinking skills, but each classroom within the school might go about contributing to this aim in a different way, accounting for learner and subject matter differences. The development of objectives is useful in drawing out this more specific strategy. The distinction between goals and objectives can sometimes be blurred because the level of specificity required to conduct the classroom is ultimately in the teacher's hands.

Likening the idea to objectives to a target is an incomplete analogy. Closer targets are not always better ones by virtue of being easier to hit. In fact, we sometimes deliberately set targets at a calculated distance. Furthermore, finding equivalence between an aim (a target well-off in the distance) and multiple goals and objectives (multiple shorter targets) can be tricky. Finally, the metaphor implies that once aims or goals are struck, we have succeeded and completed our work, when in fact, in the context of a curriculum, the achievement of goals and aims represents new and expanded opportunities for continued growth. Learning to read, for instance, not only represents an achievement of a goal, but also opens up new possibilities for the achievement of other previously unattainable goals.

Because Dewey (1916) understood that the formation of aims has ripple effects in the curriculum, he outlined what he called "the criteria for good aims." He thought that three important factors had to be weighed. First, the formation of aims had to rise up from the educational situation, "based on a consideration of what was already going on; upon the resources and difficulties of the situation" (Dewey, 1916, p. 104). In other words, to effectively set broad purposes in the school requires knowing the school, knowing what might be realizable in terms of resources and capacities, as well as what might be especially valued in the school community and needed in the light of evaluative data. The formation of aims or purposes is always affected by social and political realities and as well as by resource limitations and various other nuances in the nature of the school community. External normative aims, given by state directive, can be problematic in this sense, especially if they result in rendering the work of teachers, to use Dewey's characterization, "slavish or mechanical." Directives that arise from the state departments of education could violate one criterion of Dewey's good aims if they are imposed without due consideration of the local educational situation, and if they carry with them a rigid instructional will.

The second criterion of good aims refers to the tentative and flexible character of aims. To Dewey, good aims are elastic enough to allow for some range of interpretation as well as some flexibility in shifting course, or making other modifications as circumstance dictates. Aims help form a tentative plan and give the teacher a vision of the whole school experience, but they must be amenable to adjustments as conditions develop.

The third and final criterion of good aims is a variation of the second, and represents a kind of paradox. Aims clearly have a role to play in delimiting the school experience—refining, focusing, and simplifying it in a way that gives it deliberate purpose and meaning. But Dewey reminds us that the third criterion of good aims demands that aims produce a freeing or releasing of activities. This should not be viewed as a contradiction. The school curriculum should find a balance between giving direction and allowing for the exercise of professional judgment. A good aim should not close down the options for the teacher but open them up in a focused and directive way.

Curriculum Standards

The setting of standards also plays a fundamental role in the design of the school curriculum because it usually gives us an answer to the question of what should be taught. Some advocates of standards want them set at a national level, while others, understanding the decentralized nature of the public school system, would prefer to see them set at the state level. Interestingly, some states, such as Iowa, mandate standards but see their development as an exclusively local concern.

Most of the arguments in support of standards speak to a public accountability rationale. Advocates of standards assert that the skills and knowledge that reside in the normative agenda of the school (common knowledge in math, science, literature, and so forth, as well as the common skills of reading, numeracy, and writing) should be identified and codified, integrated in the curricula of all schools, and monitored with testing measurements whose results are regularly conveyed to the public. Such accountability is itself motivated by anxieties over the national implications of low achievement in the normative agenda, as well as over equity concerns and the possibility that certain school districts, absent the strong arm of standards, will deny certain children the opportunity to learn key knowledge and skills (Ravitch, 1995).

The idea of standards is not especially complex. It has a familiar and comfortable place in common life events. Standards are important to us largely because they usually have had some hand in helping to ensure levels of quality, safety, reliability, and efficiency in our lives. The regulation of our institutions are almost always moved by some enforcement of standards—environmental standards, health and safety standards, manufacturing standards, and licensing standards all have some ring in our lives.

The curriculum standard, of course, has a similar function. Supporters of standards claim to bring a measure of quality control to the school experience and to ensure that whatever the schools deem as most worthy is distributed fairly and equitably to all its charges. In its most common application, the curriculum standard is usually equated with something that we might also call a content standard. A content standard is little more than a goal that stipulates what should be taught. It does not speak to how it should be taught and it does not provide counsel on where it must be integrated in the fabric of the whole of the school experience. Content standards denote standardization in what is taught but no real standardization beyond it, except to the extent that the organization of the standards themselves might influence the organization of knowledge and even the organization of course work in the curriculum. Content standards usually fall under the province or dominion of state and local directives. Because the content of the curriculum is a normative concern, states often exercise some authority in setting forth content requirements for the schools.

Content standards sound innocuous enough, but their use in the curriculum usually has wide consequences. The fact of the matter is that content standards are rarely offered as only content standards. Schools typically get a package deal with content standards because such standards are often accompanied by what are known as performance and proficiency standards. Content standards might be uncontroversial if all they did was outline what should be taught. When accompanied by what are known as performance and proficiency standards, content standards take on a different life in the curriculum. Performance standards describe how students will show that they achieved the content standards, and proficiency standards provide criteria to scale or measure the degree of progress on the performance standards. The three orientations can usually be found wherever standards are discussed. State Departments of Education across the nation, for instance, have used the three components as a framework for subject specific standards. Consider the language of the Wisconsin Model of Academic Standards, which is endorsed by the Wisconsin Department of Public Instruction (1998). It defines an academic standard as "what students should know and be able to do (content standards), what they might be asked to do to give evidence of standards (performance standards), and how well they must perform (proficiency standards)." The partnering of content standards with performance and proficiency standards is an essential part of accountability routines. What is important to note here is that content standards, when tied to performance and proficiency standards, begin to do more than simply outline the content of the curriculum. They actually begin to get tied into ways of testing. This raises the possibility that the content standard could become less important than the proficiency standard, causing the teacher to look first to the test rather than to the content.

The recent implementation of the *No Child Left Behind* (NCLB) legislation dramatizes the point. In the context of NCLB, the adoption of curriculum standards represents the first step in the design of statewide yearly progress examinations in reading, mathematics, and science. The federal law explicitly states that each state shall adopt "challenging student academic achievement standards" and that such standards shall, among other things, include some specification of what "children are expected to know and be able to do" (Public Law 107-110; 20 USC 6311. Sec 1111 (b-1-a and b-1-c). The NCLB requirement for the adoption of standards is seen as the essential prerequisite for the development of a single statewide accountability (testing) system. To promote standards, in this context, means to demand accountability through the use of a single test.

The linkage of standards to tests and measurements was actually a worrisome matter to early progressive thinkers. In an essay titled, *Education Direct and Indirect* (1904), John Dewey noted that the idea of the standard was "by the necessity of the case a mechanical and quantitative thing" (p. 244). By being a "quantitative thing," the standard, in Dewey's eyes, risked bringing the nature of instruction down to its least common conceptual denominator, mostly because low or simple cognitive items were well-suited to measurement efforts. Thus, any learning experience that aimed to meet standards could find itself restricted to an unambitious list of objectives. Ideas that are not easily embodied in standards, often ones representing an enlarging and higher cognitive experience, could be lost or devalued in the school experience.

Much of the present-day response to standards, however, rejects this line of thinking. Diane Ravitch (1995), for instance, has been active in pleading a case to the American people for the place of national standards in education. She openly expresses the view that "a standard is not useful or meaningful unless there is someone to measure whether it is reached" (p. 11). Underscoring the idea of measurement, Ravitch (1995) continued to assert that "some state's boards of education think that they have standards when all they really have are hortatory or obscure statements about aspirations that are inherently unmeasurable" (p. 11).

Ravitch's position on standards is very much embodied in the work of the Fordham Institute, which, for over a decade now, has taken it upon itself to publish a rating system that grades the quality of standards developed in the states. The criteria used by the Fordham Institute reflect an accountability rationale and a very specific idea of what it means to construct good standards. Essentially it employs two criteria: 1) an index for intelligibility, which includes a screen to determine whether the standards are specific, measurable, free of jargon, and unambiguous; and 2) an index for coverage, which includes a screen to determine whether the standards capture a complete range of essential skills (Cross, Rebarber, & Torres, 2004). Of course, progressives such as John Dewey might ask how the demand to impose the criterion of measurability on a standard could be reconciled with the demand to cover a full range of essential skills. In other words, how can all essential skills be measurable?

Instructional Methods

A tendency exists among educators today to declare some instructional strategies as intrinsically good for all children in virtually all times and places. As discussed earlier, such thinking is flawed because teaching cannot and does not follow a generic best methods approach. If a generic best methods approach were used, we would not expect much independent judgment from teachers and could even view teacher creativity and teacher innovation as out of alignment with best methods.

It is true, however, that some methods, even in their decontextualized state, are on more solid theoretical ground than others. Most of us would probably agree that some instructional strategies are, by their nature, better attuned than others to the life of the learner and to the kind of society we value.

For instance, instructional methods that encourage student discussion might have some general claim as methods well-situated in the lives of learners. Similarly, instructional methods that encourage cooperation, group participation, and group deliberation have some general resonance with the values and aims of our democracy. From the standpoint of the learner and society, these are generally sound instructional approaches. Nevertheless, we should remember that instructional judgments are made primarily in the interests of achieving specified aims, goals, and objectives in the curriculum. Thus, we cannot sensibly pursue instructional strategies that are good without also contemplating what they are good for.

One can classify instructional methods in any number of ways. The broad outlines used here represent a repertoire of direct instruction, discussion-based instruction, inquiry-based instruction, and independent and differentiated instruction. These are, by no means, mutually exclusive and in no way represent the entire instructional vista.

Direct instruction is among the most familiar methodologies to the classroom scene. It is the traditional form of what we might view as teacher-initiated and teacher-directed instruction and usually takes on the form of lecture and demonstration, followed by some schedule of practice and review. It is usually targeted at the whole class, with a built-in provision for questions, for guided and independent practice, and for the employment of corrective measures. The aim of direct instruction is to help students achieve mastery of key ideas, facts, or skills.

The presentation of a lecture or a demonstration, which is the first phase of direct instruction, is probably the most commonplace (and most maligned) instructional approach used in the schools. Many educators are heavy-handed in their criticism of the lecture method because they tend to believe that any instructional position that privileges teacher-talk over student discussion is not educationally sound. Lectures can be intellectually thrilling learning experiences. They, in fact, can accomplish certain purposes more effectively than other methods and thus have their place in the classroom. Of course, like any other method, they can be misused or overused, poorly-conceived, or poorly-conducted.

As a first matter, we should note that the lecture method is best suited for older children. We know from a developmental standpoint that asking children to sit and listen attentively to what often amounts to an exposition of ideas and facts is not a wise way to teach children who have not yet achieved formal operations and whose attention spans are still relatively short. This cautionary point is an example of what we mean when we say that the instructional strategy must be attuned to the nature of the learner. But, absent the limitations posed by the learner, if the exposition of various facts, ideas, and skills is a key component to a curriculum purpose, a lecture method might prove to be a useful strategy. It is, after all, an effective way to transmit knowledge, especially if the teacher is confident in her lecturing skills. Lectures can also prove to be useful where note taking skills, listening skills, and various thinking skills take a prominent role in the instructional strategy. Lectures are perforce pedagogical acts that bring together an array of skills related to the use of voice, inflection, drama, emotive language, rate of delivery, and conceptual structure.

In direct instruction, the teacher presentation phase is followed by guided practice, which means that the teacher must try to distill the lecture or demonstration into some identifiable form of facts, skills, or knowledge that can, in effect, be practiced or otherwise manipulated for an educational effect. This is not independent work, but work done under the eye of the educator who uses it as an opportunity to check for understanding and to correct or remediate any emergent problems. The focus on feedback and correctives comes into play as the educator works on individual cases. The very last steps of the direct instructional model include a phase for independent practice (seatwork or homework), and ultimately an effort at assessment.

Direct instruction is not suited for every objective in the school curriculum. It is, in fact, best equipped to handle objectives that target skill-based needs. This makes it a good candidate for reading and mathematics instruction and also potentially for discipline-centered instruction, such as in science, where particular mechanisms, skills, and processes need to be learned. Direct instruction does not have a monopoly on skill-based objectives. Remember that multiple instructional approaches can be used to achieve singular objectives. Because the teacher ultimately puts instructional plans into action, the presentation phase of direct instruction does not always need to be followed by any of the review and practice mechanisms described above. It could instead ease into another kind of experience altogether, including discussion-based or inquiry-based instructional approaches, which could, in their own way, serve as practice and review opportunities.

Direct instruction tends to be driven by the instructional desire to describe and explicate. Discussion-based instruction, however, is more closely related to the instructional purposes of exploring, extending, probing, analyzing, clarifying, and evaluating. Discussion-based instruction obviously requires small-sized student groups. This naturally enhances the prospects for discussion. Smaller gatherings of students simply make it possible for individuals to discuss, share, and otherwise engage each other at a level of intimacy not easily accomplished in the larger group setting. As a result, discussion-based instruction is a more likely choice for curriculum objectives that stress oral expression, social mutuality, critical mindedness, and the development of various social skills.

If the instructional orientation of direct instruction is teacher demonstration and student practice, then the instructional orientation for discussion-based methodologies is teacher facilitation and student discovery. In other words, most discussion-based models try to limit teacher-talk and to encourage meaningful conversational engagements between students and between students and teachers. Where direct instruction offers knowledge from the teacher, discussion-based instruction puts the student to the challenge of contextualizing and conversing about the knowledge. Because discussion is influenced by the student's perspective on matters (student interests, aptitudes, and questions), it works in the interests of developing important appreciations.

Multiple options are available to the teacher who is interested in bringing discussion-based instruction into the classroom. Some options, such as the Socratic questioning method, still very much depend on teacher direction, but most of the others simply try to find a way to offer students an idea-oriented context within which they can pursue questions and problems that will require conversation and the active exchange of viewpoints and insights. A few of the general approaches that work within the tradition of discussion-based instruction include role playing, simulations and games, and cooperative learning.

The instructional implications of role playing activities are to try to get the students to psychologize the main features of whatever they might be studying. The technique demands an emotional and cognitive involvement with the assigned role. This is an approach that is especially useful in the study of history, or even in the study of contemporary social problems, and with younger children, in the examination of human relations problems, including interpersonal conflicts, inter-group relations, and individual dilemmas (Joyce & Weil, 1986).

The performance of a role-playing activity requires the application of a wide range of skills, including dramatic presentation skills, memorization work, and some empathetic attachment to the role. The educational benefits of role playing activity, however, do not cease with the presentation or performance. Because role playing is viewed as discussion-based instruction, its primary educational benefit is rooted in the debriefing session scheduled after the presentation. This is especially critical because debriefing allows students to ask questions, seek clarifications, offer opinions, and suggest improvements.

The use of role play in the classroom is yet another reminder of the importance of keeping the conception of the learner in mind when we make instructional selections. If, for instance, a role play activity requires the student to act out or otherwise identify with a racist, sexist, or bigoted role, the teacher, before proceeding, should account for the age and the maturity levels of the learner and the class, as well as individual factors related to ethnic, racial, or religious sensitivities. Asking a Jewish child to play the role of Hitler, or African American children to act in a slavery role may not be a professionally prudent decision. Such choices have to be approached with sensitivity to the learner and to the wider community. Similarly, teachers need to be keenly aware of the language used in the role activities produced, and decide whether the use of the language is appropriate, given the sensitivities of the student and community population.

Classroom simulations and games represent yet another discussion-based approach. With simulations, the idea is to artificially reproduce the real life conditions of a particular situation or event and to put the student into the vortex of the simulation, where key decisions need to be made. Thus, the simulation is really an instructional approach that features the application of decision-making skills. This makes it particularly appealing where the skills of problem solving or decision making are featured in the curriculum. An educational game, on the other hand, usually has no designs on simulating reality, and can integrate any number of other purposes, including drill practices and knowledge acquisition. Because the use of a game (and sometimes a simulation) are justified by a competitive task structure (tasks or activities that require students to compete against each other), they should be used judiciously, especially in settings that attach great importance to cooperative activities.

In most cases, teachers will use the simulation as an application and synthesizing activity that helps to bring together the content of the curriculum into a working reality-based scenario. Again, especially in the case of the simulation, much can be gained from a scheduled debriefing session that follows the conclusion of the simulation. This allows the teacher to put an analytical lens on the simulation itself, giving students the opportunity to discuss and reflect upon what they learned and to draw connections to subject matter. If we look at the simulation as the journey, the discussion that follows is the destination; it is the place where the activity culminates in a well-regulated and sharply analytical debriefing experience.

The very definition of game implies fun, so there is a tendency to equate the application of games in the classroom with fun-filled experiences that build important appreciations. Although all games are not created equal (and many are about as much fun as watching paint dry), the appeal to the idea of playing games, especially to young children, cannot be denied. This gives the game strategy an important advantage in assisting with the development of appreciations. Teachers sometimes recognize this and use games to compensate for activities that may not have much of an intrinsic appeal to students.

Cooperative learning is often seen as a reprieve from the traditional whole-class and individual seatwork model that still dominates the classroom. It is an especially attractive instructional option in any classroom that values the development of social skills and that aims to encourage problem-solving skills, inquiry skills, and the development of pro-social behaviors.

We often find that cooperative learning proceeds through small groups, put together by the teacher, with a task structure that requires a cooperative group effort and ultimately some group consensus. The task could be something as simple as getting together to brainstorm on a topic or as sophisticated as pursuing a specific research question that calls for a lengthy and nuanced (and well-researched) group response. Often cooperative groups are limited to a heterogeneous mix of four or five students, with each participant taking on a specific role in the group process. The idea is for the group to organize and manage itself, to have an opportunity to engage in discussion and debate, to find ways to reconcile internal differences of opinion and to ultimately offer a single group product. The actual task structure of the group assignment is central to the success of the cooperative group. The approach to the task has to be organized conceptually and in terms of labor allocations. Thus, if the assignment is to evaluate the application of a proposed new law, or to create new ideas on how to combat a crime, or to write and dramatize a play depicting an important historical event, or to offer a review of a great work of literature, some group structure (roles and functions) should be in place to handle the task structure. Johnson and Johnson (1991) suggest, at least with younger children, that the cooperative group can be best managed by identifying seven key functions: summarizing, checking, researching, running, recording, supporting, and troubleshooting. These roles could be appointed to individuals or to small subsets within the overall group.

The cooperative learning experience is monitored closely by the teacher, who has some obligation to be sure that the group is on task and to otherwise assist the group with advice on both practical and conceptual concerns, including problems that might surface from social frictions. As with the other discussion-based approaches mentioned, the cooperative learning experience is also subjected to a debriefing session that allows the groups to discuss how well everything functioned, to distill and summarize the key ideas taken from the different groups, and to reflect on what exactly made some groups more effective than others.

If discussion-based methods seek to create an informed conversation, inquiry-based methods seek to put the student into the role of a researcher. Rather than being the receiver of transmitted knowledge from the teacher, the learner is more like a discoverer guided by the teacher's map. The use of an inquiry-based strategy is obviously appropriate if the skills of inquiry take center stage in the curriculum. If skills related to observing, measuring, predicting, inferring, interpreting data, evidence collection, hypothesis formation, and experimenting are at all a part of the curriculum plan, then inquiry-based instruction will likely have some presence in the school experience.

The processes of inquiry-based instruction are put into motion when a discrepant event needs to be addressed or when a dilemma or problem or puzzling situation needs to be resolved. Inquiry-based instruction is simultaneously problem-based or problem-driven instruction. The presentation of a discrepant event, or the creation of what some educators call cognitive dissonance, is the initiating condition for inquiry-based instruction. This can be a "what if?" problem or a real life school or community-based problem; it can be an ethical dilemma or question that asks the student to evaluate or analyze ideas and topics.

Once the problem is on the table, as it were, the task of the teacher is to supply an experience that allows the learner to become better acquainted with the problem and with the various issues surrounding it. This could result in independent research work, in various reading requirements, and in structured discussion groups. An important feature to this part of the instructional process is for the student to collect relevant evidence and to evaluate the collected evidence, looking with a critical eye at the nature and credibility of the source and other factors attesting to the veracity of the evidence. This phase of the inquiry process also provides a context for the learning of the subject matter built into the instructional design.

After all the evidence is collected and evaluated and the nature of the topic is understood from its context in the subject matter, the inquiry process returns to the original discrepant event by addressing possible solutions, explanations, or hypotheses (depending on the nature of the problem). Obviously, good communication and argumentation skills are required. The inquiry process finally comes to a close with an illustration of conclusions and implications, which gets at the issue of just what was learned and what else might now be pursued to further the line of inquiry initiated.

Inquiry-based instruction obviously makes use of other instructional models. Direct instruction might play a role in helping to explain the problem, small discussion groups might be at the core of the research and data gathering stage, and cooperative learning might very well be the best way to forge and test hypotheses.

Finally, it is important to acknowledge that much of the work done by students in class is accomplished without the direct assistance of the teacher. The practical logic of the classroom obviously points to the need for children to often be working independently, if only because their teacher simply cannot be at their side at all times. Therefore, the nature of independent work in the classroom is an important part of the instructional repertoire, so much so that we find it built into other instructional approaches. One might recall, for instance, that the last phase of direct instruction advises independent practice activities and that much of the cooperative learning technique relies on independent social and decision-making interactions.

Independent work also possesses the advantage of individualization. That is, to the extent that independent work is associated with individualizing causes, it could account for pacing differences and other forms of differentiation related to aptitude, achievement, and interest levels. In this way, independent instruction represents an important procedure for individualization in the curriculum.

Some instructional approaches toward individualization do little more than set different paces or speeds for learning. Mastery learning programs, for instance, allow children to work through a common series of self-instructing workbook exercises at different rates of speed. This is not the most dynamic form of instructional individualization.

A more progressive concept of independent and differentiated instruction is embodied in the idea of the project method. Project-based learning has had a long history in the elementary school and is sustained by a desire to encourage self-directed learning by providing students with an idea-oriented and problem-focused project. The project could obviously extend into any number of subject areas, reinforce any number of skills, and develop important appreciations for what is being learned and how it is being learned.

The project method was first popularized by William Kilpatrick, whose 1918 treatise on the topic served as an impetus for a new progressive tradition of active and experience-based learning. The idea of the project method was partly designed as a counter against the then-established mentalistic conventions of schooling. So rather than engaging in learning that was book-bound and rooted in the disciplinary traditions of the formal subjects, Kilpatrick designed a method that was active and that aimed to explore problems and ideas that transcended the formal subject matter lines. The strength to the method was its capacity to bring any number of different activities to the classroom. Drawing, constructing, reading, viewing, and any number of other activities could all become part of a project. The intention was to try to make schooling coterminous with life itself.

The project method gives the teacher enormous flexibility in responding to individual differences and desires because it expects students to pursue purposeful activities independently. In fact, the key feature to the project method is self-initiation, meaning that what children want do to in school is a big factor in deciding what they should do in school. The project method has no real methodological profile. Activities that create something, that cultivate an appreciation, that rectify some intellectual difficulty, or that acquire some degree of skill or knowledge could all qualify as projects if moved by the spirit of purposefulness (Kilpatrick, 1918).

Evaluating the School Experience

We evaluate or otherwise try to understand our world as we live in it. Our abilities to pass thoughtful judgments, to draw reasonable conclusions, to establish a sense of what is worthwhile and to understand what needs to be changed (as well as conserved) are all rooted in the act of evaluation. To evaluate the world means to think actively about it and to ultimately problematize it in a way that sets the conditions for its progress. Evaluation, in effect, allows us to know what we have done well and to find a way to convert what we have not done well into corrections and improvements. It is the feedback loop in the design of the curriculum, which is to say the procedure we use to note whether certain purposes have been achieved. But it is also entangled in other curriculum-based factors, such as individual student performance, teacher performance, and other quality concerns related to the organization and mission of the school.

The term evaluation itself is unique and uniquely positioned in the process of curriculum development. The big overarching question behind it is to know whether the curriculum has produced experiences that have demonstrably attained the main purposes of the school. As Tyler (1949) put it, "the process of evaluation is essentially the process of determining to what extent the educational objectives are actually being realized by the program of curriculum and instruction" (p. 105–106).

Many educators do not understand that evaluation is an essential component to the act of curriculum development. This is partly understandable, given the high political priority placed on testing as an end in-and-of-itself. But no design of evaluation can be understood outside of its moorings in the curriculum. We evaluate in order to understand whether we have reached the purposes we explicitly sought to attain—notice I used the term evaluate, not test.

The term evaluation means something distinct from other terms (such as testing, measurement, and assessment) with which it is often associated. Ralph Tyler hit on the idea of evaluation because of his frustration with the use of tests as single point appraisal mechanisms. The early development of testing in the public schools was accompanied by a tendency to reduce the judgment of the curriculum to a single test score. Tyler saw this as a dangerous misuse of testing—one that threatened to distort the nature of the school curriculum itself. Today, of course, the problem is still with us. The handiwork of our failure to make any good distinction between testing and evaluation has given rise to what James Popham originally called high stakes testing, which are tests that are linked to high-stakes events, such as graduation requirements, grade-retention decisions, enrollment in various curriculum tracks, and even to the use of special label classifications, such as gifted and talented. When testing has this kind of influence in the curriculum, the consequences are predictable in that we can expect the test to displace the core purposes of the curriculum as the driving factor in the development of the curriculum.

Tyler's idea of evaluation was to link it to purposes and to force a form of thinking about judging effects in the curriculum that transcends the instrumentation of a test. In this manner, Tyler actually was among the first to think of evaluation along the lines of using a variety of strategies to document some judgment of what students have learned. In other words, Tyler constructed evaluation as an evidence collection process that made use of any variety of useful appraisal tools relevant to the curriculum's main purposes. Thus, if we consider core purposes x, y, and z, and provide responsive instruction to x, y, and z, we inevitably also have to look for ways to evaluate x, y, and z, which means that we must find the tools needed to demonstrate whether our purposes were indeed attained. Rather than use only a test for such a task, we might instead embrace any number of devices, including observational data, interview data, behavior inventories, rating scales, student products, and any other possible range of tools that teachers (or school-wide authorities) might find, including, of course, tests.

The instrumentation used in evaluation has to worry about validity and reliability concerns. That is, educators have to be sure that the tools they use to discern effects are valid (meaning that they actually give us the evidence that they are designed to produce) and are reliable (meaning that the evidence collected is internally consistent and consistent over time). Some instruments of evaluation, such as achievement tests, might be compromised by validity issues, especially if, for instance, they are not appropriate to the age and maturity level of the child or if they test something that the teacher has not even taught. Observational data, on the other hand, might be compromised by reliability concerns that turn out fundamentally different judgments based on who is doing the observing. Of course, to the extent that some components of evaluation are not valid, they will also likely be unreliable, and vice versa.

The traditional way to look at evaluation is to see it as a summative phenomenon, as something that occurs at the logical conclusion of a unit, chapter, or semester. The purpose of a summative evaluation is to get feedback on the curriculum experience at the completion of some logical phase of instruction. Summative evaluations are important precisely because they provide us with a completed sense of the curriculum experience. But no evaluation should become an exclusive, one-time only procedure that occurs at the end of a program. Hence, curriculum developers should see evaluation as a process that also has a formative point of reference. Formative evaluation is what we call ongoing evaluation. It might be given before the start of a new chapter, or unit, or semester (possibly to be used to gauge growth over time) or at any other time during the instructional phases. Formative evaluation gives the curriculum a way to negotiate changes and to appraise emerging problems, deficiencies, and strengths.

The evaluative component of curriculum development is obviously the one way we can determine where changes might be in order for the curriculum. If achievement test scores are lower than expected or than can be tolerated, then the school might look for solutions in the instructional component of the curriculum. If the evaluation shows that many students hate school, dislike learning, rarely read a book on their own, or rarely use a library, the school might redesign its purposes to strengthen the commitment to the realization of certain positive attitudes and appreciations in learning.

THE LATENT CURRICULUM

The implementation of the school curriculum always carries various latent or implicit meanings that teach children crucially important things. Thus, when educators teach something like multiplication skills, they might also be teaching children something about liking or disliking math, about liking or disliking learning, or even perhaps something about what it means to work hard, to persevere, to have patience, or to be honest. It is unlikely that any teacher would manifestly design lessons dedicated to making children more honest, but it is likely that many aspects of the school experience will communicate latent messages to children about honesty and other important values and attitudes. Such messages can be transmitted to the student in multiple and highly nuanced ways—in the rectitude of the teacher's own behaviors (both inside and outside of the classroom), in the manner in which teachers respond to student questions and concerns, and in the general interactive pattern between teachers and students (the tone of a teacher's voice, the style of her body language, the language used and favored in the classroom, the forms of affection, if any, conveyed, and so forth). We call this the latent curriculum, also sometimes known as the implicit curriculum, the covert curriculum or the hidden curriculum. The latent curriculum lives in the thousands of interactions that occur between teachers and students each school day.

The idea of the latent curriculum has fascinated scholars for many years because it widens the sense of the school experience by looking beyond traditional concerns over meeting behavioral objectives, covering content, keeping order, and raising tests scores. Because the early progressive movement in education took part of its identity from a commitment to broadening the focus of the school beyond its explicit commitment to developing skills and teaching knowledge, the latent curriculum became a front and center concern for progressives. Consequently, the school came under new and provocative questions about the kinds of effects it was having on teaching of critical values, attitudes, and dispositions. What effect, for instance, did schools have on the student's disposition to enjoy learning, to derive pleasure from inquiry, and to be practically empowered by the wider world of knowledge brought forth in the school? What did the schools do to construct the self-esteem of youth, to influence their leisure-time habits, and to sway their attitudes and actions toward community, society, and government? Referring to the latent curriculum as collateral learning, John Dewey (1938) understood the implications the implicit lessons taught in school. "Perhaps the greatest of all pedagogical fallacies," he wrote, "is the notion that a person learns only the particular thing he is studying at the time. Collateral learning in the way of formation of enduring attitudes, of likes and dislikes, may be and often is much more important than the spelling lesson, or lesson in geography or history that is learned" (p. 48).

The latent curriculum is important to the school because it shapes important values and outlooks, including critically important values related to independent learning and independent thinking. Learning to read, for instance, is undeniably important, but it is essentially a lost cause if the learner who can read ably hates to read altogether and rarely engages in a book independently. The latent curriculum is the main influence in producing the kinds of values and outlooks (negative or positive) we embrace toward schooling and toward learning. What schools teach implicitly can also strongly influence the makeup of the cultural norms conveyed and reinforced in the school, sending signals about what is worthy to know, worthy to do, and worthy to read, as well as indirect lessons about various common values and mores.

The latent curriculum is largely in the hands of a teacher's pedagogy. If a teacher of English, for instance, regularly uses writing assignments to punish poor behavior in class, she must understand that the latent curriculum is at work, sending a less than constructive message to the student about the act of writing. If a teacher can always be seen reading in the library after school hours and is publicly know to be a voracious reader, an important pro-reading latent message is projected. If the social studies teacher gives an unpopular viewpoint in class the same level of critical respect and appreciation that popular views enjoy, an important latent message about critical consciousness and dissent is conveyed. If a socially-unpopular or socially-clumsy student receives the same degree of attention and respect from the teacher as the academic star or the sports star, a latent social lesson is communicated. If disrespect, dishonesty, shoddiness, and laziness are treated with consistent intolerance by the teacher, again the latent lessons are clear. In none of the above cases was there ever a need to design a lesson plan. The teaching was in the subtext of the interactive pattern between the teacher and the student.

From the standpoint of the curriculum, the main implication of latent learning is to be conscious of its presence and its possibilities, and for educators to try to think deliberately about how their behavior results in offering latent lessons. The other important key is to valorize the latent curriculum by privileging its effects in the evaluation of the curriculum, so that all of the attitudinal factors that play into the latent curriculum make their way into the evaluative mechanism.

THE NULL CURRICULUM

Finally, educators would be wise to also think about an analytic feature of the school curriculum known as the null curriculum. Because the school curriculum is comprised of decisions related to what to include or privilege in the school experience, some insight can be derived from understanding what the curriculum has excluded from the experience of school children. In other words, because the school curriculum cannot teach everything, much can be learned about what the school has not chosen to include in the experience of school children. The null curriculum represents what the school has decided to not teach (Eisner, 1998) and thus becomes an analytical device for understanding the nature of bias in decision making. It also provides a useful contrast that allows educators to weight the relative importance of what they are teaching against what they are not teaching.

The null curriculum, for instance, can certainly help us understand the effects of legislation such as the No Child Left Behind Act, which has required states to design testing regiments that account for achievement in only reading, mathematics, and science education. By placing reading, math, and science at the forefront of the school's concerns, the legislation creates a null curriculum that is worth discussing. What does the school lose when it dedicates its resources unduly to matters that are only reflected in the all-important testing programs? Could the commitment to developing interpersonal skills, inquiry-based skills, the exercise of imagination, and socio-personal attitudes toward learning and toward the institution of school be lost to the null curriculum? What happens to citizenship, to the arts, to reading poetry, to learning how to get along, and other key realms of learning? What can we generally say about the desirability of such losses in light of what the legislation is offering?

Often school decision-makers don't know what they don't know, meaning that their ignorance of the full range of possibilities do not allow them to properly weigh all the key factors in a decision. The null curriculum helps to prevent such a condition by bringing to full light what the school is not doing and by forcing a discussion of the advisability of such exclusions. Think about what your own school experience did not cultivate. Hopefully, it is a long list of unwholesome or unhealthy matters, but there is likely a fairly long list of important skills and values as well. For instance, schools today generally recognize the importance of thinking skills in the curriculum, but they do not typically reflect all forms of thinking. Take the exercise of analogical thinking, which is the use of figurative language that might include the ability to use metaphors, similes, personification, and other literary forms to gain a clearer understanding of abstract or complex ideas, or the exercise of imagination, which moves beyond what is factual and logical and into the realm of informed speculation and the production of novel expressions of insight. Neither of these has much presence in schools and almost no presence in testing regiments. Think about the use of non-verbal skills of communication, including the exercise of a variety of musical, visual, theatrical, dance, and mathematical forms. When was the last time anyone danced an answer to a question in school? These typically constitute the null curriculum and by virtue of being there, they require examination and debate.

The design of the school experience is a zero sum game. A new inclusion into an existing curriculum likely means that something has to be excised to make space for it. If computer literacy, for instance, prevails as an important skill in the curriculum, some thought has to go into determining its place in the organization of the curriculum. One likely effect will be that something else will be pushed out of the explicit curriculum and pushed into the null curriculum. Thus, there will always be a null curriculum and there will always be a need to keep an eye on what we decide to not teach.

SUMMARY

The school curriculum is the teachers' blueprint for action. It outlines a normative (or institutional) agenda by detailing and organizing the overarching aims of the school, including the content, skills, and values that are expected to be taught. The teacher is the main operator of the curriculum and has to be given enough liberty to actualize the explicit curriculum in a way that is sympathetic to the unique and dynamic conditions of the classroom situation. Thus, the curriculum directs or channels instructional judgment but does not dictate it. Teachers also understand that much of what happens in the school curriculum is not always publicly rationalized or acknowledged. Many of the most important influences on student attitudes and values are conveyed latently, through interactive patterns of conversation and other forms of engagement. These interactions leave impressions on student attitudes toward school, toward learning, toward the construction of self-esteem, and other essential attitudinal dimensions. As a result, perceptive educators are deliberately conscious of the potential latent effects that occur through the explicit curriculum. Finally, the school curriculum can also be understood by what it does not teach. Using the null curriculum as an analytical tool, teachers can contemplate what is lost or otherwise neglected by virtue of its absence from the curriculum, and weigh it against what is favored by its inclusion.

REFERENCES

Cross, R. W., Rebarber, T., & Torres, J. (2004). *Grading the systems: The guide to state standards, tests and accountability policies.* Washington, DC: Thomas B. Fordham Foundation.

Dewey, J. (1904). Education Direct and Indirect. In Boydston, Jo Ann (ed.) *John Dewey, The Middle Works, 1899–1924.* Volume 16. Carbondale, IL: Southern Illinois University Press.

Dewey, J. (1916). *Democracy and education.* New York: Macmillan Co.

Dewey, J. (1938). *Experience and education.* New York: Macmillan Co.

Eisner, E. (1998). *The educational imagination.* New York: Macmillan Co.

Johnson, D. W. and Johnson, R. T. (1991). *Learning together and alone.* Englewood Cliffs, NJ: Prentice-Hall.

Joyce, B., & Weil, M. (1986). *Models of Teaching.* Englewood Cliffs, NJ: Prentice-Hall.

Kilpatrick, William. (1918). The Project Method. *Teachers College Record* 19(4):319-335.

Public Law 107-110. *The No Child Left Behind Act of 2001,* from http://www.ed.gov/policy.

Ravitch, D. (1995). *National standards in American education.* Washington, DC: The Brookings Institution.

Taba, H. (1962). *Curriculum development: Theory and practice.* New York: Harcourt, Brace and Javanovich.

Tyler, R. (1949). *Basic principles of curriculum and instruction.* Chicago: University of Chicago Press.

Wisconsin Department of Public Education. (1998). *Wisconsin Model of academic standards,* from http://www.dpi.state.wi.us.

Zais, R. S. (1976). *Curriculum: Principles and foundations.* New York: Crowell.

KEY QUESTIONS

1. How is the metaphor of "running a race track" useful to understanding the concept of the school curriculum. How is it a flawed metaphor?
2. What do you think of the metaphor that likens the framing of aims, goals, and objectives to setting targets? Where are the flaws in the metaphor? Can you think of a better one?
3. What is the essential message sent to the curriculum developer in Dewey's "criteria for good aims"?
4. What is the difference between a content standard, a proficiency standard, and a performance standard?
5. Do you agree with Diane Ravitch when she says that all standards should be measurable, specific, and exceptionally clear? Why or why not?
6. Do you believe that research can produce widely applicable best methods for teaching?
7. What is meant by the argument that one cannot pursue instructional strategies that are good without contemplating what they are good for?
8. Why is a role-playing instructional approach viewed as discussion-based instruction and what are some of the cautionary points to consider with a role-playing strategy?
9. What is meant by the reference to evaluation as "an evidence collection process"?
10. What is the latent curriculum? Describe examples of how implicit messages or meanings are taught to children through the latent curriculum.

RESEARCH EXERCISES

1. Ask any number of educators for their definitions of curriculum and analyze them according to the principles discussed in the chapter. Compare these definitions to ones drawn from the literature or the ones shared in the beginning of the chapter.

2. Survey teachers, asking them if their school district or school principal imposes any strict instructional regulations on their teaching. In other words, are they required to follow any particular method or lesson approach? Does the school have an instructional program that they must follow? Describe their attitudes and reactions to such programs.

3. Reports on the state of state standards in science, math, and English can be found on the Thomas B. Fordham Institute website (www.edexcellence.net). All of the 2005 reports can be downloaded and read in their entirety. Conduct your own analysis of the grading system used by the Fordham reviewers. Contrast the grades that they gave to each state on the quality of their standards against the documented achievement gains of the state. For instance, I took the NAEP reading scores for 8th graders, disaggregated by state, from 1998 and contrasted them against the scores achieved in 2002, noting average raw score declines and increases. I then looked to see how each of the states did on Fordham's grading criteria on reading standards, contrasting the grade given in 1998 to the grade given in 2000, and again noting declines and increases. The figure below shows the results. What might this say about the way Fordham reviews standards?

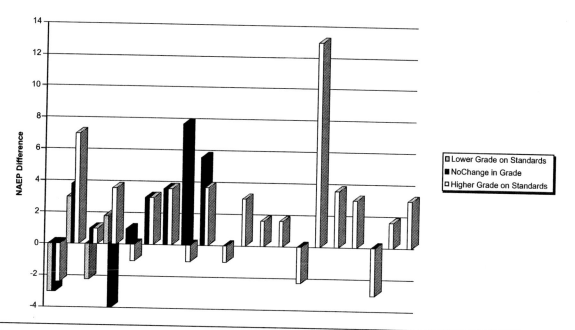

Difference in Average NAEP Score for 8th Grade Reading from 1998 to 2002 (by State) Against Difference in Grade Given for Quality of Standards.

CHAPTER 4

The Emergence of a Profession

The formation of a teaching profession in the United States is a century-old project. Historically speaking, the making of a profession of teachers is centered on producing educators who could bring specialized knowledge to the task of teaching the normative mission of the public school. At a minimum, these professionally-trained teachers are expected to possess specialized knowledge of children and to have particular subject matter knowledge and instructional know-how. They are also expected to understand the unique features of the public school agenda and to be capable of making independent judgments responsive to the conditions of the local educational situation. Thus, part of a teacher's professional development includes learning how to make and implement lessons, how to weight different motivational and pedagogical techniques, how to organize classroom events, maintain classroom control, evaluate learning outcomes, and in the most general sense, how to fulfill the mission of the school curriculum while still conducting oneself in accordance with the values of society and the nature of the learner.

WHO EDUCATES THE MASSES?

Who are the people that society has entrusted with the formal education of youngsters? What are their lives like in school and what do we expect from them in the classroom?

One of the interesting characteristics of the teaching profession is its gender distribution. Over 78 percent of the nation's 2.5 million public school teachers are women (National Education Association, 2003, p. 91). The disproportionately high representation of women in the profession has been in place since about 1900, when about 70 percent of the teaching was comprised of women (NCES, Digest of Education Statistics, 1995). In fact, in recent decades, the trend has moved in the direction of higher proportions of women, up from 74 percent in 1996 and from 69 percent in 1986 (National Education Association, 2003, p. 91). In the elementary school, hiring assignments are overwhelmingly given to women (over 90 percent), but women also take up about 65 percent of the teaching jobs in the secondary school. These are the highest proportions of women witnessed in the profession in decades. These are also very high rates by international standards (National Center for Education Statistics, 2000).

The dominance of women in the teaching profession of the American schools has something to do with the early development of normal schools in the United States, which were teacher training schools that highlighted the use of teaching methodologies as opposed to subject matter expertise. In early parts of the nineteenth century, receiving an education in the academic subject matter, which was embodied in course work at the university or college level, was viewed as appropriate for only men. It was a man's intellect, not a woman's, that was considered to be equal to the task of learning the academic subject matter. Long denied access to higher education, women could, by and large, only look to the normal school as a realistic outlet for professional education. Although normal school graduates were required to learn the subject matter that they were responsible to teach, the normal school's commitment to the "lightweight" task of teaching methodologies posed no threat to and evinced little interest from males. The old maxim of "those who can't, teach" had real life application in the minds of many males. Such a prejudice, combined with an emerging popular cultural perspective that viewed teaching as an extension of mothering, as a gentle job for a gentle sex, helped to make teaching women's work.

With respect to race and class, the nation's teaching force remains the work of mostly white, middle-class women. During the 2002 academic year, black (non-Hispanic) children represented about 17 percent of the public school enrollment, while the Hispanic enrollment stood closer to 18 percent, a combined population that exceeds one-third of the overall student enrollment (National Center for Education Statistics, 2004). At the same time, only about 11 percent of all public school teachers were drawn from these two minority groups (National Education Association, 2003, p. 89), see Figure 4–1. Indeed, as the public schools' student population is becoming increasingly diverse, the race-ethnicity characteristics of teachers are lagging behind, and the situation does not show many signs of improving. About 19 percent of all black non-Hispanic teachers are beginning teachers (three years of experience or less), but over 36 percent have twenty more years of experience. With retirement looming for a large share of black teachers, the representation of black non-Hispanic teachers in the teaching force will not likely improve soon, short of a dramatic and almost immediate influx of new teachers. For Hispanic teachers, however, the situation looks better, as about 26 percent of all Hispanic teachers are beginning teachers, while about 21 percent have at least twenty years of experience. Young beginning Hispanic teachers are in greater proportion to the whole teaching corps of Hispanic teachers than are veteran Hispanic teachers (NCES, 2003). At the same time, however, the student enrollment of Hispanic children is expected to also proportionally increase from about 18 percent in 2002 to over 20 percent by 2010 (United States Census Bureau, 2006).

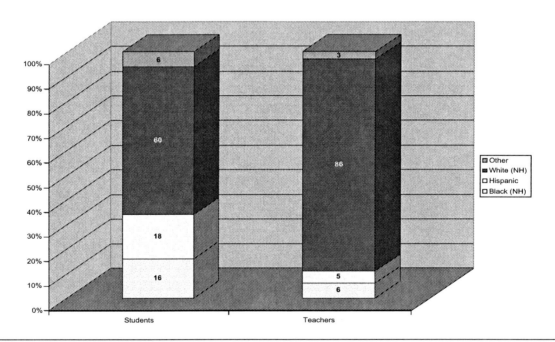

FIGURE 4–1   Public School Students v. Public School Teachers, by Race and Ethnicity, 2001. Data taken from NEA (2003) and NCES (2003).

Few would dispute the need of all children in the public schools to be exposed to the vast racial and ethnic diversity represented in the nation's population. Some have argued that it is especially important for minority children to be exposed to minority teachers, largely because of a belief that such teachers are living role models for minority children and are better attuned to the motivational and performance-related needs of minority children (Ladson-Billings, 1994). The evidence for such a contention, however, is not definitive. Using data from the National Educational Longitudinal Study of 1988 (NELS), Ehrenberg, Goldhaber, and Brewer (1995) found that the match between a teacher's race, gender, and ethnicity and those of their students did not affect student achievement. It did, in some instances, affect a teacher's subjective evaluation of a student, but there was little evidence that such evaluations had any long-term consequences. Dee (2004), however, found evidence that "own-race" teachers did affect student achievement among both minority and non-minority elementary school-aged children. This remains an important area of inquiry, largely because Dee's findings could suggest that increased racial segregation between teachers and students is a way to improve student performance, a position that is contrary to the normative policies of the public school.

Interestingly, we seem to find that minority teachers, although overall under-represented in the teaching ranks, are nevertheless heavily represented in schools where more than one-half of the student population belongs to a minority group (see Figure 4–2). Sixty-eight percent of all black non-Hispanic teachers, for instance, work in largely minority schools. This could be interpreted as both good and bad news. Although minority teachers seem to be teaching where they might be most needed, their presence in all the schools of America is still a benefit waiting to be reaped. Moreover, where there are high minority student enrollments, there are often high poverty levels among the children, and as it turns out, high levels of limited English proficiency (LEP) students. Thus, the lack of representative

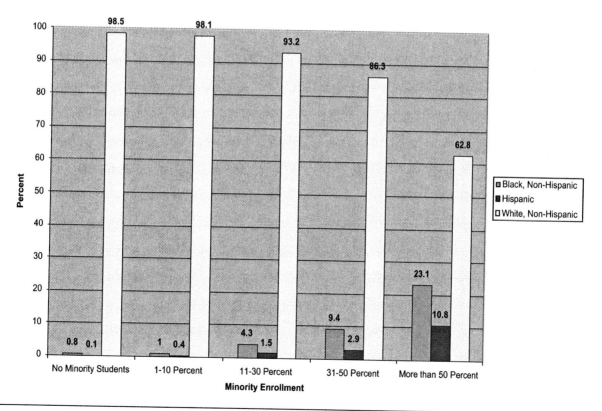

FIGURE 4–2 Percentage Distribution of Teachers According to Race-Ethnicity, by Sector and Minority Enrollment in Their Schools, 1993–94. Data taken from: NCES (1993–94), Schools and Staffing Survey.

diversity not only cuts across the student population by race and ethnicity, but also by income level and English language ability. If the public schools are schools of democracy, then it seems axiomatic that the ethnic and racial composition of America's schoolteachers will need to reflect America's student population. It currently does not and the remediation of this problem is viewed by many to be at the very core of any future school reform.

Public school teachers are a highly educated group of professionals. About 56 percent of all public school teachers have a Master's degree; less than 1 percent does not hold a Bachelor's degree (NEA, 2003). Teachers are often encouraged to pursue graduate education by school districts that design their salary schedules in a way that rewards teachers who continue to advance their education. In several states, a Master's degree is considered the professional diploma for a public school teacher. In New York, for instance, a Master's degree is required for permanent certification as a teacher. Unfortunately, across the nation, the distribution of teachers with a Master's degree is significantly lower in high poverty schools, standing at around 37 percent (as measured by schools that report 60 percent or more of their student population on free and reduced lunch), than in low poverty schools, where it is about 57 percent (National Center for Education Statistics, 1998) (see Figure 4–3).

The political and religious character of the teaching profession is balanced, if not slightly tilted, to the political right. According to the National Education Association (2003), 44 percent of public school teachers characterize themselves as liberal or moderately liberal, while 56 percent characterize themselves as conservative or moderately conservative. This contradicts the popular image of a politically

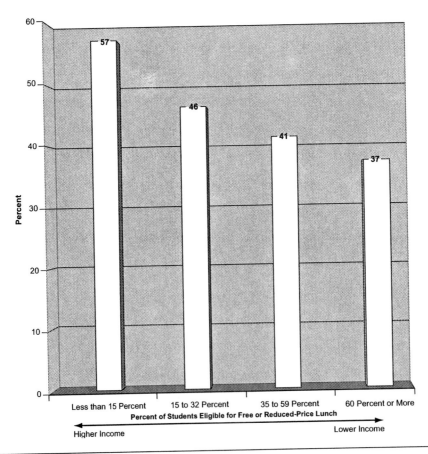

FIGURE 4–3 Percent of Full-Time Public School Teachers Who Hold a Master's Degree, by Students Eligible for Lunch. Data taken from: NCES (1998), Fast Response Survey System, Teacher Survey on Professional Development.

liberal profession that marches to the orders of the Democratic political party, although 45 percent of the teaching profession affiliates with the Democratic political party, against 28 percent with the Republican party (NEA, 2003). The Carnegie Foundation for the Advancement of Teaching (1990) reports that about one-fourth of all teachers see themselves as deeply religious and another 62 percent see themselves as moderately religious. Altogether, 88 percent of the public teaching force sees itself as deeply or moderately religious. This is an important finding because many conservative critics of the public school like to describe it as a cold institution operated by people who have no religious depth. The irony is that the secular nature of schooling is protected and served by largely religious individuals. Only 12 percent of teachers stated that they were indifferent to religion, and only 1 percent was opposed to it.

THE STATUS OF THE TEACHING PROFESSION

Participation in a profession typically requires credentials gained through some state sanctioned method of certification whereby individuals are judged able to perform a particular set of specialized professional skills. This process of certification is usually associated with a training program and is, more times than not, consummated through an official licensing examination. Other characteristics of a profession include: 1) presence of an induction program to help bring new professionals into the field; 2) ongoing in-service training programs designed to help keep professionals vital and on top of any emerging changes in their field; 3) expectation of authority to exercise decision-making in the workplace; 4) good compensation, largely through salary and benefits, throughout the span of a professional career; and 5) relevance of the credentialing process to job assignments, meaning the extent to which hiring practices are based on credentials earned in professional training programs (National Center for Education Statistics, 1997a). Not surprisingly, statistical analyses done by the National Center for Education Statistics (1997b) found that professional indices, such as teacher autonomy and teacher influence, higher end-of-career salaries, and assistance for teacher induction were all positively associated with higher levels of reported teacher commitment, and the related traits of engagement, enthusiasm, and satisfaction toward the profession.

How does teaching fare when judged as a profession against the above criteria? In terms of salaries, public school teachers across the country report an average annual salary of about $46,000 (American Federation of Teachers, 2005). Adjusting for inflation, the average pay scale for teachers has been historically flat. Using 1995 dollars, no real increase has been witnessed in the average pay for public schools teachers since at least 1995 (see Figure 4–4). In fact, when the real wages of teachers are scaled against the increases of all workers since 1995, teacher salaries have simply not kept up.

Public school teachers beginning their careers can expect to earn an average annual salary of about $32,000, although the number varies considerably across the states. The average salary, however, is still considerably lower than the salary offered to all other college graduates. Because teachers are typically given a ten-month contract, they have an opportunity to augment their annual salary. In some schools, teachers can receive supplementary pay for coaching sports, teaching during the summer months, working in after-school programs, or performing administrative jobs in the school, which on the average results in about $2,500 in supplemental earnings (National Center for Education Statistics, 1997a, p. 73).

Teacher's salaries are often determined by negotiated salary schedules that account for the education levels of the teachers and their years of experience, without, in most cases, any consideration given to

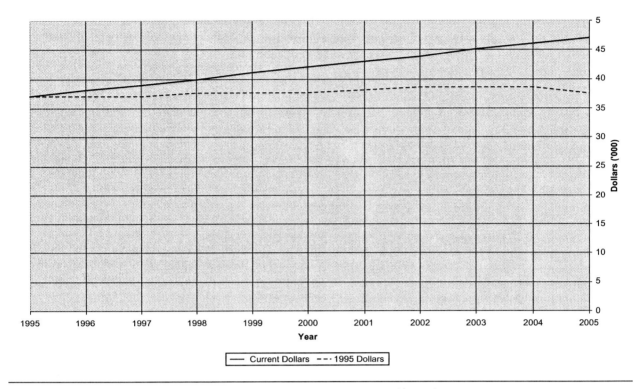

FIGURE 4–4 **Average Classroom Teacher Salary, 1995–2005 ($'000).** Data taken from National Association of Colleges and Employers; American Federation of Teachers (2005).

grade level or subject taught. Teachers can usually expect pay raises based on an accumulation of experience and additional education, not on any judgment of classroom performance, although some urban school districts have embraced performance pay for teachers by defining performance narrowly as raising student test scores (Blumenthal, 2006). Over 90 percent of public school districts still use a step-wise salary schedule that accounts for experience and education (NCES, 2002).

Teachers continue to earn less than many other college graduates, despite being no less academically able. The negative stereotype of a teacher is one that is built on the image of a low-achieving and poorly educated college graduate. Popular media outlets have featured these unfair portrayals with some regularity (Hlebowitsh, 1996). But the evidence demonstrates a fundamentally different conclusion. Educational Testing Service (ETS) released a study in 1999 (Bruschi & Coley, 1999) that documented the prose, document, and quantitative skills of teachers, showing their scores in prose and document literacy to be equal to college graduates in general. Teachers with graduate degrees also compared favorably with the general population of adults who have attained a graduate degree)(see Figure 4–5). In the words of the researchers, "What we can take away from this analysis is the assurance that our teachers measure up well with those in other professions and those with similar levels of education. This is contrary to the national view that has developed, proving that we need to abandon the currently negative stereotype" (Bruschi & Coley, 1999, p. 25).

Contrary to popular opinion, teachers do not work a shortened workweek. Teachers spend about 37 required hours per week at school, where their time is dedicated largely to teaching their class, preparing lessons, attending staff meetings, and fulfilling any number of school-related responsibilities. This amounts to only about three-quarters of the teacher's workweek, because in addition to the required time in school, teachers devote approximately 12 more hours per week to activities involving students

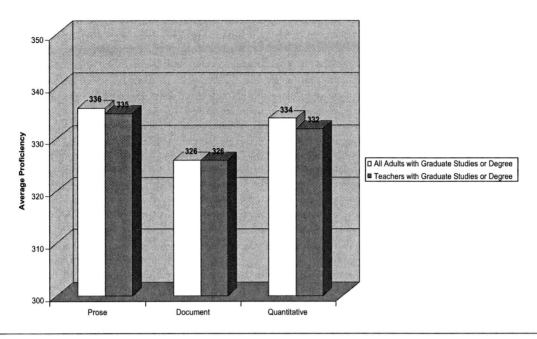

FIGURE 4–5   Average Prose, Document, and Quantitative Literacy Scores of Teachers with Graduate Studies or Degree Compared to Those of the Total Adult Population with Graduate Studies or Degree. Data taken from NCES (1992) National Adult Literacy Survey.

or involving school-related work, such as grading and lesson preparation. These numbers are more or less consistent between elementary and secondary schoolteachers. Thus, teachers, on average, spend about 49 weekly hours performing all of their teaching duties (NEA, 2003, pp. 40–43). This contrasts with the image of a reduced workweek. Other professions do not have a significantly longer workweek. Medical and law professionals report an average workweek of 49 hours. But in the case of, say, dentists, the average annual pay is $132,000 against approximately $46,000 for an elementary school teacher (United States Department of Labor, 2004).

The mentoring of the beginning teacher, which is a fundamental feature of professionalism, occurs on a formal basis with about half (58 percent) of all teachers who have three or less years of experience (National Center for Education Statistics, 1999a). Such programs seem to have had their desired effect. New teachers report that induction programs that include frequent common planning periods and regularly scheduled collaborations with veteran teachers, inside and outside of school, improved their teaching (National Center for Education Statistics, 1999b, p. 34). About 45 percent of teachers with 3 or fewer years of experience who reported to be mentored, claimed to benefit "a lot" from the experience. Only 5 percent claimed not to benefit at all (National Center for Education Statistics, 1999b) (see Figure 4.6).

The idea of teacher induction, or formal mentoring, is obviously well-established in the professions. Medical doctors, for instance, go through a three-year period of residency, during which they are under the supervision and mentorship of a senior doctor. Besides acting as an investment in producing good teachers, formal mentoring also has the effect of helping to retain teachers. Teachers with no induction experience are more likely to leave the profession than those who were formally mentored. They are also more likely to have management problems in the classroom (Darling-Hammond, 1997). Over the last twenty years, the states have taken an active interest in helping to establish the place of

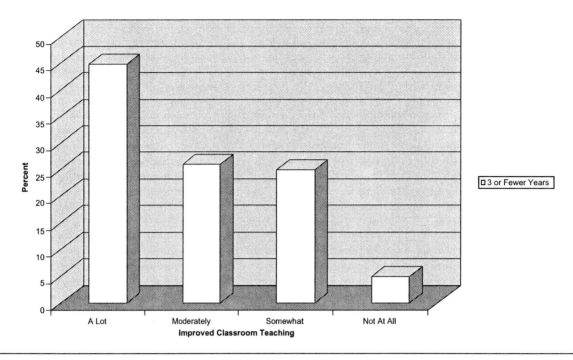

FIGURE 4–6 Percent of Beginning Public School Teachers Indicating the Extent to Which Being Mentored Improved their Classroom Teaching, 1998. Data taken from: NCES (1998), Fast Response Survey System, Teacher Survey on Professional Development.

induction in the professional development of teachers (American Federation of Teaching, 2001). Twenty-two states now mandate some formalized induction programs, another 11 have some policy on induction. Some of these states have statutory language on release time for beginning teachers, which could include time to observe or attend professional development activities; others advise some restriction on the novice teacher's duties and extracurricular involvement. A number of states mandate a standard stipend for the mentor teacher and sometimes provide language on the selection and training of the mentor teacher. Oklahoma appropriated the term "teacher resident" and designed an induction program that involves a committee made up of a mentor teacher, a school administrator, and a teacher educator, who together support the new teacher through her first year of teaching. Several states mandate a reduction on course load for mentor teachers.

In-service training for educators has a much longer and a better-established tradition in the school than induction programs. During the 2000–2001 academic years, 77 percent of all public school teachers reported participating in system-sponsored professional development activities during the school year (NEA, 2003). In-service programs that concentrated on using technology in the classroom and on grade-level/subject-matter concerns were the most popular. Other key areas of professional development dealt with topics related to the assessment of students' work, school safety, parental involvement, curriculum alignment, and classroom management. The data on in-service programs suggest that they can have a significant effect on a teacher's instructional conduct. In 1998, a strong majority of teachers reported that in-service programs improved their teaching to some degree, especially programs that committed more than 8 hours to a topic (National Center for Education Statistics, 1998). As Table 4–1 indicates, in-service programs that committed more than 8 hours of time to a topic were consistently observed by teachers to have improved their teaching in all the reported content areas.

TABLE 4–1   Percent of full-time public school teachers indicating the extent to which participation in professional development activities in various content areas improved their classroom teaching, 1998.

| | Improved My Teaching | | | |
Content Area	A Lot	Moderately	Somewhat	Not at All
State or district curriculum and performance standards	20	39	31	10
Integration of educational technology in the grade or subject you teach	38	43	17	2
New methods of teaching (e.g., cooperative learning)	39	41	18	2
In-depth study in the subject area of your main teaching assignment	41	41	17	1
Student performance assessment	35	41	20	3
Classroom management, including student discipline	40	41	14	5
Addressing the needs of students with disabilities	42	32	23	3
Addressing the needs of students with limited English proficiency or from diverse cultural backgrounds	38	34	23	5

NCES (1998) Fast Response Survey System, Teacher Survey on Professional Development and Training, 1998.

Efforts by school districts to support the ongoing or continuing education of teachers in post-bachelor settings could also be viewed as in-service education. In 2001, close to one-half of all public school teachers were reported to have earned some college credit (NEA, 2003). Although about one-third of public schools provided reimbursement to teachers for the costs (tuition and course fees) associated with furthering their education (National Center for Education Statistic, 1997a, p. 18), in 2001, teachers who earned college credits reported an average expenditure of almost $3,000 of their own money (NEA, 2003). These figures, however, have to be understood in relation to a teacher's salary schedule, which typically provides some financial rewards for the number of post-bachelor credits (or degrees) earned by a teacher. Other professional development options available to teachers include activities sponsored through other professional development organizations, work on curriculum committees or other special assignments, and even educational travel.

Teacher authority in the workplace, as demonstrated by teacher involvement in the critical affairs of the school, does not show the hallmarks of a profession. Data from the National Center for Education Statistics (1997a, p. 53) show that only 38 percent of teachers reported to have a good deal of influence over setting discipline policy and establishing curriculum (which might include activities such as choosing textbooks and instructional materials, shaping curriculum standards and objectives, and determining school-wide evaluation mechanisms). Only 31 percent of public school teachers claimed to have a good deal of influence over determining in-service content and only 8 percent claimed a lot of influence in hiring new teachers (National Center for Education Statistics, 1997a, p. 53). From other accounts, we find an overwhelming majority of teachers claiming not to be at all involved in selecting new teachers, in evaluating teacher performance and in selecting new administrators (Carnegie Foundation, 1990).

In contrast, teachers did report having extensive control of their classrooms. Teachers claimed to have extensive authority over practices such as evaluating and grading students, determining the amount of homework, selecting teaching techniques, and disciplining students. However, only a small majority of teachers viewed some classroom practices, such as selecting the content, topics, and skills to be taught in school and selecting tests and materials, as matters largely under their control (National Center for Education Statistics, 1997a, p. 52). The fact that many teachers believe that they either are not allowed or not expected to make critical judgments about what is taught in the schools most likely speaks to the influence of state-mandated content requirements in the curriculum.

Finally, a profession must, under all conditions, offer a credentialing experience that has a meaningful place in the professional workplace, meaning that a strong congruence should exist between the qualifications of the teacher and the teacher's job assignment. All teachers, for instance, should be knowledgeable of teaching and learning theory, of ways to design and apply good lessons, and of the developmental and psychological nature of the learner to which they have been assigned. Teachers with specific subject matter obligations must be deeply knowledgeable in the relevant subject matter. Thus, teachers of mathematics should have a demonstrable understanding of mathematics and so forth.

Unfortunately, the issue of credentialing remains a problem for the teaching profession because of the significant numbers of teachers who perform "out-of-field teaching" in the public schools (see Table 4–2). Out-of-field teachers can be defined as teachers who do not have an academic major, an academic minor, or certification in the teaching or subject area to which they are assigned. In the middle school grades, for instance, about 17 percent of the students enrolled in English courses were led by a teacher without a major, minor, or certification in English; for mathematics courses, the number rises to 22 percent (NCES, 2004a). In high school, 11 percent of students in foreign language courses were taught by a teacher who was without either a major, minor, or certification in foreign language. In high school English, out-of-field teachers affected over 5 percent of the student population, and in high school mathematics it was over 8 percent. If we use a more professionally-intensive criterion to define out-of-field teachers by limiting it to teachers who are without a major or certification in their field (eliminating the reference to the academic minor), the number of students exposed to out-of-field teachers rises precipitously. Approximately 70 percent of the students in middle-grade mathematics classes had teachers who did not report a major or certification in mathematics. In middle school English classes, foreign language classes, and science classes, approximately 60 percent of the student population was taught by out-of-field teachers. These high numbers in the middle school are partly the historical effect of extending the elementary certification, which does not always have a subject matter major associated with it, upward into middle school teaching.

If we apply our expanded definition to the high school, we find that approximately 30 percent of student enrolled in mathematics, English, and social science were in classrooms with an out-of-field teacher (NCES, 2004a). If a profession's credentialing process has less than a pervasive effect on professional hiring practice, one could argue that the profession is still struggling for recognition. The credentialing process in medicine, for instance, would not tolerate using doctors trained in, say, dermatology, to perform open heart surgery. Yet in teaching, credentialing still does not yet have good congruence with hiring assignments.

Table 4-2 Percentage of public school students by grade levels taught and teacher's qualification status in course subject area: 1999-2000.

Subject Field	Middle Grades 1999-2000		High School Grades 1999-2000	
	No Major & Certification	No Major, Minor, or Certification	No Major & Certification	No Major, Minor, or Certification
English	58.3	17.4	29.8	5.6
Foreign Language	60.7	13.8	47.6	11.1
Mathematics	68.5	21.9	31.4	8.6
Science	57.2	14.2	27.3	5.5
Social Science	51.1	13.3	27.9	5.9
ESL/Bilingual Education	72.9	36.1	70.8	31.1
Arts & Music	15.0	2.5	19.6	5.0
Physical Education	18.9	3.4	19.1	4.5

Middle level teachers include teachers who taught students in grades 5-9 and did not teach any students in grades 10-12; teachers who taught grades 5-9 who identified themselves as elementary or special education teachers were classified as elementary teachers. High school teachers include all teachers who taught any of grades 10-12, as well as teachers who taught grade 9 and no other grades.

NCES, Schools and Staffing Survey, 1999-2000. Public Teacher Survey and 1999-2000, Public Charter Teacher Survey.

Unfortunately, the problem of credentialing disproportionately affects schools that enroll high numbers of minority and low income children. Using the more intensive definition of out-of-field teaching, we find that the children attending high minority schools (schools with 75 percent or more minority enrollment) and high poverty schools (schools with 75 percent or more students eligible for free or reduced lunch) are much more likely to be taught by out-of-field teachers than children in low minority (10 percent or less) and low poverty (10 percent or less) settings. To the extent that we see credentialing as a problem facing the profession, we have to admit that it disproportionately affects children in high minority and high poverty school settings (see Figure 4-7). This is yet another example of how a general problem of professionalism tends to become more acute and visible in the education of low income and minority children.

Unfortunately, the teaching profession is not yet receiving passing grades on the central characteristics normally associated with professions. Accounting for inflation, salaries are generally flat and still seriously lag behind other professions. Induction and in-service programs are better designed, better funded, and more pervasive than in the past, but they are still very much in development and only have spotty support from the states. Teacher authority seems to have a solid standing in the classroom, but at the school-wide level, teacher authority is weak, having largely a sideline status to the authority of the school administration. It is important to emphasize, however, that teachers, despite being pinned with a negative stereotype about their competency, clearly represent a highly educated group with literacy and quantitative skills equal to those found in other professions, including more highly educated physicians. New forms of state (and even national) licensing examinations seems to be on the horizon for the profession as are forms of compensation that reward performance, rather than raw experience.

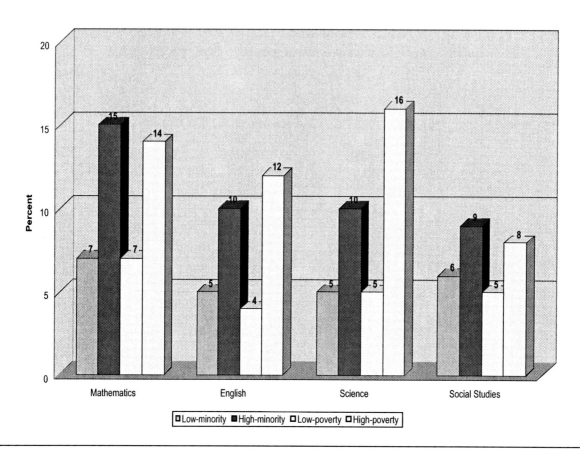

FIGURE 4–7   OUT-OF-FIELD TEACHERS: Percentage of Public High School Students Taught Selected Subjects by Teachers without Certification of a Major in the Field they Teach, by Minority Concentration and School Poverty, 1999–2000. NCES, Schools and Staffing Survey, 1999–2000. Public Teacher Survey and 1999–2000, Public Charter Teacher Survey.

TEACHER EDUCATION AND TEACHER LICENSURE

All of the states in the nation require licensure as a condition of employment for a public school teacher. Private schools are usually exempt from licensure standards, but they still tend to require a bachelor's degree as a requirement for employment. Teacher licensure is a state phenomenon, usually operationalized through the State Board of Education according to guidelines set down by the state. One can find some differences between the states, but generally speaking, regular licensure requires the completion of a bachelor's degree and a set of teacher training courses that culminate in a supervised student teaching experience. Some states also require the attainment of a minimum grade point average in college course work and the attainment of a minimum passing score (also known as a cut score) on subject matter exams and basic skills exams in reading, mathematics, and/or general knowledge. In a few states, the completion of a Master's degree is mandatory before permanent certification is granted. The common nature of the teacher training programs across the states usually makes it easy for states to forge reciprocity agreements that allow teachers licensed in one state to become licensed in another. In fact, on the average, 22 percent of the teachers certified in a state completed their teacher training in another state. In some states, the percentage goes as high as 40 percent (United States Department of Education, 2004 (see Figure 4–8).

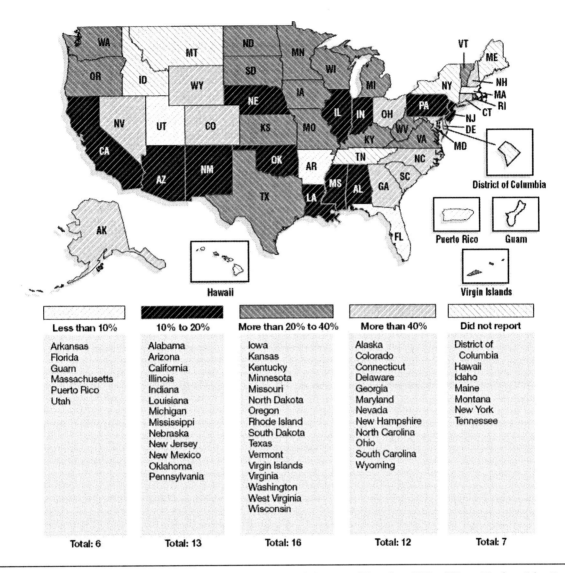

FIGURE 4–8   Percentage of Teachers Receiving Initial Certification Who Were Trained in Another State, by Percentage Reported by State: 2002–03. Note: This map reflects persons receiving initial state certification only. For purposes of this figure, the term "state" referes to the 50 states, the District of Ccolumbia, Puerto Rico and outlying areas. From U.S. Department of Education. (2004). *The Secretary's Fourth Annual Report on Teachers.* Washington, DC: United States Government Printing.

Many states allow for what are known as alternative licensure programs, which are specifically designed for college graduates who did not take the necessary courses in teacher training during their college years but who still have an interest in pursuing a teaching career. Such alternative programs are typically designed to develop new teachers in subject areas that have clear shortages (notably in math, science, and vocational education) and/or to supply teachers to low income urban and rural schools that have had difficulty hiring and retaining licensed teachers. Depending on the program, candidates in alternative licensure might be brought into the classroom immediately through a provisional license and be asked to enroll in teacher education courses on their own time. After their coursework in teacher training is complete and their professional progress in the classroom is noted to be satisfactory, alternative certification candidates can be granted full licensure. About 5 percent of the current teacher force entered through the alternative route (American Federation of Teaching, 2001).

Teacher education programs across the nation usually commences during the sophomore or junior year of college. Many teacher education programs require students to apply for admission. At many universities and colleges, teacher education is viewed as a professional training program, not an academic major. Thus, students are required to take a major in the liberal arts and sciences in tandem with their participation in teacher education. This is absolutely the case with secondary school pre-service teachers, who must major in their subject area of teaching (math for math teachers and so forth). But it is increasingly the case with elementary school teachers also, although many universities still offer an Elementary Education major. Courses in teacher education are typically comprised of methods courses in each of the relevant subject areas, core foundational courses in school psychology, human relations, special education, the philosophy and history of schooling, and ongoing field experiences in the school. Self-reported data from teachers indicate some satisfaction with their pre-service and in-service preparation. As noted in Table 4-3, over 90 percent of teachers reported that they felt at least somewhat prepared on measured classroom activities, except teaching LEP students.

Some critics of teacher education, however, would like to see the whole process of teacher preparation deregulated. Rather than moving in the direction of tightening the regulations surrounding licensure and teacher preparation, critics at the Fordham Foundation, for instance, argue that states would be wiser to loosen regulations in order to open the profession up to well-educated individuals who may not be inclined to go through the considerable set of requirements associated with certification, but who otherwise might prove to be successful teachers (Kanstoroom & Finn, 1999). A deregulated profession would mean that a wider pool of candidates could be available to school leaders to hire as they see fit. In the end, each appointment would be held accountable to one overarching criterion, which is evidence speaking to whether the teacher's students actually learned. Such a commitment to deregulating the profession does put a lot of faith in the capacity of the school to comprehensively demonstrate what students have learned. It also seems to signal a position on teaching that seemingly cares less about what teachers actually do in the classroom than what the actual measured gains of achievement have been. In fact, those who take a deregulative position of teacher education cite research demonstrating that alternatively certified teachers perform as well as traditionally-certified teachers, when measured by the performance of their students (Ballou & Podgursky, 2000). The problem is that measured student performance is usually reducible to a single shot test score rather than some comprehensive gauge of educational accomplishment, inclusive of both cognitive and non-cognitive effects.

Despite its push to bring highly qualified teachers to schools, the United States Department of Education (2002) has also taken a deregulative position on teacher training, believing that "traditional teacher training programs do not necessarily produce graduates with superior teaching skills" (p. 19) and openly stating that the alternative certification route represents the best idea for the future reform of teacher education. The Department of Education's position is that highly qualified teachers must be able to demonstrate academic and content area skills and be in possession of a bachelor's degree in an area relevant to their teaching assignment, but that they do not necessarily need to be produced in a traditional teacher training program.

However, professional groups, such as the American Federation of Teaching (AFT), have looked to find ways to strengthen what actually happens in the education of a pre-service teacher. The AFT (2000) has argued that seven essential steps should be followed in the design of all teacher education programs. These steps include supporting a core of liberal arts and science requirements to be taken during freshman and sophomore years; mandating rigorous entrance requirements; designing a comprehensive set of courses in teaching; requiring the completion of an academic major in the arts and sciences; widening the exposure to pre-service clinical experiences; exercising rigorous exit licen-

Table 4–3 Percent of public school teachers indicating how well-prepared they felt for various activities in the classroom, 2000.

Activity	How Well-Prepared Teachers Felt			
	Very Well-Prepared	Moderately Well-Prepared	Somewhat Well-Prepared	Not at All Prepared
Meet the overall demands of teaching assignments	61	35	4	NA
Maintain order and discipline in the classroom	71	24	4	1
Implement new methods of teaching (e.g., cooperative learning)	45	42	12	2
Implement state or district curriculum and performance standards	44	39	15	2
Use student performance assessment (e.g., methods of testing, applying results to modify instruction)	37	40	20	3
Address the needs of students from diverse cultural backgrounds	32	39	23	6
Address the needs of students with disabilities*	32	38	24	5
Integrate educational technology in the grade or subject taught	27	38	27	7
Address the needs of students with limited English proficiency*	27	33	28	12

* Data are based on teachers who reported that they taught students with these characteristics at the school—86 percent taught special education students with Individual Education Plans (IEPs), and 42 percent taught students with limited English proficiency.

NCES, Fast Response Survey System, "Survey on Professional Development and Training in U.S. Public Schools, 1999-2000," FRSS 74.

sure requirements at the completion of the program; and thinking about ways to work in collaboration with school districts on induction programs for graduates.

The commitment to licensure examinations for teachers is relatively new and is mostly the function of federal pressures. States, of course, have the final authority to determine the type of test used to grant licensure and the pass rate required. As matters stand now, most states ask teachers who are initially certified to take at least a basic skills exam (37 states) and a subject matter exam (37 states); a fewer number of states also require a general knowledge exam (12 states) and a knowledge of teaching exam (26 states; NCES, 2005). Only ten years earlier, states requiring basic skills and content area exams numbered in the mid-twenties (NCES, 1996). Because of federal mandates, licensure testing for teachers will likely become a more pervasive feature of the professional profile of teachers.

Most critics of teacher licensure exams argue that little is known about the relation between licensure testing and actual teacher effectiveness. The main criticism revolves around the nature of the tests, which generally fail to target mastery of college level work, and instead opt for lower levels of performance (basic skills). The other problem is the arbitrary manner in which minimum passing scores are chosen by the states. Because the states understand that cut scores affect the labor supply of teachers, they tend to set them quite low, ensuring very high pass rates. But there is still no good consensus on exactly what represents valid proficiency scores or even what such a score means in relation to teacher effectiveness.

NCLB AND HIGHLY QUALIFIED TEACHERS

Among the many changes put forth in recently enacted federal legislation, known as the No Child Left Behind Act, is a demand that all teachers of the core academic subjects of the school become "highly qualified." The law views the core academic subjects as English, reading or language arts, mathematics, science, foreign language, civics and government, economics, arts, history and geography. Thus, any teacher involved with any of the above subject areas must be highly qualified and the law directs schools to notify parents if unqualified teachers are being used. The question naturally becomes, what is a highly qualified teacher?

Highly qualified involves three major criteria: 1) the teacher must hold full licensure and have any requirements waived on an emergency or provisional basis; 2) the teacher must be in possession of at least a bachelor's degree; and 3) the teacher must demonstrate subject matter competence in each subject area in which she teaches. This last criterion is the most ambiguous because it requires some operational definition of what it means to demonstrate subject matter competency. For middle school and secondary school teachers, this is mostly straightforward because if teachers complete an academic major or graduate degree in the subject area (or coursework equivalent to it), they are clear of the requirement. But what about elementary school teachers who teach in multiple subject areas? To meet the subject matter competence component of the law, elementary school teachers are usually required to pass a state exam that tests subject knowledge and teaching skills in reading, writing, mathematics, and other areas. Secondary and middle school teachers who did not complete a graduate degree or an academic major in the subject area that they teach can also opt to take a subject test to satisfy this last criterion.

The states also have an option to apply something known as the "high, objective, uniform, state standard of evaluation (HOUSSE)" for teachers who have veteran status in the field but who do not have a college major in the field of teaching assignment. The intention here is to allow for some accounting of experience in the classroom as certification of content expertise. Depending on the state, the HOUSSE system ascribes point values toward some combination of variables, usually associated with professional development and leadership activities, college coursework, years of experience in the classroom, and other measures. The states are free to design their own HOUSSE system. Figure 4-9 displays the one used in Alabama. A teacher who can accumulate 100 points on the HOUSSE system used in Alabama meets the federal standard for highly qualified.

The supply of highly qualified teachers available in a state is influenced by any number of factors, including pay levels for teachers and the conditions of licensure. A study conducted by the CCSSO found that variables related to student enrollment and class size could also play a role (Blank, 2003).

FIGURE 4–9

HOUSSE Component	Measure	Point Value	Total Points	Verification (local/state)
College Coursework in Content Area	Semester hours 40 hours maximum	1 point for each semester hour **1**	40 points maximum	
College Coursework in Professional Studies Related to Content Area	Semester hours 35 hours maximum	1 point for each semester hour **1**	35 points maximum	
Professional Development Related to Content Area	Number of activities 12 activities maximum	3 points for each activity **3**	36 points maximum	
Professional Activities Related to Content Area	Number of activities 5 activities maximum	4 points for each activity **4**	20 points maximum	
Years of Public School Experience in the Content Area	Years of public school experience in content area	2 points each year for most recent 10 years. 1 point for each year over 10 years. **2 or 1**	30 points maximum	
Recognition in Content Area	Number of recognitions 2 recognitions maximum	2 points for each recognition **2**	4 points maximum	

Alabama Department of Education, http://www.hsv.k12.al.us/dept/forms/highlyqual.doc.

Table 4–4 lists the 11 states that experienced the greatest decline in the proportion of highly qualified teachers in math and science from 1994 and 2000. One can see that in almost all states, student enrollments have climbed and class size has shrunk during this same period of time, resulting in an increased demand for teachers and thereby making it that much more difficult for these states to meet the conditions of employing only highly qualified teachers. This is another way of saying that compliance with the rules on highly qualified teachers is obviously easier to do when class sizes are kept high, when student enrollment is stable, and when the proficiency cut scores of the teacher exams are kept low.

Federal regulations have openly stated that there will be a highly qualified teacher in every classroom in the nation. This, of course, will not likely occur. The law does not specify any particular penalty for schools out of compliance with HQT standards, but the United States Secretary of Education does have the right to withhold federal funding.

TABLE 4–4 States with Decrease in Highly Qualified Math and Science Teachers (7–12) (1994 to 2000) By State Education Demographics.

State	7–12 Total Enrollment % Change	Math, Sci. Teachers % Change	Avg. Class Size Change	Avg. Class Size 7–12 Math
Arizona	+23	NA	−0.7	27
Connecticut	+18	+16	−0.4	20
Kansas	+8	NA	−0.5	20
Louisiana	−0.1	−8	None	22
Massachusetts	+15	+15	−1.0	22
Mississippi	−4	+3	−2.7	20
Missouri	+8	+13	−1.5	23
Nevada	+40	+5	None	27
New Mexico	+6	NA	+0.9	24
Texas	+15	+60	−2.0	20
Vermont	+13	+36	+0.8	21
National Avg.	+10	+9	−0.5	23

Note: states listed had more than 5 percent decline in highly qualified teachers and were below 80 percent highly qualified in 2000. National average was 5 percent decline in math teachers with major in field.

Blank, R. (2003). Meeting *NCLB Goals for Highly Qualified Teachers: Estimates by State from Survey Data.* Washington, DC: Council of Chief State School Officers.

PROFESSIONAL TEACHER ORGANIZATIONS

Professional teacher organizations have historically maintained a dual commitment to improving the welfare of the profession and the welfare of the public school. These are, after all, complementary aims. Thus, the development of teacher groups often runs parallel with historical improvements in the workplace. One inevitably finds teacher groups entangled with political advocacy efforts, legislative initiatives, and electoral politics. The National Education Association (NEA) and the American Federation of Teachers (AFT) are the nation's two visible teacher groups, both possessing wide and often well-funded agendas. Their work intervenes in virtually all aspects of a teacher's professional life, ranging from local labor negotiations to the shaping of state and national school policies.

The National Education Association

The founding of the National Education Association (originally known as the National Teachers' Association) was an event moved by a desire to bring national identity to the cause of public education, especially as it related to the professionalization of teachers. In 1857, a national call, written by the President of the New York State Teachers Association, went out to "the teachers of the United States," inviting them to attend a meeting in Philadelphia dedicated to organizing a new National Teachers' Association. The call was also sent to other presidents of state teachers' associations. When the meeting concluded that same year, a new national group of educators, known as the National Teachers' Association (NTA), was born (Wesley, 1957). The name of the group was largely a misnomer because school administrators, eager to use the influence of the new organization to improve the profession of teaching, dominated the membership and power base of the organization.

As described in the preamble to the NEA's Constitution, the mission of the NEA was to "elevate the character and advance the interests of the profession of teaching, and to promote the cause of popular education in the United States" (National Education Association, 1997, p. 170). Early support for the NEA (or the NTA, as it was originally known) and its constitutional charge emerged from many quarters. Educational luminaries, such as Horace Mann and Henry Bernard, were impressed with the group's desire to make teaching a profession (as opposed to a vocation) and were happy to see efforts made to bring public education under the influence of professional leadership, instead of lay leadership. Groups, such as the American Normal School Association, which concerned itself with teacher preparation, and the National Association of School Superintendents, saw benefits in joining ranks with the NTA. Various independent groups, all connected to schooling in some way, also joined in the new national cause. The result was an expansive collection of educational personnel that represented a new coalition of educationists. It included school administrators, teacher educators, university personnel, and, of course, public school teachers. In 1870, the NTA group changed its name to the National Educational Association and then again to the National Education Association of the United States in 1905, but the original mission still stands as the fundamental purpose of the NEA.

Early membership in the NTA was limited to "gentlemen." Women could be elected to honorary memberships but were not allowed, under any circumstances, to address the floor at the annual conventions or to hold office in the organization. This was eventually changed in 1866, when a constitutional amendment was passed, changing the defining term for membership from "gentleman" to "person." Naturally, this change would affect the membership rolls of the NTA positively and would later set the stage for the election of Ella Flagg Young as its first female president in 1910. Young, who was a career educator with experience as a principal, teacher, and professor of education (at the University of Chicago), was the superintendent of the Chicago Public Schools when she was elected NEA president in 1910. Her election was controversial because she was originally denied the support of the nominating committee for the presidency of the NEA, which was a group overwhelmingly composed of men. But maneuverings through the protocols governing the floor at the annual conference allowed some women to substitute the majority report of the nominating committee, which contained the nomination of a man, with the minority report, which contained the nomination of Young. The convention then voted 617 to 376 in favor of the minority report, thus electing Young as the first female president of the NEA (Wesley, 1957).

There were no early racial restrictions on membership in the NEA, but because of the custom of "separate but equal," many state affiliates with white members barred blacks from membership. This, however, did not stop the NTA from seeking affiliates with both black and white state teacher associations.

As a national association, at least up until about 1892, the NTA was essentially a convention organization. In fact, the annual national convention of the NTA had actually become an important forum for the discussion of school programs, and educational practice and principles. With publications scarce and TV and radio not yet available, it was an event of some significance to the educational community (West, 1980). In 1892, the NEA had widened its work in the schools by appointing a series of very visible and highly prestigious committees charged with the responsibility of delivering recommendations for the resolution of specific school problems. The most notable committee was probably the Committee of Ten, which published a report in 1893 that, in effect, designed the coursework for high school education in America. The Committee of Fifteen, which followed the Committee of Ten report, was dedicated to the same task, but for the elementary school. The well-known Cardinal Principle report, which was published in 1918, was also the fruit of NEA sponsorship. We will study these reports and their influence on education in a later chapter.

Eventually the NEA took on legislative causes, working actively to pass federal legislation supporting the public school, a task it has maintained with a full compliment of lobbyists and political allies, into the 21st century. The legislative accomplishments of the NEA are, historically speaking, impressive. They include the founding of the Office of Education, which through NEA efforts, eventually evolved into the United States Department of Education, now headed by a secretary with a cabinet-level appointment. The NEA has also been at the forefront of advancing federal monetary support for education and continues to affect legislative initiatives at the state level, working through its affiliates, where most of the action related to the actual operation of the school, and to the improvement of teacher salaries and teacher work conditions, remains.

Today, the National Education Association (NEA) is the country's largest organization of educators, claiming a membership of about 2.3 million (close to 70 percent of all public school teachers) and an annual budget approaching 200 million dollars. Headquartered in Washington, DC, the NEA is the base for a vast network of activity that is realized through a large group of state and local affiliates. These affiliates are active in labor negotiations and ultimately work to influence and affect school policy and school practice in their respective states.

The NEA's involvement at the local and state level is heavily involved in labor and collective bargaining negotiations with school districts. It is constantly on the lookout for opportunities to combat restrictions on teacher tenure, teacher autonomy, and teacher professionalism, and to support initiatives that lead to better-funded schools and more professionally actualized teachers. At the national level, it has a large publication mill that produces a considerable mass of literature dealing with a vast assortment of professional issues. It works intimately in the halls of Congress to sway federal legislation in the direction of school improvement and to ally itself with various politicians and special interest groups sympathetic to NEA objectives.

The NEA has, over time, established the reputation of being a considerable heavyweight in the political process. Although the NEA claims to have a bipartisan outlook, it does not shy away from endorsing candidates that it believes support its objectives. In the early 1970s, the organization put itself headlong into the political process by establishing a political action group (NEA-PAC), an internal committee devoted to directing membership money toward political action, namely toward the support of favored political candidates and political issues. By following the PAC money, one discovers that the NEA is deeply seated in the Democratic Party. In the 1992 elections, for instance, 92 percent of its PAC money went to Democrats, amounting to about a 40 million dollar distribution (Lieberman, 1997). The basic explanation for this has to do with the historical attachment the NEA has had to the objective of garnering federal monies for public school causes, a position that is historically at odds with the Republican view of less government and less federal intervention in schools.

The NEA has endured quite a bit of criticism over the years. Among the prevailing criticisms has to do with the perceived view that its actions are, first and foremost, unionist in orientation and are guided only secondarily by a desire to improve public schools. Critics maintain that the NEA cannot accept any idea, even if it promises to be good for schools and school children, until it first passes through a screen that determines its suitability from the standpoint of employee (teacher) welfare. If, say, performance pay for teachers were found to be an idea that might prove to reward better teachers and create a more professional climate for teaching and learning, the NEA, its critics assert, could never support it because it would be counter to the "union" objective of increasing pay for all teachers. Lieberman (1997) cites the reorganization of the NEA in 1972 as evidence of the shift made by the NEA in the direction of a union. Prior to 1972, the NEA was organized along departmental lines that reflected interests in curriculum and instruction concerns. These included departments dedicated to, among many other things, business education, nursery education, rural education, supervision and curriculum, and so forth. They were all wiped out in 1972, replaced by a more legalistic and bureaucratic organizational structure reflecting, according to Lieberman, employee welfare issues. This criticism is further supported by the fact that approximately one-third of the NEA's 200 million dollar budget in 1997 was dedicated to a program known as Uniserve, which is operated through the state affiliates, that puts the NEA in the middle of labor negotiations with local school districts. Money made available by the NEA through Uniserve usually goes to providing a Uniserve director to a school district, whose job, depending on the desires of the local district members, is to serve as a negotiator, grievance representative, and/or general labor consultant to the local teachers (Lieberman, 1997).

The NEA has clearly put considerable resources into the advancement and defense of the public school and public school children. Although some might see its actions as self-serving, few organizations have been more vocal and more singularly committed to lobbying for public school resources. At a time when arguments for the privatization of schools have taken on a bipartisan political caste, the NEA has held to its guns and has actively opposed any initiative that even hints at the idea of using public money for private schooling purposes. Its critics might see this action as unionist, while its advocates might see it as part of its historic dedication to "promote the cause of popular (public) education."

The American Federation of Teachers

Unlike the NEA, a spirit of unionism moved the original founding of the American Federation of Teachers (AFT). At the turn of the twentieth century, some teachers, disenchanted by their work conditions and by their general lack of influence in negotiations with school boards, sought to organize gatherings of educators by reaching out to the American Federation of Labor (AFL) for union affiliation. Because of nonunion pressures exerted by administrators and school boards, many of these local chapters did not survive very long (Campbell, Cunningham, McPhee, & Nystrand, 1970). But a growing current for a national teachers' union did begin to take shape. The cradle for this teacher unionism was in the Chicago area, where in 1915, four separate local unions were engaged in embittered negotiations with their school boards. The problem came to a head when the Chicago School Board attempted to prohibit membership by teachers in any labor union. It was in this context that a handful of educators from the Chicago area, all representatives of their local union chapters, got together in 1916 to form what one might very well view as the nation's first national teachers union—the American Federation of Teachers (AFT). The idea was to find a way to organize a federation of teachers that could retain its ties to the labor movement and bring considerable resources to the local labor struggles of teachers.

Although the NEA was in existence at the time, its operations could not be characterized as union-like yet. It is important to recall that, although the NEA was concerned about teachers, it was very much dominated in its early years by male administrators, who saw the professional service base of the organization to be largely a matter of offering advice and expertise to school teachers. Thus, the AFT, with its grassroots contacts in the workplace, and its more visible female leadership, had a populist appeal to teachers. In the 1910s, membership in the AFT exceeded that of the NEA (Lieberman, 1997). But antiunion activities after World War I, coupled with an active teacher recruitment campaign led by school administrators in the NEA, brought the membership numbers back up for the NEA, and as teachers moved into the NEA, its more union-like stance began to take form.

The early difference between the two groups is perhaps best expressed historically, in the clashes witnessed between union representatives and NEA officials at the annual conventions of the NEA. Under the leadership of Margaret Haley, teachers from the Chicago Teacher Federation, a teachers union folded into the AFT (and later removed from it), had tried to petition the NEA officials for recognition on points they wanted to raise against some NEA policies and resolutions. Among the more aggravating issues to the union was the NEA's support for the idea of centralizing administrative control in the financing of the school and the supervision of teachers. While the NEA was looking for ways to solidify administrative control over teachers, the union argued that real problems related to corruption in state and local politics, inadequate school revenues, and deplorable work conditions for teachers were going ignored. Haley and her union forwarded a hard-knuckled agenda to the NEA, portraying the problems facing teachers as a worker's struggle to win justice and equity for teachers and school children. The more-gentile NEA could only interpret this position as heresy to its belief of working within the system. The AFT had clearly found its own unique place in the historical struggle to professionalize teaching.

Today, we can still see the remnants of the founding differences between the two groups. The NEA, for instance, has kept its membership open to school administrators, seeing them as part of the same professional body, while the AFT has closed the door on membership to top level administrators, believing that they cannot be trusted to look after the best collective bargaining interests of teachers.

Currently the two groups principally carry the same agenda, so much so that some of the NEA and AFT state affiliates have merged. What is interesting is that the NEA has moved solidly into more union-like activities and the AFT has moved, with equal conviction, into more professionally-based activities. The AFT is still proudly and securely committed to union activity, working directly to better salaries, working conditions, and job security for teachers, but it also carries a social agenda reflecting a commitment to public schooling, democracy, and social justice, one that looks similar to the NEA's agenda. The AFT, like its counterpart, is legislatively conscious and politically active. Its membership approaches 1 million, including nurse and health care workers, as well as non-education personnel, a vestige of its early identification with workers. In 2001, it could count approximately 17 percent of all public school teachers among it membership (NEA, 2003).

SUMMARY

The gender, race, and ethnic distribution of the teaching profession represents a misalignment with the demographic distribution of the student population. When compared to the student population, male teachers, black teachers, and Hispanic teachers are all significantly under-represented in the teaching corps. The teaching profession in the United States is also somewhat hurt by its failure to achieve high grades on known indices of professionalism. Although the rise of formal induction programs and licensing exams demonstrate some signs of maturity for the field, salary issues, and the irrelevance of the credentialing process to actual job assignments point to obvious problems. The reality is that very large percentages of children who attend middle schools and high schools continue to be taught by teachers who did not major in the very field that they were contracted to teach. The problem is more acute in high poverty and high minority schools. Not surprisingly, a new federal emphasis on teacher quality has brought on a number of changes in licensure requirements and increased attention to the testing of teacher knowledge. Using the federal definition, highly qualified teachers must be college educated and knowledgeable in their teaching subject area. Furthermore, a new debate has emerged on just what qualifies as good teacher education, with a number of critics opting for deregulation while emphasizing teacher knowledge of subject matter and teacher accountability to student test scores. Finally, the growth of two historic professional groups (the NEA and the AFT) has allowed teachers to influence various workplace concerns (salaries, benefits, preparation time, and so forth) and school policy concerns (federal and state legislation).

REFERENCES

American Federation of Teachers. (2000). *Building a profession: Strengthening teacher preparation and induction.* Washington, DC: AFT.

American Federation of Teachers. (2001). Beginning teacher induction: The essential bridge. *Educational Issues Policy Brief,* 13:5–6.

American Federation of Teachers. (2005). *Survey and analysis of teacher salary trends, 2003–2004.* Washington, DC: AFT.

Ballou, D., & Podgursky, M. (2000). Reforming teacher preparation and licensing: What does the evidence show? *Teachers College Record,* Vol. 101(1):5–26.

Blank, R. (2003). *Meeting NCLB goals for highly qualified teachers: Estimates by state from survey data.* Washington, DC: Council of Chief State School Officers.

Blumenthal, R. (2006). Houston ties teachers' pay to test scores. *New York Times.* January 13.

Bruschi, B. A., & Coley, R. J. (1999). *How teachers compare: The prose, document and quantitative skills of America's teachers.* Princeton, NJ: Educational Testing Service.

Campbell, R. F., Cunningham, L. L., McPhee, R. F., & Nystrand, R. O. (1970). *The organization and control of American schools.* Columbus, OH: Charles E. Merrill Publishing.

Carnegie Foundation for the Advancement of Teaching. (1990). *The condition of teaching.* Princeton, NJ: Carnegie Foundation for the Advancement of Teaching.

Darling-Hammond, L. (1997). *Doing what matters most: Investing in quality teaching.* New York: National Commission on Teaching and America's Future.

Dee, T. S. (2004). Teachers race and student achievement in a randomized experiment. *The Review of Economics and Statistics,* 86(1):195–210.

Ehrenberg, R. G., Goldhaber, D. D. & Brewer, D. J. (1995). Do teacher's race, gender and ethnicity matter? Evidence from the National Educational Longitudinal Study of 1988. *Industrial and Labor Relations Review,* 48(3):547–561.

Hlebowitsh, P. S. (1996). *Cries of crisis: Assessments of the public schools in the national newsprint.* In Peter S. Hlebowitsh and William Wraga (eds.) Annual Review of Research for School Leaders. New York: Scholastic.

Ingersoll, R. M. (2002). Teacher shortage: A case of the wrong diagnosis and wrong prescription. *The National Association of Secondary School Principals Bulletin 86,* June:16–31.

Kanstoroom, M., & Finn, C. E., eds. (1999). *Better teachers, better schools.* Washington, DC: The Fordham Foundation.

Ladson-Billings, G. (1994). *The dreamkeepers: Successful teachers of African-American Children.* San Francisco: Jossey-Bass.

Lieberman, M. (1997). *The teachers unions: How the NEA and AFT sabotage reform and hold students, parents, teachers and taxpayers hostage to bureaucracy.* New York: The Free Press.

National Center for Education Statistics. (1995). *Digest of education statistics.* Washington, DC: United States Government Printing.

National Center for Education Statistics. (1996). *Digest of education statistics.* Washington, DC: United States Government Printing.

National Center for Education Statistics. (1997a). *America's teachers: Profile of the profession, 1993–94.* Washington, DC: United States Government Printing.

National Center for Education Statistics. (1997b). *The status of teaching as a profession.* Washington, DC: United States Government Printing.

National Center for Education Statistics. (1998). *Fast survey response system, teacher survey on professional development and training.* Washington, DC: United States Government Printing.

National Center for Education Statistics. (1999a). *Teacher quality: A report on the preparation and qualifications of public school teachers.* Washington, DC: United States Government Printing.

National Center for Education Statistics. (1999b). *The condition of education.* Washington, DC: United States Government Printing.

National Center for Education Statistics. (2000). *Elementary and secondary education: An international perspective.* Washington, DC: United States Government Printing.

National Center for Education Statistics. (2002). School and staffing survey: overview of the data. *Education Statistics Quarterly,* 4(3):7.

National Center for Education Statistics. (2003). *The condition of education.* Washington, DC: United States Government Printing.

National Center for Education Statistics. (2004). *The NCES common core of data (CCD), state nonfiscal survey of public elementary secondary education, 1992–93 and 2002–03.* Washington, DC: United States Government Printing.

National Center for Education Statistics. (2004a). *Qualifications of the public teacher workforce: Prevalence of out-of-field teaching, 1987–88, 1999–2000.* Washington, DC: United States Government Printing.

National Center for Education Statistics. (2005). *Digest of education statistics.* Washington, DC: United States Government Printing.

National Education Association. (1997). *Handbook, 1997–98.* Washington, DC: National Education Association.

National Education Association. (2003). *Status of the American public school teacher.* Washington, DC: NEA.

United States Census Bureau. (2006). *Statistical abstract of the United States statistics.* Washington, DC: United States Government Printing.

United States Department of Education. (2004). *The secretary's fourth annual report on teachers.* Washington, DC: United States Government Printing.

United States Department of Education. (2002). *Meeting the highly qualified teachers challenge.* Washington, DC: United States Government Printing.

United States Department of Labor. (2004). Bureau of Labor Statistics. *Occupation Statistics,* 2004, http://www.bls.gov/oes/current/oes_stru.htm.

Wesley, E. B. (1957). NEA: *The first hundred years.* New York: Harper and Brothers.

West, A. M. (1980). *The national education association: The power base for education.* New York: The Free Press.

KEY QUESTIONS

1. Why is the teaching profession still mostly comprised of women?

2. Do you agree that the teaching force needs to reflect the demographic composition of society? Do we hold other professions to the same standard? Does this mean that bringing males into the profession has the same urgency as bringing racial and ethnic minorities into the profession?

3. Should teacher salaries be determined by classroom performance, as opposed to more educational credits and additional experience? What are the fundamental concerns about performance pay for teachers?

4. What are some of the factors that make it difficult for teachers to exercise independent professional authority in the workplace?

5. Should teachers have some role to play in affecting school-wide decisions, such as setting disciplinary policy, determining in-service content, and hiring new teachers?

6. Why is "out-of-field teaching" more prevalent in the middle school than in the high school and more prevalent in high poverty schools than low poverty schools?

7. What do you think of the Department of Education's definition of "highly qualified teachers"? Why is the department pursuing a policy to bring only highly qualified teachers into the classroom?

8. What is the ideal way to educate teachers? Is a more deregulative approach sensible—one that is flexible enough to bring talented people into the profession without the encumbrance of teacher education courses, or should the focus be on making teacher education more comprehensive and obligatory for all prospective teachers?

9. Explain the fundamental difference in outlook or orientation between the NEA and the AFT.

RESEARCH EXERCISES

1. Investigate the portrayal of teachers in the major national media outlets, including national news journals and newspapers, over the past several decades. What conclusions can you draw?

2. Explore the nature of the affiliation or connection that the NEA and the AFT have to the Democratic political party.

3. According to a report filed by the National Center for Education Statistics (1997a), a profession can be evaluated against six main levels of performance. These include the following:
   - *Credentials:* the extent to which hiring practices are based on credentials earned in professional training programs
   - *Induction:* the extent to which mentoring programs are in place to serve as effective inductions for newcomers into the profession
   - *Professional Development:* the extent to which provisions and experiences are provided that allow for the continuing growth and development of the professional
   - *Authority:* the extent to which professionals are able to influence decisions in the workplace
   - *Compensation:* the extent of compensation offered through salary and benefits

   How would you begin to use these criteria to grade the profession of teaching? Some evidence is provided in the text, but what other kind of evidence would you look for to make a judgment on each criterion? How might you apply these criteria to other professions and how might they score?

4. Research the data on the self-reported job satisfaction rating of teachers and report your general findings. Both the NCES (1997a) and the NEA (2003) collect data on job satisfaction.

5. Research the data on teacher attrition, starting with Ingersoll (2002). Based on your finding, how might you design a strategy to combat teacher attrition?

6. Research the literature on "own race" teaching and design a small study to test the main proposition that teachers are more effective with children of their "own race" than teachers who do not share the same race.

7. How do the demographic patterns of the professional teaching force in other advanced nations compare and contrast to the demographic patterns in the United States? Pick one nation and analyze the similarities and differences.

CHAPTER 5

The Philosophy of Teaching

The act of teaching is not a mechanical or objectively neutral process. It is an undertaking deeply embedded in a set of values that helps dictate the nature of the experience brought to the classroom. Tyler (1949) likened the role of philosophy in the curriculum to a screen through which ideas are filtered. The screen of philosophy helps to crystallize and focus the purposes and objectives of the classroom, ultimately sharpening the teacher's sense of why she is doing what she is doing. Because a philosophy is tied to wider epistemological questions, such as what it means to lead a good life in a good society, it has a defined perspective on what is worth knowing and doing. Certain restrictions naturally limit the possibilities for the expression of philosophy in the school. To start, a philosophy of teaching has to be responsive to the three professional sources of decision-making discussed in an earlier chapter (the learner, the society, and subject matter). A teacher does not have the right to exercise, say, a fascist school philosophy in an institution expressly dedicated to educating youth for participation in a democracy. Such a philosophy would violate the obligation to secure the values and aims of society in the experience of the school. Different educators might use different arguments to justify whether certain actions and experiences in the school are responsive to democracy, but an overtly anti-democratic philosophy cannot stand. Similarly, no philosophical justification could be accepted for experiences that are not age-appropriate or that are viewed, in any way, as harmful to the mental, emotional, and physical well-being of the child. A teacher, for example, who has an earnest philosophical commitment to bringing the hard realities of the life experience to the classroom has to be careful not to overstep certain boundaries. Obviously, one does not teach children that fire burns by forcing their hands into the flames.

Formulating a school (or classroom) philosophy is not just a ritualistic exercise designed to reassure the public that the school is moved by high-minded purposes, but a serious commitment to a standard of conduct. School mission statements often make reference to objectives in the public mandate, such as fostering democratic values, assuring equal opportunities to learn, and nurturing an attitude for lifelong learning. Such statements are in effect statements of philosophy and are useful if they are viewed as commitments to practice. A philosophy, in this sense, represents a kind of resolution on the part of the school to not only reflect its expressed ideals in the classroom but to also be judged against them. It is easier to have ideals than to live by them. A philosophy of teaching is a matter of living by an ideal; it is a compass that orients the instructional or pedagogic methods in the school.

TEACHING IN THE CONSERVATIVE TRADITION

The conservative philosophical position on the school curriculum is essentially a subject-centered one. It holds that teaching is largely a matter of maneuvering through the considerable accumulation of wisdom embodied in organized knowledge. The purpose of the school is primarily a matter of cultural transmission, the conveying and the preservation of common cultural knowledge. Students are believed to be well-served as citizens by this purpose because the school will have exposed and socialized them in the essential dimensions of civilization. Among young children, the focus of education is devoted to the preparation of the basic skills used for later mastery of the subject matter. This general orientation is viewed as conservative because it is committed to the conservation of humanity's wisdom as it is believed to be found in particular academic disciplines.

Perennialism

The value of learning from a perennialist perspective is unalterably tied to the subject matter. Learning is primarily a matter of immersion in a set of subjects believed to be endowed with the verities and virtues of western civilization. Grammar, reading, rhetoric, logic, mathematics, and the great literary books of humanity (the historic core of the liberal arts) have long stood as the main columns of content for perennialists. Hutchins (1936) referred to them as the permanent studies. The choice of the term permanent studies is revealing because it holds to the assumption that the educating powers of these studies persist over time. In other words, the studies are perennial—everlasting through time. This is the strongest way of saying that the subject matter itself and the powers that transfer from it represent the main ends of education. Learning arises from the activity generated in the learner's mind by the subject matter. Teachers might seek ways to guide, stimulate, and assist it, but the subject matter is the true teacher.

A perennialist maintains that one must have a wholly exclusive experience in the permanent studies to be educated. Thus, there is a kind of one-size-fits-all mentality to the perennialist, a belief in posing one uniform curriculum experience to all students in virtually all places and all times. This insistence is born in the desire to educate all youth, not just the elite, in a form of education believed to be essential to democracy. All youth not only benefit intellectually from experiences that discipline the mind, but their studies also grant them their cultural inheritance. Through the eternal truths and virtues of perennial studies, a new generation can share a bond with previous generations and carry with it the common outlook it will need to advance itself. As Hutchins (1972) stated, "the primary aim of the educational system in a democratic country is to draw out the common humanity of those committed to its charge" (p. 209). To Hutchins and other perennialists, this common humanity dwells in the permanent studies.

The commitment to the mind is justified by the doctrine of mental discipline and is so intense that other areas of study in the school that have less of a claim to the mind (including vocational studies, elective studies, physical education, and the performing arts) are often viewed as anti-intellectual pursuits. This is especially the case when it comes to vocational education, which in the eyes of a perennialist has no place in the school. Any regard for vocational education is interpreted negatively, as taking time and resources away from the central cause of developing one's mind and character. During the 1980s, Mortimer Adler, a long time proponent of the perennialist position in the schooling, argued for the elimination of all electives in the upper six years of schooling, with the exception of a choice of a second language, and the elimination of all specialized job training throughout. "The kind of vocational training that now goes on in schools is worse than useless . . . it is undemocratic in the extreme" observed Adler (1988, p. 281). Adler could see no value in job training when the important task of mind training was before the school. Vocational education took time away from the intimate tutoring that Adler believed each student needed in order to be brought through the canons of high western thought. This privileging of matters pertaining to the mind over matters and pertaining to the body leaves a mentalistic mark on the schooling experience, a mark that stresses a rational, contemplative, abstract, bookish, and subject-centered approach to learning. To Adler, physical education could only be justified from the standpoint of its contribution to mindful learning. In 1984, for instance, he described two purposes for physical education: "1) to develop the knowledge and habits requisite for the care of the body throughout life, and 2) to provide some physical relief from the taxing brain work of schooling" (p. 161).

For the elementary school teacher, the perennialist view means that serious attention is given to the management of basic skills education, especially reading instruction. At this level of schooling, the development of the basic skills tends to take on a life of its own. It is viewed as the key needed to unlock the doors to civilization, the very skills that will enable students to eventually read and think their way through the omnipotent subject matter. Thus, the instructional repertoire of the perennialist is unabashedly supportive of skill-drill strategies. As Adler (1984) observed, "often painful, usually boring, drill is necessary. . . . Students have to develop error free habits. Repeating the act (i.e., experience) is indispensable" (p. 42).

The elementary school is also the place students get their first instructional experiences in reading and understanding the literary classics. This is where the "great books" curriculum, the centerpiece to perennialist thinking, first takes hold. As one perennialist phrased it, "There should be no school in which the young mind fails to receive, like seeds destined to germinate in later years, a full sowing of sentences great men have spoken" (Van Doren, 1943, p. 95). The responsibility of the teacher, from elementary school to college, is to use the "great books" to bring the meta-narrative of civilization to the student. This could call for a varied set of instructional actions. One role for the teacher could be that of a seminar leader (Adler, 1984), one who draws out the powers of the literature through questioning techniques that "catch the mind" and promote virtue. Another could be that of the coach, the vigilant tutor who pays close attention to the work of the student, offering immediate feedback, "shrewd" criticism, and hard-driving repetitions of skill.

The duty to coach or to attend to the intellectual skills of the individual is often used by perennialists as the main justification against a more comprehensive school design. The argument is that when the school tries to take on too much, the teacher cannot offer a close hand in the intellectual education of a student. The perennialist might ask: Why see education as an endeavor that is, metaphorically speaking, miles wide and inches deep when one can focus on mindful learning with precision and depth?

And what about the fact that, until the nineteenth century, all great books were written by white European males? Adler's response is that the intention of studying the great books is neither to study Western civilization nor to acquire knowledge of historical facts, but rather to understand great perennial ideas. The fact that only great ideas could be had from the "great books" is unproblematic to Adler because the hand of history drew the repertoire of the great books. The issue of diversity does not calculate because learning is not about diversity; it is about training the mind, the will, and the character through the permanent studies.

During the 1980s, the U.S. Secretary of Education, William J. Bennett, often displayed his perennialist colors. In 1986, for instance, he helped to author a report on elementary education in the United States, entitled *First Lessons*, which outlined general curricular conditions for reform (Bennett, 1986).

Ideal of the Learner
A disciplined mind immersed in the highest traditions, values, and wisdom of Western humanity.

Ideal of the Society
A democracy moved by its western inheritance and the eternal truths and virtues that accompany it.

Ideal of the Subject Matter
A core of permanent studies, resembling the core of the liberal arts, that can discipline the mind and embody the wisdom of humanity.

FIGURE 5–1   Conceptual Features of Perennialism.

The report bore an unmistakable, if not proud, resemblance to the 1895 National Education Association's "Committee of Fifteen" report. William Torrey Harris, a well-known mental disciplinarian, authored the nineteenth century document. In framing the curriculum, Bennett called on the 1895 report stating, "grammar, literature, arithmetic, geography and history are the five branches upon which the disciplinary work of the elementary work is concentrated" (p. 20). In 1987, Bennett proposed a similar report but this time on the American high school. The report, entitled "James Madison High School," represented another retrogradation to the nineteenth century. Stating that "schooling in the full set of core academic disciplines should be central to the true purposes of American secondary education," Bennett (1987, p. 2) proposed a set of courses that looked very much like the general course requirements found in the 1893 "Committee of Ten" report, which itself featured a classic mental disciplinarian approach to high school education.

After his tenure as Secretary concluded, Bennett continued to be a national presence in education as an indefatigable critic of the public school, repeatedly alleging that the school had neglected basic education and failed to give proper deference to the literary works of western civilization. He also helped to popularize perennialist causes by editing the *Book of Virtues* (Bennett, 1993), a compendium of "great" essays, poems, and stories chosen for their enduring relevance as stories of virtue.

Irrespective of what one might think of it, perennialism certainly makes its argument on practical school grounds. Its most dramatic educational claims are tied to its advocacy of a well-defined sense of subject matter. It also holds to a well-developed theory of society, asserting an egalitarian position by contending that civilizing outcomes are accorded to all who are properly taught by its methods. The perennialist view has also carved out its own image of the learner, putting its emphasis on the mentalistic and the intellectual. Some readers might claim that the perennialist position is at odds with the literature on the nature of the learner, especially to the extent that mental discipline still prevails as a rationale for teaching, but wrongheaded or not, it can stake its claim along the three factors and thus earn its status in the curriculum.

Essentialism

Essentialists and perennialists are brothers under the same skin. They share a basic commitment to training the intellect through subject-centered knowledge. The dividing line, however, is mostly drawn in an argument over what is the most worthy form of knowledge. The perennialist's preference is to showcase the timeless intellectual virtues of our western cultural heritage, as it exists in the Great

Books and the liberal arts, while the essentialist's preference is to support a more fundamentally modern outlook on the academic disciplines. The effect with the essentialist is a more strictly academic and disciplinary experience than one might find in the humanities approach of the perennialist.

Essentialist thinking, as implied, is rooted in the learning doctrine of mental discipline. Thus, the focus of the school is very much subject-centered, academic, and mentalistic. A core of knowledge and skills, residing in logically organized academic disciplines (the very kinds of traditional disciplinary lines that one typically sees in the organization of a high school or even college curriculum), is the headline performer in the curriculum. The general educational plan is disciplined study in language and grammar, mathematics, the sciences, history, and foreign language. The primacy of the subject matter in learning is justified as a perennialist might justify it. The subject matter not only trains the mind but it also provides the basis for a common universe of discourse and understanding in society. Essentialism, in this way, asserts to be on the side of democracy.

The connection to democracy is important. At the turn of the century, William Bagley (1907) took an essentialist position by arguing that school curriculum should be "a storehouse of organized race experience, conserved against the time when knowledge shall be needed in the constructive solution of new and untried problems" (p. 2). This statement touches on some of the main principles of the social theory behind the essentialist argument. Essentialism aims to provide an education in the "essentials" of our civilization, the indispensable features of our core cultural knowledge as it is organized in the academic disciplines. Bagley's reference to the race experience should be translated to mean the experience of the human race (humanity), which he believed was warehoused in the academic disciplines. This body of core knowledge is brought to the experience of learners for the purposes of cultivating the faculties of thinking and reasoning, and of promoting a common or shared culture. This is the essentialists' way of offering a general education to the population, an education in the knowledge one needs to lead an informed life in a democracy.

The heyday of essentialists, however, was less influenced by democratic factors than by nationalistic ones. During the Cold War period in the United States, the discipline-centered traditions of the essentialists looked to be the perfect foil against the perceived imperialistic designs of the Soviet state. The education of engineers, scientists, and mathematicians (the main workers in the technological and space-related defense of the nation), required a highly academic disciplined-centered experience. This was a position strenuously maintained in the federal sponsorship of discipline-centered curriculum projects in the high school during the Cold War period. The provision of intellectual training in the fundamental disciplines became the first duty of the school because it was viewed as crucial to the defense of the nation. Anything that could not find a justification within this duty was likely to be excluded from or at least relegated in the school curriculum. Such a view, of course, fit hand and glove with the academic orientation of the essentialist curriculum.

During the late 1980s, the essentialist position turned to the idea of general education in an argument that was no longer about nationalistic concerns but about the kind of public education students needed for participation in a democracy. The impetus for the refocus was a widely read and controversial book by E. D. Hirsch (1987). The gist of Hirsch's argument was centered on a belief that a spiraling decline in the shared knowledge of the citizenry was threatening the livelihood of American democracy. The book, entitled *Cultural Literacy*, was a kind of call-to-arms for the essentialist position. Hirsch attempted to draw attention to the fact that much of the power of the content in the traditional academic disciplines had been lost in the school. Students, Hirsch argued, did not know anything especially penetrating about their own cultural history and cultural literature. They did not benefit from the inner powers of scientific and mathematical knowledge. They were simply not culturally literate. This conclusion was buoyed by NAEP data documenting embarrassingly poor student performances on historical and literature-based knowledge tests (Finn & Ravitch, 1987). From the standpoint of the essentialist, two vital factors in the education of youth were being neglected. First, the students' minds were not being effectively trained or disciplined, but more importantly the students were failing to gain the cultural background knowledge (the shared knowledge and shared vocabulary) they needed to forge a national identity and to participate in a common universe of understanding and insight. The antidote, of course, was to bring back the academic disciplines and place them front and center in a no-nonsense curriculum.

Hirsch has continued in his quest to revitalize the high academic tradition of the essentialist in the school and in society. He has emerged as a critic of what he views as "contentless" teaching in the school and has made his own contribution to fill this perceived void by publishing a series of cultural-literacy dictionaries, cultural-literacy workbooks, and cultural-literacy tests. He has also founded the tellingly titled, "Core Knowledge Foundation," which is a group that offers insight to schools on ways to encourage learning in the core knowledge areas.

In many ways, the American school, especially the high school, has continued to operate in the wake left by the essentialists during the Cold War, supporting discipline-centered graduation requirements, discipline-centered curriculum organization, and discipline-centered testing. And increasingly, advocates for the establishment of national standards and uniform content standards could be heard using a classic essentialist rationale: the need to give students a standard or uniform program of disciplined intellectual training in core academic areas.

Advocates of the essentialist view have a well-defined position on the school curriculum, which is featured in their insistence to bring the integrity of the subject matter back to the schools. By working on the point of subject matter, essentialists are working with a key factor in curriculum development. But the essentialist's concerns over the subject matter really represent a broader and more important purpose, which originates in their social theory of democracy. The essentialist assertion is that an intellectual and cultural core of skills and knowledge is needed to bring insight and stability to our democracy. This emphasis makes it clear that essentialist thinking is working within the lines of the curriculum, offering clear value judgments on the purposes and the experiences of the school.

Ideal of the Learner
A rational mind immersed in the fundamental academic disciplines.

Ideal of the Society
 A democracy dependent on a common or shared core of academic knowledge.

Ideal of the Subject Matter
A strictly academic and discipline-centered curriculum, attendant to the inner designs and intellective powers of the individual disciplines.

FIGURE 5–2   Conceptual Features of Essentialism.

TEACHING IN THE PROGRESSIVE TRADITION

To the degree that a conservative perspective on schooling aims to preserve and transmit a core culture, a progressive perspective aims to change it. The root word of progressive is progress, which implies change for the sake of betterment or improvement. This shift in focus takes the progressive vision of schooling directly into some estimation of the actual skills, attitudes, knowledge, and competencies needed to respond to and improve upon the problems of living. Talk of mind training is replaced with discussion of relevance to the life experience. Because progressives do not believe that subjects carry internal mind-training capacities, the subject matter loses it exalted status in the curriculum, although it retains its importance as a key variable in the curriculum.

Experimentalism

The experimentalist variant to the progressive perspective is embodied in the work of John Dewey. The controlling aim of the philosophy is to conceive of the school as an agency for democracy, as the place where children are taught the values, skills, attitudes, knowledge, and general competencies needed to lead a good life in a good society. Dewey is widely known as a philosopher of American democracy who took an unusually strong interest in schooling. Philosophers have historically made their marks by writing their views on ethics, logic, religion, aesthetics, truth, and even reality, but very few have exercised their analytical acumen on the topic of schooling. Dewey, however, could not escape the connection that schooling had to his philosophical views, especially in relation to the concept of democracy, and exhibited an interest in schooling that went as far as directing his own laboratory school at the University of Chicago, a rare activity for a philosopher indeed!

How does experimentalism begin to represent a philosophy that identifies with democracy? Why the term experimentalism, which seems to connote some strange association with specialized laboratory techniques? The answer to these questions starts with an understanding of what Dewey (1916) saw as the main basis of all education, which he described as that "reconstruction or reorganization of experience which adds to the meaning of experience and which increases ability to direct the course of subsequent experiences" (pp. 89–90). To understand experimentalism, one must understand this idea. To simplify matters, the "reconstruction or reorganization of experience" is really just a way of saying that one must learn from one's experience in a way that avoids repeating mistakes and that contributes to one's ability to make more informed decisions in the future. The implication is that learning is a process of experiential growth, always in the state of becoming and, if properly managed, improving, but never achieving completeness or finality. Such view of experience, however, does not emerge idiosyncratically. Some method of thinking has to be used to help regulate it.

To Dewey, this method of intelligence could be found in the scientific method. The scientific method applied to learning in school has several advantages from the standpoint of an experimentalist. First, it holds all truth up to ongoing inspection, a principle running counter to the conservative belief in the eternal value and truths of the western canon. The tentative nature of truth puts extra emphasis on the process of inquiry and the use of evidence and reasoned argumentation in decision-making. Second, the scientific method is designed to be responsive to the improvement of existing conditions. It is a problem-resolution method that tests new ideas in the interests of producing improvements. This makes it an elegant method for democracy because it poses problems as opportunities for new understanding and insight. Finally, a scientific method of thinking hones the very important skills of reflective thinking, a required condition for informed participation in a democratic society. Thus Dewey's insistence in seeing education as a "reconstruction of experience" could be seen as motivated by a desire to teach students a method of intelligence that gives them an effective handle on their personal and public lives. Inculcating students in the attitudes, habits of mind, and methods of scientific inquiry, could not only give students, as Dewey (1938) phrased it, "freedom from control by routine, prejudice, dogma, unexamined tradition, (and) sheer self-interest," but also "the will to inquire, to examine, to discriminate, to draw conclusions only on the basis of evidence after taking pains to gather all available evidence" (p. 31).

The practical consequence of positioning the "reconstruction of experience" in the center of the school experience is a problem-focused curriculum that highlights the importance of inquiry-based learning. This obviously calls for a very different conception of subject matter from what one might witness in a more conservative philosophy. No single body of content has a warrant on intelligence among experimentalists, as it does with perennialists and essentialists. In fact, to the experimentalist, traditional subject matter lines are dissolved and are reconstituted topically, according to the problems and the purposes of the educational situation. Because life problems are not easily placed in disciplinary subjects, a premium is put on the interdisciplinary construction of subject matter. The aim of knowledge (or the subject matter) is not the contribution it makes to one's mind, but the contribution it makes to one's behavior. To know that poor eating habits, for instance, increase the odds of certain illnesses, can be interpreted as mindful knowledge (one could know it, but still eat poorly) or as knowledge that exists in the actions of life (one knows it and acts accordingly). The experimentalists stake their claim with the latter.

The focus on behavior is especially important because as a philosophy of democracy, experimentalism ultimately judges the effects of schooling against some standard of betterment or progress in the life experience. This is a principle associated with the roots that experimentalism has in a broader philosophical tradition known as pragmatism. The pragmatist's prejudice is to affect the here and now, to look at life as a matter of present significance, and not as a matter that has some ultimate judgment in some transcendental place. This is a way of keeping the focus on experience and on the kind of intelligent conduct that will produce the prize of progress. As Dewey (1938) observed, "We always live at the time we live and not at some other time, and only by extracting at each present time the full meaning of each present experience are we prepared for doing the same thing in the future" (p. 51). Even the study of the past only has relevance as it grants understanding to the present. "The present," stated Dewey (1916), "generates the problems which lead us to search the past for suggestion, and which supplies meaning to what we find when we search" (p. 89).

Thus, we return to the primacy of experience in the school. Schooling, to paraphrase Dewey, is not a preparation for life but is life itself, and in the case of American schooling, life in a democracy. This means that the whole child must be educated, not just his or her mind. The curriculum, as a result, is comprehensive in its ambition, interdisciplinary in its overall organization, and activity-based in its sense of experience. Because the school is the engine of democracy, considerable emphasis is placed on the value of the shared experience and the communion of values, outlooks, and problems that help to amalgamate the people of the nation.

Experimentalism has real life application in the school curriculum. The nature of the learner and the nature of the subject matter have definitive shape in the experimentalist tradition. The focus on social consciousness and problem solving sends strong signals in the curriculum as does the reconceptualization of subject matter as an interdisciplinary construct. The latter point often proves to be problematic in the school curriculum because subject matter still tends to be organized within discipline-centered lines, and teachers are typically not trained to handle interdisciplinary inquiries. The implications for practice include a more experiential, democratic, and inquiry-based

Ideal of the Learner
A socially-conscious, democratically-inspired and intellectually-empowered problem-solver.

Ideal of Society
A democracy whose citizenry is engaged in a common universe of social discourse and social understanding.

Ideal of Subject Matter
A problem-focused, idea-oriented curriculum directly responsive to the personal and socio-civic experience.

FIGURE 5–3   Conceptual Features of Experimentalism.

classroom than might otherwise not be the case, but also one that might give short shrift to key content knowledge.

Romantic Naturalism

The first signs of a progressive movement in the schools of the United States occurred at the turn of the twentieth century and were largely child-centered in orientation. Because the school was so deeply ensconced in a conservative subject-centered view of learning during the late nineteenth century, the conditions were conducive for a counter-reaction that could undo the extreme of subject centeredness. The child-centered movement in America *was* the counter-reaction, offering a philosophy of learning unabashedly dedicated to providing children with joyful, open-ended, activity-based education. Where the subject-centered view was mentalistic, the child-centered view was active; where the subject-centered view staked its claim in a uniform, subject-based, and planned experience, child-centered proponents countered with an individualistic, emotional, and spontaneous experience. Where teacher-directed instruction, teacher authority, and a structured curriculum ruled in the school, child-centered advocates aimed for reforms that allowed children to direct their own learning and to determine for themselves what they will learn and how and when they will learn it.

These expressions of child centeredness unfolded under the influence of a romantic naturalist philosophy. The story of romantic naturalism begins with the peculiar manner in which the nature of the learner is understood. Taking its philosophical leanings from Rousseau, whose disdain for institutions and adults was legendary, romantic-naturalism forwarded the idea that children are best educated in a free and largely unhampered environment, with only minimal adult intervention. Professing a commitment to the innate goodness and innocence of children, romantic naturalists put little stock in the relevance of uniform experiences in the school or even in the act of curriculum or instructional planning. The philosophy embraced the natural self-educating powers of the child—the notion that learning is so much a matter of individual choice and individual direction that it is best to allow it to be dictated by the preferences and pleasures of children. Romantic naturalists believe that nature provides the inner processes needed to produce virtuous and self-actualized human beings, but that schools tend to ruin this natural process by imposing an "educational" agenda on children that undermines their self-educating inclinations. Thus, the teacher's role is to help create a classroom environment that facilitates individual expressions and the pursuit of individual interests. One author put it this way: "What we need to do, and all we need to do, is bring as much of the world as we can into the school and the classroom; give the children as much help and guidance as they need and ask for, listen respectfully when they feel like talking; and then get out of the way. We can trust them to do the rest" (McCraken, 1973, p. 16).

The romantic progressives sometimes represent their position by flying under the banner of "learning by doing," arguing that there is educational virtue in essentially any task that the child is committed to perform in the classroom. In short, having an experience moved by student desire or student decision is ipso facto educational. This idea drew opposition from experimentalists, who argued that all experiences (doings) were not necessarily educational and that great many were, in fact, miseducative. While we might learn by doing, all doings are not necessarily educational (Hook, 1973). The distinction very much exemplifies the difference between experimentalist and romantic naturalist thinking.

Put in historical context, one could appreciate the early appeal of romantic naturalism. Many early progressives were keen to repudiate the assumption that children were innately evil (or ordained as originally sinful). They were attracted to any idea that opened up possibilities for the child to gain due consideration in the curriculum and that provided a foothold for active learning experiences in an institution that had long equated formal education with a stale uniformity of mental exercises and repressed physical motion. By anointing the child in their educational theorizing, romantic progressives brought activity and life to the school, freeing the student from the abstract and lifeless quality of early timeworn methods of schooling. Moreover, the progressive impulse to personalize schooling held possibilities for the outward extension of schooling, making it not a matter aligned to some elitist conceptions of high western thought but a matter that resided naturally in all human beings. As Bode (1938) stated, "the emphasis of progressive education on the individual, on the sinfulness of imposition, and on the necessity of securing free play for intelligence, is a reflection of the growing demand, outside of the school, for recognition of the common man" (p. 11).

This, however, did not prevent romantic naturalism from suffering early attacks from both conservative and progressive quarters. Critics targeted several theoretical problems. First, child-centered progressives were accused of advancing a form of education that denied children the central source of all learning, which was the wisdom of adults and the extended wisdom of the race experience. To conservatives, this meant that the power of the subject matter was eviscerated from the experience, an inexcusable failing. To the experimentalists, this meant that the learning would somehow proceed in a free form without any engagement to the agenda of democracy. The combined criticisms argued that the romantic naturalists failed to offer any vision of subject matter and any vision of society. The effect is that the school is removed from its historic role as an agency for democracy. In other words, because the romantic school program supports no social agenda, in the interest of advantaging only individualistic endeavors, it runs the risk of failing to systematically teach students the kinds of skills they will need to avoid being victims of anti-democratic and authoritarian forces. Bode (1938) put it another way: "If democracy is to have a deep and inclusive human meaning, it must have also a distinctive educational system" (p. 26).

Romantic naturalism was the by-product of progressive thinkers who were absorbed with the individual and threatened by the boundaries implied in any social theory or social mission of schooling. Although romantic naturalism sounds like a philosophy with little application or basis in the realities of schooling, it did have its day in the educational sun both during the early stages of its development and later during the 1960s. The late 1960s and the early 1970s brought forth school reforms touting the value of open-ended experiences, self-directed learning, and facilitative teaching. Open education and the open classroom became educationally fashionable because they encouraged a free form of teaching and learning, often in an open physical environment that resulted, in some cases, in classrooms without walls or doors. Popular best-selling authors preached a gospel of school renewal that

Ideal of the Learner
A self-educating force of nature whose education is best served with only minimal adult intervention.

Ideal of Society
Multitudinous egoistic and individualistic pursuits.

Ideal of Subject Matter
A content neutral curriculum emphasizing free activity.

FIGURE 5–4   Conceptual Features of Romantic-Naturalism.

portrayed emergent acts of love and compassion as the main basis for school improvement. Free schools, alternative schools, and concepts such as de-schooling society (which implied that one could receive an education simply from freely chosen experiences in the wider society) gained popular currency. Much of this writing produced a criticism of public schooling that featured images of repressive schools.

From the standpoint of the curriculum, romantic naturalism breaks some of the rules. As indicated earlier, the theoretical foundation for curriculum development demand some view on the learner, society, and subject matter. If any of these factors are ignored or rejected, the curriculum development process is likely flawed. Romantic naturalists have a clear vision of the learner. It is, in fact, the *sine quo non* of the philosophy. The curriculum is of, for, and even by the child; from it, all else flows. That leaves it with no clear perspective on society other than one that values egoistic pursuits and no clear vision of subject matter, other than that which emerges from the quixotic experience of the child.

Social Efficiency

Yet another group of thinkers was also intent on bringing life activity to the curriculum. However, they differed substantively from other progressive groups by supporting a factory model of schooling intent on standardizing experiences in the curriculum while also sorting and slotting the student population in a way that aimed to adjust everyone to their station in life. Advocates of such a view sought to use the curriculum to strike the chord of order, control, and social harmony in the school. Out of this group of thinkers arose a conception of curriculum that was management-oriented, efficiency driven, and highly prescriptive in its detail. In the literature, it is commonly referred to as the tradition of social efficiency, but more contemporary formulations of it can also be seen in competency-based or mastery-learning instruction.

The commitment to social efficiency in the curriculum was historically preceded by a commitment to social efficiency in the society. During the 1900s, the business community led the way with a new efficiency strategy known as scientific management. Developed by an engineer named Frederick Taylor (1911), scientific management promised to provide a method for businesses, particularly factories, that would increase production while also lowering costs.

The key to the idea had to do with identifying and then standardizing the action of the most productive workers. The premise was that there was one best way to do any job, and that such a way could be discerned through careful study. To Taylor, if the most productive worker had an output of x, then there was no reason why all workers could not meet the same output figure. By using various incentives,

Taylor identified the very best workers, meaning those who produced the most in the least amount of time. Taylor then analyzed their actions, and tried to note, in behavioral terms, what made them so productive. After having identified the practices central to the success of the most productive workers, Taylor standardized them, so that other workers could be taught to do the same.

The lesson that Taylor provided to businesses soon reached the schools. Applied to the curriculum, scientific management was deceptively simple: find the best practices, standardize them, and make them part of the school routine. The "best" practices under Taylor's conditions, however, were always those that managed to secure the highest productivity with the least amount of effort. There were going to be complications if the same rationale was to prevail in the schools. It was one thing to note the productivity of an assembly line worker, but it was quite another to make similar judgments with something as complex and dynamic as the education of children. To make it work, substantive changes had to be made in the way that the curriculum was to be conceived. Generally speaking, a factory model had to be embraced for the curriculum. The idea of productivity in the school meant that actual learning outcomes needed to be identified and that measurements needed to be taken to determine whether they had been reached. The Taylorian regard for efficiency had in fact set the wheels in motion for a whole new science of school measurement, a numerical way of demonstrating achievement and mastery.

The implications of Taylor's work were very clear in the early curriculum design work being promoted by like-minded thinkers in the burgeoning field of curriculum studies, the most prominent being a University of Chicago professor named John Franklin Bobbitt. For the curriculum to be manageable and operative, Bobbitt believed that learning had to take on a character of specificity that it had never seen before. Many social progressives had built the school experience on the ground of generalizability, talking of the need for broadly framed objectives that were more statements of principle than specific actions to be undertaken. Bobbitt, however, thought such thinking was unrealistic and irresponsible and he wanted to change it:

> Objectives that are only vague, high-sounding hopes and aspirations are to be avoided. Examples are: 'character building,' 'the harmonious development of the individual,' 'social efficiency,' 'general discipline,' 'self-realization,' 'culture,' and the like. All of these are valid enough; but too cloud-like for guiding practical procedure. They belong to the visionary adolescence of our profession—not to its sober and somewhat disillusioned maturity. (Bobbitt, 1924, p. 32)

Out of this demand for a new level of specificity arose a method of curriculum development known as activity analysis. An admirer of Taylor's work, Bobbitt believed that the school curriculum was best served by preparing the learner for specific activities in adult life. He wanted the school to survey all of the relevant activities in the lives of adults (as they related to occupations, family, society, and so on) and then, similar to Taylor's standardized production model, teach directly to each activity. Bobbitt (1918) expressed his theory in clear terms:

> The central theory is simple. Human life, however varied, consists in the performance of specific objectives. However numerous and diverse they may be for any social class, they can be discovered. This requires only that one go out into the world of affairs and discover the particulars of which these affairs consist. These will show the abilities, attitudes, habits, appreciations and forms of knowledge that men need. These will be the objectives of the curriculum. They will be numerous, definite and particularized. The curriculum will then be that series of experiences which children and youth must have by way of attaining those objectives. (p. 42)

The intention was to be as specific as possible in the framing of activities because the job of the curriculum was to prepare the learner for specific tasks through a process of habit formation. "The most significant feature of the work of practical curriculum making today," stated Bobbitt (1921), "is the tendency first to particularize with definiteness and in detail the objectives" (p. 607). As a result, Bobbitt's curriculum was filled with thousands of skills and behaviors that were, by the function of their specificity, often fixed at rather low, mechanistic levels. Here is a list of objectives taken from a reading program designed for the Los Angeles schools (Bobbitt, 1921, p. 609):

You will be ready to undertake A-1 reading when you can do the following things:

1. When you are spending at least sixty minutes a day on reading and phonetics.
2. When you know at sight one hundred words from the list of one hundred and twenty-five on flash cards chosen from the main list.
3. When you can use any of the one hundred words in sentences with the following word phrases: This is, I see, I have, We have, I can, We can, Can you, Have you, I like, We like; a, the, an.
4. When you can read the first, second, fourth and fifth stories in the Free and Treadwell Primer.
5. When you are able to read no less than ten pages of your Supplementary Unit primer.
6. When you can speak the English language well enough to understand the work of the next grade intelligently.
7. When you read a sentence as a whole and not word by word. If a sentence is long, you will phrase it properly.
8. When you can read print from the flash cards or from your books, also standard script as written on the blackboard by your teacher.
9. When you can read silently and interpret sentence units with our required vocabulary as "Was the cat black?" or "Can a dog fly?".
10. When you have read the Jack Straw Stories (optional).

The idea of atomizing the activities of the school applied to virtually every facet of the school curriculum, including reading, arithmetic, spelling, language, and penmanship. As Bobbitt (1924a) claimed, activity analysis was intent on discovering the specific forms of behaviors for humans to follow. "It would discover the five or ten thousand words they spell, the several score mathematical operations they perform, the several hundred specific practical home activities in which they engage, the main things they do in the care of their health, the specific things involved in managing a checking account at the bank, and the like" (p. 50). Readers should note that Bobbitt worked out of a functionalist perspective, trying to train the student population for the performance of functions or activities that contributed to and ensured a stable and secure society. He did not concern himself much with the nature of the learner or with the ideals of society.

Bobbitt believed that the curriculum could be reduced to a conveyor-like process that yielded a completed product. Bobbitt (1913) was not subtle about such matters. "Education," he declared, "is a shaping process as much as the manufacturing of steel rails" (p. 11). The factory metaphor captured the essence of education that Bobbitt promoted. Students were the raw products, the school was the assembly-line, and the society the consumer. The world of philosophy and concerns for social reform and socio-personal growth were simply not important considerations. The charge of the school was to fit individual into life, into a slot that ensured order and stability.

To its advocates, the method of activity analysis carried certain positive results. By virtue of the method, for instance, the school curriculum was undoubtedly more closely connected to life. After all it was based on activity. This was not an insignificant claim because Bobbitt believed that activity analysis worked out the progressive regard for "learning as doing." He felt activity analysis presented a good working alternative to the tradition of mental discipline which placed misdirected attention, to use Bobbitt's phrase, on "the memory reservoir" of students, on the idea of "subject storage" and the image of a student "as knower." Armed with activity analysis, Bobbitt could claim that he was interested in conduct, action, behavior, and the construction of the learner "as doer." Activity analysis also presumed to be better suited for teachers because it offered pre-fashioned and ready-made activities that did not require the teachers to think independently. "The burden of finding the best methods," stated Bobbitt, "is too large and too complicated to be laid on the shoulders of the teachers" (1913, pp. 51–52). Activity analysis also pointed to new promises in the area of waste elimination and institutional order by making it clear that some scale of measurement was needed for assessment purposes. Lastly, social efficiency, by aiming to teach children according to their needs and abilities, was a victory for differential experiences in the school, ones that led to different social and vocational destinies. This willingness to differentiate in the school curriculum presumably helped to secure a world where everyone could find their place, where the individual was adjusted to a social order that stabilized society.

Job analysis had it share of critics. No one's critical remarks, however, were more penetrating than Boyd Bode's (1927). Bode attacked Bobbitt for the manner in which Bobbitt discerned his objectives, noting how Bobbitt drew largely from adult activities. He contended that Bobbitt had set into motion a condition for education that simply served the status quo (things as they already existed). To Bode it was clear that job analysis was little more than training for adjustment to existing social conditions. In a democracy, Bode continued, society is better served if education proceeds from the level of general training, targeting abilities that cut across particular conditions and particular problems. Individuals (and by implication, the collective society) could only grow and develop if they had the skills needed to deal with emergent problems and issues, as opposed to being adjusted to and knowledgeable of particular existing conditions. Specific activities change over time. The activities of being a citizen or a farmer are different now from what they were decades ago. Thus, to look at specificity as the answer to the curriculum was to promote outdated training that would not likely have much relevance beyond the immediate present.

The general conceptual components of social efficiency can still be found today in its hybridization with behaviorist psychology. The stimulus-response connectionism inherent in behaviorism was friendly to the demand for specificity that the social efficiency perspective valued. The effect was the use of instructional forms that relied on finely-specified objectives, including prominently known approaches such as competency-based instruction, mastery learning, and programmed instruction. Each of these instructional approaches was designed around a sequential and hierarchical pattern of highly specific learning objectives. The purpose was to offer a tightly designed sequence of objectives integrated into pre-designed instructional exercises (often workbook exercises), which if followed properly, were guaranteed to result in an individual's mastery of the skills and knowledge built in to the objectives. The presumption was that anything worth knowing was measurable and reducible to a working sequence of objectives.

Under the demands of competency-based strategies, the curriculum developer itemizes exactly what needs to be taught and eventually evaluates it for mastery. A competency-based reading program, for instance, usually represents a specific set of competencies, organized by grade levels. It directs the teacher to teach each competency directly, and regulates each student's movement through the curriculum with mastery tests of each competency. The result is a highly skill-based school experience commonly marked by rather low level activities. What could not be effectively measured (and demonstrated as mastered) is not taught. Skills in oral communication, in writing, in argumentation, in

Ideal of the Learner
Individual needing to be adjusted to the tasks of adult life.

Ideal of Society
A functionalist theory advancing a harmonious and well-ordered society.

Ideal of Subject Matter
Particularized life activities required to adjust individual to life roles.

FIGURE 5–5   Conceptual Features of Social Efficiency.

problem solving, in cross-disciplinary insight, and in research skills (to name just a few), are simply not part of the instructional picture.

The social efficiency perspective obviously does not do much to advance the professional development of educators. Most of the important judgments in the curriculum are already made for the teachers, who are left with following directions and handing out pre-developed worksheets. The idea of "teacher proof" materials was born and came into favor in this philosophical climate. Teacher proof materials were typically comprised of programmed learning workbooks, some varieties of computer-assisted instruction, and highly prescriptive learning packages that scripted what teachers should say and do. Their orientation was to find a way to protect the curriculum from the teacher; hence, the term "teacher-proof."

The philosophy of social efficiency is clearly defined and positioned in relation to at least two of the three factors for professional decision making. It has marked out a functionalist view of society and an activity-based view of subject matter, and largely views learners in relation to the talents and skills they can bring to their functionalist role in society. As indicated, such a philosophy of schooling tends to ignore important generalizable skills, such as problem solving, that allow the learner to adjust to changes rather than to be simply adjusted to the status quo.

EDUCATION IN THE RADICAL TRADITION

The radical philosophies discussed in this section are radical in a political sense, taking their pledges mostly from an overtly ideological or political way of thinking that is, more often than not, explicitly designed to revolutionize, overthrow, and generally subvert the existing system of schooling. The social reconstructionist perspective, born during hurly-burly days of the Great Depression, was largely an attempt to inject American schooling with a socialist ideological outlook. Current radical thinking, often loosely categorized as postmodern in orientation, operate on a similar basis, although within a wider range of attendant political viewpoints.

Social Reconstructionism

To understand social reconstructionism one must understand the fundamental social class analysis that gave it its start. During the 1920s and into the 1930s, a number of scholars vented their frustration with what they perceived as rampant class-based bias in the leadership and operation of the public schools. George Counts, who would emerge as the main historical voice of social reconstructionism, had preached this message throughout the decade of the Great Depression. His early work helped expose some of the problems, showing, for instance, that disproportionately high numbers of student dropouts were from low-income families. He also examined school board memberships and found that the membership base was mostly comprised of men drawn from the middle and upper classes. These general conditions, according to Counts (1922), encouraged the school to see its interests not in the widest public good but in the education of the wealthy and the accompanying promotion of the values of competitive and individualistic capitalism. Counts stood firm with his accusation. The school, he alleged, was systemically, even ideologically, designed to perpetuate the socio-economic status quo. It was the handmaiden of the ruling economic class, sustaining, instead of combating, the evils of extreme poverty and social inequities.

Progressive thinkers had not given the problem of social class much standing in their philosophies. The child-centered romantics had no social theory behind their thinking and the experimentalists, although concerned about socio-economic disparities, were not interested in posing an educational experience specifically designed to remedy specific social problems. Education with the experimentalists always sided with democracy and with the expectation that the schools will produce an enlightened citizenry that could take charge of its own social problems. But they did not view the school as an instrument for dislodging or reforming a specific social ill.

It did not take long for the social class analysis offered by Counts and others to yield an educational philosophy that saw itself as an antidote to the crisis of classism in the schools. To the scholars who were earnestly offended by the failing of the school on the socio-economic front, the thinking took shape in acutely ideological ways. Because the educational institution was itself accused of being ideological (deeply situated in the back pockets of business interest and socially conservative groups), some scholars had no reservation about flipping the ideological switch in the school and teaching in a direction that favored radical social transformation. One had to fight ideological fire, they claimed, with ideological fire.

Thus, social reconstructionism was born as a philosophy openly and unapologetically dedicated to educating youth in socialist doctrine and the new social order it demanded. The duty of the teacher was to teach in a way that made a contribution to the social reconstruction of the society, which, in the view of its proponents, needed to lean heavily in the direction of a collectivist socialist society. Teachers had to understand that they were now caught in a revolutionary struggle to wrest the control of the school away from the ruling upper classes. This would call for abrupt and confrontational educational tactics. George Counts (1932) stated the matter rather bluntly. Education must:

> emancipate itself from the influence of the (ruling upper classes), face squarely and courageously every social issue, come to grips with life in all of its stark reality, establish an organic relation with the community, develop a realistic and comprehensive theory of welfare . . . and become less frightened than it is today at the bogeys of imposition and indoctrination. (pp. 9–10)

The educational plan was simple. Schooling must not fear indoctrination; it must embrace it as a way to drive a stake through the heart of the capitalistic nature of schooling. In this way, education could become an enterprise dedicated to influencing students to accept the collectivist ideals of socialism, a position completely at odds with the experimentalist thinking of John Dewey. The social reconstructionists believed that this form of education was most suitable for democracy because their ideal of society depended on a citizenry prepared to defend the worthiness of a utopian socialist arrangement.

Thus, the teacher became a kind of ideological missionary who emphasized the importance of economic equity, worker's rights, class analysis, and the other collectivist ideals.

The social reconstructionists never gained much currency in the schools, but their criticism of the schools has continued to be a source of ongoing commentary. Today, the line of argumentation started by Counts continues to be played out by scholars claiming to embrace a critical theory of education. Critical theory aims to disclose all forms of injustice and inequity in schooling by revealing the interests served by the knowledge and the human action brought to bear in the school setting. Needless to say, critical theorists find that corporate ideology (capitalism) is behind the acts of injustice and inequity in schooling, although they also offer accusations of cultural hegemony or cultural imperialism, male authority, and white racism. The thesis is that the main function of schools is wedded to the reproduction of the socio-economic order (and associated dominant groups). The school is said to offer knowledge and skills that empower the most privileged in a way that keeps social class divisions in tact. Thus, the mode of analysis in this philosophy is to look closely for signs of how, not if, the school carries out its repressive mandate. Because schools do not openly tout their repressive actions, one has to look for them and make a case for them as they might exist in the curriculum.

Critical theory is largely a theory or philosophy of protest, although some educators claim that they are involved in something known as critical pedagogy (Wink, 2000). McLaren (1989) states that critical pedagogy is about "how and why knowledge gets constructed the way it does, and how and why some constructions of reality are legitimated and celebrated by the dominant culture while others are clearly not" (p. 169). One could appreciate the legacy of the social reconstructionists in McLaren's statement. Concerns over dominant groups inevitably leads to a highly politicized form of teaching that encourages students to be more conscious of class, race, ethnic, and even gender differences, and more able to see their own victimization at the hands of society, or as the case with children from dominant groups, their own role as victimizers. Ideology stills prevails as the main educating force in the school.

The social reconstructionist point of view has some merit from the standpoint of the curriculum. It abides by a strongly worded and highly politicized view of society, which allows it to shape the natures of the learner and the subject matter accordingly. One should keep in mind that, although social reconstructionism possesses a social theory, it is not exactly a democratic social theory. It puts emphasis on an a priori vision of society and it has no qualms about imposing a hard political stamp on the school curriculum, which really can be interpreted as violations to the factor of society. The politicized nature of truth in this arrangement also has ripple effects in politicizing the school experience by making hard-line distinctions between the politically virtuous and their doctrinal enemies.

Ideal of the Learner
Guardian of the highest principles of a collectivist doctrine.

Ideal of the Society
A utopian social arrangement stressing economic and social equality.

Ideal of Subject Matter
Politicized knowledge designed to promote the utopian causes of the society.

FIGURE 5–6   Conceptual Features of Social Reconstructionism.

Postmodernism

The best way to start a discussion of postmodernism is by exploring the modernist assumptions it aims to combat. A modernist view could be encapsulated with a few central principles. These might include demonstrating a faith in the idea of scientific progress, in rationalist thinking, in the power of evidence, in the reliability of social labels, and in the power of a common culture. The postmodern perspective not only does not accept such assumptions but actively seeks to explode them in the interests of "decentering" our way of examining the world. The effort to "decenter" is moved by a decidedly anti-western sentiment and by a desire to expose and undermine "the privileging of Western patriarchal culture with its representations of domination rooted in a Eurocentric conception of the world" (Aronowitz & Giroux, 1991, p. 64). In its place, the postmodernist seeks to stress the value of individual initiative, the recognition of human intention, the unmasking of political ideology in knowledge, the taming of social-control mechanisms in the school, and the general belief that society is marked by conflicting interests of class, gender, and culture.

The postmodern commitment is deeply involved in providing what one might call oppositional thought in the school experience, a pledge of negativity that helps to deny the validity of any grand claims on what is worth knowing and that also helps to preserve the dynamism of the lived experience in school. Thus, traditions or conventions are subjected to deep criticism. By taking up the role of criticism (or negativity), the postmodernist hopes to bring forth more self-consciousness and a better view of the plurality of thought in our lived experience. The school, which is perceived to be historically involved in transmitting established norms, becomes a place where knowledge is challenged and its linkage to political ideology and sources of power and domination is exposed. Such efforts are viewed as empowering because they lead to eye-opening moments that allow students to see themselves in a more authentic context. Oppositional thought also demands that the schools take an active role in revealing the interests served by the knowledge and the human action taken up by the school.

Postmodernists also believe that individuals need to escape from the forces of rationality in school. As a result, they are wary of the methods of science, believing that science is really just an ideological cloak draped over acts of oppression. One could see this, they claim, especially well in the manner in which science is used to create social categories or social labels in school. For example, special education labels, which typically include designations such as behaviorally-disordered, emotionally-disturbed, or learning disabled, might be viewed by most as instructional categories designed to assist special-needs children by helping to justify remedial education or other extra educational services. To the postmodernist, however, such categories must be "deconstructed" and understood from the position they might play in the oppression of a disproportionately large number of minority and low-income children who comprise them. Yet as an instructional endeavor, special education is legitimated by a science of test sources, research findings, and other so-called objective data. Science validates its existence and its utility. But from the perspective of the postmodernist, special education should be viewed from its less obvious effects, which might include acknowledging how children in special education settings endure psychological messages that could lead to the deterioration of their academic competencies and life skills.

One could also find a very strong emphasis among postmodernists on what one might loosely call the hidden or latent curriculum, which is, to recall, school action justified by certain articulated intentions that gives rise to latent or covert effects. Postmodernists are very attracted to the idea of the hidden curriculum because it allows them to make certain claims about the subtext of schooling, about unstated and latent effects. When a teacher, for instance, reminds children in a low-income school that they are all "such good workers," a postmodern analysis might deconstruct such a phrase as a latent reminder to the children that they are ordained to be workers in a class-based society. When the "great books" are given to students to read, the latent message is that only the writing and thinking of white European males have a claim on greatness. When schoolwork results in keeping children busy with drudgery and away from their heart-felt desires, the school could be interpreted as practicing a kind of breaking down of spirit in a person for the purposes of preparing them for low-level work.

Postmodernism also focuses on difference, a position decidedly at ends with conservatives and virtually all other philosophical views of the school, except romantic naturalists. Because there are different ways of knowing, experiencing, and even labeling the world, the focus of learning is dedicated to these differences, what is sometimes referred to as "otherness." To the postmodernist, the failing to the conservative embrace of the Great Books is fundamentally a failing inspired by ethnocentrism and class-bias (Aronowitz & Giroux, 1991). If the task of postmodernism is to assist with student identity, then this identity must be subjected to the full variance of experience, highlighting narratives taken from varied views of race, class, and gender. Marginalized or subordinate groups (usually women and minority groups), are especially important to the postmodern position because they represent a group struggle that could be used against the dominant ideology. Such groups become a potential source of subversion, opposition, and ultimately transformation. The sympathy toward so-called subordinate groups, coupled with an uncontested denial (if not hatred) of dominant thinking, has sometimes resulted in the accusation of politically correct thinking among postmodernists.

Because schools (and society in general) are believed to be heavily layered with corporate ideology, often peddled to the masses through the popular media, teachers are expected to keep an eye out for such incursions in the purposes and materials of the curriculum. Students must not be subjected to the transmission of knowledge, but should be taught to question knowledge, see the misrepresentation in it, and search for the imperialism, patriarchy, racism, and vulgar capitalism that have shaped it and continue to sustain it.

Postmodernism, in the end, offers an escape for the student from the social repressions inherent in knowledge and in the experience of living. Part of this freedom resides in the active questioning of everything that presumes to pass as truth or reason. But the process also embraces the idea of asking learners to look introspectively for a more authentic sense through meditative ponder, intuition, imagination, and the active interpretation of everyday events. This is part of the existentialist nature of postmodernism.

The educational route in postmodernism is sometimes so personal that much of the school experience resembles the features of romantic naturalism. For instance, in attempting to describe how a postmodern high school might begin to conduct its own version of education, Aronowitz and Giroux (1991) grant authority to only teachers and students; none is granted to even legislative or governmental agents. "Students and teachers," they assert, should "negotiate which courses, if any, are to be required" (p. 21). Teachers discuss and "try to persuade" students into engaging in a certain regiment of courses. "The normal classroom now resembles an open classroom where small groups of students are simultaneously studying different aspects of the course of subject matter, and others are engaged in individual tutorials with the teacher or other knowledgeable persons" (p. 21). The nature of these tutorials is decidedly political, which is where the comparison to the romantic naturalists begins to fray.

Because postmodernism features a cultural criticism of the school, it is difficult to completely understand its standing in the curriculum. When one examines the practical implications of the criticisms, postmodernism operates in the school much in the way that we might expect romantic naturalism to operate, with one important difference. The postmodern position has an ideological prod that pushes the student in a direction of confronting the dominant ideology and ultimately understanding the

Ideal of the Learner
An emancipated individual seeking an authentic meaning and identity in an ideologically-layered world.

Ideal of Society
Emancipated individuals and subordinate groups finding identity and understanding in a repressive society.

Ideal of Subject Matter
Deconstructed knowledge, understood in relation to its linkage with dominant ideology.

FIGURE 5–7   Conceptual Feature of Postmodernism.

oppression inherent in dominant thinking. Fundamentally, the problem with the postmodern position from the standpoint of the curriculum is that it is decidedly non-normative in orientation, while the public school curriculum is, at its very core, a normative project.

SUMMARY

Philosophy has an undeniably profound place in the classroom and school. It is the defining source behind the considerable variation in teaching style one sees across classrooms and schools. This is not to say, however, that all philosophies necessarily have equal standing in the school. Fascist or authoritarian views, for instance, are obviously not reconcilable with the schools of a democracy. Where a philosophy wants to make a stand in a classroom, it must have some insight to offer on the three fundamental factors in the educative process (the learner, the society, and subject matter). In this way, a philosophy acts as a kind of screen through which ideas are filtered.

Three traditions of philosophical insight encapsulate the main positions on the purpose and practice of the schooling. Conservative views are deeply subject-centered, still associated with the psychology of mental discipline and very much wedded to the idea of transmitting the culture through the knowledge embodied in the traditional academic subjects and the "great books." Progressive-experimentalist views are less mentalistic than the conservative views and are more attached to teaching the very skills, competencies, and attitudes needed to conduct an intelligent life in a democratic society. Essential to this process is the involvement of the scientific method applied to social thinking. The romantic variant of the progressive education movement is child-centered and allegiant to the naturalist views of Rousseau. The social efficiency tradition, although furnishing progressive credentials in support of activity and engagement to life conditions in the curriculum, violates a tenet of progressivism by advocating what is in effect education for life adjustment. Finally, the radical tradition offers a social reconstructionist view that embraces a politicized curriculum as the best way to rid the nation of capitalist oppression as well as a postmodern position that seeks inner understandings through the dislocation and deconstruction of dominant views.

REFERENCES

Adler, M. (1984). *The paideia program: An educational syllabus.* New York: Macmillan Publishing Co.

Adler, M. (1988). *Reforming education: The opening of the American mind.* New York: Macmillan Publishing Co.

Aronowitz, S., & Giroux, H. (1991). *Postmodern education: Politics, culture and social criticism.* Minneapolis: University of Minnesota.

Bagley, W. (1907). *Classroom management.* New York: Macmillan Publishing Co.

Bennett, W. J. (1986). *First lessons: A report on elementary education in America.* Washington, DC: United States Department of Education.

Bennett, W. J. (1987). *James Madison High School.* Washington, DC: U.S. Department of Education.

Bennett, W. J. (1993). *Book of virtues: A treasury of great moral stories.* New York: Simon & Shuster.

Bobbitt, J. F. (1913). The supervision of city schools: Some general principles of management applied to the problems of city-school systems. *Twelfth Yearbook of the National Society for the Study of Education, Part I.* Bloomington, IL: Public School Publishing Co.

Bobbitt, J. F. (1918). *The Curriculum.* Boston: Houghton Mifflin Co.

Bobbitt, J. F. (1921). A significant trend in curriculum-making. *Elementary School Journal* 21 (April):607–15.

Bobbitt, J. F. (1924). *How to make a curriculum.* Boston: Houghton Mifflin Co.

Bobbitt, J. F. (1924a). The new technique of curriculum-making. *Elementary School Journal* 25 (September):45–54.

Bode, B. H. (1927). *Modern Educational Theories.* New York: Macmillan Publishing Co.

Bode, B. H. (1938). *Progressive education at the crossroads.* New York: Newson and Co.

Counts, G. S. (1922). *The selective character of American secondary education.* Chicago: University of Chicago Press.

Counts, G. S. (1932). *Dare the schools build a new social order?* New York: The John Day Co.

Dewey, J. (1916). *Democracy and education.* New York: Free Press.

Dewey, J. (1938). *Experience and education.* New York: Macmillan.

Finn, C., & Ravitch, D. (1987). *What do our 17-year-olds know?* New York: Harper & Row.

Hirsch, E. D. (1987). *Cultural literacy: What every American needs to know.* Boston: Houghton Mifflin.

Hook, S. (1973). John Dewey and His Betrayers. In C. Troost (ed.) *Radical school reform: Critique and alternatives.* Boston: Little, Brown and Company.

Hutchins, R. M. (1936). *The higher learning in America.* New Haven: Yale University Press.

Hutchins, R. M. (1972). The great anti-school campaign. In Robert Hutchins and Mortimer Adler (Eds.). *The great ideas today.* Chicago: Encyclopedia Britannica.

McCraken, S. (1973). Quackery in the Classroom. In C. Troost (Ed.) *Radical school reform: Critique and alternatives.* Boston: Little, Brown and Company.

McLaren. (1989). *Life in schools: An introduction to critical pedagogy in the foundations of education.* New York: Longman.

Taylor, F. W. (1911). *The principles of scientific management.* New York: Harper and Brothers.

Tyler, R. W. (1949). *Basic principles of curriculum and instruction.* Chicago: University of Chicago Press.

Van Doren, M. (1943). *Liberal education.* New York: Henry Holt and Co.

Wink, J. (2000). *Critical pedagogy: Notes from the real world.* New York: Longman.

KEY QUESTIONS

1. Of the seven orientations discussed in this chapter, where might your own views begin to settle? Is there a way to shape a kind of eclectic approach to philosophy, taking the best of each tradition?

2. What do perennialists mean when they declare the need for youth to be engaged in the permanent studies?

3. Conservatives share a commitment to the development of a common culture with experimentalists. Explain the connection and the vital difference within it.

4. Explain the term experimentalism and its association with the work of John Dewey.

5. What is the reconstruction of experience and how is it vital to the work of John Dewey?

6. How is the following quote taken from Rousseau emblematic of his view of schooling? "God makes all things good; man meddles with them and they become evil."

7. In 1932, George Counts helped to author a report titled *A Call to the Teachers of the Nation*. The report maintained that "teachers will have to emancipate themselves from the dominance of the business interests of the nation, cease cultivating the manners and association of bankers and promotion agents, repudiate utterly the ideal of material success as the goal of education, abandon the smug middle-class tradition on which they have been nourished in the past, acquire a realistic understanding of the forces that actually rule the world, and formulate a fundamental program of thought and action that will deal honestly and intelligently with the problems of industrial civilization" (p. 20). Do you believe that such matters should be part of a teacher's responsibility? Why or why not?

8. In what ways does postmodernism lead to child-centeredness?

9. What are the basic similarities between postmodernism and social reconstructionism?

RESEARCH EXERCISES

1. Ralph Tyler referred to philosophy as a screen through which ideas are filtered. Try another metaphor to explain the role of philosophy in teaching. In what way is philosophy like an engine, a foundation, a compass, or a recipe? How adequate are these metaphors? Construct your own metaphor.

2. Observe a teacher and make some determinations about the philosophical prejudices that might underpin his teaching. Interview him about why he does what he does.

3. Examine one phase of the school curriculum (i.e., multicultural education, the reading program, and the math program), and analyze the philosophical tradition behind it.

4. Get a copy of a school's mission statement and analyze it against the seven orientations described in the chapter.

5. Observe a classroom with an eye toward looking for evidence that supports or contradicts the social reconstructionist's view that public education serves capitalist interest.

6. Examine the literature used to teach English in middle or secondary school (language arts in elementary school) as it is used in a classroom with which you are familiar. Conduct a postmodern analysis, looking for the dominant ideology used to color the worldviews of children, especially children from minority or subordinate groups.

7. Here is a short questionnaire that can help you gauge the extent to which a person's philosophical position is tilted in the direction of either child-centeredness or subject-centeredness. For research purposes, think about giving it to teachers or principals from different school settings. Interpret the results in relation to variables such as grade level; years of experience; ethnicity, race, and gender; and the income level or percentage of minority students. What might be the significance of finding different levels of commitment to child-centered or subject-centered views in different school settings?

Rate each of these statements according to this scale. Compare your answers to the key below to determine your orientation.

Strongly Disagree	**Somewhat Disagree**	**No Opinion**	**Somewhat Agree**	**Strongly Agree**
1	**2**	**3**	**4**	**5**

1. The education of children would be better served if we abandoned objectives and simply allowed children to explore their own heartfelt needs and interests.
2. Students should always be permitted to determine their own rules in the educational process.
3. The most important kind of education is one that is expressly dedicated to the cultivation of the mind.
4. Exposure to the strict academic disciplines is the most essential aspect in the education of youth.
5. Self-improvement and self-actualization are the most important components to a good public education.
6. Schools are primarily designed to maintain and preserve certain established values and ideas.
7. Memorization is the most important key to learning.
8. The most effective learning is usually unstructured and spontaneous.
9. Academics are most important to the education of youth; everything else is, more or less, a frill.
10. Good teachers try not to impose any cultural values on the student.

Key: 1. child-centered (C-C); 2. C-C; 3. subject-centered (S-C); 4. S-C; 5. C-C; 6. S-C; 7. S-C; 8. C-C; 9. S-C; 10. C-C.

Tally your score for each category and average them (divide by 5) to see where you stand.

CHAPTER 6

The Laws and Ethics of Teaching

Teachers obviously shoulder certain legal and ethical obligations. They have a legal duty of care to their students, which includes the responsibility to secure the safety of the classroom, to attend to the individualistic needs of the students, and to ensure that everyone is provided with an equal opportunity to learn. Teachers are also expected to represent themselves as role models to school children, to make professionally defensible instructional decisions, and to abide by a code of professional ethics in their school behaviors. These matters of professional conduct are no less important than knowledge of subject matter or expertise in pedagogy and classroom management. Being aware of some of the fundamental issues in this area gives educators a working sense of how they might proceed with their own actions and behaviors, and how they might react to the actions and behaviors of others. Knowledge of the law allows the teacher to err on the side of caution, to think twice before acting, and to know when to seek professional advice. The reality of lawsuits often looms in the school setting and teachers should be aware of general legalistic expectations governing their behavior.

PROFESSIONAL ETHICS

The nature of professional ethics in the classroom is very much influenced by legal considerations. A teacher's freedom of expression in the classroom, for instance, is restricted by legal guidelines. Public school teachers cannot advocate religious or political views in their classrooms and they cannot use language or display behaviors that might be viewed as immoral or professionally unbecoming. Even a teacher's personal life (what he or she does away from the school) can come under scrutiny by the school if it can be shown to be relevant to the teacher's performance in the classroom. Because school communities expect teachers to be role models to their children, a teacher's personal life can be evaluated, under certain qualified conditions, against some community standard of ethics and morality.

Legal Ethics and the Idea of "Conduct Unbecoming"

The idea of "conduct unbecoming" is a legalistic one. It can be used to make a case against a teacher who has presumably violated a professional code of ethics, usually in relation to a moral issue.

School communities have historically expected chaste behaviors from their teachers, viewing them as epitomes of morality and virtue. Teachers who violated the moral norms of a community often found themselves without a job. At the turn of the twentieth century, some of the moral restrictions placed on teachers, especially female teachers, bordered on the absurd. They included restrictions against dancing, immodest dressing, and dating. Today, the restrictions are much more reasonable but they are no less important.

The working principle in dismissing a teacher for immoral behavior or for conduct unbecoming is showing a nexus or connection to the teacher's performance in the classroom (Fischer, Schimmel, & Kelly, 1999). If a particular moral or ethical violation can be judged to adversely affect a teacher's potential to fulfill the teaching mission of the school, dismissal proceedings can go forward. Such a criterion for dismissal leaves any number of behaviors open to judgment. Serious criminal convictions, such as felonies, can quickly and easily result in a teacher's dismissal because they represent what is known as *prima facie* (face value) evidence of unfitness to teach. Any violent crime, and especially any serious crime involving a child, is, de facto, by its very nature, viewed as immoral and evidence of an unfitness to teach. Any serious criminal conviction involving sexual or physical assault, the use of a gun, or any crime specifically targeted toward children would be treated similarly.

Judgment of unfitness to teach in relation to lesser criminal offenses, however, requires more interpretation. Can a teacher, for instance, be dismissed on grounds of immorality or conduct unbecoming, if he or she is convicted of drunk driving? The question immediately goes to the issue of whether such a crime could be established to negatively affect the performance of the teacher in the school (Fischer, Schimmel, & Kelly, 1999). Thus, the extent to which the drunken driving charge is publicly known is an important consideration. A drunk driving arrest in another state, say, during the summer months might not even become an issue for a teacher, but one that occurs in broad daylight, say, in front of the school and that eventually hits the front page of the local newspaper, is another matter altogether. Second, the degree to which the offense represents an established pattern of behavior, speaking to a defect in the character of the teacher, is another important factor; it makes a difference if we are talking about a fifth drunk driving charge, as opposed to a first. Other contextual factors also come into play. Was this a high school mathematics teacher or a teacher with a specific charge, as some health and physical education teachers carry, to teach about the dangers of drunk driving? If it is the latter, the teacher's publicly known problem with drinking and driving could be viewed as directly undermining his or her chances of conducting an effective educational experience with the children. Is there evidence that the parents have lost trust in the educator? Has a cloud of fear, distrust, and disrespect settled over the relationship between the teacher and the parents? Or is this a widely beloved and admired teacher whose skills in the classroom cannot be easily replaced?

Can these rules about the personal moral conduct of teachers also be applied to the personal lifestyle of the teacher? Should, for instance, homosexual or transsexual teachers actually fear for their jobs? The fact is that some school districts still might find homosexuality to be a moral or ethical breach. But, it is only a breach with consequences if the district can demonstrate it to be a matter that might undermine the teacher's ability to effectively teach in the classroom (Fischer, Schimmel, & Kelly, 1999). In 2003, the Supreme Court ruled that states cannot classify homosexual sex as a crime, thus making it impossible to dismiss homosexual teachers on the grounds that they violated state sodomy laws (Imber & Van Geel, 2004, p. 408). Thus, the issue of a teacher's sexual orientation goes to the relation of the teacher's conduct with teacher effectiveness. The legal argument would need to demonstrate how particular patterns of "homosexual" behavior might be construed as contributing to, say, a disruptive climate for teaching, or distressed relations with parents. The transgendered teacher is in a similar legal situation. A male teacher who undergoes a sex change over the summer and returns to school in the fall as a female, is open to an accusation of unfitness to teach. Obviously, there is no way for such a physical operation not to gain public notice. In the few cases tested on this issue, the main argument made against the teacher was that students and parents were confused, and in some cases frightened, by the sex change, making healthy and educative engagements between the teacher and the students (and parents) difficult to achieve.

The issue of a teacher's moral suitability, as it relates to sexual matters, manifests in other ways as well. For instance, school districts have attempted to dismiss unwed mothers, arguing that the condition of pregnancy outside of the institution of marriage violates the community's moral values and represents a living contradiction to the school's sexual education message (Fischer, Schimmel, & Kelly, 1999). From the legalistic point of view, the unwed status of the teacher would have to be publicly known but other contextual factors would also be weighed. It would likely matter, for instance, if the teacher had an appointment on a high school faculty, as opposed to a elementary school faculty, or if the teacher actually had responsibilities to teach sex education. It would also likely matter if parents and students came to the support of the teacher. The very same issues prevail if the school sought to dismiss a teacher, on moral grounds, for unwed cohabitation or for conducting an open extra-marital affair. The public performance of sexual acts, however, is generally viewed as ipso facto immoral and prima facie evidence of unfitness to teach (Imber & Van Geel, 2004, p. 408).

Generally speaking, conduct unbecoming only bears consequences when it can be shown to adversely affect the ability to teach. Public intoxication, drunk driving, fighting, and small-time shoplifting, do not stand alone as justifiable grounds for dismissal (Fischer, Schimmel, & Kelly, 1999). If the teacher's competence in the classroom cannot be connected to any of these actions, the teacher will not likely face dismissal. As mentioned, felonious crimes are automatically seen as negatively affecting a teacher's fitness to teach. The assumption is that a teacher with a felony represents a potential danger to the school and a disruption to the learning environment, automatically making him or her unfit to teach students (Imber & Van Geel, 2004, p. 409). Any immoral conduct involving a student, including sexual advances or drug or alcohol use with students, is usually viewed in the same light.

Classroom Issues

Teachers, as a matter of ethics, have an obligation to conduct themselves in the classroom in a way that realizes the school's educational mission and that abides by professional standards of behavior. This essentially means that teacher judgment needs to be attentive to the nature of the learner, to the overall purposes and policies of the school, to various state demands and capitol laws, and to a sundry of other factors related to the values of our society and the nature of the subject matter taught. These are a few of the main sources that help to shape and define professionally justifiable action in the classroom.

Professional educators, however, are also expected to hold some respect for parental views on schooling and to reflect, within certain limits, on various community prerogatives. The exercise of local/community control is, after all, one of the unique hallmarks of America's decentralized system of public schooling. But this can get complicated if community-supported desires, as parents might shape them, are at ends with what one might view as a professionally grounded argument for the education of school children. A teacher could find herself in a position of advancing a professional cause without community support, or rejecting a community cause that fails to meet a professional standard of performance. If teacher judgment is found to be out of alignment with community wishes, the problem has to find some resolution in determining the professional worth of the teacher's position. This is an easy decision if the community priority is outrageously misguided—for instance, if it is racist in its orientation, and demands racist kinds of behaviors from teachers. But the schisms between teacher judgment and community desires are usually more subtle than this.

For instance, as a general matter, teachers cannot conduct themselves in the classroom in a manner that might be construed as supporting a religious or denominational point of view, even if the community desires it. We will discuss this issue more thoroughly in another chapter, but teachers must be conscious about avoiding any entanglement with religious doctrine. The same rule applies to partisan political views. Teachers are, by professional code, not allowed to proselytize or indoctrinate students into supporting or disdaining particular political perspectives. A teacher, for instance, may not openly endorse political candidates in the classroom or support particular political positions on controversial public issues, without running the risk of being accused of and punished for unprofessional conduct. The teacher has an obligation to remain as neutral as possible on political matters and present multiple points of views in the interests of widening and informing student understanding. With regard to religion, the obligation is to maintain a secular line of inquiry when dealing with religious matters. It is important to note that these rules apply only to the classroom and school, and not to the teacher's personal life. Unlike issues related to "moral behavior," the personal religious and political views and actions of teachers, when exhibited outside of school, are basically protected rights.

The tension between community mores, ethical restrictions against proselytizing, and a teacher's view of an educationally sound experience was evident in a case in Idaho (Richardson, 10 February, 1993). Three high school teachers were suspended by the school board for allowing lesbian parents to speak to a group of students. The suspension unleashed deep community divisions over the incident, including the mobilization of action groups defending the teachers, as well as groups defending the school board action. The problem was that some parents were very much against any interaction between their children and avowed adult homosexuals. One parent stated that "the majority of the school is Christian and Mormon and they're opposed to homosexuality. [The lesbian speakers] just shouldn't have been brought in" (Richardson, 10 February, 1993). Other parents viewed the teachers' decisions to invite homosexuals to the classroom, without their prior consent, as a failure to be responsive to parental rights. Do parents actually have a right to tell teachers what their children can or cannot experience in the school? Can a community carrying a particular religious or political stamp actually filter the public school classroom? Does a teacher have an ethical responsibility to get approvals from parents before proceeding with an instructional strategy? Of course, the school must be sensitive to parental views or demands. And schools, in fact, often draft excusal policies that allow students to opt out of certain experiences in the interest of community responsiveness and are required, under most conditions, to allow excusals that have religious merit.

What is interesting in this case is that the teachers' decision to invite a group of lesbians to their classroom, which was viewed by some parents as unprofessional and unethical, could also be viewed as fundamentally professional and ethical, inspired by a principle to widen and broaden the school experience of the students in a way that could strengthen their understanding of differences in their society. A key component in judging the teacher's success in doing this is determining whether the experience had educational merit or whether it involved promotion of a homosexual lifestyle, which some parents alleged. The course taught by the teachers was called "American Character" and the topic of homosexuality, as it turned out, had a valid place in the textbook that was used in the class and was covered in the social-studies curriculum. The teachers were eventually reinstated to their positions. The topic of homosexuality was judged to be within the educational purposes of the school curriculum and no evidence could be found to support the idea of promoting a homosexual lifestyle.

Ethical considerations always pervade the classroom. Teachers, for instance, cannot use vulgar or hateful language, nor can they verbally abuse students. Teachers are expected to protect the moral sanctity of the classroom, and be vigilant about any student-to-student harassment and the use of inappropriate language or behaviors from students in the classroom. Their teaching methods are also subject to ethical screenings. Controversial teaching methods that walk the line between ethical and unethical judgment provide interesting insight in this area. For example, what if an English teacher wants to encourage youngsters to be honest with their language and to openly express themselves in their writing assignments, with no fear of punishment or consequence? What if such a policy resulted in a long line of essays written by students that were rife with vulgar and highly offensive language? The teacher here is ostensibly working within professional lines, trying to respond to the learner's life and voice, and trying to find a way to enhance good writing. Can the teacher be charged with an ethical or professional infraction?

This is essentially the question that was tested in a suburban high school outside of St. Louis (Diegmueller, 21 June, 1995). An English high school teacher with a reputation for using creative and innovative methods of teaching gave her students an assignment to write and later produce a script for a play. The teacher abided by a long-held "no censorship" policy in her classroom, believing that it is important to encourage students to write freely and creatively from the basis of their experience and imagination. As the playwriting assignment went forward, the students decided that they wanted to videotape their plays being performed. The tapes eventually showed 11th grade students, all African-Americans, acting out their plays, using a steady stream of profanity in their work. The plays dealt with themes such as sex, teenage pregnancy, gangs, drugs, killings, and imprisonment, and the tapes showed the students using words like "motherfucker," "bitch," and "nigger" with some regularity. When the principal discovered the tapes, the teacher was suspended and eventually fired (Diegmueller, 21 June, 1995).

Where controversy prevails in such an instance, it is incumbent on the teacher to demonstrate the educational viability of the classroom-based experience, making a case for it from the standpoint of its educational purpose and the maturational age of the student. It is also probably wise, as a matter of ethics and good instruction, to try to anticipate any problems that might arise under such circumstances and to apprise parents and students beforehand of the educational purpose of the experience. The educational intentions of the teacher in this case were not in question. The teacher had gotten positive reviews for her teaching in the past and had been praised widely in professional quarters for her student-centered techniques. Although the teacher's action formally broke the school's policy on student profanity, this case was really about ethical and professional judgment. Could this particular activity be viewed as educationally sound, from the standpoint of encouraging good writing and communication skills, while allowing, if not privileging, the use of vile language among the students? In a case such as this one, the answer to the question of professionalism is argumentative. The teacher, in this case, was not reinstated.

Teachers often find themselves and their teaching caught up with potentially controversial matters. What if another high school teacher assigned an essay or book laced with profane language or showed an R-rated movie in class? In 1999, Chicago school officials recommended the dismissal of a teacher who showed a 4th grade class the R-rated movie "Striptease" (Class Sees 'Striptease', 28 May, 1997). In the movie, the actress who plays a stripper in the movie appears partially nude. In this case, the teacher's actions could not be determined to be moved by any educational purpose, and the movie itself, with its bawdy title and its R-rating, was fundamentally inappropriate to the age level of the children. This was an experience that could not be justified from the standpoint of educational purpose or the nature of the learner. In the same year, a school district in Oklahoma settled a claim by students who alleged that a teacher put them in a shower stall smeared with feces as part of a history lesson on slave ships ('Slave Ship' Case Settled, 8 July, 1998). If the allegations were true, the teacher might have been motivated by some perverse desire to offer a realistic historical experience to the children. But here, the educational purpose was overwhelmed by the violation done to the children in subjecting them to a callous and unnerving experience.

In contrast, teachers have used techniques that offended the ethical sensibilities of some administrators and parents, but that proved, in the end, to be educationally worthy. One well-known case (*Keefe v. Geanakos*, 1969), again involving a high school English teacher, concerned an assignment that required the student to read an *Atlantic Monthly* essay containing repeated references to the word "motherfucker." Some parents complained and the teacher, after refusing conditions placed on his teaching, was eventually dismissed. This eventually resulted in legal action. When the courts examined the assignment in relation to the educational purposes of the school and reviewed the actual usage of the word in the essay, which was characterized by the judge as "scholarly and thoughtful," the teacher's action was supported. Interestingly, the judge concluded that "the sensibilities of offended parents are not the full measure of what is proper in education" (Fischer, Schimmel, & Kelly, 1999, p. 166), a point that returns us to the original tension explored between community (parental) views of learning and professionally-argued views of learning.

Among the newer ethical problems being raised in classrooms today has to do with the ethics of testing. Increasingly, efforts at accountability have often resulted in equating good teaching with high-test scores. This has, unfortunately, lead to growing incidences of teacher involvement in test-related misconduct.

Some teachers, for instance, were found to have copied test booklets for the purpose of using them to help prepare students for upcoming exams. For example, in Rhode Island, state officials temporarily canceled English and mathematics exams after discovering teachers had used previous tests to prepare their students (Archer, 17 March, 1999). A few teachers apparently had gotten into the habit of photocopying the exam from the previous year and using it as a platform for test preparation. If this resulted in actual test items being given to the students in preparation for the exam, there would be little question about the unprofessional behavior of the teachers, because such an occurrence would actually invalidate the exam.

Some teachers have also been found to be less than vigilant in following proper testing protocols, and in some cases, have been accused of altering student exams, erasing wrong answers and replacing

---

1. The private life and private actions of teachers can be viewed as a professional concern, if they can be linked in any way to the classroom performance of the teacher.
2. Felonious criminal charges against a teacher are typically viewed as *prima facie* (at face value) grounds for dismissal; misdemeanor charges against a teacher can result in dismissal if they show some nexus or connection to the teacher's performance in the classroom.
3. The sexual orientation of a teacher and the lifestyle choices of teachers, including the decision to cohabitate outside of marriage, are private matters unless they can be shown to negatively affect the teacher's performance in the classroom.
4. The use of vulgar, hateful, or obscene language in the classroom by the teacher can be viewed as grounds for dismissal; the use of vulgar, hateful, or obscene language in the context of a school assignment or school activity can also be grounds for dismissal, unless it can be shown to have a linkage to an expressed educational purpose that is within the boundaries of the school's mission and appropriate to the maturational level of the student.
5. Proselytizing a religious, political, or lifestyle point of view on the classroom is grounds for dismissal.

FIGURE 6–1   Generalizations About Conduct Unbecoming.

them with correct ones. In the Houston Independent School District, a nine-month inquiry found irregularities at six of the system's 280 schools. Investigators found that students were given oral prompting during the state exam, that answer keys were used to correct student answers, and that general test security was lacking (Johnson, 17 March, 1997). State officials in Texas also put 11 school districts on notice, asking for an explanation for the high number of erasures found on their state tests over the years. Erasure mark analysis is often used to raise a flag of suspicion. The state apparently has data on the number of erasures that can be reasonably expected on its tests. Anything falling outside those expectations could raise suspicions of tampering and becomes grounds for investigation.

TEACHER LIABILITY

The dismissal of teachers on the grounds of immorality or conduct unbecoming is one matter, but what legal liability do teachers carry for their behavior if a child is injured at school under their watch? If a child breaks an arm during a physical education routine, can the physical education teacher be held liable? If a student is injured during a mugging on a class trip, can the teacher be found to be legally accountable?

Generally, a four-step process is followed when teachers are implicated in liability cases in school: 1) Did the teacher have a duty of care to the student at the time of the injury?, 2) Was this duty breached by negligence?, 3) Was there a casual connection between the purported negligence and the resulting injury?, and, 4) Did an actual injury result?

The concept of duty of care goes directly to determining who is responsible for the supervision of the student at the time of a given incident. Because teachers and administrators are, in most states, considered "in loco parentis" (in the place of the parents), they have a general duty of care to all students. They are expected to act with the same level of discretion and authority that a "normal" parent would display in a similar situation. Where students are gathered together for any stretch of time in the school, school personnel have a general duty of care. School personnel typically supervise study halls, recess periods, and even parking lots. The author is personally aware of a middle school that fails to provide any teacher supervision in its girls' locker room because of the fact that there are no female physical education teachers on staff. If a serious injury occurs in the locker room, the school will clearly be in danger of being found liable because the duty of care was not fulfilled. Some public high schools have been sued by parents whose children were killed or injured in lunchtime car crashes, after being allowed to leave the school campus during the lunch hour. The school, in this case, is accused of breaching its duty of care by keeping its campus open during lunchtime and allowing student to travel (Richard, 9 December, 1999). The implication is that only a vigilantly supervised closed campus can fulfill the duty of care. The courts, however, have not been clear in determining how much responsibility is accorded to the school once students leave campus.

With regard to specific negligence, however, there must be an individual or individuals specifically charged with duty of care. If an injury occurs under the territorial watch of a teacher—whether in the teacher's classroom, study hall, or on the playground—there is little question about where the duty of care resides. Children are not expected to be supervised at every moment and in every situation and circumstance of schooling. When a child goes to the bathroom, teachers are not expected to accompany them, although this might be the case with a special needs learners or very young children. If an incident occurs as a student is moving between classrooms or on the way to the bathroom, the issue of "duty of care" may not apply to a particular teacher.

But if duty of care is established, how is negligence determined in liability cases? The basic question asked here goes to the evidence speaking to a teacher's lack of vigilance, lack of action, or lack of foresight related to the occurrence of the injury. For example, could the teacher have reasonably foreseen the collapse of a bookshelf that broke a student's arm? Were there early signs that the bookshelf might have collapsed? Did the teacher take action to remedy the problem or protect students from potential injury, such as roping off the area until the shelf could be dismantled or repaired? Similarly, if a student is injured during recess, was the injury a function of the normal events associated with playground activity, or was it due to a foreseeable problem that the teacher ignored, or to a lack of proper supervision or instruction?

Determining proper supervision depends on the circumstances of the school and weighs factors related to age, maturity, and prior history with the student. It also weighs the nature of the specific activity. Obviously, teachers working in vocational education shops, gymnasiums, and even science labs are expected to provide increased supervision and more safety instructions, because there are known dangers in these settings that the teacher must anticipate, specifically caution against and vigilantly guard against. Any knowledge of special danger requires direct supervision from the teacher, as opposed to general supervision (Valente, 1998). This extends to the playground or to other contexts involving students known to have violent tendencies. Stricter supervision is also expected from teachers working with very young children, special-needs children, and students who have a history of problematic or recalcitrant behavior. Children age 7 and under are considered incapable of determining the degree of care necessary to prevent injury, and are therefore rarely considered libel for their own injuries (Jasper, 1998. p. 74).

In short, teachers are expected to be able to prevent foreseeable problems, weighing factors related to the nature of the learner, to the special circumstances of the classroom, and any other emergent conditions. In their classrooms, they are expected to be on the scene and to be watchful. If a group of students is left unattended and something happens, the teacher is clearly at risk of being found liable. But if a student, in clear violation of specific safety instructions and repeated interventions of the teacher, sets his shirt ablaze when fooling around with a Bunsen burner during a science experiment, the teacher would have a good defense against an accusation of negligence. The law essentially demands reasonable and prudent supervision—meaning that there is no expectation of telepathic powers or of superhuman ability, only a reasonable presence of supervision and preventative action.

The third factor in assessing liability goes to the principle known as proximate cause, whereby a given injury can be clearly established as resulting from negligence. Sometimes, events can occur in a classroom that have less bearing on teacher negligence than to other factors. For example, if a fight breaks out in a classroom, and someone gets injured, some determination will have to be made about whether the fight was spontaneous and not foreseeable, or whether the teacher should have been able to foresee and prevent it. Even if it occurred in an unsupervised classroom, the courts would look to determine if it was the lack of supervision that was the proximate cause of the injury. Perhaps no amount of supervision could have prevented the event from occurring. Perhaps the injury that ostensibly resulted from the fight was a preexisting injury suffered under circumstances that had nothing to do with the fight. Or, perhaps another event occurring just outside the class required the teacher's intervention and exit from the classroom, whereby the proximate cause was not the teacher's exit but the event that compelled her to leave. As Jasper (1998, p. 73) puts it, the courts use a "but for" test: Would the injuries have occurred "but for" the negligence of the teacher?

Finally, without real injury there is no real negligence. Therefore, establishing the validity of an injury is a crucial part to the general analysis used to determine liability. A manifest injury, such as a broken

1. School personnel have a legal duty of care to all students to the fullest extent possible.
2. Duty of care means that reasonable and prudent decisions need to be made to ensure the safety and security of the school environment.
3. The standards of reasonableness change depending on the characteristics of students and the nature of the school activity. Very young children and special needs learners require tighter supervision. School environments where there are special dangers, such as vocational education shops and science laboratories, also require tighter supervision.
4. To avoid the accusation of negligence, teachers need to demonstrate reasonable foreseeability in preventing the circumstances that might have led to the injury of a student.
5. There is no negligence and no liability unless a real injury has been demonstrated.

FIGURE 6–2   Generalizations About Teacher Liability.

arm, is not an issue, but complications arise when students claim to suffer from ambiguous medical ailments.

In some states, judgment of comparative negligence is allowed, which means that the courts could determine proportional negligence between both the plaintiff and the defendant. Thus, if a sixteen-year-old boy breaks his leg playing a game of tackle football against school rules, the teacher could be found to be comparatively negligent, if for instance, he had duty of care and failed to see or stop the game. However, the boy could also be found to be comparatively negligent if the courts are convinced that he was old and mature enough to understand the obvious physical risks involved in playing tackle football (Imber & Van Geel, 2004, p. 509). Comparative negligence could attribute a certain proportion or percentage of fault to each party, which would then be applied to any monetary damages given to the plaintiff. Thus, a finding of 10 percent negligence against the teacher would mean that the teacher would pay only 10 percent of any monetary recovery.

School districts are cognizant of their potential liability. They often provide liability coverage for their teachers. Local teacher unions often offer teachers inexpensive personal liability coverage. School districts commonly ask parents to sign consent forms releasing them from liability when students are engaged in activities outside of the school, such as field trips and sporting events. However, there is still a legal expectation, irrespective of the waiver, that the school will protect and secure the safety and welfare of the children. If negligent, the school and any involved teachers can still be found liable.

FREEDOMS OF EXPRESSION

Once professional educators walk into a school, their First Amendment rights are subject to some restriction. The protection of the teacher's expressed views is always weighed against factors pertaining to the maintenance of quality educational experiences in school. In other words, teacher speech is not protected if it is viewed as counter to the promotion of the central educational services of the school. Academic freedom is curtailed in the same way, as are certain freedoms of association, personal speech, and even freedoms of choice in personal appearance.

Teachers' Academic Freedom

Let us start with the concept of academic freedom, which is a European idea born in the context of German higher education, where scholars were given the freedom, unconstrained by government interference, to search for and teach the truth (Hudgins & Vacca, 1995). In America, academic freedom is a derivative of the First Amendment right to free speech. It allows educators to make decisions about reading materials, teaching methodologies, and study topics that may not always be popular with local community or governmental viewpoints. It encourages experimentation with ideas and supports an open climate of criticism and debate. Academic freedom is a cornerstone of higher education in America, and it has also been applied, in a highly qualified way, to the K-12 setting.

Teachers, as indicated, are expected to exercise some independence and control in their classrooms. They need to have the freedom to select different instructional strategies, and make adjustments in the operation of the classroom based on a diagnosis of emergent problems and needs. This, however, does not translate into allowing teachers to assign any topic or reading material that they desire or to try any unconventional or radical form of pedagogy that pleases them. All teacher action has to meet a standard of professionalism. Teachers are essentially free to choose topics, materials, and teaching strategies, as long as their decisions are professionally defensible. This means that teacher judgment on these matters must be within the boundaries of the school's expressed educational purposes, appropriate for the age and maturity of the students, and not disruptive to the teaching/learning process of the school. For instance, a teacher will not have much of a leg to stand on if he insists on using readings from a pornographic magazine to motivate adolescent boys to become better readers, or if he uses blatantly racist materials without having a clear and high-minded instructional purpose or objective. In the former case, there are obvious standards of morality that would be violated as well as issues pertaining to the appropriateness of the material based on age and maturity factors. In the latter case, there are also issues of morality, linkage to school purposes, and the potential for disruptive classroom interactions.

Similarly, teachers cannot use the concept of academic freedom to justify ignoring or omitting prescribed course content. The courts have ruled that the content of the curriculum (not the teaching methodology or usually not curriculum materials) is largely a matter of local school board authority, typically granted by the states. Some schools tolerate or even encourage teachers to take a more daring attitude toward the content base of the curriculum than others, advocating different ways of capturing and even supplementing the content. But the content itself cannot be ignored in the name of academic freedom. Controversial topics and ideas have a place in the classroom, as long as they are related to the subject matter that the teacher has been assigned to teach.

The authority of local school boards' courts over the curriculum was strengthened in the 1988 Supreme Court ruling in the case *Hazelwood v. Kuhlmeier* case. Although the case dealt with student free-speech rights, the ruling gave public school authorities wide discretion in dealing with controversial content in the school. But, the school board cannot act idiosyncratically. For example, any decision to exclude material from the curriculum must be rooted in an educational argument. Restrictions on what teachers teach and what materials they use must be based on arguments over the educational viability of the topics or materials.

In a manner of speaking, the courts have tried to define the difference between the idea of censorship and the idea of exclusion by educational judgment. School boards that insist on the removal of certain materials because they are offensive to certain political or religious standards in the community are engaging in censorship if their argument does not extend to the educational value of the material. Teachers are held to the same standard. Thus, if a teacher refuses to teach a certain book or deal with certain topics because it conflicts with her personal political, religious, or philosophical belief system, she is engaging in censorship. A school board can decide to not allow the use of certain materials if it can show that the students do not have the emotional maturity needed to deal with the materials, that the materials themselves advance no palpably significant educational objectives, that the materials might create a condition that undermines the entire educational process of learning in the school, or that the materials violate basic standards of civility. When decisions are made for educational legitimate reasons, they are not acts of censorship, they are acts of educational judgment.

Most schools like to leave these decisions to their teachers, but differences in opinion can occur. In Alabama, an English teacher assigned her high school junior class the novel *Welcome to the Monkey House*, by Kurt Vonnegut. The controversial assignment led the principal to dismiss the teacher, who believed that the story was "literary garbage"' condoning "the killing off of elderly people and free sex" (Thomas, Sperry, & Wasden, 1991, p. 162). But the teacher fought the dismissal. In *Parducci v. Rutland, (1970),*the issue before the Court was to determine whether the dismissal was an act of censorship that violated the teacher's academic freedom, or a valid educationally-defensible judgment by the principal attesting to the unprofessional behavior of the teacher. Was the story out of alignment with the maturity level of the students? Was it outside the educational purposes of the school? Did it cause a disruptive environment for learning? The Court eventually ruled in the favor of the teacher, observing that, "Since the board has failed to show either that the assignment was inappropriate reading for high school juniors, or that it created a significant disruption to the educational processes of this school, the Court concludes that the teacher's dismissal constituted an unwarranted invasion of her First Amendment right to academic freedom" (Thomas, Sperry, & Wasden (1991), p. 162).

Teachers' Personal Views

There are, of course, other forms of freedom that involve teachers. Among the more controversial ones is the teacher's right to express her personal views in public and in school. If a teacher is upset about a certain school reform strategy or a particular funding referendum, does she have the right to express her views?

As indicated, teachers' rights to express themselves can be curtailed if their views have a negative effect on their performance in the classroom or on the overall educational operation of the school. In the famous *Pickering v. Board of Education* (1968) case, a teacher wrote a highly critical letter to a local newspaper about the manner in which the school board and superintendent were handling some school financing issues. The strongly-worded letter contained some false statements that were damaging to the reputations of certain school board members and school administrators (McCarthy, Cambron-McCabe, & Thomas, 1998, p. 272). The teacher was fired because the school district maintained that his relationship with his superiors was so damaged by the letter that he could no longer effectively carry out his teaching responsibilities. The teacher responded by arguing that his First Amendment right to free speech had been violated. Eventually the case made its way to the Supreme Court, which sought to reconcile the issue by balancing the teacher's interest to express his views against the school's interest in providing effective educational services. The Court recognized that if the fallout from the teacher's letter made it impossible for the teacher to work effectively with administrators and other key school leaders, with clear negative effects in classroom performance, his dismissal could be upheld. In the end, however, the court sided with the teacher, stating that the teacher's letter did not hinder the performance of the teacher's classroom duties or otherwise obstruct the educational operation of the school. Although the teacher prevailed in *Pickering*, schools understand that teacher expression on matters of public concern is protected and can only be curtailed in the face of evidence that such speech has hampered the educational operations of the school or the classroom performance of the teacher.

Student Expression

Students also live with clear limits on their expression. Generally speaking, students' right of expression is also moderated by whether their viewpoints disrupt the educational process of the school. This typically is the strongest and most frequently used justification for restricting student speech, but it is not the only one.

In *Bethal School District v. Fraser* (1986), a high school student was suspended from school after he presented a cleverly written campaign speech at a school assembly that employed frequent sexual innuendo. The reaction from the student body was predictably boisterous. Some students in the audience hooted and yelled, others made graphic gestures mimicking sexual activities, while others appeared baffled and embarrassed (Imber & Van Geel, 2004, p. 141). Some of the students in the audience were as young as age 14. The student who gave the speech claimed that his suspension from school was illegal because it violated his First Amendment right to free speech. The Supreme Court, however, disagreed, observing that the speech had the effect of creating a disruptive environment and that lewd and indecent speech is not protected in a school environment. According to the Court, the school was well within its right to punish the student and to protect a captive student audience from lewd or vulgar speech, even if there was no evidence of a disruption.

In similar cases, the courts upheld the suspension of students whose speech posed disruptive threats to the school, including the suspension of a boy who persisted in wearing a confederate flag on his sleeve in a racially-tense school environment, and students who have made threatening or menacing remarks to teachers (McCarthy, Cambron-McCabe, & Thomas, 1998, p. 117). The confederate flag patch was considered symbolic speech, which can be readily restricted if it is determined to be potentially disruptive or otherwise lewd or inflammatory. Similarly, any "fighting words" (words that by their very utterance inflict injury) can be restricted.

Threats offered in the context of a legitimate school assignment can be especially difficult to decipher. In 1998, a student at a high school in Washington State handed in a poem to his English teacher for extra credit. The poem depicted a lonely student who roams the school and eventually draws a gun and kills 28 people. "As I approached the classroom door, I drew my gun and threw open the door. Bang, Bang, Bang-Bang. When it was over, 28 were dead, and all I remember was not feeling any remorse, for I felt, I was, cleansing my soul..." (Walsh, 9 March, 2000). The boy was expelled from school. The question was whether, in the context of a poem written to an English teacher, the boy's poem could be viewed as a credible threat or simply fiction. In the absence of any evidence that the poem actually posed a threat, a lower court eventually ruled in favor of the boy. In another case in Wisconsin, an 8th grade boy, who was disruptive in class, was asked to go in the hallway to do his writing assignment. Upset at being asked to leave the room, he wrote an essay that described a student who beheads his teacher with a machete (Walsh, 12 January, 2000). The school suspended the student for a year. The court in this case, however, saw credibility in the student's threat. There was linkage between the teacher depicted in the essay and the actual teacher, and the written essay itself was a by-product of an assignment given by the teacher.

It should be made clear, however, that a school cannot restrict a student's speech simply because it does not like what the student is saying. The famous *Tinker v. Des Moines Independent School District* (1969) case concerned students who wore arm bands in protest of the Vietnam War. The Supreme Court upheld their right to conduct this silent method of protest, largely because it was found that it did not disrupt classwork or otherwise impede the educational operation of the school. The Court stated that school officials must have "more than a mere desire to avoid discomfort and unpleasantness that always accompany an unpopular viewpoint" in justifying a curtailment of student expression (McCarthy, Cambron-McCabe, and Thomas, 1998, p. 123). This was a strong signal that students enjoy First Amendment rights in the schools as they pertain to the expression of opinions on controversial issues.

Do schools have to wait for a disruption to occur before acting on it? As it turns out, the school may try to "forecast substantial disruption" based on credible evidence pertaining to an event. In the wake of the 1999 Columbine school shooting, many schools were quick to prohibit students from wearing black trench coats, the very type of coats used by the students who committed the murders in Columbine. The schools were able to forecast substantial disruption by showing that the wearing of such coats was associated with the strong media images of the killings at Columbine. The thinking was that such coats could create a very real atmosphere of nervousness in the school, enough to disrupt its educational operations.

Written Expression

Student writings can also be curtailed in the school, especially if they emerge from school-sponsored programs and give the appearance of representing the school. In *Hazelwood v. Kuhlmeier* (1988), the Court found that written student expression can indeed be regulated if it at all impedes on the educational process or if it otherwise does not have educational value or merit. High school journalism students at Hazelwood East High School, in Missouri, contended that their First Amendment rights were violated when the principal of their school did not allow two articles to be published in the school's newspaper. The articles dealt with sensitive topics, including a story about pregnant teenage girls and another about the effect of divorce on teenagers. They included stories about real students in the high school whose names were changed to protect their identities. The principal objected to the articles on educational grounds. He felt that the topics, which made references to sexual activity and to birth control, were inappropriate for most of the students attending the high school. The Supreme Court ruled in favor of the principal's action, maintaining that school officials can regulate material when it involves a legitimate educational interest. In the words of the Court, the First Amendment is not violated if educators "exercise editorial control over the style and content of student speech in school-sponsored expressive activities so long as their actions are reasonably related to legitimate pedagogical concerns" (Fischer, Schimmel, & Kelly, 1999, p. 182).

Exceptions to the *Hazelwood* principle exist in states that have drafted Freedom of Press laws, which give students wide editorial control and relieve school administrators from any legal actions that might be taken against the school paper. Under Freedom of Press laws, schools still have the responsibility to advise students and educate them in the techniques of proper journalism, but final editorial decisions belong to the students and may not be censored by administrators, unless the publication of the paper poses a material disruption to the learning environment of the school (Imber & Van Geel, 2004, p. 140). Moreover, *Hazelwood* only applies if the school paper, either by policy or long-standing practice, is not considered to be a public forum—that is, a publication regularly read by the general public (Imber & Van Geel, 2004, p. 137). In the *Hazelwood* case, the publication of the paper was explicitly linked to the school curriculum and to two standing journalism courses in the school. The student paper was a by-product of educational purposes embedded in the curriculum, not a publication with public forum status.

An important legal distinction emerges under the discrete influences of *Tinker* and *Hazelwood*. The Court's rulings have created a distinction between the nature of school authority over school-related student expression and personal student expression. Personal speech falls under *Tinker* (and *Bethal*) and simply means that only speech that is disruptive or manifestly vulgar can be restricted. Thus, an underground student newspaper, operating without school funds, constitutes personal speech and enjoys more constitutional protection because of it. The school cannot prevent an underground paper from discussing controversial topics, or from criticizing school officials or school policies, just because it does not see the educational merit in it. The school can regulate the distribution of the paper, but the publication itself cannot be banned from the school unless it is found or is forecasted to cause substantial disruption in school or endanger the health and safety of students. School-related speech, on the other hand, falls under *Hazelwood* and says that speech that is tied to instructional concerns can in fact be curtailed for pedagogical purposes, even it is not disruptive to the school (Valente, 1998, p. 178).

Symbolic Speech

Another area of concern is symbolic expression, which gets into modes of expression embodied in the way one dresses and grooms. Among teachers, clear regulations are in place against wearing palpably religious clothes and religious jewelry. These are discussed in more detail in a later chapter. The courts have also given school districts wide latitude in enforcing grooming and dress codes for teachers. Among students, however, the regulations are slightly more complicated. Religious dress, for instance, is protected by the Constitution when worn by students. Unless the dress shows some affiliation to a disruptive event in the school or is in open violation of a school policy, it cannot be regulated.

Schools are, of course, well within their right to regulate student clothing, but the regulations cannot be arbitrarily designed. Generally speaking, dress that is unsanitary, unsafe, obscene, or vulgar or that is associated with a disruptive element in the school can be regulated. Sanitation issues are fairly straightforward, as are clothes viewed as obscene, which typically apply to scantily clad students, who (especially in the context of a high school), by their very lack of dress, might pose a disruptive threat to the school. Safety issues might lead to the regulation of certain clothes in certain settings (i.e., loose-fitting clothes might not be permitted in a laboratory or vocational education setting).

More interesting are the efforts to regulate T-shirts containing various written and symbolic messages. Because *Bethal* made it clear that schools can punish students for lewd or indecent speech, a T-shirt or sweatshirt containing a lewd or indecent message can be regulated. This is an easy call to make if the shirt is manifestly vulgar, as in one case where a student wore a shirt containing a cartoon-like caricature of three school administrators boozing on alcoholic drinks (Fischer, Schimmel, & Kelly, 1999, p. 464). But what if the message is more subtle? For instance, can a shirt containing the message "Drugs Suck" be regulated? It carries an anti-drug message and is not as obviously vulgar as the earlier example. The answer has to do with how the word "sucks" is interpreted. Other examples of pro-educational messages conveyed in a less-than-civil light run up against the same problem.

The Courts have upheld the right of students to convey personal political messages on their T-shirts if they are not disruptive and not vulgar. Ironically, a T-shirt containing a picture of a marijuana plant with the wording "Legalize It" beside it is easier to support as a free expression right than a T-shirt that reads "Drugs Suck" because of its association with a vulgar word. But any T-shirt that carries a religious message (e.g., "Jesus Saves"), assuming that it is free of any association with a disruptive circumstances, is clearly protected.

Finally, schools can prohibit any clothes viewed as gang-affiliated or affiliated with any potential for disruption in the school. Some schools have banned the wearing of certain sports apparel, saggy pants, and jewelry, because of known associations with gang or criminal activity. In such cases, however, a clear and factually-based linkage has to be shown between the wearing of such clothes and gang activity. Interestingly, some public schools are now experimenting with school uniform policies, arguing that school uniforms can make a positive contribution to a more conducive learning environment in schools. Some urban schools are using school uniform policies as a preemptive strike against gang activity, as a way to protect against the use of gang colors and gang affiliations in the school. The case law on school uniform policies has yet to play itself out. One way of looking at it is to say that under *Hazelwood*, school uniform policies could have a solid place in the school if they can be justified as essential to the maintenance of a legitimate educational interest. This would be an easier argument to make in a school threatened by recurrent gang or criminal activity than in one that has no such problems. Civil libertarians, however, are active in arguing that required uniforms violate students' free expression rights.

1. Teachers have limited academic freedom. They are generally accorded academic freedom to choose teaching methodologies, curriculum materials, and certain topics, as long as these choices can be justified as within the educational mission of the school and be judged to be appropriate to the age and maturity level of the student. Their professional judgments must also not result in any disruption in the school environment. Choices based solely on political, religious, or lifestyle beliefs are not allowed.
2. Teachers do not have the right to not teach state- or district-mandated curriculum.
3. Local school boards have legal authority over what can be taught, as long as they do not contradict state directives and as long as their decision has educational merit. This means that decisions should be responsive to the manifest purposes of the school and the age level of the students, and must not result in any disruption to the educational process.
4. A teacher's right to free speech outside of school can be curtailed or punished if his speech can be connected to an inability to conduct an effective teaching/learning environment in school.
5. Student personal speech can be curtailed or punished if it is manifestly vulgar, lewd, or inflammatory, or associated with some form of disruption in the school.
6. School-related student speech, associated with the school-sponsored programs, such as school newspapers, can be regulated if it cannot be justified to have educational merit.
7. A school does not need to wait for a disruption to occur in order to regulate the conditions causing it. It may foresee disruption in the speech of teachers and students, making an argument for the standpoint of the available evidence.
8. Symbolic student speech, in the form of dress, may be regulated if it is unsanitary, unsafe, disruptive, and/or vulgar.
9. Any clothes associated with gang affiliation or any element potentially disruptive to the school may be regulated.
10. Religious clothes worn by students may not be regulated unless they prove to be disruptive, unsanitary, unsafe, or vulgar.
11. School uniforms in public schools have yet to be adjudicated as freedom of expression violations, but public schools have argued for such policies as a means toward maintaining a conducive educational environment in school.

FIGURE 6–3   Generalizations about Freedom of Expression.

TEACHER TENURE AND TEACHER DISMISSAL

The employment process for teachers is a matter that is managed at the local school level. The building principal, sometimes working with a committee of teachers and parents, will typically make the final hiring decision, contingent on the approval or sanction of the local school board. Local districts can require teachers to become residents of the district as a condition of appointment. They can also ask for a medical examination, and a screening for physical fitness, vision and hearing, psychiatric conditions, and even, although this is controversial, drug use.

Two types of employment contracts are offered to teachers: term contracts and tenure contracts. Term contracts are usually offered to new teachers for a fixed period of time, usually one or two years. After the contract expires, the school board can choose to not renew it for any or for no reason—except, of course, for reasons that represent an infringement of constitutional rights (i.e., a decision based on a teacher's race, religion, gender, or protected speech, or that involves a "liberty" concern). The only requirement in a decision to not renew a term contract is timely notification of the terminal year of the contract. Note that this is not a dismissal proceeding against a teacher, but a decision to not renew a contract after it expires. If a non-tenured teacher is dismissed during the term of a contract period, the school must provide a formal and timely notice of the termination, detail its justification for termination and hold a formal hearing or other forum so the teacher can hear and respond to the grounds for dismissal. This is known as due process, a procedure that will be detailed a little later. No due process is accorded to a nonrenewal, however, unless stipulated by state law or by union agreement, or triggered by a constitutional violation. Because the school district is under no legal obligation to provide a reason for the nonrenewal of a teacher's contract, the burden of proof in arguing that a nonrenewal was illegal resides with the probationary teacher.

Tenure contracts, on the other hand, have an entirely different legal status and provide teachers with considerable job security. Virtually every state has drafted laws supporting tenure contracts. The idea of tenure, one should remember, is not a constitutionally protected right; it is a statutory provision (a matter of state law). The idea of tenure was originally designed to eliminate the role of political patronage in government hiring processes, to guarantee to teachers some right to academic freedom, and to otherwise protect good teachers from arbitrary or capricious actions by school officials.

In most cases, tenure contracts are offered to teachers only after they have successfully demonstrated their professional worth during a fixed probationary period, usually after about three years. During the probationary period, teachers work under term contracts. Once a tenure contract is offered, however, the teacher is automatically granted a contract renewal each year and comes under a new set of regulations governing disciplinary or dismissal decisions. Tenure grants "property right" status to the teacher's employment, which means that due process must be followed in any disciplinary proceedings or any attempt to terminate a teacher's employment.

Every American citizen has a constitutional right to due process. According to the Fourteenth Amendment to the Constitution: "no state may deprive a person of life, liberty, or property without due process of the law." Such a right protects the accused from irresponsible and unwarranted punitive actions. Due process essentially means that a set of rules and principles has to be followed when an individual is accused of an act that might lead to his dismissal or that might otherwise affect his livelihood or reputation. In the context of the school, this usually means that a teacher who is subjected to serious charges must be informed in a timely manner of any proceedings or accusations and must be given a fair opportunity to answer the charges. The teacher also has the right to legal counsel, a right to mount a defense against the charges, and a right to appeal.

With due process to consider, school districts cannot behave whimsically in their actions against teachers. The school has to be sure to abide by due process if the problem involves a liberty, life, or property concern. The courts have defined a liberty concern broadly, as a concern involving the reputation, honor, or integrity of a person. Thus, if a non-tenured teacher were facing a disciplinary action or even a nonrenewal that might implicate his character or subject him to pubic scorn, due process would have to be followed. For non-tenured teachers, accusations pertaining to drinking problems, sexual misconduct, mental instability, and extensive professional incompetence would likely result in due process, given the stigmas associated with them (McCarthy, Cambron-McCabe, & Thomas, 1998, p. 368). However, no liberty concern applies, and hence no due process follows for non-tenured teachers who face criticism on a lesser scale of infamy. Due process would likely not be needed if a teacher were accused of a less serious job-related criticism, such as an inability to get along with others, poor work habits, tardiness, absenteeism, and aggressive behavior. For tenured teachers, any disciplinary action is granted due process. Moreover, any decision to terminate a tenured teacher requires evidence of what is known as "dismissal for cause," and in such a case, the burden of the proof rests with the district, which often must pull together a long and exhaustive record of documentation. Grounds for "cause" include incompetence, immorality, insubordination, financial exigency, and an elastic phrase known as "other good and just cause."

The most common reason for dismissal is incompetence, which is a charge with multifaceted characteristics. As indicated previously, many cases of incompetence revolve around issues of classroom management and classroom control. A teacher who cannot maintain order and discipline cannot move forward with an educational mission—hence the charge of incompetence. The charge of incompetence could be sustained in other ways as well. For example, an elementary school teacher whose teaching of spelling is compromised by his own inability to spell, or a high school mathematics teacher who is obviously deficient in math skills can each be fired on the charge of incompetence. But the burden of proof is with the school district if the charge involves a tenured teacher. Other grounds for dismissal due to incompetence could include a failure to work effectively with colleagues and parents, excessive absenteeism, and an inability or unwillingness to teach district or state curriculum mandates (Essex, 1999, p. 182).

Some states require that the school district first give the teacher an opportunity to correct deficient behavior; only after such steps have been taken can the district move forward with a charge of "irremediable incompetence" (Thomas, Sperry, & Wasden, 1991, p. 93). Thus, for a teacher with classroom management problems or with a deficiency in a particular skill, or with a poor absentee record, the district will provide assistance and look for improvements in the teacher before taking dismissal actions against her. This preliminary action, in fact, often becomes part of the documented record eventually used in a teacher's dismissal proceeding. Naturally, some behaviors are so wrong and so completely unprofessional, especially if they involve unambiguous moral indiscretions, that they are viewed, *prima facie* as irremediable.

Because school administrators are responsible for supervising the staff of a school, the failure of teachers to follow a valid and reasonable directive from an administrator can be viewed as insubordination and thus grounds for dismissal. The key here is that the school district has to document that the administrator's directive was reasonable and valid, and not moved by any purpose other than a professional one.

Other grounds for dismissal include the common argument of financial exigency, which has nothing to do with a teacher's performance and everything to do with the financial realities of supporting school programs and the faculty who teach them. Thus, a school that is experiencing dramatic drops in enrollment is well within its right to reduce its teaching force, including tenured teachers. Here

1. Term contracts are offered to non-tenured teachers. Once the term of the contract expires, the school district can choose to not renew the contract for any or for no reason, except ones that evoke a constitutional violation. The burden of proof for a constitutional violation resides with the teacher.
2. A tenure contract represents an expectation of automatic renewal each year and gives the teacher a legal property right to her job.
3. All tenured teachers are granted due process if disciplinary or dismissal proceedings are undertaken against them; non-tenured teachers are granted due process if they are being dismissed from a job while still under contract, but they can expect no due process in a nonrenewal decision, unless a constitutional principle is involved, including "liberty" concerns, as interpreted by the courts.
4. Tenured teachers can only be dismissed for cause. The burden of proof resides with the school district. Cause means that a district would have to prove incompetence, insubordination, conduct unbecoming, financial exigency, or other good and just causes.

Figure 6–4   Generalizations About Teacher Tenure and Teacher Dismissal.

again the school must follow due process, demonstrating a bona fide financial crisis and explaining how the reduction will alleviate the crisis (Essex, 1999, p. 193). If a reduction in force action is being undertaken, most state tenure laws give tenured teachers priority over non-tenured in retaining their jobs. Sometimes school districts keep a recall list if new jobs open up as a result of improved financial conditions, retirements, or leaves of absence.

SEARCH AND SEIZURE

All American citizens have a constitutional protection, guaranteed by the Fourth Amendment, against unreasonable search and seizure. The basic purpose of the amendment is to safeguard the privacy and security of individuals against arbitrary invasions by government officials. The problem is that the amendment does not indicate what exactly constitutes an unreasonable search. As a result, we have a long line of case law that has helped to define the boundaries of reasonableness. In most cases, the Fourth Amendment applies to police actions, requiring the police to abide by a principle known as probable cause, which means no search of an individual's property or possessions is allowed unless the police can document a probable suspicion that a crime was committed by the individual. To search someone's home, the police need to gather a warrant that the court certifies within the boundaries of probable cause.

In the context of school, however, probable cause generally does not apply. Students, of course, do not give up their constitutional rights in school, but the school is unique because of the balance needed between individuals' Fourth Amendment right and the school's duty to provide a safe and secure learning environment. As a result, the courts have eased the search and seizure requirement in the context of the school from probable cause (probable suspicion that a crime has been committed) to reasonable cause (reasonable suspicion that a crime or transgression has been committed). This easing of the requirement reflects the unique standing of school officials in the lives of schoolchildren. In most states, school officials are viewed as *in loco parentis* (in the place of parents) to students, which grants them certain liberties that, say, the police do not have. In fact, any police action in the school still falls under probable cause requirements, and any student coming under suspicion off school property is also protected by probable cause.

What are the general parameters of reasonable cause? An answer began to emerge in the 1985 landmark case, *New Jersey v. TLO.* In 1980, a teacher at a New Jersey high school had determined that two girls were smoking cigarettes in the school lavatory, which was a violation of school rules. The teacher brought the girls to the vice-principal of the school, who questioned the girls. One of the girls admitted to the transgression, but the other, a 14-year-old freshman known as TLO in the court documents, offered no admission of guilt. Suspecting that the girl was not telling the truth, the vice-principal searched TLO's purse, where he found a pack of cigarettes and some rolling paper. This confirmed the teacher's claim about smoking in the bathroom, but the discovery of the rolling papers raised new suspicions about potential marijuana use by the girl. In the vice-principal's mind, there was a strong association between rolling paper and marijuana use. Thus, he continued with his search of TLO's purse and quickly discovered a small amount of marijuana, a considerable sum of one dollar bills, an index card appearing to detail the names of students owing TLO money, a pipe, and a few other incriminating items (Essex p. 38). Later the girl admitted to police that she was selling drugs in the school, but when the school took punitive action against the girl, her defense was that the school's search was not warranted. Her claim was that there was no probable cause and no court certified warrant to justify the principal's search of her pocketbook. The Supreme Court, however, interpreted the matter differently and offered a new standard of reasonable suspicion as the basis for school-related search and seizure.

Reasonableness means that the search had to be justified at its inception and limited in its scope. The accusation of smoking from the teacher and the denial by TLO justified (at its inception) a search of the girl's purse. If all that the principal found at that point was simply a pack of cigarettes, the search would stop, which speaks to the issue of scope. But because new evidence was uncovered in the original search, the scope of the search legitimately widened. The school, the Court reasoned, cannot be expected to get a warrant every time it needs to deal with issues concerning the safety of the learning environment. The school simply has to have reasonable grounds, with pertinent evidence, to believe that a student violated a school rule or policy. It cannot be a hunch or some intuitive feeling. Moreover, the school cannot decide to search everyone because of one violation of school rules. The determination of reasonableness also involves factors related to the student's age, history, record in school, the seriousness of the potential problem, the reliability of the information drawn from informants, the degree of urgency to search without delay, and the type of search (McCarthy, Cambron-McCabe, & Thomas, 1998, p. 219). Ultimately, students have a reasonable expectation of privacy, but school personnel certainly can search their personal property if reasonable suspicion prevails. This means that their lockers, book bags, purses, and other property are subject to searches based on reasonable suspicion.

In the case of physical searches, however, including either a physical pat down or, at its most extreme, a strip search, the rules change. The school not only has to document a reasonable suspicion but it only has to conduct a reasonable search, accounting for the nature of the crime, the age of the student, and other factors. In other words, a strip search of a student accused of stealing five dollars from the teacher's lounge is not a reasonable search even if there were reasonable suspicion. Similarly, no one will strip search a kindergarten student, unless there was truly imminent danger, knowing that a 5-year-old child has no criminal culpability. Generally, physically intrusive searches demand a higher standard of suspicion, approaching probable cause. As one court phrased it, "We are of the view that as intrusiveness intensifies, the standard of the Fourth Amendment reasonableness approaches probable cause even in the school context" (Essex, 1999, p. 42).

Given the requirements in making a particularized case of reasonable cause against a student, is the school still allowed to conduct general searches of all students, using devices such as metal detectors, sniffing dogs, urine tests for drug use, or mere visual searches of lockers? The answer is yes, provided that the school can demonstrate a need for such searches to protect the general safety of the school

---

1. School officials need to have reasonable suspicion to perform a search and seizure of an individual's property and possessions.
2. Reasonable suspicion is affected by a number of factors, including the age of the student, the school history of the student, the reliability of informant information, the seriousness of the problem, and the nature of the search.
3. An individualized search must be justified by its origin and limited in scope by the emerging evidence.
4. More invasive searches, such as strip searches, require a higher standard of suspicion, approaching the police standard of probable cause.
5. Police actions in school fall under probable cause.
6. Blanket or general search policies, involving metal detectors or sniffing dogs, can be conducted if they are part of a general plan to protect the school from a known and documented harm.

FIGURE 6–5 Generalizations About Search and Seizure.

environment. Thus, one will find metal detectors in schools where gun violence can be documented to exist in the surrounding neighborhood or within the student population itself. In 1998, an elementary school in Indianapolis took the unusual step of installing metal detectors after three students from the school, between the ages of 7 and 8, were arrested for gun possession in three separate incidents (Portner, 3 June, 1998). A similar rationale applies to other forms of general searches. For instance, drug sniffing dogs may be brought in for a general sweep of student automobiles and lockers, but only in relation to a general safety plan to protect students from an established threat in the school or community of drug abuse. Because the dogs represent a much more intrusive search of one's person, than, say, metal detectors (which are minimally intrusive), they cannot be used on individual students unless individualized reasonable suspicion exists. Finally, with all general searches, every effort has to be made to make the search truly general, not simply directed at a particular segment of the school population.

However, searches conducted against segments of the population are allowable, if there is a reasonable suspicion of rules violations within the group. For example, one school learned from reliable sources about serious drug use among its student athletes. The school enacted a policy asking participating students to submit a urine sample that would be tested for drug use. One student, who was never under any suspicion of drug use, refused to take the test, arguing that the test was an unreasonable invasion. The school suspended him and he took the school to court *(Vernonia District v. Acton, 1992)*. The Supreme Court adjudicated the case and ruled that the school could institute such a policy as a measure against known drug use because it was conceived as a strategy to protect the general welfare.

SUMMARY

The extensive body of case law on the legal and ethical behaviors of teachers helps to give the school some general guidelines on dealing with teacher indiscretions. Regarding conduct unbecoming, apart from a felonious crime or a blatantly immoral act, teacher behavior is only actionable if it negatively affects the performance of the teacher in the classroom. Regarding teacher liability, a straightforward process, involving four critical analytical steps, is used to determine negligence and eventual liability. Although the process is straightforward, determination related to duty of care, reasonable foresight, and proximate cause are deeply contextual and argumentative. Regarding academic freedom, public school teachers must understand that it exists in a limited and qualified form in the K-12 setting.

School authorities can curtail what teachers are teaching and even how they are teaching, if their actions can be justified from a valid educational or teaching perspective, or if they are associated in any way with some disruption in the school environment. School authorities can also discipline the personal speech of teachers if that speech demonstrably undermines the teacher's performance in the classroom. Student expression in the school can also be restricted. Personal student speech can be censored if it is vulgar or if it results in a disruption; school-related student speech can be regulated if it does not fulfill a valid educational purpose, even if it doesn't cause a disruption.

Regarding employment issues, teachers generally are hired under two types of contracts: term contracts and tenure contracts. Terms contracts typically run for a year or two and require the school to offer no explanation for the nonrenewal of the contract at its expiration (unless the reasons represent a constitutional infringement, which the teacher would have to prove). By contrast, tenure contracts, which are granted to teachers after a trial or probationary period, provide automatic yearly renewals and mean that teachers can only be dismissed for "cause," (for incompetence, insubordination, immoral behavior, or financial exigency), with the burden of proof resting on the school's shoulders.

Finally, with regard to search and seizure regulations in school, school officials must have reasonable suspicion of rule-breaking activity, not the police standard of probable suspicion, to conduct a search of the student's property or possessions. The standard of reasonableness shifts in the direction of probable cause as the nature of the search becomes more intrusive. General searches or sweeps of student possessions and property (lockers and book bags) are allowable if the school can demonstrate a need for such measures to protect the safety and security of the school environment.

REFERENCES

Archer, J. (17 March, 1997). Rhode Island halts exams in wake of wide-scale security breaches. *Education Week.*

Class sees 'Striptease'. (28 May, 1997). *Education Week.*

Diegmueller, K. (21 June, 1995). Expletives deleted. *Education Week.*

Essex, N. L. (1999). *School law and the public schools: A practical guide for educational leaders.* Boston: Allyn Bacon.

Fischer, L., Schimmel, D., & Kelly, C. (1999). *Teachers and the law,* 5th ed. White Plains, NY: Longman.

Hudgins, H. C., & Vacca, R. S. (1995). *Law and education.* Charottesville, Virginia: Michie Law Publishers.

Imber, M. & Van Geel, T. (2004). *Education law.* Mahwah: NJ: Lawrence Earlbaum.

Jasper, M. C. (1998). *Education law.* Dobbs Ferry, NY: Oceana Publications.

Johnston, R. C. (17 March, 1997). News: Texas presses districts in alleged test-tampering cases. *Education Week.*

McCarthy, M. M., Cambron-McCabe, N. H., & Thomas, S. B. (1998). *Public school law: Teachers' and students' rights.* Boston: Allyn Bacon.

Portner, J. (3 June, 1998). Indianapolis uses metal detectors on elementary pupils. *Education Week.*

Richard, A. (8 December, 1999). Policies on lunchtime scrutinized after deadly crashes. *Education Week.*

Richardson, J. (10 February, 1993). Lesbian parents' school visit sparks a clash of cultures in Boise suburb. *Education Week.*

'Slave Ship' case settled. (8 July, 1998). *Education Week,* Vol. 17(42):4.

Thomas, G. J., Sperry, D. J., and Wasden, F. D (1991). *The law and teacher employment.* St. Paul: West Publishing.

Valente, W. D. (1998). *Law in the schools.* Upper Saddle River, NJ: Merrill.

Walsh, M. (12 January, 2000). Law Update: Violent essay. *Education Week.*

Walsh, M. (8 March, 2000). A fine line between dangerous and harmless student speech. *Education Week.*

Cited Law Cases

Bethel School District No. 403 v. Fraser, 478 U.S. 675 (1986)

Hazelwood School District v. Kuhlmeier, 484 US 260 (1988)

Keefe v. Geanakos, 418 F.2d 359, 362 n. 9 (1st Cir. 1969)

New Jersey v. T.L.O, 469 U.S. 325 (1985)

Parducci v. Rutland, 316 F. Supp. 352, 355 (M.D. Ala. 1970)

Pickering vs. Board of Education, 391 U.S. 563 (1968)

Tinker v. Des Moines Independent Community School District, 399 U.S. 503 (1969)

Vernonia School District v. Acton, 515 U.S. 646 (1995)

KEY QUESTIONS

1. Can a teacher who preaches his politics and religion in class be dismissed? Why or why not?
2. Can a teacher accused of drunk driving be dismissed? Why or why not?
3. Can a teacher be fired for using vulgar or profane language? Why or why not?
4. Can a teacher show an R-rated film in class without fearing repercussions?
5. What criteria do the courts use to determine liability? Explain each characteristic of the criteria.
6. Explain how student age and various special dangers associated with various classroom or teaching environments factor into the determination of negligence and liability.
7. What are the limitations that a teacher must observe in considering the use of unconventional or controversial teaching methods?
8. Explain the implication of the Pickering case on teacher speech.
9. Describe the idea of *in loco parentis* and explain how it factors into search and seizure regulations in school.
10. Explain the distinction between school-related student speech and personal student speech.
11. What was the essential implication of the ruling in *Bethal v. Fraser*?
12. How is the *Hazelwood* ruling significantly different from the *Tinker* ruling?
13. What are the general grounds for regulating student dress in school?
14. If a student wore an anti-drunk driving T-shirt which read "See Dick Drink, See Dick Drive. See Dick Die. Don't be a Dick" would the school be within its right to ask the student to change?
15. What are the main differences between term and tenure contracts?
16. What is due process?
17. Under what conditions can a probationary teacher claim a liberty right in asking for due process?
18. What are the main grounds for dismissal of tenured teachers and why is it relatively difficult to dismiss a teacher once he or she is granted tenure?
19. Can probationary teachers not have their contracts renewed for no reason once their term contract expires?
20. What are the main characteristics of reasonable suspicion when conducting a search of a student's property or possessions?
21. Are general sweeps for drug use allowed in school? If so, what are the particular conditions allowing it?
22. Are strip searches legal in school? If so, what are the particular conditions allowing it?

RESEARCH EXERCISES

1. Research newspaper accounts related to teacher firings and analyze any one of them in relation to the principles discussed in the chapter. A good source for up-to-date accounts include local newspapers as well as *Education Week* (www.edweek.org).

2. Research newspaper accounts in relation to alleged school censorship efforts and analyze any one of them in relation to the principles discussed in the chapter.

3. Research newspaper accounts related to teacher liability and analyze any one of them in relation to the principles discussed in the chapter.

4. Research in detail one of the historic legal cases cited in the chapter, providing fresh detail and insight into the cited case.

5. Design a survey, based on the generalizations offered in the chapter on conduct unbecoming, teacher liability, teacher expression, and/or search and seizure, that tests teacher knowledge on any or all of these areas. Give the survey out and report on the findings.

6. Survey state teacher tenure laws from a state or two of your choice.

7. A pair of editorials that had been written about a new club for heterosexual and homosexual teens called the Gay Lesbian and Straight Society had been pulled from the school newspaper, the "Liberty," at the direction of Berkmar Principal Kendall Johnson. Gwinnett County school officials said Johnson ordered the student editorials removed because he believed they could have caused a stir at Berkmar during exam time. The paired editorials, written as a "point-counterpoint" debate, were to appear in the December issue. "The point/counterpoint was inflammatory in nature and could be disruptive," said Gwinnett Schools spokeswoman Sloan Roach. "People have very strong feelings about this issue. Mr. Johnson was not going to allow there to be distractions from what they are about—teaching and learning."

Find our more about this case and take a position supportive or critical of the principal's decision.

PART 2

The History of the American School Experience

Knowledge of the past is the key to understanding the present.
History deals with the past, but this past is the history of the present.

John Dewey

CHAPTER 7

The Early Development of the Public School

Public education in the United States arose out of an early union between the church and the state. Because the dominant motivation in the founding of colonial America, especially in New England, was religious freedom, the school became an important part of the orchestration of institutions used to serve a church-based society. Interest in mass public education was based on the desire to inject religion into the life of the state. The Puritans took the first direct steps in this direction during the seventeenth century, when they offered laws promoting state-sponsored schooling. To them, publicly-funded schools were simply public extensions of the church. The religious homogeneity of the Massachusetts Bay Colony made such an arrangement between church and state interests easy to accomplish. What was good for the Puritan faith was also good for government; there was no real separation. Colonial New England, after all, was a settlement that, in the words of Lawrence Cremin (1977), was founded in the unsettlement of Europe, in a movement to find new expression for religious conviction, and in a general mood of adventure that was believed to be guided by God's grand design.

But elsewhere in the colonies, the idea of commingling state and church concerns, as well as the idea of using public monies for public schools, was problematic. The hurdles were obvious. For example, if publicly funded schools were to be church-based, which church, which doctrine, and which ecclesiastical slant on learning would be best for all of the children living in a religiously diverse region? Given the difficulties inherent in resolving such questions, much of the education of children outside of New England occurred in nonpublic places, including the church and the household. The Puritan belief in using the public school for denominational purposes was simply not portable to other regions, and would, in time, become increasingly difficult to manage even in New England. In the South, social castes (ranging from black slaves, to white indentured servants, to white masters) made the idea of publicly-funded mass education inconceivable.

In the post-revolutionary period, however, the school acquired a new public agenda. Secular sociocivic obligations made their way into the school curriculum. The shift was influenced by the writing and the ratification of the Constitution and by the growing belief that the new American nation had to find itself by building common political communities, not pluralistic religious ones. No longer able to support sectarian views, the publicly-funded school had to aim at a wider mark, at a mandate that stressed the inclusivity of a wider range of youth. This meant that the public school had to examine its place as an agency that ensured national unity, that strengthened opportunities for economic and social mobility, and that ultimately socialized a new generation of youth into the skills and dispositions needed to conduct an intelligent life in a democracy. This did little to practically advance the education of women and Blacks, but it did set the conditions for the growth a school system that would, over time, extend itself upward and outward.

COLONIAL SCHOOLING AND THE IDEA OF LOCAL CONTROL

The history of American education dates back to the early seventeenth-century settlements in New England. The center of the action was in colonial Massachusetts where the Puritans took an active hand in promoting publicly-funded education at virtually every level of school organization. The Puritans were well-known for their efforts at providing a beginning education, up to about age 7, to all the children in their communities, as well as for providing continued education, up to about age 15, to a select group of boys. They also founded a number of colonial colleges, the first and most famous being Harvard College, which was chartered in 1636. Ultimately, they built an educational structure that set the basis for a town-controlled system of compulsory education that, by the close of the seventeenth century, could boast of having produced higher literacy rates than those achieved in England (Cohen, 1974).

The Puritan's attraction to public education was not moved by democratic or egalitarian principles, but by a desire to use the school as an agency for the advancement of church doctrine. Despite escaping religious harassment in Europe, the Puritans had no intention of establishing a New World community open to all religious creeds. To the Puritans, such an arrangement would inevitability lead to anarchy and a serious falling away from God (Cohen, 1974). They were strong-headed about these matters, denying suffrage to non-church members and tolerating no dissent against the church. The Puritans' embrace of the state in establishing schools was motivated by a transparent desire to create and sustain a government in the image of their church.

Because the Puritans believed that mass education was needed to bring the gospel of Christian faith to all of their children, they committed themselves, with the urging of the church, to publicly-funded schools. To the Puritans, the road to personal salvation was always traveled through the Bible, and unlike other colonial Americans, they were willing to collectively fund schools to serve as one of the main vehicles for this most important journey. The Puritan idea of using the state to enforce and otherwise support a tax-based public education for all youth set an early pattern of organization and governance for American public education that was sustained long after the State and Church went their separate ways (Cubberley, 1947).

As in most colonial settlements, the Puritan home or family unit was considered to be the well-spring for moralistic and religious education. A family, in fact, was not considered very civilized if it did not attend properly to the religious education of its children (Rippa, 1984). Given the hardships of life in the New World, however, many parents proved to be neglectful of their duties, so much so that the Puritans enacted legislative statutes compelling families, under the threat of fines or removal of custodial rights, to teach reading and religion to their children. The result was the Massachusetts Law of 1642, passed at the behest of the church, which made education compulsory for all youth in the Massachusetts Bay Colony. No distinction was made in the law between the education of both boys and girls. To the Puritans, the eternal souls of both boys and girls were at stake.

The law empowered town officials, also known as selectmen, with the responsibility to check and certify that each child in the community was literate and knowledgeable of the laws of the land and of the main principles and texts of the church. The officials periodically paid visits to homes, where they expected parents or masters (hired teachers) to account for the education of the children in the household. Thus, the 1642 law made education compulsory, but it did not necessarily establish schools. Education was a requirement, but its operation was still largely a family matter, conducted in the home.

It being one chiefe project of that old deluder, Satan, to keepe men from the knowledge of the Scriptures, as in former times by keeping them in an unknowne tongue, so in these latter times by perswading from the use of tongues, that so that at least the true sence and meaning of the originall might be clouded by false glosses of saint seeming deceivers, that learning may not be buried in the grave of our fathers in the church and commonwealth, the Lord assisting our endeavors,—

It is therefore ordered, that every towneship in this jurisdiction, after the Lord hath increased them to the number of 50 householders, shall then forthwith appoint one within their towne to teach all such children as shall resort to him to write and reade, whose wages shall be paid either by the parents or masters of such children, or by the inhabitants in generall, by way of supply, as the major part of those that order the prudentials of the towne shall appoint; provided, those that send their children be not oppressed by paying much more than they can have them taught for in other townes; and it is further ordered, that where any towne shall increase to the number of 100 families or householders, they sall set up a grammer schoole, the master thereof being able to instruct youth so farr as they may be fited for the university, provided, that if any towne neglect the performance hereof above one yeare, that every such towne shall pay £5 to the next schoole till they shall performe this order.

Shurtleff, N. B. (1853–54) Records of the governor and company of Massachusetts Bay in New England. In Cohen, S. (1974) *Education in the United States: A documentary history* (New York: Random House) p. 394

FIGURE 7-1   Massachusetts Law of 1647.

Within five years, however, the Puritans took an even larger step toward establishing a public system of schooling by passing a law, known as the Massachusetts Law of 1647, which specifically required townships of a certain size to maintain schools and hire teachers. Figure 7–1 reproduces the law. The actual maintenance of some type of school represented a much stronger commitment to public education because it required public monies and enforced public accountability. Again, the driving force behind the legislation was the church. As far as the church was concerned, children could not be expected to understand the Bible unless they possessed the basic rudiments of reading. The thinking was that the Old Deluder (Satan) was always among the people, looking for opportunities to exploit them, and that direct measures had to be taken to protect them, especially the children, from his clutches. The best protection, of course, was to be charged with the word of the Lord, and at least to the Puritans, the best way to secure this effect was to erect a school system that imbued all youth with the stories and principles of the Bible and the skills needed to read the Bible. In the words of the law, schools had to be maintained to thwart the "chief project of the old deluder Satan to keep men from the knowledge of the scriptures" (Meriwether, 1907).

Thus, the Massachusetts Law of 1647, also known as the Old Deluder Act, authorized, depending on the size of the town, the provision of schools and the employment of teachers. For towns with at least fifty households, a teacher of reading and writing had to be employed at a wage determined by the town; for towns with at least 100 households, the same requirements applied, but a Latin grammar school (a secondary school) was required as well (Colony of Massachusetts, 1853). The Massachusetts law was copied in Connecticut in 1650, although compliance to the law became increasingly problematic as populations spread along the frontier (Noble, 1959).

School Life

The Puritans essentially had two types of schools: dame schools and Latin grammar schools. Dame schools were elementary, or primary, schools typically conducted out of the home. Early in their development they were either private neighborhood schools that survived off of small weekly fees paid by parents or semipublic schools that received marginal assistance from the town treasury (Small, 1969). Without the compulsion of law, dame schools emerged rather idiosyncratically. As a mother taught her own children the rudiments of reading, other neighborhood children might be included for a small fee (Small, 1969). As the dame schools began to receive some public support, they took on a sharper focus. With the passage of legislation compelling the establishment of schools, the dame schools garnered more substantive support from town sources and some developed into town elementary schools.

The town schools, in effect, became the elementary schools of New England, providing an essential education in the ABC's and in elementary reading up to the age of about 7 or 8, an age limit slowly extended upward over time. Such schools were moved out of the household and into their own facilities. These town schools ultimately set the early tradition of instruction in the three R's and compelled the increasing use of local taxes to support of public education.

As reported by Rippa (1984), the dame schools were characterized by a harsh and dogmatic atmosphere. The teaching revolved around the letters of the alphabet and the scriptures in the Bible. As indicated, in most cases the formal education of children in the dame school was concluded by age seven, and for the overwhelming majority of the population no other opportunity for further public education existed. Household duties awaited the girls and various apprenticeships or work on the farm awaited the boys (French, 1964). The household continued to be the strongest source of education for both boys and girls (Cremin, 1977).

For a small group of boys, however, formal schooling continued in an institution known as the Latin grammar school, a school design imported from England. The sole purpose of the Latin grammar school was to provide pre-ministerial training to a small elite group of boys. Latin was at the center of instruction because it was the sacred language of religion, which presumably made it good for the mind and for the soul. Education in the Latin grammar school among the Puritans started at about age seven and ran until approximately age fifteen. Upon graduation, the boys in the Latin grammar schools were expected to enroll at Harvard College, where their education for the ministry would begin in earnest.

Girls were excluded from the Latin grammar schools and from higher education. Many males believed that higher education would come at the cost of a female's health, reveal their innate mental inferiority, deprive them of their most effeminate qualities, and lead to the neglect of children (Douglas & Grieder, 1948). Few male colonists saw the contradiction between their religious views and the manner in which they disregarded the education of girls beyond the most rudimentary levels (Harris, 1899). French (1964) cites work that claims very high illiteracy rates for women in the colonies, especially in relation to the illiteracy rates of men. Woman would only begin to benefit from the opportunity for a higher education during the early nineteenth century.

As with the dame schools, the Latin grammar school also featured religious exercises and a rote/recitation style of learning. Educators placed faith in the act of memorization, which was encouraged through skill-drill exercises and repeated recitations. Memorizing grammatical rules and a multitude of Latin equivalents for English words, and translating Latin passages to English and back again to Latin, constituted a good share of the instruction (Cohen, 1974). Students also read noted classical authors, such as Cicero, Horace, Tully, Ovid, and Virgil, and received rigorous religious training, including daily recitation of prayers and catechisms, and translation of the New Testament from Latin (Cohen, 1974). Writing and the fundamentals of arithmetic were optional, but in most cases were ignored (French, 1967). Class discussions were abhorred, and a climate of control and order, with all of its attendant punishments and regulations, pervaded the school. The entrance requirements for Harvard College testified to the instructional priorities of the Latin Grammar schools. In 1642, the entrance requirement read: "When any scholar is able to read Tully, or such like classical Latin author *extempore,* and make and speak true Latin in verse and prose, *suo (ut aiunt) Marte:* and decline perfectly the paradigms of nouns and verbs in the Greek tongue, then may he be admitted into the College" (Mayer, 1964, p. 55).

Graduates of the Latin school were essentially innumerate and unable to write with much fluency, but they usually were quite literate in Latin (Cubberley, 1947). No allowance was made in such schools for technical, business, or commercial education, or for what were viewed then as "polite accomplishments" such as music or dancing (Cohen, 1974). Ultimately, the failure of the Latin grammar school to be in touch with the matters and demands of colonial life led to its demise (Tanner & Tanner, 1987). Life in a New World, on a new frontier, surely called for more useful knowledge than Latin.

The teachers in the colonial schools were poorly trained and the conditions for teaching did not encourage very thoughtful experiences in the classroom. Everyone followed the same instructional pattern in the classroom, as all the children memorized and recited their ways through their lessons. Except for some reading materials, there was no classroom equipment to facilitate instruction. Paper and individual desks were rare and slates would not appear in school until the early 1800s.

The buildings themselves were undersized and often decrepit (Cohen, 1974). For instance, the most common building design was a simple carpenter box, usually 25 feet × 25 feet, 6 to 9 feet high, and presumably big enough for sixty pupils (Small, 1969). These schools, more often than not, were built cheaply and hastily, and were known to fall into quick and dramatic disrepair. One complaint was recorded by a Roxbury citizen in 1681. "The inconveniences I shall instance no other than that of the schoolhouse, the confused and shattered and nasty picture that it is in, not fitting for to reside in; the glass broken and thereupon very raw and cold; the floor very much broken and torn up to kindle fires; the hearth spoiled; the seats, some burnt and others out of kilter, so that one had as well nigh as good keep school in a hog-sty as in it" (Small, 1969, p. 258).

In most cases, the furnishings in the school buildings were threadbare, consisting of planks on barrels or stakes for desks, and benches for seats (Small, 1969). In the winters, many schools went unheated and those that were heated relied on poorly ventilated fireplaces or stoves, such that it sometimes became difficult to breathe (Small, 1969). The heating of the school building also consumed much wood, which was the only available heating fuel, and frequently led to a wood tax levy on families with children attending school (Small, 1969).

Some of the schoolrooms were equipped with whipping posts, which were used with unruly students (Cubberley, 1947). But even the use of the whipping posts had an ecclesiastical rationale. Because children were believed to be born sinful, they periodically had to have "old Adam beaten out of them" (Knight, 1951, p. 127). The wisdom of the schoolmasters was that children were better off whipped than eternally damned, which gave easy justification to their punitive methods in the classroom.

Small (1969) cites an example of a boy who made a bad recitation, causing his teacher to flog "another boy for not exercising a better influence over the delinquent" (p. 386). Other teachers were more creative in their offerings of punishment. One schoolmaster, after securing several offenders, asked one to get on all fours, the other to mount his back, and the third to whip the other two around the room. Then they changed positions until each boy had his turn at whipping once and being whipped twice (Small, 1969). Milder forms of punishment included forcing students to sit on air or to stand in the corner with their face to the wall, tapping them on the head with a steel-thimbled finger, and slapping them with a rawhide ruler (Small, 1969).

Throughout colonial America, the curriculum materials used in the various schools were wedded to the notion of building knowledge in reading as a way to build knowledge in religion. To this end, the hornbook was among the earliest instructional devices used in colonial America. Brought from England, the hornbook, which was used widely in colonial America, was not really a book in the sense that we might know it today. It was made out of a thin piece of wood with a handle, looked much like a paddle, and was by some accounts, periodically used for the purpose of hitting children (Meriwether, 1907). On the top of the wood laid a paper that usually contained the alphabet, various letter combinations, and the Lord's prayer. The paper was covered with a thin sheet of cow's horn, made transparent by boiling and scraping that protected the book and made it quite durable for use in school. The hornbook kept instruction fixed on phonemic representations of letters (B as in bear, H as in horse) and on nonsense jingles that represented the sounds that the letters made (Art we add, Ben is bad, Cat she can, Dad or Dan, Ear and eye). Some hornbooks also carried the emblem of Christ's cross at the very top of their front side. Once the children finished all of their lessons on the hornbook, they were ready for catechism, which entailed the memorization and recitation of various religious texts. During catechism lessons, the children were subjected to texts such as the Westminster Catechism and Reverend John Cotton's Spiritual Milk for American Babes Drawn out of the Breasts of Both Testaments for Their Souls' Nourishment (Callahan, 1963).

The most influential text used in the education of young colonists, which eventually replaced the hornbook, was the New England Primer, a book that embodied much of the Puritan view of moral depravity in humankind (Ford, 1899). The primer, which first appeared in 1690, was saturated with religiosity (with moral maxims, hymns, and prayers). It dutifully reproduced the language of the Bible—the commandments, the Lord's Prayer, various samples from the Old Testament, and unique verses that taught literacy within the story of Christianity. The primer used rhymes and poems to help children learn the phonetic sounds symbolized in the letters and letter combinations of the alphabet. These rhymes were also used to teach children something about their own innate proclivity toward sin. The book, for instance, covered the alphabet in the following manner: A: "In Adam's Fall, we sinned all"; B: "Thy life to mend, this book attend" (a pictured Bible); and so on (Rippa, 1984). One particularly popular poem, reproduced in Alexander Rippa's (1984, p. 39) history of the schools, captures the miserable moralistic tone to which children were subjected. The poem reminded the children of their sinful nature and of their destiny with the fires of hell. Children often memorized and performed the poem in school.

> You sinners are, and such a share
>   as sinners many expect
> Such you shall have, for I do save
>   none but mine own elect.
> Yet to compare your sin with their
>   who liv'd a longer time,
> I do confess yours is much less,

though ev'ry sin's a crime:
A crime it is; therefore in bliss
you may not hope to dwell;
But unto you I shall allow
the easiest room in hell.

The merging of reading instruction with the moralistic preachments of the Puritan faith was the rule of thumb in The New England Primer. Proper child-rearing values at the time promoted the need to instill children with fear, obedience, and discipline (Karier, 1967). However, with changing social conditions, later editions of the New England Primer deemphasized stories about sin and eternal punishment and instead stressed patriotic themes and the practical values of learning to read (Butts, 1955). The New England Primer was used in school for well over a century, with an estimated three million copies sold. It was said to have "taught millions to read, and not one to sin" (Callahan, 1963, p. 116).

The education of black and Native American children in New England was an outgrowth of missionary work. Some early missionaries even managed to have the Bible translated into Algonquin, which resulted in small numbers of Algonquin converts settling in Puritan towns (Cohen, 1974). Depending on the town, separate schools could be found for Native American children at virtually all age levels. Even Harvard College opened a college for Native Americans, housed in a separate building, in the 1650s. Because of the nature of life in New England, chattel slavery never took hold in the north. As a result, there were few Blacks in New England during the seventeenth and eighteenth centuries. Cohen (1974) estimates that Blacks made up slightly more than 2 percent of the total population during the late eighteenth century. There were no laws against educating Blacks, but there was discrimination. Thus, although compulsory school laws covered black children, most were educated in separate sectarian schools, with no real opportunity for an education beyond the town elementary school.

Regional Differences

Not all of the colonies were as strongly committed to establishing a public school as were the Puritans in New England. In the southern colonies, for instance, religion was simply not as strong a factor in daily life or in schooling. The character of life in Virginia, with its dispersed plantations, as opposed to towns, and its general lack of good transportation made public schooling a difficult institution to realize (Cubberley, 1947). Moreover, the South was much slower to establish local colleges and to set up printing presses that might have provided printed matter to the populace (Cremin, 1977). Wealthy parents relied on tutors and private schools for the education of their children, while the children of the poor were left to the largess of charity, which often led to church-sponsored pauper schools.

In most cases, the children of the poor, whose parents were under no legal compulsion to educate their children, were left to labor in the fields without an education. In 1642, the Virginia legislature passed a law providing apprenticeship education for the children of the indentured servant classes and children who were orphaned or otherwise indigent. But there were no guarantees that any apprenticeship program would offer anything other than vocational training; no stipulation was made for reading or religion education.

The societal fabric of the South was also quite different from the more homogeneous North. Black slaves and white indentured servants working on the plantations were considered too lowly to deserve even the most basic education. Such a population was not likely to win legislative support for the public schooling of its children. Thus, there was little motivation, from the standpoint of public policy, for free and common public schools in the South. The idea that one school could be fashioned to serve these antagonistic social classes was simply unthinkable. As a result, literacy education in the colonial south resided neither with the state nor with the church, but with private tutors and private schools for the wealthy, and charity schools for the poor.

The education of girls was more restricted in the South than in the North because the Anglicans did not share the Puritan zeal for bringing the Christian creed to both sexes (Cohen, 1974). As in the North, however, the southern attitude toward women and education rarely went beyond expectations of knowledge in cooking, sewing, and the basic rudiments of reading, writing, and arithmetic. Depending on the region, girls were able to gain an education through charity schools, dame schools, private schools, and for the wealthiest, boarding or finishing schools. Most girls, however, were taught at home to do the things that contributed most directly to their roles as wives and housekeepers, with some emphasis also on teaching the values of modesty, gentleness, and piety (Cohen, 1974).

The education of slave children had, by and large, no legislative support in the South during the seventeenth century. And by the early parts of the nineteenth century, the southern states were actively drafting laws prohibiting the education of slaves. As the slave markets grew in size and as the margins of profits increased, due in part to new farming technologies, the institution of slavery became especially vicious. Where slaves in the seventeenth century once found some support for their education as a matter of Christian salvation and even, in some cases, economic benefit to the slave master, the nineteenth century brought nothing but educational deprivation to Blacks. During the early nineteenth century, slave owners were keen to create a submissive and obedient labor force. They understood that education could prove to be a liberating force, and thus a menace to their slave-based economy. The ability to read might give slaves "dangerous" ideas about their own abilities, and ultimately reveal new life possibilities (Beale, 1975). Many southerners also held to the idea that black slaves were uneducable, and acted on this conviction by forbidding the teaching of Blacks throughout most of the region. Slaves, especially on the larger plantations, had to rely on their own wit and will to educate themselves, often using family or community storytelling and various clandestine meetings that focused on black folklore, on know-how with some agricultural and artisan skills, and on Christian precepts (Cremin, 1977).

Prior to the development of the chattel slavery markets that marked the nineteenth century, Blacks in the South had found some educational opportunities in the evangelical activities of the Society for the Propagation of the Gospel in Foreign Parts (SPG), in the work of the Quakers, and in the activities of various northern abolitionist societies. SPG, which was chartered in England, was dedicated to conducting missionary work in English colonies. The missionaries targeted the southern colonies of America, seeking converts, distributing Bibles, and founding churches in the hope and the intention of bringing Blacks, Indians, and poor Whites into the Episcopal faith (Cohen, 1974). Like the Puritans, the SPG believed in the importance of education in bringing the Word of God to the people. Thus, the SPG established a network of charity schools. Taught by missionaries, the schools emphasized Episcopal religious tenets and basic instruction in literacy and numeracy. Ultimately, the SPG succeeded in providing some semblance of a centrally administered system of schooling for black children in the South (Cohen, 1974).

The middle colonies also made no strong claim for the role of public education. As in the Southern colonies, the middle colonies had no identifiable ethnic or religious monopoly that could make such a claim without enduring religious frictions. Thus, in the middle colonies, the state played a rather marginal role in the education of youth—no single church dominated its political landscape (Cubberley, 1947). Although the belief in educating youth for personal salvation existed among the middle colonists, these educating obligations were handed to the church and to private schools. The result was that families had to depend on the church or private advantage to receive even a rudimentary education. The State was, for all intents and purposes, out of the picture. The laissez-faire attitude toward public education in the middle colonies continued into the nineteenth century, and was not surmounted until the migration of New Englanders created a critical mass that helped to agitate for free school legislation (French, 1964).

Various church-affiliated groups did provide an important educational service to the children in the colonies. Quakers, for instance, provided literacy education to both sexes and admitted poor and minority children to their schools free of charge. They also sponsored a network of charity schools throughout the colonies for the education of black and Indian children. Most Quakers did not own slaves, and dedicated themselves to abolitionist causes as well as to the educational causes of black children. As Button and Provenzo (1983) put it, "The Church of England had hoped to save souls . . . abolitionist Quakers aimed to save men and women" (p. 38).

All in all, the colonial educational scene was marked by three rather different movements (Cubberley, 1947). In New England, particularly in Massachusetts, efforts were directed at establishing state-sponsored common schools that carried a clear religious mandate. The preponderance of towns and the lack of religious diversity made it easy for the citizens of Massachusetts to conduct such schools. The United States inherited its present system of governance, with some obvious changes, from the Puritan New England model. In the middle colonies, which were populated mostly by Protestants and Catholics, the church stood alone as the main player in the education of youth. Education proceeded along denominational lines, and the role of the state in such affairs was viewed as repugnant to the people. In the South, the attitude toward education favored private tutoring or private schooling, and church-sponsored pauper schools for the poor.

Of course, the New England tradition eventually prevailed nationwide. Had the middle colonists had their way, the structure of schooling in the United States might have evolved into a partnership between private and public schools; had the Southern colonists' views become popular, the nation's schools might have developed into an openly private and parochial system (French, 1964). Clearly, the events of the colonial period were central to the development of how we see the public school today.

THE MOVEMENT TOWARD A SECULAR MANDATE

As American-born colonists began to expand their settlements inland during the mid-1700s, new attitudes toward schooling and religion began to prevail. Never having borne the yoke of religious oppression in Europe, this new generation of colonists was less zealous about religion and more civic-minded in its approach toward government and business. To these early Americans, the hard work of frontier settlement life pointed to a more practical outlook toward life in general and toward schooling in particular. Influenced by a revolutionary tempest, the colonists were also beginning to develop a sense of national identification. One major consequence of the American Revolution was that schooling had to play a larger role in the area of civic affairs and economic needs. Knowledge of Latin and Greek was simply not going to take the new generation of youth far enough in dealing with the nation's growing economic, political, and social demands. A new method of schooling was on the horizon.

BRINGING THE SCHOOL TO THE PEOPLE

By 1750, an entirely new vision for a secondary institution, known as the academy school, was beginning to take shape. First advanced by Benjamin Franklin, the American-style academy was designed to make the curriculum more utilitarian than the Latin grammar school and more responsive to emergent economic and social needs. The academies did not abandon the traditional courses in Latin and Greek, but they gave such courses a less exalted status in the curriculum. Franklin believed that the coursework had to be broadened to include scientific inquiry and practical instruction in utilitarian pursuits, such as writing, bookkeeping, gardening, and surveying. Even physical education had some currency in the curriculum. Of course, the curriculum also retained all of the traditional academic disciplines. Franklin also wanted to avoid religious or sectarian instruction in the academies, except as it might be related to other academic studies. In essence, his idea for schooling in the academy marked an early movement toward a new and comprehensive form of education.

Not only was the curriculum different, but those admitted into the school were different as well. For the first time, girls were being freely admitted into post-elementary education. The Latin grammar schools, we should remember, excluded girls, largely because they were designed as preparatory education for the ministry, which girls could not pursue. The academies, by contrast, were often coeducational, as well as openly utilitarian in their curriculum orientation. Household skills, along with the academic traditions of grammar, mathematics, foreign languages, and English had a place in the curriculum. The curriculum offerings, in other words, were relevant to both boys and girls.

However, the academies were still not truly public institutions. They were open to the public but they were not free. Nor did they always operate as Franklin had hoped or expected. The classic traditions provided in the curriculum provided too strong an undertow for the utilitarian brand of education that Franklin promoted, and some academies actually became breeding grounds for college-bound elites (Butts, 1955), much to Franklin's dismay.

Still, the academies were a significant step in the development of a new philosophy of schooling that was more useful and more attentive to real life issues and experiences than was the convention (Butts & Cremin, 1953). The actual range of subjects offered in the curriculum represented a more free-wheeling and practically-minded perspective on learning than what was typically provided in the Latin grammar schools. By the end of the Eighteenth century, Latin grammar schools had more or less expired or transformed themselves into institutions resembling academies. A new curriculum prototype was born in the academy design, one that underscored the significance of comprehensive schooling.

Changes were also occurring at the level of school governance. During the early phases of the colonial settlement, the typical New England town was organized around facilities for public meetings and public schooling. The requirements for universal church attendance and the fear of Indian attacks had kept most settlements within one-half mile of most towns (Cremin, 1951). In time, more inland settlements arose at the peripheries of the central town. For those living in the removed areas, the centrally located church and school became difficult to reach and were less widely used. Because they supported the school with their taxes, those living in the outlying sections asked town officials to provide some school services to them. The original solution was something known as a moving school. The town sent an itinerant schoolmaster to each of the more rural communities for a designated period of time. This meant that a schoolmaster might arrive to teach in a particular precinct for an agreed period and then leave to go teach in another part of town for an agreed period, and continue with such a schedule until completing a rotation that covered all of the town's territory.

This practice, however, eventually gave way to the proportional sharing of property taxes so that each subdivision could independently govern its own schools. Soon, these districts opened their own dame schools and private tuition schools and the education of children began to be framed as a district, as opposed to a town, concern. The districts, in essence, rediscovered the dimension of local school governance that was once fundamental to the central town. For the purposes of schooling, these districts typically were restricted to the distance one could reasonably expect children to walk to school (Button & Provenzo, 1983, p. 93). Such an arrangement, however, did not have legal sanction until the passage of the Massachusetts Law of 1789, which established the district as the basic unit of organization for the public school and reconfirmed the essential logic of the Massachusetts Law of 1647, which assigned the function of the school to local governance (Cremin, 1951). Each town or district was now more or less free to proceed along its own individual lines. Like the Law of 1647, the new legislation also encouraged the local inspection of schools by town or district officials, stressing the responsibility that ministers had in supervising the curriculum and in encouraging attendance (Cremin, 1951).

One important difference, however, is that the functional governance of the school was entrusted to civil authorities, not religious ones. Town funds, not church funds, were used to finance the schools. The Puritans actually had few objections to the change because they understood that in assigning the governance of the school to civil authorities still meant that religious instruction had a sound advocate (Cubberley, 1947). The priorities of the church, whether in the hands of civil or religious authorities, were still superordinate in the conduct of the school.

New England and some of the middle colonies made great strides in providing a basic and religious education to youth. However, with the exception of Massachusetts, the colonies made little progress toward universalizing even a primary education for children. The state laws were permissive, and the local districts were not equally committed to the provision of common schools. Those who had means could find schools for their children, but for the majority of the population, life was still marked by illiteracy. However, whatever strides that might have been taken in the seventeenth century toward the provision of a public education in the colonies were essentially reversed with the start of the Revolutionary War. Many colony schools closed under British occupancy and in the midst of military engagement, many others fell into disarray and disrepair. Educational options decreased and illiteracy increased.

Education in the New Nation

After the colonists emerged from the war against England and achieved independence, their new nation was impoverished and was faced with the daunting task of establishing an independent government amid a society growing in cultural and religious diversity. The United States Constitution seemed to provide no indication of how the public school might evolve in the new nation. The framers of the American Constitution, virtually all privileged men of the colonial aristocracy, made no mention of education in the document. This has led to speculation about what role they envisioned for the school in society (Butts, 1978), with some scholars arguing that the framers wanted to leave schooling to the private sector. The fact that no direct reference to education or schooling can be found in the nation's most important legal document is not exactly an endorsement of the centrality of public education to the workings of the new democracy (Power, 1991).

But the framers' views on education were couched in other positions, the most prominent being the position taken on the separation of church and state. When the attendees of the Constitutional Convention contemplated some of the growing pains of the new nation, they were quickly drawn to the question of how the state and church might be able to reconcile their agendas. Among the problems that the new nation was experiencing was a growing religious diversity. The writers of the Constitution posed a solution by supporting the free exercise of religious faith for all and by banning federally-sponsored religion. The government and the church could no longer be intimates, as they had been in some of the more homogeneous colonies. Moreover, when the Tenth Amendment to the Constitution, which declared that any powers not specifically delegated to the Constitution become the property of the states, was ratified in 1791, public education secured a place as a state function, as opposed to a federal one. To this day, the public schools are marked by a state-specific strategy of governance that allows for the exercise of local district views.

Taking religion out of the governance of the state set the course for a common, nonsectarian, state-funded public school. Public monies could no longer be used to support sectarian religious education, although it would take some time to fully realize this prohibition. With the apparatus for publicly-funded education already in place in states like Massachusetts, the public school had begun its transformation from an institution dominated by religiosity to one charged with enlightening a diverse citizenry for civic participation. The development of a new democracy was now dependent on a public school system that could help build functioning political communities (Butts, 1978). The very system that had its beginnings in religion was now conceived as a form of protection against it. The new mandate for the school was civic in character and was generally associated with the need to socialize good citizens.

Many of the early advocates of a public system of schooling referred to the need for education to become a source of general enlightenment for the citizens of a new democracy. These were essentially the sentiments expressed by early statesmen like Thomas Jefferson, Thomas Paine, John Adams, John Jay, James Madison, and George Washington. The dominant themes of religious fervor were now replaced with more secular rhetoric about equity, liberty, individualism, and reason. Thomas Jefferson, more than anyone in his time, directly appealed to the logic of allying democracy with public education. In a famous statement, he declared that "if a nation expects to be ignorant and free in a state of civilization it expects what never was and never will be..." (Callahan, 1963, p. 125). As early as 1779, Jefferson proposed a plan for public education in the state of Virginia that mandated free public schooling for all free white children, at public expense, for three years, after which the best and brightest would be chosen for secondary education at state expense, with the aim of eventually enrolling at the College of William and Mary, again at public expense (Callahan, 1963).

Many southerners resented state-supported education and even a statesman with the credentials of Jefferson could not convince the legislature to accept his proposal. Jefferson's dream of a state-funded system of schooling in Virginia that provided a primary education for all free children and a more advanced education for the meritorious, including what he hoped would be the first state university, was rejected and not realized until after his death.

Universal basic elementary schooling was still many decades into the future, but Jefferson and others planted the idea for it. By the end of the eighteenth century, state governments throughout the colonies, with some regional variations, were beginning to confront the reality of funding public education. In 1776, for instance, Pennsylvania and North Carolina expressed a commitment to publicly-funded education in their state constitutions, and several other states followed (Butts, 1978). By the late 1780s, states such as Vermont, Massachusetts, and New Hampshire instituted general state school laws, mandating compulsory public education (Cubberley, 1947). Not only were elementary and Latin grammar schools supported in New England, but new colleges were also being founded, including Yale and Dartmouth. Thus, in New England and, eventually, in New York and

Ohio, the belief in state-sponsored schooling continued, even after the religious justification for it had eroded (Cubberly, 1947).

The middle Atlantic states, however, were much less attuned to the objectives of general education in the population. Some legislative support for the public financing of pauper schools could be found, but the tradition of privately-funded education continued to prevail. Similarly, the southern states, as well as Rhode Island (which was the first state to legislatively support the freedom to exercise any religion) essentially maintained that the state had no business in the affairs of educating children.

Even as various states incorporated a commitment to public schooling in their constitutions and laws, the federal government was underscoring the importance of public education through its regulation of the westward migration (Cubberley, 1947). As settlers moved to land in Ohio and other territory west of Ohio, Congress demanded that land surveys be conducted and that one section of the land surveyed (640 acres) in every township be reserved as a place for the maintenance of a school (Butts, 1978). Land grants provided by the Land Ordinance of 1785 enticed settlers from New England to migrate to the Midwest and helped create the conditions for the rise of publicly funded schools.

Despite the efforts to support education through land grants, state laws, and state constitutional protections, the free public school in America was still largely an abstraction at the turn of the nineteenth century. The country was quite poor and had not worked out how public education could be funded. Moreover, the agrarian life style, the relative isolation of villages, and the fact that education was not yet central to the political or business practice of the time gave education a rather low priority.

The Struggle for the American Public School

As the nation entered the nineteenth century, a philanthropic movement to offer free education to children of the poor was thriving in the cities of the North. This movement had its roots in Europe, where public education was considered to be an act of alms for the poor (Power, 1991). To wealthy Europeans, who could afford to educate their own children, public schools were constructed as pauper schools. To give public money to such schools was viewed as unnecessary and unwise. Despite the considerable legislative support given to the public school in the United States, the tradition of education as alms appealed to many wealthy Americans. At the turn of the nineteenth century, for instance, one could find public schools funded by various agencies and philanthropists, including some free schools for black children, which existed in New York City as early as 1787. Many of these charity schools were later absorbed by the public school system and got their charter from the state (Cubberley, 1947).

During the early 1800s, among the more significant events emanating from the philanthropic school movement was a pedagogical innovation known as the Lancaster method (sometimes also known as monitorial instruction). Named after the philanthropist Joseph Lancaster, the method originated in England and was popular in many of its pauper schools. The major appeal to the method was that it was a cheap and efficient way to educate large numbers of children in an equal and common manner. The idea was rather simple: the school congregated a large class into a room, anywhere from 200 to potentially 1,000 students, and then sorted them into even rows. One student, usually a boy, was then chosen as the monitor of the row or a portion of it, and with the other chosen monitors was instructed by the teacher in the lessons for the day. The monitor's responsibility was to return to his group or row and instruct it in the very lesson that he had just completed with the teacher—hence the phrase "monitorial instruction." This system was used for the teaching of reading, catechism, simple computations, writing, and spelling. It usually took on a competitive edge, as different groups of children, led by their monitor, competed for various rewards (Button & Provenzo, 1983, p. 69).

The beauty of the practice was that hundreds of youth presumably could be educated in one room by one teacher, with results that were no worse than those achieved in the Latin grammar schools or dame schools. With the Lancaster method, students no longer had to wait their turn at their teachers' desk to read or recite their lessons. Moreover, the method protected against student idleness and offered a climate of order and control. Used on a wholesale basis, the Lancaster method greatly reduced the costs of providing a public education (Cubberley, 1947). With classroom sizes literally in the hundreds, per-pupil expenditures could be kept low. In the words of one admirer, "When I behold the wonderful celerity in instruction and economy of expense and when I perceive one great assembly of a thousand children, under the eye of a single teacher, marching, with unexampled rapidity and with perfect discipline to the goal of knowledge, I confess that I recognize in Lancaster the benefactor of the human race" (Clinton, 1809, p. 121).

Another idea inspired by a philanthropist and brought to the colonies from England began to take hold at the level of primary education. In nineteenth century England, it was not uncommon for children as young as five to be employed in factories, working up to 14 hours a day. One manufacturer, Robert Owen, attempted to help remedy this situation by offering an education to children between the ages of three and five, partly to provide them with some enjoyment and play before entering factory life and partly to offer them moral and intellectual training. These schools were known as infant schools. In the cities on the northeastern shores of America, infant schools were supported by various philanthropists for the same purposes they served in England. The infant schools were especially popular in Boston, New York, and Philadelphia.

The infant schools signified an early organizational distinction between primary and elementary education. Unlike the Lancaster schools, the infant schools actually tried to advance a new theory of teaching that was driven by a psychological view of children (Cubberley, 1947). With the introduction of the infant school to America came the introduction of the learner (his or her needs and interests) into the teaching/learning equation. This was fundamentally different from the Lancaster effort, which was influenced entirely by business values and efficiency concerns.

The growth and stabilization of the country during the early stages of industrial development helped the public school to identify with national goals and needs. The school's normative agenda was no longer reducible to its local, district, or regional priorities. It now aimed at a wider mark, conceived, particularly among various social reformers interested in bringing better equity to the social landscape of America, as a leveler of economic differences, as an agency that provides social and economic opportunities and a place where students can learn what it means to be an American.

One of the first steps taken in the direction of developing a national consciousness was tied to the goal of using the school to build a common language and a common history. Lexicographer Noah Webster (1739) took this task on as a matter of national urgency:

> It will be readily admitted that the pleasures of reading and conversing, the advantage of accuracy in business, the necessity of clearness and precision in communicating ideas, require us to be able to speak and write our tongue with ease and correctness . . . [We] must gradually destroy the differences of dialect which our ancestors brought from their native countries. (p. 89)

Webster helped the schools serve the objective of fashioning a national culture by publishing his Grammatical Institute of the English Language, a three part book containing sections on spelling, grammar, and readings. The spelling section, which was published separately as the American Spelling Book, eventually superseded the New England Primer as the most widely used text in the schools in the late 1700s and into the 1800s. Figure 7–2 shows a sample lesson from the book. It was said to

Of the Boy that stole Apples.

An old Man found a rude Boy upon one of his trees stealing Apples, and desired him to come down; but the young Sauce-box told him plainly he would not. Won't you? said the old Man, then I will fetch you down; so he pulled up some tufts of Grass and threw at him; but this only made the Youngster laugh, to think the old Man should pretend to beat him down from the tree with grass only.

Fable I.—Of the Boy that stole Apples.
From a Webster's speller dated 1789.

Well, well, said the old Man, if neither words nor grass will do, I must try what virtue there is in Stones: so the old Man pelted him heartily with stones, which soon made the young Chap hasten down from the tree and beg the old Man's pardon.

MORAL

If good words and gentle means will not reclaim the wicked, they must be dealt with in a more severe manner.

FIGURE 7–2   Sample Lesson from Webster's *American Spelling Book* (1789).

have gone west with the settlers, often being the first book printed by the local presses in the small frontier towns (Pangle & Pangle, 1993). Webster, of course, later wrote and published the Dictionary of the English Language but it was his speller that gave impetus for a common language without accents and that contributed to the ideal of a common classless society. Throughout, Webster's work stressed the Puritan values of thrift, diligence, and work. But Webster disdained the rather stern style used in the New England Primer and used images of animals and other childhood pleasantries to convey his messages to children, although moralistic proclamations were in constant use in the text (Pangle & Pangle, 1993). The influence of Webster's work in shaping a national culture earned him the title of "Schoolmaster to America" from his biographer (Drake, 1955, p. 153).

The rise of the industrial age also influenced the renewed call for public education. Industrial development brought factory work into the life of the new American, and many of these factories led to the rapid growth of cities, particularly in the northeastern and north central regions. In the North, as manufacturing facilities developed in the cities, a concentration of capital and labor followed. Where the colonial village was once homogeneous and tied to work on the land, the new cities brought together a wide mix of people who earned a living in the factory (Cubberley, 1947).

As the United States continued to attract diverse populations to its shores, it became clear that some type of amalgamating institution was going to be needed to build political communities in the nation. The common public school was one way to promote a common national experience. By the 1850s, the annual immigration rate exceeded 500,000 with immigrants representing a wide range of national origins. Between 1840 and 1870, the population of the country doubled, and doubled again between 1870 and 1900. At the dawn of the new century, one out of every seven Americans was foreign-born (Butts, 1955). No other nation had faced the challenge of socializing a largely unedu-cated pluralist population into a unified entity. The argument that children needed basic reading skills to do manufacturing work and to become enlightened enough to stay away from crime and other socially undesirable behavior also gained credence. Thus, the school increasingly was taking on the role as a leveler of economic differences, assimilator of ethnic differences, and communicator of what it means to be an American.

The idea of a publicly funded school system for all youth had its share of detractors. Many argued that state-supported education was a luxury that the nation could not afford and that such a system would simply result in the industrious people of the nation supporting the education of the stupid and the lazy. Critics also asserted that state had no business in schooling; that such an institution was best left to the influences and desires of the church and the family. One could even encounter the aristocratic claim that the poor did not need an education because they had no time to use it (Callahan, 1963).

Given the opposition to publicly-funded schooling, gaining public support for a school tax repre-sented a significant challenge. The result was that many states first looked to other financial sources, including lotteries, occupational taxes, bank taxes, and money taken from license fees. Some states also used rate bills, another practice inherited from England, which were charges levied on parents whose children were in school.

These sources proved to be inadequate and the argument for public schooling could not escape the prospect of funding by taxation. The argument for school taxation rested on the same principle that equated taxation with the price a society must pay for social order (for courts, jails, roads, police, and so on). According to this rationale, free public schooling was an investment in the stability and progress of society, in making people more civilized and enlightened.

Not surprisingly, support for the use of local property taxes to fund schools was strongest in New England. In Massachusetts, the legislature passed the Law of 1789, which gave local districts full and complete power to tax and control their own schools. Such a system was well-aligned with the struc-ture of the school organization established in early New England and was popular in several north-ern states. "For the purpose of public instruction," declared Daniel Webster, "we have held, and do hold, every man subject to taxation in proportion to his property; and we look not to the question whether he himself have or have not children, to be benefited by the education for which he pays" (Harris, 1907, p. 44). The idea of local taxes was begrudgingly accepted, but permissive state laws gave local school districts all kinds of leeway. Districts not disposed to funding public schools, for instance, were really under no compulsion to do so and there was little in the way of organized authority at the state level to compel them to do otherwise. Local decision making thrived but not always in ways that were in the interests of the public school. Clearly, the universalization of the public school could not be accomplished under circumstances that allowed local districts to do anything they pleased, includ-ing doing nothing. Local concerns were important, but the state clearly needed to take an active hand in developing, facilitating, and supervising public education.

Eventually, the state moved in on the public school by establishing forms of state aid, which led to the establishment of criteria used to secure these funds and then to supervisory roles in accounting for the use of these funds. States often forced local taxes on schools by making state monetary commitments to local districts contingent on some ratio of in-kind monetary commitments at the local level. In order to accomplish all of its new functions, the state had to create an administrative structure, led by a state school officer, which would be responsible for the supervision of the public schools. In the 1830s, James Carter, an educator and an activist for preschool legislation, argued long and hard for a more direct state role in the public schooling in Massachusetts. He wanted to establish a state board so that efforts to create public high schools and normal schools (training institutes for teachers) could be linked to some central authority. In 1837, Carter succeeded in winning approval for a state board and proceeded to help select Horace Mann as the first state Secretary of Education in Massachusetts in 1837. The appointment would prove to be historic.

Horace Mann and the Rise of State Authority

Probably more than anyone who lived in the nineteenth century, Horace Mann used his new office to reawaken the Jeffersonian concept of mass education for the benefit of social, political, and economic progress. The effect of Mann's leadership in Massachusetts broadened schooling opportunities in the state, elevated the base of tax support for schools, upgraded the hygienic standards of schoolhouses, supported the training of teaching in normal schools, brought more women into the profession, increased the number of school libraries, and generally improved the pedagogical practices of teachers. During his tenure, Mann increased teacher salaries, lengthened the school year, and generally increased the appropriations to schools (Rippa, 1984).

Mann studied the emerging educational theories of his time, and attempted to apply the best of these ideas to the schools in Massachusetts. For instance, he was among the first to try to improve on reading instruction by considering what was then known as the whole-word method of teaching reading, which essentially rejected the phonetic breakdown of words in favor of whole word recognitions (Tanner & Tanner, 1987). In his Second Annual Report, in 1838, Mann displayed remarkable sensitivity, for his time, toward the needs of learners. In fact, his regard for learners was logically connected to his desire to develop a statewide teacher training system.

Although Mann understood the limitations to what he could accomplish in the school, he was nonetheless an activist in his own right. Mann was clearly unhappy with the district system in Massachusetts that was ushered in with the passage of the Massachusetts Law of 1789. Local schools had gotten used to regulating themselves and were not held accountable to any concerns that transcended local matters. To Mann, the district school needed to be given a center of gravity that brought things together under a common civic mission and that provided an overseeing agency devoted to maintaining standards of quality in the education of all children. Mann saw little more than anarchy in the idea of local school control (Power, 1991). In his Fourth Annual Report, 1840, he asked for a consolidation of small districts into larger ones, with the ultimate goal of bringing them under state authority.

To the chagrin of many citizens, Mann also sought to keep the functions of state-funded schools separate from sectarian religious instruction. He wanted to use the school to promote a civic community that would give children a common discourse for mutual understanding and tolerance. Although Mann was highly critical of the way schooling was conducted in Massachusetts, he understood its promise and was optimistic about the powers of free common schools, thinking that they could help eliminate poverty and class distinction and become "the great equalizer of the conditions of men."

Mann also had a keen political sense and generally avoided matters in the curriculum that might divide the population (Butts, 1978). Religion was generally avoided in the school, although Mann advised that the Bible be read without commentary. Potentially fractious political issues were also avoided. Mann understood that the common public school was a fragile institution and he did not want to imperil its future by generating controversies in the curriculum that might spill into the community. Thus, he tried to hold the line on controversies by focusing the curriculum on literacy instruction, moral training, and knowledge of government (Butts, 1978). As Karier (1967) explains, Mann also viewed the American public school as a form of protection against social revolution and as an important contrast to the European model of schooling that accepted the inevitability of class differences.

Because of his many progressive ideas, Mann was not the most popular man in Massachusetts. We should remember that the early history of Massachusetts upheld the right of the Church to dictate school practice, and Mann was breaking from tradition by trying to erect a wall of separation between the two. Critics accused Mann (and the State Board of Education that he led) of trying to take God out of the public school, to make them Godless, which in the eyes of many citizens, made them worthless. Mann was subjected to attacks from the pulpit and through the press. In his third year in office, Mann had to face the indignity of two legislative attempts, led by religious groups, to abolish the State Board of Education (Rippa, 1984). But the attempts failed and Mann kept his position as Secretary of Education for 12 years.

Mann also made quite a few enemies among school masters, mostly because he was so unabashedly critical of their work. A skilled writer, Mann used his annual reports on the state of education in Massachusetts to comment on the many educational problems of the day. In the Seventh Annual Report, Mann took direct aim at the poor teaching in the schools and spoke admiringly about how education in Prussia, which he visited for a period, could provide some thoughtful lessons for educators in Massachusetts. In the Prussian schools, Mann (1844) observed, "I never saw a blow struck, I never heard a sharp rebuke given, I never saw a child in tears. . . . I heard no child ridiculed, sneered at, or scolded, for making a mistake" (p. 187). Could a visitor, Mann added rhetorically, spend six weeks in our schools and walk away with the same impressions?

Mann also accounted for the style of instruction in Prussia, noting the scholarly insight of the teachers, whose books (to paraphrase Mann) were in their heads not in their hands. He recounted classroom observations that allowed for student questions, classroom discussions, and more humane and empathic treatments of youth. Not surprisingly, his report drew a harsh response from the Principal's Association in Boston and set off a year-long written debate between Mann and the principals.

The genius of Horace Mann had to do with his perception of the changing social landscape of Massachusetts and America. Although he was personally a deeply religious man, he knew that battles over which religious creeds to read and study in the school would eventually undermine any chance of establishing a universally-accessible common public school. Thus, Mann worked out of a socio-civic tradition that stressed democratizing themes in the schools and the professionalization of teaching. It was largely through his work that a strong model for free common schooling developed during the 1840s in Massachusetts, a model that not only influenced other states but other countries as well. Mann and his ideas traveled widely. He advised other state authorities on matters of school administration and counseled the development of public schools in such distant places as Chile and Argentina (Noble, 1959).

The Cause of Teacher Education

Teacher education was part and parcel of the general effort made to elevate the common public school experience during Horace Mann's tenure as Secretary of Education. Under Mann's leadership, the State Board of Education in Massachusetts funded and operated three teacher education schools, each located in a different region of the state. Because there was no legislative support for teacher education schools (known as normal schools at the time), Mann had to solicit private donations in addition to state money to get the schools opened and operating.

Horace Mann was militantly committed to the idea of teacher education. It was, to him, the single most important variable in sustaining the common public school experience. The argument supporting normal schools was not complicated. As Mann phrased in his Twelfth Annual Report, "Common schools will never prosper without normal schools. As well might we expect to have coats without a tailor, and hats without a hatter, and watches without a watchmaker, and houses without a carpenter or mason, as to have an adequate supply of teachers without normal schools" (Mangun, 1928, p. 412). Mann knew from firsthand experience how bad, even abusive, some of the teachers were in the schools. He also understood how very deficient many teachers were in their own academic knowledge and skill. As indicated, he was not hesitant about criticizing public education officials in the Massachusetts schools. Mann wanted to help cure the problem by giving teachers preparatory experiences with children, by strengthening their academic educations, and by encouraging the participation of women in the education of young people. Because the number of students attending the common schools in Massachusetts was growing precipitously (jumping 50 percent between 1840 and 1860), teacher training was especially critical.

The term "normal school" was imported from the Prussian system of schooling, which Mann visited and which featured teacher training. The idea of teacher education, however, existed in the colonies before Mann's efforts to popularize it. James Carter presented the idea of teacher seminaries in his *Essays of Popular Education,* as did others, such as Thomas Gallaudet in his essay, *Plan for a Seminary for the Education of Instructors of Youth* (1825). In 1827, Carter went one step further and attempted to win legislative support for the idea, to no avail, in the State of Massachusetts. Moreover, some private academies had included teacher training in their curricula. This was especially the case in New York, where a law drafted in 1827 provided state subsidies to academies establishing teacher training courses (Drake, 1955, p. 374).

What Mann had in mind, however, was a state-sponsored network of normal schools, governed by the state in the service of the state's schoolchildren. He did not want teacher training to be folded into the curriculum of the academy. He wanted it to stand on its own, as an experience requiring the wholesale time and energy of its student population. "In Massachusetts," Mann stated, "the business of the normal school is to possess the entire and exclusive occupancy of all the instructors and all the pupils; to have no rival of any kind, no incidental or collateral purposes..." (Williams, 1937, p. 202).

The town of Lexington, Massachusetts, agreed to the conditions for the operation of the state's first normal school in July of 1839. Another normal school was opened in Barre, Massachusetts, in September of 1839, and a third in Bridgewater, one year later. The Lexington school restricted attendance to women and focused on elementary education teaching. Several factors weighed into this decision. First, men typically were not interested in teaching young children because other means of advancement were available to them. Second, and probably more important, much of the leadership on the State Board of Education, Horace Mann included, believed that women were, by their very nature, better suited to teach young children than were men. Mann saw women as freer from political ambitions and from vulgar habits, "more mild and gentle" with "stronger parental impulses" and "purer morals" (Williams, 1937, p. 203). Because of the need for qualified elementary school teachers, the education of female teachers was a critical mission for Mann. At the other two normal schools, Barre and Bridgewater, the enrollment was open to both sexes because of the teacher training extended to teaching in the high school.

The curriculum of the normal school required prospective teachers to learn the course of study for the common school in its entirety and to practice the art of imparting instruction to youth, usually by means of a model school experience. Normal school attendees were graduates of the common district schools, but were unevenly schooled. Thus, some attention had to be paid in the normal school to the actual knowledge and skills that the teacher was responsible to teach. Mann also felt that it was especially important for the normal school to offer experiences in practice teaching, under the eyes of an experienced teacher critic. Mann was said to be fond of telling the story of a skillful eye surgeon, who, when asked how he learned such amazing skills of surgery replied, "By practice, but I spoiled a bushel basketful of eyes in learning how" (Williams, 1937, p. 191). To Mann, this trial and error method was comparable to what schoolteachers were doing to children. The normal school was designed to prevent such abuse.

In time, state-sponsored normal schools were also established in New York and in many western and southern states. In the western-most states, normal school studies began to find a place in the university curriculum, leading to the development of teachers' colleges and teacher education or normal school studies' departments. Normal school studies were established in many of the leading western public universities, including the University of Indiana (1852), Wisconsin (1856), Missouri (1856), Kansas (1876), and Iowa (1855). This was partly a function of dissatisfaction with the work of normal schools and a desire to elevate the status of teaching. The first university department of education was founded at the University of Iowa in 1855 (Drake, 1955). Over time, state normal schools evolved into regional multi-purpose colleges. In the South, normal schools first appeared in the 1870s, many of which were black normal schools established during the Reconstruction.

THE UPWARD AND OUTWARD EXTENSION OF SCHOOLING

The upward and outward extension of public school in the United States was dependent on finding a way to fund education beyond the childhood years and on designing a post-elementary school experience that would have wide student appeal.

Like many aspects of public education, the American high school had its roots in Massachusetts. As indicated earlier, by the mid-1700s, the Latin grammar school was waning as an institution and the academy was on the rise. By the mid-1800s, the Latin grammar school had essentially disappeared, supplanted by the tuition-based academy. In Massachusetts, where free public schooling at the elementary school level was becoming a reality, public schooling was also being extended into the secondary school years. The academies were still tuition-based, but Massachusetts was ahead of its time by enacting legislation in 1827 that required the establishment of tax-supported high schools in towns with 500 or more households. Over the course of the next two decades, at least 100 public high schools were maintained in Massachusetts. By 1860, a free public school system existed at the elementary school level in Massachusetts, while free public high schools were becoming more popular, even in more rural areas.

The first public high school was opened in Boston in 1821. It was designed more in the image of the academy than the Latin grammar school. Latin and Greek were not part of the school's curricular offerings. Instead, the center of the curriculum was comprised of English, mathematics, science, logic, and history (Boston Records, 1820, p. 134). In 1826, a separate high school for girls was opened in Boston, which became so oversubscribed that the mayor closed it down after two years, fearing its cost to the city's coffers (Rippa, 1984).

The idea for public high schools spread to other states, especially in the North. But the development of the public high school in other states was hindered by a district system that allowed local districts to decide whether they would erect such schools. Lenient state laws did not always compel compliance to the state's wishes. Districts sometimes abused their power, which led to uneven tax support for the schools and uneven access to schooling.

It was only a matter of time before the constitutionality of tax supported high school education was tested. The most prominent court case occurred in Kalamazoo, Michigan, where a citizen tested the school board's right to levy taxes in support of high schools (Tanner, 1972). The complainant argued that high schools were not institutions designed to educate all of the children and so should not be supported by tax dollars. But the State Supreme Court ruled that tax monies could be used to support high school education if they aimed to provide an education to rich and poor alike (Butts, 1955). Although the high schools were not widely attended, they had to be equally accessible to all. This was a significant ruling because it gave the high school a secure place in the common, publicly supported school system.

The growing popularity of public school across the cities and towns of the nation meant that fundamental changes had to occur to the structure of school organization. The evolving common elementary school, which had long practiced non-graded instruction, was undergoing divisional changes that separated primary education from intermediate education (Douglas & Grieder, 1948). Soon, actual grade divisions followed. This change was facilitated by the construction of new school buildings that tried to accommodate smaller groups and by the provision of smaller classes, with classes reduced to 50 and 75 students (Cubberley, 1947). Moreover, the American system of schooling created one unified pathway for schooling (kindergarten to college) that all students could theoretically access, as opposed to the dual ladders that existed in Europe (one for the college-bound and one for the vocational-bound). Even higher education received a boost with the Congressional passage of the Morrill Act of 1862, which authorized federal subsidies and land grants for the endowment of state universities. Many of these early land grant universities, which sometimes featured education in agriculture and mechanics, have since become among the largest and most comprehensive universities in the world. The land grant act also represented a new pedagogical priority in the education of young adults because practical studies, as opposed to classical studies, now had a justifiable place in the post-secondary curriculum.

SUMMARY

Public education in colonial America reflected regional differences in attitudes toward the idea of publicly-funded schools. In homogeneous New England, the public school was conceived as an extension of the church, as an institution that could broaden and secure the agenda of the church in the community. Uniformly committed to the cause of building a church-based society, the Puritans passed legislation that resulted in public funding for a compulsory school system. In the middle and southern colonies, geographic and demographic conditions did not allow for a uniformly supported system of public schooling.

The character of instruction in the common schools of New England and the northwest expansion would eventually change. The founding of a new nation had to bring forth a new way of doing school, one that aimed at the development of national consciousness and the integration of utilitarian studies in the curriculum. A new comprehensive vision of schooling had to be found, which included teaching the rules of arithmetic and grammar, the conventions of spelling and reading, various occupational skills, as well as the holdover academic studies from the Latin grammar school.

The American school began to look to Europe for new ideas, focusing largely on the advances made in the Prussian system, which included the development of teacher training institutes, known as normal schools, and new theoretical outlooks on the classroom and the curriculum. Horace Mann's tenure as the State Superintendent of Education in Massachusetts set many of the early precedents for the relation between state and local school interest. He led the way for the development of a state-regulated system of schooling, showing others how to balance state and district concerns in ways that ensured properly-funded and properly-managed schools, while stressing the role of the educated teacher. Teacher education, in this sense, was an especially important development because it helped to plant the seeds for the professionalization of teaching.

The early development of the public school in New England has indeed pointed the way for public education in America. On principle, the foundation for tax-supported public education was secure at the turn of the twentieth century. Opportunities for an education were no longer dependent on the philanthropy of industrialists and other elites, or on the church. A new democratic vista was before the nation—public schools, free and open to all, supported by the public, regulated by the state, free from sectarian control, and still responsive to local conditions.

REFERENCES

Beale, H. K. (1975). The education of Negroes before the Civil War. In J. Barnard & D. Burner (Eds.) *The American experience in education.* New York: New Viewpoints.

Boston Records. (1820). Proceedings of town meeting, XXVII, 168–171. In D. Calhoun (1969). *Educating of Americans: A documentary history.* Boston: Houghton-Mifflin Company.

Button, H. W., & Provenzo, E. P. (1983). *History of education and culture in America.* Englewood Cliffs: Prentice Hall.

Butts, R. F. (1955). *A cultural history of western education: Its social and intellectual foundations.* New York: McGraw-Hill.

Butts, R. F. (1978). *Public education in the United States.* New York: Holt, Rinehart, and Winston.

Butts, R. F., & Cremin, L. A. (1953). *A history of education in American culture.* New York: Holt, Rinehart, and Winston.

Callahan, R. (1963). *An introduction to education in American society.* New York: Alfred A. Knopf.

Clinton, D. W. (1809). "Address on the opening of a new school building." In D. Calhoun, (1969). *Educating of Americans: A documentary history.* Boston: Houghton-Mifflin Company.

Cohen, S. S. (1974). *A history of colonial education, 1607–1776.* New York: John Wiley and Sons.

Colony of Massachusetts. (1853). *Records of the governor and company of the Massachusetts Bay in New England.* Boston: William White.

Cremin, L. A. (1951). *The American common school: A historic conception.* New York: Teachers College, Columbia University.

Cremin, L. A. (1977). *Traditions of American education.* New York: Basic Books.

Cubberley, E. B. (1947). *Public education in the United States.* Boston: Houghton-Mifflin Company.

Douglas, H. R., & Greider, C. (1948). *American public education.* New York: The Ronald Press Company.

Drake, W. E. (1955). *The American school in transition.* New York: Prentice-Hall.

Ford, P. L. (1899). *The New England Primer*. New York: Dodd, Mead.

French, W. M. (1964). *America's educational tradition*. Boston: DC Heath and Co.

French, W. M. (1967). *American secondary education*. New York: The Odyssey Press.

Harris, W. T. (1899). *Education in the United States*. New York: D. Appleton and Co.

Karier, C. J. (1967). *Man, society and education*. New York: Scott Foresman and Co.

Knight, E. W. (1951). *Education in the United States*. Boston: Ginn and Company.

Mangun, V. L. (1928). *The American normal school: Its rise and development in Massachusetts*. Baltimore: Warwick and York.

Mann, H. (1844). Seventh annual report of the board of education. In D. Calhoun, (1969), *Educating of Americans: A documentary history*. Boston: Houghton-Mifflin Company.

Mayer, F. (1964). *American ideas and education*. Columbus, OH: Merrill.

Meriwether, C. (1907). *Colonial curriculum 1607–1776*. Washington, DC: Capital Publishing Co.

Noble, S. G. (1959). *A History of American education*. New York: Rinehart and Company, Inc.

Pangle, L. S., & Pangle, T. L. (1993). *The learning of liberty*. Lawrence, KS: University Press of Kansas.

Power, E. J. (1991). *A legacy of learning*. Albany, NY: SUNY Press.

Rippa, S. A. (1984). *Education in a free society: An American history*. New York: David McKay Company, Inc.

Small, W. H. (1969). *Early New England schools*. New York: Arno Press and the New York Times.

Tanner, D. (1972). *Secondary education*. New York: Macmillan Co.

Tanner, D., & Tanner, L. N. (1987). *History of the school curriculum*. New York: Macmillan Co.

Webster, N. (1739). The call for a national culture. In Calhoun, D. (1969). *Educating of Americans: A documentary history*. Boston: Houghton-Mifflin.

Williams, E. I. F. (1937). *Horace Mann: Educational statesman*. New York: Macmillan.

KEY QUESTIONS

1. Why did regional differences exist in the colonies toward the provision of publicly-funded schooling?
2. How did the Lancaster method of teaching contribute to the argument for publicly-funded education?
3. How do you account for the slight attention given to the education of woman and girls in the colonies?
4. Explain the decline of religious bodies in the control of education.
5. Characterize the overall nature of teaching in a New England dame school or Latin grammar school.
6. Explain the shift from religious instruction to socio-civic objectives in the historical development of the public school.
7. Why was the Massachusetts Law of 1647 also known as the Old Deluder Act?
8. Explain the methods of and the justification for discipline in the schools of the Puritans.
9. In what way was the American public school born out of a religious mandate?
10. In what way was the Massachusetts Law of 1647 a greater stride toward the development of the public school than the Massachusetts Law of 1642?
11. What was meant by the observation that the New England Primer "taught millions to read and not one to sin"?
12. In what ways was Ben Franklin's academy a reaction against the Latin grammar school?
13. How did the national government support the development of the public school through its

regulation of westward settlements?

14. As the nation grew in number and diversity, what were the more important mandates facing the schools?

15. What were some of the early arguments made against the support of publicly-funded education?

16. In what way was the virtue of the district system also its fundamental weakness?

17. What was Horace Mann's main argument for more active state control over public schools?

18. Why did Mann not support the introduction of controversial topics in the school curriculum?

19. Why was Mann not always the most popular public official in Massachusetts?

20. How could Noah Webster be viewed as "Schoolmaster to America"?

RESEARCH EXERCISES

1. Research the requirements for admission into a particular American university today against its stated admission requirements in an earlier decade, or even an earlier century. Describe the differences and the likely consequences on the formation of the graduates.
2. Compare the actual language of the Massachusetts Law of 1647 to the Massachusetts Law of 1827. Note differences and similarities.
3. Research the curriculum offerings in the early academy schools and compare and contrast them to what one might typically find in an American high school today.
4. Read one of Horace Mann's twelve Annual Reports as Secretary of Education in Massachusetts and discuss its relevance today.
5. Examine any combination one of the state constitutions for their wording on compulsory schooling and discuss similarities and differences.
6. Research the nature of the curriculum offerings in the early normal schools.
7. Despite the lack of educational opportunity, several Blacks achieved distinction in various areas of endeavor during the late eighteenth and early nineteenth century. Benjamin Banneker (1731–1804) was a well-known writer, astronomer, and scientist; Ira Alderidge (1807–1867), a widely-known actor; Martin Delaney (1812–1885) was a graduate of Harvard Medical School; and Isabella Baumfree (1797–1883), also known as Sojourner Truth, was an abolitionist and orator, as was Harriet Tubman (1820–1913). Research one of these distinguished African Americans, focusing on their early education. Where were they schooled? Who provided the schooling?

CHAPTER 8

Defining the School Experience at the Turn of the Twentieth Century

A new day was dawning for the public school at the turn of the twentieth century. The school gates were just beginning to swing open and the very idea of pedagogy was taking on new scientific and philosophical slants. A new progressive force of reformers was gaining visibility in American education, setting a counterbalancing to traditionalist thinking and raising new questions about curriculum content and instruction practices. The American public school was poised to get an injection of new ideas that would set the course for an entirely new way of looking at teaching and learning. At the same time, traditionalist measures of teaching were themselves gaining support, especially from advocates in the liberal arts who were pushing for a highly academic, subject-centered curriculum. The conditions were set for a debate over the practices of the American school, a clash of ideas that featured a child-centered form of progressivism and a subject-centered traditionalism (Dewey, 1902; Bode, 1938).

THE ASCENDANCY OF THE TRADITIONAL LIBERAL ARTS

The progressive backlash witnessed in the schools at the turn of the century was due in part to the ascendancy of traditionalist thinking. In most of the schools at this time, traditional approaches to teaching youth, which stressed the Old World methods of rote and recitation, were still quite popular. In fact, advocates for such instruction emerged from the ranks of the liberal arts, equipped with a new psychology and an associated doctrine of learning that justified the old pedagogy. Many of these thinkers could be classified as traditional humanists (Kliebard, 2004)—scholars who believed that a good education entailed an immersion in the disciplines and the great works of the liberal arts. In an earlier chapter, this broad group was described as representing essentialist and perennialist perspectives on the school. During the early stages of development in the American high school, from the late nineteenth century into the twentieth century, such thinkers dominated the educational scene.

The Doctrine of Mental Discipline

The type of schooling supported by the traditional humanists is probably best understood by explaining the learning doctrine that underscored their thinking about teaching. The traditionalists rationalized virtually everything that was done in the school through a learning doctrine known as mental discipline. The central principle of the idea was derived from faculty psychology, which held that the mind was made up of separate faculties that collectively comprised the human mind. According to faculty psychology, responses related to emotions, affections, the will, and the intellect all had their compartmentalized place in the mind. More progressive thinkers used faculty psychology to argue for a more holistic approach to education that encompassed all of the so-called faculties (mental, physical, moral, emotional). By contrast, supporters of the doctrine of mental discipline used it to justify a preoccupation with the task of finding a way to train the intellectual faculties. In instructional terms, according to the doctrine of mental discipline, the intellectual faculties could be developed and improved only through certain mental exercises. Proponents believed that such exercises could so strengthen the mind that the benefits to learners would be transferable to virtually all life situations, making them better able to live intelligently.

The key to the teaching/learning process, under these assumptions, was to ensure that students were exposed to subject areas believed to be intrinsically empowered with the capacity to cultivate the mind's intellectual faculties. This meant that students needed to be trained in the study of certain subjects. Skills of memory, judgment, imagination, and other mental processes could only be sharpened if students were regularly immersed in the proper mix of academic subjects. The "mind as muscle" metaphor came to be associated with the doctrine of mental discipline because it captured the idea that the mind, like a muscle, had to be rigorously exercised. Such a workout, however, could only be accomplished with the heavy mental equipment that the traditional academic disciplines provided. Thus, Latin, Greek, mathematics, rhetoric, grammar, and the "great books" were at the core of a good mental routine.

Mental discipline was an early expression of a classical dualism in education that placed the power of the mind over the power of the body. It fostered a bias favoring "mindful" intellectual activity, as it might be construed in its most puristic academic sense, over vocational and experiential activity. This would seemingly have made it an untenable idea for the prevailing institution of public schooling, which was increasingly committed to broadening its scope of learning opportunities. But the doctrine of mental discipline also represented a pulling back from the ideal of the comprehensiveness and a movement away from the academy design. In fact, as previously mentioned, the academies themselves were drawn to the doctrine of mental discipline, so much so that many became purely scholastic centers for highly discipline-centered learning.

Mental disciplinarians could argue effectively for their place in the school experience because they had addressed two essential curriculum questions: They had a ready answer to the question of what should be taught in the school curriculum and an equally clear, though less obvious, answer to the question of how it should be taught. What one taught in school from the standpoint of mental discipline was a traditional body of academic knowledge built largely on the liberal arts. Because the subject matter did the "teaching" through its inherent intellective capacities, mental disciplinarians did not believe that any particular instructional methodology was needed to actualize the connection between the subject matter and the mind. Teachers, of course, had to be well-schooled in the subject matter, but their prime role in the classroom was as purveyors and guardians of the liberal arts tradition. Thus, the teacher, who frequently came into the classroom with little professional training, was not expected to do much more than maintain order in the classroom, fulfill the primary need for basic skills instruction (which was typically approached through rote and repetition procedures), represent an example of moral rectitude to the school community and secure an exposure to the academic traditions.

Adherents to the doctrine of mental discipline were convinced that they had identified a central core of studies needed to develop the human mind. But they also hit upon an even more important revelation. They maintained that this core of studies was appropriate for the education of all youth, not simply for those aiming to go to college. The mental training afforded to the individual by academic studies represented the best preparation not only for college-bound students but also for ordinary citizens. This egalitarian principle in the traditional humanist position turned out to be crucial for the school curriculum. It gave the traditional humanists a platform upon which the education of all youth could be maintained. At the level of the high school, this position was made quite clear in a curriculum document sponsored by the NEA and published in 1894 by a committee of traditional humanists, known as the Committee of Ten.

The Committee Reports and the Identification of the Curriculum

The Committee of Ten report (1893) was written under the chairmanship of Charles Eliot, who was, at the time of the writing of the report, president of Harvard University. Funded by the National Education Association for the purpose of providing some curriculum direction to the American high school, the Committee of Ten fashioned a clear statement on what should be taught. Many secondary schools, which served less than 5 percent of the student population in the 1890s, were facing a dizzying set of requirements from different universities and colleges, and were quite confused over how to prepare their students to succeed. Moreover, participation in public secondary education was on the rise, forcing many to think about high school as not only a preparation for college but as a preparation for life itself. The Committee (1893) took note of this trend, stating that "A secondary school programme tended for national use must be made for those children whose education is not to be pursued beyond the secondary school. The preparation of a few pupils for college . . . should in the ordinary secondary school be the incidental, and not the principal object" (p. 481).

The Committee of Ten was dominated by believers in the doctrine of mental discipline. The membership included five college presidents, one professor, two private school masters, a principal of a public school, and the sitting U.S. Commissioner of Education (Rippa, 1971). The actual report provided a single curriculum prescription for the high school, advancing what was, in effect, a highly traditional set of studies, rooted in the liberal arts, believed to be essential to disciplining the mind. The Committee supported nine broad subjects: Latin, Greek, English, modern languages, physics, astronomy and chemistry, natural history, history, and geography. The inclusion of science courses was unconventional for its time and was the result of Charles Eliot's influence, who, as a former professor of chemistry, believed that there were mind training possibilities in studies not traditionally conceived in the liberal arts. The report made no provision for physical education, the fine arts, or for any vocational subject, which were thought to have no relevance to the strengthening of the mind.

Thus, by virtue of what it included and excluded, the Committee of Ten helped to erect a high school curriculum on nine subjects conceived as equally able to train the mind. As indicated, these nine subjects were upheld as appropriate for the education of all youth, including those who did not plan to attend college. Although the committee asked for four different curriculum tracks (classical, Latin-scientific, modern languages, and English), there was little difference between them, as Figure 8–1 shows. Each track or program represented a slight variation on the nine core subjects.

Interestingly, the chair of the Committee of Ten, Charles Eliot, did not give full support to the Committee's work. Eliot had already been on record for his support of free electives in the curriculum, a cause that he championed at Harvard University during his tenure as president (Rippa, 1971). Eliot accepted the value of mental training, but he did not think that only certain subject areas had a monopoly on mind development. Eliot thought, in fact, that virtually all subjects had value in this regard as long as they were taught in a manner that cultivated reason and morality. This was an unconventional departure from the orthodoxy of mental discipline. Thus, when the Committee of Ten limited its recommendations to nine essential subjects, Eliot had to face up to a compromise. But the committee had a little bit of compromising to do as well because without Eliot it probably would not

Year	Classical. Three foreign languages (one modern).		Latin-Scientific. Two foreign languages (one modern).	
I.	Latin...................	5p.	Latin	5p.
	English................	4p.	English................	4p.
	Algebra.................	4p.	Algebra	4p.
	History................	4p.	History................	4p.
	Physical Geography........	3p. ——— 20p.	Physical Geography........	3p. ——— 20p.
II.	Latin...................	5p.	Latin	5p.
	English................	1p.	English................	lp.
	¹German (or French) begun .	4p.	German (or French) begun ..	4p.
	Geometry...............	3p.	Geometry...............	3p.
	Physics.................	3p.	Physics.................	3p.
	History................	3p. ——— 20p.	Botany or Zoology.........	3p. ——— 20p.
III.	Latin...................	4p.	Latin	4p.
	¹Greek	5p.	English................	3p.
	English................	3p.	German (or French)	4p.
	German (or French)	4p.	Mathematics $\begin{cases} \text{Algebra 2} \\ \text{Geometry 2} \end{cases}$	4p.
	Mathematics $\begin{cases} \text{Algebra 2} \\ \text{Geometry 2} \end{cases}$	4p. ——— 20p.	Astronomy ½ yr. & Meteorology ½ yr.	3p.
			History.................	2p. ——— 20p.
IV.	Latin...................	4p.	Latin	4p.
	Greek................	5p.	English $\begin{cases} \text{as in Classical 2} \\ \text{additional 2} \end{cases}$	4p.
	English................	2p.	German (or French)	3p.
	German (or French)	3p.	Chemistry	3p.
	Chemistry	3p.	Trigonometry & Higher Algebra or History $\Big\}$	3p.
	Trigonometry & Higher Algebra or History $\Big\}$	3p. ——— 20p.	Geology or Physiography ½ yr. and Anatomy. Physiology. & Hygiene ½ yr...........	3p. ——— 20p.

FIGURE 8–1 Committee of Ten Program for Secondard Schools, 1893. From Committee of Ten (1893), *Report of the Committee of Ten on secondary school studies* (Washington, DC: National Education Adssociation).

Year	*Modern Languages.* Two foreign languages (both modern).		*English.* One foreign languages (ancient or modern).	
I.	French (or German) begun . .	5p.	Latin, or German, or French .	5p.
	. . . . English	4p.	English.	4p.
	Algebra.	4p.	Algebra	4p.
	History.	4p.	History.	4p.
	Physical Geography	3p.	Physical Geography	3p.
		20p.		20p.
II.	French (or German)	4p.	Latin, or German, or	
	English.	2p.	French . . . . 5 or 4p.	
	German (or French) begun . .	5p.	English. . . . . 3 or 4p.	
	Geometry.	3p.	Geometry.	3p.
	Physics.	3p.	Physics.	3p.
	Botany or Zoology.	3p.	History.	3p.
		20p.	Botany or Zoology.	3p.
				20p.
III.	French (or German)	4p.	Latin, or German, or French .	4p.
	English.	3p.	English { as in others 3 / additional 2 } . .	5p.
	German (or French)	4p.		
	Mathematics { Algebra 2 / Geometry } . . .	4p.	Mathematics { Algebra 2 / Geometry 2 }	4p.
	Astronomy ½ yr. & Meteorology ½ yr.	3p.	Astronomy ½ yr. & Meteorology ½ yr.	3p.
	History.	2p.	History { as in the Latin- / Scientific 2 / additional 2 } . .	4p.
		20p.		20p.
IV.	French (or German)	3p.	Latin, or German, or French. .	4p.
	English { as in Classical 2 / additional 2 }	4p.	English { as in Classical 2 / additional 2 . . . } .	4p.
	German (or French)	4p.	Chemistry	3p.
	Chemistry	3p.	Trigonometry & Higher Algebra	3p.
	Trigonometry & Higher . . . . . Algebra . . . . } . . or History . . . . } . . Geology or Physiography } . .	3p.	History.	3p.
	If yr: and Anatomy, Physiology, & Hygiene ½ yr..	3p.	Geology or Physiography ½ yr. and Anatomy, Physiology, & Hygiene ½ yr.	3p.
	. . . .	20p.	. . . .	20p.

FIGURE 8–1   Continued.

have supported even as many as nine core areas of study. Eliot's lobbying helped to secure a place for courses in the modern sciences in the curriculum, which was a breakthrough for the time.

Still, frictions with the Committee underscored a fundamental issue in the development of the school experience. Eliot had raised an interesting and important question: Should the school stand by a uniform academic curriculum that treats every student more or less the same, or should it aim to widen its offering beyond the scope of core academic subjects? That is, should the school experience be linked to the acquisition of a formalized body of knowledge, or should it look more comprehensively at student and societal needs? At the secondary school, the Committee of Ten had opted for uniformity and for focused instruction in nine academic areas.

The Committee of Ten report was widely accepted and was generally followed by American high schools for forty years (Tyler, 1988, p. 270). Historical enrollment and registration data confirm the emergent place of traditional subject matter in the school experience at the turn of the century. As reported by Kliebard (2004, pp. 223–232), by 1910 about half of the high school enrollment took classes in Latin and in algebra, while rhetoric captured about 60 percent of the enrollment. In the science, the proportion of the high school enrollment taking science classes was lower, mostly in the 20 to 25 percent range, and mostly embodied one of three classes (either in physiology, geology, or physics).

Before the dust settled from the Committee of Ten report, another NEA-sponsored committee, known as the Committee of Fifteen, offered a reconsideration of elementary education in America. Charles Eliot again emerged in the middle of the debate. Although not a member of the Committee of Fifteen, Eliot (1893) used various forums to argue that the elementary school curriculum had to be broadened and enriched with more diverse offerings. This was a matter of considerable significance to Eliot. He believed that too much time and energy were being spent on a narrow range of subjects, including hold-over subjects from the Latin grammar school, such as Latin and grammar. He also thought that it was wrong to conceive of elementary education as a single program of studies for all students, and that it was important to recognize the value of some individualization in the curriculum. Eliot wanted to integrate a new science course in the elementary school and to reduce the time devoted to traditional courses.

When the Committee of Fifteen submitted its recommendations in 1895, however, it was clear that Eliot's views had only gained partial acceptance. The report of the Committee of Fifteen (1895) supported the inclusion of some new courses, including one dedicated to "Natural Science and Hygiene." Overall, however, the report sanctioned the status quo and helped to solidify the traditionalist's grasp on the curriculum (Tanner & Tanner, 1987). Even where new courses were added, the time devoted to them, relative to the traditional subject-centered courses, was slight. The central subjects that the committee recommended for the elementary school were those that the traditionalists viewed as most worthy—grammar, literature, arithmetic, geography, and history.

The central figure in the story of the Committee of Fifteen's work was its chair and main author—William Torrey Harris, then United States Commissioner of Education. Harris had a respected background in philosophy and once held the job of superintendent of schools in St. Louis. At the turn of the century, he was emerging as one of the most outspoken and articulate proponents of the traditionalist viewpoint. Harris, in fact, had cultivated a new rationale for the subject-centered thinking that dominated the curriculum for years to come. He believed that public education had everything to do with transmitting the race experience (as in human race experience) of the nation. Further, he was convinced that this could best be accomplished by elevating the importance of five central academic areas (grammar, literature and art, mathematics, geography, and history), which he likened to the five windows of the soul. To Harris' (1888) thinking, the schools could best serve the nation by actively transmitting the high accomplishments of humanity, which were embodied in "the five windows." The windows, the argument went, gave the learner a view of all that was worthy in our culture (Cremin, 1988). Hence, it was through the windows that society became civilized and enlightened; life was in the subject matter.

Due, in part, to his high standing as Commissioner, Harris strongly influenced the deliberations of both the Committee of Ten and the Committee of Fifteen. Because of his regard for subject-centered study, Harris became an active critic of anyone who argued for the inclusion of course work (at the post-primary school level) in the natural sciences, the vocational arts, physical education, and any other "nonacademic" pursuits.

Because the traditional humanists were not averse to privileging matters pertaining to the mind over matters pertaining to the body, they left a mentalistic mark on the schooling experience—a mark that stressed a rational, abstract, bookish, and subject-centered approach to learning. Any reference to vocational education in the context of the school was interpreted negatively, as taking time and resources away from the central cause of developing the mind. William Torrey Harris, for instance, spared few words in expressing his contempt toward what he called manual training in schools, believing that, "the great power of education . . . was not gained by repeatedly performing an action, such as sawing wood or welding two pieces of iron," but from "the ability to think, reason and generalize" (Ravitch, 2000, p. 37). To Harris, these latter abilities represented a well-trained mind and were fundamentally rooted in an exposure to a certain selection of subject matter. The stakes were nothing less than the very inheritance of civilization because as indicated, Harris believed that the wisdom of the ages (the human race experience) could be best captured and conveyed to youth through five essential features of subject matter or knowledge—arithmetic, geography, history, grammar, and reading.

THE CHILD-CENTERED COUNTERREACTION

As mentioned, part of the reaction against traditionalist thinking in the schools had to do with a desire to locate the child at the center of teaching and learning formulations. Many of the early impulses on this front came from Europe. The philosophical discourses of Rousseau, the practical work supported by Robert Owens in the infant schools, and the new pedagogical theorizing offered by Pestalozzi and others all delivered messages about the importance of recognizing the life of children in schools. Educators in America tapped into these influences and launched a movement dedicated to giving learners their due consideration in the school. This commitment, however, also had the overreaching effect of glorifying learners and their innate capacities to decide what was best for their own education.

The Doctrine of Original Goodness

The major philosophical voice helping to clear the way for more expressly child-centered views in education was Jean Jacques Rousseau. His thinking was rooted in a desire to undermine the doctrine of original sin promulgated by the Calvinists and other religious groups. Children were not born sinful, proclaimed Rousseau. Quite the contrary, they were born good and innocent, and made sinful and depraved by adults and the social institutions to which adults subjected them. Rousseau was, in effect, proclaiming a doctrine of original goodness. Rousseau's thinking on these matters was likely influenced by the manner in which children were exploited in eighteenth century France, and by his own unhealthy upbringing (Rippa, 1971). It is not so much that Rousseau had trouble envisioning healthy and active interactions between children and adults. Rather, he thought that nature's original construction of children was flawless and that adults had to follow its lead and not interrupt or undermine its work with too frequent or too prescriptive interventions (Thayer, 1960). Thus, spontaneity and natural interests were very important to any education justified by Rousseau.

Throughout his works, Rousseau glorified the early or primitive savagery of humanity as a natural and good period, a time when humankind was in a state of equilibrium with nature. "Civilized" man, according to Rousseau, severed this connection and corrupted itself through its social inventions of greed and power. Because children were born as one with nature, without the contamination provided by society, Rousseau celebrated their innocence and their beauty. His message was that children, as raw products of nature, were born good, but that society corrupted them and eventually made them evil. This was a recurring theme in his work. For example, in Emile, originally published in 1762, he stated: "Everything is good as it leaves the hands of the Author of things; everything degenerates in the hands of man . . . He turns everything upside down; he disfigures everything; he loves deformity, monsters. He wants nothing as nature made it, not even man" (Rousseau, 1979, p. 37).

According to Rousseau, the pedagogical antidote to the depravity of "civilized" man was for adults to take a limited and distance role in the education of children—to regulate, if the need arose, the education of children from afar, but to always allow children to unfold and develop under their own initiative, will, and interests. It was the child, not the church and not the state, that was at the center of Rousseau's universe.

Rousseau's theorizing had a dramatic influence on the thinking and actions of a small group of school reformers in Europe, whose ideas eventually traveled across the ocean and reached America during the mid-1800s. This group, comprised, most prominently, of Johann Pestalozzi, Johann Herbart, Friedrich Froebel, and Maria Montessori, helped to set an early condition for the rise of an important branch of the American progressive education movement.

Early European Influences on Classroom Practice

In elementary education, the colonial style of rote and recitation was challenged directly by a view of teaching developed in the late seventeenth century by a European reformer named Johann Pestalozzi. Inspired by the child-centered thinking of Rousseau, Pestalozzi (1894) experimented with new forms of teaching that focused on what he believed to be the natural inclinations of children. Pestalozzi viewed learning from the standpoint of faculty psychology. Unlike the traditional humanists, however, he argued for a school experience that nurtured all of the mind's discrete faculties (emotional, intellectual, physical, and moral), which he believed could only be accomplished through experiential or sensory learning. He vested the teacher's authority in the activities of learning, rather than in external prodding, and saw motivation as emerging out of the inner instincts and desires of children. Pestalozzi could not abide the Calvinist view of child depravity, arguing instead that all children should be disciplined gently. It was these Pestalozzian principles that so impressed Horace Mann during his visit to the Prussian schools in the 1840s.

According to Pestalozzi, teaching/learning had to move way from the act of memorizing and reciting, which he likened to "empty chattering," and toward the acts of sensing, interpreting, observing, and questioning. Teaching had to engage students in language and thinking; it had to proceed along the lines of children's organic development and be planned and organized ahead of time. In this manner, Pestalozzi emancipated teachers, not only by liberating them from the dreary recitation style of instruction that bound them and their students to the text, but also by giving them a reason to consider their own ideas in the light of the learner's needs. As Power (1991) observed, an implication of Pestalozzi's work was that "teachers could no longer be regarded as mere hearers of lessons" (p. 203). This amounted to a virtual sea change in the school curriculum. Observations, investigations, discussions, individual expressions, and activity, all ignored in the early American schools, now had a legitimate place in the classroom.

Pestalozzi also stressed the role of objects in teaching. He wanted children to study real objects found in nature to cultivate their sense of observation and their overall understanding of objects in the world. Relying on his own observations of children, Pestalozzi believed that sense perception was the most important pathway to good learning for children. This, of course, was the opposite of the memorization exercises regularly witnessed in the colonial schools and the instructional reliance that such schools put on reciting from books. Pestalozzi wanted to connect the sights, sounds, and touch of learning into the development of language and thought.

Pestalozzi's perspective on learning had specific implications for the school curriculum. In the teaching of science, for instance, it led to a higher regard for nature study, observational insight, and outdoor learning (Cubberley, 1947). It also led to the inclusion of drawing, modeling, music, and general physical activities in the school. With Pestalozzi, the schools now had a way to justify a break with the instructional tradition of memorization exercises and to offer activities that encouraged expression and sense perception. Ironically, over time, Pestalozzi's object lesson lost its sensory and observational slant (Meyer, 1975; Cubberley, 1947). As stated by Thayer (1960), Pestalozzi's object teaching did indeed "open the door of the classroom to the outside world of objects and events, but, in the course of time, it also degenerated into a barren verbalism" (p. 230). Today, of course, we can still find the legacy of object teaching in classroom efforts to offer demonstration lessons and in the continuing custom of "show and tell" in early education.

Another European thinker who gained some ascendancy in the American schools during the nineteenth century was a German professor of philosophy named Johann Herbart. Herbart was highly sympathetic to the work of Pestalozzi, fundamentally agreeing with his open rejection of the rote and recitation approach to instruction, with his regard for the use of real objects in teaching, and with his belief that schooling was a process of social and moral development. Herbart, however, asked new and different questions, and approached the problem of developing an educational theory and method with novel insight.

First, Herbart shed the Pestalozzian concern for the faculties of the mind. To Herbart, it was not individuals' minds that needed to be developed, but their social character and morality, of which the mind was but a part. Thus, the purpose of the school was not to cultivate the different faculties of the mind, but to cultivate the social powers of the individual. This meant that schooling had to be more obviously social and less tied to the content of the academic traditions. Herbart maintained that school experiences had to be framed around the problems and concerns of the social environment and he contended that studies in history and literature, which were not popular at the time, were absolutely vital to the fulfillment of such a purpose.

As a result, Herbart (1901) sought to use history and literature to synthesize the subject matter in school so that it could be better linked to the social environment. He viewed the convention of organizing knowledge along strict disciplines as illogical and not attendant to the living conditions of individuals. No single subject area had a monopoly on the interests and needs of a child, and thus no single subject could be promulgated as most appropriate for all children. The solution was to find focal points of concentration or convergence among different disciplines that took on a historical focus and that conveyed a literary tradition.

These units of subject matter were known as correlations or concentrations. A concentration was simply a general topic on which the work of a whole school or grade or class could be focused for an extended period of time. American supporters of Herbart, for instance, frequently used *Robinson Crusoe* as a way to unify all inquiry in the third-grade classroom, which traditionalists derided as bad pedagogy. But to a Herbartian, such an activity had all the essential ingredients of a good education. *Robinson Crusoe*, after all, was a literary work that represented a simple level of culture, highlighting the problem of survival, and it offered multiple correlations to various subject areas.

Charles McMurray, an American proponent of Herbart, reported on a way that the elementary school could use basic historical topics as correlations in the curriculum. In the fifth grade, for instance, McMurray identified the story of John Smith, the founder of Jamestown, as the synthesizing correlation. For planning purposes, the correlation could be seen as carrying a geography component that might highlight the study of Chesapeake Bay (its climate, its main crops, and natural resources), a science component that might focus on the flora and fauna of Virginia, a mathematics ingredient that might offer mathematical queries into the production, marketing, and consumption of vital crops in Virginia, and a language component that might focus on the adventure of Smith's life (McMurray, 1946). Butts (1955) believed that the Herbartian effort to bring a sense of convergence to literature, history, and the social environment helped to develop the role of social studies in the school curriculum.

Herbart was, in effect, the first to argue for a more integrated and interdisciplinary curriculum. Such a belief was anathema at the time, given the the dominance of the traditional humanists' views in the curriculum. In fact, when Herbart's ideas began to attract a following in the United States, they were vigorously attacked by William Torrey Harris, who as the defender of the liberal arts tradition in the schools, felt that more integrated schemes contemplated by the Herbartians could not effectively transmit American culture. The correlations advanced by the Herbartians eviscerated Harris' five windows of the soul. Obviously, this was no small problem to Harris, who thought that Herbart's views threatened the school's capacity to bestow children with the cultural treasures of the past, with the very tools that Harris believed children needed to understand themselves and their society. Harris was not shy about expressing his disdain for Herbartian thinking, referring at one point to the integrated use of Robinson Crusoe in the curriculum, as "shallow and uninteresting" (Krug, 1964, p. 103).

Out of Herbart's work also arose an unusual theory of teaching that equated the maturational development of the individual with the evolutionary stages of human culture. Known as the cultural-epoch theory, this idea implied that the proper instruction of children had to be connected with a period of development in the human race that loosely corresponded with their age. Hence, the youngest school children might be given activities dealing with primitive life and with the hunting and gathering period of human history. Slightly older children (grades 2 and 3) might engage in activities related to early agricultural life and early civilization. Children in the later elementary grades might engage in activities rooted in the medieval period, the early explorers and settlers, and so on, until the industrial age was reached. Thayer (1960) described these stages of human evolution as: 1) prehistoric, 2) patriarchal, 3) tribal, 4) feudal with absolute monarchy, 5) revolutionary, with constitutional monarchy, and 6) republican or self-governing. The corresponding stages in the development of the learner were: 1) infancy, 2) childhood, 3) preadolescence, 4) early adolescence, 5) middle adolescence, and 6) late adolescence (pp. 234–235). Followers of Herbart saw a wonderful sense of unity between the individual and the race experience in cultural epochs theory. To them, the theory contained the vast character building potential of historical study, and the actual cultural epochs provided focal points for a more unified arrangement of the subject matter in the curriculum.

Herbart also spoke directly to the issue of teaching methodology. Like Pestalozzi, he did not want to resort to external devices to inspire motivation; he wanted it to emerge out of the conditions of learning. Using principles taken from Pestalozzi, Herbart developed a method of instruction based on the notion that all learning is a process of assimilating knowledge of what one already knows, of connecting new knowledge to existing conditions, and existing understandings. According to Herbart, if such a connection were properly made, the learner would be in an ideal learning situation; his or her interests would be aroused, and his or her mind would be prepared to absorb the new material.

Herbart tried to formalize this process into five steps (Butts, 1955). First, (1) the teacher had to make formal preparations by recalling or otherwise stimulating prior ideas and experiences in the child (to which the new material can be related). Following the step of preparation, (2) the teacher presented all of the new material to the student, which was then followed by (3) an effort to build associations (through comparisons and contrasts) between the old and the new. The final two steps called for the teacher (4) to draw generalizations from the individual cases discussed in class, and (5) to find examples and practical situations highlighting the generalizations. This method lent some sense of standardization to instruction, and dominated the training given in the American normal schools in the 1890s. In fact, American Herbartianism made its greatest inroads in American education via the normal school. During the late nineteenth century, several Americans traveled to Prussia, where they studied with the disciples of Herbart at the University of Jena. This group included Charles DeGarmo, Charles McMurray, and his younger brother Frank. DeGarmo and the McMurray brothers went on to popularize Herbart through their own writings, which focused on teaching methods that could be used in normal schools. The steps of instruction in the Herbartian method and the idea of curriculum concentration gave young teachers a ready handle on what to do in the classroom.

Whereas Pestalozzi influenced instruction at the elementary school level and Herbart at the secondary school level, two more important European figures emerged to influence instruction at the primary school level: Friedrich Froebel and Maria Montessori. Froebel's interest in education was also piqued by the work of Pestalozzi. He visited his schools in Switzerland and was impressed with the value Pestalozzi placed on play and on "nonacademic" pursuits, such as art and music. Froebel, however, formulated his own views on schooling by merging the sense perceptions fundamental to Pestalozzi with a philosophy of romantic idealism.

Through idealism, Froebel (1887) saw his work, in kinship with the spirit of God, as drawing out the innate gifts given to children by God—gifts that allowed children to closely identify with the divine spirit. Froebel felt that his instructional efforts awakened the inner strengths of children, which in turn, allowed them to find an essence of unity under the service of the divine. Liberating children's "gifts" and encouraging their spontaneous and natural curiosity was the way that teachers took children down the path toward perfect unity (Butts, 1955). This was Froebel's way of facilitating the work of God. "Education," he observed, "consists in leading man, as a thinking, intelligent being, growing into self-consciousness, to a pure and unsullied, conscious and free representation of the inner law of Divine Unity and in teaching him ways and means thereto" (1887, p. 2).

Froebel opened his own school for very young children in 1840, in which singing, drawing, painting, coloring, dancing, dramatics, and self-selected activity were all encouraged. He called the school Kindergarten, which means a garden where children grew. Froebel advanced beyond Pestalozzi in several ways. Froebel, for instance, awakened the spirit of "learning by doing," the physical/motor side of learning, and the ideal of directing the desires of children in socially satisfying ways. He was not preoccupied with the faculties of the mind, nor with the Herbartian idea of finding unity between the child and cultural history. What he wanted most was for children to find themselves through play, and he envisaged growth as a social concept, as part of the quest to find the whole. The next chapter will detail some of the main programmatic characteristics of the Froebelian kindergarten.

Under Froebel's influence, children gained new authority and respect in the school experience. The child, after all, was anointed with the inner spirit of God, and play, liberated from the exigencies of survival, represented a high spiritual form. Education, then, could not revert to prescriptive or coercive measures; it had to engage the student in a facilitative role that enlivened the inner spirits of play and self-activity. Moreover, the child itself, a kind of replica of God, was to be revered and his inner spirit cherished as the main pathway toward growth and understanding.

Over time, the metaphysical justifications Froebel used to sanction his kindergarten had to give way to different criteria. Curriculum planning could not revolve around a mystical explanation about how the child's consciousness was part and parcel of the Divine spirit. As a result, Froebel could only advance the curriculum so far. The legacy of Froebel, however, can still be appreciated in the design and function of the kindergarten today, where children, by and large, are still allowed to play, where social activities are viewed as educative and where the embrace of the child, especially relative to the upper grades, continues to be warm and protective.

Maria Montessori worked along the same lines as Froebel, but she brought a different level of analysis to the problem of teaching children. Trained in the field of engineering, medicine, anthropology, and experimental psychology, Montessori had a comprehensive lens with which to view the problem of educating children. She started her work in education in 1898 by focusing on the education of "idiot children" housed in the insane asylums of Italy. After spending two years preparing methods of instruction for these children, she discovered that many of their problems were environmental, not biological, in nature. The children, in other words, were in many cases victimized by poor environmental experiences; they were deprived of the early stimuli needed to develop into intellectually and emotionally healthy individuals. Montessori validated her thesis by teaching these "deviants" to read and write, and to compete successfully with so-called normal children. Montessori's success with these children, which to outside observers bordered on the miraculous, inspired her to move forward with formulations on early education for all children (Rippa, 1971).

After years of advanced study in experimental psychology, Montessori opened a preschool in 1907 for the education of children living among the slum tenements of San Lorenzo, a poverty-stricken section of Rome. She noted how these poor children, like the feeble-minded children in the asylums, were at a considerable disadvantage because they were not benefiting from any of the basic early childhood experiences that were preparatory to later success and health.

In her school, which was called "Casa dei Bambini" (The Children's House), Montessori set out to help correct the early environmental problems of the poor. She formulated a pedagogical model that worked off of Pestalozzi's idea of sense impression, which aimed at fostering the growth of intelligence through the senses. She developed quite a few original games and tasks that highlighted the sense experience. These activities came with certain "didactic apparatus"—blocks, cylinders, and other manipulatives that children could select at their discretion. The didactic materials represented a form of sensory gymnastics to Montessori. Children could engage in their use freely, which meant that individual youngsters could occupy themselves by selecting into and out of various tasks associated with the materials. Thus, a new level of individualization was recognized in the Montessorian classroom. Montessori also designed and developed children's furniture for the classroom in order to encourage real social interactions among the children, which included social events such as preparing lunch and cleaning up afterward. She asked teachers to be cognizant of the particularities of each child and to encourage free choice among the children.

Montessori's work made it clear that early education was fundamental to the sound development of humans. She countered the argument for biological determinism by showing what a good early educational environment can do. Historically, her work has been criticized for being too programmatic and for relying too much on the didactic apparatus, which tended to be reducible to the completion of predesigned tasks. She was also criticized for not reflecting social needs and collective group actions in her teaching. The individual was always the central variable to Montessori and the importance of the group project and social intercourse were not stressed by her. To this day, Montessori's ideas are still vital in early education programs throughout the nation. The idea of providing youth with early sensory experiences as an investment in later development has stayed vital, long after Montessori's death.

AMERICAN CHILD CENTEREDNESS

As indicated, the Americans showed considerable interest in some of the more progressive educational ideas being tested in Europe. As applications of these new ideas were attempted on American soil, European thinkers like Pestalozzi and Herbart began to enjoy professional recognition among American educators. This gave learners a new priority in the American schools and set the conditions for uniquely American innovations based on learners' interests.

The Americanization of Johann Pestalozzi

The Americanization of Pestalozzi was largely realized in the operation of the early normal schools. As indicated, the proliferation of elementary schools put a great deal of emphasis on the education of elementary school teachers during the mid-1800s. Education in the subject matter was an uncomplicated affair in the normal schools, but education in pedagogies was something that could proceed down any number of philosophical avenues. The ideas of Pestalozzi, and later of Herbart, found a warm welcome in the American normal schools because they were framed with the teacher in mind. Finding new ways to teach, grounded in a new way of running the school, was the central effect of the ideas. For Pestalozzi, other signal events in the dissemination of his ideas in America included the endorsements he received from Horace Mann in his efforts to reform the Massachusetts common schools and from various disciples working in private schools throughout America.

In 1861, a teacher training school opened in upstate New York that openly claimed to apply the teachings of Pestalozzi. Led by E. A. Sheldon, the Oswego (New York) Normal School quickly became the main American preparation center for teachers interested in Pestalozzian methods. Sheldon had established a local reputation in Oswego as a distinguished educator, founding a school there in 1848 for poor and neglected children and rising to the position of superintendent of the Syracuse schools in 1851. In 1853, he returned to Oswego as its superintendent of schools. He first encountered Pestalozzi's ideas not in Europe, but in Canada, where he was visiting some schools in 1859. There, he purchased a set of materials produced by the Home and Colonial Training Institution in London, a group that openly promoted Pestalozzian principles in the education of children in England (Barlow, 1977, p. 94). Sheldon contacted the institution and arranged to have an instructor, Margaret E. M. Jones, travel to Oswego to begin training teachers. This eventually led to the opening of the Oswego Normal School.

The teaching at the school proceeded along classic Pestalozzian lines, with students taught the following principles:

> 1) Begin with the senses; 2) Never tell a child what he can discover for himself; 3) Activity is a law of childhood. Train a child not merely to listen, but to do. Educate the hand; 4) Love of variety is a law of childhood—change is rest; 5) Cultivate the faculties in their natural order. First form the mind, then furnish it; 6) Reduce every subject to its elements, and present one difficulty at a time; 7) Proceed step by step. Be thorough. The measure of information is not what you give, but what the child can receive; 8) Let every lesson have a definite point; 9) Proceed from the simple to the difficult, i.e., from the known to the unknown, from the particular to the general, from the concrete to the abstract; 10) Synthesis before analysis—not the order of the subject, but the order of nature. (Barlow, 1977, p. 96)

As Oswego's graduates went far and wide, so did Oswego's reputation. The Oswego school graduated and sent teachers to classrooms across America with the expectation that they would use teaching methods that represented a clear departure from the widespread memorization and mentalistic techniques used in the schools. As Cubberley (1947) observed, "What Pestalozzi tried most of all to do was to get children to use their senses and their minds, to look carefully, to count, to observe forms, to get, by means of their five senses, clear impressions and ideas as to objects and life in the world about them and then to think over what they had seen and be able to answer his questions because they had observed carefully and reasoned clearly" (p. 390). This was a long way from the mental school tradition of colonial America.

The Child Study Movement

The emerging recognition of the child in school deliberations was also advanced by a burgeoning child study movement in America. The movement was especially vital during the 1890s and 1900s, steered by the able hand of G. Stanley Hall, an American psychologist who brought credibility to the task of child study by making it accountable to modern scientific methods. The purpose behind the child study movement was to examine the nature of the child in ways that might inform the practical judgments of the school teacher. Hall, for instance, conducted studies on the muscle use of children in school and concluded that very young children needed to have opportunities for large muscle development, a finding that had very clear and practical use in the school (Tanner & Tanner, 1987). He even went as far as developing a systematic survey of what primary school children knew about common animals, insects, plants, and other phenomena, which he wrote up in an essay titled, "The Contents of Children's Minds" (Hall, 1883). This was the style of the child study movement—to find insight about children that might lead to better teaching. Even teachers got into the act by beginning to study children for the purpose of improving their practice, by questioning them, keeping observational notes on them, and checking their vision and hearing.

Hall's influence in education, however, transcended his work in the child study movement. As Harvard's first doctoral graduate in psychology, Hall had the credentials and the intellectual prowess to speak directly to a newly developing theory of instruction, one that accounted for the natural development of the child. At the turn of the twentieth century, he was indeed emerging as one of the new titans in education, as one who spoke for the causes of children in education from the stage of science (Cremin, 1961). In this way, Hall represented a position that was diametrically opposed to the work of William Torrey Harris, the great defender of the centrality of the liberal arts in the curriculum.

Hall, in fact, made quite a spirited criticism of the Committee of Ten report through which he helped to frame an important counterposition to the traditional liberal arts argument (Kliebard, 2004). The

Committee of Ten report, he stated, was faulty in fundamental ways. First, Hall observed that the report failed to understand the importance of individual differences among students by trying to adjust them uniformly to preexisting subject categories. Second, he simply did not see or appreciate the so-called transferable life skills that were supposedly being affected in the kind of studies supported in the report. Hall was no mental disciplinarian, and he did not accept the view that certain subjects had mind training powers that were transferable as life skills.

Clearly, Hall wanted to scuttle the traditionalist version of learning that treated children as passive receptors in need of having their heads filled with disciplinary knowledge. In its place he wanted to see a curriculum that showed some responsiveness to the individual, a desire that inevitably led to the idea of curriculum differentiation or individualization in the school experience. Hall (1901) argued that the curriculum had to be differentiated so that each individual could be given the chance to grow and unfold according to his or her own potential.

Hall's commitment to individualizing the curriculum was justified paradoxically by a Social Darwinian view of the world, where heredity, not the environment, was the ruling law. To Hall, the school curriculum had to be determined by student needs, but because he believed these needs were native, the school had to encourage, through curriculum differentiation, the development of the most gifted students ("the best blood"). This also meant that all "nongifted" could be treated in a more simple manner—all in the name of the learner. To know children, then, was to appreciate their native endowments, something that Hall believed would become obvious to teachers as they allowed their students to develop freely. In this way, Hall helped to tow the Rousseauian line about the virtues of a laissez-faire education, as he encouraged teachers and parents to stay out of nature's way and to act only as guardians of the child's health and natural endowments (Cremin, 1988). Ironically, such an attitude contradicted the very role and purpose of child development, which would presumably encourage teachers not to leave students alone but to take an interventionist role attuned to their developmental nature. This, however, was not a contradiction from Hall's standpoint. Because child study pointed to certain development patterns in all learners, Hall argued that such patterns might help teachers foster certain learnings for children, but that ultimately it was the child's unique endowments that would determine his or her progress. Teachers could facilitate the growth of the child, but without native endowments, certain potentials could not be realized. Growth was largely preordained.

By examining the process of development among children, Hall also became a proponent of the culture epochs theory supported by American Herbartians. The theory, to recall, was tied to the notion that the development of the individual recapitulates the course of human history (from pre-savagery to civilization). The more sophisticated way of putting this is to say that ontogeny (the development of the individual) recapitulates phylogeny (the evolution of the race). To Hall, the natural development of children went through the various stages of race experience. Making the connection between the two was essential to good instruction. Such ties helped the student along an already predetermined path. Cultural epochs theory also helped to justify the indulgent treatment they received at the hands of teachers working with Hall's ideas. As young children recapitulated the experiences of the human race, they could not be asked, in any way, to meet adult standards of punishment and adult prohibitions; they had to be treated at their level of race development (Cremin, 1988).

Although culture epochs theory had its share of problems, it still represented a breakthrough in the curriculum that favored the child. The content of the curriculum could now be argued to be with and in the child (part of his natural development), and not in the liberal arts. Furthermore, the right of education, which was long seen as a luxury or privilege, was now naturally embedded in the child (Cremin, 1961).

The Progressive Criticism of Child Centeredness

All in all, proponents of the child-centered approach had done a fairly successful job of securing the place of the child in the curriculum equation. The problem was that, too often, the thinking started and stopped with the child. A good share of the school community embraced romantic naturalist reasoning, as many of the private and university schools of the 1920s highlighted a curriculum that encouraged children to follow their momentary interests and wishes. Many of these progressive schools concentrated on the education of young children. In 1928, Rugg and Schumaker published a book that appraised the first quarter century of child-centered education in the schools, showing how teacher initiatives were frequently supplanted by a desire to reflect children's interests in the school. Others critics, including John Dewey, eventually offered more strident criticism of the child-centered perspective.

The notion of child-centeredness, as expressed in its most Rousseauian form, would eventually be sullied by both traditional and progressive critics. John Dewey, for instance, could not fathom how any form of education can deny children the wisdom and maturity of experience offered to them by adults, especially ones professionally trained to deal with children. He was usually a gentle critic, but in this case, Dewey (1929) was strong-worded in condemning child-centeredness.

> There is a present tendency in so-called advanced schools of educational thought to say, in effect, let us surround pupils with certain materials, tools, appliances, etc. and let pupils respond to these things according to their own desires. Above all let us not suggest any end or plan to students; let us not suggest to them what they shall do, for that is an unwarranted trespass upon their sacred individuality since the essence of such individuality is to set up ends and aims. Now such a method is really stupid. For it attempts the impossible, which is always stupid; and it misconceived the conditions of independent thinking. (p. 153)

Dewey believed in the need to reflect the nature of the learner in school decisions, but he also believed that the learner, as an immature organism, could not be effectively socialized into the canons and the learnings of the social group (the culture) without the active intervention of adults. Boyd Bode, who was among the most penetrating progressive critics of his time, sided with Dewey in assailing the thinking of those who opted for child-centeredness and in worrying about the negative effects that such a view might have on the progressive movement.

> The failure to emancipate ourselves completely from Rousseauism . . . is responsible for most, if not all, of the weaknesses of the progressive movement in education . . . The insistence that we must stick uncompromisingly at all times to the 'needs' of childhood has bred a spirit of anti-intellectualism, which is reflected in the reliance on improvising instead of long-range organization, in the overemphasis of the here and now, in the indiscriminate tirades against 'subjects' [and] in the absurdities of pupil planning. (Bode, 1938, p. 70)

Dewey and Bode were at the forefront of a very different version of progressivism, one that honored the child but that also brought other fundamental variables to the act of teaching and learning. In the eyes of Dewey and other like-minded progressives, child development could not be contemplated without thinking about the child in the context of the society. They believed that it was ridiculous to think about the child in terms that were independent of the society or of the skills, attitudes, and knowledge one needed to be successful in society. This new attitude pervaded the progressivism explained in the next chapter.

SUMMARY

The early struggle to influence the course of the American school experience was won by the traditional humanists, whose views represented an extension of the old colonial idea of mental learning in the context of selected subject areas. The Committee of Ten and Committee of Fifteen reports made it clear that the first pattern of course work to be established in a more universalized version of public schooling would be subject-centered. But there were changes in the air, blowing mostly from the continent of Europe.

The European notion of child-centeredness began to take hold in America in the 1860s and left an indelible impression on the American school scene. Because of it, normal schools found real opportunities to teach teachers about children, rather than simply subject matter. The recalculation of the curriculum with the child in mind also gave way to new visions of subject matter organization, such as the Herbartian notion of concentration, and also set the conditions for the study of the learner as an important component in the teaching/learning process. Some of these elements helped to form the pillars of the progressive education movement.

At the same time, child-centeredness ran the risk of reaching too far in the direction of the child, creating schools openly dedicated to the romantic/naturalist view of learning. In this sense, child-centered thinking represented a classic counterreaction to the traditionalism that dominated the schools at the end of the nineteenth century. The traditional school, long a bastion of order and control, had deliberately squelched student expression and initiative, and showed little regard for the interests and welfare of learners. Child-centeredness found its way as a palliating force against traditional extremes. But by casting its floodlights on the child, the child-centered school created its own counterextreme. Thus, much of the early twentieth-century debate over the school curriculum was waged between subject-centered (traditionalist) views and child-centered views. This was an inadequate framing of the curriculum problem because it posed the curriculum in dual terms—as either subject-centered or child-centered. As we will see in the next chapter, another progressive group demanded that both factors (the learner and the subject matter) be integrated with yet another important factor (the society).

REFERENCES

Barlow, T. A. (1977). *Pestalozzi and American education.* Boulder, CO: Este Press.

Bode, B. H. (1938). *Progressive education at the crossroads.* New York: Newson and Co.

Butts, R. F. (1955). *A cultural history of western education: Its social and intellectual foundations.* New York: McGraw-Hill.

Committee of Fifteen. (1895). *Report of the Committee of Fifteen.* New York: Arno Press [1969].

Committee of Ten. (1893). "Report of the Committee of Ten on secondary school studies." In D. H. Calhoun. (1969). *Education of Americans: A documentary history.* New York: Houghton-Mifflin.

Cremin, L. A. (1961). *The transformation of the school.* New York: Alfred A. Knopf.

Cremin, L. A. (1988). *American education: The metropolitan experience.* New York: Harper and Row.

Cubberley, E. (1947). *Public education in the United States.* New York: Houghton-Mifflin.

Dewey, J. (1902). *The child and the curriculum.* Chicago: University of Chicago Press.

Dewey, J. (1929). Individuality and experience. In J. Dewey, *Art and education.* Merion, PA: The Barnes Foundation Press.

Eliot, C. (1893). Can school programs be shortened and enriched? *National Education Association Proceedings.* Washington, DC: The Association.

Froebel, F. (1887). *The education of man.* New York: Appleton [translated from German and originally published in 1826].

Hall, G. S. (1883). The contents of children's minds. In D. Calhoun, (1969) *Educating of Americans: A documentary history.* New York: Houghton-Mifflin.

Hall, G. S. (1901). The ideal school as based on child study. In D. Calhoun, (1969) *Educating of Americans: A documentary history.* New York: Houghton-Mifflin.

Harris, W. T. (1888). What shall the public schools teach? *The Forum,* 4:573–81.

Herbart, J. F. (1901). *Outlines of educational doctrine.* New York: Macmillan.

Kliebard, H. (2004). *The struggle for the American curriculum,* 3rd edition. New York: Routledge Kegan.

Krug, E. A. (1964). *The shaping of the American high school.* New York: Harpers and Row.

McMurray, D. (1946). *Herbartian contributions to history instruction in American elementary schools.* New York: Bureau of Publications, Teachers College, Columbia University.

Meyer, A. E. (1975). *Grandmasters of educational thought.* New York: McGraw-Hill.

Pestalozzi, J. H. (1894). *How Gertrude teaches her children.* Syracuse: C. W. Bardeen.

Power, E. J. (1991). *A legacy of learning.* Albany, NY: SUNY Press.

Ravitch, D. (2000). *Left back.* New York: Simon and Schuster.

Rippa, A. (1971). *Education in a free society: An American history.* New York: David McKay Co.

Rousseau, J. J. (1979). *Emile.* New York: Basic Books [translated from French and originally published in 1762].

Rugg, H., & Schumaker, A. (1928). *The child-centered school.* New York: Arno Press and the *New York Times,* (1969).

Tanner, D., & Tanner, L. N. (1987). *The history of the school curriculum.* New York: Macmillan.

Thayer, V. T. (1960). *The role of the school in American society.* New York: Dodd, Mead and Co.

Tyler, Ralph. (1988). Progress in dealing with curriculum problems. In L. Tanner, ed. *Critical issues in curriculum: The 88th yearbook of the national society for the study of education.* Chicago: University of Chicago Press.

KEY QUESTIONS

1. What was the doctrine of mental discipline, and how did it help to give rise to a subject-centered view of learning?
2. What was the central recommendation of the Committee of Ten report and how did such a recommendation influence the character of high school education?
3. In what ways did Charles Eliot, the Chairman of the Committee of Ten report, differ with the Committee's recommendations?
4. Describe the fundamental differences between the way that William Harris and Charles Eliot conceived of the school curriculum.
5. Both Pestalozzi and mental disciplinarians used faculty psychology to justify their school actions. Explain how this could be so.
6. What was the central message that Pestalozzi wanted to send to the school?
7. Why were supporters of Herbart turning toward thematic treatments in the curriculum, using, as described, the novel *Robinson Crusoe* as a way to unify all studies in the third grade classroom?
8. Describe how the Herbartian idea of correlations might be used in an elementary school?
9. Why was William Harris utterly distressed at what the Herbartians were advocating in the curriculum?
10. Describe culture epochs theory and explain why many Herbartians were attracted to the idea.
11. Explain how Froebel believed that he was facilitating the work of God through the way that he was educating small children.
12. How did Maria Montessori's work with "feeble-minded" children lead her toward early childhood instruction?
13. In what ways was Maria Montessori's work in early childhood education criticized?
14. How did the philosophical work of Jean Jacque Rousseau contribute to the child-centered movement in education?
15. Explain the significance of G. Stanley Hall in the development of the child-centered movement in education.
16. In what ways did Hall's Social Darwinism arguably contradict his work in the area of child development?
17. What was the essential argument that Dewey and some other progressives made against child-centered thinking?
18. In what ways was the child-centered movement a counteraction to the traditionalist curriculum?

RESEARCH EXERCISES

1. Read the Committee of Ten report and imagine its application in the American high school today. What in the report might be viewed as anachronistic? What might be viewed as still relevant?
2. Find contemporary advocates or supporters for the teaching of Latin in the schools today. Evaluate their rationale for teaching Latin against its historical association with the doctrine of mental disciple.
3. Research the applications of Pestalozzi's idea on object teaching. What were the actual lessons like? Evaluate the lessons against today's standards of instruction.
4. How did Marie Montessori's work eventually find such widespread popularity in the American preschool tradition? What were the sources of her popularity?
5. Read Steven Selden's *Inheriting Shame: The Story of Eugenics and Racism in America*, 1999 (New York: Teachers College Press) and report on the role that Social Darwinism played in the eugenics movement in the United States.
6. Read Rugg and Shumaker's well-known "The Child Centered School" and report on what they found in the various child-centered schools they visited.
7. Research and report on the curriculum used to teach teachers in the Oswego Normal School during the late nineteenth century.
8. Research and report on an example of a Herbartian correlation design for the elementary school curriculum.
9. Read G. Stanley Hall's *The Contents of Children's Minds* and examine how it comports with the ideals of the child study movement.
10. Research Dewey's views on the works of Froebel, Rousseau, and/or Montessori. What did he have to say about each of these child-centered reformers?

CHAPTER 9

Defining the School Experience into the Twentieth Century

While much of the early debate between progressives and traditionalists was mired in a contest between child-centered versus subject-centered views, some progressive thinkers tried to get outside of the dispute. Believing that school reform could not be reduced to a dualism between child-centered and subject-centered thinking, these progressives wanted the school to also see itself in relation to the values and aims of society—to, in effect, consider its role in building a good society. Of course, this was always an implicit concern, as both child-centered and subject-centered advocates felt that their own brand of education would yield well-educated individuals who could contribute to a better society. Yet the new progressive focus aimed to make it an explicitly formulated concern, directly attached to a social democratic theory, and to the use of the school as a tool for social reform. Thus, the struggle over the school curriculum became part of a broader struggle over how the school would factor into the causes of social progress. Varieties of progressives had different ideas on how to develop the school along these lines.

PROGRESSIVISM AND THE CAUSE OF SOCIAL REFORM

Led by the work of John Dewey, a new group of progressives aimed to temper the conception of the child in the development of the school curriculum with a vision of schooling that proposed to improve social conditions, advance democratic principles, and develop common democratic communities. The child-centered movement focused on individualistic pursuits of self-expression, self-meaning, and self-development. By contrast, the progressivism of Dewey emphasized the importance of developing social insight and community consciousness. Dewey conceived of schooling as a miniature unit of democracy, immature in its development, but nevertheless consciously conceived to produce a comprehensive and enlarging social experience, where children learned about their differences and their commonalities, where vocational pursuits coexisted with academic ones, and where the ideals of tolerance and social mutuality commingled with critical mindedness.

Dewey and the Educative Process

Philosophers build their reputations by writing on a conventional set of topics. Most continental philosophers have produced substantive work on logic, ethics, religion, politics, and aesthetics. Few, however, exercised their analytical acumen on the topic of schooling. John Dewey, of course, was the exception to the rule. The idea of schooling had a profound connection to Dewey's wider philosophical universe, largely because it was an essential piece to his concept of democracy. The seriousness of this matter is underscored by the fact that Dewey directed his own laboratory school at the University of Chicago, a rare activity for a philosopher indeed!

In 1902, based on his work in his laboratory school, Dewey put forth what he believed to be the main factors in the learning process. "The fundamental factors in the educative process," he declared, "are the immature undeveloped being; and the certain social aims, meanings and values incarnate to the matured experience of the adult" (Dewey, 1902, p. 4). He continued along this line of thinking by also linking subject matter to the interactive consideration of the learner and the society, leaving school reformers with a useful framework. Because of Dewey, professional educators had a way to begin to define good teaching. At a minimum, good teaching meant that some thought had to be given to 1) the nature of learners (their interests, problems, developmental nature), 2) the values of the society (democratic principles of cooperation, tolerance, critical mindedness, and political awareness), and 3) the representation of the subject matter as it interacts with the nature of learners and the values of society. Such factors were not discrete entities, but worked together as interrelated and complementary elements. Thus, the needs of learners living in a democracy had to be considered. Similarly, the choice of subject matter in the curriculum had to be based on what was most worth knowing for someone living in a democracy.

Lester Ward and the Founding Progressive Principle of Environmentalism

Dewey was not alone in his effort to create a new form of education openly devoted to the idea of using the school for social democratic purposes. Other scholars were advocating the very same idea, the most notable being Lester Ward.

Ward was trained as a geologist, but he used his analytical talents to test the prevailing social doctrines of the day. His most important work, a two-volume book entitled *Dynamic Sociology*, took direct aim at the assumptions of social Darwinism, which presumed that a "survival of the fittest" attitude was the best policy in the schools and in society. Even G. Stanley Hall, the champion of the child study movement, had bowed to social Darwinism, believing that children were genetically wired for success. Ward, however, had come to quite a different conclusion. He believed that environmental factors were at the forefront of an individual's chance to succeed in life, and that the uneven distribution of wealth and all of its concomitant inequalities (access to knowledge, to nutrition, to the fulfillment of material needs) ensured the continued poverty of underclass citizens. Intelligence, to Ward, was evenly distributed across social, economic, and gender lines. The trick was to develop a system of education that distributed equal qualities of experience. There was no lack of intelligence among poor people or among women; there was only the lack of opportunity (Tanner & Tanner, 1987).

To Ward, the quality of the learning experience was the precondition for securing the opportunity to learn, and ultimately, to improve oneself. There could be no learning without a systematic opportunity to learn. And this could not occur by happenstance. Dewey (1916), whose work followed in the intellectual tradition of Ward, understood this very well, referring to the school environment as a "purified medium of action"—a place that deliberately eliminated, as much as possible, the unworthy (miseducative) features to the environment, that simplified the environment in the interests of advancing various important effects and that broadened the living experience in the school. According to Dewey this required, in part, that schoolchildren learn together in one unified setting, in a common universe of knowledge and problems, where equal opportunities could be assured and where common bonds of understanding could be formed.

Ward, not surprisingly, also put his faith in the public school, believing that it was the most important function of government—the main engine for social correction and social improvement. Through the school, he wanted to lay to rest the idea of biological inheritance in intelligence, and to operationalize the idea that healthy environmental interventions were the key to improving the lives of people. He was also not shy about encouraging government intervention to help close the chasm of inequity in people's lives, a view that led some to describe him as "the prophet of the welfare state" (Kliebard, 2004). While Ward underscored the sociological need for schools to lend themselves to social progress and social change, Dewey put the flesh on the bones, as it were, by specifying how schools should conduct themselves based on these priorities. Ward helped to cripple the inherent laissez-faire attitude of social Darwinism and provided the main rationale and conceptual foundation for a method of schooling that looked to prepare a rising generation for social insight and social gain.

PROGRESSIVE IDEAS IN ACTION

The progressive education movement in America was partly a protest movement. The movement, after all, originated from an effort to reconcile the untenable dualism that prevailed between subject-centered and child-centered views. The progressive education movement also had a full supply of practical proposals. For instance, progressives had their say in the practical struggle to build a new public school system for emancipated blacks and in the cause of extending the reach of schooling in poor communities. A new progressive way of looking at subject matter brought reforms to the high school curriculum and new ideas on how to teach kindergarten. The school, in fact, would change in all kinds of ways because of the hands-on work of the progressives.

Booker T. Washington, W. E. B. Du Bois, and the Black American Struggle for Schooling

Although four million black Americans gained their constitutional freedom following the Civil War, they did not gain freedom from private discrimination nor obtain much in the way of social or economic stability. Largely destitute, they had to find their way to a new life with limited assistance. One important legislative mechanism that existed, however, was the Bureau of Refugees, Freedmen and Abandoned Lands, or simply the Freedmen Bureau. The agency operated from 1865 until 1872, carrying out a comprehensive mandate to help resettle blacks. Its work addressed a variety of concerns, but among its more successful endeavors was the building and operation of public schools for black children. Under the leadership of General O. O. Howard, the Freedmen Bureau combined moneys collected from various private aid agencies and benevolent societies and applied them to the development of a schooling infrastructure for black American children. This included the purchase of buildings and curriculum materials and the hiring of teachers for the schools. The Bureau had no appropriations from Congress during its first several years of existence. Instead, it relied on the benevolence of northern aid societies and O. O. Howard's creative way of extracting rent money from abandoned lands given to the Bureau (Harlan, 1988).

Money, however, was not the main obstacle standing in the way of the movement to bring schooling to the children of former slaves. Aggressive white racism in several southern states resulted in threatened and real violence directed at blacks and at their school personnel and facilities. The "problem of the color line" was just beginning to take form. Jim Crow laws prevailed, and overt racism in the private management of restaurants, hotels, trains, and theaters, which were not illegal under the provisions of the Fourteenth Amendment, oppressed blacks. In the South, "separate but equal" became the dominant social doctrine of the time, eventually receiving the sanction of law under the *Plessy v. Ferguson* Supreme Court ruling in 1896.

Booker T. Washington was likely the most important African American figure to influence the education of blacks during this turbulent historical period. Because of his inclination to accommodate to racism, Washington became a controversial figure in black struggle to achieve freedom and equal opportunity.

Born in 1856, Washington was the child of a white father and a black mother. His mother's duties as a slave cook placed her and her child in relatively close proximity with the master class. As a result, Washington's early socialization was marked by frequent and immediate interactions in the home and with the family of the slave master. Historians speculate that this gave Washington an early orientation in the skills of accommodation and compromise (Harlan, 1988). His mother subsequently married Washington Ferguson, a black slave on a neighboring farm, and in 1865, the family was given its freedom and found wage-earning work in a mining town in West Virginia. Here Washington experienced the hardships of laboring in the mines, but because of the efforts of the local black Baptist church, he also experienced his first lessons in reading and writing. He, however, did not stay with his family very long. At about the age of 10 or 11, he took a job as the servant in the home of a well-to-do general in town. Again Washington found himself in the close company of paternalistic racists. The general's wife, who was from New England, was a strict disciplinarian who was scrupulous about cleanliness and order. Living in the house allowed Washington to personalize some of these same values, but access to books in the home also gave him the opportunity to further his own education (Harlan, 1988).

Washington eventually made his way to the Hampton Normal and Industrial Institute, where he came under the influence of General Samuel Armstrong, the founder of the Hampton Institute. Armstrong, who had a missionary background and who was a commander of black troops in the Civil War, was committed to providing an industrial education for blacks and Native Americans. His focus on industrial education was moved by a mixture of racism and well-meaning concern for the livelihood of southern blacks. At one level, by saying that blacks (and Native Americans) could best advance themselves by getting trained in a set of industrial skills, Armstrong was implying such groups were incapable of performing in higher education (in the true collegiate tradition) and in the professional class jobs that awaited its graduates. Armstrong, however, tried to portray the idea of industrial education for black Americans as a dignified pursuit and as a reasonable first step to assist blacks in the post-slavery transition period. He tried to convince business interests that blacks educated through the industrial model could become an important force in the economy, which, in the end, could also contribute to their assimilation. Moreover, to Armstrong, industrial education carried the collateral effect of teaching blacks the attitudes and morals of industriousness (i.e., thrift, abstinence, order, and cleanliness).

Washington submitted to Armstrong's philosophy and promoted the idea of industrial education for blacks throughout his life. Armstrong's views were criticized by no less a figure than William Torrey Harris, who saw little promise in any educational idea that strayed from the intellectual traditions that he held so dear (Morgan, 1995). But the real debate on this issue would take shape in a long-running feud between Washington and his most dogged critic, W. E. B. Du Bois.

Washington is probably best known for his association with the Tuskegee Institute, which he was appointed to lead in 1881. The Tuskegee Institute was a school dedicated to the improvement of the life condition for blacks in America. Supported by both public and private moneys, the Tuskegee Institute was established as a normal and industrial school that trained teachers, farmers, and tradesmen. Washington encouraged its graduates to return to their communities, where they could become beacons for the next generation (Harlan, 1988). Bringing educated teachers back to the communities from which they came was Washington's way of multiplying the effects of a Tuskegee education. As he stated, "We wanted to give [the students at Tuskegee] such an education as would fit a large proportion of them to be teachers and at the same time cause them to return to the plantation districts and show the people there how to put new energy and new ideas into farming, as well as into the intellectual and moral and religious life of the people" (Washington, 1901, 347–348). But education at Tuskegee, as Washington phrased it, was not only of the hand, it was also of the heart. Washington aimed to shape the character of Tuskegee graduates with certain attitudes toward thrift, honesty, hard work, cleanliness, and racial conciliation, all of which, Washington believed, were needed to facilitate the social assimilation of black Americans and the establishment of a firm economic foundation for their futures. "We wanted to teach the student how to bathe; how to care for their teeth and clothing. We wanted to teach them what to eat, and how to eat it properly, and how to care for their rooms. Aside from this, we wanted to give them such a practical knowledge of some one industry, together with the spirit of industry, thrift and economy, that they would be sure of knowing how to make a living after they had left us..." (Washington, 1901, p. 347). The school started with 30 students in 1881, but by 1916 over 1,000 were enrolled.

Washington abided by what many view as a pragmatic and politically realistic vision for the improvement of black Americans. The problem, however, as many of his critics saw it, was that his vision for a good life in America did not aim as high for blacks as it did for whites. He tended to see the improved future for blacks in America as a long-term battle that had to be won in small increments. The main methods for improvement included a qualified version of educational opportunity, full economic participation and the embrace of Puritan virtues toward God and work. He did not see full participation in the political life of the country as an especially important asset and discouraged blacks from recognizing the act of voting or the holding of political office as a working solution to their problems (Anderson, 1978). Washington wanted blacks in America to be armed with a practical education that would give them a decent and dignified living, and that, in the end, would help show the world how very capable they were of achieving their own high standard of independence and livelihood. With this in mind, he hoped that a practical industrial education would light the way for black Americans as they climbed out of the depths of generational experiences in slavery. "Tuskegee," he declared, "emphasizes industrial education training for the Negro, not with the thought that the Negro should be confined to industrialism, the plow or the hoe, but because the undeveloped material resources of the South offer at this time a field peculiarly advantageous to the worker skilled in agriculture and the industries, and here are found the Negro's most inviting opportunities for taking on the rudimentary elements that ultimately make for a permanently progressive civilization" (Washington, 1905, p. 356). Washington's own story of rising up from slavery to become a national political figure reflected what he thought could happen to all blacks, if given an education and an opportunity to show the world their talents and values.

In his senior years, Washington become an advisor to several United States' Presidents and to philanthropists seeking to donate money to advance causes benefiting blacks in America. If there ever was a black political broker at the turn of the twentieth century, it was Booker T. Washington. He personally dispensed a large share of the endowments that came from philanthropists like Andrew Carnegie and emerged as the favored choice by white patrons in virtually all matters of philanthropy involving blacks (Harlan, 1988).

Washington encouraged a kind of peaceful apartheid between blacks and whites. He declared, "In all things that are truly social, we are as separate as the fingers, yet one as the hand in all things essential to mutual progress" (Washington, 1895, p. 350). This kind of language, with its clear separatist implications, satisfied many whites, but it also rankled some black intellectuals looking for a very different solution to the problems associated with skin color in America.

To this end, black social thought was also influenced by the work of W. E. B. Du Bois, who articulated a much more ambitious social agenda for black Americans. Specifically, Du Bois demanded full political and civil gains (including voting rights), access to liberal education (not industrial education), and equal economic opportunities for all blacks. Du Bois' familial background was quite different from Washington's. Born and raised in the North in a family of means, Du Bois traveled to Germany for graduate studies and ultimately earned a Ph.D. from Harvard University. Du Bois' broader and more revolutionary perspective on social reform in America was embodied in an intellectual movement known as the Niagara movement. Comprised of a small group of black intellectuals educated in elite northern universities, the Niagara movement emerged as the countervoice to Washington's, as the foil that represented "the talented tenth" of the black population (the very subpopulation that would be stifled by Washington's insistence on an industrial education for blacks). Du Bois' idea was that, at a minimum, 10 percent of the black population had to receive a classical education at the leading universities of the country, much like the education he received. Du Bois (1903) was strongly worded in his condemnation of Washington. "Mr. Washington came, with a definite single programme.... His programme of industrial education, conciliation of the South, and submission and silence as to civil rights and political rights, was not wholly original....But Mr. Washington...put enthusiasm, unlimited energy and perfect faith into this programme and changed it from a by-path into a veritable Way of Life" (p. 352).

The main battleground for the debate between Washington and Du Bois emerged in the constitution of the National Negro Business League, which Washington founded in 1899. In the hands of Washington, the League pressed the case for a segregated black economy, which, from Washington's viewpoint, would eventually achieve its own high status and make it clear to whites that broader social changes had to follow (Harlan, 1988). The League's message stressed the power of the purse in bringing new improvement to life of blacks. Black money had to be directed toward black merchants, who, possessing a first-rate practical education, could provide attractive goods and services to consumers. Earning, saving, and ultimately spending dollars was to become a political activity for black Americans. Washington believed that to the extent that blacks were able to demonstrate the virtues of conducting a good business, of working hard, of gaining private property, even within separatist lines, the demand for more extended gains in civil rights would inevitably follow. In a way, the natural segregation that manifested after the emancipation of blacks was to Washington a natural business opportunity for them. This was the chance to work within the cracks of a system designed to keep them down and to transcend it by proving to the world that there was no way of keeping down a people who worked hard, lived thriftily, and sided with Godly virtues.

Du Bois, however, continued to move in the direction of full equal rights for all blacks, and in 1909, founded the National Association for the Advancement of Colored People (NAACP). The original members of the group included the leading black intellectuals of the day and other intellectual activists, including John Dewey and Jane Addams (Morgan, 1995). The NAACP, has, of course, achieved legendary status as an agency in the historic fight for civil rights.

Some critics have looked upon Washington's leadership as one that was too willing to compromise and too unwilling to agitate for radical change. Despite the fact that Washington was born into slavery, he is nevertheless viewed by some as a bourgeois conservative who accommodated white supremacist views and sent racists exactly the wrong message, which was that blacks could settle for a humble segregated place in society and learn to live with the hostility that existed toward their social mobility and improvement. Others argue that his methods were appropriate for the time and that his single-minded focus on self-improvement through education carried a lasting legacy. In either case, we could consider both Washington and Du Bois as working in the progressive tradition of social change, making different arguments, but still both seeing the school and educational opportunity as the basis for the improvement of social conditions for black Americans.

Jane Addams and the Settlement House Movement

Lester Ward's idea of environmentalism got an early test at the hands of educational progressives, some of whom worked from an agenda even wider than the school. Driven by the need to take direct action against the poverty and squalor of city life, social activists, like Jane Addams and Lillian Wald, opened settlement houses for the indigent. Located in the poorest city neighborhoods of the cities, the settlement houses were community centers that provided local residents, including children, with educational experiences that helped them deal with the emergent needs of their difficult and often painful lives. The key to their function was to deal with neighborhood needs. Cremin (1961) describes the kinds of questions that moved the spirit of the settlement house. "Were the streets dirty and the tenements infested with vermin? Settlements founded antifilth societies to induce people to rid their rooms of bedbugs, lice, cockroaches, and rats. Were gangs of street urchins a menace to life and property? Settlements established boys' and girls' clubs to channel the ebullient energy of adolescence into athletics, arts, and crafts, and constructive recreation. Were death and disease rates in the slum pitifully high? Settlements became first-aid centers, clinics, headquarters for visiting nurses, and schools of preventive medicine. Were young men unable to obtain jobs? Settlements experimented not only with trade education but with devices for fitting individuals to the trades for which they were best suited. Were mothers required to work? Settlements introduced kindergartens and day nurseries. Were workingmen illiterate? Settlements taught them to read. Was summer oppressive in the city? Settlements established playgrounds and vacation centers." (pp. 60–61)

Jane Addams was the most prominent name associated with the settlement house movement in America. She established her house in 1893 in a Chicago neighborhood populated by immigrants living under terrible conditions of poverty. At her settlement, called the Hull House, Addams placed education at the center of all of the action. There was a kindergarten for toddlers and clubs for boys and girls. For adults, there were classes in English, cooking, nutrition, dress making, childcare, the trades, and the like (Cremin, 1961). There were also various music and drama clubs; the Working People Social Science Club, which looked into issues of social justice; a club for young working women called the Jane Club; the Electrical Club, which taught about electricity; a Men and Women's Club; and clubs devoted to the work of Shakespeare and Plato. In addition, there were public forums, an art gallery, college extension courses, free concerts, a reading room, a coffee shop, a nursery, a gymnasium, a Labor Museum, and a branch of the Chicago Public Library on the grounds (Colky, 1987). For the children, Addams tried to provide a comprehensive education that went beyond the 3Rs offered in the schools, stressing the study of art, literature, and history in ways that related to industrial life. Moreover, Addams agitated for reform in factory legislation and for improved city services for the poor. Here was an example of progressive ideas in their full bloom of practice.

Addams worked directly with people needing help, using the very problems of their lives as targets for instruction and improvement. She was driven by the ideal of developing and liberating the communities to work in the interest of political reform and social reconstruction. Whereas Dewey turned to the school to fulfill his hopes for social reform, Addams remained anchored in the community, living amid the very problems and perturbations that plagued poor people. John Dewey was a frequent visitor to the Hull House even before he opened the doors to his own school. He became a great admirer of the Hull House and of Jane Addams herself. He and Addams, in fact, became the closest of friends, so much so that Jane Addams became the namesake for John and Alice Dewey's daughter, Jane Dewey. Dewey himself acknowledged a deeper faith in the guiding forces of democracy by witnessing Addam's work at the Hull House (Cremin, 1988). Jane Addams eventually achieved world-wide recognition for work, winning the Nobel Peace Prize in 1931 for the humanitarian causes that she championed in the Hull House (Lagemann, 1985).

Addams philosophy was clearly on the side of progressivism and very much committed to the provision of comprehensive educational services well into adulthood, predating the idea of adult education as it is known today. Addams once declared that the settlement house was a protest against a restricted view of education (Cremin, 1961). To Addams, schooling was a matter of socialization for participation in democracy, which required a widely encompassing form of education.

The Conception of Subject Matter as Activity

The question of what content or what knowledge is most worthwhile in the experience of the school has been an enduring one for educators. Students, after all, need to be taught something, and selectively choosing what knowledge to teach in school is not an easy task. During the early decades of the twentieth century, some progressives developed an innovative approach to the organization of subject matter that was partly a reaction against the mentalistic tradition described earlier and partly an independent conceptualization of a new progressive vision for schooling. The change, however, was unmistakable. The subject matter of schooling that unfolded in progressive circles aimed at making a direct link to life experiences. It broadened the organization of subject matter into topical focal points (or what others might properly interpret as interdisciplinary schemes) and extended itself into vocational realms rarely embraced by mental disciplinarians. The result was profound because, compared to its mentalistic counterpart, the new progressive vision of subject matter was more comprehensive in its reach, less preoccupied with traditional academic subject matter boundaries, and, most significantly, more committed to the identification of the actual skills, attitudes, knowledge, and competencies needed to deal with the problems of living.

Few embraced this new outlook more conspicuously than John Dewey. As he phrased it, "anything which can be called a study, whether arithmetic, history, geography or one of the natural sciences, must be derived from materials which at the onset fall within the scope of ordinary life-experience" (Dewey, 1938, p. 48). No single body of content had a warrant on intelligence in Dewey's scheme. His intention was to dissolve the traditional subject matter lines and reconstitute them topically, according to the problems and the purposes of the life experience. Because life problems were not easily placed in disciplinary subjects, a premium was placed on the interdisciplinary construction of subject matter. Furthermore, the aim of knowledge (or the subject matter) was not limited to its mind training possibilities, but was instead focused on the effect that such knowledge had on behavior. In other words, the act of knowing was not interpreted as mindful knowledge but as knowledge that existed in the actions of life.

The main implication for educators was that the subject matter of the curriculum was not viewed as the starting point of the school experience. "When education is based in theory and practice upon experience," Dewey (1938) noted, "it goes without saying that the organized subject-matter of the adult and the specialist cannot provide the starting point" (p. 56). The idea of subject matter could not be put forward as an end in-and-of-itself, as was the case with mental disciplinarians or other traditional humanists. Rather, the subject matter became a traveling partner in the achievement of more broadly stated goals that spoke to broader judgments and behaviors. As Dewey (1897) observed,

> there is no fixed body of facts which, in itself, is externally set off and labeled geography, natural history or physics...Only as we ask what kind of experience is going on, what attitude some individual is actually assuming, what purposes or ends some individual has in view, do we find a basis for selecting and arranging the facts under the label of any particular study. (p. 361)

The practical consequence of such a view was a problem-focused curriculum that highlighted the importance of inquiry-based learning. Thus, in the Dewey laboratory school, one finds that much of the school curriculum was built around what Mayhew and Edwards (1936) referred to as social occupations—cooking, carpentry, sewing, and weaving. Out of these occupations children could learn more traditional pursuits in arithmetic, reading and writing, and the sciences. But the subject matter came to the occupations, as it were, which gave the subject matter new meaning. The occupations themselves were worthwhile only to the extent to which they informed problems and needs in experience. For instance, the 12-year-olds in the laboratory school had at one time made it clear to their teachers that they needed their own independent physical space in school, where they could hold meetings without interruption and where materials could be kept for their ongoing projects. Out of this need arose a plan to design and build a clubhouse.

> Committees on architecture, building, sanitation, ways and means and interior design were formed, each with a head chosen because of the experience in directing affairs. The site for the building was chosen under the guidance of the teachers in the different departments; plans were made and the cost estimated. A scheme for decoration was worked out, designs for furniture made. The choice of a location was prefaced by a study of the formation of soil, the conditions of drainage, climate exposure to light or wind, which must be taken into account in building a house. (Mayhew & Edwards, 1936, p. 229)

The areas of study encircling the clubhouse project included the study of geological formations and its effect on drainage (even examining the relation of good drainage to a healthy and secure building), the study of physiography and the physical geography of Chicago, and the study of various architectural forms. In other instances, the curriculum in the Dewey Laboratory School offered, for the younger children, experiences in the scientific and educational uses of cooking, which highlighted the teaching of fractions, knowledge of nutrition, and the application of the scientific method. Cooking, in fact, was used in other contexts as well, including the teaching of foreign languages. As reported by Laurel Tanner (1997), one laboratory school teacher taught French to fifth graders by conducting their cooking lessons in French. Emphasizing ear-memory and pronunciation, the teacher made the event of cooking into a French language exercise. Efforts to teach mathematical concepts also prevailed in various occupational contexts, including in classes where children were knitting and woodworking, while history was taught in a biographical fashion, focusing on biographies that allowed students to confront the same problems that historical figures faced, with an eye toward reconsidering historical judgments and behaviors (Tanner, 1997).

The idea of subject matter as activity was the featured innovation in many experimental schools. Among the most notable experimental efforts was the Gary School Plan, which took the idea of subject matter as activity to new heights. The Gary School, which was led by William Wirt (who was a student of Dewey's), was essentially dedicated to recasting the nature of schooling from a desk-bound classroom event to a community-life event. Wirt aimed to link the experiences in school to the operational needs of the school. Thus, the shop classes actually maintained the physical plant of the school, the science labs handled the operation of the cafeteria, students handled all the bookkeeping, and general efforts were made to connect whatever was taught to individual and social needs (Cremin,

1961). The intention was to make schooling part of life itself rather than some preparation for life. But the popularity of the Gary Plan, and various other experimental school endeavors, would be relatively short-lived mostly because of a failure to find a balance between what Dewey called the logical and the psychological organization of subject matter.

Dewey's distinction between the logical and the psychological features of subject matter is instructive. The *logical* is familiar enough. It represents the systemic organization of important facts and principles. The *psychological*, however, means that subject matter could be used to inform an individual's way of examining and thinking about the world; that subject matter could reside in one's psychical operating system in a way that affects one's decisions, values, dispositions, and outlooks. Thus, the psychological organization of subject matter always has to be rooted in life experiences. To Dewey, it was the *psychological* that gave the *logical* meaning and it was the *psychological* (the reach into one's life) that was so sorely missing from more traditionalist constructions of subject matter.

Dewey's distinction is important because various critics claimed that any effort to select subject matter on the basis of its relevance to life applications was doomed to becoming a low cognitive exercise, mostly because it would tend to honor only the *psychological*. By doing so, it would fundamentally fail to capture what the mentalistic tradition saw as the very purpose of schooling—immersion in the vast accumulation of insight stored in the organized edifices of the academic subject areas. Unfortunately, some of these fears were realized among child-centered educators who privileged whatever seemed to attract the interests of students often at the expense of the logical organization of subject matter. This was a problem that worried Dewey. "No experience is educative," he noted, "that does not tend both to knowledge of more facts and entertaining of more ideas. . . . It is not true that organization is a principle foreign to experience. Otherwise experience would be so dispersive as to be chaotic" (Dewey, 1938, p. 55).

The truth was that some progressives schools, especially those self-identifying with the child-centered movement, had only gotten half of Dewey's message, the half urging that attention be given to the life activities of children. The other half, which accounted for the logical organization of the subject matter, went missing. In their well-known exposition on the early rise of child-centered schools in the private school sector, Rugg and Schumaker (1928) illustrated the nature of this child-centered shift and showed how very different its construction of subject matter was from conventional or traditionalist thinking. Table 9–1 demonstrates how the child-centered schools turned away from the traditionalist commitment to *a priori* subject matter in favor of the subject matter of experience.

In the hands of the child-centered advocates, the Deweyan construction of subject matter as activity had shifted to an argument for "learning by doing," which was an argument that maintained there was educational virtue in essentially any task chosen by children. In short, having an experience moved by student desire was, ipso facto, educational. Learning-by-doing, in fact, became the driving notion behind William Kilpatrick's (1918) well-known effort to integrate the subject matter in school through what he referred to as the Project Method. Kilpatrick's method aimed to support as educative any activity that students were committed to perform (those moved by what he referred to as "wholehearted purpose") and to make such activities the main focal points for the organization of subject matter. In the elementary school, the Project Method led to the development of "teacher units" that favored student activity with no clear linkage to the logical organization of subject matter. Kliebard (2004) described one project developed in 1927 for a second-grade classroom in Lincoln School, an experimental laboratory school at Teachers College, Columbia University.

> In a Study of City Life, ...children began with the study of the city's transportation, one boy making a model of Grand Central Station while others made trains, trucks, buses, taxis, and boats.

TABLE 9-1 Typical Captions of the Educational Programs.

The Child-Centered Schools	The Conventional Schools
(These are representative centers of subjects).	*(These are representative school interest or units of work).*
A food study—fruits and vegetables	Algebra
A study of trees and tree making	Arithmetic
History play—"Following Columbus"	Bookkeeping
A knight study—making and giving a play	Economics
A play city	English Composition
A study of milk	Geography
Study of Holland	Grammar
A study of wool	History
Water transportation	Latin
A study of boats	Manual training
How man has made records	Nature study
A study of tree people	Reading
Care of a flock of chickens	Rhetoric
Story of the growth of Chicago	Science
The study of Greek life	Spelling
Colonial life	Writing

> Next they constructed buildings—a wholesale market, a bakery, a post office, a fire station, a bank and so on.... Eventually, the project led to a six week study of foods, where various food stuffs were prepared and sold at various market prices (p. 168).

The subject matter followed no logical pattern of organization and was often conflated as activity.

The progressive commitment to subject matter as activity also helped to find a place for manual arts or vocational education in the curriculum. Few realms of the curriculum could equate activity with subject matter as harmoniously as the vocational realm. The progressive ardor for subject matter as activity meant that subject matter specifically linked to making a living or performing a paying occupation would necessarily have high value in schools. The problem associated with the idea of vocational subject matter as activity was its association with the eventual monetary benefit it provided to the student. One needs to remember that the social occupations central to Dewey's laboratory school were used not as ends in and of themselves, but as ways to help psychologize subject matter—to connect the *logical* to life experiences. The problem with much of the emerging view of vocationalism, however, was its preoccupation with vocational function, with representing a form of education for adjustment to a particular way of making a living. Dewey (1916) sought education through occupations, not for occupations. As he phrased it:

> there is doubtless...a tendency for every distinction vocation to become too dominant, too exclusive and absorbing in its specializing aspect. This means emphasis upon skill or technical method at the expense of meaning. Hence it is not the business of education to foster this tendency, but rather to safeguard against it, so that the scientific inquirer shall not be merely the scientists, the teacher merely the pedagogue, the clergyman merely the one who wears the cloth and so on. (p. 308)

Kliebard (1999) argues that the vocationalism in the progressive response produced a form of education that unabashedly aimed to adjust students to existing social conditions. The inclusion of vocational subject matter as activity also had the effect of broadening the school offerings and appealing to a broader swath of the school-age population, of recasting the curriculum in a way that considered both common and differentiated forms of instruction and of consecrating the design of the comprehensive high school, which aimed to keep all school-age children, irrespective of their post-school destinations, under one common school roof. In this way, the idea of subject matter as activity was a feature of a more egalitarian social policy toward public schooling.

Dewey's effort to find reconciliation between the logical side of subject matter, which was the preoccupation of the traditional humanists, and the psychological side of the subject matter, which was the preoccupation of child-centered advocates, has since given us an analytical tool to understand the nature of the different approaches to subject matter and to ultimately find a new balance in the construction of subject matter as activity.

The Cardinal Principles Report of 1918

Serious changes in the composition of the secondary school curriculum were affected in yet another famous NEA-sponsored committee report. Like its 1898 counterpart (the Committee of Ten Report), the *Cardinal Principles Report of 1918*, more than any document of its time, led to a national call to change the high school curriculum. Unlike the earlier report, however, it asked for sweeping changes that resulted in broadening the scope of the schools' curriculum offerings. As mentioned, the Committee of Ten and Fifteen reports had kept the schools centered largely on academics, within the limits of a very few subject areas. The Cardinal Principles report changed this radically.

In 1913, the National Education Association appointed a committee, aptly named the Commission on the Reorganization of Secondary Education, to reconsider the pattern of course work in the high school. After five years of deliberation, the Committee offered its recommendations in a report known as the *Cardinal Principles Report of 1918*. Whereas the Committee of Ten report itemized subject areas to be taught, the *Cardinal Principles Report* itemized practical objectives to be met. These objectives included the command of the fundamental processes (basic skills), worthy home membership, health, vocation, citizenship, worthy use of leisure time, and ethical character.

The listing of seven objectives for the school foretold a whole new sense of a school. If the report was to be taken seriously, secondary education now had to shift from its academic emphasis in the traditional liberal arts to a more comprehensive emphasis that included academic, vocational, socio-civic, and socio-personal concerns. It was precisely in the context of these recommendations that the blueprint for the comprehensive high school was fashioned.

Under the influence of the Cardinal Principles report, the American comprehensive high school acknowledged two main functions: 1) the provision of specialized studies for the purpose of dealing with issues related to individual interests and talents in areas of college and vocational preparation and personal development; and 2) the provision of unifying studies for the purpose of dealing with the vital problems of social life in a democracy as they relate to citizenship, ethical character, and worthy home membership. Thus, individualized programs, including specific career or vocational preparation programs and courses related to student interests and aptitudes, were part and parcel of the specialized facet of the curriculum. At the same time, the school provided common courses, also known as unifying studies, that taught a common core of knowledge, values, and skills to all youth. Together, the two functions educated the whole student.

The notion of providing new breadth in the course work of the curriculum had very direct effects on the way that the school had to be organized. Differentiation in the curricular program was going to be needed to allow students to pursue their own plans, interests, and needs. The curriculum could no longer be seen as one monolithic block of courses, a problem that hounded the Committee of Ten report from its inception.

The *Cardinal Principles Report* has often been cited as a turning point in American education, primarily because it offered a comprehensive school model as an alternative to the strictly academic curriculum. Partly as a result of the report, the idea of mental discipline was rejected and the search for life activities responsive to individual and social needs was enacted. As Butts (1955) put it, "What the seven cardinal principles did was shift the emphasis in schooling away from the preoccupation with the academic and intellectual disciplines and to broaden the social role of education almost beyond recognition" (p. 194). The report can be viewed as a uniquely American effort to educate youth in a unified setting in ways that allowed for both common learning and specialized individualized learning. Such a system diverged markedly from the separatist, dual system that existed in Europe. Instead of going to separate trade schools, American students interested in vocation education found a hospitable climate in the unified cosmopolitan school. Vocational education was, after all, one of the cardinal principles. Yet, no matter what their specialization might be, students were always required to participate in heterogeneously grouped common learning, which aimed to build common communities along common knowledge and common values.

The ideal of the comprehensive school would run into its share of some problems. Although the specializing function of the curriculum was designed to respond to key individual differences, it sometimes resulted in a system of curriculum tracking that came at the expense of lower achieving students. Although the idea of common leaning was designed as a school experience in common democratic living, it sometimes resulted simply in the drafting of core academic courses required for graduation. Still, the commitment to educating all high school students under one roof, irrespective of their background and their career expectations, has remained vital in the United States.

The American Kindergarten

Securing a publicly supported kindergarten in the ladder system of American education was an important achievement. The kindergarten, invented by Friedrich Froebel, found its first American expressions in several Midwestern German American homes and schools. Most scholars acknowledge that Mary Schurz was the first American practitioner of the kindergarten. In 1856, she opened a private, German-speaking school for friends and family in Watertown, Wisconsin (Ross, 1976).

The most visible source of advocacy for the *public* kindergarten came from William Torrey Harris, who used his authority as superintendent of the St. Louis public schools to support the introduction of the kindergarten in his district. Harris shared Froebel's commitment to the philosophy of romantic idealism, which stressed the importance of bringing individuals into conformity with the absolute perfection or wholeness embodied in the divine spirit. But Harris and Froebel had different ideas about the pathway toward the achievement of that perfection. In 1873, Harris asked Susan Blow, a trainee in Froebelian methods, to oversee an experiment of kindergarten education in a school within the St. Louis district, the Des Peres School. Her job was to teach the kindergarten and to prepare a report on her experiences.

The arguments against including the kindergarten in the school structure were fairly well entrenched at the time. The major complaint was that the "nonacademic" mission of the kindergarten would not generate much public interest and would only waste money. Critics maintained that, if the kindergarten was going to emphasize the importance of play, as Froebel demanded, then few parents would regard it as necessary. The resulting limited enrollment would probably not justify the expense. Other critics pointed to the actual types of experiences that the kindergarten supported. Because Froebelian notions were child-centered, many believed that the kindergarten would spoil young children and ruin their chances for later success in school. Some critics, for instance, cited the importance of silent study in the primary school experience and pointed to the kindergarten's philosophical opposition to silence. They maintained that socializing young children one way during the kindergarten years, only to reverse direction during the post-kindergarten years, was educationally unsound.

As director of the experimental kindergarten in St. Louis, Susan Blow had a response to these assertions. In 1878, after her first year, she reported data showing very high attendance rates, relatively low financial expenditures, and evidence that the children outperformed primary school children on primary school tasks (Ross, 1976). St. Louis would soon become known as the center of the kindergarten universe, employing 131 paid kindergarten teachers by 1879. Blow would make a name for herself as an expert teacher and practitioner of the kindergarten. Before long, the St. Louis schools became the prime training grounds for young teachers in the kindergarten method.

Blow's work clearly convinced Harris that the kindergarten was a wise investment. Harris, in fact, believed that the development of certain nonacademic skills in the kindergarten would later make it easier for primary school teachers to attend to the essential academic tasks he so valued. If kindergarten teachers could focus their efforts on the development of good manners, cleanliness, handicrafts, and manual dexterity, then primary grade teachers would be freer to direct their attention and energy to an education in the academic disciplines. As it turned out, Froebel's romantic idealism would have its way in the kindergarten, while Harris's more traditional conception of schooling would apply to the post-kindergarten years. Harris observed, for instance, that:

> the kindergarten should be a sort of sub-primary education. . . . The disciplines of reading and writing, geography and arithmetic, as taught in the ordinary, primary school, are beyond the power of the average child not yet entered upon his seventh year. And beyond the seventh year the time of the child is too valuable to use it for other than general disciplines . . . He must not take up his school time with learning a handicraft (Blow, 1900, p. 9).

Harris also believed that the kindergarten represented an early school intervention that would eventually pay a positive social dividend. With children enrolled in school at the ages of four and five, Harris was convinced that kindergarten classes could become early weapons against the poor habits and low-mindedness that many children inherited from their families (Blow, 1900). In fact, this was the same basic rationale offered by many advocates of private charity kindergartens. With so many young children living in slum conditions, the kindergarten was viewed as a kind of child-saving agency (Vandewalker, 1971). Harris, however, saw public kindergartens not only benefiting the children of the poor who would be spared from the experiences of vice, crime, and neglect at an earlier age, but also the children of the rich, who would be saved "from the ruin of self-indulgence and the corruption ensuing on weak management in the family" (Blow, 1900, p. 9).

The early American kindergarten was deliberately Froebelian in its purpose and procedures. As mentioned, Froebel placed a high premium on play, but in forms that would develop the physical, intellectual, and moral nature of the child. He worked out a system for educating very young children by requiring them to manipulate a set of playthings, which he called gifts, and various handiwork activities, which he called occupations. He also stressed the importance of telling certain stories and singing certain songs. The kindergarten, in this sense, was not only a philosophy for early schooling but also a procedure for early schooling.

The playthings, or gifts, were chosen and devised by Froebel, and included different-colored balls, a wooden sphere, different-sized cubes and triangles, a cylinder, a square, small sticks, and wire rings. These materials, when manipulated by children, allowed them to develop important observational capacities and to begin to understand ideas associated with the handling of the gifts, such as presence, absence, clasping, rolling, and falling (Ross, 1976). The gifts also enabled teachers to introduce concepts such as gravity and space to children (Kilpatrick, 1916).

The balls had the added power of representing a perfect form of unity, a geometric form that reminded children of the sense of unity that they needed to find in themselves. In the words of Froebel, "The child . . . perceives in the ball the general expression of each object. . . . Even the word ball, in our significant language, is full of expression and meaning, pointing out that the ball is, as it were, an image of All" (quoted in Kilpatrick, 1916, pp. 111–12). The cubes, in sharp contrast to the balls, gave the child the chance to develop an understanding of contrast and variety. By playing with the cubes, cylinder, and balls, the child could develop the verbal skills needed to describe the distinguishing characteristics of the unified world (Ross, 1976).

Understanding the contrasting and opposing conditions of the universe was important to Froebel because such understandings helped children conceive of the endpoints of the whole. All of the gifts, in some combination, could also be used to build different geometric forms. Children, in fact, were encouraged to use different geometric parts to form different geometric wholes. Throughout the learning/playing process, the idea was to show the child the constituent parts comprised in the whole, a symbolic message that recurs in Froebel's kindergarten.

The handicraft activities, or occupations, were also vital to Froebel's kindergarten procedure. The occupations entailed a variety of activities with different materials, including sewing, drawing, paper twisting, weaving, paper folding, paper cutting, and clay modeling (Ross, 1976). These activities gave children the chance to ponder their world, to engage in a creative and productive process of learning, and to see geometric forms as the building blocks of the world. The goal here was to give children the opportunity to synthesize and integrate the general geometric elements of the world, to find the whole (the Allness) in the synthesis of the parts. As a devotee of Froebel, Blow (1908) characterized the idea behind these kinds of activities: "As we learn the phonetic alphabet in order to get at the sense of what is written in books, so we learn the alphabet of form, in order to get at the sense of what is written in the great book of nature" (p. 41).

Where reading and writing were prominent in the early dame schools and Latin grammar schools, Froebel sought to replace these activities with experiences in song, storytelling, games, conversation, and outdoor events such as gardening. The goal, again, was to show children their place in the whole of the social group. The teacher, for instance, might sing the following rhyme as she engaged children in the manipulation of eight small cubes: "Look here and see! One whole, two halves; One half, two fourths; Two halves, four fourths; One whole, four fourths; Four fourths, eight eights; Eight eights, one whole. Here are many, here are few; It's a magic way to do" (Kilpatrick, 1916, p. 141). Froebel also developed a series of games and often stressed the significance of the circle.

Not surprisingly, criticism of the kindergarten method soon followed. The most basic criticism emerged from John Dewey (1916), who, despite admiring Froebel's contribution to education, felt that the kindergarten method had become too prescribed and too dependent on a particular set of materials and activities. William Kilpatrick (1916) questioned the foundation of symbolism in

Froebel's theories, asking how a ball or any other object could have any special claim on an organic or social construction of unity. Kilpatrick also asserted the need for the kindergarten to move beyond Froebel's pre-occupation with symbolism in favor of dealing with real-world issues and problems.

G. Stanley Hall, whose own work underscored the importance of making adjustments in the learning environment based on the emerging knowledge of the learner, made a similar point. He attacked some kindergarten training schools for their uniform and programmatic approaches toward teaching. For instance, he argued that because some gifts were too small for young children, they would only frustrate the children and undermine the learning experience (Ross, 1976). As founder of the child study movement, Hall argued that kindergarten teachers had to be receptive to the new knowledge available on the nature of the child and be prepared to make appropriate changes in classroom materials, curricula, and methods. Thus, kindergarten teachers had to be less concerned with using the particular gifts and materials developed by Froebel, and more concerned with making intelligent adjustments to the learning environment in light of the latest available knowledge on learners.

Hall's message reached a receptive audience, as kindergarten training sites began to acknowledge the importance of the child study movement in creating new insights for kindergarten teachers. However, it also galvanized a group, led by Susan Blow, committed to the orthodox interpretation of the Froebelian system. Blow claimed that the kindergarten represented a uniform plan of action based on the materials developed by Froebel. Meanwhile, other emerging scholars in the field, particularly Patty Smith Hill, argued that the kindergarten classroom had to retain some flexibility to best serve the interests of children.

Because she challenged Blow directly, Hill emerged as an important thinker in the kindergarten movement. Her early appointment to Teachers College in Columbia University as a lecturer on kindergarten and preschool education gave her views a visible platform. Having studied at some level with Dewey and Hall, Hill was less ideologically attached to the work of Froebel than was Blow. Hill acknowledged the significance of Froebel by crediting him with helping to bring the child into the center of curriculum formulations and with making the school a happier place marked by play, games, music, and well-educated teachers. Hill believed that the school environment had to be open to change based on the best available knowledge. New songs, games, materials, and methods had to be continuously considered as new demands on and insights into learners and the society emerged.

By the 1890s, kindergarten teachers were being trained nationwide. Naturally, Froebelian gifts and the principles governing their application in the classroom were an important part of the training (Ross, 1976). But the debate that loomed between Blow and Hill pointed to two very different kindergarten training programs. Blow wanted attention to be directed at the true Froebelian procedures; Hill wanted these procedures to be reevaluated and amended not only in light of new knowledge about learning but also in relation to the unique social context of America. Hill, for instance, moved away from teaching teachers how to use the stories and songs that Froebel chose for the kindergarten and toward encouraging teachers to create their own stories, using the issues and demands of the day to make them more suitable for American children. Because Froebel's stories and songs were originally conceived for and used with German children, Hill wanted the stories and songs used in the American kindergarten to be composed specifically for American children. Because of Hill's influence, early kindergarten teachers would, in fact, become authors of children's stories and original composers of simple children's tunes. For instance, Hill, with her sister, composed the traditional birthday song "Happy Birthday to You" (Rudnitski, 1994). Hill also preached the selective and adapted use of the gifts, arguing that they should be bigger, as dictated by child study findings, and that many other types of objects should be brought into the school, including dolls and bean bags. She believed that the symbolic commitment to teaching children their place in a unified world took precious time away from other important objectives in the curriculum, including the development of social skills. She turned the gifts into means serving broader ends as opposed to ends in themselves.

Blow saw these developments as little more than contaminants to the true Froebelian method. To her, modifications in the Froebelian approach testified to the weakening of the kindergarten ideal. Blow disdained, for instance, the manner in which some kindergarten teachers were building their curricula around Herbartian themes, or concentrations, and using the gifts and occupations to advance the knowledge and ideas inherent in the study of the concentrations (Blow, 1908). Such an approach, in Blow's view, destroyed the special value of the gifts and the occupations. Froebelian instruments, she asserted, should not be used for non-Froebelian aims.

In the end, the progressive views of Patty Smith Hill won the day. The American kindergarten would have to acknowledge the special vision of Froebel and the dedication that he inspired among its early practitioners. The growing strength of the child study movement and the awakening of the progressive commitment to the social aims of schooling led the school away from Froebelian procedures and their mystical rationales. The American kindergarten would instead support a form of practice better attuned to the nature of the learner and to the values and aims of democracy.

SUMMARY

Many child-centered thinkers in American education viewed themselves as on the side of progressivism, largely because they opposed the subject-centered and mentalistic views of the traditional humanists. Other progressives saw as much danger in the child-centered perspective as in the subject-centered view it was designed to counter. Chief among these was John Dewey, who succeeded in galvanizing a new progressivism that deliberately shaped the school as an agency of and for democracy. The school, as a result, was moved, as never before, by a new theoretical outlook that accounted for the learner, the subject matter, and the society. Such an outlook also brought a renewed faith in the powers of the environment. The effects were palpable. Booker T. Washington and W. E. B. Du Bois offered views on how the school could act as a corrective agency in the lives of recently emancipated blacks. The settlement house movement, popularized by Jane Addams, gave hope to poor and immigrant populations. A new reconfiguration for the secondary school curriculum, as set forth in the Cardinal Principles Report, created the early pattern for the American comprehensive high school. A new idea for kindergarten education, influenced by the child study movement, brought relevant activity into the school experience. And a completely new conception of subject matter, which aimed to reach into personal/social dimensions of the learner's life, took the edge off the mentalistic tradition of teaching that had commandeered the school.

REFERENCES

Anderson, J. D. (1978). The Hampton model of normal school industrial education, 1868-1900. In Vincent P. Franklin & James D. Anderson (1978), *New perspectives on black educational history.* Boston: G. K. Hall and Co.

Blow, S. (1908). *Educational issues in the kindergarten.* New York: Appleton.

Blow, S. (1900). Kindergarten education in Butler, N.M. (1969). *Education in the United States.* Albany: Lyons.

Butts, R. F. (1955). *A cultural history of western education.* New York: McGraw-Hill Co.

Colky, M. (1987). Jane Addams' Hull House: Early contributions to adult education. *Journal of Midwest History of Education Society,* 15:32–43.

Commission on the Reorganization of Secondary Education. (1918). *The cardinal principles of secondary education.* Washington, DC: U.S. Government Printing Office.

Cremin, L. A. (1961). *The transformation of the school.* New York: Alfred A. Knopf.

Du Bois, W. E. B. (1903). The souls of black folk. In Daniel Calhoun (1969), *Educating for Americans: A documentary history.* New York: Houghton-Mifflin.

Dewey, J. (1897). The psychological aspect of the school curriculum. *Educational Review,* 13:356–369.

Dewey, J. (1902). *The child and the curriculum.* Chicago: University of Chicago Press.

Dewey, J. (1916). *Democracy and education.* New York: Macmillan Co.

Dewey, J. (1938). [original publication date]. Experience and education. In J. Boydston (1988). *John Dewey: The later works, 1925–1953, Vol. 13.* Carbondale, IL: Southern Illinois University Press.

Harlan, L. R. (1988). *Booker T. Washington in perspective.* Jackson: University of Mississippi Press.

Kilpatrick, W. (1918). The Project Method. *Teachers College Record,* 19(4):319–335.

Kilpatrick, W. (1916). *Froebel's kindergarten principles.* New York: Macmillan.

Kliebard, H. M. (1999). *Schooled to work.* New York: Teachers College Press.

Kliebard, H. M. (2004). *The struggle for the American curriculum,* 3rd edition. New York: Routledge and Kegan Paul.

Lagemann, E. (1985). *Jane Addams on education.* New York: Teachers College Press.

Mayhew, Katherine C., & Edwards, Anna C. (1936). *The Dewey school.* New York: Atherton Press.

Morgan, H. (1995). *Historical perspectives on the education of black children.* Westport, CN: Praeger.

Ravitch, D. (2000) *Left back: A century of failed school reforms.* New York: Simon and Schuster.

Ross, E. D. (1976). *The kindergarten crusade.* Athens: Ohio University Press.

Rugg, H., & Schumaker, A. (1928). *The child-centered school.* Yonkers-on-Hudson, World Book Company.

Rudnitski, R. A. (1994). Patty Smith Hill and the progressive kindergarten. *Current Issues in Education,* 11(1):25-34.

Tanner, L. N., & Tanner, D. (1987). Environmentalism in American pedagogy: The legacy of Lester Ward. *Teacher College Record,* 88(4):537–548.

Tanner, Laurel. (1997). *Dewey's laboratory school.* New York: Teachers College Press.

Vandewalker, N. C. (1971). *The kindergarten in American education.* New York: Arno Press and the New York Times [1908].

Washington, B. T. (1895). The Atlanta compromise. In Daniel Calhoun (1969), *Educating for Americans: A documentary history.* New York: Houghton-Mifflin.

Washington, B. T. (1901). Up from slavery. In Daniel Calhoun (1969), *Educating for Americans: A documentary history.* New York: Houghton-Mifflin.

Washington, B. T. (1905). Tuskegee and its people. In Daniel Calhoun (1969), *Educating for Americans: A documentary history.* New York: Houghton-Mifflin.

KEY QUESTIONS

1. Describe in general terms what Dewey supported as the main factors in the educative process.
2. What was Lester Ward's main contribution to the progressive movement?
3. What were settlement houses and how did they fit into Lester Ward's thinking about school and society?
4. What was the general nature of the debate between Washington and Du Bois?
5. What was Washington's rationale for supporting industrial and normal school education for blacks?
6. Why did the Cardinal Principles Report of 1918 represent a proverbial tidal change in the way that high school education was conceived?
7. What are the two main curricular functions of the school according to the Cardinal Principles Report?
8. What were the main principles distinguishing the Froebelian kindergarten from the one supported by Patty Smith Hill?
9. Explain Dewey's distinction between the logical and the psychological organization of subject matter in the curriculum?

RESEARCH EXERCISES

1. Read *Experiencing Dewey*, edited by Breault and Breault, in which leading scholars from educational studies choose their favorites quotes of Dewey and offer some commentary on them. Select your own favorite quote from the group and make your own case for it.

2. Conduct an analysis of the way that subject matter or content is organized in a particular school or school district. Is there evidence of the progressive conception of subject matter as activity? Are there differences across grade levels, ability groups, or curriculum tracks?

3. Search the curriculum offerings of the Hampton School at its founding, or any other historically black school that was dedicated to industrial and normal education. Was the curriculum, in your view, empowering or simply a way to help keep blacks oppressed?

4. Read Diane Ravitch's *Left Back*. In it, she argues that the issue of subject matter stands at the very center of the historical struggle over the nature of school reform in the United States. In fact, Ravitch believes that the history of school reform in the United States was largely reducible to a dispute between those who were supportive of the place of rigorous subject matter in the curriculum, defined in its most disciplinary and traditional form, and those who were against it. Do you agree?

5. Research the history of the Froebelian kindergarten in America, focusing mostly on the application of the gifts and occupations in the experience of the school children. Provide examples of how the gifts were used in particular schools by particular teachers.

6. Research the work of Patty Smith Hill and Susan Blow. Compare and contrast their views on kindergarten education.

7. Research Dewey's laboratory school and provide particular examples of the kind of teaching that was provided to its students.

8. Research the kind of educational activities provided in any of the settlement houses across the United States during the early twentieth century.

9. Organize a pictorial essay of any of the laboratories school, settlement houses, normal schools, black industrial/normal schools, and/or kindergartens at the turn of the century.

PART 3

The School and Society

The conception of education as a social process and function
has no definite meaning until we define the
kind of society we have in mind.

John Dewey

CHAPTER 10

The Structure of American Education

The organization of the American school represents an interplay between state and local jurisdictions. Early state school laws gave local school districts considerable liberties, but as the nation developed and as the teaching profession began to gain some professional legitimacy, states became increasingly adamant about the establishment of public schools in local districts and more focused about how such schools should go about educating youth. As discussed, the historical model for the state supervision of local schooling was established by Horace Mann during his tenure as the first state superintendent of Massachusetts. The very notion of allowing the state to guide the school is rooted in the Massachusetts laws of 1642 and 1647. The legislators of the Massachusetts Bay Colony were the first to mandate public education, the first to require the maintenance of town schools, and the first to use public taxes to fund public schools.

The role of the federal government in the governance of the school was decided in the 1791 ratification of the Tenth Amendment to the Constitution, which gave the state full powers in the operation of the public schools. Although the Constitution delegated no duties to the federal government in the arena of public education, the federal government still had a legislative role to play. In fact, the nature of federal intervention in schooling was set early. Congress drafted the Land or Northwest Ordinance of 1785, which demanded that federal grants of land be contingent on the parceling of land for local public schools. Here the federal government enacted legislation aimed at promoting the general welfare of the nation by encouraging public schools without stipulating how such schools should be conducted (Cremin, 1951).

GRADE- AND SCHOOL-LEVEL ORIENTATIONS

The American system of education, which is structurally organized as one path (or one ladder) from kindergarten to college, came into existence through various sources of influences. In the eighteenth century, the public schools in America were organized without a grade-level structure. Dame schools and common elementary town schools were largely ungraded and made no effort to connect themselves to more advanced schools, such as the Latin Grammar schools or the academies (Douglas & Grieder, 1948). In other words, the elementary school did not flow curricularly into the secondary school; they were not component parts of one larger unit. Eventually the growth in participation rates in school led to the use of age segregated classes that had to articulate with each other and to the establishment of a graded educational ladder that gave the whole system of schooling a unified focus (see Figure 10–1).

Almost all American public schools use grade levels to organize instruction, but the grade configuration that comprises each school varies (Jones, Salisbury, & Spencer, 1969). Many school districts use a 6/3/3 configuration, which includes six years of elementary school (not counting kindergarten),

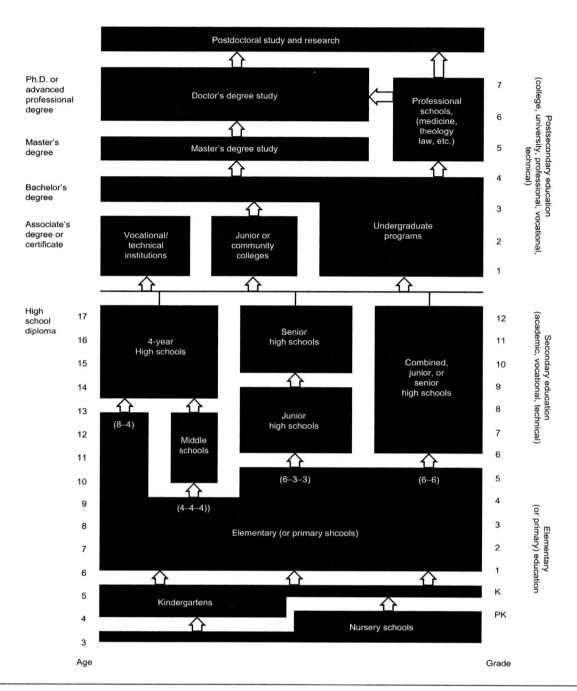

FIGURE 10–1 Composite of the American Ladder System. National Center for Education Statistics. (2005). *Digest of education statistics*. Washington, DC: Department of Education, p. 7.

three years of junior high school, and three years of high school. Increasingly, however, school districts are recognizing the value of a middle school, as opposed to a junior high school, for the education of preadolescents. School districts so inclined lean toward the adoption of a 4/4/4 or 5/3/4 pattern, which demands the placement of the ninth grade in high school and the sixth grade in middle school.

Middle schools were developed in response to the accusation that traditional junior high schools were little more than imitations of senior high schools (Tanner, 1972). Focused on the needs of preadolescents in the curriculum, middle schools promised to provide learning experiences that went beyond the curricular concerns of the college-bound. The junior high school was originally rationalized as a transition or intermediate institution between the self-contained classroom setting of elementary school and the departmentalized setting of the senior high school. It had failed to become a distinctive institution for preadolescents. Moving the course work for the ninth grade out of the middle school setting was significant because ninth grade course work is recorded on the high school transcript used for admission to college. The effect is a departmentalizing pressure on the ninth grade curriculum that makes it difficult for the middle school to fully express its commitment to the education of preadolescents. Similarly, moving the sixth grade into the middle school setting better captured the developmental period of preadolescence. As a result, the 5/3/4 configuration is ideal for the middle school because it allows for the exploration of curriculum options that are attuned to the early adolescent. Under such a configuration, the school could stress interdisciplinary themes, exploratory learnings, and more multi-age grouping strategies, all without worrying about the disciplinary priorities of a college preparatory education (Wiles & Bondi, 1993).

For every rule in American education, there are always notable exceptions. Because the American schools are decentralized (without a single federal or national authority), it is difficult to make a generalization about them. Small rural districts, for instance, might organize their schools with a 6/6 configuration, and where the population is especially small, the district might adopt one unified K-12 setting. Moreover, the manner in which a school district structures its grade levels may have nothing to do with educational principles and everything to do with institutional factors, such as the size of its facilities and its projected enrollment distributions.

Still, there are some common threads. For instance, with some small exceptions, most school districts recognize the divisions of elementary, middle or intermediate, and secondary schools. In doing so, they recognize the accompanying instructional and pedagogical orientations of each division. As a result, the secondary school and the junior high schools have traditionally been institutions openly departmentalized in how they organize the curriculum, while elementary schools and middle schools have been less inclined toward departmentalization.

Much teaching in the elementary school continues to occur along traditional subject lines (math, science, language arts, and so on). However, the actual elementary school classroom is often self-contained, meaning that one educator is responsible for teaching all of the standard academic subjects in one heterogeneously grouped classroom. The self-contained classroom design used in elementary schools is ideal for group-centered learning that promotes interdisciplinary visions. It is also seen as the best arrangement for educators to conduct a classroom that is responsive to the comprehensive development of each young child. By being together in one place for extended periods of time, the teacher and the students can get to know one another quite well and the teacher can dedicate herself to finding a way to individualize each student's program. Removed from subject-centered concerns, the teacher working in a self-contained classroom can focus her instructional intentions on the social, physical, sensory, and academic development of each child.

Some critics, however, see the touted strength of the self-contained classroom as its main weakness. They argue, for instance, that teachers working in self-contained heterogeneously mixed classrooms really have to deal with too much variation, leaving them with no good way to deal with individualizing needs. The self-contained classroom, they claim, is usually set at the pace of the slowest learner, which results in compromising the education of the most academically-inclined. In response to these problems, elementary school educators are known to make use of instructional ability groups, especially in the areas of reading and mathematics instruction. Note that intraclass grouping (within the self-contained classroom) is a practice different from ability-based interclass grouping, something also known as curriculum tracking, which is discussed in the next chapter.

In some school districts the self-contained system in the elementary schools has been abandoned in favor of departmentalization. Today, some elementary schools are teaching children within an organizational scheme that is not unlike what one might expect at a high school level. Specialized teachers are being used to teach specialized subjects, sometimes in ability-grouped settings. Some elementary schools employing specialized teachers have tried to temper the arrangement by using heterogeneous groups taught by a team of teachers, sometimes known as a house or unit. This team teaching arrangement allows for collaborative curriculum planning, some articulation across the subjects and grades, and combined group meetings. This arrangement is also used in large-sized middle schools and high schools to preserve the smallness and intimacy of the school experience.

Middle schools have, by and large, featured curriculum designs that more closely resemble those found in self-contained elementary schools than those found in high schools. The middle school ideal seeks connections between subject areas for the purpose of providing integrated and socio-personal learning opportunities. Like the elementary school, the middle school is not under direct college preparatory pressures. Under ideal circumstances, the curriculum in the middle school should focus on the psycho-social development of the early adolescent and deal with items related to health, social responsibility, basic communication, and human relation skills. The development of more complex thinking skills should also be at center stage because, developmentally speaking, many preadolescents are just entering into the Piagetian stage of formal operations, which stresses hypothetical thinking. The academic subject areas of the middle school curriculum should not be disciplinary, but should aim at socio-personal issues that speak to life interests, peer relations, questions of social identity, and the like. Exploratory learning should be valued as a way to open up the world to the preadolescent and to develop early interests in various new ideas and subjects.

At the secondary school level, public education follows two different approaches. Most high schools are comprehensive institutions that provide educational programs for both college- and non-college-bound students in a unified setting. Thus, college preparatory programs are offered to students on a college track, and vocational programs are offered to students destined for blue collar work. All youth, however, are also given opportunities in exploratory, enrichment, and general education programs, with the latter representing a chance to educate the whole student population in a common, heterogeneously-mixed instructional setting. The other secondary school approach is the specialized high school, which, depending on the school, offers specialized training in a particular academic or vocational area. Specialized vocational schools, in fact, are popular in some school districts. Specialized magnet schools, which can offer unique academic or trade programs for students, have also grown in stature and popularity in school districts across the nation, especially in large urban districts.

School Governance

Today the unified system of American pubic education is governed through three interrelated sources of influence: the federal government, the state government, and the local school board. The legal governance of the school falls entirely into the hands of the state. Each state conducts its schools as it sees fit, as long as it abides by the laws of the nation. Thus, in effect, 50 states translates into 50 different systems of schooling. Although each state is, of course, influenced by certain centralizing influences including the federal government and other national sources (including the testing and textbook industries), there is no centralized national or federal control of public education. The public school system in the United States is, in fact, among the few in the world to be governed by an openly decentralized system. Other advanced nations, such as Japan, China, Russia, and most European nations, have central ministries of education that dictate national policy and practice for schooling.

Ultimately, state legislatures are responsible for the general operation of public schools. They authorize funding and contemplate legislative support for the schools. The actual day to day supervision of the state system, however, is done by a state board of education and its main administrative unit—the state department of education. Almost all the states have state boards of education. Their services extend into the areas of policy development, school personnel, budget appropriations, curriculum, and the law. Among other duties, state boards of education appoint and supervise the chief state officer or state superintendent of education and oversee budgetary appropriations for school spending, licensure regulations for teachers, standards for accreditation, and compliance with state school laws. Some state boards of education are more interventionist than others. In Texas, for instance, the state is involved in appointing a committee to screen school textbooks for the purpose of identifying an adoption list from which schools can make their selections. Contrast this to Iowa, where the state not only eschews textbook adoption policies, but also any dictation of state standards and state graduation requirements to local school districts.

In most states, the members of the state board are appointed by the state governor. In 15 states membership is by popular vote, and in a small group of five states, the state legislature appoints school board members. Still other states use some combination of these methods. In most cases, the board is comprised of lay people. Membership rarely requires professional educator status, although in Indiana four of the 11 members of the board must be educators. Different states attach different conditions to the composition of the Board. In Georgia, a board member must be a resident of the state for at least five years; in Kentucky, board members must be at least 30 years old and hold at least an Associate's degree; in Delaware, at least two school board members must have local school board experience; and in New Jersey, at least three of the 13 Board members must be women. The number of voting members on a state board ranges from seven, which is the case in ten states, to 16, which is the membership size of the New York State Board of Education. The length of term ranges from three years in Rhode Island to nine years in West Virginia and Mississippi.

The chief officer of the state typically answers to the state board of education, especially if he is an appointed official. Frequently, the chief officer of education is also the executive chairperson of the state board. The chief officer makes the decisions on appointments in the state department, offers budgetary and legislative recommendations to the state board, and is responsible for determining the status and the needs for public education, particularly as they relate to improving the conditions of schooling. The state superintendent is also responsible for the function of the state department of education, which often operationalizes the work of the state board with regard to regulate teacher certification, school accreditation, financial authorizations, and other pertinent issues. The state department of education is often active in compiling statistical data on the schools and in filing an annual state report on educational progress. It is the main administrative agency for public education in the state.

The chief school officer is an elected position in 18 states, and an appointed position in the remaining states. The appointment can come from the state board of education or from the governor, which, in 32 states, represents two sides of the same coin because state boards of education in such states are also appointed by the governor. Only a small handful of states require the superintendent to have had experience as a professional educator.

Often overlooked is the influence that state governors have in this arrangement of authority. In most cases, the governor appoints the executive state officer of education and the state board of education.

It is also the governor who gives final approval to the state school budget. The governor can propose bills to the legislature, veto bills forwarded by the legislature and use the office as a platform for the promotion of reform.

Except in the state of Hawaii, which has one statewide school district, every public school in America is part of a local school district arrangement, and in this sense, local communities still have a voice in their schools. In fact, one can consider the local district the basic administrative unit for the implementation of state policy. Because the local district is an agent of the state, it needs approval from the state to carry out its functions. The state can intervene virtually as it wishes in local school matters. For example, it can change a district's boundaries, authorize an evaluation of its curriculum, or if warranted, entirely usurp its governing powers.

Each local district also has its own local school board whose members, again depending on the district, might be appointed or elected, but the overwhelming majority is elected. Although local school districts, in most cases, have some latitude in decision making, they must comply with state requirements, especially in areas of institutional regulation. State laws and regulations might specify the length of the school year, the standards of preparation required of teachers, minimal teacher salaries, required subjects areas to be taught, and other essential aspects of the school's operation. Within this framework of regulations, the local school district usually has an opportunity to follow its own prerogatives. Local school boards, after all, authorize the funds raised through local taxes and make the decisions related to personnel and property. Within certain boundaries, local school boards plan school policy and appraise the work of the personnel that they hire, especially the superintendent. They also approve budgets, determine school and attendance boundaries, enter into labor negotiations, and make numerous curriculum-related decisions. Their work, however, is bound to the formation of policy, not to its implementation. They are comprised of lay citizens, most of whom serve without pay and who are under a state directive to operate as a public body in deliberate discussion with the public.

The actual implementation of the local board's policy wishes is typically delegated to the superintendent of schools. Thus, the superintendent is the main representative of the board when it is not in session, as well as its official executive agent, making decisions in accordance with board policy and in close contact with board personnel. But, the superintendent also acts in an advisory capacity. As the chief officer of the school district, the school superintendent makes recommendations to the local board on various fronts, including the appointment of personnel, the drafting of labor policies, curriculum reform actions, physical plant issues, and public relations concerns. The local school superintendent is also responsible for submitting a budget to the board for its analysis and eventual approval.

The idea of the local school district is distinctively American. Advocates of localism have long hailed the idea of keeping the school close to the people. Local school control also carries its share of problems. As we shall find, the district system tends to lead to funding inequities between schools, a problem that many states have been unable to solve. Too often, local school boards overstep their responsibilities and attempt to micromanage their schools, which sometimes results in the promotion of narrow political or even religious agendas. The state, of course, oversees these actions and can apply remedies.

The federal government also has a place in the governance of the school. Historically, its role has been to implement any federal legislation related to the functioning of the school, which has frequently meant providing monies to schools through federal programs sanctioned by Congress. The federal government is responsible for evaluating the status of American education at the national level. However, it has little jurisdiction in the area of policy or practice.

Most of the educational actions of the federal government are operationalized through the Department of Education, which is led by a cabinet-level Secretary of Education. The secretary has no power to dictate educational changes or prescriptions to the states. There is no centralizing national power for school policy and school practice. The secretary, however, can be enormously persuasive and influential on state-level school policy, largely because of the national visibility of the position, the federal grant money underpinning Department of Education causes, and the easy access that the secretary has to national media sources.

The Department of Education and the Secretary also oversee the Office of Educational Research and Improvement, which assumes all of the main responsibilities for reporting and analyzing national measures of school achievement. This office conducts the National Assessment of Educational Progress (NAEP), which provides measurements of the levels of proficiency achieved by American students in various subject areas, including math, science, reading, and writing.

The federal government has traditionally played a prominent role in promoting public education. Its prominent legislative initiatives include the Morrill Act of 1862, which was largely responsible for the development of the nation's state universities, and the Smith-Hughes Act of 1917, which provided massive funding for the support of vocational education in secondary schools. More recently, the federal government has sponsored a variety of initiatives and programs. For example, the GI Bills supported the cost of post-secondary education for military veterans. The National Science Foundation maintained a presence in the area of math and science education. The National Defense Education Act of 1958 funneled federal monies for the improvement of instruction in math, science, and foreign language, and for the development of early instructional technologies. The Elementary and Secondary Act of 1965 targeted the education of children in low income brackets. The National Merit Scholarship program recognized and supported the post-secondary education of the most academically talented students in the nation, and a host of other initiatives addressed special education, bilingual education, vocational education, and compensatory education. Various areas of the federal government, including the Department of Defense, the Department of Justice, the Department of the Interior, and the Department of Labor, have also, at one time or another, provided federal education programs for youth at some level of the educational ladder.

FUNDING PUBLIC EDUCATION

The education of the American school child is supported by taxes that are collected at the local, state, and federal levels. The average breakdown of school funding by state is, more or less, evenly split between the local district and the state, with each taking on between 40 and 50 percent of the obligation. In some states, such as Hawaii, there is full state funding, and in others, such as New Hampshire, there is heavy reliance on locally raised revenues. Nationwide, the federal government averages less than 10 percent of school funding. Figure 10–2 shows the national breakdown of school revenues and Table 10–1 shows the state-by-state profile of the sources used for school expenditures.

The typical pattern for financial support in the American schools follows the governance structure discussed earlier. The state creates the local school districts and authorizes levy taxes in order to raise funds for the support of public schools. The local districts raise these funds through property taxes. Obviously, the value of real estate properties will affect how successful a district is in finding the

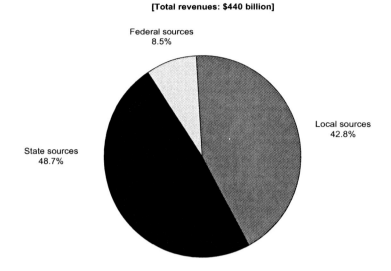

[Total revenues: $440 billion]

Federal sources
8.5%

Local sources
42.8%

State sources
48.7%

FIGURE 10–2 Revenues for Public Elementary and Secondary Education, by Source. SOURCE: Data reported by states to the U.S. Department of Education, National Center for Education Statistics, Common Core of Data (CCD), "National Public Education Financial Survey," 2002–03.

proper level of financial support. The basic capacity of a local school district to raise monies for the school is always a function of the property wealth of the district combined with the tax burden that the community is willing to accept. This can lead to remarkable disparities in spending between different local districts.

Differences in funding at the local level usually result from differences in the value of commercial and residential property zoned to a district. A district wealthy in property value can raise more revenue for its students, and often at a lower tax rate, than a property-poor district. When local districts have no state restrictions over their school budgets, the differences in spending between high- and low-spending districts can reach astounding proportions. For example, the highest-spending district in some states has a per pupil expenditure rate eight times greater than that of the lowest-spending district. Table 10–2 shows the differences witnessed in the states between per pupil district expenditures at the 95th percentile in the state, and district expenditures at the 5th percentile during the 2002-2003 academic year. The ratio for the United States reflects about a one-and-one-half average difference (1.40) between school spending at the 95th and 5th percentiles, but significantly higher disparities can be found in individual states. Arizona, Montana, and Nevada, for instance, all display about a two-and-one-half fold difference. If one does the math, this practically means that, over the course of a 13-year career of going to school, students attending a school district at the 95th percentile of funding in Arizona will likely have about $130,000 more spent on their education than students attending schools at the 5th percentile of funding.

 Although the local district has to rely almost exclusively on property taxes, states can turn to a number of sources for revenue. State funds for the schools are typically drawn from sales and income taxes, but many states engage special programs, such as state lotteries, to raise funding for education. In Georgia, for instance, lottery income is used to fund a scholarship program that pays for the tuition, fees, and books of any Georgia high school graduate who has maintained a B average or better and attends a public university or college within the state. Although there is quite a bit of variance, on average 33 percent of state tax revenue for public schools is from sales or gross receipt tax, 30 percent from personal income tax, 8 percent from corporate tax, and the remainder from excise

Table 10-1 State by State Distribution of Revenues for Public Schools by Source.

Percentage Distribution of Revenue for Public Elementary and Secondary Schools, by Source, and Outlying Areas: School Year 2002-03.

State	Within-State Percentage Distribution		
	Local	**State**	**Federal**
United States[1]	42.8	48.7	8.5
Alabama	30.9	57.6	11.6
Alaska	25.5	56.8	17.7
Arizona[1]	40.2	48.4	11.4
Arkansas	33.0	55.2	11.7
California	31.3	58.9	9.9
Colorado	50.4	43.1	6.5
Connecticut	57.4	37.4	5.2
Delaware	28.0	63.4	8.6
District of Columbia	86.2	†	13.8
Florida	45.8	43.6	10.5
Georgia	43.7	48.2	8.1
Hawaii	1.7	90.1	8.2
Idaho	31.1	59.1	9.8
Illinois	58.5	33.0	8.5
Indiana	33.5	58.8	7.6
Iowa	46.0	46.6	7.4
Kansas	33.8	57.1	9.1
Kentucky	30.7	58.8	10.6
Louisiana	37.7	49.1	13.2
Maine	48.1	42.9	8.9
Maryland	55.0	38.3	6.7
Massachusetts	53.1	40.9	6.0
Michigan	28.9	63.3	7.8
Minnesota	20.2	73.8	5.9
Misslsslppl	30.8	53.8	15.4
Missouri	56.2	35.8	8.0
Montana	39.2	46.3	14.5
Nebraska	56.7	34.4	8.9
Nevada	62.8	30.2	7.0
New Hampshire	45.9	48.9	5.2
New Jersey	52.2	43.5	4.3
New Mexico	12.9	72.1	15.0
New York	47.5	45.6	7.0
North Carolina	26.7	63.7	9.6
North Dakota	47.9	36.8	15.3
Ohio	48.7	44.8	6.4
Oklahoma	32.6	54.7	12.7
Oregon	40.0	50.9	9.1
Pennsylvania	55.6	36.6	7.7
Rhode Island	51.5	42.0	6.5
South Carolina	42.1	48.1	9.8
South Dakota	50.6	33.7	15.7
Tennessee	46.1	43.8	10.0
Texas	49.2	40.9	9.9
Utah	34.3	56.4	9.3
Vermont	25.3	67.8	7.0
Virginia	53.8	39.6	6.6
Washington	29.2	61.8	9.0
West Virginia	27.9	61.4	10.6
Wisconsin	40.6	53.4	6.1
Wyoming	40.3	50.9	8.8

SOURCE: Data reported by states to U.S. Department of Education, National Center for Education Statistics, Common Core of Data (CCD), "School District Finance Survey" (F-33), FY 2003, version 1a.

TABLE 10–2 Revenues Per Student for Public Elementary and Secondary School Districts, by State: School Year 2002–03.

State	Revenues Per Sudent			
	5th Percentile	Median	95th Percentile	Federal Range Ratio[1]
United States	$6,340	$8,891	$17,078	1.69
Alabama	6,200	6,942	8,589	0.39
Alaska	7,684	16,333	34,753	3.52
Arizona	5,167	7,647	17,272	2.34
Arkansas	6,227	6,826	9,416	0.51
California	6,765	8,669	15,261	1.26
Colorado	7,003	8,890	15,521	1.22
Connecticut	9,872	11,729	17,203	0.74
Delaware	9,335	10,302	13,742	0.47
District of Columbia	†	16,499	†	†
Florida	6,684	7,515	10,268	0.54
Georgia	7,170	8,429	11,499	0.60
Hawaii	†	11,309	†	†
Idaho	5,710	7,527	14,641	1.56
Illinois	6,422	8,150	13,686	1.13
Indiana	6,355	7,439	10,287	0.62
Iowa	7,586	8,764	13,251	0.75
Kansas	7,417	9,102	12,388	0.67
Kentucky	6,424	7,224	8,888	0.38
Louisiana	6,522	7,499	9,987	0.53
Maine	8,603	11,261	23,824	1.77
Maryland	8,441	9,436	11,066	0.31
Massachusetts	9,130	11,253	18,613	1.04
Michigan	7,521	8,708	11,996	0.59
Minnesota	8,003	9,350	12,993	0.62
Mississippi	5,682	6,659	8,813	0.55
Missouri	6,184	7,551	11,255	0.82
Montana	5,632	8,869	19,005	2.55
Nebraska	5,792	9,151	19,980	2.28
Nevada	7,115	8,592	20,122	1.83
New Hampshire	8,150	11,234	23,636	1.90
New Jersey	10,557	13,458	22,705	1.15
New Mexico	7,066	10,602	23,687	2.35
New York	10,766	13,428	21,971	1.04
North Carolina	6,408	7,422	10,221	0.59
North Dakota	6,323	8,919	17,882	1.83
Ohio	7,017	8,135	13,357	0.90
Oklahoma	5,529	6,965	11,231	1.03
Oregon	6,725	7,968	18,313	1.72
Pennsylvania	8,075	9,688	13,185	0.63
Rhode Island	9,094	10,900	16,442	0.81
South Carolina	6,830	8,399	10,685	0.56
South Dakota	6,635	7,944	14,318	1.16
Tennessee	5,540	6,298	7,816	0.41
Texas	7,116	8,581	16,636	1.34
Utah	5,368	6,845	12,129	1.26
Vermont	8,970	15,470	26,040	1.90
Virginia	7,205	8,315	11,748	0.63
Washington	7,105	8,657	19,000	1.67
West Virginia	7,850	8,627	10,061	0.28
Wisconsin	8,800	10,104	12,872	0.46
Wyoming	9,562	12,463	22,442	1.35

SOURCE: Data reported by states to U.S. Department of Education, National Center for Education Statistics, Common Core of Data (CCD), "School District Finance Survey" (F-33), FY 2003, version 1a.

and business taxes. Once the state collects its money for public education, it has to decide how the monies will be allocated.

Because one of the functions of the state is to help equalize differences in per pupil expenditures across school districts, local districts that are less wealthy and less able to invest large sums of money in the education of their children are supposed to find relief from the state. Many states tackle this problem by applying a minimal provision philosophy of funding, whereby each district in the state must meet a minimal baseline investment. The baseline represents a commitment of monies that will supposedly ensure an adequate education for all youth in the state (Guthrie, Garms, & Pierce, 1988).

For several decades now, several lawsuits have been filed against states alleging a failure to provide equality of educational opportunity. As of 1998, sixteen states have had their method of financing public schools declared unconstitutional by their state supreme courts (Linn, 1998). The list includes Alabama, Arizona, California, Connecticut, Massachusetts, Missouri, Montana, New Hampshire, New Jersey, Ohio, Tennessee, Texas, Vermont, Washington, West Virginia, and Wyoming.

This litigation is in the state courts because the U.S. Supreme Court does not view public education as a right protected under the federal constitution. The U.S. Supreme Court took this position in 1973 when it heard the case of *San Antonio Independent School District v. Rodriguez,* in which the plaintiffs charged that the inequities in the funding of the local schools violated their children's equal protection guarantees under the Fourteenth Amendment to the Constitution. The allegation was that the disparities represented the denial of a fundamental civil liberty to an offended group of citizens. The equal protection clause of the Fourteenth Amendment reads that "No state shall . . . deny to any person within its jurisdiction the equal protection of the laws." The Supreme Court, however, did not see a constitutional violation in *San Antonio,* holding that no particular group was damaged by the system of funding (the property-poor district was not wholly comprised of a single homogeneous group). The interdistrict differences in funding did not undermine the adequacy of education provided to schoolchildren in different school districts, but were, in fact, a reasonable byproduct of the state's interest in maintaining local control. In other words, children in poorer districts were likely getting an inferior education to children in wealthy districts, but they were still getting an adequate one. The effect of this ruling shifted school finance litigation to the states' courts. Justice Thurgood Marshall, in fact, almost encouraged challenges at the state level when he asserted in *San Antonio* that "nothing in this court's decision today should inhibit further reviews of state educational funding schemes under state constitutional provisions." Unlike the federal constitution, most state constitutions have explicit constitutional language or clauses referring to free public education as a fundamental right.

Litigation challenging the state constitutionality of state funding schemes was already underway in California in the late 1960s, as documented in the well-known *Serrano v. Priest* case. John Serrano, a parent of a child in a Los Angeles area school, noticed the poor quality of school services made available to his child. When he protested to the school, he was told that the school simply could not afford to make improvements. The principal of the school actually advised the father to move to a wealthier school district if he wanted better instruction for his child (Guthrie, Garms, & Pierce, 1988). At the time of the trial, the disparities in the per pupil expenditures between Los Angeles area school districts were striking. Serrano, who could not afford to move, brought suit against the state, arguing that the method of school funding, which was heavily dependent on a district's local wealth, violated provisions of the state constitution.

Acknowledging education as a fundamental right and allowing property wealth to stand as an aggrieved or suspect class of "individuals," the State Supreme Court of California pronounced the entire system of financing schools in California to be in violation of the state's constitution. The problem was that educational opportunities were too closely tied to the taxable wealth of a given school district. This was not an argument, as in the *San Antonio* case, over the adequacy of the educational provisions offered in an inequitable system, but over the actual fiscal inequalities in the funding structure of the state system. The court could not tolerate a system of school funding that allowed district spending to be related to district wealth. The new catchword would become fiscal neutrality, which meant that no relation could exist between per pupil spending and local district property wealth. In other words, the quality of education has to be a function of the entire state's wealth, not of the local district's. California, like many other states, relied on property taxes as a major source of local school revenue for the school. Because of the *Serrano* ruling, this had to change. Either local school revenue had to be equalized through state aid or a state system of funding had to be explored.

Historically, when states began to give money to schools, the thinking was that each district, irrespective of its local investment, should be given a flat rate grant of money sufficient for a minimally adequate education (Swanson & King, 1991). These were known as flat grant programs. Schools spending in excess of the flat grant rate were believed to be indulging in a luxury that was their right. The minimal guarantees of an adequate education were thought to be supported under this scheme; basic equalization, in this sense, was upheld. The problem, of course, was that minimal support was an arbitrary amount, especially because the conditions of learning across city and rural landscapes varied so widely. Some schools, moreover, were already vested with local monies at a rate well above the flat grant line drawn by the state. Because the flat grant provided an equal amount of money for each district, it had little to no impact on the variance in spending across districts. Flat grant programs were eventually abandoned by most states in favor of what is known as the foundation program.

The foundation program is driven by a minimal provision philosophy, but it is a wiser way of setting an adequate minimal level of funding for each school district. As with the flat grant program, the foundational program sets a minimal funding level that represents what each district must provide to ensure an adequate education. It also requires, in most cases, each district to levy a property tax at a fixed rate. If a property-rich local district meets the baseline or foundational figure with its own local monies, it receives nothing from the state in general aid, but if a less wealthy district falls short of this figure, the state makes up the difference. Some states also have a recapture clause that requires any districts that spent above the foundational level to return those monies to the state for redistribution (Guthrie, Garms, & Pierce, 1988). Under the foundation program, the state does not provide money to districts spending above the minimal provision. Thus, it can usually set the minimal provision at a higher rate than what was possible with flat grants. Today, some form of foundation programs are in operation in about 40 states.

The problem for foundation funding, however, is that local funding disparities are often so wide that many states simply cannot afford to bring the lower districts up to a competitive level. Further, the typical state action in closing the funding gap is to ensure that students in lower spending districts receive a fair and basic education, which means that they aim at a minimal compensation figure rather than at a full and comprehensive one. In Montana, litigation was filed against the state for operating a foundation program that equalized at a level below the average spending of districts. Table 10–3 shows the cost and need adjusted foundation level for each of the 50 states.

Even if average levels were met, the poorest districts would still be at a disadvantage because in most cases their needs and problems are not average. In many cases, the problems resulting from poverty make public education in such places more costly, and thus require an above-average investment.

Table 10-3   Nationally Adjusted Implicit Foundation Levels (Ranked).

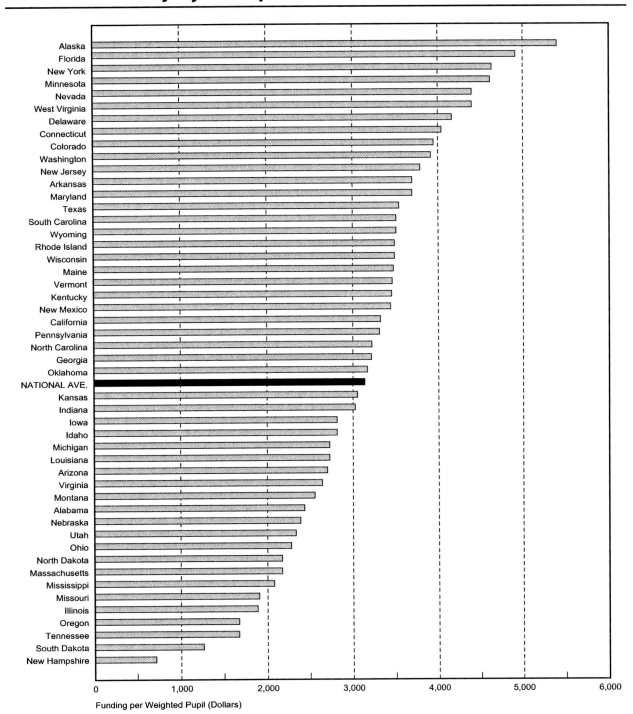

Funding per Weighted Pupil (Dollars)

Researchers concerned about the equity of school finance systems have tried to account for this problem by developing the idea of vertical equity. According to this concept, some students, such as those who are disabled, or are limited in their English proficiency, need additional educational services that are going to be more costly to the district than would normally be the case. Thus, when school funding is calculated with vertical equity in mind, adjustments have to be made to give added weight to those students who need extra or special educational services. With vertical equity, funding levels are calculated as a *per-weighted pupil* figure. Thus, weighing schemes could be used in foundation programs by recalibrating the way special needs students are counted. An educable mentally retarded student might be counted at 1.5, meaning that the associated costs with educating such a student would be 1.5 times the cost of educating a non-classified student; the weigh factor for the education of a deaf student could go to 4 and for a home- or hospital-bound student to 10 (Guthrie, Garms, & Pierce, 1988).

Vertical equity issues are also accounted for through categorical aid programs. Each school district, irrespective of its wealth, will usually receive some funds from the federal government, often as a result of categorical aid programs that designate monies for special purposes such as the education of disabled students or the education of students from low income backgrounds. States also provide categorical aid to school districts, as well as supplemental funding for special education programs. A significant number of states also provide categorical monies for limited English proficiency programs and for compensatory education programs. It is fair to say that the highest poverty schools receive more categorical aid than low poverty schools, but these do not always eliminate inequities.

Increasingly, there is also talk of embracing full state funding in the war against funding inequities. This would mean that each state would assume the full costs of running each of its school districts. Local revenues, in such a case, would likely become state property and be redistributed on an equitable level. Of course, such a scenario might also result in the forfeiture of local decision-making and local preferences and priorities. Currently, Hawaii is funded as one state-wide system and Washington uses a modified form of full state funding by collecting from local districts, pooling the revenues with state funds and redistributing to schools on an equal per pupil basis (Linn, 1998).

Over the past decade, the states have taken a more active hand in the financing of schools (see Figure 10-3). State presence will likely increase because a reliance on state taxes will probably be the only way to equalize the resources of the schools. This fact has been made quite clear in Michigan, whose citizens decided to opt for a revamped tax structure that puts much of the financial burden for public schooling on the state. In 1993, Michigan voters supported a school finance reform plan that diminished the state's reliance on local property taxes as a source of school funding. In 1993–94, the statewide average millage rate for the operation of local schools was just under 34 mills on all property, which is another way of saying $3.40 for every $100 of assessed property value or $34 for every $1,000. The mill is a denomination used in school finance, associated with an old English coin long out of use, which represents a tenth of a cent (.001). The local school operating millage rate is now 6 mills on all property in Michigan and 18 mills on non-homestead property (mostly business and industry). This money remains within the school district and serves as part of the district's foundation allowance. The schools in Michigan were able to shift away from a reliance on local property taxes by increasing the sale tax in the state from 4 to 6 percent and tripling the tax on cigarettes. Under the new funding conditions, all of the schools in the state now draw most of their monies from state coffers and are guaranteed by a minimum or foundational level of $5,000 per student, giving most poor districts in the state about $1,000 more per student than they had been used to spending. Wealthier school districts in the state can spend above the foundation level but their capacity to generate the kind of local revenue that created earlier disparities has been curtailed.

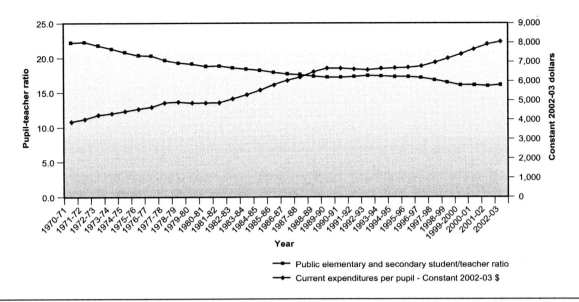

FIGURE 10–3 Sources of Revenue for Public Elementary and Secondary Schools Since 1970
SOURCE: U.S. Department of Education, National Center for Education Statistics, Statistics of State School Systems; Revenues and Expenditures for Public Elementary and Secondary Education; The NCES Common Core of Data (CCD), "National Public Education Financial Survey," 1987–88 through 2000–01; and Projections of Education Statistics to 2013.

Funding inequities also occur between states, but these rarely get as much attention. The issue of disparities is no less an issue simply because it is happening between states rather than within them. Because public schooling is controlled at the state level, most of the research interest is focused on variations within states. From an inter-state perspective, however, one finds that school funding revenues differ considerably. The funding disparities between states are so wide in some cases that if we compare the per-pupil expenditures in the highest spending districts of a low-revenue state to per-pupil expenditures in the lowest spending districts of a high-revenue state, we find that the school-children in the latter situation are probably better off. In Mississippi, for instance, students in the highest revenue districts ($4,180 per pupil, which is at the 95th percentile) still receive less than the children in the lowest revenue districts (5th percentile) in 29 states. Students in the lowest revenue group in New York (5th percentile), benefit from a higher per-pupil revenue than in the majority of other states, including states whose school funding systems were found to be more equitable than New York's. As noted on Table 10-3, district revenue at the 5th percentile in Connecticut, New Jersey, and New York (adjusted for cost and need) is higher than spending at the 95th percentile in Tennessee, Utah, and Mississippi. Thus, children in low-equity, high-revenue states still might be better off than children in high-equity, low-revenue states (NCES, 1998).

Despite the changes occurring at the state level in school funding, the role of the federal government in the economic arrangement of schooling will likely remain the same. The federal role in school financing is essentially limited to aid enacted by Congressional legislation. This includes direct grant programs, compensatory aid for children of poor families, as well as indirect categorical aid given to states or geographical regions, which trickles down to school districts. As indicated, the overall financial investment in a public school amounts to less than 10 percent of the total financial commitment. With such a limited role, the federal government's effort to assist districts with large concentrations of poor students has not had a significant impact on the funding disparities between schools.

Historically, the federal government has invested in the expansion of educational opportunities, playing a prominent role in the education of handicapped children and in bilingual instruction and compensatory education. It has also been active where compelling national defense interests have been involved and where the economic livelihood of the country has been in question.

Church and State

One of the fundamental legal principles regulating the relation between the church and the state derives from the First Amendment to the Constitution: "Congress shall make no law respecting an establishment of religion, or prohibiting the exercise thereof. . . ." The purpose of the principle ensures religious freedom for all by prohibiting any governmental establishment of religion (The Establishment Clause of the First Amendment) and by protecting against government restrictions of any individual religious expression (The Free Exercise Clause of the First Amendment). The Fourteenth Amendment to the Constitution extended these restrictions to state and local governments, including public school districts.

In 1947, the Supreme Court, in *Everson v. Board of Education*, offered its first ruling on the relation between church and state. Its judgment spoke to the meaning of both the Establishment and Free Exercise Clauses of the First Amendment. *Everson* concerned a New Jersey law that allowed for the payment of transportation for students attending parochial schools. Although the Court upheld the law, in doing so it also outlined broad separationist lines between church and state, harkening back to the words of Jefferson, arguing that there must be a "wall of separation between Church and State." The Court stated outright that the government cannot set up a church, that it cannot pass laws aiding one religion or even aiding the religious over the nonreligious, and that no tax can be levied to support religious activities. These were all Establishment Clause issues. At the same time, it also offered safeguards for the rights of people to practice religion without state interference, stating that no persons can be forced to remain away from church or to profess a belief against their will, that no persons can be punished for professing a religious thought or engaging in a religious action, and that the government cannot participate in the affairs of religious organizations. These were all Free Exercise Clause issues. Embodied in these ideas was the brick and mortar for the wall of separation. According to this notion of separation, the state is prohibited from favoring any religious belief system but it is also compelled to protect the rights of people to practice their religion without government interference.

The metaphor of a wall of separation has endured for many years. It has helped the courts to offer important prohibitions against certain religious activity in the school. But the image of a wall of separation between church and state does not capture the actual relation between schooling and religion very precisely. The school, in fact, cooperates with the church in the interests of the student's free expression rights (Power, 1991). Jefferson's famous metaphor notwithstanding, the relation between church and state, in the words of Justice Warren Burger, is represented by a "blurred, indistinct and variable barrier, depending on the circumstances of a particular relationship" (Patrick & Long, 1999).

Contrary to popular belief, schools are not designed to be religion-free. Although there have been episodes in public schools, especially in the development of curriculum materials, where religion has been systematically and unreasonably culled from the learning experience (Vitz, 1986; Nord, 1995), many, if not most, public schools have been accommodating to religion. Students, for instance, have the right to pray individually or in groups when attending public school, as long as they do so without disrupting the school environment. In fact, student prayer groups enjoy some popularity in the public schools. According to some estimates, 12,000 Bible clubs are operating in American public schools (Prayer in Public Schools?, 1994). Students may also carry and read religious materials in school and, within certain boundaries, even distribute religious material in school. They also have every right to be excused from school in order to attend to religious obligations or desires, and with certain qualifications, to be excused from classroom activity if it is viewed by them or their parents as offensive to their religion. Many high schools offer comparative religion courses and many of the new content standards developed for the teaching of history, social studies, and civics include references to teaching about religious beliefs and practice.

The place of religion in the curriculum, in fact, cannot be denied if it is placed within established secular purposes. One, for instance, cannot effectively study the history of early America without understanding how religious faith drove much of the actions and thinking of the early settlers. Similarly, one cannot effectively understand the Civil Rights movement in America without learning that much of the prominent leadership came out of the Southern Leadership Christian Conference, or that the concept of nonviolent civil disobedience was partly justified by Christian doctrine. In such cases, religion is justly integrated within a secular instructional purpose.

The Establishment and Free Exercise Clauses

In adjudicating cases that test the interference of government in the religious lives of citizens, the courts target two main questions. One is whether there is excessive government involvement in supporting a particular religion, which as indicated, is something known as the Establishment Clause. The other, which is less well-known but equally important, is whether an individual's faith has been handicapped or burdened by the government, which involves the Free Exercise Clause.

To deal with the Establishment Clause, the Supreme Court has, since the 1970s, advanced a three-part framework, sometimes known as the Lemon test, which is based on the 1971 *Lemon v. Kurtzman* ruling. In the *Lemon* case, the Supreme Court did not allow public money to be used to support instruction in secular subjects at parochial schools. The law that the Court struck down aimed to assist religious schools with the education of low-income children by offering a partial reimbursement to the schools for the costs of educating such children in secular subjects.

The test used by the Court in the *Lemon* case asks the following: 1) Does the government's action (in this case, the public school's action) fulfill a clear secular purpose? If it does not, a Constitutional violation may result; 2) Does the government's action advance religion as a primary effect? If it does, again, a Constitutional violation may be the consequence, and; 3) Does the effect of the government's action foster an "excessive entanglement" with a religion? Entanglement, in the context of schooling, can mean any number of things. For instance, if important school personnel, such as the teacher or a principal, display behaviors that can be interpreted as being strongly associated with a religious point of view, one could argue that the effect is entanglement. The Courts are especially concerned about the actions of teachers because of the influence they have on pupils and because of the role-model expectation placed on teacher behavior. If a teacher, for instance, offers a sectarian prayer in class, she clearly becomes entangled with a sectarian view and by implication, privileges, or advances a sectarian view in the presence of students. This would be tantamount to the establishment of a religion in the school. The idea of entanglement, as a criterion for judging establishment issues, emphasizes the importance that the Court places on government neutrality. As Chief Justice Burger stated, "The general principle is that we will not tolerate either government established religion or government interference with religion. Short of those expressly proscribed government acts, there is ample room for play in the joints productive of a benevolent neutrality which will permit religious exercise without sponsorship and without interference" (Witte, 1999, pp. 157–158).

In recent years, the Supreme Court has criticized and even departed from the Lemon Test. Although today's Supreme Court has not entirely rebuffed the *Lemon* test (and its commitment to neutrality and separation), it has explored other criteria for legal interpretation. One is known as the coercion test, which says that there must be evidence of government coercion in moving individuals to profess or accept a religion for a violation of the Establishment Clause to exist. Such a test, which is largely supported by political conservatives and others favoring the widened role of religion in schooling, would open up new channels between the school and church, making "a lack of coercion" the defining element for the release of religious views in the school. The question, of course, gets into legal nuances over operational definitions of coercion—whether, for instance, something such as audible school prayer could represent a form of indirect or subtle coercion, as it might arise from social pressures and the desire to yield to school-sponsored norms. Supreme Court Justice Kennedy has argued that permitting the noncoercive endorsement of religion in school is fundamentally constitutional, because it is the only way to prevent the unconstitutional practice of state hostility to religion (Finkelman, 2000, p. 96).

Another way of judging Establishment Clause concerns is through something known as the endorsement test, which essentially says that government action must be struck down if it has the purpose or effect of endorsing a religion (McCarthy, Cambron-McCabe, & Thomas, 1998). The endorsement standard is similar to the *Lemon* framework. In fact, it is a kind of reinterpretation of the *Lemon* test that says that even if the school causes, as a primary effect, the advancement of a religion (one prong of the Lemon test), in the end, its action has be to judged by whether there is evidence that the effect is governmental endorsement of a religion. The endorsement test could be viewed as the weaker sister of the Lemon test, because it leaves open the possibility that schools could be entangled with religious points of view without necessarily endorsing them. The endorsement test was conceived by Justice O'Conner in her effort to make a distinction between government actions that advance religion and government actions that advance and endorse a religious point of view. "What is crucial," O'Conner stated, "is that government practice not have the effect of communicating a message of government endorsement of disapproval of religion" (Finkleman, 2000, p. 287).

Yet another way to judge Establishment concerns involves what is known as nonpreferentialism, or equal treatment. This position recasts the relation between church and state by saying, in effect, that religion can be given active government support as long as it does so equally and non-preferentially to all denominations (Patrick & Long, 1999). Thus, financial aid to religious schools, under non-preferentialism, is no problem as long as it is equally and non-preferentially distributed. Just how nonpreferentialism would deal with concerns such as school prayer is not clear. Under such a doctrine, the school might have to offer any number of denominational prayers on an equal opportunity basis.

Establishment issues represent only half of the problems in the realm of church/school relations. Schools also need to be conscious about not showing hostility toward or interfering with the personal religious convictions of students. This is the central concern of the Free Exercise Clause. To deal with the Free Exercise Clause, the courts have to weight the interests of the school to conduct its normative mandate against the religious expression rights of the individual.

In cases where the school is viewed by certain parents as impeding the free exercise of their children's religious beliefs, an excusal policy or alternative assignment is typically used. If a certain book or school assignment, for instance, offends an individual's religious view, the teacher will find another book or assignment. The school might not always be able to offer alternative experiences, due to any number of reasons, or it might believe that an excusal from a particular assignment or book is inappropriate and educationally unsound. Imagine, for instance, in the extreme case, a request to prohibit a child from experiencing reading instruction on the grounds of religious offense. The school would clearly have the right to claim a state interest in advancing the literacy of a child, even in the face of a Free Exercise challenge.

The well-known *Mozert v. Hawkins County* case illustrates the tensions involved in dealing with Free Exercise exemptions. The case raised questions about how far schools must go in order to protect individual religious expression.

It all started when a group of fundamentalist Christians objected to the required reading materials used in the elementary school, materials that the group claimed were in violation of the Free Exercise Clause of the Constitution. Their children, they asserted, were being forced to read materials objectionable to their religious faith. They further claimed that the reading series used in the school promoted a secular religion that supported world government, nontraditional gender roles, moral relativism, nonreligious views of death, critical views of the founders of the country, socialism, universal communication, magic, environmentalism, disarmament, gun control, kindness to animals, vegetarianism, negative views of hunting and war, and several other unacceptable perspectives (DelFattore, 1992).

The parents offered many examples. They objected, for instance, to the reading and teaching of Jack London's story, *To Build a Fire*. The main character in London's story is a Yukon traveler who accidentally gets his feet and legs wet, which in the Yukon, is a life-threatening condition. The traveler had to build a fire to survive, but when the man ultimately failed to build a fire, due to a series of bad decisions, his death was inevitable. The parents complained that the man in the story failed to recognize that God was responsible for the physical survival of individuals. In fact, he failed to pray for wisdom and salvation. Thus, the children who read the story will not learn that it was the will of God, not the failed decisions of the man, that dictated his destiny. The complainants also objected to the fact that the man's death made no reference to an afterlife. This lack of reference taught children to accept a humanistic view in which there is no God and no hereafter—a view highly offensive to the parents (DelFatorre, 1992). Similar complaints were made against the *Wizard of Oz* and *Cinderella*, in which, it was alleged, the satanic practice of witchcraft is condoned. Clearly, the plaintiffs did not want their children to be exposed to any ideas that went against their particular religious views. The issue was whether the school had to accommodate such views.

The school's reaction to these complaints was to say that it was simply conducting reading instruction, well within its secular mandate, and that it could not, given the importance of reading instruction to all academic achievement, excuse the children from reading instruction. It further maintained that critical reading was one of the key components to the reading program, a skill that would allow all children to read all the material with a critical eye. Finally, the school claimed that it could not provide an alternative reading program because of the number of students involved and because of the integrative nature of reading instruction in the subject matter of the curriculum. The school consequently asserted that any accommodation would be disruptive to the whole school and would result in considerable financial duress to the school.

A circuit court eventually agreed that there was indeed a free exercise violation and that the reading stories did indeed pose a trespass on the religious sensibilities of the children. Observing that a uniform series of books and stories was not a necessary condition for teaching children to read, the court looked for a solution in some accommodation strategy. It understood, however, that asking the school to provide an alternative assignment in alignment with the religious views of the children could be potentially viewed as an establishment violation. So, instead, it ordered the school to provide an option out of the reading program and suggested that the children be taught privately. This meant that the complainant's children would now be reading at home or in some other private setting, apparently in accordance with their religious faith.

This ruling, however, was eventually overturned by an appeals court panel. The judges on the panel argued that the mere exposure to beliefs in books did not constitute an active advocacy for or, in this case, against a particular religion. All areas of learning, after all, carried the potential of communicating values that might offend a student's or parents' religious beliefs. The court also stated that because reading was integrated into other aspects of the curriculum, the removal of students from reading class would seriously undermine the whole educational process. The court further ruled that even if the school offended the religious views of the plaintiffs, it was done with a compelling state interest in mind.

In the end, the plaintiffs lost the case, but there were lessons learned for public school authorities. The *Mozert* case made it clear that the school district should honor excusal requests from parents as long as such requests did not produce an unreasonable financial, pedagogical, or administrative hardship on the school, and as long as the overall educational environment of the school was not disrupted.

School Prayer

Historically, the schools used biblical texts and invoked Christian prayers with some frequency. Over the years, however, school prayer has been litigated as a First Amendment violation, and the courts have, by and large, judged that the conditions of the Establishment Clause ("to make no law respecting the establishment of a religion") could not be met when one considered the place of prayer in the school (Sendor, 1988). Generally speaking, the courts found that, by allowing audible prayer and Bible reading, the school district (the government) was no longer acting toward a clear secular purpose and was advancing religion as a primary effect *(Engel v. Vitale, 1962; Abington v. Schempp, 1963)*.

In *Engle v. Vitale,* the landmark case on school prayer, the Court ruled that the State of New York cannot require the daily recitation of a state-composed prayer in its public schools. The schoolchildren in the state started each school day with the following prayer: "Almighty God, we acknowledge our dependence upon Thee, and we beg Thy blessing upon us, our parents, our teachers and our country." Even though the prayer was voluntary and nondenominational, it was nevertheless publicly practiced and was ultimately viewed by the Court as promoting religious practice. The Court, in effect, declared that any state-sponsored prayer (voluntary or not, denominational or not) was a violation of the Establishment Clause. In writing the majority opinion, Justice Hugo Black observed that "it is no part of the government to compose official prayers" (Patrick & Long, 1999, p. 162). *Engle* unleashed widespread public fury, causing the Court to engage in the unprecedented event of explaining the decision to the press (Finkleman, 2000, p. 442). In *Abington v. Schempp,* the Court extended the logic of Engel by not allowing Abington High School to dedicate any school time to prayer or to Bible readings. The school selected various biblical verses to read over the public address system, but the Court found these to be purely religious exercises. These early rulings tended to show the Court's inclination to demand neutrality from the school on issues related to religion.

In a dissenting statement, Justice Stewart asserted that prohibitions against prayer were less of a manifestation of state neutrality and more representative of state hostility and discrimination against religious exercises. Stewart outlined the basic elements to the coercion test, arguing that voluntary non-coercive prayer, free from embarrassment and pressures, should be allowable. Stewart went further and maintained that the refusal to permit non-coercive religious experiences in school resulted in the establishment of the religion of secularism.

The majority opinion in *Abington v. Schempp* took this accusation seriously and stressed the fact that prohibitions against sectarian prayer and the reading of sacred text could not be interpreted as an endorsement of a secular religion. There was nothing in the two cases that precluded the study of the Bible or religion in the school experience. Such study was allowable if it fulfilled a manifestly secular school purpose. Because there is protection for the freedom to hold religious beliefs, the school cannot prevent individuals or groups from engaging in private prayers, as long as such prayers are voluntary, nonofficial, and nondisruptive. Private prayer, in fact, is a protected right in the public schools.

The courts have treated so-called "moments of silence" differently from prayer, mostly because they are less easy to interpret as Establishment Clause violations. If the school designates a "moment of silence" or "silent meditation" without formally sanctioning prayer or any other denominational method of reflection, it will likely be on more constitutional ground than if it refers to a period of "voluntary prayer." This was the case in *Wallace v. Jaffree*, which highlighted a father's effort to stop the school from practicing voluntary devotional exercises in his daughters' school. In 1978, the Alabama legislature passed a law mandating that each school day begin with a moment of silence for meditation purposes. In 1981, the legislature added the option of voluntary prayer to the law, and in 1982 it added that willing students could be led in prayer by teachers. Jaffree, a resident of Mobile County and an avowed agnostic, had complained to the school about the ridicule his daughters had endured as a result of their nonparticipation. Eventually, he took his concerns to court. The Court struck down all of the exercises except the 1978 stature because it was the only provision in the law that was free from any reference or entanglement with official prayer.

A period of meditation does seem to be resonant with secular purposes. It has no real connection with advancing a religion because youth who are asked to participate in moments of silence (or meditation) can presumably think about or meditate on anything they choose. All this assumes that there is no compulsion in the school to embrace a particular form of reflection or meditation. This means, however, that teachers have to be scrupulous about their own behaviors during official moments of silence. Some school districts have instructed their teachers not to bow their heads, fold their hands, close their eyes, or provide any hint that they may actually be praying (When Quiet Is Pervasive in School, 1994). The concern here is over the issue of perceived teacher entanglement with a religious or prayerful view. Laws mandating a moment of silence at the beginning of the school day exist in Alabama, Georgia, South Carolina, and Tennessee. Several other states allow for a moment of silence but do not require it.

A variation of this problem is the issue of prayer held at special school ceremonies. The Supreme Court, in *Lee v. Weisman*, held that prayers at graduation ceremonies advance religion, noting the importance of the event in the lives of the students and the coercive elements at work in attending and participating (or passively listening) to an explicit state religious exercise *(Lee v. Weisman, 1992)*. But some legal arguments favor school prayer at graduation ceremonies. The claim is that there should be little concern over the Establishment Clause because the exercise is not officially part of the school curriculum program and can be viewed as ceremonial rather than educational in purpose. Moreover, because attendance at such events is typically voluntary and because there is usually a strong gathering of parents and other mature adults at such events, there is not as much of a concern over potential proselytism. This is a fundamentally different scenario from, say, prayer at a mandatory public school meeting (pep rallies, assemblies, homeroom activities, and other special school events) without the buffeting presence of parents. The use of devotional or prayerful student speech at graduation

1. School-sponsored prayer is unconstitutional. Prayers cannot be offered in classrooms, or in opening morning exercises.
2. Moments of silence, as long as they are voluntary and not part of any devotional activity, are usually constitutional.
3. Individual or group prayer is protected as long as is done in private and does not disrupt the school.
4. Prayers offered at school-sponsored events outside school hours are judged by the context of the event. Prayers offered at graduation ceremonies are typically viewed as less problematic because they are ceremonial events that attract many adults. They are easier to protect if they are student-led than if they are part of the school's program.

FIGURE 10–4   Principles and Guidelines on School Prayer.

ceremonies is easier to protect because it is harder to argue that such speech is government speech that endorses religion, which the Establishment Clause forbids, and as opposed to private speech that endorses religion, which the Free Exercise Clause protects (McCarthy, Cambron-McCabe, & Thomas, 1998).

Several school districts, understanding the distinction between school-sponsored and personal speech, found a way around the prohibition of prayer at graduation ceremonies by allowing students to vote on whether to include student-delivered invocations. The reasoning was such elections removed the speech from school sponsorship and put it purely in the realm of private speech, thereby giving it Free Exercise protections. This tactic was tested in the courts in the *Santa Fe Independent District v. Doe* case when the school district authorized student elections to determine whether to have student-led devotionals during the pre-game ceremonies of its high school football contests. In a 5–4 vote, the Supreme Court concluded that such a practice was nonetheless school sponsored because the election was organized, authorized, and ultimately supervised by the school. The degree of involvement of the school in the actual election process gave the impression that the school sanctioned the devotionals.

Schools can change the conditions of their involvement in graduation ceremonies by explicitly designating the event as a forum for student expression. This would mean, however, that the process for choosing the speaker is student-led without any conditions attached to the content of the speech and that the student's speech is not reviewed by the school and does not bear the imprimatur of school approval. Under these circumstances, student speech would have standing as private speech and religious expression would be less encumbered by Establishment concerns (Cambron-McCabe, McCarthy, & Thomas, 2004, p. 32).

Religious Holidays and Religious Symbols

The observation of holidays that have clear religious overtones is also an area that has required legal clarification from the courts. By applying the three conditions of the *Lemon* test, a school cannot observe religious holidays if such observations advance a religious belief or fail to reflect a clear secular purpose. Thus, holidays such as Christmas can be observed in the school as long as the practice is clearly secular in its orientation. Teachers can discuss the commercial aspects of the holiday, the cultural folklore surrounding the holiday, and the festival traditions of the holiday, but if they raise ideas related to the celebration of the birth of Jesus, who is seen by Christians as the savior of the world, they will likely be on less steady Establishment Clause grounds.

Classroom and school displays fall under the same principle. During the winter holiday season, displays of snowflakes, wreaths, and even Santa Clauses usually reflect a secular intention to enjoy the gaiety of the season and can be offered without much problem. Displays that come closer to sanctioning the actual sacred character of Christmas, such as Christmas trees, which despite being a paganistic rite historically, could still be symbolically viewed as a place where gifts are offered in celebration of the birth of Jesus, are more problematic. Actual portraits of Jesus and the birth of Jesus in the manger are likely out of the question, unless, again, they are offered with a clear secular purpose in mind.

A case in Kentucky tested whether the public schools of Harlan County could display a copy of the Ten Commandments on their walls. Knowing that a secular purpose must be secured to allow such a display, the school showcased the Ten Commandments with other important historical documents, claiming that the display was little more than a way to show the history of American government. A district court judge did not agree with the school's position, saying that the inclusion of the Ten Commandments served no secular purposes, was patently religious in nature, and issued an order to have the display removed (Federal Judge Orders Religious Codes out of Kentucky Schools, 8 May, 2000).

Music teachers who direct school choir and band performances during various holiday seasons have sometimes fallen into controversy in this area. Can "Silent Night," for instance, be sung without violating the Establishment Clause? Unambiguous references to a "holy night" and to "Christ, the Savior" seem to suggest a religious intent. But the use of a song, such as "Silent Night," can in fact be offered with secular intent. The teacher simply has to demonstrate that the choice of songs to be performed by the students advances a secular learning purpose. The singing of "Silent Night" might be justified along these lines by arguing that the song has secular artistic value (many of the world's greatest musical compositions are religious in orientation). But the more likely rationale for the singing of "Silent Night" would be to appreciate and recognize festival songs typically sung during the winter holiday season. To make such an argument, however, requires the teacher to teach the students to perform other festival songs, including perhaps Hanukkah and Kwanza songs. Thus, the performance of "Silent Night" might not be viewed as an Establishment issue if the teacher can show that it was one of several important festival songs sung by the choir in the interests of fostering the appreciation and recognition of winter holiday songs. If, on the other hand, the song was sung for devotional purposes or without any palpable secular purpose in mind, it could be viewed as an Establishment violation.

Similar issues are raised when a teacher openly wears religious apparel to school. As with most issues, there is no consensus on this issue. Some courts have reasoned that attire itself is not objectionable because it represents an affiliation with a faith but not the open promotion of a faith. As long as the attire is not part of an open plan to inject personal religious views by the teacher, it is not a problem. Other courts have maintained that the wearing of religious attire, if occurring on a daily basis, represents a subtle signal about religious faith and leads to clear associations between state authority (the teacher) and a particular religious faith, which itself would be indicative of an excessive entanglement of school personnel with a religion (Sendor, 1988).

Students, of course, generally have no regulations on their religious apparel, unless their clothes are found to disrupt the learning climate of the school. This was precisely the problem that surfaced in an interesting case that occurred in California. Three elementary school students of the Sikh faith were banned by their school principal from carrying their sacred knives, known as kirpans, to school. The students, who are mandated by their faith to carry their kirpans as a sign of their devotion to God, were in violation of the schools' weapons policy and created, at least in the mind of the principal, an

1. Religious holidays that have some basis in secularity may be treated in the school experience as long as a secular school purpose is being fulfilled.
2. Religious symbols and displays are allowable if used for a legitimate secular school purpose. For instance, religious songs might be used in music classes and religious statures in art class, but only if a clear secular school purpose justifies their use. Classroom displays fall under the same criterion of judgment.
3. Teachers may not wear religious garb or religious jewelry if it is found to have the effect of promoting a religious faith. Teacher dress may not be stridently and obviously religious in its visual effect. A small pair of earrings symbolizing a cross is one matter; a 6 inch x 6 inch crucifix necklace is another. The key is to determine the proselytizing impact of the religious garb.
4. Schools must make reasonable accommodations to student religious views, including accommodations related to religious dress and the wearing of religious symbols. Only if the school can demonstrate or anticipate that the student dress will have (or has had) some disruptive impact on the school, can student religious dress be limited.

FIGURE 10–5   Principles and Guidelines on Religious Holidays and Religious Symbols.

unsafe condition for learning. The knives were four-inch blades that could cause appreciable injury in the event of an accident or deliberate mischief. The question was whether the safety and security of the student population was compromised by the presence of kirpans and whether the Sikh students were being subjected to an unreasonable burden on their freedom of religious expression. A circuit court ruled in the favor of the Sikhs and stated that every reasonable accommodation had to be taken to allow the Sikh youngsters to wear their knives. In this case, the Court, using a balancing test, was convinced that the Free Exercise Clause could be secured without harming the educative environment of the school. The Court, in fact, suggested that certain safeguards be taken, such as blunting the knives and sewing them into their cloth sheaths (Sihk Students Return, 21 September, 1994).

In a more recent case, a pair of high school students in an Indiana school fought for their right to wear a pentagram because they claimed it as a symbol of their Wiccan religion. The girls were working in a junior teaching program that brought them in contact with third grade students when they were dismissed from the program over fears that the symbol they were wearing was satanic and therefore a disruption to the school. The court ruling, however, failed to find any evidence of disruption caused by the wearing of the pentagram and held for the students, telling them that they can return to the program wearing the five-pointed star (Federal Judge Upholds Indiana Students' Right to Wear Wiccan Symbols, 1 May, 2000).

The Teaching of Creationism

In recent years, objections have been raised over the manner in which science educators have privileged the theory of evolution over Biblical accounts of the origin of human life. The controversy dates back to the Scopes Monkey trial of 1925, when it was argued that even in science class, teaching should not conflict with the Bible. As late as the 1960s, several states had laws on the books prohibiting the teaching of evolution. In 1968, a school teacher in Arkansas challenged the antievolution law in her state on the grounds that it existed for the sole purpose of privileging a sectarian view of human origin. In *Epperson v. Arkansas* (1968), the Supreme Court agreed with the teacher's position and ruled the Arkansas law unconstitutional.

But the issue was still not resolved. Believing that the courts would uphold a balanced treatment of creationism with evolution, some states sought to gain standing for two competing views in the science curriculum. The belief was that if the secular purpose was to teach the origins of humankind, creationism had a legitimate place in the school curriculum. Creationism, after all, certainly had no less to say about the topic than evolutionary theory. Thus, from the standpoint of those supporting its place in the curriculum, creationism found the secular argument it needed to exist on an equal treatment basis in the curriculum.

As a consequence, Tennessee introduced a 1971 law requiring an "equal amount of emphasis" on alternative theories, including, of course, the Genesis account, and in 1981, Arkansas and Louisiana followed suit (Fraser, 1999). It was not long, however, before the courts were involved. In 1982, in *McLean v. Arkansas Board of Education,* a federal court found that Arkansas' balanced treatment statute violated the Establishment Clause. Specifically, the court flatly asserted that creation science was not a science. The teaching of a scientific theory, such as evolution, had to be sanctioned by a method of science, not by a preexisting religious faith. The fact that the National Academy of Science, a distinguished association of scientists, did not recognize creationism as science added weight to the argument. The court also noted the emphasis given in the statute to creationist literature as an alternative to the theory of evolution, which it took as evidence that the law was less interested in posing alternative views than posing a particular alternative view, one with clear linkages to the Bible.

A similar situation prevailed in Louisiana. In the Louisiana law, known as the Creationism Act, the school was obligated, as a matter of fairness and neutrality, to teach evolution on an equal basis with creation science, or not teach it at all. In *Edwards v. Aguillard* (1987), the state portrayed its mandate for equal time as reasonable because evidence could be brought into the science classroom to support and refute both evolutionary and creationist views of the world. The legal challenge offered against the Louisiana law also claimed that state's effort was moved by the singular purpose of promoting a sectarian view in the science curriculum. Few could deny the fact that creationism was an unambiguous Christian version of truth that the school was being asked to legitimate as science. Teaching of the origins of humankind was indeed a secular purpose, but the place of creationism in fulfilling such a purpose could not be justified on secular (scientific) grounds. Using the *Lemon* test, the Supreme Court struck down the Louisiana law, arguing that the law was intended primarily to benefit or advance one particular religious belief (one prong of the Lemon test).

In 1995, the issue was again tested, but this time in the context of the school. In Capistrano, California, a schoolteacher refused to follow the district's requirement to teach evolution in science class. The teacher claimed that evolution was a religion and that the requirement to teach evolution was a patent infringement of the Establishment Clause. Yet again the courts disagreed, ruling that in biology class evolution has a legitimate secular claim, while creationism does not (Fisher, Schimmel, & Kelly, 1999).

Despite these rulings, creationism continues to find its way into the news. In 1999, the Kansas State Board of Education adopted state-approved standards for science education that conspicuously left out any reference to evolution. The lack of state sanction for evolution allowed (even encouraged) local school districts to ignore evolution in their science curriculum (Kansas Evolution Controversy Gives Rise to National Debate, 8 September, 1999). Critics asserted that this turned out to be little more than an effort to impose a de facto prohibition on the teaching of evolution. The Kansas State Board later reversed itself, but other forms of resistance against the teaching of evolution continued to materialize.

In 2005, for instance, a suburban school district in Georgia took it upon itself to place a sticker on its science textbooks that read as follows: "This textbook contains material on evolution. Evolution is a theory, not a fact, regarding the origin of living things. This material should be approached with an open mind, studied carefully and critically considered." The sticker was challenged in the courts on Establishment grounds. Using the *Lemon* test, a federal judge concluded that the use of the sticker was indeed moved by secular purposes, as it encouraged critical thinking about theories of origin and even strengthened the possibilities of teaching evolution to all students by removing any offense certain religious subgroups might feel toward it. The problem, however, was not in the purposes but in the effect of the purposes, which according to the judge, put the school in the position of endorsing a viewpoint entangled with Christian fundamentalist and creationist thought. By denigrating what is the *dominant* scientific theory of origin, the school district had endorsed the well-known alternative theory—creationism. In the long running debate between supporters of evolution and their religious detractors, the school district had decided to side with proponents of religious theories of origin, which constituted enough of an entanglement to declare an Establishment violation.

In a similar case, the school board for the Dover School District in Pennsylvania adopted a policy that required a statement to be read to students in 9th grade biology classes. The statement said that evolution is "still being tested" and it alleged that "gaps in the theory exist for which there is no evidence." It then presented intelligent design as "an explanation of the origin of life that differs from Darwin's view." (*U.S. Judge Rules Intelligent Design Has No Place in Science Classrooms*, 20 December, 2005). The reference to intelligent design, as opposed to creationism, was believed to give the school a chance at securing a secular rationale, as it only claimed that some unidentified supernatural had played a role in shaping the development of humans and other living things. The federal court, however, concluded that the purpose of such a policy was transparently religious in orientation, that intelligent design was not a science, and that it could not uncouple itself adequately from creationism. The judge wrote that it was acceptable to have intelligent design "studied, debated, and discussed," but that it could not be presented as an alternative to evolution in the science classroom. In November 2005, after the court rendered its judgment, the residents of Dover ousted the eight incumbent school board members who supported the intelligent-design policy, and replaced them with eight challengers who opposed the policy.

The upshot of all the wrangling in court is that creationism can be taught in the school, but under a secular objective that makes no claim to science. If schools want to teach it in a comparative religion class, or in a class dedicated to religious views on the origins of humanity, no Establishment violation would apply. But, as a science, creationism poses an Establishment violation because it offers a religious message to a decidedly nonreligious purpose.

---

1. Creationism may be taught in the school when justified by a reasonable secular purpose. In a comparative religion class or a class that explores different views of human origin, it could be taught without posing an establishment violation.
2. State laws prohibiting the teaching of evolution have been struck down as establishment violations because their intent have been found to be influenced by a desire to erect an alternative sectarian view on the origin of humankind.
3. State laws mandating equal treatment of evolution with creationism have been struck down as establishment violations because their intent has been found to be influenced by a desire to support an alternative sectarian view on the origin of humankind.
4. Evolution has been declared to be a legitimate scientific theory in the context of science education and not a secular religion posing an establishment threat.

FIGURE 10–6   Principles and Guidelines on the Teaching of Creationism.

State Aid to Religious Schools

Public money has long gone to the aid of children attending private schools, including religious or parochial schools. The design of the aid structure has been based on something known as the child-benefit doctrine, which in effect says that public monies may be used in the education of children attending private school if the children are the primary beneficiaries of the money (*Board of Education v. Allen*, 1968). If the aid, however, is viewed as primarily benefiting the religious institution, it would be deemed impermissible. Thus, public transportation aid and aid in the form of loaned textbooks and other instructional materials are generally permissible under the child-benefit doctrine, but aid in the form of physical space and certain instructional services is viewed as an advantage to the religious enterprise per se.

Even under the child-benefit doctrine, state aid to religious schools can be offered only under certain conditions. In the 1985 *Aguilar v. Felton* ruling, the Supreme Court barred public school teachers from being sent into parochial schools to provide federally-sponsored remedial education to disadvantaged students (a program justified under Title 1 of the Elementary and Secondary School Act). The prohibition against public school teachers working on parochial school grounds did not mean that parochial school children would be denied Title 1 services. Such services were their right through the child-benefit doctrine. But it did affect where such services would be provided. Because of the *Aguilar* ruling, the federal government spent 100 million dollars building and operating off-site mobile classrooms for the purpose of providing Title 1 services to children attending parochial schools (Fraser, 1999).

In *Aguilar*, the Court found that because the Title 1 remedial instruction put public school employees on parochial school grounds, it created a symbolic link between religion and schooling (an entanglement) that had the effect of advancing religion. Even though participating teachers in the program had been instructed to avoid involvement in religious activity and were monitored in an attempt to guard against the dissemination of religious views, the Court believed that their presence in the religious setting of the school (and the accompanying mechanism of state supervision) constituted state sanctioning of a religious point of view. Under the conditions of the partnership between the school systems, public and private school personnel worked together to resolve issues related to scheduling, classroom assignments, and instructional implementation. This amounted to excessive entanglement.

In the same year, the Supreme Court struck down a Michigan law aiming to publicly fund special education programs (remedial and enrichment programs) in nonpublic parochial schools, arguing that direct aid to an instructional program had the primary effect of advancing religion (*School District of the City of Grand Rapids v. Ball*, 1985). In this case, public subsidies went to funding public school teachers who came into private schools and parochial school teachers working in after-school programs. The Supreme Court was convinced that neither program could certify that it was neither advancing nor inhibiting a religious point of view in the education of the participating children.

The Supreme Court fundamentally changed its outlook on both cases in 1997. The *Aguilar* and the *Ball* decisions were overruled in *Agostini v. Felton*. In the new ruling, the Court moved away from the *Lemon* test, with Justice O'Conner arguing that not all entanglements (one prong of the *Lemon* test) have the effect of advancing a religion. Because Title 1 services had to be offered to parochial school children, either off parochial school grounds or on, there would have to be some entanglement (Patrick & Long, 1999). The question was whether the entanglement was excessive. O'Conner felt that the safeguards in place related to the monitoring of teachers in the parochial settings and to the teacher's obligation to remain neutral on matters of religion protected against an excessive entanglement. In dissent, Justice Souter observed that any state-sponsored instruction on parochial school grounds was excessive entanglement, and certainly more of an entanglement than would otherwise be the case. The setting, he argued, tempted the teacher to reflect the religious mission of the school.

State aid to parochial schools was also adjudicated from another angle. In 1972, New York State proposed a tuition reimbursement program for parents of children attending private schools (of which 90 percent were parochial schools), along with a financial program designed to give money to private schools for the maintenance and repair of their facilities. The law was challenged in the 1973 case of *Committee for Public Education and Religious Liberty v. Nyquist*. The Supreme Court's response to the law was to determine whether the two programs constituted an Establishment Clause violation. In examining the tuition reimbursement program, the Court could not find assurances that the money given to the parents would be used for exclusively secular purposes. To the Court, giving money to parents for the religious education of their children was tantamount to state sponsorship of the religion. Similarly, the facilities maintenance fund was struck down because it too resulted in aid that had the primary effect of subsidizing and advancing the religious mission of sectarian schools.

The image of school vouchers now appears on the horizon for state aid to religious schools. The *Agostini* ruling makes it clear that the Court is willing to entertain the prospect of church/state entanglements that do not result in the endorsement of a particular religious point of view, or church/state entanglements that are noncoercive in nature. This might be a short step away from allowing public monies to be used for the purpose of empowering parental choice in a school voucher program that includes religious schools. On the other hand, the *Nyquist* case stands as a ruling that explicitly denies public money to parents for the religious education of their children. It seems, however, that the conceptual tide is moving more in the direction of the *Agostini* judgment.

In Wisconsin, in *Jackson v. Benson* (1998), the State Supreme Court allowed public monies to be used for the education of a limited group of low-income children in private schools, including private religious schools. The court ruled that the Milwaukee-based program, known as Milwaukee Parental Choice Program (MPCP), was upholding the principle of neutral and indirect aid to religious schools, the defining idea in the *Agostini* ruling. The state court decided that giving a public voucher, worth over $4,000 per child, to a limited group of low-income parents, simply allowed parents to decide which school best benefited the education of their own children (*Jackson v. Benson*, 1998). The parents could use their voucher to send their children to a private nonsectarian school or a private parochial school. They also, of course, had the nonvoucher option of the neighborhood school. If their child attended a religious school with public money, the child could not be compelled to participate in school-based religious activities. Given the range of choices available, the court believed that the program in no way skewed the decision toward religion. To the court, the primary effect of the program was secular—to expand educational choice opportunities for low-income children in a low-performing school district. It is noteworthy that the ruling made no reference to entanglements, but to the maintenance of neutrality, a slight shift away from one prong of the Lemon test.

In 2002, the Supreme Court spoke directly to the issue of participation of religious-based schools in state-funded voucher programs. In *Zelman v. Simmons-Harris*, the Supreme Court ruled that a $2,250 voucher in the Cleveland City School District could be used in a scholarship program designed to provide school choice opportunities to low-income families. Styled after the Milwaukee program, the

Cleveland City School District voucher program is made up of only private schools, most of which are manifestly church-based. In a 5–4 decision, the Supreme Court found that because the program gave choice to low-income families in a particular geographic location, it was neutral on the question of religion and fulfilled a secular purpose. The decision, however, marked a separation from the *Lemon* test, as over 96 percent of the participants in the program chose a religious school, making it clear that even if the primary effect of the program was a religious-based education, it was nonetheless constitutional. As Chief Justice Rehnquist observed, "where a government aid program is neutral with respect to religion, and provides assistance directly to a broad class of citizens who, in turn, direct government aid to religious schools wholly as a result of their own genuine and independent private choice, the program is not readily subject to challenge under the establishment clause" (*Supreme Court Upholds Cleveland Voucher Program*, June 27, 2002).

In 2004, Florida's voucher program, which is similar in character to the Cleveland and Milwaukee programs, ran afoul of state strictures against using public money for religious education. Florida's Constitution explicitly states that "no revenue of the state . . . shall ever be taken from the public treasury directly or indirectly in aid . . . of any sectarian institution." In 1999, Florida Governor Jeb Bush helped to pass legislation that gave a choice to families with students in "chronically failing" schools. The program gave parents of the children in "failing" schools the option to either transfer their kids to another public school or take a scholarship from the state that could be used in any private school of their choice. Many parents used the money to purchase a religious-based education for their children. A District Appeals Court ruled that the "no aid" provision of the state constitution made such legislation illegal. The next likely stop for the case is the Florida Supreme Court, and there is even talk of a voter's initiative to change the wording of the "no aid" provision in the state constitution. Interestingly, considerable legal challenges against the use of public money in voucher programs will likely prevail in the states in the future because of much more aggressive language against church/state entanglements in their constitutions.

1. Under the doctrine of child-benefit, state aid may be offered to the direct benefit of a child schooled in a parochial setting. This would include transportation costs, certain instructional services, and any federally-sponsored program designed to serve legislatively-targeted student populations.
2. Title 1 services to parochial school children, as taught by public school teachers and supported with public money, may be offered in parochial schools. Certain monitoring safeguards are used to insure that religion is not being advanced in such programs.
3. Limited voucher programs, which give low-income parents an opportunity to choose a school for their child from a menu of sectarian and sectarian schools, have been upheld in some states. The Supreme Court has also upheld voucher programs that fulfill the secular purpose of giving choice to low-income families.

Figure 10–7 Principles and Guidelines for State Aid to Religious Schools. United States General Accounting Office (1997) *School Finance: State Efforts to Reduce Funding Gaps Between Poor and Wealthy Districts* (Washington, DC. GAO) p. 94.

SUMMARY

The governance structure of the American public schools resides within the states, as guaranteed by the Tenth Amendment to the Constitution. Despite the decentralized nature of the system, the nation's schools have some semblance of commonality. They are organized broadly along elementary, intermediate, and secondary school lines, and within a unified system of education that, in most cases, represents one progression from the elementary school to post-secondary options. The main administrative base for almost all public schools is the State Board of Education (and its partner—the State Department of Education), which regulates the extent and the nature of local participation and involvement in public schooling. Schools are funded mostly from state and local coffers, with the state monitoring financial disparities among districts and implementing monetary distribution plans designed to keep the gaps in spending between districts within a reasonable range. The federal government's financial role in schooling is limited largely to categorical aid for special needs students.

The relation between church and state priorities in the schools is defined by two clauses in the First Amendment to the Constitution: "Congress shall make no law respecting an establishment of religion, or prohibiting the exercise thereof...." The Supreme Court has adjudicated many cases that posed a threat to the First Amendment, as summarized in Table 10–4. Since the 1970s, a guiding legal mechanism, known as the *Lemon* test, has been used to determine violations. The *Lemon* test, which underscores the importance of government neutrality and separation from religious concerns, has in recent years fallen out of favor with the Court. It still remains, with some modifications, the main test for determining First Amendment violations.

REFERENCES

Cambron-McCabe, N. H., McCarthy, M. M., & Thomas, S. B. (2003). *Public School Law: Teacher's and Student's Rights.* Boston: Allyn Bacon.

Cremin, L. A. (1951). *The American common school: A historic conception.* New York: Teachers College, Columbia University.

DelFattore, J. (1992). *What Johnny shouldn't read.* New Haven: Yale University Press.

Douglas, H. R., & Greider, C. (1948). *American public education.* New York: The Ronald Press Company.

Federal judge orders religious codes out of Kentucky schools, courthouses. (8 May, 2000). By the Associated Press, *Freedom Forum Online* (www.freedomforum.org).

Federal judge upholds Indiana students' right to wear Wiccan symbols. (1 May, 2000). By the Associated Press, *Freedom Forum Online* (www.freedomforum.org).

Finkelman, P. (2000). *Religion and American law.* New York: Garland Publishing.

Fischer, L., Schimmel, D., & Kelly, C. (1999). *Teachers and the law,* 5th ed. White Plains, NY: Longman.

Fraser, J. W. (1999). *Between church and state.* New York: St. Martins Press.

Guthrie, J. W., Garms, W. I., & Pierce, L. C. (1988). *School finance and education policy.* Englewood Cliffs, NJ: Prentice-Hall.

Jones, J. J., Salisbury, G. J., & Spencer, R. L. (1969). *Secondary school administration.* New York: McGraw-Hill.

Kansas evolution controversy gives rise to national debate. (8 September, 1999). *Education Week.*

Linn, D. (1 September, 1998). Financing America's public schools. NGO *Online:* The National Governor's Association and NGA Center for Best Practices.

TABLE 10–4 Important Supreme Court Cases Related to Religion and Schooling.

Everson v. Board of Education. 330 U.S. 1 (1947)

Can the cost of public transportation for children attending parochial schools be supported with public money? The Court supported the public payment for transportation under the child benefit doctrine, but in doing so, it described broad separationist lines between church and state.

Engel v. Vitale. 370 U.S. 421 (1962)

Can audible and public nondenominational prayer be offered in school by school officials? The Court found any official public prayer (denominational or not) to be unconstitutional.

Abington School District v. Schempp and Murray v. Curlett. 374 U.S. 203 (1963)

Can Bible verses or the Lord's Prayer be publicly read or recited in school under official school sanction? The Court found such Bible readings unconstitutional.

Epperson v. Arkansas. 393 U.S. 97 (1968)

Can the state of Arkansas uphold a law prohibiting the teaching of evolution? The Court found such a law to be an establishment violation and, thus, unconstitutional.

Lemon v. Kurtzman. 403 U.S. 602 (1971)

Can public subsidies be used to support the teaching of secular subjects in parochial schools? Such support was found unconstitutional because of the entanglement of religious personnel in the teaching of secular subjects. It also outlined a framework against which future establishment challenges could be judged.

Aguilar v. Felton. 473 U.S. 402 (1985)

Can public school teachers, supported by Title 1 funds, teach parochial school students on the grounds of the parochial schools? The Court ruled that such an arrangement was unconstitutional. Title 1 funds to support the remedial education of children attending religious schools must occur off grounds.

Grand Rapids School District v. Ball. 473 U.S. 373 (1985)

Can public monies be used to support the special education of parochial school children (remedial and enrichment) in a shared time program with public school teachers? The Court rules the program unconstitutional because its primary effect was to advance religion.

Wallace v. Jaffree. 472 U.S. 38 (1985)

Can a state pass a law requiring a moment of silent meditation or voluntary prayer at the beginning of the school day? The court struck down such a law in Alabama as unconstitutional.

Edwards v. Aguillard. 482 U.S. 578 (1987)

Can a state pass a law requiring the equal or balanced treatment of creationism with evolution in the science curriculum? The Court struck down such a law in Louisiana as unconstitutional.

Lee v. Weisman. 505 U.S. 577 (1992)

Can school prayers be offered at graduation ceremonies? The Court sees school-sponsored prayer at graduation ceremonies as unconstitutional.

Agostini v. Felton. 521 U.S. 203 (1997)

Is the original *Aguilar v. Fulton* ruling still valid? The Court overturned the original *Aguilar v. Fulton* ruling, clearing the way for public school teachers to offer federally-sponsored remedial education to school children attending religious schools.

McCarthy, M. M., Cambron-McCabe, N. H., & Thomas, S. B. (1998). *Public school law.* Boston: Allyn Bacon.

National Center for Education Statistics. (1998). *Inequalities in public school district revenues.* Washington, DC: National Center for Education Statistics.

Nord, W. (1995). *Religion and American education.* Chapel Hill: University of North Carolina Press.

Patrick, J. J., & Long, G. P. (1999). *Constitutional debates on freedom of religion: A documentary history.* Westport, CN: Greenwood Press.

Power, E. J. (1991). *A legacy of learning.* Albany: SUNY Press.

Prayer in public schools? It's nothing new for many. (22 November, 1994). *New York Times.*

Sendor, B. B. (1988). *A legal guide to religion and public education.* Topeka: National Organization on Legal Problems of Education.

Sikh students return. (21 September, 1994). *Education Week.*P

Supreme Court Upholds Cleveland Voucher Program. (27 June, 2002). *Education Week.*

Swanson, A. D., & King, R. A. (1991). *School finance.* New York: Longman.

Tanner, D. (1972). *Secondary education.* New York: Macmillan Co.

U.S. judge rules intelligent design has no place in science classroom. (20 December, 2005). *Education Week.*

Vitz, P. (1986). *Censorship: Evidence of bias in our children's textbooks.* Ann Arbor: Servant Books.

When quiet is pervasive in school. (4 September, 1994). *New York Times.*

Wiles, J., & Bondi, J. (1993). *The essential middle school.* New York: Macmillan.

Witte, J. (1999). *Religion and the American constitutional experiment: Essential rights and liberties.* Boulder: Westview Press.

Other Cited Law Cases

Board of Education v. Allen, 392 U.S. 236 (1968)

Committee for Public Education & Religious Liberty v. Nyquist (1973)

Jackson. v. Benson, 578 N.W.2d 602 (Wis. 1998)

McLean v. Arkansas Board of Education (1982)

Mozert v. Hawkins County Public Schools, 765 F.2d 75 (6th Cir.1985)

San Antonio Independent School District v. Rodriguez, 411 U.S. 1 (1973)

Santa Fe Independent School District v. Doe, 120 S.Ct. 2266, 68 USLW 4525 (2000)

Serrano v. Priest, 5 Cal.3d 584 (1971)

Zelman v. Simmons-Harris, 536 U.S. 639 (2002)

KEY QUESTIONS

1. Why is the 9th grade typically excluded from the middle school arrangement?
2. Why is the self-contained classroom more popular in elementary schools than in secondary schools?
3. What is the fundamental difference between a comprehensive high school and specialized secondary school?
4. What makes a governor of a state especially influential in public education?
5. Explain the relation between local and state school authorities.
6. What were some of the more significant initiatives sponsored by the federal government over the years?
7. What is the main difference between flat grant and foundation financial programs?
8. Why do foundation programs often fail to have much impact on local funding differences?
9. How does a reliance on property tax help create funding equities in public education?
10. What is a minimal provision philosophy in the area of school finance?
11. Explain the Establishment and Free Exercise Clauses as they relate to church and state.
12. Describe the main features of the *Lemon* test.
13. What other ways has the Court used to determine Constitutional violations of the First Amendment?
14. Why is a moment of silent meditation probably an easier case to make against the accusation of an establishment violation than public prayer?
15. Defend the position of the plaintiffs in the *Mozert v. Hawkins* case. Make the case for a Free Exercise violation.
16. How have the courts dealt with the place of creationism in the science education?
17. How have the courts handled the presentation of prayers at graduation ceremonies and other school-sponsored events?
18. Can religion be properly and honestly integrated in the school curriculum? If so, how?
19. What are the rules governing "religious dress" among teachers and among students?
20. How can a music teacher get away with teaching a song, such as "Silent Night," during the winter holiday season?
21. What is the child benefit doctrine?
22. Explain the fundamental shift in thinking that occurred in the Supreme Court between the first ruling on *Aguilar v. Felton* and the later ruling on *Agostini v. Felton.*

RESEARCH EXERCISES

1. Investigate any of the cases listed on Table 10–4. Focus on whether the violation was an Establishment or Free Exercise issue. Explain the rationale behind the thinking of both the majority and the dissenting opinions.

2. Examine the school curriculum between two different schools in two different districts. To what extent can you attribute any of the differences to local control influences?

3. Contact a district-wide curriculum director or superintendent to discuss the rationale behind the district's rationale for it grade level configurations.

4. Report on a present day church/state challenge involving a school. Analyze it from the standpoint of what you know about establishment and free exercise guidelines. If the courts haven't ruled on it yet, what decision might you anticipate? If it hasn't gone to court yet, how might you advise the school? If the court has rendered a ruling, do you agree with it?

5. Interview students who experienced instruction in creationism while in a science classroom. Ask whether they felt establishment kinds of pressures or effects in their experience.

6. Report on how a governor's state educational policy has made a difference in the practice of the state's public schools.

7. Interview a local or state school board member in the interests of reporting what they actually do over the course of an academic year.

8. Interview an appropriate state department official in the interests of reporting on how the state attacks funding disparities between school districts.

9. Design a simple exam that tests for some of the basic guidelines that teachers should know on the topic of church and state. Administer it to a group of teachers and disaggregate some of the results by subgroups (e.g., veteran teachers v. beginning).

CHAPTER 11

The Condition of American Education

One does not have to go very far or dig very deep to encounter less than complimentary commentary on the American public schools. The national media have been especially quick to remind the public of deficiencies in the public schools. In recent years, for example, the public has been advised that SAT scores are declining dangerously, that dropout rates are embarrassingly high, and that measures of reading and math achievement are disturbingly short of proficient. The media have often infused their reportage with attention-commanding language about an educational crisis, which has matched the rhetoric of school failure favored by most politicians.

Interestingly, the institution of schooling has had to endure this kind of criticism with some regularity. Since at least mid-century, the public schools have been blamed for virtually every perceived nationalistic failure or decline. During the late 1950s, for example, when the Soviet Union was believed to hold some militaristic and technological advantage over the United States, the public school was blamed for not producing enough quality scientists, mathematicians, and engineers to meet the Soviet threat. During the early 1980s, when the Japanese economy was thriving and taking the lead in the development of global technological advancements, the presumed lack of American competence to compete with the Japanese was publicly attributed to failings in the American public school. A spate of popular books followed, advising Americans to imitate the success of the Japanese educational system, only to stop after the Japanese economy found its own way into a deep and debilitating recession. In 1983, a national commission appointed by President Reagan to study the condition of public education in America was so appalled by the alleged low state of achievement in the public school that it declared the "nation at risk" (NCEE, 1983). Today, government-sponsored school reform efforts converge around a perception of widespread crisis in the literacy and numeracy skills of American school children and, by implication, in the quality of teaching to which they are exposed. Critics often cite the less than impressive performance of American school children on cross-national studies of achievement, all of which call attention to what they believe to be a widening learning gap between the United States and its competitors in Europe and Asia.

The public school has always been a favorite whipping boy for politicians and media critics. Historically, the schools seem to always be perceived as central to any failures in society, but somehow insignificant or incidental to any signs of societal progress or success. Where there have been economic, technological, and military successes in society (and there have been many), the schools have received little or no public credit. Perhaps this is good psychology, as it prevents complacency and inertia born of self-congratulation. The truth is that if one were to judge the schools according to the nation's success on various nationalistic and techno-industrial scales, one would necessarily have to make a positive assessment about public education.

Indignant about the barrage of criticism mounted against the school, some commentators have tried to correct *the big lie* that they believe has been told to the American people about public education

(Bracey, 2004; Berliner & Biddle, 1997). For instance, the SAT score has indeed been on the decline, but its drop is mostly attributable to a rise in the number of students taking the exam (and going on to college) from low-income and minority group settings. This is an effect that could be viewed, in its largest democratic context, with some qualified satisfaction. Similarly, international test data might not always point to a superior performance by American students, even though they sometimes do, but few understand that the basis of comparison between the United States and other advanced nations is not always fair and that the extension of public schooling in America sometimes results in secondary and post-secondary enrollments not imaginable in the schools of many other advanced nations. Complaints about the school dropout rate in public education persist, often associated with nostalgic views about earlier times, but the American public school's holding power has never been better and the number of minority and low-income children staying in school has never been higher. Although it is fashionable to talk about the low state of achievement in the public schools, the federal data not only show no appreciable decline in national achievement over the past decades, but modest signs of progress in selected areas.

The school, of course, has its share of problems. It is no more perfect than any other social institution. Clearly, much still needs to be done to make it a more enlightened and thoughtful place. It has, in fact, failed to adequately serve all youth, especially students from inner-city minority and low-income settings. Even these deficiencies, however, can only be fully understood after taking various sociological factors into account.

UNDERSTANDING SCHOOL ACHIEVEMENT

School achievement is typically understood in reference to some form of standardized test, such as the Iowa Test of Basic Skills (ITBS), or for college-bound seniors, the SAT or ACT. Each of these tests is an attempt to gauge what students have learned from what was taught to them in school. Thus, determining what children are taught (or what they are supposed to have been taught), is the first step in the design of valid and reliable measurements of achievement. An achievement test is only valid to the extent that it actually tests what has been taught. It is not only a gauge of what students have learned, but also a gauge of how effectively they have been taught.

Understanding that achievement is a function of teaching is important because it helps to clarify the difference between the constructs of achievement and aptitude. Aptitude speaks to a student's intrinsic ability in a particular area of knowledge or set of skills. Thus, a musical aptitude exam might attempt, among other things, to determine an individual's ability to discern different pitches or tones, while a musical achievement exam might attempt to target, say, an individual's knowledge of music theory or music history. The former is more of an intrinsic ability (although it can be taught) and the latter is strictly achievement because knowing the terms and principles of music theory or music history requires some form of instruction; they cannot be spontaneously apprehended. IQ tests are aptitude exams; basic skill tests and teacher-made subject area tests are achievement exams. To most school districts, school achievement is largely concerned with reading and mathematical skills in the elementary school and discipline-centered subject matter in the secondary school. Obviously, aptitude influences achievement because having an innate skill in a particular area makes it easier to achieve in that area.

Almost all classroom teachers worry about properly "covering" all the content and skills that are associated with the curriculum of a particular course or grade level. When thinking about achievement, the idea of coverage is important because achievement is directly related to a student's instructional exposure to the various content and skills tested. Differences in instructional exposure could very much affect differences in achievement and help explain some of the achievement disparities witnessed between various subgroups. Some of the achievement differences found between low-track and high-track ability groups, between the sexes, between children from different income and racial backgrounds, and between various school districts (or even whole countries), could be attributable to differences in the opportunity to learn (OTL) the tested material.

OTL factors can manifest in a number of ways. For instance, the degree of commonality that exists between what is covered in a textbook and what is actually tested, speaks to an OTL issue. Commercial publishers of texts are cognizant of this and often tout the linkage their books have to various important tests. The availability of coursework, especially advanced placement courses, that could extend a student's exposure to knowledge, is an OTL factor. Students exposed to more advanced coursework, not surprisingly, have higher achievement levels. The overall linkage between a school's curriculum and the test is another OTL factor. This, in fact, has become so much of a concern in school districts that school-wide curriculum alignment strategies have been used in many districts to bring the whole of the school curriculum into alignment with state-mandated tests. The liberties that teachers take with course materials and the extent to which they emphasize or de-emphasize certain content and skills also influence OTL.

Berliner and Biddle (1997) have emphasized the power of OTL as it relates to achievement by half-humorously articulating the "Berliner and Biddle's Student Achievement Law," which states that "regardless of what anyone claims about student and school characteristics, opportunity to learn is the single most powerful predictor of student achievement") (p. 55). This is another way of saying that one cannot expect students to know something that they have never been taught and that achievement, in some cases, can be improved by simply providing more equitable opportunities to learn.

When achievement data are used to compare groups, whether it is by classrooms, school buildings, school districts, or even national school systems, it is important to understand the role of OTL. Because the governance structure of the public school in the United States is decentralized, the linkage between a school's curriculum and any standardized test is generally unknown and is not always likely to be tightly coordinated. Different states have different graduation requirements, different subject area mandates, and different means of regulating local districts. Some states have strict curriculum requirements, while others have hardly any. In fact, the movement to embrace state-wide standards is often stirred by a desire to better centralize the curricular presentation of the public school in the interests of securing more equitable OTL standards, which will, many believe, help to elevate achievement. Many other advanced nations have a centralized system of school governance, often regulated by a national ministry of education that mandates a national curriculum and sometimes even national examinations. The result, in the most extreme cases, is a uniform school experience where every student is, in effect, on the same page, in the same text, doing the same thing, at around the same time. If these standardized national systems are closely coupled with an achievement test, as they often are on international tests, one could imagine the advantage on measured indices of achievement. As it turns out, this is one of the key reasons why achievement in the United States is sometimes lower than in other advanced nations.

THE NATIONAL ASSESSMENT OF EDUCATIONAL PROGRESS

Part of the responsibilities of the United States Department of Education is to provide a national picture of the state of achievement in the public schools. As a result, the National Center for Education

Statistics (NCES) has been engaged in collecting data on criterion-based measures of achievement in reading, mathematics, science, writing, literature, geography, history, civics, art, music, and computer skills. These tests are collectively known as the National Assessment of Educational Progress (NAEP), the results of which are popularized by the NCES as "the nation's report card of educational progress." The tests are ongoing and congressionally mandated.

NAEP is not designed to compare individual achievement or the aggregate achievement of school districts. No individual student- or school-specific results are collected or reported. Instead, the NAEP is designed to track longitudinal achievement on a set of skills and knowledge in various subject domains. NAEP reports state-by-state results and, of course, national composite scores. The results of the exams are analyzed against any number of variables, including gender, race, income level, OTL factors, home environment conditions, and attitudes. NAEP is administered to a national representative sample of students, usually fourth, eighth, and twelfth graders.

NAEP is known as a criterion-referenced exam, which means that it assesses students across a range of increasingly complex criterion levels. The exam yields what is known as an absolute measure; that is, the measurement is made against some predefined criteria of knowledge or skills. The criterion levels for the NAEP indicate who has achieved or mastered a basic, intermediate (often equated with proficiency), and advanced level of understanding within a subject area. The items on the exam are deliberately linked to these criterion levels.

This makes the NAEP exams different from the norm-referenced standardized exams that are so popular in the schools today. The Iowa Test of Basic Skills, the SAT and the ACT, and most other standardized achievement exams, are norm-referenced exams. They are designed to measure student performance, not against criterion levels, but against (or relative to) the performance of other students. Thus, norm-referenced exams can be described as relative measures. Results on a norm-referenced exam are used for comparability purposes, in situations where it is important to know how the performance of student x compares to that of student y. Such tests usually have percentile rankings associated with the raw scores. They are referenced against the norm (average) established by the test takers.

A norm-referenced exam is based on the idea of creating an average as a central tendency, with more or less equal numbers of students below and above the average. Each of the items on a norm-referenced exam must make some contribution to a normative distribution, meaning that each item has to help create a Bell-curve distribution of scores. Items with very low or very high difficulty levels have some trouble producing the variance needed to build a norm-referenced exam. As a result, measuring progress with a norm-referenced exam can be tricky because of its demand to maintain variance in the score distribution. This, of course, contrasts with a criterion-referenced exam, such as the NAEP, which aims to design low difficulty items for low criterion levels and high difficulty items for higher criterion levels that, in the end, allows for an expression of progress against set levels of content and skill.

The Reading Report Card

The NAEP reading exam, which has been in operation since 1969, is a comprehensive measure of reading ability. It is given to a national sample of 9-, 13-, and 17-year-olds, and is based on a wide range of reading appraisals, from simple narrative passages to complex articles dealing with specialized topics. Reading selections in the NAEP include poems, essays, reports, passages from selected texts, and stories. Comprehension is judged with multiple-choice measures and with open-ended questions.

Reading achievement is especially important to our society because it is the main pathway to intelligent and informed participation in society. Reading, after all, is a widely-applicable skill that, once mastered, provides independent access to ideas, knowledge, and information. It is a skill that transcends all subject areas, in that reading is required for the study of mathematics, science, social studies, and so forth. Reading education is arguably the most important feature of the school's normative mandate.

As indicated, NAEP examinations are built on criterion measures of achievement. In reading, three criterion levels are used to delineate the sophistication of reading abilities: basic, intermediate (proficient), and advanced. Each level is calibrated to the three age groups tested. Figure 11–1 describes the reading achievement level description for the eighth grade group. Figure 11–2 is an item map that displays the knowledge and skills associated with the various items asked on the eighth grade exam, as well as the scale score at which students have a high probability of successfully answering the question.

Because NAEP tests are longitudinal, the scores can be examined in relation to past performances. NAEP measures of reading performance existed since the early 1970s, so there is some basis for comparability over time. Over the course of the last three decades, the overall NAEP reading scores have held steady. Students at two of the tested levels are significantly better readers today than their counterparts in 1971. The 17-year-olds, however, are lower achievers today than their counterparts from 1988–1992. The scores of the 13-year-olds have held steady since 1975 and only the nine-year-olds achieved an average score in 2004 that bettered all of the previously tested years (National Center for Education Statistics, 2005).

Basic: Eighth-grade students performing at the *Basic* level should demonstrate a literal understanding of what they read and be able to make some interpretations. When reading text appropriate to eighth grade, they should be able to identify specific aspects of the text that reflect overall meaning, extend the ideas in the text by making simple inferences, recognize and relate interpretations and connections among ideas in the text to personal experience, and draw conclusions based on the text.

Proficient: Eighth-grade students performing at the *Proficient* level should be able to show an overall understanding of the text, including inferential as well as literal information. When reading text appropriate to eighth grade, they should be able to extend the ideas in the text by making clear inferences from it, by drawing conclusions, and by making connections to their own experiences—including other reading experiences. *Proficient* eighth-graders should be able to identify some of the devices authors use in composing text.

Advanced: Eighth-grade students performing at the *Advanced* level should be able to describe the more abstract themes and ideas of the overall text. When reading text appropriate to eighth grade, they should be able to analyze both meaning and form and support their analyses explicitly with examples from the text; they should be able to extend text information by relating it to their experiences and to world events. At this level, student responses should be thorough, thoughtful, and extensive.

FIGURE 11–1   Achievement Level Description for Eighth Grade Reading. National Center for Education Statistics (2005). *The Nation's Report Card—Reading 2005.* Washington, DC: United States Department of Education) p. 29.

Grade 8 Item Map

This map describes the knowledge or skill associated with answering individual reading comprehension questions. The map identifies the score point at which students had a high probability of successfully answering the question.[1]

NAEP Reading Scale

500

340

330
- 336 Use examples to compare poetic language to everyday speech
- 332 Negotiate dense text to retrieve relevant explanatory facts
- 327 Explain action in narrative poem with textual support—**Sample Question 3**
- 325 Provide specific explication of poetic lines

Advanced

323

320
- 323 Explain the meaning of an image in a poem
- 318 Explain text information to generate related question

310

300
- 301 Describe difficulty of a task in a different context
- 300 Provide support for judgement
- 299 *Recognize author's device to convey information*
- 297 *Recognize meaning of poetic comparison*—**Sample Question 4**

290
- 295 Use metaphor to interpret character

Proficient

281

280
- 284 Apply text information to hypothetical situation and explain
- 284 *Recognize what story action reveals about character*
- 279 Relate text information to hypothetical situation
- 278 Infer character's action from plot outcome

270
- 275 Use task directions and prior knowledge to make a comparison
- 267 Provide supporting details to explain author's statement
- 262 *Use context to identify meaning of vocabulary*
- 261 *Identify causal relation between historical events*

260
- 260 *Identify appropriate text recommendation for a specific situation*
- 254 Explain reason for major event

250
- 253 Make inference based on supporting details to identify feeling
- 248 *Recognize information included by author to persuade*
- 248 Provide specific text information to support a generalization

Basic

243

240
- 247 *Locate specific information in detailed document*
- 237 *Recognize significance of article's central idea*

230
- 234 Provide partial or general explication of poetic lines
- 232 *Identify characterization of speaker in poem*
- 228 *Recognize an explicitly stated supporting detail*

220

0

1 Each grade 8 reading question in the 2005 reading assessment was mapped onto the NAEP 0–500 reading scale. The position of a question on the scale represents the average scale score attained by students who had a 65 percent probability of successfully answering a constructed-response question, or a 74 percent probability of correctly answering a four-option multiple-choice question. Only selected questions are presented. Scale score ranges for reading achievement levels are referenced on the map. For constructed-response questions, the question description represents students' performance at the scoring level being mapped.
NOTE: Regular type denotes a constructed-response question. Italic type denotes a multiple-choice question.
Source: U.S. Department of Education, Institute of Education Sciences, National Center for Education Statistics, National Assessment of Educational Progress (NAEP), 2005 Reading Assessment.

FIGURE 11–2 Item Map for the Eighth Grade Reading NAEP Exam. National Center for Education Statistics. (2005). *The Nation's Report Card–Reading 2005.* Washington, DC: United States Department of Education, p. 30.

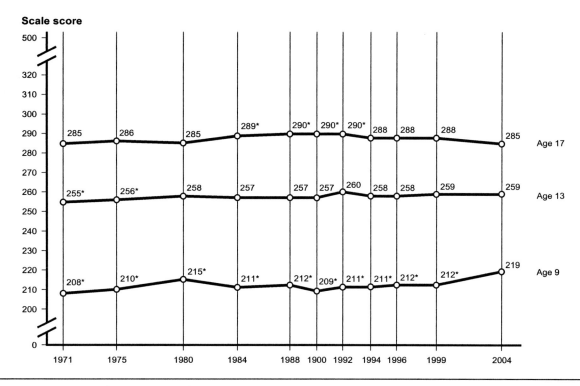

FIGURE 11–3   National Trends in Reading by Average Scale Scores. National Center for Education Statistics. (2005). *NAEP 2004 Trends in Academic Progress.* Washington, DC: U.S. Department of Education, p. 10.

The relative steadiness of the NAEP reading scores disguise the gains achieved in the overall composite scores of minority group populations, particularly African American students. Since 1971, the overall improvement in the reading score of white students has been smaller than the overall reading improvement documented for black students. The result is some reduction in the gap or the difference in the average reading performances between white and black students. Although the narrowing of the differences was interrupted in the 1990s, it is still a notable achievement, especially in light of the fact that the dropout rate had decreased among black students. Minority students who might have dropped out in previous school years are now staying in school. This being the case, the average score might be expected to drop, but the opposite has been the case. As displayed in Figure 11–4, the reading achievement gap between 17-year-old white and black students, while still significantly wide, is narrowing. The gaps have also closed in both fourth and eighth grades, a trend that holds some hope for continued future progress.

Lest the NAEP race/ethnicity subgroup data are misinterpreted, it should be made clear that the underperformance of black and other minority children is likely a function of several interrelated factors. Disproportionately high numbers of minority children live below the poverty line and the legacy of racism against minority children, black children especially, has sometimes resulted in the denial of equal opportunities to learn. Moreover, some evidence suggests that there are lower quality teachers in predominately black schools. Others have pointed to cultural explanations, noting that stereotyping and racism in society have encouraged some black children to disassociate from school. The high incidence of single-parent homes in the black population and the relatively low involvement of black parents in the schooling enterprise might also be factors (Johnson & Viadero, 2000). The gap between

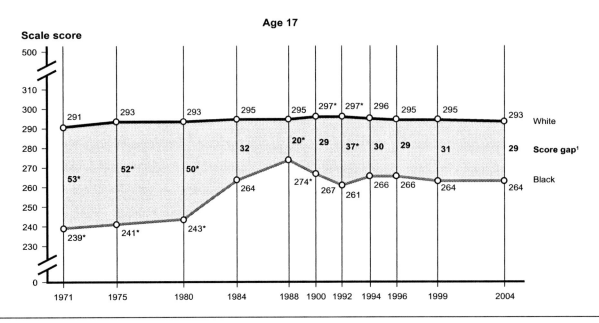

Age 17

FIGURE 11–4 Trends in Average Reading Scale Score and Score Gap Between White Students and Black Students, Age 17: 1971–2004. National Center for Education Statistics. (2005). *NAEP 2004 Trends in Academic Progress.* Washington, DC: U.S. Department of Education, p. 33.

black and white children, it should be said, exists in early reading and math-related skills, even before they enter kindergarten. The vocabulary development scores of a typical black four-year-old fall below the twentieth percentile of the national distribution (Jencks & Phillips, 1998; Lee & Burkam, 2002). This points to factors in the early life of black children, with the preschool and the home environment being likely places to look for some explanation.

Reading achievement scores along the scale of gender also reveal some interesting trends, with females showing an advantage. Although the difference of the reading achievement between boys and girls at all three levels of NAEP reporting is significant, it is not nearly as profound as the differences witnessed between the races and between income levels. This is probably because gender is not confounded by poverty. Equal numbers of boys and girls live below and above the poverty line. Yet the differences in reading achievement between boys and girls are especially persistent, as little progress has been made in closing the gap among 17-year-olds. The reading achievement gap has closed somewhat among nine-year-olds, but it has not produced a commensurate effect eight years later, when the fourth graders are tested again as 17-year-olds. As we will discuss in a later chapter, female superiority in reading achievement is a world-wide phenomenon in advanced industrial nations.

The differences between average reading scores among students eligible for free/reduced lunch and ineligible for free/reduced lunch, which is a way that the government distinguishes between children living near or in poverty against those living outside of poverty, are also quite wide. Because of the disproportionate representation of minorities in lower income settings, achievement differences by income contribute to the achievement differences between the races. The data on low-income children also testify to the fact that, irrespective of race or ethnicity or gender, considerable achievement differences exist between the school children living near or in poverty and those living outside of it. To be eligible for free lunch, students must be in families whose income is at or below 130 percent of the poverty level, which translates to an annual income of about $24,000 for a family of four. Students

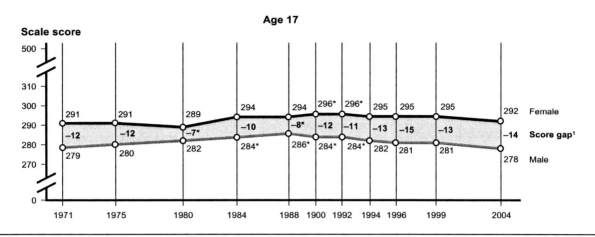

FIGURE 11–5 Trends in Average Reading Scale Score and Score Gap Between Females and Males, Age 17: 1971–2004. National Center for Education Statistics. (2005). *NAEP 2004 Trends in Academic Progress.* Washington, DC: U.S. Department of Education, p. 31.

eligible for reduced lunch costs are from families whose income is between 130 and 180 percent of the poverty level, which tops out at an annual income of $34,783 for a family of four. Reading achievement differences by income are dramatically large and are similar to the 20- to 30-point differences found in the White/Black test gap (National Center for Education Statistics, 2005).

NAEP data also reveal some of the home conditions supporting reading and literacy and confirm the long-standing belief that the home-reading conditions are associated with reading achievement (National Center for Education Statistics, 2005a). NAEP found, for instance, that a negative association exists between television viewing and reading achievement, meaning that children who watch a lot of TV are less likely to be good readers than children who watch less TV. The reason for this likely has to do with the fact that frequent TV watching might displace activities in the home that might make a stronger contribution to literacy (such as going to the library, reading for leisure, telling stories, and conversing about things read). It also might be that homes with less TV watching might be homes with higher parent education levels, which itself might explain the association.

NAEP found a variety of associations between reading achievement and home conditions. For example, children from homes with more literary material (home-magazines, newspapers, encyclopedias, and books) were more likely to have higher NAEP reading scores than children from homes with less literary materials. The difference, in fact, between students who reported four types of literary materials in the home and those who reported two or less was 30 scale points on the NAEP. Again the association probably speaks to the importance of students having early and easy access to a wide range of reading materials, from which to draw, explore, and pursue interests. It might also simply be explained as a variable that acts as a proxy for income. Families that are wealthy in reading materials might also be wealthy families in general, so income could be the factor that is driving the achievement. Still other associations continue to build a strong case for the support of reading at home. Students who engage in leisure time reading (reading for fun) and who spend time discussing their readings with family members and friends are likely to be higher achievers in reading. We cannot know for sure if students who read for leisure gain more reading practice and therefore become higher achievers, or if students with higher achievement are simply more inclined to read for leisure. Probably both factors are at work. Nevertheless, it seems incumbent on the school and the family to

TABLE 11.1   Average Scale Score of Fourth Graders on NAEP Reading Against Various Home Reading Factors, 2000.

	NAEP Reading Scale Score	**% Reporting**
Read for Fun:		
Every day	223	43
Once or twice a week	218	32
Once or twice a month	216	12
Never or hardly ever	202	14
Discussed Studies & Talked About Reading:		
Almost every day	221	54
Once or twice a week	219	23
Once or twice a month	217	6
Never or hardly ever	201	17
Types of Reading Materials in the Home:		
Four	229	34
Three	219	34
Two or fewer	203	32
Amount of Time Spent Watching TV:		
6 hours or more	196	18
4–5 hours	213	17
2–3 hours	224	40
1 hour or less	224	25

National Center for Education Statistics. (2005). *The Nation's Report Card: Fourth Grade Reading 2000.* Washington, DC: U.S. Department of Education, pp. 48–61.

encourage and support leisure-time reading and to be responsive to opportunities to discuss what students have read. All in all, the job of teaching children to read seems to be shared by the family and the school in a way that is different from virtually any other aspect of the school curriculum. As displayed on Table 11–1, NAEP data bear out the fact that where families or homes support reading, the achievement dividend is significant (National Center for Education Statistics, 2005a).

The Mathematics Report Card

The NAEP math assessment also covers a comprehensive set of skills, using the same criterion levels used for the reading measurement: basic, proficient, and advanced. The content areas in each of the tests for the three age groups are listed as: Number Sense, Properties, and Operations; Measurement; Geometry and Spatial Sense; Data Analysis, Statistics, and Probability; and Algebra and Functions. The exam includes multiple choice items and questions requiring students to construct responses. More than half of the overall items for the exam are constructed-response questions. Figure 11–6 provides an outline of the topics covered with items used on the NAEP test for eighth graders.

Like the reading data, the NAEP math results suffer from serious achievement differences between the races and between income levels. As indicated in Figure 11–8, among 17-year-olds, the difference between white and black students in 2004 was 28 scale points. Among 9-year-olds, the gap stood at 26 scale points. These scale point differences are quite large, representing the equivalent of about two or three grade levels (Grouws & Cebulla, 2000).

Grade 8 Item Map

This map describes the knowledge or skill associated with answering individual mathematical questions. The map identifies the score point at which students had a high probability of successfully answering the question.[1]

NAEP Mathematics Scale

500 _____

370 _____

365 Reason about pattern on a grid using concept of slope

360 _____

353 Determine a probability (calculator available)

343 Determine effect of increasing the value of one variable

340 _____

Advanced
323

350

335 Reason about properties of a parallelogram

330 _____   330 *Determine median price for a gallon of gasoline*

320 _____

319 *Estimate the x-coordinate from the graph of a curve*
317 *Solve a story problem involving percent increase*
315 *Determine the 6th term in a pattern—**Sample Question 3***

310 _____   311 *Predict results of experiment using probability*

306 *Determine an equation given a table of x and y values*

Proficient
281

302 Solve a story problem with multiple operations

300 _____   301 Extend a pattern on a grid

294 *Determine coordinates to complete a rectangle*
294 *Identify piece of information not needed*

290 _____   291 *Solve problem involving square root (calculator available)*

283 *Shade a grid to form symmetric pattern—**Sample Question 4***
282 *Determine how many angles are less than 90 degrees*

280 _____   282 *Convert a written number to decimal form*

274 *List angle measures from smallest to largest (protractor available)*

270 _____

Basic
243

260 ....

253 Draw the reflection of a figure

250 _____   252 *Determine area of shaded region on a grid*

247 Solve a multi-step story problem

240 _____

0

1 Each grade 8 mathematics question in the 2005 mathematics assessment was mapped onto the NAEP 0–500 mathematics scale. The position of a question on the scale represents the average scale score attained by students who had a 65 percent probability of successfully answering a constructed-response question, or a 74 percent probability of correctly answering a four-option multiple-choice question, or a 72 percent probability of correctly answering a five-option multiple-choice question. Only selected questions are presented. Scale score ranges for mathematics achievement levels are referenced on the map. For constructed-response questions, the question description represents students' performance rated as completely correct.
NOTE: Regular type denotes a constructed-response question. Italic type denotes a multiple-choice question.
Source: U.S. Department of Education, Institute of Education Sciences, National Center for Education Statistics, National Assessment of Educational Progress (NAEP), 2005 Mathematics Assessment.

FIGURE 11–6   Item Map for the Eighth Grade Math NAEP Exam. The latest NAEP math results show strong progress in the overall averages scored across the nation. In 2004, the average scale score for fourth and eighth graders represent a significant statistical improvement over the original 1972 scores (see Figure 11–7). Overall, the average rate of progress, in fact, has been consistent and solid. Such improvements contradict the public perception of decline in the mathematical skills of school children.

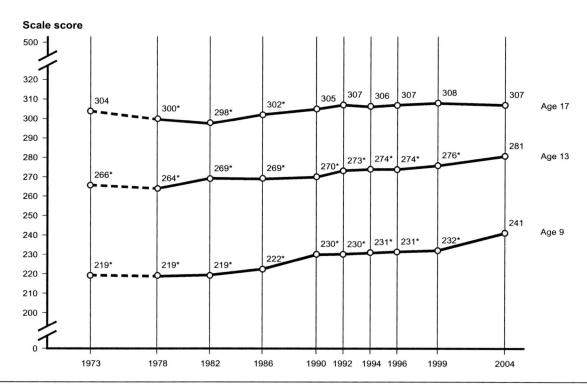

FIGURE 11-7 **Trends in Average Math Scores for Students aged 9, 13 and 17: 1973-2004.** National Center for Education Statistics. (2005b). *NAEP 2004 Trends in Academic Progress.* Washington, DC: U.S. Department of Education, p. 17.

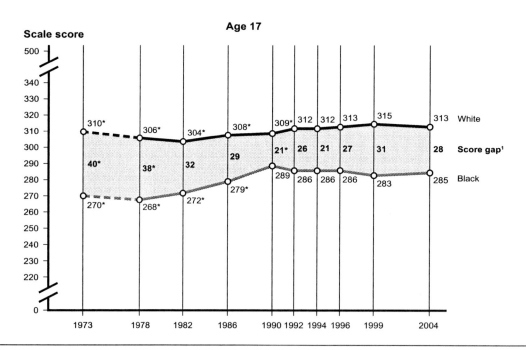

FIGURE 11-8 **Trends in Average Math Scale Score and Score Gap Between White Students and Black Students, Age 17: 1973-2004.** National Center for Education Statistics. (2005b). *NAEP 2004 Trends in Academic Progress.* Washington, DC: U.S. Department of Education, p.33.

Achievement gaps naturally pose a challenge for the schools, but the good news is that the disparities, like those witnessed on the NEAP reading results, have gotten significantly smaller over time. In 1973, the difference in NAEP math achievement, at all tested age groups, between white and black children was approximately 40 scale points (National Center for Education Statistics, 1999). By 2004, the differences were reduced, after some slippage in the 1990s, to about 27 scale points for both 17-year-olds and 9-year-olds.

OTL could be a factor in the math achievement gap problem because the participation rates in the most advanced mathematics courses indicate significantly different exposures between the races. For instance, in 2004, about 19 percent of white high school graduates were enrolled in Calculus. This contrasts to approximately 8 percent of black high schoolers (National Center for Education Statistics, 2005b, p. 59). Although a larger percentage of high school youth today is taking math courses than in the past, the OTL gap between the races seems to be widening. For instance, only 6 percent of white 17-year-olds were enrolled in Calculus in 1978, against 4 percent of black 17-year-olds. By 2004, the number of whites in Calculus more than tripled (to 19 percent) but only doubled (to 8 percent) for blacks (see Figure 11–9; National Center for Education Statistics (2005b, p. 59).

Boys outperformed girls on the 2005 Math NAEP, but contrary to public perception, the advantage was not dramatic or even significant (National Center for Education Statistics, 2005c). In fact, it has never been very dramatic. In 1973, 17-year-old boys outperformed 17-year-old girls by approximately six scale points, but girls actually scored slightly higher than boys in the two other younger-aged groups. This is an interesting phenomenon in light of the amount of attention given to the matter of

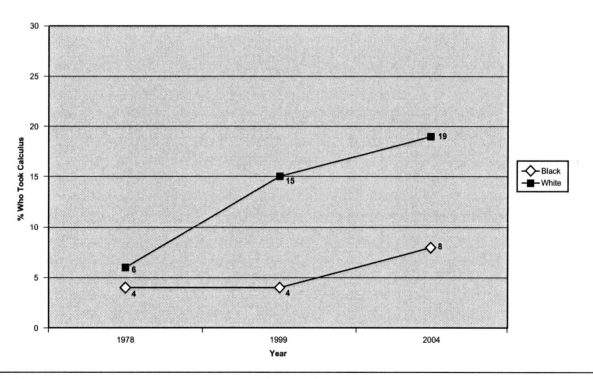

FIGURE 11–9   Percentage of Students, Age 17, Who Took Calculus as Their Highest Mathematics Course, by Race: 1978, 1999, and 2004. National Center for Education Statistics. (2005b). *NAEP 2004 trends in academic progress.* Washington, DC: U.S. Department of Education, p. 59.

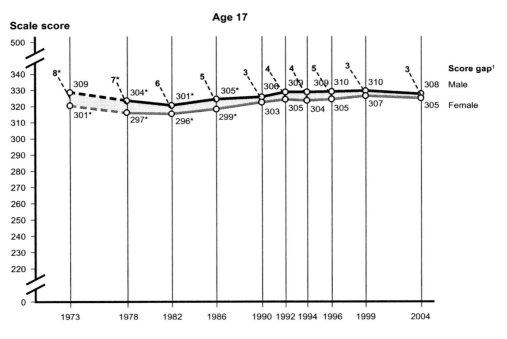

#The estimate rounds to zero.
*Significantly different from 2004.
1 Male average scale score minus female average scale score. Negative numbers indicate that the average scale score for male students was lower than the score for female students.
NOTE: Dashed lines represent extrapolated data. Score gaps are calculated based on differences between unrounded average scale scores.
Source: U.S. Department of Education, Institute of Education Sciences, National Center for Education Statistics, National Assessment of Educational Progress (NAEP), selected years, 1973–2004 Long-Term Trend Mathematics Assessments.

FIGURE 11–10   Trends in Average Mathematics Scale Scores and Score Gaps for Students Age 17, by Gender: 1973–2004. National Center for Education Statistics. (2005b). *NAEP 2004 Trends in Academic Progress.* Washington, DC: U.S. Department of Education.

gender bias in math and science, although it is somewhat understandable because of the unwillingness of girls to pursue math/science-related careers. In 2004, 17-year-old boys outscored the same aged girls by three scale points.

Interestingly, the course-taking patterns in mathematics between the sexes demonstrate equal access to all math courses, even the more advanced ones. Figure 11–11 shows the percentage of 17-year-old males and females by the highest mathematics course taken in high school. The participation rates are more or less even, with a slight advantage given to females.

The role of course taking has proven to be essential to mathematical achievement. As Berliner and Biddle's Student Achievement Law suggests, students with greater opportunities to learn mathematics tend to learn more mathematics. The average NAEP math score of a student is very much associated with the highest mathematical course taken (see Figure 11–12). The difference between students taking Pre-Calculus or Calculus as their highest math course and students taking Algebra I as their highest math course is over 50 scale points on the Math NAEP (National Center for Education Statistics, 2005b). There may, in fact, be wisdom in the recent calls to increase graduation requirements, to include more academic courses in the curriculum and to standardize the curriculum in a way that equalizes OTL. The data suggest that simply taking a course might contribute to overall achievement, although one cannot take this too far. We are still left with the dilemma of associational evidence. Are students who are good in mathematics inclined to take more math courses or are students who take more math courses better at math? In either case, the mandate should be to widen the opportunities

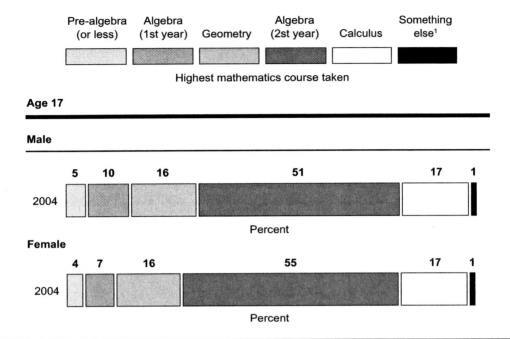

FIGURE 11–11   Percentage of Students Age 17, by Gender and Highest Mathematical Course Taken: 2004. National Center for Education Statistics. (2005b). *NAEP 2004 Trends in Academic Progress.* Washington, DC: U.S. Department of Education.

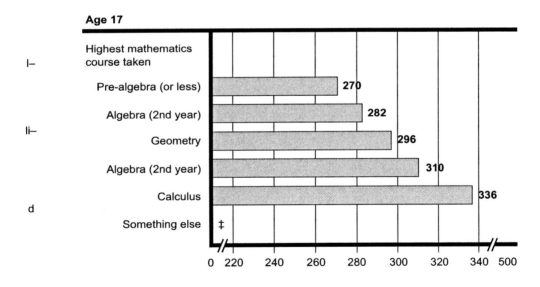

‡ Reporting standards not met. Sample size is insufficient to permit a reliable estimate.
SOURCE: U.S. Department of Education, Institute of Education Sciences, National Center for Education Statistics, National Assessment of Educational Progress (NAEP), 2004 Long-Term Trend Mathematics Assessments.

FIGURE 11–12   Average NAEP Mathematics Scale Score, Age 17, by Highest Mathematics Course Taken, 2004. National Center for Education Statistics. (2005b). *NAEP 2004 Trends in Academic Progress.* Washington, DC: U.S. Department of Education, p. 33.

to learn mathematics. In 2004, the reality nationwide was that only 70 percent of all high school students took at least three years of mathematics in high school, while 86 percent completed at least two years (National Center for Education Statistics, 2005b, p. 58). The percentage of students who actually took Calculus was about 17 percent in 2004 (NCES, 2005b).

INTERNATIONAL COMPARISONS

The operating characteristics of a nation's public school system are usually the function of a unique blend of cultural, political, historical, and linguistic influences. Many advanced nations are ethnically homogeneous and are governed by a central ministry that supports a national curriculum—with national standards, national exams, and national licensing regulations for teachers. As mentioned earlier, the historical traditions and pluralistic backdrop of the United States resist such nationalizing tendencies. Nevertheless, some school initiatives are more likely to prevail in the American context than in, say, the public schools of Europe or Asia. Matters related to second language learning and second culture assimilation, for instance, have a presence in the mandate of the American schools that are rare in more culturally and linguistically homogeneous nations (such as Japan, for instance). In fact, the commingling of religious, political, class, and ethnic differences in the life of the school is a signature feature of American education.

Factors outside of the institution of public schooling, such as home and family life conditions, are similarly variable across nations. Rates of recreational reading, school homework, community involvement, and television viewing vary by considerable measure across the world. Belief systems related to effort, interest, expectation, and ability are all mediated by cultural and ethnic conditions. The prevalence of poverty, crime, and various social maladies (such as racism, sexism, and/or teenage pregnancies) is obviously not equally distributed among nation states and could also affect the nature of the schooling experience. Teacher salaries, teacher prestige, investment commitments, and various legislative initiatives also have their influence. Legislative edicts related to the education of children with disabilities in different countries result in different percentages of children receiving additional resources for defined disabilities and in completely different instructional settings for the teaching of children with disabilities (OECD, 2004). In terms of the effects of poverty on schooling, the United States, despite its standing as one of the wealthiest nations in the world, has a larger percentage of children living in poverty than in most other industrialized nations. In Finland, for instance, close to three percent of children are documented as living in poverty; in the UK, the number is closer to 16 percent, while in the United States it reaches to almost 22 percent (Berliner, 2005). Not surprisingly, the United States also has comparatively high numbers of children born to drug-abusing parents, single-parent families, and homelessness (Berliner, 2005). Furthermore, as one can note in Figure 11–13, variables sensitive to school success, such as the percentage of students who speak a non-tested language, are foreign-born and/or live in non-two-parent families, vary widely across nations. All of these factors should give us pause when we compare schools on an international basis.

Cross-National Outcomes

Various agencies are engaged in conducting research on school effects in the cross-national educational context. The results of such research usually demonstrate a less than impressive performance by the public schools in the United States. This tends to play into the hands of public school critics, especially politicians, who tend to see the international data as reliable measures of school quality. The problem, however, is that cross-national data are not easy to interpret and the standing of the United States in the international context may not always be as mediocre as it tends to be portrayed.

For more than a decade, the United States has participated in several international projects designed to yield important information on the performance of its schools against the schools of other advanced nations. Among the more recent initiatives is the United States' participation in the OECD's

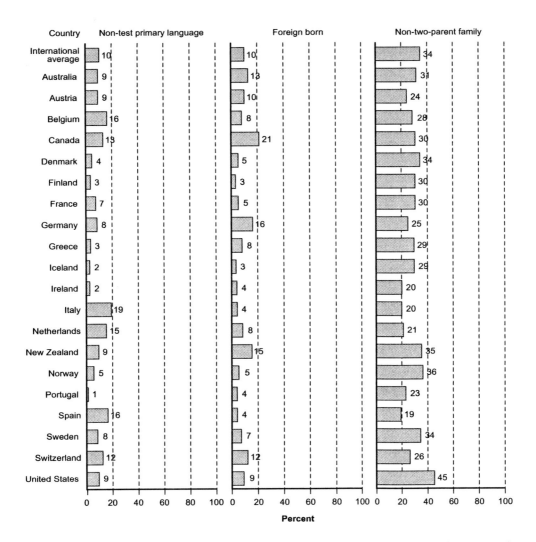

NOTE: The international average is the weighted mean of the data values for the 20 countries included in the analysis. Language spoken at home, immigrant status, and family structure are based on students' reports. "Test-language" students reported speaking the language in which the test was administered always or most of the time at home while "non-test-language" students reported using another language always or most of the time at home. Students from a "two-parent family" reported living with both their mother and father. The category "non-two-parent family" encompasses all other responses.
SOURCE: Hampden-Thompson, G., and Johnston, J.S. (2006). *Variation in the Relationship Between Nonschool Factors and Student Achievement on International Assessments* (NCES 2006-014), table 1. Data from Organization for Economic Cooperation and Development (OECD), Program for International Student Assessment (PISA), 2003.

FIGURE 11–13   Percentage of 15 Year-Olds Who Spoke a Non-Test Language, Were Foreign Born and Were From Non-Two Parent Families, By Country, 2001. National Center for Education Statistics. (2006). *U.S. Student and Adult Performance on International Assessment of Educational Achievement.* Washington, DC: U.S. Department of Education, p. 7.

Program for International Student Assessment, also known as PISA, which assesses reading, math, and science achievement among 15-year-olds. The PISA studies are primarily limited to 30 industrialized nations with membership to the Organization for Economic Cooperation and Development (OECD). These could be considered among the wealthiest nations in the world. Of particular note is how the United States fared against the G8 group of nations, the eight nations of OECD that represent two-thirds of the world's economy.

As reported by PISA, the participation rates of the population in the institution of school at both the upper secondary and the tertiary levels clearly says something important about the American effort to extend the school upward into the lives of its citizens. None of the G8 nations reported in the PISA

Percentage of the population ages 25 to 64 that has completed at least an upper secondary education,
by age group and country: 1999

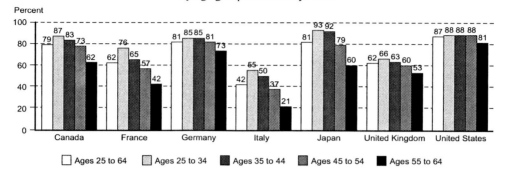

NOTE: The United Kingdom includes England, Northern Ireland, Scotland, and Wales. Data for the United Kingdom exclude individuals who have completed short programs that do not provide access to higher education, since these programs do not meet the minimum requirements to qualify as upper secondary education based on the international standard (ISCED). Data for the United States include individuals who have completed both a high school diploma and a General Educational Development (GED) award.
SOURCE: Organization for Economic Cooperation and Develoment, Education at a Glance, 2001, Table A 2.2a.

Percentage of the population ages 25 to 64 that has completed at least a first university degree,
by age group and country: 1999

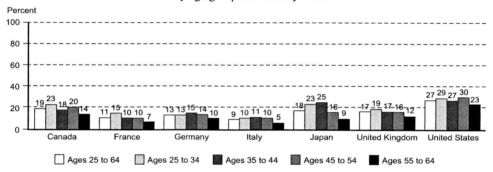

NOTE: The United Kingdom includes England, Northern Ireland, Scotland, and Wales. Data for the United Kingdom exclude individuals who have completed short programs that do not provide access to higher education, since these programs do not meet the minimum requirements to qualify as upper secondary education based on the international standard (ISCED).
SOURCE: Organization for Economic Cooperation and Develoment, Education at a Glance, 2001, Table A 2.2b.

FIGURE 11–14   Percentage of the Population, Ages 24–64, that Has Completed an Upper Secondary Education: 1999. National Center for Education Statistics. (2002). *Comparative Indicators of Education in the United States and Other G8 Countries.* Washington, DC: U.S. Department of Education, p. 19.

study demonstrates the generational participation of the masses in the institution of schooling at the high school and college levels that one witnesses in the United States. As noted in Figures 11–14 and 11–15, both high school completion and college completion rates are generally higher and more widespread through all the age groups of the population than in most other G8 nations. Although the secondary graduation rates in the United States might be artificially high because of the inclusion of GED (test equivalency) diplomas (a point we will revisit later), there is no denying the generally high participation levels in college.

When one examines the measures of average achievement on the PISA exams, however, the United States is a comparatively poor performer. As depicted in Tables 11–2, 11–3, and 11–4, the average math, science, and literacy achievement scores of 15-year-olds in the United States were relatively low. The different shaded bands used in the following tables indicate statistical differences in the scores. Thus, the average United States' score in math was statistically lower than all the G8 nations, except Italy (NCES, 2004a). The science averages showed a similar pattern. The news was slightly better on literacy scores, as only Canada posted a statistically higher score than the United States.

TABLE 11–2   Average PISA Mathematics Literacy Scores of 15-Year-Olds, by G8 Nations: 2003.

Country	Average Score
Japan	534
Canada	532
United Kingdom (2000)	529
France	511
Germany	503
United States	**483**
Italy	466
Russian Federation	468

NCES. (2004). *International Outcomes in Learning Mathematics Literacy and Problem-Solving.* Washington, DC: U.S. Department of Education, p. 14.

TABLE 11–3   Average PISA Science Literacy Scores of 15-Year-Olds, by G8 Nations: 2003.

Country	Average Score
Japan	548
United Kingdom (2000)	532
Canada	519
France	511
Germany	502
United States	**491**
Russian Federation	489
Italy	487

National Center for Education Statistics. (2006). *U.S. Student and Adult Performance on International Assessment of Educational Achievement.* Washington, DC: U.S. Department of Education, p. 22.

TABLE 11–4   Average PISA Reading Literacy Scores of 15-Year-Olds, by G8 Nations: 2000.

Country	Average Score
Canada	534
United Kingdom	523
Japan	522
France	505
United States	**504**
Italy	487
Germany	484
Russian Federation	462

National Center for Education Statistics. (2006). *U.S. Student and Adult Performance on International Assessment of Educational Achievement.* Washington, DC: U.S. Department of Education, p. 11.

The averages noted in the PISA studies, however, represent central tendencies that may not always tell the whole story of achievement, largely because they fail to capture how students are doing in particular school settings and in particular subgroups. Measures of average collapse the differences that exist between middle-class, wealthy, and low-income students in the United States, as well as between students with different linguistic backgrounds and different state-influenced school experiences. This is a point that is especially relevant in a decentralized system that allows for differentiated levels of school expenditures and assorted sets of statewide standards and accountability mechanisms. Thus, to report only on a national average conceals the fact that students in some settings and from some sub-groups are doing very well compared to their foreign peers. In 1992, for example, the National Center for Education Statistics (1991) conducted studies to compute average achievement levels of 13-year-olds in the 50 states against averages taken from nation states. Hungary reported significantly higher average scores than the United States in mathematics proficiency among 13-year-olds, but five states outperformed Hungary. Thirteen-year-old students in Taiwan and Korea ranked first and second, respectively, on the international mathematics test, but students in Iowa and North Dakota did just as well as the Korean students. These comparisons demonstrate that there is greater variation in the mathematics proficiency scores of students within countries and states than across countries and states. The difference between the 10th and 90th percentile was 90 scale points in Mississippi and 96 scale points in Taiwan, but the difference in average proficiency between Taiwan and Mississippi was 39 scale points (NCES, 1991).

Differences in international achievement scores can also be accounted for by weighing the influence of opportunity-to-learn measures (OTL). As indicated earlier, such measures can be understood by trying to compute the degree of commonality between what is taught in the school experience and what is actually tested (in this case, on an international test). In a decentralized system, the possibilities for significant differences on opportunity-to-learn scales among the student population are much greater than in a centralized system that imposes a uniform national curriculum. The reality of international testing is that choices and preferences expressed at the state and local levels on matters related to what gets taught likely contribute to the high variability of achievement witnessed across state and local lines. These differences in OTL can be a factor in lowering average national achievement scores because they likely mean that certain students were not exposed to the tested material. Adding to the dynamics of OTL are the clear differences documented in the length of the school day and school year and in the time devoted to the teaching of various subjects between nations, and in the case of the United States, between its 50 states. This is another way of saying that where there is no necessary centralized linkage between what gets taught and what get tested, achievement may be depressed because of the increased odds that some students will not have an instructional encounter with tested material.

Finally, one should note that public schooling in America has long embraced the vision and the rhetoric of putting the school in the egalitarian role of reducing or leveling economic and class differences in the population. The comprehensive and unified system of schooling witnessed in the United States today testifies, at least in part, to the veracity of this rhetoric. Everyone, of course, knows that the American schools still have a long way to go to bring equally enriching and satisfying school experiences to all youth—irrespective of their class, ethnicity, or race. By international standards, however, the United States shows less class-based stratification in its schools than do the schools of most OECD nations. In many Western European nations, students are sorted into four or more school types at age 15, meaning that 15-year-olds physically go to different schools with different social and career predestinations—the college-bound to the college-bound high schools and so forth. In some European nations, such as Austria and Germany, curriculum tracking, which is the preliminary mechanism to later school type placement, occurs as early as age 10. The results from the PISA studies show that countries that separate students at an early age into different types of schools experience a greater degree of socioeconomic or class bias (Figure 11–15). In other words, disadvantaged students are more likely to be placed in low status schools, with lower expectations and a less demanding curriculum, while the socially advantaged benefit from higher status schools. The effect is a reproduction of the social and economic status quo. In nations that keep students in comprehensive schools, of which the United States and the Scandinavian nations are leaders, the relation between social class and achievement is weaker.

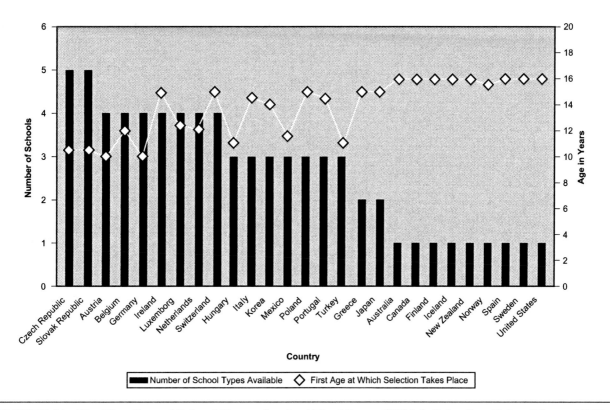

FIGURE 11–15   Number of School Types Against First Age of Which Selection Takes Place. OECD. (2005). Education at a Glance, p. 62.

SCHOOL DROPOUTS

A high school diploma has long been valued as an achievement in America—and for good reason. For young adults, documented lifetime benefits accrue from staying in school. The lifetime earning power of an individual and the general indices of quality in an individual's life are profoundly tied to education levels (NCES, 1995). The average dropout will, over a lifetime, earn about $212,000.00 less than a high school graduate and $812,000.00 less than a college graduate (Schwartz, 1995). Those who stay in school are less likely to be unemployed, less likely to land in jail, and less likely to be victims of crime. Girls who drop out are more likely to become pregnant at a young age and more likely to become single parents (NCES, 1993).

The holding power of the school also pays broader societal dividends. A democracy is obligated to commit itself to the widest levels of enlightenment in the population. In this sense, access to and completion of a high school education is a societal requirement, not a luxury or privilege. No advanced democratic society can expect to sustain itself without extending the education levels in the general population. The historical effort to universalize secondary education in the United States has been driven by the belief that the greatest public good will be served. Little wonder that there is often great upset over the dropout rate in America. There is a lot at stake.

Historically speaking, the United States has made significant gains in keeping students enrolled in school and extending their education upward into college. Nostalgia for the good old days of public education often ignores the very high dropout rates that were common only 40 years ago. As noted in Figure 11-16, a larger proportion of the young adult population goes to and stays in high school and college today than in any recent time on our nation's history.

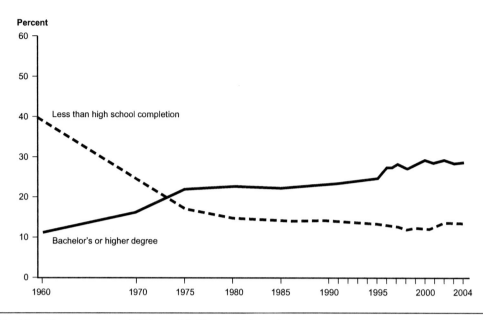

FIGURE 11–16 Percentage of 25- to 29-Year-Olds Who Have Not Completed High School and Percentage Who Completed a Bachelor's or Higher Degree: Various Years, 1960 to 2004. SOURCE: U.S. Department of Education, National Center for Education Statistics, *Digest of Education Statistics, 2004,* based on U.S. Department of Commerce, Census Bureau, Current Population Surveys (CPS), March, various years.

Yet in many public schools, especially in the cities of America, the dropout rate remains tragically high. Understanding the meaning of the dropout rate is not as cut and dried as it might seem. Dropping out of school, for example, is not always a final condition. Students who drop out sometimes return to school or decide to pursue a high school equivalency diploma, also known as the General Education Development certificate (GED). Accounting for the GED brings the traditional dropout rate down by a considerable measure. A study using a national sample of longitudinal data showed that 84 percent of the high school sophomore class graduated on time in 1982, but that two-thirds of the remaining 16 percent completed high school over the next ten years, the vast majority over the first four years. Over the ten-year period, the graduation or completion rate of the class of 1982 went up to 93.7 percent (NCES, 1995a). This is not to say that a GED is an effective replacement for a high school diploma. Various studies found that GED recipients do less well than high school graduates in their earnings, employment, wage rates, and progression into postsecondary education (National Library of Education, 1996). The compelling evidence points to the power of the school experience embodied in the attainment of a high school diploma.

Different dropout counting procedures can also confuse matters. The National Center for Education Statistics measures the dropout rate in three fundamentally different ways. The most straightforward and perhaps most trustworthy method of counting is known as the on-time (or freshmen) graduation rate. This measures the proportion of ninth graders who actually completed or graduated from high school with a regular diploma over their scheduled 4-year period in high school. The key to this measurement is high school completion, as certified by a diploma. Students who were awarded alternate credentials, such as a GED equivalency diploma, are not counted as graduates. Such a measure provides a real indicator of graduates who actually attended high school and took advantage, for better or worse, of the whole of their school experience. The sad news is that, across the country, about one out of every four high school freshmen fail to graduate on time, leaving a virtual army of adolescents unconnected to the school. The state rates vary considerably, as noted in Table 11-5.

TABLE 11–5 Averaged Freshman Graduation Rates, by State: School Years 2002–03 and 2003–04.

State or Jurisdiction	2002–03	2003–04
United States[1]	73.9	75.0
Alabama	64.7	65.0
Alaska	68.0	67.2
Arizona	75.9	66.8
Arkansas	76.6	76.8
California	74.1	73.9
Colorado	76.4	78.7
Connecticut	80.9	80.7
Delaware	73.0	72.9
District of Columbia	59.6	68.2
Florida	66.7	66.4
Georgia	60.8	61.2
Hawaii	71.3	72.6
Idaho	81.4	81.5
Illinois	75.9	80.3
Indiana	75.5	73.5
Iowa	85.3	85.8
Kansas	76.9	77.9
Kentucky	71.7	73.0
Louisiana	64.1	69.4
Maine	76.3	77.6
Maryland	79.2	79.5
Massachusetts	75.7	79.3
Michigan	74.0	72.5
Minnesota	84.8	84.7
Mississippi	62.7	62.7
Missouri	78.3	80.4
Montana	81.0	80.4
Nebraska	85.2	87.6
Nevada	72.3	57.4
New Hampshire	78.2	78.7
New Jersey	87.0	86.3
New Mexico	63.1	67.0
New York	60.9	–
North Carolina	70.1	71.4
North Dakota	86.4	86.1
Ohio	79.0	81.3
Oklahoma	76.0	77.0
Oregon	73.7	74.2
Pennsylvania	81.7	82.2
Rhode Island	77.7	75.9
South Carolina	59.7	60.6
South Dakota	83.0	83.7
Tennessee	63.4	66.1
Texas	75.5	76.7
Utah	80.2	83.0
Vermont	83.6	85.4
Virginia	80.6	79.3
Washington	74.2	74.6
West Virginia	75.7	76.9
Wisconsin	85.8	–
Wyoming	73.9	76.0

SOURCE: NCES. (2006). *The averaged freshman graduation rate for public schools from the common core of data: School years 2002–2003, 2003–2004.* (Washington, DC: U.S. Department of Education, p. 5.

Another method used by the National Center for Education Statistics to measure dropouts is known as the event dropout measure. Event dropouts are students in grades 10–12 who dropout of high school between the beginning of one year and the beginning of the next. These are students who have neither completed high school, nor a GED. The event dropout measure gives us the closest approximation of a real time dropout rate, one that occurs over a relatively short and identifiable period of time. The advantage here is that the school can examine the dropout rate in relation to particular events and initiatives.

The most comprehensive and most frequently reported measure of dropouts is the status dropout measure, which tracks the proportion of 16- to 24-year-olds, who have either not completed high school, not completed a GED or are not currently enrolled in high school. This statistic widens the scope of the dropout construct by giving us a sense of the overall retention power of the school with the added effect of accounting for GED equivalency recipients.

Such a comprehensive measure is useful for reporting general trends over time and in relation to various subgroups. If one examines status dropout rates against categories of ethnicity and race, for instance, one can see that considerable progress has been made to close the dropout gap between white (non-Hispanic) and black (non-Hispanic) youth. The dropout rate for Hispanic youth, however, remains quite high. In 2001, approximately 11 percent of all 16- through 24-year-olds had not completed high school (or its equivalent) and/or were not enrolled in school. Whites were better than the national average with about a seven percent status dropout rate against an 11 percent rate for blacks and a 27 percent rate for Hispanics (see Figure 11–17). Disaggregated by gender, the status dropout rate was 12 percent for males in 2001 and nine percent for females. The most dramatic sta-

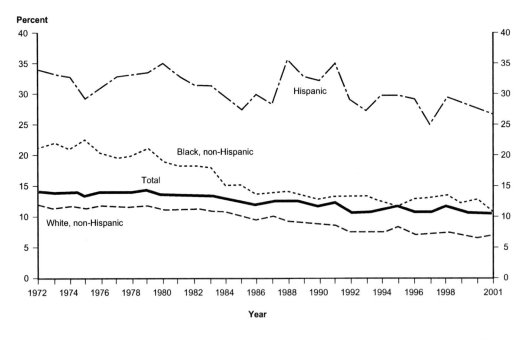

NOTE: Due to small sample sizes, American Indians/Alaska Natives and Asians/Pacific Islanders are included in the totals but are not shown separately. In addition, the erratic nature of the Hispanic status rates reflects, in part, the small sample size of Hispanics in the CPS. Numbers for years 1987 through 2001 reflect new editing procedures instituted by the U.S. Census Bureau for cases with missing data on school enrollment items. Numbers for years 1994 through 2001 reflect changes in the CPS due to newly instituted computer-assisted interviewing and the change in population controls used in the 1990 Census-based estimates, with adjustment for undercounting in the 1990 Census. See appendix C for a filler description of the impact of these changes on reported rates.
SOURCE: U.S. Department of Commerce, Census Bureau, Current Population Survey, October 1972–2001.

FIGURE 11–17 **Status Dropout Rates of 16- Through 24-Year Olds, by Race/Ethnicity: October 1972 Through October 2001.**

tus dropout disparities are based on income levels. In 2000, students from the lowest quartile of family income posted a status dropout rate of over 20 percent (20.7 percent), while those in the highest quartile reported a status dropout rate of 3.5 percent, approximately a 600 percent difference (NCES, 2001). As depicted in Figure 11–18, income levels represent significantly wider gaps in the status dropout rates than either of the differences reported on the categories of race or gender (not accounting for the Hispanic rates). Although poverty levels negatively affect the graduate rates of all racial and ethnic subgroups, the relation between poverty and graduation rates is the strongest for black students (see Figure 11–19). The gloomy reality is that graduation rates for black students living in low poverty settings are still lower than the graduation rates of whites and Asian students in high poverty settings.

As indicated, the Hispanic status dropout rate represents a troubling anomaly in the national trends. Researchers in the National Center for Education Statistics, however, believe that the reported Hispanic dropout numbers are artificially ballooned by demographic factors related to immigration. NCES found that about one-half of all Hispanic dropouts are foreign-born and that about 70 percent of this foreign-born group does not even enroll in a school in the United States. Many foreign-born Hispanic youth come to the United States in pursuit of a job, not an education, and usually have limited or no English proficiency skills. Because of their age (16- to 24-year-olds), these foreign-born youth are included in the status group calculation and hence are counted as dropouts. The effect of immigration can be especially appreciated by examining the status dropout rate for first-generation and second-generation Hispanics, which is 15 percent and 14 percent, respectively. These are still significantly higher than the dropout rates for first- and second-generation non-Hispanics, but not nearly as high as the overall reported status dropout rates.

Researchers have tried to find the variables around which dropouts might cluster and have asked why some students find the choice to leave school attractive. Interesting work has been done at the state

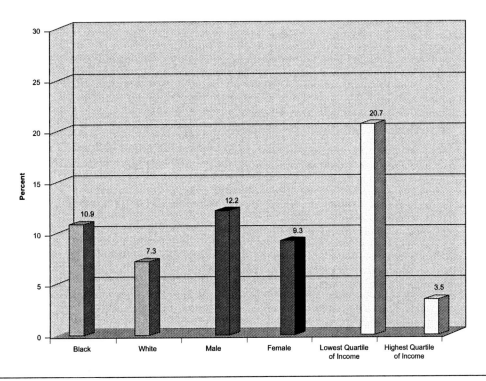

FIGURE 11–18   Differences Between Status Dropout Rates, by Various Subgroups: Black/White, Male/Female, and Lowest Quartile of Income/Highest Quartile, 2001.

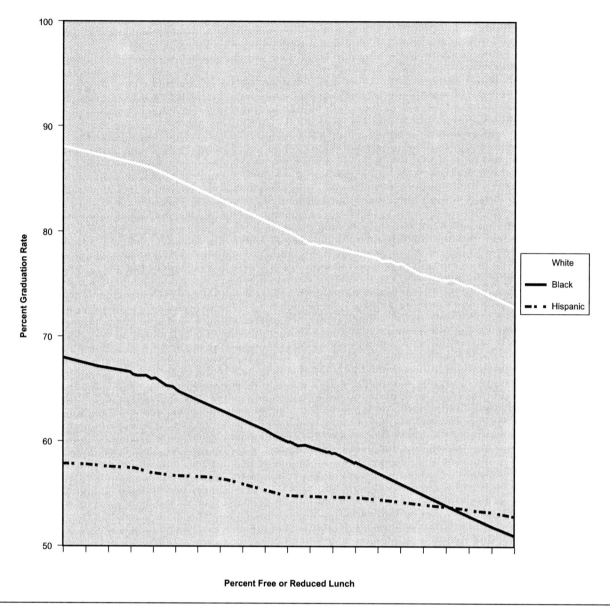

FIGURE 11–19   Estimated Graduation Rate Trajectory by District Poverty for the Average Student of Three Major Racial-Ethnic Groups. Swanson, C. B. (2004) Sketching a Portrait of Public High School Graduation. In Orfield, G. (ed) *Dropouts in America*, Cambridge, MA: Harvard University Press, p.31.

level in this area. Many states provide comprehensive statewide data on the characteristics of dropouts. In Texas, for instance, about 50 percent of the dropouts were not identified as "at risk" the year they dropped out, showing how daunting it is to anticipate just who might be a candidate for dropping out. Seventy-five percent of the dropouts in Texas were also over age and most dropouts occurred in urban areas, irrespective of school size (TEA, 1995). In North Carolina, almost 70 percent of the dropouts were enrolled in the general education curriculum; less than five percent were enrolled in college preparation. The majority of dropouts in North Carolina were in grades nine and ten, more than 60 percent of the total, and about 75 percent of the pool was performing below the 50th percentile on standardized tests. Most of the students cited "academic problems" and "choosing work over school" as their main reasons for leaving school (NCSD, 1994).

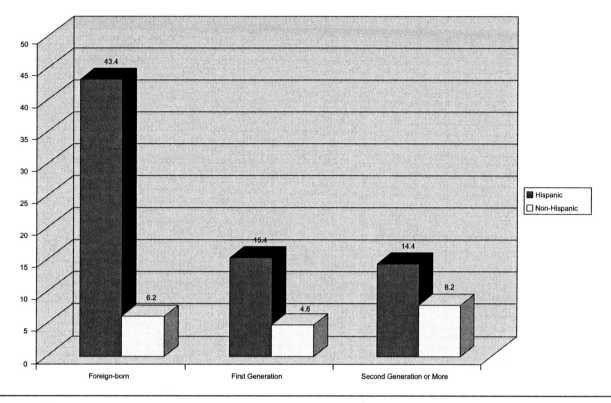

FIGURE 11–20   Status Dropout Rates, by Recency of Immigration: Hispanic and Non-Hispanic, 2001. NCES. (2004). Dropout Rates in the United States. Washington, DC: U.S. Department of Education, p. 14.

The national data are similar. Based on a national data base, researchers found that about one-fifth of all status dropouts (ages of 18–24) were married, living with someone, or divorced, with females more likely to be married than males. Forty percent had a child or were expecting one. More than one-half moved during their high school years. One-fourth, in fact, changed schools two or more times. Twelve percent, twice as many as school graduates, ran away from home. One-half were enrolled in a general high school program; very few were in college preparatory studies. One-half missed school at least ten days; one-third cut class at least ten times and one-third was either suspended or put on probation. Students who repeated one or more grades were twice as likely to drop out as those who had never been held back (Schwartz, 1995).

Studies conducted by the National Center for Education Statistics (1993) found that, when dropouts were asked why they left school, many simply reported that they did not like school. Other popular reasons included not being able to keep up with the academic work, not being able to get along with teachers, and not performing well in school (see Table 11–6).

One could conceive of the school-related reasons for dropping out as factors that push students out of schools, and the job/family-related reasons as factors that pull students from school. Factors internal to the school, such as poor teaching, unfair disciplinary policies, and unresponsive curriculum offering can contribute to pushing students out of school. Schools must be aware of how they might contribute to school failure and to student resentment toward schooling. This involves being aware of OTL factors, as they might be differentially distributed across curriculum tracks and ability groups, and being aware of grade promotion policies that leave over-age students in difficult, if not humiliating, classroom situations. Schools have less influence on the factors outside the school environment,

Table 11–6 10th to 12th Grade Dropouts Who Reported Various Reasons for Dropping Out of School.

| Reasons for Dropping Out | Total | Sex | | Race-Ethnicity | | |
		Male	Female	Hispanic	Black, Non-Hispanic	White, Non-Hispanic
School-related:						
Did not like school	42.9	43.6	42.2	48.0	28.8	45.5
Could not get along with teachers	22.8	24.6	21.1	24.6	27.8	21.5
Could not get along with students	14.5	17.7	11.6	15.6	18.4	13.6
Did not feel safe at school	6.0	7.0	5.1	8.3	8.5	4.8
Felt I didn't belong	24.2	25.8	22.7	16.0	25.9	26.6
Could not keep up with schoolwork	31.3	32.7	29.9	35.0	25.6	30.3
Was failing school	38.7	43.4	34.5	40.6	39.5	36.6
Changed school and did not like new school	10.6	10.5	10.7	12.3	9.1	10.2
Was suspended/expelled from school	15.5	21.6	10.0	10.1	24.4	15.4
Job-related:						
Could not work and go to school at same time	22.8	26.9	19.1	20.4	15.4	24.6
Found a job	28.5	35.9	21.8	34.1	19.1	27.5
Family-related:						
Had to support family	11.2	10.4	11.9	15.8	11.8	9.9
Wanted to have family	7.5	6.4	8.4	9.1	4.6	8.2
Was pregnant*	26.8	–	26.8	30.6	34.5	25.6
Became parent	14.7	7.7	21.0	19.6	21.0	12.4
Got married	12.1	3.7	19.7	13.4	2.0	15.1
Had to care for family member	11.9	9.5	14.0	8.5	14.7	10.7
Other:						
Wanted to travel	8.1	8.2	8.0	6.6	7.3	7.1
Friends dropped out	8.0	8.5	7.5	7.6	6.7	8.6
Had a drug and/or alcohol problem	4.4	6.1	2.8	1.8	2.1	5.9

–Not applicable.

*Females only.

SOURCE: U.S. Department of Education, National Center for Education Statistics, National Education Longitudinal Study of 1988 Second Followup Survey, 1992, unpublished data.

but they can still offer services to prevent students from being pulled away from the school. In this regard, ancillary services, such as after-school programs, special summer programs, counseling services, mentoring programs, homework assistance centers, and work-study programs could be used. Given the role that pregnancy plays in school drop outs, comprehensive sex education and community outreach programs that deal with issues of sexuality could be viewed as contributing to dropout prevention. Finding ways to accommodate and support a student's situation once she or he becomes a parent might also be viewed in a similar light.

TECHNOLOGY AND SCHOOLING

Over the past decade, the American public schools have made a considerable investment in the use and the application of technologies in the classroom. These technologies are inclusive of a full range of computer, networking, and software applications. To what extent are such tools and services fulfilling an important educational mandate in the school and garnering the support of classroom teachers?

Nearly all public schools can now boast of having the technologies that provide access to the Internet. This is no small achievement because only ten years earlier, Internet access was available in only about one-third of the public schools. Over 90 percent of instructional rooms in the public schools currently have access to the Internet, up from a minuscule three percent in 1994. This is largely good news because few educators question the opportunities that the Internet provides to enhancing teaching and learning in the classroom. In 2001, 61 percent of practicing teachers reported that classroom access to the World Wide Web was essential to their teaching.

The emerging centrality of computers and Internet access in the instructional life of the school raises important questions about the differences that exist in computer and Internet access and use against socioeconomic status, household characteristics, and race/ethnicity. Among children between the ages of 5–17, close to 77 percent use a computer at home, in contrast to 41 percent of black and 41 percent of Hispanic children. Only 39 percent of children from families whose income is less than $20,000 use a computer at home, in contrast to 89 percent of those living in families earning over $75,000 annually. The gap between a two-parent household (74 percent) and a female-headed household (44 percent) is similarly wide. These numbers only speak to access and use of the computer. To fully appreciate the impact, one has to examine the use to which the computer is being applied.

Data from the NCES indicate that more than half of all children with home access to a computer use it for school assignments (67 percent), about half also use it for e-mailing and word processing, and that an overwhelming 90 percent use it for gaming purposes. These usage rates suggest that the technology is not incidental to school success, notwithstanding the very high use for playing games.

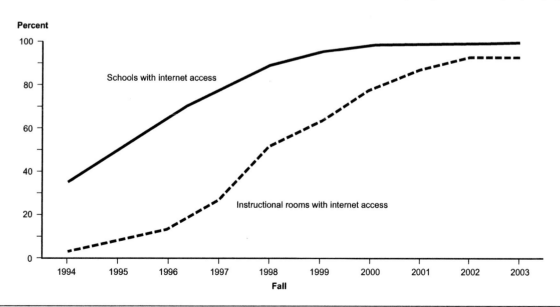

FIGURE 11–21   Percent of All Public Schools and Instructional Rooms with Internet Access: 1994–2003. SOURCE: U.S. Department of Education, National Center for Education Statistics. Fast Response Survey System, *Internet Access in Public Schools and Classrooms: 1994–2003.*

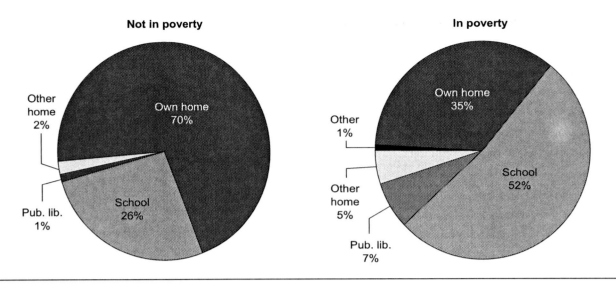

FIGURE 11–22 Percent of Children and Adolescents, Age 5–17, Who Use the Internet at Only One Location and Poverty Status: 2001. Note: Estimates may not sum to 100 percent because of rounding. SOURCE: U.S. Census Bureau, Current Population Survey, September 2001.

Fortunately, the school has taken up the slack for children without home access to the Internet. Among the children who use the Internet in only one location, students living in poverty make disproportionate use of the school location. The most frequently reported use of the Internet, irrespective of income, or race/ethnicity, was completing school assignments. Almost all public schools provide after-school access to computer resources and close to 90 percent also provide before-school access.

SUMMARY

The condition of public education in America is marked by mixed results. Most achievement measures are stable, as are the national dropout rates. If anything, slight but significant improvements can be found in the achievement and dropout data. Low achievement can at least be partly traced to poverty and home environments.

The NAEP achievement indices in reading and mathematics show no appreciable decline in overall performance. The composite averages, however, mask differences that exist between the performances of various subgroups. Although the achievement gap in reading and math that exists between white and nonwhite children has improved considerably over the past several decades, it is still quite wide. Some of the differences might be explained by the disproportionately high representation of minority groups living in poverty and perhaps by differential OTL factors in the school. Some of the achievement gaps can be detected among 4-year-olds, which points to family and preschool environments as contributing factors. The achievement differences witnessed against the variable of gender, although significant in the area of reading, are significantly smaller than anything witnessed across income and race categories.

The differences in the dropout rates between white and black children have been closing and demonstrate enormous historical improvements in the graduation rates of black children in the public schools. The Hispanic population, however, has not experienced the same kind of improvements. The Hispanic population is unique because it is very much affected by immigration factors. Most of

Hispanic status dropouts, for instance, were born outside of the United States and are counted as dropouts, even though in many cases, they never attended public school. The evidence on dropping out of school indicates that there are factors internal to the school that tends to pull students out. The internal factors seem to play a more significant role than the external ones. The number one reason cited for leaving school, for instance, was "not liking school."

Although much has been written about the poor performance of the United States schools in comparison to other advanced nations, the data show that the basis for comparison is complicated by OTL factors and by various cultural and governance differences. The U.S schools clearly have lower aggregate average scores on most international tests of achievement, but the variance between states is often wider than the variance between nations, meaning that some states perform better than some of the highest performing nations. Moreover, the U.S schools are documented to have wider participation levels and less class bias in secondary and tertiary school enrollments.

REFERENCES

Berliner, D. C. (2005). Our impoverished view of educational reform. *Teachers College Press*.

Berliner, D. C., & Biddle, B. J. (1997). *The manufactured crisis: Myths, fraud and the attack on America's public schools*. White Plains, NY: Longman Publishers.

Bracey, G. W. (2004). *Setting the record straight: Responses to misconceptions about public education in the U.S.* Portsmouth, NH: Heinemann.

Grouws, D. A., & Cebulla, K. J. (2000). Elementary and middle school mathematics at the crossroads. In T. Good (Ed.), *American education: Yesterday, today and tomorrow*. The Ninety-Ninth Yearbook for the National Society for the Study of Education. Chicago, IL: University of Chicago Press.

Jencks, C., & Phillips, M. (1998). America's next achievement test: Closing the black-white score gap. *The American Prospect Online, 40* (Sept.–Oct.).

Johnson, R. C., & Viadero, D. (15 March, 2000). Unmet promise: Minority achievement. *Education Week*.

Lee, V. E., & Burkam, D. T. (2002). *Inequality at the starting gate*. Washington, DC: Economic Policy Institute.

National Center for Education Statistics. (1991). *Education in States and Nations*. Washington, DC: Department of Education.

National Center for Education Statistics. (1993). *Dropout rates in the United States*. Washington, DC: U.S. Department of Education.

National Center for Education Statistics. (1995). *Digest of education statistics*. Washington, DC: U.S. Department of Education.

National Center for Education Statistics. (1995a). *Dropouts and latecomers*. Washington, DC: U.S. Department of Education.

National Center for Education Statistics. (1999). *The condition of education*. Washington, DC: U.S. Department of Education.

National Center for Education Statistics. (2001). *Digest of education statistics*. Washington, DC: U.S. Department of Education.

National Center for Education Statistics. (2002). *Comparative indicators of education in the United States and other G8 countries*. Washington, DC: U.S. Department of Education.

National Center for Education Statistics. (2004). *Dropout rates in the United States: 2001*. Washington, DC: U.S. Department of Education.

National Center for Education Statistics. (2004a). *International outcomes in learning mathematics literacy and problem-solving.* Washington, DC: U.S. Department of Education.

National Center for Education Statistics. (2005). *The nation's report card: Reading 2005.* Washington, DC: U.S. Department of Education, 2005.

National Center for Education Statistics. (2005a). *The nation's report card: Fourth grade reading 2000.* Washington, DC: U.S. Department of Education, 2005.

National Center for Education Statistics. (2005b). *NAEP 2004 trends in academic progress.* Washington, DC: U.S. Department of Education.

National Center for Education Statistics. (2005c). *The nation's report card: Mathematics, 2005.* Washington, DC: U.S. Department of Education, 2005.

National Center for Education Statistics. (2006). *U.S. student and adult performance on international assessment of educational achievement.* Washington, DC: U.S. Department of Education.

National Center for Education Statistics. (2006a). *The averaged freshman graduation rate for public schools from the common core of data: School years 2002–2003, 2003–2004.* Washington, DC: U.S. Department of Education.

National Committee for Excellence in Education. (1983). *A nation at risk.* Washington, DC: U.S. Department of Education.

National Library of Education. (1996). *Educational and labor market performance of GED recipients.* Washington, DC: U.S. Department of Education.

North Carolina State Department of Mental Health. (1994). *Dropout data report and program summary.* Raleigh, NC: North Carolina State Department of Mental Health.

Organisation for Economic Co-operation and Development. (2005). *Education at a glance.* Paris: OECD Publishing.

Organisation for Economic Co-operation and Development. (2004). *Students with disabilities, learning difficulties and disadvantages: Statistics and indicators.* Paris: OECD Publishing.

Schwartz, W. (1995). School dropouts: New information about an old problem. *ERIC/Cue Digest, #109 ERIC.* New York, NY: Clearinghouse in Urban Education (ERIC document 386515).

Texas Education Agency. (1995). *Public school dropouts, 92–93.* Austin, TX: Publications Distribution Division of Texas Education Agency (ERIC 384685).

KEY QUESTIONS

1. What is school achievement and how does it differ from the school aptitude?
2. Explain how opportunity-to-learn factors play into achievement and how OTL factors can explain differences in achievement between various groups.
3. What is the NAEP?
4. What is the fundamental difference between a criterion-referenced and a norm-referenced test?
5. What are the overall trends to report on NAEP reading results?
6. What is the general relation between reading achievement and home reading conditions?
7. Speculate on why there is a wide difference on reading achievement measures between white and black children, between boys and girls and between children living above and below the poverty line.
8. What are the overall trends to report on NAEP math results?
9. Do course-taking patterns in mathematics suggest OTL differences between boys and girls?
10. What is the difference between event dropouts and status dropouts?
11. Outline a strategy to further improve the holding power of the school given the data presented on dropouts.
12. Explain how dropouts can be pushed out of school as well as pulled out of school.
13. How are home literacy experiences affected by poverty levels?
14. How might OTL affect the results of the international education exams?
15. How does the unified/comprehensive system popular in the United States and Scandinavian nations differ from the bipartite or tripartite systems popular in most of Europe?
16. What does it mean to say that the variance in measured achievement within a country is greater than the variance between countries?

RESEARCH EXERCISES

1. Research the history of the SAT. Discuss its purpose and its historic trends, looking especially for explanations for its recent decline.
2. Trace NAEP's history or report on a recent NAEP study from a subject area other than reading or math.
3. Research any of the achievement gaps discussed in the text (race, income, and gender) and look to provide some explanation for their existence.
4. Distribute the home reading survey listed in Table 11–4 to a classroom of school children and then correlate the results against another variable or two (teacher's judgment of reading facility, grades achieved in school, income levels, and so forth).
5. Report on the educational governance structure of any of the OECD nations. Compare and contrast with the United States.
6. Report on any of the recently disseminated international education studies published by the NCES or OECD.
7. Compare the status and event dropout rates, or the on-time graduation rates of two or more different school districts. Examine, through interviews, why the differences exist.

CHAPTER 12

School Equity

A democratic society obviously demands a democratic school system—one that aims to create intelligent, socially responsible, and autonomously thinking individuals. This means that the schools need to exercise some consciousness over how equitably and effectively the normative mandate of the school (the essential knowledge, skills, and values needed for participation in society) is taught.

In some ways, the news on school equity in America is encouraging. Because of the early American commitment to the universalization of secondary schooling and to an openly accessible system of higher education, enrollment rates in American high schools and colleges are, relative to international standards, quite large. Although the school is rightfully criticized for some of its equity failings, there are also signs of significant progress. For instance, the percentage of degrees obtained by women and minorities in the United States (in both technical and non-technical fields), is quite high by international measures. As indicated in the previous chapter, the United States schools, relative to the schools of other advanced nations, have a low factor of class stratification and socio-economic bias (OECD, 2005).

However, there is also a dark side to the American school that runs counter to its egalitarian and democratic ideals. American schools continue to suffer from clear inequities both across and within public school districts. Many of these inequities disproportionately affect children from low-income families. Many schools are inequitably funded, racially stratified, and curricularly sorted in ways that work against students from low-income families. Many schools still reinforce gender stereotypes that are damaging to the education of both boys and girls. This chapter will explore issues of inequity in four parts—from the standpoint of curriculum tracking, school segregation, gender bias, and poverty.

CURRICULUM TRACKING

Curriculum tracking is a phase of the school that sorts students into instructional groups according to various judgments of academic performance, all for the purpose of providing a homogeneous instructional target to the teacher. In essence, tracking represents an encompassing use of grouping designed to structure an entire classroom according to an ability or achievement level.

Ability Grouping and Tracking

Ability grouping is widely practiced in the schools. Imagine a self-contained classroom of fourth graders whose reading achievement levels range from a primer level of reading to a high school equivalency. The teacher in such a class would likely have no choice but to explore differentiated ways to teach reading. The most common approach to accommodate such variation is to form ability groups that receive separate (usually small group) instruction. In the elementary school, at least in most cases, the use of such reading groups occurs *within* a mixed-ability classroom. A student might go to an ability-based reading group, but still experience mixed-group instruction in every other phase of the school curriculum. In fact, the elementary school teacher usually only uses ability-based instruction in reading education and occasionally in math education, while keeping the inclusive nature of the self-contained classroom intact. Thus, where *within class* ability grouping prevails, the majority of the instructional time in the wider self-contained classroom experience is still usually conducted without ability grouping.

Tracking, however, is not about *within class* grouping. The best way to define tracking is to see it as the wholesale grouping of students into instructional programs, *between* (not within) classrooms. Tracking, in fact, is marked by the absence of wider heterogeneously-grouped experiences and by clear high- to low-ability (and status) designations between entire classrooms. Sometimes known as an XYZ approach, tracking looks to divide students by ability and achievement, using something like a top 20 percent, middle 60 percent, and bottom 20 percent distribution.

Because of the predominance of the mixed-ability self-contained classroom in elementary education, widespread curriculum tracking is rarely witnessed in the early grades. Of course, it can (and sometimes does) occur in elementary schools, especially if the school does not embrace the self-contained classroom arrangement. If reading instruction, for instance, is sorted by ability and taught in separate classrooms, and if this same or a similar sorting system is also used to teach science, math, and language arts in separate ability-based classrooms, then it would be fair to say that the elementary school is tracked. As mentioned, this is an uncommon arrangement for the elementary school. The elementary school is more likely to see a limited tracking system, dedicated only to reading and perhaps math education, where ability groups are taught in separate classes, even sometimes across grade levels.

Tracking usually starts in the middle school and increases its profile in the curriculum into the high school years. Although middle schools are, by philosophical disposition, designed to keep the learner away from tracked experiences, often in the interests of keeping them involved in exploratory and general education, national survey data suggest the persistent presence of tracking in schools serving preadolescents. According to Braddock (1990a), close to one-fourth of middle-level schools (grades five through eight) engage in a rigid form of tracking by using *between-class* ability grouping in all subject areas. Approximately one-third of the middle schools (depending on the grade level) report no *between-class* ability grouping and the remaining percentage report *between-class* ability grouping in some subjects. Rates of tracking in English, math, science, and social studies increase substantially from fifth grade to eighth grade, while the percentage of schools using no *between-class* ability grouping decreases substantially between these grades. These data do not apply to ability groups formed within classrooms, only to the designation of whole classes by ability. See Table 12–1 for a complete breakdown of the national survey.

At the high school level, tracking tends to grow in scope, but not necessarily in intensity. According to another study by Braddock (1990b), only about 8 percent of the nation's comprehensive high schools used *between-class* ability grouping in all subject areas, but the remaining 92 percent used *between-class* ability grouping in some subjects. Curriculum tracking is most popular in English, with 59 percent of the comprehensive schools using it. Approximately 42 percent of the schools engage in tracking math/science instruction and 38 percent social studies instruction (Braddock, 1990b). In most high schools, only one or two academic tracks can be found (usually math and English) with the remainder of the school curriculum left undifferentiated.

Table 12–1 Grouping Practices in Middle-Level Schools

	GRADE			
	5	**6**	**7**	**8**
All Subjects	23	22	22	23
Some Subjects	40	44	47	50
Reading	96	86	63	54
English	24	44	54	54
Math	57	77	84	88
Science	4	5	14	16
Social Studies	4	4	10	10
No Subjects	37	34	31	21

SOURCE: Braddock, J. H. (1990a). Tracking in the middle grades: National patterns of grouping for instruction, *Phi Delta Kappan, 71*(6), 445–49.

Two basic forms of tracking exist in the schools. One approach identifies whole ability groups irrespective of the subject matter taught, with entire classes marked by a high, middle, and low designation. Thus, students in each group will be tracked together for instruction in English, math, social studies, science, and so on. Consequently, a high track might represent some honors or advanced placement group (or groups) bound for college; a middle track might contain a smattering of college-bound and vocational education students with middle range academic aptitudes; and a low track will likely enroll low-functioning students (low aptitude and/or low motivation) who are often not college bound. The other approach to tracking reconstitutes the ability levels according to the subject matter, making it possible for one student to be placed in a high level math course but a low-level English course, and so on. However, even this form of tracking typically results in the same students being placed in the same levels across the board. A national survey, for instance, indicated that 60 to 70 percent of tenth graders who were enrolled in honors math were simultaneously enrolled in honors English; a similar pattern held between remedial math and remedial English (Oakes, Gamoran, & Page, 1992). Carey and others (1994) found considerable overlap between ability levels in math and English courses offered in the tenth grade.

Curriculum tracking in the high school also has to be understood in relation to the school's obligation to provide enrichment and remediation experiences. The availability of honors or advanced placement courses at the secondary school level for a small percentage of high-ability or high-achieving students is clearly a form of tracking. The nature of the track could be very much affected by the enrollment criteria and by the positioning of the coursework in the curriculum. Thus, if self-selection is allowed into the honors and AP courses (which is increasingly the case with school districts) or if access to these courses is based on course performance in a set of heterogeneously grouped prerequisites, the nature of the curriculum track has changed from being based on ability to being based on interest and achievement. Contrast this to a more traditional track design, in which an honors or advanced placement group is identified as high ability as early as the ninth grade (sometime earlier with the assistance of the middle school). The group then moves en mass through the school curriculum, experiencing coursework preparatory for admission into top colleges and universities and clearly distinguished from coursework offered to lower track groups.

Why Is Tracking Used in the Schools?

Tracking is used in the schools for several reasons. First, as mentioned, tracking is expressly designed to be responsive to the divergent ability and achievement levels of students. Thus, students who may not be as skilled as others in, say, mathematics, are believed to be served by a slower pace and a more deliberate and detailed approach, while those who are more skilled are free to go forward without as much restraint and with more opportunities for enrichment. Many believe that it is simply too much to expect teachers to be responsive to a wide range of student skills in one classroom—that teachers can very much benefit from having a more precise and less wide-ranging ability/achievement target at which to aim their instruction. Second, it is commonly believed that when students of mixed abilities are all taught in one common classroom, the achievement of the high-ability student is dragged down. The thinking is that teachers pace their classrooms according to the slowest runner, and that the faster ones never get to fully stride and run far. Some evidence exists to support this conclusion, at least in the area of mathematics instruction. According to Loveless (1998), low-achieving students seem to learn more in heterogeneous math classes, while high-achieving and average-achieving students sustain achievement losses in these settings.

These reasons are, at their face value, sound and logical. But critics say that when tracking is implemented, its consequences reach well beyond its intentions of providing appropriate instructional opportunities for youth of varying ability levels. Tracking, they claim, becomes a way of rationalizing differential *qualities* of experience, in that students in high groups, when compared to their peers in low groups, benefit from higher teacher expectation, more idea-oriented learning engagements, more meaningful curriculum materials, a better classroom climate, and a more challenging teaching methodology. The fact that this differential in quality cuts across racial and economic lines, in that low-level tracks are disproportionately represented by minority and low-income children, places tracking at the center of our discussion on equity.

Inequities in Tracking

Much of the best work done on the inequitable nature of tracking was drawn from a national sample of schools (Oakes, 1985). Taking her data from Goodlad's landmark study of schooling, Jeannie Oakes documented the qualitative differences witnessed between the various tracks of a school curriculum. Oakes, for instance, reported on how the content of the curriculum varied at different track levels. Higher track levels were marked by a sharp focus on college preparatory topics and were not likely to emphasize basic skills instruction. Generally speaking, higher level students engaged in higher cognitive work than their counterparts in the lower tracks—making judgments, drawing inferences, and engaging in idea-oriented forms of instruction. Low track levels were dedicated primarily to rote learning and to basic skills instruction, including in English class, and functional literacy skills, such as filling out a job application (see Table 12–2).

Although one would naturally expect ability tracks to vary in cognitive intensity and perhaps somewhat in content, the existing situation between high- and low-track settings can be more properly distinguished as two *qualitatively* different experiences, one that provides high-cognitive experiences for the academically-inclined and low-cognitive experiences for those with lesser academic skills. This is verified also in what teachers report to be the desired behavioral outcomes for students in the different tracks. Teachers, for instance, were more likely to describe behaviors like self-direction, critical thinking, creativity, and active involvement in learning as appropriate outcomes for the high track, while openly aiming at characteristics like working quietly, punctuality, conforming to rules, and getting along with others for the low track (Oakes, 1985). Such disparities reflect base inequities in the way we educate youth; they cannot be justified as outcomes appropriate for varied levels of ability.

Not surprisingly, teacher expectations for the children in the different tracks also vary. This results in considerable instructional advantage to the students in the high track, not only because of the obvious benefits of being marked as having ability, but also because of the nature of instruction that occurs

TABLE 12–2 Selected Student Responses to Curriculum Tracking

Students' written responses to the question: "What is the most important thing you have learned or done so far in this class?"

Mathematics

HIGH-TRACK STUDENTS

1. Learning to change my thought processes in dealing with higher mathematics and computers. —Senior High
2. Inductive reasoning.—Senior High
3. Learned many new mathematical principles and concepts that can be used in a future job. —Senior High

LOW-TRACK STUDENTS

1. Really I have learned nothing. Only my roman numerals. I knew them, but not very good. I could do better in another class.—Junior High
2. I have learned just a small amount in this class. I feel that if I was in another class, that I would have a challenge to look forward to each and every time I entered the class. I feel that if I had another teacher I would work better.—Junior High
3. How to do income tax.—Senior High

English

HIGH-TRACK STUDENTS

1. I have learned things that will get me ready for college entrance examinations. Also, many things on how to write compositions that will help me in college.—Junior High
2. To me, there is not a most important thing I learned in this class. Everything or mostly everything I learn here is IMPORTANT.—Junior High

LOW-TRACK STUDENTS

1. I learned that English is boring.—Senior High
2. Job applications. Job interviews. Preparation for the above.—Junior High
3. To spell words you don't know, to fill out things where you get a job.—Junior High

SOURCE: Oakes, J. (1985). Keeping track: How schools structure inequality. (New Haven, CT: Yale University Press).

in the higher track. High-track experiences, for instance, were reported to be less punitive in nature, less inclined to be preoccupied with discipline and control, and more environmentally friendly than the low tracks. Students in high-ability tracks observed their teachers to be more concerned with their personal needs and interests, and their own peers to be more friendly than those in the low tracks. The high track also outscored the low track on scales of teacher clarity, organization, and enthusiasm (Oakes, 1985).

Oakes (1990) also examined how race and class affect a student's opportunity to learn in a tracked math and science program, asking particularly whether such factors affect access to programs and to qualified teachers. Oakes again uncovered several disturbing trends. Using a national sample of schools, Oakes (1990) found, for instance, that the basic qualification patterns of teachers were not only noticeable across schools, varying according to race and social class, but within schools as well. Regarding the qualifications of the teachers assigned to teach math and science in the various ability tracks of the secondary school, a clear trend emerged. The lower tracks, when compared to the higher tracks, attracted significantly more uncertified teachers, significantly fewer teachers with a B.A. or B.S., significantly fewer teachers with Master's degrees, and significantly fewer teachers carrying the

TABLE 12–3 Teacher Qualification Differences Across Ability Tracks and Socioeconomic Status (SES) Levels

	LOW-ABILITY CLASSES		HIGH-ABILITY CLASSES	
	Low-SES, Minority, Urban	High-SES, White, Suburban	Low-SES, Minority, Urban	High-SES, White, Suburban
Certified in Science/Math	39	82	73	84
Bachelor's in Science/Math	38	68	46	78
Master's in Science/Math	8	32	10	48
NSTA* Qualified	11	36	5	47
NCTM† Qualified	23	26	4	16
Computer Course Work	41	61	69	62

Source: Oakes, J. (1990). Multiplying Inequities (Santa Monica, CA: Rand Corporation) p. 67.

endorsement or qualification of the National Science Teachers Association. In general, teachers working in lower tracks seem less academically and professionally prepared than their colleagues in higher track settings, at least in secondary math and science instruction. When one examines these same concerns across social class and race, the picture worsens. As noted in Table 12–3, the qualifications of teachers working in the tracks of a low-income, largely minority school are at a considerable distance from the qualifications of teachers working in the high tracks of a high-income, largely white school.

Supporters of tracking have responded to these findings by observing that such a mal-distribution of qualified teachers has less to do with tracking than with critical shortages in the teaching profession. Loveless (1998), for instance, argues that if the teaching staff is varied in its range of qualifications, a staffing distribution that brings more qualified teachers to high-level groups actually makes some sense. The most qualified teachers, especially those with advanced knowledge in their subject areas, are not necessarily best positioned to work with low-track students who have remedial needs.

Oakes' work on tracking has been widely read and cited, and has had considerable sway in turning school leaders and school commentators against the practice of curriculum tracking. Even mainstream critics have bordered on the dramatic in damning the practice of tracking. Harold Howe, Secretary of Education during the Johnson Administration, called tracking "one of the most destructive aspects of factory-model schooling," arguing that it perpetuates disadvantage, fosters racial and cultural isolation, and encourages low expectations for black and Hispanic students (Howe, 1993, p. 144). Similarly, as documented by Loveless (1998), popular journals such as *Better Homes and Gardens* and *U.S. News and World Report* have run articles criticizing the practice of tracking, while various national organizations, including the National Governor's Association, the Children's Defense Fund, the Carnegie Corporation, the College Board, and the National Education Association, have done the same. These actions have apparently had their impact, as many school districts have moved to either reduce or eliminate the practice of curriculum tracking.

Responses to Criticism of Tracking

The negative portrayal of tracking and ability grouping has not gone uncontested. Several researchers have been critical of Oakes' data on tracking, claiming that she lacked good controls and made selective use of the literature to bolster her anti-tracking sentiments (Kulik, 1993). Two groups of researchers studying the best evidence on *within-class* ability grouping claim that they carry positive achievement effects, thus validating the kind of grouping practices commonly witnessed in elementary schools (Slavin, 1990; Kulik, 1993). As far as *between-class* grouping (tracking) is concerned, Kulik (1993) claims that students in lower and middle groups have achievement scores virtually indistinguishable from similar students in mixed groups and that there are no discernible negative effects in the self-esteem of students. Kulik goes further and states that students in high-level tracks outperform similar students in mixed-group setting. His conclusion is that tracking benefits high-level students and, in effect, does no harm (or at least is no worse than mixed groups) to the education of middle- and low-achieving students.

As far as the accusation of racial bias in assignments to the curriculum tracks, Loveless (1998) claims that if controls are taken into account for the achievement status of students assigned to the high-curriculum track (their achievement scores), black students actually enjoy a 10 percent advantage over whites in being assigned to the high track. In effect, it is easier for black students to get assigned to a high track, even though their overall percentage is underrepresented. This, combined with evidence indicating that the achievement gap between white and black students reaches its widest at eighth grade, essentially before the onset of the most severe forms of ability grouping and tracking, leads Loveless to conclude that tracking has little culpability in the achievement differences that exist between white and black students. A stronger case, in fact, can be made for class discrimination, in that some evidence exists to show that students from poor families are more likely to be assigned to a low track than wealthier students with identical achievement records (Loveless, 1998).

Alternatives to Tracking

What alternatives to tracking might the school consider? All children, after all, need to be challenged at their own level, and high- and low-ability children naturally need to be free to pursue their learning needs in a climate most conducive for learning. The complete elimination of ability grouping or tracking is simply not a politically realistic option. And tracking (and ability grouping in general) have strong support from both parents and teachers.

One option for schools is to revisit the design of the comprehensive school, which is theoretically opposed to tracking. Even though curriculum tracking has often flourished in comprehensive schools (Oakes, 1985; Nasaw, 1979), one should remember that the concept of the comprehensive curriculum balances the individualistic phase of the curriculum, which provides students with opportunities for advanced and accelerated instruction, with commonly-grouped core learning experiences. At both the middle school and high school levels, ability concerns can be dealt with through self-selected advanced placement and honors courses, electives, and some expectation of individualization within heterogeneously grouped classrooms. These are all ways to deal with individual ability needs without making tracking a monolith in the curriculum.

There is also the wider question of whether tracking is systemically flawed or implementationally flawed. In other words, if tracking results in less than equitable school experiences between low- and high-track students, is the problem rooted in the very idea of tracking itself or in the manner in which it is implemented? Some of the problems related to teacher expectation, curriculum selection, classroom climate, and instructional differences witnessed between tracked classes could, in fact, be dealt with without necessarily eliminating tracking. Through in-service training and other efforts, the school could in fact raise some consciousness over the kinds of problems that prevail in curriculum tracking in the interests of bringing truly responsive and high-quality experiences to children at all ability and achievement levels.

SCHOOL DESEGREGATION

The struggle to desegregate the American public school became most visible after the Supreme Court ruled that "separate educational institutions are inherently unequal." This ruling, handed down in the 1954 case of *Brown v. the Board of Education of Topeka*, reversed the "separate but equal" doctrine supported by the Court almost 60 years earlier in another famous court case, *Plessy v. Ferguson*. Over 50 years have passed since the historic ruling in *Brown*. Its effect has been dramatic in making public education a more integrated experience. Because of the *Brown* ruling and the considerable number of legalistic rulings that followed it, one could conclude that school desegregation efforts have triumphed in America. Segregation by state-enforcement has been outlawed, the circles of interaction between the races in public schools have multiplied enormously, and courts throughout the country continue to exercise vigilance over schools that have not yet freed themselves from past discriminatory practices. The struggle for school desegregation, which has been a long and hard fought battle waged through both legalistic and legislative channels, has clearly yielded progress. But, as with all problems in a democracy, the struggle is ongoing and new challenges continue to compel the attention of educators and other school leaders in their quest to secure equal opportunities for all youth.

Legal and Legislative Influences

The story of school desegregation has a long history that has its starting point in pre-Civil War America. In 1849, in a case that foreshadowed *Brown*, Benjamin Roberts filed a lawsuit against the City of Boston and its school segregation policies. Roberts' daughter was not allowed to attend the school nearest her residence because she was "a colored person." She was forced instead to go to the Smith Grammar School for black children, which was at a considerable distance from her home and was transparently inferior in its resources to the white schools. Claiming a violation of equal rights to civil and political affairs, Roberts' lawyer, the well-known abolitionist Charles Sumner, made his case not on the grounds of inequities in the resources of the school, but in the very notion of separating the races. Using an argument that would later be appropriated by the lawyers in the *Brown* case, Sumner declared that "the separation of the schools ... tends to create a feeling of degradation in the blacks, and of prejudices and uncharitableness in the whites" (Irons, 1991, p. 15). The judge in the *Roberts* case opted to allow the segregation practices to stand, believing that elected officials had the right to decide what was best for the education of both white and black students. The case was lost, but the legal argument was not.

Unfortunately, the Massachusetts ruling gave wide berth to the installation of a Jim Crow system in the South that separated the races in virtually all facets of society. The term "Jim Crow" was coined by abolitionists to describe the segregation practices that had become common place in the South. By the late nineteenth century, the South mandated Jim Crow laws that resulted in segregated restaurants, hotels, parks, libraries, theatres, railroads, beauty parlors, barbershops, and perhaps most significantly, schools (Irons, 1991). The legal justification for segregation was founded on the principle of "separate but equal" access to facilities and resources. In other words, as long as the facilities were equal, they could also be separate. This was the legal and largely unchallenged premise of life in the Southern states.

In 1896, however, the Supreme Court would have its first opportunity to examine the legal basis of Jim Crow in the case of *Plessy v. Ferguson*. The case involved a man named Homer Plessy who was imprisoned for failing to vacate his seat in a Louisiana Railway coach reserved for white passengers. Plessy, who was Creole and 1/8 black, deliberately challenged the law, seeking to make the legal claim that separate facilities were so inferior and so humiliating that they in effect conferred "a badge of servitude" on blacks. The Supreme Court, however, upheld the Louisiana statute mandating the segregation of passengers in railroad coaches. The Court put its faith in the "separate but equal" doctrine, explaining that separate facilities for the races are constitutionally allowable as long as the facilities were equal. This line of reasoning gave Court sanction to a policy of de jure segregation (segregation by law or state-enforcement) that affected virtually every condition of life in the South. The Court reasoned that there could be no presumption of deliberate discrimination or of inferiority toward minorities in a system that maintains separate and equal standards.

The "separate but equal" standard was still vulnerable, mostly because there was little reality to the "equal" side of it. As stated by Whitman (1998), "separate but equal" was producing "grotesque inequalities," which were manifest in obvious ways, including school spending differences between white and black schools in many parts of the South. Few could disagree that the "separate but equal" doctrine was anchored in racism and intolerance, and accompanying beliefs in black inferiority. Justice Harlan, in fact, underscored this point in his dissenting statement in *Plessy*."

> What can more certainly arouse hate, what more certainly create and perpetuate a feeling of distrust between the races, than state enactments which in fact proceed on the ground that colored citizens are so inferior and degraded that they cannot be allowed to sit in public coaches occupied by white citizens? That, as all will admit, is the real meaning of such legislation as was enacted in Louisiana. (Whitman, 1993, p. 16)

Justice Harlan's dissent was a precursor to what the Court would later say in the 1954 *Brown* ruling: that the idea of "separate but equal" was inherently unequal because it was moved by racist intentions and racist projections of inferiority toward blacks. Like the nineteenth century *Roberts's* case, *Brown v. Topeka* also featured a young black female, Linda Brown, who, because of the color of her skin, was not allowed to attend the school zoned for her neighborhood. Instead she had to go across town to attend an all-black school. The Topeka School system, where Brown was enrolled, was segregated by race, an arrangement that was legal and widely practiced. When the Brown family sued on the basis that separate facilities were inherently unequal, the school district's position was that it fulfilled its obligation to maintain equal facilities. The Brown suit did not question the equality of the facilities; instead it pursued the very idea of segregation, claiming that the very existence of a segregated system had a hurtful (and inequitable) effect on the education of black children.

The argument was buttressed by psychological findings showing that young black children suffered from feelings of inferiority, self-rejection, and hostility brought on by the racism inherent in segregation. These, in fact, were the main finding that came out of Kenneth Clark's famous doll studies, in which black children preferred white dolls over black ones and self-described the black dolls as less nice and less attractive than the white ones. "The conclusion I was forced to reach," observed Clark, "was that these children . . ., like other human beings who are subjected to an obviously inferior status in society . . ., have been definitely harmed in their personalities; that the signs of instability of their personalities are clear" (Irons, 1991, p. 69). Testimony from other psychologists underscored the same concern, and emphasized the fact that state sanction of segregation gave legal certification and legitimacy to a policy that was interpreted (by both whites and blacks) as denoting the inferiority of blacks, and that ultimately had very clear negative effects on the motivation, ego identity, and other key personality factors important to learning and to the general development of black children (Irons, 1991, pp. 129–130).

The Supreme Court ultimately agreed with the Brown's position and, in a strongly-worded ruling, rejected the *Plessy* standard of "separate but equal." The *Brown v. Topeka* (1954) ruling ushered in a new day for race relations in America, outlawing de jure segregation in public schooling, using the argument that it victimized black children with feelings of inferiority that affected their minds and hearts in ways that had long-term negative consequences. In the words of the Court,

> Segregation of white and colored children in public schools has a detrimental effect upon the colored children. The impact is greater when it has the sanction of the law; for the policy of separating the races is usually interpreted as denoting the inferiority of the Negro group. A sense of inferiority affects the motivation of a child to learn. Segregation with the sanction of law, therefore, has a tendency to retard the educational and mental development of Negro children and to deprive them of some of the benefits they would receive in a racially integrated school system. (Whitman, 1998, pp. 121–122)

Because of the Brown ruling, the dual system of schooling practiced in the South had to be dismantled. Besides prohibiting de jure segregation, the Supreme Court put school districts on notice to design desegregation plans that began to undo the vestiges of racism inherent in the segregated system and that showed signs of reasonable integration, or what the Court would later call unitary status. In a ruling that came one year after *Brown v. Topeka*, known as *Brown II*, the Supreme Court attempted to articulate how and when school desegregation could be achieved. Although the message that the segregated system had to be razed was clear enough, the Court unfortunately put no timeline on the matter, advising school districts to proceed "with all deliberate speed," and giving no advice on how desegregation might be implemented or how progress might be evaluated. This gave school districts little incentive to move quickly and little sense of what the Court might be looking for in a desegregated school system.

The political fallout from the *Brown* decision was dramatic. The Supreme Court, for its part, had anticipated some of the tumult. Understanding the political gravity of the impending decision, Warren Burger, Chief Justice of the Supreme Court, actively petitioned members of the Court to find a way to make the decision unanimous. Once the decision was rendered, the Court went through the highly unusual step of explaining it to the public in a press conference setting. Still, various political officials, especially in the South, did their best to undermine the *Brown* decision. Governor Faubus of Arkansas, for instance, was one of several governors who actively resisted integration efforts, famously calling upon the Arkansas National Guard to prevent black children from entering and enrolling in Central High School in Little Rock, Arkansas. Eventually President Eisenhower had to direct 1,000 federal troops to Arkansas to protect and allow access to the nine black children seeking enrollment at Central High School.

Even in the face of massive resistance, desegregation efforts slowly came into focus. Among the more popular schemes used in schools during the early stages of desegregation was the open enrollment system, or freedom of choice plan, which allowed families to choose the school that they believed to be most appropriate for the education of their children. The thinking was that the goal of integration could be served by allowing minority (and majority) families the option of enrolling their children in a district public school of their choice. But the open enrollment system turned out to be quite problematic as a tool for school desegregation. First, black children developed some identification and intimacy with their segregated school. And black school administrators, fearing a loss of work, often did little to encourage black families to opt for the "white" school (Whitman, 1998). Second, there were clear psychological and social restraints to a black parent's desire to opt for a white school. Given the history of apartheid, many black families felt that it was not safe or in any other way wise to send their children to a school where they were not likely wanted. Harassment from racist groups, including the KKK, gave these fears a basis in reality. Third, freedom of choice allowed families to opt out of schools that were beginning to show signs of integration. In this way, freedom of choice was a mechanism that could not only serve integration but also work against it.

In 1968, the Supreme Court reviewed a case, *Green v. County School Board of New Kent, Virginia*, that centered around a freedom of choice plan that a school district had conceived as a device for desegregation. Parents in the district were allowed to send their children to either of two schools, both of which were historically segregated. After three years, the plan yielded no significant school crossover between the races. No white children enrolled in the historically black school and only a small percentage of black children enrolled in the historically white school. The district maintained that it had done its best and was free from any accusation that it was practicing segregation. The segregation that prevailed in the district, it claimed, was a function of parental choice, not district action.

The Court disagreed and stated forthrightly that the only desegregation plan it would accept was one that worked. The language in the ruling was clear: "'Freedom of choice' is not a sacred talisman; it is only a means to a constitutionally-required end—the abolition of the system of segregation and its effects. If the means prove effective, it is acceptable, but if it fails to undo segregation, other means must be used to achieve this end. The school officials have the continuing duty to take whatever action may be necessary to create a 'unitary, nonracial system'." In effect, the Court demanded that the district rethink its strategy, stating that the effect of a district's desegregation strategy had to be the "root and branch" elimination of segregation.

At the same time, the Court established criteria that helped districts determine whether they succeeded in achieving what the Court labeled as unitary (or integrated/desegregated) status. To achieve unitary status, the school district had to show that racial identification was eliminated in several key areas: in the composition of the student body, faculty, and staff; in transportation systems; and in extracurricular activities and facilities. These became known as the Green factors or Green standards. To make the grade as a unitary school system, a school district would have to demonstrate proportionality across its attendant schools in the racial identification of the student body, the faculty, and staff. Thus, the proportion of minority teachers and minority students in any one school within the district could not be out of line with district proportions. Furthermore, school districts had to ensure equal access to transportation systems, extracurricular activities, and facilities, so that all the schools within the district were equally resourceful and equally accessible. In the 1969 case of *Alexander v. Holmes County* (almost 15 years after the Court offered its infamous "with all deliberate speed" decree to schools), the Court also declared that all desegregation plans must be implemented immediately and must not stop until unitary status, as defined by the Green standards, was achieved. Its patience worn thin, the Court had become more definitive on what it wanted from desegregation initiatives.

Several events influenced the more aggressive stance taken by the Court. In 1966, the well-known Coleman report revealed that "the great majority of American children attend schools that are largely segregated . . . where almost all of their fellow students are from the same racial background as they are" (p. 4). The Congressionally-mandated Coleman report also revealed a nationwide achievement gap between white and black youngsters, one that widened as the students proceeded through the grades. It also argued, somewhat surprisingly, that the physical facilities of the schools in America were more or less equal, but that such resources were marginal to the achievement of the children. The expectation was that the study would show clear differences in the quality of the school resources used in the education of the average black child and the average white child. The report instead pointed to the family background of the children as the more significant factor in school achievement. It also claimed that school achievement among black youngsters could improve if they attended schools with white youngsters who were from homes supporting education. This finding had strong parallels to the central themes of the *Brown* ruling, which maintained that the very operation of segregation had a negative effect on the achievement and the general academic outlook of black children. Integration, it seemed, was key to equal opportunity and shared school success.

These findings, one should keep in mind, came in the wake of a broader civil rights movement, which gave notice to inequities in employment practices, social and economic mobility, and access to higher education. Approximately two years before the release of the Coleman report, the federal government undertook a series of initiatives to combat poverty and racial discrimination. The federal action commenced in 1964 with the signing of the Economic Opportunity Act, which led to the establishment of the Office of Economic Opportunity and the support of intervention programs like Upward Bound, the Job Corps and the widely publicized Head Start. In general, this act extended financial help to low-income and mostly minority students hoping to gain a higher education and sponsored instructional programs in adult education and early learning. Its ambitions were far-reaching. In the summer of 1965, for instance, Head Start enrolled close to half a million poor, mostly nonwhite children, so they could be offered early academic experiences that could translate into later academic success. The program was designed as an enhancer of equal opportunity whose intention was to bring disadvantaged children up to speed so they could compete in elementary school.

The year 1964 also marked the signing of the Civil Rights Act, which provided the funds and resources for various desegregation efforts. Title IV of the Act gave federal financial support to school districts preparing school desegregation plans and charged the Attorney General with the power to file suit against schools still practicing discrimination. Title VI threatened the loss of federal moneys to school districts found to be using federal sponsored programs in a racially discriminating manner. One year later, President Johnson signed the Elementary and Secondary Act of 1965 into law. The provisions of this law were also centered around educational programs for the underprivileged. Title I of the Act brought federal money to the cause of advancing the education of low-income children. Title II was designated for the purchasing of curriculum materials. The act also funded efforts to bring the resources of the community, and various collaborative agencies together to improve the school lives of disadvantaged children. Each of these legislative mandates gave the federal government a visible role in dealing with issues of educational opportunity, racial isolation, and underachievement.

During this period, a new voice had emerged in the South, preaching a social gospel of civil disobedience, which helped lay the groundwork for black resistance to segregation and for federal involvement in the enforcement of desegregating edicts. Martin Luther King's charismatic leadership transformed the question of segregation into the more expansive question of civil rights. He was committed to blurring the color line and bringing a sense of humanity and common decency to race relations. Reverend King did not accept any position advancing some form of peaceful or harmonious apartheid. He accepted nothing less than full and complete integration in the fabric of American society and assurances of equal rights and equal opportunities for all Americans.

Given the national consciousness over race relations and the emergence of a more aggressive Supreme Court, the prospects for desegregation had improved going into the 1970s. School districts, feeling the legal and political fire beneath them, explored various desegregation strategies. Some school districts used a tactic known as majority to minority transfer, a practice that allowed children to move or transfer from any district school in which their race was in the majority to a school in which their race was in the minority. This was a school choice option that limited transfers to only those having a desegregating effect. But these choice programs were still not producing the desired effect. To encourage more crossover, school districts designed magnet schools that offered a special curriculum or some instructional feature that would pull students (as a magnetic force pulls) to its doors. By placing well-funded, highly regarded magnet schools that served some special academic end (science education, fine arts education, and so forth) in a segregated neighborhood, school districts were convinced that they could attract non-minority participation in these schools. As it turns out, they were more right than wrong. Magnet schools undoubtedly served the purpose of desegregation by helping to put a halt to the "white flight" that many urban school districts were experiencing. They represented an important component in a multifaceted desegregation strategy.

Where such desegregation methods were not successful, the school explored other methods, such as the gerrymandering of schools zones, which sometimes involved transporting children to a school outside their neighborhoods, or the forced pairing of existing segregated schools for the purpose of swapping half of the students in one school with the other for either a partial or full school day experience. In each situation, busing was used to effect desegregation. Transportation remedies, in fact, were typical in cases where school segregation existed because of deeply entrenched segregated housing patterns. In the 1971 ruling of *Swann v. Charlotte Mecklenburg Board of Education*, the Supreme Court cleared the way for more expansive desegregation plans that included the pairing of noncontiguous school locations and the busing of students across fairly wide geographic lines. Using the *Green* factors as its formula for integration, the Supreme Court upheld the plan of a lower court to strike out against racial imbalances in the district's schools. After having experienced no success with its majority to minority plan, the Charlotte-Mecklenberg District, which was a consolidated district that included both urban and suburban schools, designed a multifaceted desegregation plan that made use of school pairings (two-way busing), the use of satellite assignments (one way busing), the consolidation of schools, and the redrawing of attendance zones (Orfield & Eaton, 1996). At some level, each of these strategies entailed the transportation of some children to a school not always in closest proximity to their home. The Court had sent the strongest signal yet that desegregation meant examining measures beyond freedom of choice plans, various transfer policies, and thematic magnet schools. Not months after the *Swann* ruling, more than a half million children in cities throughout the nation were assigned to schools outside of their neighborhoods, a remedy that was wildly unpopular with most school parents and that led to various street protests (Irons, 1991, p. 225).

By 1974, in *Milliken v. Bradley*, the possibilities for transportation remedies expanded outward after a circuit court judge ordered the desegregation of Detroit's city schools by prescribing a transportation remedy that involved 53 suburban school districts just outside of Detroit. Unlike the Charlotte-Mecklenberg District, which was a consolidated school district involving the schools of an entire metropolitan area, Detroit's outlying area was comprised of independent school districts. Thus, the *Milliken* case represented an important test for interdistrict remedies. Many of the suburban districts filed an immediate appeal, claiming that they could not be compelled to participate in an interdistrict remedy when they had no role in segregating the schools in the Detroit district. In the lower court, the judge viewed district boundaries as matters of political and administrative convenience that stood in the way of bringing equal opportunity to the school children of Detroit—boundary lines, as the argument went, that were created by state officials who had allowed the Detroit schools to build schools and draw enrollment lines that produced entrenched school segregation. The Supreme Court, however, in a close decision, did not agree. The Court stated that because segregation was occurring in the Detroit schools, the problem belonged to Detroit, not any of its contiguous school districts. Unless it could be proven that suburban schools (or the state) had engaged in discriminatory action that had a hand in creating the school enrollment patterns in Detroit, the white suburban schools could not be put under any legal compulsion to participate in the desegregation remedy. Detroit would have to go at it alone and find a way of integrating a small and dwindling white enrollment with a large and ever-increasing black enrollment (Orfield & Eaton, 1996). This was the first major sign that the Court had begun to ease off of its aggressive posture toward desegregation.

To the advocates of desegregation, *Milliken* was viewed as solid defeat of the mandate authorized under *Brown* and a virtual guarantee that segregation would continue to prevail in largely minority city school districts. Justice Thurgood Marshall, whose history with the historic *Brown* ruling is well-documented, referred to *Milliken* as "a giant step backwards" (Orfield & Eaton, 1996, p. 29). The Court, recognizing that long-term integration was not likely to occur in Detroit, returned to the *Milliken* ruling in *Milliken II*, and ordered the state to pay for educational programs that might help repair the harm created by segregation. Separate schools, the Court seemed to say, could now become equal through intradistrict compensatory programs. Interdistrict desegregation, however, could only be authorized in districts where there was evidence of constitutional violations conducted either by the districts or the state overseeing them. Moreover, unitary districts could always choose to enter into voluntary interdistrict remedies (McCarthy, Cambron-McCabe, & Thomas, 1998).

In 1991, the backslide on desegregation continued when the Supreme Court ruled in *Board of Education of Oklahoma City Public Schools v. Dowell*. A lower court stated that once a school district was declared unitary, it could be released from any obligations to further maintain desegregation. The Oklahoma City Public Schools had operated under a court-ordered desegregation plan for about five years. The plan relied heavily on transportation remedies. A federal court eventually declared the district to be in compliance (and unitary) and freed it from any further programs. The district, citing the unpopularity of the busing program, adopted a neighborhood school policy that resulted in about half of its schools becoming intensely segregated. The Supreme Court upheld the action of the district, stating that even segregated housing patterns could not compel court-ordered desegregation if such patterns existed by private choice and were not a legacy of an official segregation policy. The schools, once declared unitary, could go about their business without court supervision unless faced with the accusation of discriminatory practice. The *Oklahoma City* ruling was the clearest signal yet that *Brown* had run its course, in the sense that once a district was declared unitary, it was allowed to resegregate as long as it is not done with discriminatory intent.

Not one year later, another decision distanced the desegregation movement even further from the principles of *Brown*. In *Freeman v. Pitts*, the Court found that the Green standards used for guidance in desegregation plans and for eventual release from judicial oversight need not be strictly followed. School districts, in fact, could be partially released from their desegregation responsibilities even if they did not achieve integration along the lines specified in the Green standards. The Courts accepted the position of the De Kalb School District in arguing that it acted in good faith in bringing racial balance to its school enrollments but that changes in demographics of the district made it impossible to integrate its schools on the scale demanded in the Green standards. The new accepted legalistic mantra was that racial balance caused by private choice and demographic changes did not have constitutional implications.

Finally, along these same lines, the Supreme Court also ruled in *Missouri v. Jenkins* (1995) that compensatory efforts (Milliken II-type remedies) supported by the State to assist a school district with desegregation, could not be constitutionally supported unless there was evidence of discrimination on the part of the State. Over an 18 year period, the Courts required the State of Missouri to pay over 1 billion dollars for improvements in the Kansas City, Missouri School District (KCMSD), all for the expressed purpose of making the district attractive to non-minority students living outside the district and to district students attending private schools. The money went to the building of state-of-the-art magnet schools, various capital improvements, teacher salaries, expanded summer programs, and any number of innovative instructional programs. Because there were not enough white children living in the district, the lower courts had designed a desegregation remedy aimed at voluntarily bringing and retaining white children to the city schools. Saddled with most of the enormous costs associated with the upgrades, the State of Missouri claimed that the compensatory efforts were beyond the scope of the desegregation order. The Supreme Court, in a 5–4 decision, agreed, indicating again, as it did in *Milliken v. Bradley,* that intradistrict problems had to be solved with intradistrict remedies. The Court also noted that KCMSD had failed to demonstrate educational progress and even much desegregation, and that the state's role in investing in the desegregative attractiveness of the schools was not working and was no longer required. The Court released the State of Missouri from its court-imposed obligation, leaving the matter of desegregation to KCMSD.

In the *Oklahoma City, Freeman,* and *Missouri* cases, there was no mistaking the new legal doctrine under which desegregation practices would now be screened: racial imbalance in the schools was not unconstitutional; only racial imbalance caused by discrimination was unconstitutional. Believing that *Brown* underwrote a theory of black inferiority by casting anything as predominantly black as automatically substandard, Justice Thomas helped move the Court away from the spirit of *Brown.* "If separation is a harm," he stated, "and if integration therefore is the only way that blacks can receive a proper education, then there must be something inferior about blacks. Under this theory, segregation injures blacks because blacks, when left on their own, cannot achieve" (Irons, 1991, p. 286). The momentum away from *Brown,* however, had started even before Justice Thomas' arrival on the Supreme Court bench. Since *Milliken,* an incremental shift has occurred in the legalistic line of thinking on school segregation. All that seems left of *Brown* today is the historic debt, operationalized mostly through the conditions represented in the Green standards that school districts must still pay to *Brown.* As matters stand now, once a school district has been declared unitary, using some consideration of the factors identified in *Green,* the district is free to go its own way even if segregation again prevails, as long as the resegregation does not occur as a result of intentional discriminatory practices. The result has been unmistakable signs of resegregation. As noted in Table 12–4, the exposure rates of black children to white children has fallen in the major city districts that have been declared unitary. In Cleveland, for instance, the average black child attended a school that enrolled about 21 percent whites before it achieved unitary status; that number has now been reduced to about 9 percent whites, post-unitary status.

Table 12–4 Changes in Percentage of White Students in the School Attended by an Average Black Student in Select Districts that Have Been Declared Unitary

School District	Black/White Exposure	
	1991	2003
Indianapolis Public Schools	0.42	0.23
Boston	0.18	0.10
Detroit City	0.05	0.02
Minneapolis	0.44	0.20
Kansas City	0.22	0.08
St. Louis City	0.15	0.11
Charlotte-Mecklenburg	0.51	0.28
Cincinnati	0.29	0.16
Cleveland	0.21	0.09
Oklahoma City	0.32	0.19
Austin ISD	0.29	0.19
Dallas ISD	0.09	0.04
Houston ISD	0.09	0.06
San Diego Unified	0.28	0.19
San Jose Unified	0.40	0.28
Denver County	0.32	0.18

Adapted from Orfield, G., & Lee, C. (2006). Racial transformation and the changing nature of segregation, p. 41.

The historic trail of Supreme Court decisions on school desegregation can be understood in three epochal periods: 1) the *pre-Brown* period of "separate but equal," that certified pervasive de jure segregation across most of the South; 2) the *Brown* period, which declared segregation, even in a de facto form, as inimical to the education of all black children and which gave rise to a four-decade struggle to eradicate segregation "root and branch"—to use the term coined in the *Green* ruling; and 3) the modern *post-Brown* period, which represents tolerance for segregation uninfluenced by discriminatory intent, but only after its vestiges have been eliminated (via the Green standards). Today over 1,000 school districts are still under court supervision and many still have trouble demonstrating unitary status. Nevertheless, the stage now appears set for the reduction of judicial control in the area of desegregation and the return of school operations to local control (McCarthy, Cambron-McCabe, & Thomas, 1998, p. 486). Time will tell if the Court's movement away from *Brown* was premature.

The Effects of Desegregation

Did all the efforts to desegregate the schools have a positive effect on the lives of minority children? The national data, collected and collated by Gary Orfield, Director of the Harvard Project on School Desegregation, show some historic gains in the area of desegregation. Progress in the South, for instance, has been nothing short of spectacular. As shown in Figure 12–1, the percentage of black children attending white majority schools has climbed enormously in the South. Prior to 1954, essentially no black children attended white majority schools. State-enforced segregation made it unlawful. By 1988, however, about 43 percent of black children attended majority white schools in the South. This percentage has since retracted to about 30 percent in 2003, likely because of the Court's willingness to release districts from court supervision after being declared unitary.

This is not to say, however, that segregation is no longer a problem in the American schools. About 18 percent of all black school children and 11 percent of Hispanic children attend what Orfield and Lee (2005) call apartheid schools, defined as 99 percent to 100 percent minority schools (p. 28).

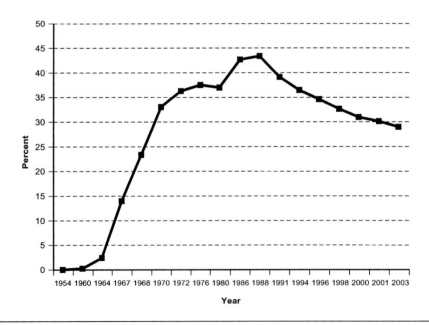

FIGURE 12–1   Percent of Black Students in Majority White Schools in the South. SOURCE: Southern Education Reporting Service in Reed Sarratt, The Ordeal of Desegregation (New York: Harper & Row, 1966); HEW Press Release, May 27, 1968; OCR data tapes; 1992–3, 1994–5, 1996–7, 1998–9, 2000–01, 2001–02, 2003–04 NCES Common Core of Data.

Table 12–5 Percent of Students from Each Racial/Ethnic Group in Predominant (50–100 Percent), Intensive (90–100 Percent), and Extreme (99–100 Percent) Minority Schools. Type of School

| Race | Type of School | | |
	50–100% Minority Schools	90–100% Minority Schools	99–100% Minority Schools
Black	73	38	18
Latino	77	38	11
White	12	1	0
Asian	56	15	1
Native American	52	27	16

Adopted from Orfield, G., & Lee, C. (2005). Why segregation matters: Poverty and educational inequality, p. 13.

Slightly more than 1/3 of all black and Hispanic children attend intensely minority schools (defined as 90 percent or more minority enrollment; see Table 12–5). Although clear historical gains have occurred in increasing the exposure of black and Hispanic children to white children, progress has been more or less stagnant since 1990.

The problem of desegregation still mostly resides in the cities and suburbs. The percentage of minority children enrolled in predominantly minority school (defined as 50 percent or more minority enrollment) is considerably higher in large metro areas than in small metro areas and towns. The communities in the cities are not only more segregated but they are obviously much larger in size than their suburban and town counterparts. Given the fact that interdistrict remedies cannot be mandated unless there is evidence of discrimination in the action of the state or the outlying communities, desegregation efforts in these areas more or less rely on magnet schools, choice plans, and in districts not yet declared unitary, transportation remedies.

Not surprisingly, in states with large urban populations, segregated schools continue to be the rule of thumb for blacks and Hispanics. For instance, in New York about 61 percent of black students attend intensely minority schools (schools with a minority enrollment of 90 percent or more); only 14 percent of the state's black student population attends a majority white school. The effect is a low exposure rate for black children to white children. In New York, the average black school-aged child attends a school with an enrollment of about 18 percent whites. Similar percentages prevail in California and Illinois, each of which possesses extremely large urban areas (Los Angeles and Chicago are among the three largest school districts in the country). See Table 12–6 for a ranking of the most segregated states for black students in the United States.

Obviously, integration is most easily served in states where the minority population is small. In the state of Iowa, for instance, intensely minority schools do not even exist, as is also the case in Montana, Nebraska, New Hampshire, Vermont, and a few other states. The New York City public schools, which carries an enrollment of over one million students (only 16 percent of whom are white), will easily serve more minority students in its schools than the entire public school system in the state of Iowa.

Many of the most highly segregated high-minority schools in the nation also enroll among the poorest children in the nation. More than 60 percent of all black and Hispanic children attend high-poverty schools (defined as 50 percent or more of children receiving free or reduced lunch). Twelve percent of black and Hispanic children attend extreme poverty schools (defined as >90 percent poor), compared to 1 percent of whites. In 2000, the average black and Hispanic child attended a school with about 45 percent of its students living in poverty—a number that is about 2.5 times greater than the

TABLE 12-6   Most Segregated States for Black Students, 2003-04.

Rank	% Black in Majority Minority Schools		% Black in 90-100% Minority Schools		Black Exposure to White	
1	California	87 New York	61 New York			18
2	New York	86 Illinois	60 Illinois			19
3	Illinois	82 Michigan	60 Michigan			22
4	Maryland	81 Maryland	53 California			22
5	Michigan	79 New Jersey	49 Maryland			23
6	Texas	78 Pennsylvania	47 New Jersey			25
7	New Jersey	77 Alabama	46 Mississippi			26
8	Louisiana	77 Wisconsin	45 Louisiana			27
9	Mississippi	76 Mississippi	45 Texas			27
10	Georgia	73 Louisiana	41 Wisconsin			29
11	Wisconsin	72 Missouri	41 Pennsylvania			30
12	Connecticut	72 Ohio	38 Georgia			30
13	Pennsylvania	72 California	38 Alabama			30
14	Ohio	71 Texas	38 Hawaii			32
15	Alabama	70 Georgia	37 Ohio			32
16	Arkansas	69 Florida	32 Connecticut			32
17	Nevada	69 Connecticut	31 Missouri			33
18	Massachusetts	67 Massachusetts	26 Florida			34
19	Florida	67 Indiana	23 Arkansas			36
20	Missouri	67 Arkansas	23 Nevada			38

Source: Common Core of Data. 1991 and 2003.

rate for white children. Given the very real effects on poverty on school achievement, the association between economic poverty and racial segregation is especially troubling.

GENDER AND SCHOOLING

In recent years, the question of gender discrimination has found its way into the public discourse on schooling. The general concern is whether boys and girls encounter sex-based differences in the school that affect the quality of their experience, and by implication, their chances at school success. Can gender bias, for instance, be found in, say, what is taught and how it is taught in the curriculum? Can achievement differences between boys and girls ever be explained by gender discrimination?

Gender Bias

Because most school teachers are women, logic might suggest that schools are places where girls might find some advantage over boys. But according to some feminist theorists, schools are designed to promote the success of males. Female teachers, as the argument goes, are largely subordinate in the structure of school power. Because the superordinates of the school (principals and superintendents) are still mostly males, "male values" (typically described as competition, individuality, and rationality) prevail in school operations. At the same time, "female values" (typically described as subjectivity, empathy, and caring), are given short shrift, all of which comes at the educational and psychological cost of girls.

This was the general line of thinking that arose from much of the research dedicated to the question of gender bias in public schooling during the early 1990s. Observational research conducted by Myra and David Sadker (1994), for example, pointed to the conclusion that boys dominated classroom processes in a way that left the education of girls compromised. Observational research revealed that the nature of student teacher interactions (at both elementary and secondary school levels) was favorable to the education of boys. The data showed that teachers tended to give boys more attention (including listening and counseling), offered them more thought-provoking questions, and rewarded them more often, although they also criticized and punished them more often (Sadker, Sadker, & Klien, 1991). A report published by the American Association of University Women (AAUW), titled *How Schools Shortchange Girls,* put added emphasis on the problem by noting the low self-esteem girls suffer in school and the low interest level exhibited by girls in math and science. The AAUW (1992) report brought national attention to the issue of gender bias, as it found its way into the popular press, and touched off a national debate over the viability of single-sex classrooms.

Among the more visible effects of the new consciousness given to gender concerns was a renewed effort to enforce prior anti-sexist legislation. During the early 1970s, the Congress passed Title IX legislation that made it illegal for any educational programs receiving federal moneys to discriminate on the basis of sex. In the words of the law, "no person in the United States shall, on the basis of sex, be excluded from participation in, be denied the benefit of, or be subjected to discrimination under any education program or activity receiving Federal financial assistance." For school systems, this meant, minimally, that a Title IX officer needed to be appointed to coordinate compliance and to handle emerging complaints regarding sex discrimination. Compliance to Title IX, however, was slow in coming and federal sanctions against offending schools were usually not very substantial (Hansot, 1993). During the 1990s, however, Title IX had new vitality. Its impact was first felt in athletic programs, where girls' sport programs had long been under-resourced and under-appreciated. In 1971, for instance, 294,000 girls participated in high school athletics against 3.6 million boys, but by 1994, the participation rates changed significantly, as 2.2 million girls participated in high school athletics against 3.5 million boys. Title IX provisions also began to alter the pattern of sex-segregated courses in health, vocational education, physical education, and some higher level courses in mathematics and science.

The gender bias debate, however, is not definitively reducible to the conclusion that schools only shortchange girls. As a group, girls earn higher grades than boys throughout their school careers in all subject areas and are less likely to be placed in special education programs than boys. They outperform boys on writing-skills assessments and outscore boys in all age groups on measures of reading achievement. Girls also drop out of school less often than boys, although the act of dropping out has a more lasting negative effect on them.

Evidence, in fact, supports the interpretation that boys are shortchanged in school too, and that gender stereotypes are at the core of the problem. The historical underperformance of boys in verbal areas, for instance, could be a function of a stereotypical view that equates reading, especially reading certain kinds of materials, with female behavior. The fact that reading skills are taught in the elementary school (where about 90 percent of the teachers are female) strengthens the possibilities for the case. Similarly, the question of why boys are disproportionately classified into special education categories could have something to do with the more aggressive and attention-commanding school behaviors witnessed in boys. The data on special education classifications clearly demonstrate that, compared to girls, boys are disproportionately labeled as "learning disabled," or "emotionally

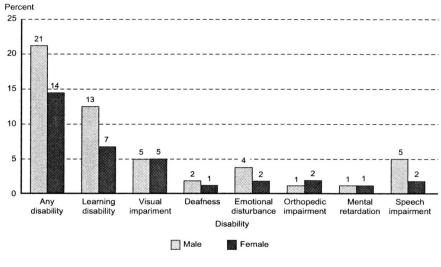

NOTE: Included in the totals but not shown separately are students with other disabling conditions. Students may be included in more than one disability category.
SOURCE: U.S. Department of Education, National Center for Education Statistics, Parent Interview Survey of the National Household Education Surveys Program (Patent-NHES: 1999).

FIGURE 12–2   Percent of First to Fifth Graders with Various Disabilities, by Disability and Sex: 1999. Adopted from NCES. (2004). *Trends in educational equity in girls and women,* p. 42.

disturbed" (by about a 2 to 1 margin). One explanation is that boys manifest greater behavioral problems in the classroom and thus find themselves more likely to be evaluated for a learning problem (Greenberg, 1985). If such an explanation were valid, the paradox is that the stereotype of quiet passivity expected from girls might save them from unfair special education classifications, although it should be said that the low female representation in the special education enrollments could also be interpreted as a sign of gender bias against girls (as a failure to be responsive to the special learning needs of girls).

According to Belenky and others, the stereotype of quiet passivity accorded to girls is a very serious educational problem. In their interviews with women and girls, Belenky and others (1986) found that many women viewed their schooling experiences as sitting in classes silently, watching and listening to other students (mostly boys) talk. Because American culture tends to value girls who are polite and quietly submissive, these women and girls felt that their voices were not valued and that their effort to exercise an opinion was often interpreted as rude behavior. Belenky and others cite the importance of verbalizing one's thoughts in the development of crucial reasoning skills to reinforce their indictment against the school. Given the role of silence in the school lives of girls, Belenky and others argue that girls tend to see themselves as receivers of knowledge in the classroom rather than as mediators of knowledge—as receptacles into which other people make "deposits" of knowledge. Receivers of knowledge tend to believe that other people have very important things to say, but that their own thoughts are unimportant.

Gender discrimination is obviously not just a school problem. Clearly many gender-based stereotypes are also perpetuated by the family and by society in general. Olivares and Rosenthal (1992) cite several studies that point to the role parents play in perpetuating gender stereotyping. Parents, for example, still encourage sex-typed activities for their children (Lytton & Romney, 1991), continue to choose stereotyped toys and colors for infants and toddlers (Pomerleau, Boldice, & others, 1990) and frequently evaluate children negatively, especially boys, when they exhibit cross-sex play or cross-sex personality traits (Martin, 1990). Some scholars believe that gender-linked toys play an important role in fashioning stereotypes. Toys, for instance, that might help children develop an attitude of caring, such as baby dolls, have too often been seen as appropriate for only girls. Young boys could obviously learn something important about fatherhood and childcare in general when they play with baby dolls. Interestingly, dolls for boys are typically superheroes that engage in fantastic physical feats and physical battle. Similarly, toys that might serve as an introduction to science and mechanics such as building blocks, have too often been reserved for only boys (Noddings, 1992).

Gender Segregated Classrooms

Gender inequities have led some schools to consider the idea of gender-segregated classes. Typically, the presumption here is that boys undermine the education of girls through their attention-getting and through competitive behaviors and by their knack at getting preferential treatment from teachers. Others believe that girls simply learn differently from boys and are best taught away from boys. Proponents of single-sex classes will cite the low self-esteem of girls, their low levels of interest in math and science, the sexual harassment they suffer at the hands of boys and the omnipresent "boys curriculum" (a la male values) that conspires against them.

Gender-segregated classes, however, are not without their own problems. First, one could argue that they violate a basic principle of the public school mandate, which is to provide integrated experiences for all youth irrespective of race, ethnicity, social class, and gender. In fact, some legal analysts have argued that gender-segregated classes are violations of Title IX. Citing the Title IX provision, some states have openly declared gender-segregated classes illegal. But Title IX provisions, it should be said, allow for some gender-based exceptions. It recognizes gender differences in relation to safety issues, privacy concerns, and ability levels. Separate classes for contact sports are allowable, separate classes dealing with specific issues of human sexuality, and musical choruses based on a particular voice range are all exempted from Title IX (Salomone, 1999). Exceptions, however, are generally not permitted in any core academic areas, notwithstanding exceptions for purposes of affirmative action, which are designed to overcome the marginalizing effects that resulted from the limited historical participation of persons of a particular sex in a particular program. This means that a school district could document a case for single-sex classes as a matter of "affirmative action," as a way to overcome past impediments on female school achievement. As a result, math and science education is obviously more likely candidates for single-sex schooling than, say, reading education.

The research findings on the topic of all-girl classes are equivocal. Some of the research suggests that girls experience more comfort, greater self-confidence and higher achievement in single-sex settings, with these effects being more pronounced with low income black and Hispanic girls (Salomone, 1999). However, critics argue that all-girl classes seem to be a peculiar response to the accusation of school-based gender bias, because they are themselves vulnerable to the accusation of sexism, implying that girls cannot compete in a classroom setting that includes boys. Other critics observe that making gender the salient factor in classroom enrollments misses out on other important factors, especially race and class-based factors, that have as much, if not more, of a claim on inequity than does gender. They also question why gender-based problems need to be necessarily remedied through class segregation when so many other solutions are available. If boys, for instance, are ridiculing girls, can a method be found to prevent such episodes without resorting to gender-based class segregation? If teachers are unwittingly providing advantages to boys, can the school seek a remedy, built on in-service training or even extra classroom programs, that keep the classroom integrated? And if segregation by gender finds a compelling argument in terms of enhancing the school performance of girls, what prevents a similar argument from being made for ethnic, class, or race-based education?

School-Based Differences

Interestingly, the achievement data, in most cases, show little evidence of a serious gender gap, with a few important exceptions. In 1997, Educational Testing Service (ETS) conducted a study that tried to bring all of the best studies together on the relation between gender and school achievement for the purpose of finding what they might have to say in the aggregate (Cole, 1997). The results point to some interesting differences. Figure 12–3 shows that most achievement categories fall within margins of difference considered to be very small (the shaded box), attesting to the fact that in most areas there is not much of a gender gap.

Notable differences did manifest in a few areas. Females in 12th grade, for instance, clearly showed some advantage over 12th grade boys in writing and language use, while boys clearly demonstrated advantage over girls in mechanical/electronic know-how. One could interpret the news in Figure 12–3 as worse for boys than girls if only because verbal-, writing-, and language-use skills all have high utility and relevance in life, arguably more so, at least, than knowledge of mechanics and electronics. On the other hand, mechanical know-how might offer boys access to higher paying jobs. Interestingly, the differences between girls and boys in math and science were small, as boys showed slightly better skills with math concepts and girls slightly better computational skills.

In most cases, the differences seen among 12th graders are witnessed as early as elementary school and get wider and more intense as students progress through the school system. As noted in Figure 12–4, the advantage girls show in writing and language-use was evident as early as fourth grade. It magnified by eighth grade and even more so by 12th grade. A similar though less dramatic pattern could be seen in the areas where male scores were higher. This could point to the possibility that schools are playing a role in exacerbating achievement differences between boys and girls, or at least in failing to make much of a contribution to preventing the differences from getting worse.

The issue of reading achievement deserves closer examination. Interestingly, international achievement data demonstrate that a female advantage in reading performance is, in fact, a worldwide phenomenon, at least among the most industrialized nations (see Figure 12–5). Each of the G8 nations (and a few others) reports statistically significant differences in the reading performance scores of 15-year-old girls over 15-year-old boys. Significant differences also exist between the sexes in the fourth-grade reading score averages in selected industrialized nations. Such a worldwide phenomenon could suggest a biological explanation, but it is also entirely conceivable that societal and school-based socializational patterns within each of the nations are similar enough to produce a female advantage in reading performance. International data also show some male advantage in math achievement among 15-year-olds, but it is only statistically significant in two of the selected nations (Korea and Germany). In the United States, the evidence on participation in home-based pre-literacy behaviors suggest that girls do not seem to have an early OTL (or environmental) advantage. Virtually equal percentages of 3- to 5-year-old boys and girls were read to and told stories in their homes. Yet boys take longer to learn how to read than girls, and possess a much less constructive attitude toward reading, in that they read less and are less enthusiastic about it.

Girls, as indicated, drop out of school less than boys and generally exceed the grade performance of boys in all academic areas. Some critics have interpreted this phenomenon to be the function of school reward structure for compliant behavior—that grades offer little in the way of reliable assessments of academic performance. Girls, in other words, get better grades because they are more compliant and even nicer to teachers than boys. There might be something to this criticism, but school grades are still one of the best predictors of academic performance after high school and are associated with produc-

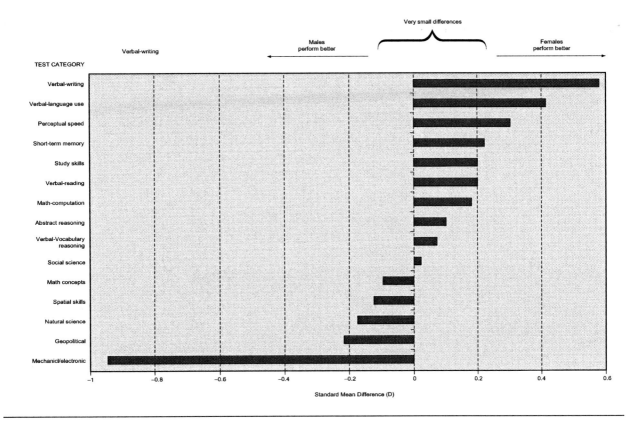

Figure 12–3   Gender Differences and Similarities for Twelfth Graders on Fifteen Types of Tests.
NOTE: Based on seventy-four tests for twelfth graders nationally. SOURCE: Cole, N. (1997). *The ETS gender study: How females and males perform in educational settings* (Princeton, NJ: Educational Testing Service), p. 12.

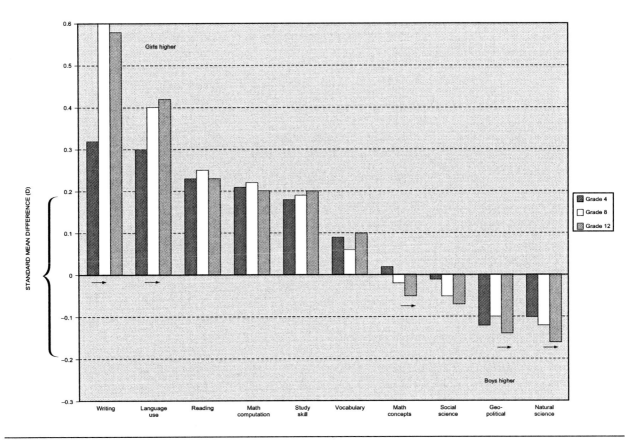

FIGURE 12–4   Trends by Subject Area, Grades 4–12. NOTE: Arrows indicate a significant grade-to-grade change in degree of gender difference. SOURCE: Cole, N. (1997). *The ETS gender study: How females and males perform in educational settings* (Princeton, NJ: Educational Testing Service), p. 5.

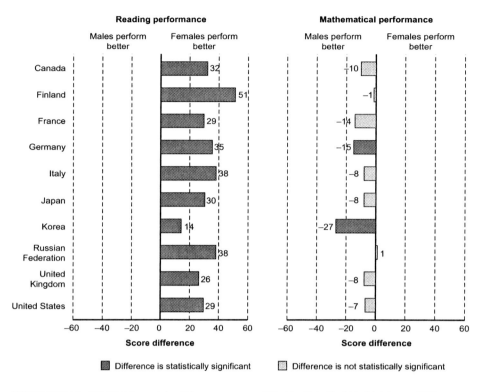

NOTE: The reading and mathematics scales were designed to have an average score of 500 points, with about two-thirds of students across OECD countries scoring between 400 and 600 points. The Netherlands is excluded due to low response rates.
SOURCE: Organization for Economic Co-operation and Development (OECD). (2001). *Acknowledge and Skills for Life: First Results From the OECD Programme for International Student Assessment* (PASA) 2000.

Figure 12–5 Sex Differences in 15-Year-Olds' Performance in Reading and Mathematics, by Selected Industrialized Nations: 2000. Adopted from NCES. (2004). *Trends in educational equity in girls and women,* p. 37.

tive skills, such as doing one's work and participating in class (Cole, 1997). Good grades clearly count for something productive.

Yet despite achieving better grades in math and science, girls typically stay clear of mathematics and science as a career. They are also less inclined to enroll in Advanced Placement (AP) courses in math and science. A multitude of factors may be at play here, including a testing bias and a potential stereotypic socialization pattern in the school (and in society in general) that upholds mathematics and sciences as less than suitable careers for women. According to some surveys, girls learn to think that they are not mathematically capable as early as the elementary grades (AAUW, 1992). Yet, as noted in Figure 12–6, the course taking patterns of girls shows no reluctance to take courses in the mathematics and sciences. Virtually equal number of boys and girls enroll in Calculus and slightly larger percentages of girls enroll in Geometry, Algebra 2, Biology, Chemistry, and AP Biology. But the AP scores of boys in Calculus and in the sciences are higher compared to females, as are the proportions of males taking the AP math and science exams.

High school-aged girls are also much more deeply involved in the extracurricular life of the school than boys. The participation rate for girls in activities such as the school newspaper, the musical and performing arts, academic clubs, and student government are significantly larger than the rate witnessed from boys. Boys only participate on athletic teams more than girls (see Figure 12–7).

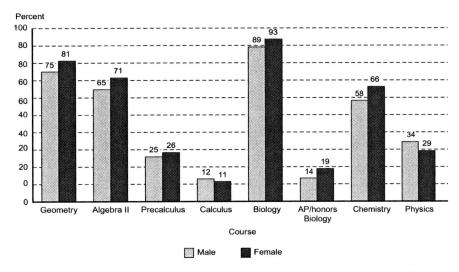

SOURCE: U.S. DDepartment of Education, National Center for Education Statistics, High School and Beyondd Longitudinal Study of 1980 Sophomores, "High School Transcript Study" (HS&B-So-80/82); 1990 High School Transcript Study (HSTS:90); National Education Longitudinal Study of 1988 (NELS:88/92), "Second Follow-up Transcript Survey 1992"; 1994 High School Transcript Study (HSTS:94); 1998 High School Transcript Study (HSTS:98); and 2000 High School Transcript Study (HSTS:00).

FIGURE 12–6   Percent of High School Graduates Who Had Taken Various Math and Science Courses in High School, by Sex: 2000. Adopted from NCES. (2004). *Trends in educational equity in girls and women,* p. 61.

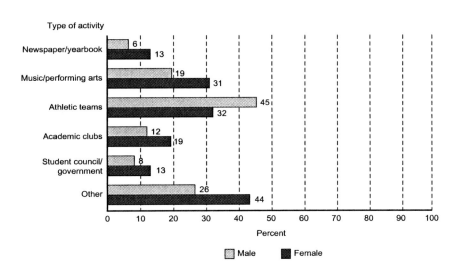

NOTE: The response notes for this survey do not meet NCES statistical standards. The response rate for this survey was less than 70 percent and a ful nonresponse bias analysis has not been done to date.
SOURCE: University of Michigan, Institute for Social Research, Monitoring the Future Study, 2001.

FIGURE 12–7   Percent of High School Seniors Who Participated in Various School-Related Activities during the School Year, by Sex: 2001. Adopted from NCES. (2004). *Trends in educational equity in girls and women,* p. 49.

Perhaps the most interesting trend to report in relation to gender is the changing face of higher education enrollments. Annual growth rates for women enrolled in higher education have been climbing steadily for the past four decades. In 1970, about 42 percent of all Bachelor's degrees awarded were issued to women; the number was slightly below 40 percent for graduate degrees. Females now represent the majority of undergraduate population (56 percent) and the graduate population (58 percent). Similar gains have been made in the professional schools. Although female presence in higher education is on good ground, there is less cause for optimism when one focuses directly on income earning. The average earning gap against all levels of educational attainment is documented in Table 12–7. In 2000, women with Bachelor's degrees earned 78 cents against the average dollar earned by a male with a Bachelor's degree. Part of the difference is accounted for by the disproportionate number of women in historically low-income jobs. Women account for 98.6 percent of all secretaries (the leading occupation overall for women), 84 percent of all elementary school teachers, and 90 percent of nurses, while 76 percent of all physicians and 89 percent of all engineers are men (U.S. Department of Labor, 1999). Differences in earnings between the sexes also exist in starting salaries within the same field (National Center for Education Statistics, 1998).

TABLE 12–7 Percent of 25- to 34-Year-Olds Who Were Employed, by Sex and Level of Educational Attainment: 1971–2002.

	Male				Female			
Year	Less than High School Completion	High School Diploma or GED	Associates's Degree or Some College	Bachelor's Degree or Higher	Less than High School Completion	High School Diploma or GED	Associate's Degree or Some College	Bachelor's Degree or Higher
1971	87.9	93.6	89.9	92.5	35.4	43.1	44.9	56.9
1973	88.8	93.8	88.5	93.5	38.4	46.5	51.0	62.7
1975	78.0	88.4	87.7	93.5	35.4	48.1	53.6	66.3
1977	81.5	89.5	89.1	93.3	41.0	53.0	58.0	69.5
1979	80.5	91.3	90.9	94.1	43.2	58.0	64.2	74.0
1981	76.7	86.9	88.5	93.7	42.7	61.3	67.6	76.4
1983	69.3	78.6	83.8	91.1	37.1	58.8	68.3	79.2
1985	76.1	86.1	89.7	92.2	40.3	63.9	71.0	80.6
1987	75.0	86.8	89.0	92.1	44.0	65.6	72.2	81.4
1989	77.6	87.8	91.1	93.7	43.0	66.9	74.0	82.1
1990	76.0	88.6	89.7	93.0	44.4	67.5	74.5	83.2
1991	69.9	84.9	88.6	91.8	42.3	67.0	73.5	82.6
1992	69.9	84.7	86.7	90.9	41.7	65.4	74.0	82.5
1993	71.0	83.6	87.2	92.3	42.2	66.0	73.0	81.6
1994	70.8	85.2	88.0	92.8	40.1	66.2	74.3	81.6
1995	71.8	86.6	89.6	92.9	45.8	67.2	73.0	83.4
1996	74.9	86.3	87.6	92.1	45.5	66.3	76.4	83.7
1997	73.0	85.6	90.0	93.0	43.1	69.6	75.3	83.1
1998	79.3	85.9	87.9	92.5	44.4	69.4	76.0	83.6
1999	77.2	88.0	87.4	91.0	47.2	69.5	76.1	82.0
2000	78.4	88.3	88.4	92.4	47.6	70.7	76.0	84.6
2001	78.8	85.5	86.9	91.3	48.8	70.9	76.4	81.4
2002	75.9	82.2	85.8	90.3	46.0	66.3	74.9	80.7

SOURCE: U.S. Department of Commerce, Bureau of the Census, March Current Population Surveys (CPS), various years, unpublished data.

Adopted from NCES. (2004). *Trends in educational equity in girls and women,* p. 92.

POVERTY IN THE HOME

In a nation as prosperous as the United States, the idea of poverty is constructed in relative, not absolute terms. Absolute poverty reflects a definition that is based on some minimal provision of food, shelter, and clothing. Much of the struggle in third-world nations is a struggle to keep people above absolute poverty levels. Under these conditions, running water, refrigeration, a roof over one's head, and basic health care provisions cannot be taken for granted. In America, poverty is determined by using an index that weighs family income with family size. In 2004, the U.S. Census Bureau reported the poverty threshold as $15,205 in annual income for a family of three (two adults and one child). The index increases by about $4,000 for each additional child living in the household. So, for a nuclear family of four, the threshold is about $19,000; for a family of five, it is about $23,000, and so on. These are before-tax numbers that do not vary geographically. Families living in relative poverty conditions typically receive support from the government in the form of food stamps, free school lunch, Medicaid, and public housing subsidies. Table 12-8 details the specifications involved in determining poverty status.

In 2002, over 34 million people lived in poverty in America, as defined by the above definition. This amounts to about 12 percent of the total population (U.S. Census Bureau, 2003). The percentage of Americans living below the poverty level has held between 12 and 15 percent of the population since 1970. Of the 34 million living in poverty in 2002, close to 12 million were children under the age of 18, which represents about 16 percent of all the children in the nation (see Figure 12-8).

The issue of poverty, as indicated earlier, intersects with race. In 2002, a little less than half of all school-aged children living in poverty in the United States self-identified as white non-Hispanics, amounting to about 15 million children. This compares to about eight million black school-age children and eight million Hispanic school-age children living in poverty. Thus, the single largest group constituting the poor in the American schools is white non-Hispanic children. But when one examines the distribution of the poor as a percentage of each race and ethnic group, a different picture emerges. About one in five of all minority children (Blacks and Hispanics) live in poverty, while less than one in ten white non-Hispanic children (8 percent) live in poverty (U.S. Census Bureau, 2003).

Poverty factors can play an especially strong role during a child's preschool years. For instance, home literacy experiences, which include activities such as being read to, being told a story, and being taught letters, words, or numbers, are less likely to occur with regularity in families living in poverty. Something as seemingly simple as going to visit the library with a family member, an experience obviously connected to literacy development, is significantly less likely to happen to a child living in poverty than to one who is not (see Table 12-9). Not surprisingly, school readiness skills, which include recognizing letters, counting to 20 or higher, writing one's name, and reading or pretending to read a storybook are, across the board, lower among children below the poverty line than those living above it (Nord, Lennon, Liu, & Chandler, 1999). Early literacy gains are also to be had through conversation, where vocabularies and contexts for reading can be developed. Evidence reported in Rothstein (2004) demonstrates stark social class differences in the linguistic intensity of home conversations. For instance, professional-class parents spoke, on the average, over 2,000 words per hour to their children, working-class parents about 1,300 and welfare mothers about 600 words per hour (pp. 27–28). Not surprisingly, as early as age five, one finds significant differences in the basic literacy skills (measured as recognizing printed words, identifying sounds, vocabulary, word reading, and reading comprehension) of children from different income levels and races/ethnicities (Lee & Burkam, 2002; see Figures 12-9 and 12-10). These early life home-based benefits for upper-income

TABLE 12–8   The Official Measure of Poverty.

The Official Measure of Poverty

Following the Office of Management and Budget's (OMB) Statistical Policy Directive 14, the Census Bureau uses a set of money income thresholds that vary by family size and composition to determine who is in poverty (see the matrix below).

Poverty Thresholds in 2002 by Size of Family and Number of Related Children Under 18 Years.
Dollars

Size of Family Unit	Related Children Under 18 Years								
	None	One	Two	Three	Four	Five	Six	Seven	Eight or More
One person (unrelated individual):									
Under 65 years	9,359								
65 years and over	8,628								
Two people:									
Householder under 65 years	12,047	12,400							
Householder 65 years and over	10,874	12,959							
Three people	14,072	14,480	14,494						
Four people	18,556	18,859	18,244	18,307					
Five people	22,377	22,703	22,007	21,469	21,141				
Six people	25,798	25,840	25,307	24,797	24,038	29,588			
Seven people	29,615	29,799	29,162	28,718	27,990	26,924	25,865		
Eight people	33,121	33,414	32,812	32,285	31,538	30,589	29,601	29,350	
Nine people or more	39,843	40,036	39,504	39,057	38,323	37,313	36,399	36,173	34,780

Source: U.S. Census Bureau.

If a family's total income is less than that family's threshold, then that family, and every individual in it, is considered in poverty. The official poverty thresholds do not vary geographically, but they are updated annually for inflation using the Consumer Price Index (CPI-U). The official poverty definition uses money income before taxes and does not include capital gains and noncash benefits (such as public housing, medicaid, and food stamps).

Example: Suppose Family A consists of five people: two children, their mother, father, and great-aunt. Family A's poverty threshold in 2002 was $22,007. Suppose also that each member had the following income in 2002:

Mother	$10,000
Father	5,000
Great-aunt	10,000
First child	0
Second child	0
Total:	$25,000

Since their total family income, $25,000 was greater than their threshold ($22,007), the family would not be considered "in poverty" according to the official poverty measure.

While the thresholds in some sense represent families' needs, the official poverty measure should be interpreted as a statistical yard-stick rather than as a complete description of what people and families need to live. Moreover, many of the government's aid programs use different dollar amounts as eligibility criteria.

Poverty rates and the number in poverty are one important way of examining people's well-being. Other more detailed measures of poverty are considered in the sections "Depth of Poverty Measures" and "Alternative Poverty Measures," and in the recent Census Bureau report, *Supplemental Measures of Material Well-Being: Expenditures, Consumption and Poverty* (P23–201).

For a history of the official poverty measure see "The Development of the Orshansky Thresholds and Their Subsequent History as the Official U.S. Poverty Measure," by Gordon Fisher, at *www.census.gov/hhes/ poverty/povmeas/papers/orshansky.html.*

Weighted average thresholds:

Some data users want a summary of the 48 thresholds to get a general sense of the "poverty line." These average thresholds provide that summary, but they are not used to compute poverty data.

One person	$9,183
Two people	11,756
Three people	14,348
Four people	18,392
Five people	21,744
Six people	24,576
Seven people	28,001
Eight people	30,907
Nine people or more	37,062

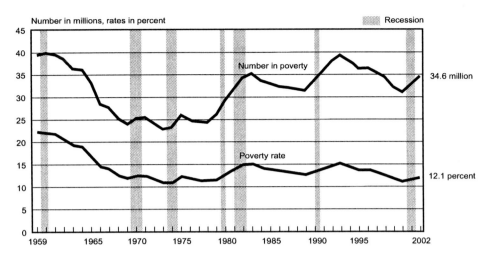

NOTE: The data points represent the midpoints of the respective years.
SOURCE: U.S. Census Bureau, Current Population Survey, 1960–2003 Annual Social and Economic Supplements.

FIGURE 12–8   Number in Poverty and Poverty Rate: 1959 to 2002.

TABLE 12–9   Percentage of prekindergarten children ages 3–5 who participated in home literacy activities with a family member three or more times in the preceding week, by selected child and family characteristics: 2005.

Child and Family Characteristics	Read to[1]		Told a Story		Taught Letters, Words, or Numbers		Taught Songs or Music	
	1993	2005	1993	2005	1993	2005	1993	2005
Total	78.3	85.7	43.0	53.7	57.7	76.6	41.0	54.4
Age								
3	79.4	86.4	46.4	54.5	57.2	75.5	45.0	60.9
4	77.8	84.7	41.2	52.8	58.1	76.8	38.9	49.7
5	75.9	86.5	35.8	54.6	57.9	80.0	33.1	47.1
Race/Ethnicity[2]								
White	84.8	91.9	44.3	53.3	57.2	75.7	40.2	52.1
Black	65.9	78.5	39.0	54.3	62.7	80.6	48.9	56.4
Hispanic	58.2	71.8	37.7	49.8	53.9	74.3	38.7	59.1
Asian/Pacific Islander	68.8	84.4	52.1	64.5	61.8	75.2	35.9	46.9
Poverty Status[3]								
Poor	67.5	78.4	39.1	50.8	59.6	76.0	45.2	53.7
Near-Poor	75.5	82.4	42.5	53.6	58.1	78.0	39.4	59.2
Non-Poor	86.8	90.2	45.6	55.0	56.2	76.2	39.5	52.5

[1]In 1993, respondents were asked about reading frequency in one of the two versions of the survey questionnaire. The percentages presented in the table are for all of the respondents who answered three or more times on either version of the questionnaire.

[2]Black includes African American, Hispanic includes Latino, and Pacific Islander includes Native Hawaiian. Race categories exclude Hispanic origin unless specified. Other race/ethnicities are included in the total but are not shown separately.

[3]"Poor" is defined to include those families below the poverty threshold; "near-poor" is defined as 100–199 percent of the poverty threshold; and "non-poor" is defined as 200 percent or more than the poverty threshold. See supplemental note 1 for more information on poverty.

SOURCE: U.S. Department of Education, National Center for Education Statistics. (2006). *The Condition of Education 2006* (NCES 2006–071), Table 33–1.

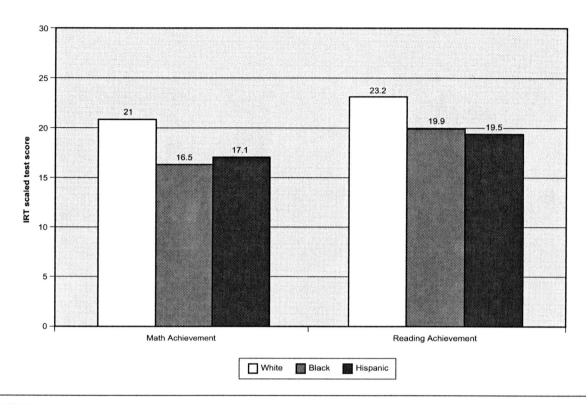

FIGURE 12–9 Math and Reading Achievement at the Beginning of Kindergarten (By Race).
Lee, V. E, & Burkam, D. T. (2002). *Inequality at the starting gate.* Washington, DC: Economic Policy Institute, p. 16.

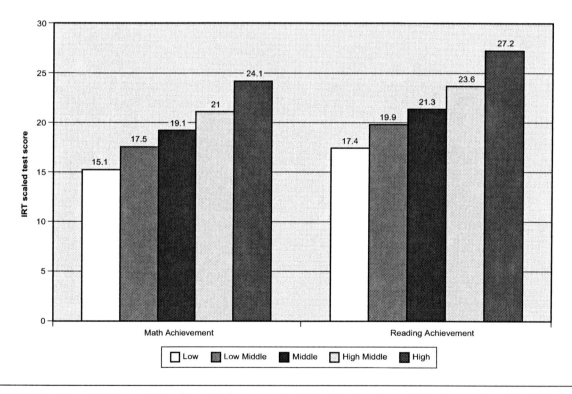

Figure 12–10 Math and Reading Achievement at the Beginning of Kindergarten (By SES Quintiles). Lee, V. E., & Burkam, D. T. (2002). *Inequality at the starting gate.* Washington, DC: Economic Policy Institute, p. 18.

children are not easily overcome. As Rothstein (2004) phrased it, "a typical middle class child who began to read at home will have higher lifetime achievement than a typical low income child who was taught only in school, even if each benefits from good curriculum" (p. 19).

The demographics of the American family have also posed new problems for the public school. Over the past several decades, a dramatic change has occurred in the nature of the family. Certainly the nuclear family is not what it used to be. Today's American family is clearly different from the American family of the 1960s and 1970s. Since 1960, the number of divorces in America has more than doubled, as has the number of births to unmarried women (NCES, 1996). As a result of these two factors, the number of single-parent families has climbed significantly over the years. Because such families are at higher risk of descending into poverty and because they often result in the decreased involvement of the father in the family life, the effects on the children in these families can be profound. The fracture of the traditional nuclear family has, in fact, affected black children more than any other race or ethnic group (see Table 12–10). It is yet another factor to consider when contemplating some of the achievement differences discussed earlier. In 2003, more than half of all black children (54 percent) lived in a single-parent household, compared to about 20 percent of white children and 34 percent of Hispanic children.

The traditional nuclear family, of course, has no monopoly on providing an enlightened and loving experience for children. Against all odds, many single-parent families provide their children with a healthy upbringing. But the association between poverty and single-parent homes cannot be ignored. In fact, the kind of differences in home-literacy activities that exist between low- and high-income families also manifest between single-parent families and two-parent families (Nord, Lennon, and others, 1999).

Another factor emerging in the literature has to do with the role of the father in the school education of children. The data show that single-parent families headed either by the father or mother are every bit as involved in their child's school education as all mothers in two-parent homes (NCES, 1999), but a nonresident father's involvement drops off considerably. Only 8 percent of all nonresident fathers displayed high involvement in their children's school education. Not surprisingly, the children of fathers with high levels of involvement in their schools (at all grade levels) were more likely than children of fathers with low-level school involvement to get better grades, to enjoy school, and to participate in extracurricular activities. They were also less likely to be expelled or suspended from school

TABLE 12–10 Percentage Distribution of Family Households by Family Status and Race/Ethnicity: 2003.

Race/ethnicity	Married Couple	Female Householder, No Husband Present	Male Householder, No Wife Present
Total[1]	**74.9**	**18.7**	**6.5**
White	79.9	14.3	5.8
Black	44.2	46.9	8.9
Hispanic	65.0	23.9	11.1
Asian/Pacific Islander	80.5	12.8	6.7
American Indian/Alaska Native	61.0	28.9	10.1

[1]Totals include race/ethnicity categories not separately shown.

NOTE: A family is a group of two people or more (one of whom is the householder) related by birth, marriage, or adoption and residing together. By contrast, a household is defined as the people who occupy a housing unit.

It includes the related family members and all the unrelated people, if any, such as lodgers, foster children, wards, or employees who share the housing unit. Detail may not sum to totals because of rounding. Race groups include persons of Hispanic origin.

SOURCE: U.S. Department of Commerce, Census Bureau, American Community Survey, unpublished data, 2003.

or to repeat a grade (NCES, 1999; see Table 12–11). Low-income children are disproportionately affected by the negative outcomes associated with nonresident, low-involvement fathers.

One must also acknowledge the association of poverty and race/ethnicity with health concerns. Significant differences across race and ethnicity levels are witnessed at the very beginning of life, as exemplified in the data on low-birthweight babies. The percentage of black, non-Hispanic, low-birthweight babies is almost double the national average (see Table 12–12). Needless to say, low birthweight is a clear risk factor for later developmental problems, including learning problems. Not surprisingly, one can find a similar disproportionate representation of black children documented with disabilities and served by special education programs (see Table 12–13). The data on the general indices of health indicate significant differences by poverty status in the percentages of children who are in very good or excellent health (see Figure 12–11). The reality is that lower income children have more hearing problems, poorer oral health, higher levels of lead exposure, greater rates of asthma, and

TABLE 12–11   Selected School Outcomes by Family Type and Level of Fathers' Involvement, 1996.

	FATHERS IN TWO-PARENT FAMILIES		NON-RESIDENT FATHERS	
	Low Involvement (47)	High Involvement (26)	Low Involvement (82)	High Involvement (8)
Child Gets Mostly A's	34	50	29	35
Child Enjoys School	33	49	34	44
Child Participates in Extracurricular Activities				
Grades K-5	73	79	73	86
Grades 6-12	79	94	75	92
Child Has Repeated a Grade	14	6	18	7
Child Has Been Expelled/Suspended				
Grades 6-12	17	9	27	14

TABLE 12–12   Percentage of Babies of Low Birthweight, by Race/Ethnicity: 2002.

Race/ ethnicity	Low Birthweight
Total	**7.8**
White, non-Hispanic	6.9
Black, non-Hispanic	13.4
Hispanic	6.5
Asian/Pacific Islander[1]	7.8
American Indian/Alaska Native[1]	7.2

[1]Includes Asian/Pacific Islanders and American Indians/Alaska Natives of Hispanic origin. NOTE: Babies of low birthweight weigh less than 2.500 grams/5.5 pounds.

SOURCE: U.S. Department of Health and Human Services, Centers for Disease Control and Prevention (CDC), National Vital Statistics Reports, *Births: Final Data for 2002,* based on CDC, National Center for Health Statistics, Final Natality Statistics, 2002.

TABLE 12–13   Number, Percentage, and Percentage Distribution of Children Ages 3 to 21 Served Under the Individuals with Disabilities Act (IDEA), by Race/Ethnicity: 2003.

Race/ethnicity	Number of children served under IDEA	Percent of children in each racial/ethnic group served under IDEA	Percentage distribution of children served under IDEA
Total	**6,633,902**	**8.6**	**100.0**
White, non-Hispanic	4,035,880	8.4	60.8
Black, non-Hispanic	1,334,666	11.5	20.1
Hispanic	1,035,463	7.5	15.6
Asian/Pacific Islander	137,544	4.4	2.1
American Indian/Alaska Native	90,349	11.9	1.4

NOTE: Detail may not sum to totals because of rounding.

SOURCE: U.S. Department of Education, Office of Special Education Programs (OSEP). *Data Tables for OSEP State Reported Data,* 2003.

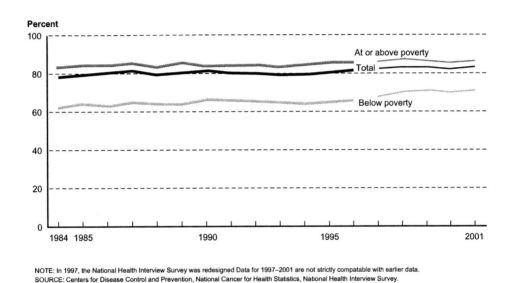

NOTE: In 1997, the National Health Interview Survey was redesigned Data for 1997–2001 are not strictly compatable with earlier data.
SOURCE: Centers for Disease Control and Prevention, National Cancer for Health Statistics, National Health Interview Survey.

FIGURE 12–11   Percentage of Children Under Age 18 in Very Good or Excellent Health by Poverty Status, 1984–2001.

poorer vision than their upper income peers. They are also more likely to be born to a mother who smoked during pregnancy and who otherwise did not receive comprehensive prenatal care (Rothstein, 2004, pp. 37–45). Each of these heath-related disparities is obviously not incidental to school success.

Poverty and its proxies are also powerfully associated with OTL factors in the curriculum. In the body of the coursework alone, considerable differences can be seen between the races in the enrollment rates to both basic and advanced courses. As displayed in Figure 12–12, the rates of enrollment in advanced coursework among white and Asian students exceed the rates observed among black and Hispanic students, especially in mathematics and English. Adding to the OTL gap are summer and after-school experiences that can be readily gained for children from families with financial means. Thus, participation rates in constructive extra-school events (such as summer camps, music lessons,

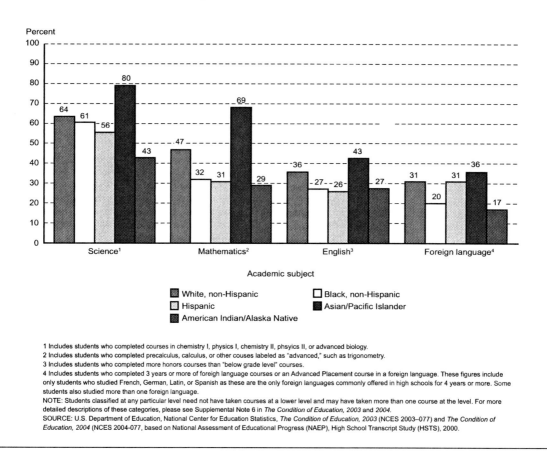

1 Includes students who completed courses in chemistry I, physics I, chemistry II, phsyics II, or advanced biology.
2 Includes students who completed precalculus, calculus, or other couses labeled as "advanced," such as trigonometry.
3 Includes students who completed more honors courses than "below grade level" courses.
4 Includes students who completed 3 years or more of foreign language courses or an Advanced Placement course in a foreign language. These figures include only students who studied French, German, Latin, or Spanish as these are the only foreign languages commonly offered in high schools for 4 years or more. Some students also studied more than one foreign language.
NOTE: Students classified at any particular level need not have taken courses at a lower level and may have taken more than one course at the level. For more detailed descriptions of these categories, please see Supplemental Note 6 in *The Condition of Education, 2003* and *2004.*
SOURCE: U.S. Department of Education, National Center for Education Statistics, *The Condition of Education, 2003* (NCES 2003–077) and *The Condition of Education, 2004* (NCES 2004-077, based on National Assessment of Educational Progress (NAEP), High School Transcript Study (HSTS), 2000.

FIGURE 12–12   Percentage of High School Graduates Who Completed Advanced Academic Courses, by School Subject and Race/Ethnicity: 2000.

and extensive travel), as well as access to privately-funded tutors, are much more likely to surface in the experience of children living above the poverty line than in the lives of their low-income peers.

As indicated, poverty is a dynamic variable that acts in concert with other variables, all of which work together to threaten a student's odds at school success. Poverty is entangled with family structure patterns, parent education levels and a whole host of other variables. Rothstein (2004), in fact, prefers to use the term socio-economic status to better capture the full complement of cultural, psychological, and economic characteristics at play. Thus, low-income families with high parent education levels and periodic, rather than sustained, experiences in poverty, carry higher socio-economic status than families caught in generational poverty with low parent education levels. The National Center of Education Statistics has designed a family risk index that encompasses many of the factors discussed here. The risk factors include living in a household below the poverty line, living in a household where English is not the primary home language, living in a single-parent household, and having a residential mother whose highest education is less than a high school diploma/GED. Each of these factors is negatively associated with reading and math achievement. In the education of very young children, we find that the family risk factors very much predict early achievement gains in reading and math. For first-time kindergarteners, a child with no family risk factors will average a gain of 84 scale points in reading by the time they reach third grade, in contrast to a 73-scale point gain among children with two or more family risk factors. The disparity is significant, as it approaches almost a full standard deviation difference and indicates that much of the problem associated with raising achievement is intertwined with factors that are often outside of the school's control.

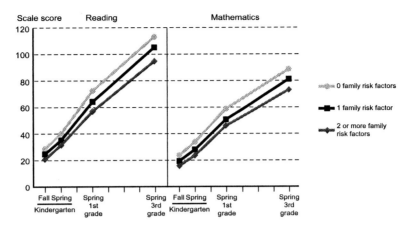

2 Family risk factors include living below the poverty level, primary home language was non-English, mother's highest education was less than a high school diploma/GED, and living in a single-parent household, as measures in kindergarten. See supplemental note 1 for more information on mother's education and poverty.

NOTE: The findings are based on children who entered kindergarten for the first time in fall 1998 and were assessed in fall 1998, spring 1999, spring 2000, and spring 2002. Estimates reflect the sample of children assessed in English in all assessment years (approximately 19 percent of Asian children and approximately 30 percent of Hispanic children were not assessed). The Early Childhood Longitudinal Study, Kindergarten Class of 1998–99 (ECLS-K) was not administered in spring 2001, when most of the children were in 2nd grade. Although most of the sample was in 3rd grade in spring 2002, 10 percent were in 2nd grade, and about 1 percent were enrolled in other grades. See supplemental note 3 for more information on ECLS-K.
SOURCE: Rathbun, A, and West, J. (forthcoming). *From Kindergarten Through Third Grade: Children's Beginning School Experiences* (NCES 2004–007), tables A-4 and A-5. Data from U.S. Department of Education, NCES, Early Childhood Longitudinal Study, Kindergarten Class of 1998–99 (ECLS-K), Longitudinal Kindergarten-First Grade Public-Use data file and Third Grade Restricted-Use data file, Fall 1998, Spring 1999, Spring 2000, and Spring 2002.

FIGURE 12–13   Reading and Mathematics Performance: Children's Reading and Mathematics Scale Scores for Fall 1998 First-time Kindergartners from Kindergarten Through 3rd Grade, by Family Risk Factors: Fall 1998, Spring 1999, Spring 2000 and Spring 2002[2].

SUMMARY

The school equity issues raised in this chapter range from the sorting of students in academic programs by ability (and de facto by race and income), to manifest race-based segregation, to the differential, if not inequitable, treatment of the sexes in school, and finally to concerns about schoolchildren who are from low-income families with low socioeconomic status. In the case of curriculum tracking, the need to manage differential abilities and talents clashes with the need to secure equitable experiences. The key to the provision of differential experiences in the school curriculum is to find a way to be responsive to individual aptitudes, interests, and remedial needs without marginalizing the quality of the schooling for low-achieving students.

In the area of school segregation, the *Brown* ruling made it clear that segregation sanctioned by the law is inherently unequal and is, in fact, state-sponsored racism. The historical trend has been to integrate the schools in districts that have traditionally practiced racial discrimination. All in all, the historical results have been impressive. Because the Court's new propensity has shifted to seeing segregation in unitary districts as problematic only when it is an outcome of discriminatory practices, some re-segregation can occur.

With regard to gender bias, the question is whether the schools have conducted themselves in a manner that has come at the expense of the education of girls. Although there is clear persuasive evidence that the school has indeed committed some gender-based offenses against girls, the school achievements of girls are impressive. They get better grades than boys, drop out of school less often, and are better readers and writers. For their part, boys show some slight superiority in math and science and considerable superiority in mechanical know-how, and select into math and science careers at a disproportionately high rate.

Finally, the factor of poverty also raises its head in the context of school achievement. Poverty is a risk factor that disproportionately affects the lives of minority children. The evidence is clear that living in poverty puts students at a considerable disadvantage, both in terms of extra-school factors (such as family life and health concerns) and factors internal to the school (such as OTL variables in the school curriculum).

REFERENCES

American Association of University Woman. (1992). *How schools shortchange girls.* Washington, DC: National Education Association.

Belenky, M., Clinchy, B., Goldberger, N., & Tarule, J. (1986). *Women's way of knowing.* New York: Basic Books.

Braddock, J. H. (1990a). Tracking in the middle grades: National patterns of grouping for instruction. *Phi Delta Kappan* 71(6):445–449.

Braddock, J. H. (1990b). *Tracking implications for student race ethnic groups* (Report no. 1). Baltimore Center for Research on Effective Schooling for Disadvantaged Students.

Carey, N., & others. (1994). *Curricular differentiation in public high schools.* Washington, DC: National Center for Education Statistics.

Cole, N. (1997). *The ETS gender study: How females and males perform in educational settings.* Princeton, NJ: Educational Testing Service.

Coleman, J., & others. (1966). *Equality of educational opportunity.* Washington, DC: Office of Education.

Greenberg, S. (1985). Educational equity in early education environments. In S. Klien (Ed.), *Handbook in achieving sex equity through education.* Baltimore, MD: Johns Hopkins University Press.

Hansot, E. (1993). Historical and contemporary views of gender and education. In Sari K. Biklen and Diane Pollard (Eds.), *Gender and Education. Part 1. Ninety-second Yearbook of the National Society for the Study of Education.* Chicago: NSSE.

Howe, H. (1993). *Thinking about our kids.* New York: Free Press.

Irons, P. (1991). *Jim Crow's children.* New York: Penguin.

Kulik, J. (1993, Spring). *An analysis of the research on ability grouping.* National Research Center on the Gifted and Talented Newsletter, 8-9 (ED367-095).

Lee, V. E., & Burkam, D. T. (2002). *Inequality at the starting gate.* Washington, DC: Economic Policy Institute.

Loveless, T. (1998). *The tracking wars: State reform meets school policy.* Washington, DC: Brookings Institution Press.

Lytton, H., & Romney, D. (1991). Parents' differential socialization of boys and girls. *Psychological Bulletin,* 109, 267–296.

Martin, C. L. (1990). Attitudes and expectations about children with non-traditional and traditional gender roles. *Sex Roles* 229(3/4):131–165.

McCarthy, M. M., Cambron-McCabe, N. H., & Thomas, S. B. (1998). *Public school law: Teachers' and students' rights.* Boston: Allyn and Bacon.

Nasaw, D. (1979). *Schooled to order.* New York: Oxford University Press. National Center for Education Statistics. (1996). *The condition of education.* Washington, DC: U.S. Department of Education.

National Center for Education Statistics. (1998). *Gender and racial/ethnic differences in salary and other characteristics of postsecondary faculty.* Washington, DC: U.S. Department of Education.

National Center for Education Statistics. (1999). *How involved are fathers in their children's school?* Washington, DC: U.S. Department of Education.

National Center for Education Statistics. (2004). *Trends in educational equity of girls and women.* Washington, DC: U.S. Department of Education.

Noddings, N. (1992). Gender and the curriculum. In Phil Jackson (Ed.), *Handbook of research on curriculum.* New York: Macmillan.

Nord, C. W., Lennon, J., Liu, B., and Chandler, K. (1999). *Home literacy activities and signs of children's emerging literacy.* (Washington: Department of Education)

Oakes, J. (1985). *Keeping track: How schools structure inequality.* New Haven: Yale University Press.

Oakes, J. (1990). *Multiplying inequalities.* Santa Monica, CA: The Rand Corporation.

Oakes, J., Gamoran, A., & Page, R. (1992). Curriculum differentiation: Opportunities, outcomes and meanings. In Phil Jackson (Ed.), *Handbook of research on curriculum.* New York: Macmillan.

Olivares, R. A., & Rosenthal, N. (1992). *Gender equity and classroom experiences: A review of research* (ED366–701).

Orfield, G., & Eaton, S. (1996). *Dismantling desegregation: The quiet reversal of Brown v. Board of Education.* New York: The New Press.

Orfield, G., & Lee, C. (2005). *Why segregation matters: Poverty and educational inequality.* http://www.civilrightsproject.harvard.edu/research/deseg/deseg05.php.

Orfield, G., & Lee, C. (2006). *Racial transformation and the changing nature of segregation.* http://www.civilrightsproject.harvard.edu/research/deseg/Racial-Transformation.pdf.

Organisation for Economic Co-operation and Development. (2005). *Education at a Glance: OECD Indicators.* Paris: OECD Publishing.

Pomerleau, A., Boldice, D., & others. (1990). Pink or blue: Environmental stereotyping in the first two years of life. *Sex Roles* 22(5/6):359–67.

Rothstein, R. (2004). *Class and schools.* New York: Teachers College Press.

Sadker, M., & Sadker, D. (1994). *Failing at fairness.* New York: Touchstone.

Sadker, M., Sadker, D., & Klien, S. (1991). The issue of gender in elementary and secondary education. In Gerald Grant (Ed.), *Review of research in education.* Washington, DC: American Educational Research Association.

Salomone, R. (1999). Single sex schooling: Law, policy, and research. In Diane Ravitch (Ed.), *Brookings papers on education policy.* Washington, DC: Brookings Institution Press.

Slavin, R. (1990). Achievement effects in ability grouping in secondary schools. *Review of Educational Research,* 60(3):471–499.

United States Census Bureau. (2003). *Poverty in the United States.* U.S Department of Commerce.

United States Department of Labor. (1999). *Labor statistics in the Women's Bureau* (www.dol.gov)

Whitman, M. (1998). *The irony of desegregation law 1955–1995: Essays and documents.* Princeton, NJ: Markus Weiner.

KEY QUESTIONS

1. What are the typical justifications given for the use of curriculum tracks in schools?
2. How have critics argued that curriculum tracking practices are inequitable and unfair to poor and minority group students?
3. What is the difference between curriculum tracking and ability grouping?
4. Why is curriculum tracking rarely considered to be a problem in elementary schools?
5. Explain the different forms of tracking that can exist in high schools.
6. What are the ways that school districts coped with the mandate to desegregate?
7. In what way was the ruling *Brown v. Board of Education* a repudiation of Plessy?
8. What are the Green factors and what role have they played in the historical struggle to desegregate the schools?
9. What were some of the strategies embraced by the federal government in the 1960s as it dealt with issues of segregation and poverty?
10. What was the essential implication behind the *Swann* ruling?
11. Why did Justice Thurgood Marshall believe that the *Milliken* ruling was a "giant step backward" for desegregation efforts?
12. Explain the significance of the *Oklahoma City v. Dovell* ruling.
13. What are the national trends in the area of school segregation? Where is segregation most intractable and where has the most progress been?
14. Make a case demonstrating how schools might shortchange boys.
15. Do you believe that schools embrace male values in their conduct in a way that compromises the education of girls?
16. What are the essential points of difference in the achievement of boys and girls once they reach 12th grade? Speculate on how these differences arose.
17. Explain the strong classroom performance of girls in math and science against their slight underperformance on standardized tests in math and science and against their lack of interest in pursuing math and science careers.
18. What are the general arguments for and against single sex classrooms? What are your personal views on the matter?
19. What is Title IX and what role has it played in regulating gender bias issues in the schools?
20. Explain how poverty intersects with race and how such an intersection might explain some of the achievement differences witnessed between the races.
21. Detail the manner in which poverty affects home environment in ways that might also affect school achievement.
22. Explain how the factor of poverty is also associated with OLT factors in school.

A Chronology of Cited School Desegregation Cases

Plessy v. Ferguson, 163 U.S. 537 (1896)
Brown v. Board of Education, 349 U.S. 294 (1955...U.S. 483 (1954)
Green v School Board of New Kent County 20 L. Ed. 2d 716 (1968)
Alexander v. Holmes County Bd. of Educ., 396. U.S. 19 (1969)
Swann v. Charlotte-Mecklenburg Board of Education, 402 U.S. 1, 32 (1971)
Milliken v. Bradley, 418 U.S. 717 (1974)
Board of Education of Oklahoma City v. Dowell, 498 U.S. 237 (1991)
Freeman v. Pitts, 112 S. Ct. 1430 (1992)
Missouri v. Jenkins, 515 U.S. 70 (1995)

RESEARCH EXERCISES

1. Sort out the way that a high school or middle school of your choice is tracked. Is it across-the-board tracking, or is it tracking in select subject areas? Who decides who gets placed in each tracked level? What is the demographic breakdown of the different tracks, by race, income, ethnicity, and gender?

2. Collect student impressions of what they have learned on a common subject from the perspective of three differentially tracked classrooms.

3. Observe what occurs in three differentially tracked classrooms with an eye on noting what gets taught, what the expressed expectations are, what the social engagements are like, what the quality of the teaching is like, and so forth.

4. Collect teacher impressions of how they view their teaching on a common subject in three differentially tracked classrooms.

5 Write a historical case study account of a school district that has not yet achieved unitary status, emphasizing what it has tried to do to desegregate its schools.

6. Write a detailed case study account on any of the following cases: *Roberts v. City of Boston; Plessy v. Ferguson; Green v. County School Board of New Kent, Virginia; Alexander v. Holmes County; Swann v. Charlotte Mecklenburg Board of Education; Milliken v. Bradley; Board of Education of Oklahoma City Public Schools v. Dowell; Freeman v. Pitts; Missouri v. Jenkins, or any other major desegregation case.*

7. Interview a school superintendent, district curriculum coordinator, or a Title IX compliance officer to discuss issues of gender that the school district is facing and trying to tackle.

8. Analyze the commercial advertising of the toy industry, looking for gender-linked toys and speculating on how these gender-linked toys may or may not result in early experiences tied to different forms of school success.

9. Observe a set of classrooms at a certain grade level with an eye on noting differences in the way boys and girls are treated. Conduct a frequency count of the number and the types of questions asked and answered, the form, intensity, and frequency of praise or punishments used, the number of children who might be considered off task, and so forth.

10. Examine the reading gender gap as it is discussed and treated in another nation.

11. Select any of the NAEP reports on achievement and report on any of the achievement gaps (by race, income, gender) and examine why such gaps might exist.

CHAPTER 13

The Culture and the Language of Schooling

Public education in the United States features a unique tension between two equally important cultural agendas. The first, which overlaps with wider normative concerns, has to do with building a common culture that includes the teaching of a common language, a common knowledge base, and a common foundation of values. Such an agenda is tied to what we might label as the amalgamating process of schooling—that part of the school experience aiming to create a unifying national identity. In a pluralistic nation such as ours, the amalgamating process must be balanced against the considerable diversity perspectives embodied in the varied traditions of race, ethnicity, religion, politics, class, and language in the population. Thus, the second cultural agenda of the school is tied to what we might label as the diversifying process of schooling—that part of the school experience showing sensitivity toward and tolerance for family-based culture and ancestral heritage. These two processes are not mutually exclusive. One could say, for instance, that the diversifying aspects of schooling are, in fact, part and parcel of our common culture. For analytical purposes, it is useful to see how the amalgamating and diversifying features of the school exist side by side and how clashes between them can result in accusations of cultural imperialism on the one side and cultural divisiveness on the other.

The tension between amalgamating and diversifying the school experience is the natural consequence of living in a pluralistic constitutional democracy that claims no nationally-identifiable ethnic, religious, or racial prototype. The United States is a nation whose ancestors were immigrants or slaves, and continues to be a nation favored by immigrants today. In the 1990s, the foreign-born population of the United States nearly doubled, to 31 million, comprising about 11 percent of the total U.S. population. In both absolute numbers and percentages, this is comparable to the historical peak immigrations of the early nineteenth century. Differences within ethnic groups (namely religious, political, geographical, and class-based differences) also speak to an important facet of diversity. For instance, low-income white children living in urban settings are likely to have more in common with other low-income children living in urban settings, irrespective of ethnicity or race, than with their higher income white suburban peers. The white coalminer's daughter likely has much in common with the black coalminer's daughter. Add religious and political flavors to the mix and one can really begin to appreciate the complexity of diversity concerns.

CULTURAL DIVERSITY AND COMMONALITY

We can say that, in many respects, the common culture in America is multicultural, and that the idea of cultural diversity exists in delicate balance with the idea of cultural commonality. In this way, the forces of assimilation, which aim to make a common culture, work together with the forces of diversity. They exist in a kind of partnership.

Consider for a moment the notion of diversity without a context of commonality; that is, try to unhinge the idea of difference from any basis in common values or common principles. The effect would likely be cultural relativity, which is the view that all cultural values and actions are equally moral and equally acceptable. Thus, racists, sexists, fascists, and anyone who opposes tolerance of differences could all be counted as contributors to the cause of diversity. These are, after all, diversifying outlooks. The paradox is that where such a climate of cultural relativity prevails, intolerance would likely grow. If there is no center of cultural gravity (and all cultural claimants are equal), ethnic or religious diversity can quickly degrade into conflicts and hostility. A vital common culture, however, helps prevent balkanization by drawing a line between the tolerable and the intolerable, between the type of diversity that contributes to the common good and the type that destroys it. It helps us to say no to racism and sexism even in the face of the diversity that such views bring to school.

Similarly, the idea of fashioning a common culture without any appreciation for diversity is equally unhealthy because it can result in a form of imperialism and undermine the important school purpose of enlarging and enriching the experiences of youth. A common culture that is unmediated by diversity concerns is often a repressive culture. The former Soviet Union, for instance, was a nation that tolerated little religious or political diversity and imposed rigid guidelines on the thoughts and actions of its people. It, like other totalitarian regimes, was a historical example of a nation without consciousness for its diversifying agenda. In the United States, any effort to fashion a common culture in the school has both an intellectual and a moral obligation to reflect the deep diversities of its people (Gutmann, 2000).

In 1908, Jane Addams wrote a short essay titled, "The Public School and the Immigrant Child," in which she argued that immigrant traditions were fundamental to the process of assimilating foreign-born children into American culture. To Addams, our differences were at the very heart of our commonalties; who we were individually had everything to do with creating who we were collectively. She believed that, at some level, our differences had to be circulated, understood, and accommodated into a community of common concerns and common principles. Hence, Addams had little tolerance for those who aimed to educate children in a manner that ignored the cultural dynamics of the child's family life. She wanted to use these dynamics to give children a global and multi-ethnic view of society in a way that related to the problems, issues, and values of American democracy. She expressed this idea clearly in her 1908 essay:

> Can we say, perhaps, that the schools ought to do more to connect these [immigrant] children with the best things of the past, to make them realize something of the beauty and charm of the language, the history, and the traditions which their parents represent. It is easy to cut them loose from their parents, it requires cultivation to tie them up in sympathy and understanding. The ignorant teacher cuts them off because he himself cannot understand the situation, the cultivated teacher fastens them because his own mind is open to the charm and beauty of that old country life. In short, it is the business of the school to give to each child the beginnings of a culture so wide and deep and universal that he can interpret his own parents and countrymen by a standard which is world-wide and not provincial. (Addams, 1908, p. 138)

Addams, of course, was unique for her time, but the problem of forging a common culture without disrupting the pluralistic elements of American society is one that continues to be debated by policymakers and practitioners today. How is it possible, after all, for the public school to acculturate school children (whose identification with ethnicity, class, language, religion, and politics is overwhelmingly varied) into an American culture without destroying the very essence of diversity that makes our democracy so vital and interesting? Historically speaking, immigrant and first-generation American students of various ethnic and language traditions have always had to learn to reconcile their family culture with the broader societal culture. But did these youth necessarily have to reject their own family or community culture or language in the interests of assimilating into a larger or more dominant national culture?

The truth of the matter is that the schooling process has not always resulted in a happy resolution between the forces of amalgamation (qua, assimilation) and diversity. The by-products of assimilation (and cultural unity) can sometimes lead to the severing of community- or family-based cultural connections for some children, which in the context of the school could mean that students might give up the use of their first language in school or even lose some identification with cultural traditions in the home. Students sometimes come to school with value systems not typically associated with what we might see as American culture, some of which may even be at odds with the overall goals of democracy. Differences in outlook between the school and the family exist toward sex roles, language usage, career choices, and racial tolerance (to name just a few areas). How should these cultural differences be treated in the curriculum? Are sexist views to be tolerated because they have the sanction of family or ethnic culture? Is Ebonics or Black English a form of communication that should be respected in the school? Should the school teach children to take pride in their ethnic or racial identity or teach about the holidays and traditions of different cultures around the world? Should schools also be prepared to provide a forum for the discussion, analysis, and criticism of cultural differences? Is it sensible or otherwise appropriate to engage in critical discourse over matters sensitive to family-based and church-based belief systems? These are difficult questions that do not always have definitive answers.

THE CULTURE OF SCHOOLING

The concept of culture is complicated. Acceptable definitions are hard to frame. For our purposes, we will examine the notion of culture in terms of the forces that it exerts in binding people together and in establishing rules, norms, and customs for behavior. In other words, how does the school contribute to the formation of American culture—to the making of rules, knowledge, and traditions with which we can all identify? It seems clear that the "culture" of the school should reflect the wider culture, but how can the school apprehend this culture and give it life in its daily operations?

Sources of a Common Culture

In *The Interpretation of Cultures*, Clifford Geortz (1973) writes that "cultural patterns are programs: they provide a 'template' or 'blueprint' for the organization of social and psychological processes" (p. 216). The words template or blueprint are metaphors for the way culture guides a group of people. They suggest that, despite individual variations, those who share a culture are guided by a set of underlying "directions" for living. This so-called set of directions depends on a foundation of commonality—a common language, common values and principles, common knowledge, and even a regard for common problems. Dewey (1916) stated that humans live in communities by virtue of the things that they have in common, and they communicate as a way to share and eventually possess things in common. Community is indeed a common unity.

Language, of course, is our best way of ensuring some basis of commonality, although it is obviously not enough. We are all endowed with the capacity to speak, but the kind of language we speak is obviously culturally derived—it includes us in one culture and necessarily excludes us from another. People consistently use language and other cultural commonalties to help define who they are, and equally importantly, who they are not. Thus, societies always have some semblance of a common language. The political debates witnessed over the place of English in the school experience are really debates about defining a common culture.

This was exactly the situation when the Oakland Unified School District declared its intention in 1997 to teach the African-derived language of ebonics in the school curriculum, asserting that it was the unique "genetically-based" language of the descendants of slaves. It called for African-American students to be taught in their "primary language" of ebonics. Criticism of the District's new policy was swift and set off a national argument over the place of English teaching in the curriculum. Advocates of teaching English-only believed that the teaching of ebonics would not only fail to properly assimilate black children into American culture, but would create deeper divisions between the races, fissures that would go as deep as language. The Oakland Unified School District eventually retracted from its original position and redefined the place of ebonics in the school curriculum as a means to assist in the education of English language proficiency, a tradition of teaching well-established in bilingual education programs (Schnaiberg, 22 January, 1997).

A common culture is also created through the teaching of a common history. The history of America testifies to a struggle to build what is now the world's oldest democracy, but much of this history is contentious because of arguments over whether the whole story is being told and whether the story reflects the true diversity embodied in the American experience. Here again the diversity agenda arises to complicate our sense of commonality. The founding of America, from the perspective of Native Americans and black Africans, was not the call to freedom or self-government that it was for early European-Americans. The vantage points of women, minorities, laborers, gays, various ethnic groups, and the poor all provide a different historical perspective on living in America. Our common history is marked by interesting and telling subtexts.

Obviously, socialization in a common set of values and a common basis of knowledge also contributes to the development of a common culture. The axiology of American democracy speaks to clearly delineated constitutional freedoms and principles, and to a social democratic theory of understanding. These include, to select a small list, a belief in government by the consent of the governed, a commitment to group cooperation, critical tolerance of differences, an appreciation for the constitutional freedoms of assembly and expression and other key principles, including most fundamentally, a willingness and an ability to deliberate about relevant disagreements (Gutmann, 2000). A willingness to engage in discourse over differences is a hallmark common value of democracy. Only the school is deliberately designed to fulfill the task of conveying many of these common values in the lives of children.

Some evidence suggests that, despite the considerable diversifying elements in society, American youth embrace a common core of values. People for the American Way (Schmidt, 25 March, 1992) released a study that found widespread consensus among all youth on core values, including the significance of the family, the importance of personal responsibility and the belief in equity. It also showed that the school was still the one place where youth have regular contact with people of other races and ethnicities—more so than work, the neighborhood, sports activities, and church or house of worship activities. The overwhelming majority of youth in the survey study approved of interracial dating and more than 70 percent said they have had a "close personal friendship" with a person of another race.

Percentage saying that each statement is very close or somewhat close to their own view:

Percentage saying that each statement is very close or somewhat close to their own view:

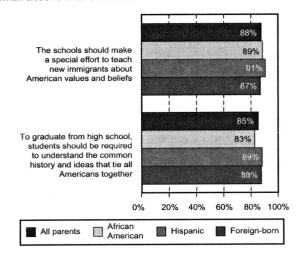
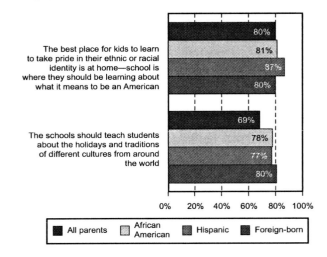

FIGURES 13–1 and 13–2   Large Numbers of Both U.S. and Foreign-born Parents Expect the Schools to Teach all Children About the Ideals and History of the Country. Source: Public Agenda 9/98.

Parent surveys of common American values taught in the schools reflect a similar pattern. In 1998, Public Agenda asked parents to respond to various questions that sought to determine whether parents across the nation held any number of key American values in common. Its report, titled *A Lot to Be Thankful For,* found clear evidence of patriotism among pluralities of parents and a desire by parents for the school to teach history in a way that was fair to all subgroups without becoming divisive. Parents also roundly supported the ideals of personal freedom, tolerance toward others, and hard work, and wanted schools to teach the common values of American society. In fact, vast pluralities of parents believed that the school had been paying too much attention to what separates different racial and ethnic groups, and not paying attention to what they have in common. Figures 13–1 and 13–2 express some of the views.

The teaching of a common body of knowledge and a common cultural vocabulary that might help to bind the nation is also an indisputable feature of building a common culture. As indicated in an earlier chapter, conservatives and progressives alike have argued that the notion of shared common knowledge is essential to generating the quality of social discussion and a sense of community required to educate good citizens. What they cannot agree on is the nature of this shared knowledge. The National Assessment Educational Progress (NAEP) data on students' knowledge of history seems to indicate that students do not have a common grounding in historical knowledge (NCES, 2002). NAEP civics data indicate a similar problem. According to the 1998 report on NAEP Civics, only 42 percent of fourth graders reported studying how their government works; only 55 percent studied the laws of government, and only 50 percent studied the rights and responsibilities of citizenship (NCES, 1999). The percentages are slightly better at the eighth- and twelfth-grade level but still indicate that a core of civic topics, related mostly to citizenship, does not have an ongoing presence in the curriculum (see Table 13–1). Given what we know about OTL factors, this is not a promising sign for building a common core of civic values and knowledge.

TABLE 13–1

Percentage of students, average civics scale scores, and percentage at or above *Proficient* by type of content studied this year as reported by students, grades 8 and 12: 1998.

This Year Studied	GRADE 8						GRADE 12					
	Yes			No			Yes			No		
	Percentage of Students	Average Scale Score	Percentage at or above *Proficient*	Percentage of Students	Average Scale Score	Percentage at or above *Proficient*	Percentage of Students	Average Scale Score	Percentage at or above *Proficient*	Percentage of Students	Average Scale Score	Percentage at or above *Proficient*
U.S. Constitution	79	152	23	14	152	25	71	151	26	27	15.4	28
Congress	75	152	23	17	151	24	71	151	26	27	15.4	29
President and Cabinet	55	156	26	32	149	21	63	152	28	32	152	27
How Laws are Made	67	151	23	24	155	26	64	150	26	32	155	30
The Court Systems	60	152	23	30	153	25	64	150	26	32	155	30
State and Local Government	67	151	22	22	155	28	69	150	25	28	156	32
Political Parties, Elections, Voting	69	152	23	22	153	25	70	150	26	27	155	29
Other Countries' Government	40	146	19	45	158	29	48	150	26	44	155	29
International Organizations	33	146	18	43	160	32	45	150	26	45	155	31

NOTE: A small percentage of students responded "I don't know" to each of the topics.

SOURCE: National Center for Education Statistics, National Assessment of Educational Progress (NAEP), 1998 Civics Assessment.

Melting Pot Versus Salad Bowl

In most cases, the thinking on the making of a common culture in the school embraces either of two frameworks. One view conceives the school's role in the acculturation of youth as providing the heat for a "melting pot" society, where our differences are dissolved into a uniform mold. Under such conditions, exclusive immersion in the English language is required, and finding ways for children to fit into one cultural design is the purpose of schooling. The "melting pot" perspective typically upholds the western canon in the school curriculum, usually through the presentation of academic disciplines in the liberal arts. Its main purpose is to transmit western culture in the interest of teaching a foundation of knowledge that can be used for common understanding and common discourse.

The "melting pot" perspective might lead to a common culture, but critics have argued that it fails democracy because it carries no diversifying strategy. In fact, the very idea of unity in the context of the melting pot metaphor can be construed as having imperialistic qualities because all differences are melded away and recast in the image of only one privileged culture, which historically speaking, has been one that resides in the traditional liberal arts (with its attendant emphasis on so-called Euro-centered Western thinking and Western literature). Howe (1993) accentuates this point by arguing that the melting pot metaphor approach produces outcomes that contradict its original intentions by creating the conditions for ethnic divisiveness, not unity, as subgroups seek to huddle together in order to protect their cultural identity from dominant forces.

Another way of looking at acculturation is to frame it as a process that cultivates a dual identity—one with the larger American tradition, and the other with the more community-based or familial tradition. This can be expressed in terms of a "salad bowl" metaphor, where differences are essential to the overall composition and quality of the whole. Thus, national identity does not come at the expense of an ethnic identity, but is vested in a multitude of ethnic identities—an idea that stresses democratic principles of tolerance and understanding. To be different then, is to be normal, as long as our differences have some center of gravity: Some see this as a more appropriate way of handling the acculturation process in the American schools, although there are potential dangers here as well because diverse elements often represent deep contrasts that cannot be easily incorporated into a harmonious whole.

MULTICULTURAL EDUCATION

The call for multicultural education has been reverberating in the discussions on public education for at least three decades. The strength of the current movement to bring multicultural education into the school curriculum is, in some ways, indicative of the problem that the school has had with diversifying its experiences. The purposes of multicultural education include preventing prejudice and stereotyping, promoting a better understanding of the different ethnic groups in society and ultimately finding some enriching center of common understanding.

Various scholars have argued that the systematic bias favoring a so-called European culture in the school has damaged the ability of minority youth to succeed in schools. Not many years ago, the treatment of nonwhite groups in the curriculum materials and textbooks of the American schools were not only infrequent but were often negligent or even outright offensive toward minority groups. These kinds of abuses have led to a call for the dislodging of western dominance in the school curriculum and for the widening of school experiences along different cultural lines. The claim is that if white children with European ancestry can experience a Euro-centered curriculum in the school, then children from other ethnic groups should retain the same type of benefit.

Consequently, some advocates of multicultural education have argued for ethnocentric forms of instruction, meaning, in effect, that black youth should receive an Afro-centric education, Latino youth a Latino-centered education, and so on. Supporters of these views do not see any contradiction in advancing a form of multicultural education that encourages ethnic separatism. Their thinking is that children need to be given a deep exposure to their ancestral culture, and be taught to respect and admire their own heritage. The result, they claim, is raised self-esteem and a more honest awareness of their ancestors' role in the experience of the human race. This has resulted, in some cases, in the ethnicizing of mathematics and science education, as well as the advocacy of ethnic-based schools for ethnic subgroups of students.

Criticism of this view has emerged from various quarters. In *The Disuniting of America*, Arthur Schlesinger (1991) shows how ethnocentric views on multiculturalism have given rise to an educational multiculturalism that is most interested in finding ways to make children feel good about their ancestry. The effect, he claims, is the glorifying of one often-historically marginalized perspective, and a repudiation of the widest conception of a common core of knowledge. As Schlesinger documents, ethnic separatists often treat their ancestral cultures in felicitous terms, while assuming the worst from the so-called white European western tradition. Ultimately, they ask minority children to study their ethnicity with more intensity than their own common American culture. Thus, African-American youth are believed to be able to learn more by studying African culture than by studying American culture.

Ravitch (1990) has labeled this perspective as particularistic multiculturalism. Rather than focusing on the broadest interpretation of the common culture in America, in the interests of creating a more enriching common discourse, particularistic multiculturalists reject the very idea of an American common culture. Ravitch argues, that if taken seriously, particularistic multiculturalism can lead to a proliferation of culturalized or ethnicized versions of what gets taught in school and how it gets taught (African math with African pedagogical techniques for African American children, ethnic science for immigrant children, history from the Japanese perspective for Japanese American students, and so forth). Such a development would undermine the key purpose of public schooling, which is to provide a common and enlarging experience in the values, problems, and pluralistic dimensions of American culture. Progressive educators have long argued that the school curriculum should provide countervailing experiences to the more parochial (particularistic, if you will) experience in the home, widening the common basis for ethnicity, racial, religious, and political understandings.

To this end, multicultural education can obviously have an important place in the school curriculum. The study of our nation's history, for instance, cannot be properly managed unless it embraces its many multicultural aspects. This means not only recounting the considerable hardships sustained by members of various ethnic groups through stories of discrimination and xenophobia and bigotry, but also recounting the successes of assimilation, tolerance toward others, and the considerable body of legal, political, and social struggles that eventually made America the pluralistic democracy that it is today.

To do this, effective ways have to be found to conceive and operationalize multicultural education in the school. Banks and McGee-Banks (2006), in fact, have detailed a hierarchy of approaches. Among the least ambitious but most popular multicultural education methods is known as the contributions approach, sometimes also labeled as the heroes and holidays approach. The intention here is to inject diversifying content in the curriculum as it relates to the study of selected ethnic holidays and heroes.

The limitations here are obvious, as the idea of multiculturalism is given only a spotty place in the curriculum and is treated mostly in a cheery way rather than in a manner that confronts the ugliness of victimization and oppression. More ambitious is an ethnic-additive approach, which is more comprehensive than the contributions approach because it seeks to supplement the school experience by adding ethnic content throughout the curriculum, although without fundamentally changing the structure of the curriculum. Thus, a high school might develop a long list of elective studies that relate to minority cultures and groups. In the classroom, a teacher using an ethnic-additive approach might add an ethnic feature onto a conventional unit in an effort to be more attendant to diversity needs, or might make a classroom event of presenting students with the food, language, and music of a particular culture, or might simply offer a multicultural reading list to students. The point is that with an ethnic-additive approach, multiculturalism becomes periodically plugged into the curriculum. Such a plug-in tactic is not ideal because it tends to fragment multiculturalism, giving it the appearance of popping up here and there in the curriculum.

Another form of multicultural education, known as the transformative approach, aims at a wider and more integrated mark. Here the thinking is that multiple cultural perspectives need to be folded into most, if not all, school studies. The idea is to integrate the curriculum with multiple perspectives, to make it the overarching theme in the design of the school experience. In history, for example, the teaching of a major historical event, such as the founding of the nation, would require opening the learning experience to various perspectives not usually presented. The role of the women, blacks, and indigenous people would be brought into the curriculum. Students might be asked to examine the petition brought against slavery to the General Court of Massachusetts by free African-Americans in 1777, or the letter from three Seneca leaders to President Washington in 1790 expressing concerns about the effects of revolutionary war on native populations, or the letter composed by Benjamin Banneker to Thomas Jefferson in 1791 outlining the obvious discrepancies between the ideals of the American revolution and the life conditions of blacks (Patrick, 2000). Banks and McGee-Banks (2006) also identify a decision-making approach to multiculturalism that puts students in the role of researching social problems and eventually taking social action for their remediation.

CULTURE AND CRITICAL THEORY

Over the past several decades, a group of radical scholars in education has examined schools from the standpoint of socioeconomic and minority-group interest (Apple, 1990; Giroux, 1983; McLaren, 1994). These scholars have tried to reveal the injustices and inequities of public schooling, focusing on practices such as "low ability" curriculum tracks and special education labels that affect disproportionately large numbers of minority children and children living in poverty. They have also examined the nature of culture perpetuated in the schools and have accused the public school of practicing cultural hegemony, which is the enthroning and imposing of one cultural tradition onto the vast diversity of ethnic and cultural groups that make up the American public school.

Such an outlook can be said to be informed by critical theory, which is in essence, a neo-Marxist view of schooling that holds to the belief that schools reproduce, rather than ameliorate, socio-economic conditions (Gibson, 1986). Schools, in this way, are believed to be instruments of oppression, designed to keep certain groups down while lifting a few others up. This process of reproduction is said to be operationalized in various ways. Differential access to knowledge, differential opportunities to think and use language, and the basic privileging of different subject matter are all part of the process. Critical theorists claim, for instance, that the decision to teach English in high school with a list of readings drawn from Western traditions is indicative of an open privileging of one set of writings over another and the concomitant privileging of one cultural perspective over another. Table 13–2 presents the results of the most popularly adopted book length works taught in American high school English classes. Shakespeare is clearly the big winner, as four of his works surface on the top ten list. A critical theorist might ask why Shakespeare should have a prominent place in the English curriculum and also ask whose interests are being served by such a phenomenon. Why is the reading list in an American English high school class representative mostly of white, male, European voices? A critical theorist might also ask why certain types of students seem to find their way into low-ability curriculum tracks, again wanting to know why and how certain groups are affected by this.

One of the ways that critical theorists seek to slay the so-called cultural hegemony in the school is to question the rationalizations used by the school to justify its various actions so that any "truth" offered by the school cannot be accepted without analysis. Thus, when a school determines whether a student should be labeled "emotionally disturbed, learning disabled" or even gifted, the critical theorist questions the truth of these labels, reminding us that they are not real in nature but man-made and vulnerable to all kinds of problems and prejudices in judgment. Critical theorists observe that special education, although legitimated by statistical procedures and research findings, is not only ineffective at serving special needs students but actually leads to the further deterioration of their academic competence and life skills. The problem is that once given the label, the student becomes the label, irrespective of whether he or she really fits it. The label might provide access to various special instructional services but at the same time it also sends a psychological message to the students about their own low skills and about the school's low expectations toward their education.

In this way, scientific or rational explanations of social phenomena in schools are met with considerable skepticism by critical theorists. Science, as the argument goes, is a weapon of control. It uses tech-

TABLE 13–2   Percentage of Public Schools Assigning Each Book in English Class Grades 7–12, 1988

1.	*Romeo and Juliet*	Shakespeare	90%
2.	*Macbeth*	Shakespeare	81
3.	*Huckleberry Finn*	Twain	78
4.	*To Kill a Mockingbird*	Lee	74
5.	*Julius Caesar*	Shakespeare	71
6.	*The Pearl*	Steinbeck	64
7.	*The Scarlet Letter*	Hawthorne	62
8.	*Of Mice and Men*	Steinbeck	60
9.	*Lord of the Flies*	Golding	56
9.	*The Diary of a Young Girl*	Anne Frank	56
9.	*Hamlet*	Shakespeare	56
12.	*The Great Gatsby*	Fitzgerald	54
13.	*Animal Farm*	Orwell	51
13.	*Call of the Wild*	London	51
15.	*A Separate Peace*	Knowles	48
16.	*The Crucible*	Miller	47
16.	*The Red Badge of Courage*	Crane	47
18.	*Great Expectations*	Dickens	44
18.	*Our Town*	Wilder	44
20.	*A Tale of Two Cities*	Dickens	41

SOURCE: Applebee, A. (1989). A study of book-length works taught in high school English. Report Series 1.2. Albany: Center for the Learning and Teaching of Literature, State University of New York..

nical and often dazzling numerical methods to hide the social realities of oppression and inequities. It is not the neutral or nonpolitical method that it claims for itself. Rather, it is a highly ideological method that imposes rational solutions to social problems, disguises socially repressive conditions with technical showmanship, and sees imaginative and more subjective judgments as essentially unworkable. These alleged effects play into the radical belief that science itself is responsible for creating an amenable social arrangement for dominant economic groups. The role of standardized examinations in the school is a prime example. Standardized exams often hold the key to unlocking the doors to scholarships, to being admitted to well-known universities, and procuring various certifications. They are supported by a technical science of reliability and validity that reminds everyone of their fairness and objectivity, and that creates the impression of a level playing field. But the exam itself and the system in which it operates rarely gets interrogated for its role in blocking the pathways of access to knowledge for certain children from marginalized populations.

Some critical theorists also believe that the repressive force of the school is exercised in the economic arena. Much has been written by critical theorists about the alleged correspondence between the needs of capitalism and the methods of public schooling. The school, according to their argument, exists to serve capitalism. Specifically, it acts to stratify the labor force by creating low-level and high-level workers, and by socializing youth to accept a class-based system as an inevitable feature of living in America. The schools, in this way, not only produce the needed variance of skills for the workforce, including nonskilled workers, but also inculcate the habits and personality traits that must accompany such skills—such a docility for the low-level worker and self-direction for the high-level worker. As noted by Bowles and Gintis (1976), the heart of this reproduction is found in the social encounters of the school, encounters that "closely correspond to the social relations of dominance, subordination and motivation in the economic sphere" (p. 265).

One of the more interesting and popular scholars who has written on the topic of how schools might provide handicapping experiences to students from marginalized groups is Brazilian educator, Paulo Friere. As a social activist with Marxist leanings, Friere has worked to help historically oppressed people in Latin America to rise up against a system that had been holding them down. Freire (1982) formulated a theory that took a direct look at how the education of peasant-class children in Latin America was preoccupied with the transmission of facts and information that, at least to Freire's thinking, prevented these children from learning how to think well and to live politically and intellectually empowered lives. Freire argued that public schooling in Latin America often abided by what he called banking education, which he described as an instructional preoccupation with conveying facts and information to students in ways that stunted their thinking capacity. To learn through banking education meant to memorize information and to be the uncritical recipient of someone else's knowledge and words. Such a bias in learning gave the teacher dominance over the student, making the teacher "the teller" and the student "the receiver." Banking education, as Friere (1982) stated it, is "an act of depositing, in which the students are depositories and the teacher the depositor. Instead of communicating, the teacher issues communiqués and makes deposits which the students patiently receive, memorize and repeat" (p. 58). The main effect of banking education is that it keeps the students passive and quiet. Its main effects are in the null curriculum, in that it does not encourage dialogue or any use of language in the action of learning and therefore diminishes the opportunity for students to form the skills and dispositions needed to become socially-responsible and critically-minded citizens.

Although Freire was speaking of the manner in which indigent peasant-class children are socialized in Latin American schools, his idea can also be used as a critique against some of the ways that American children are taught, especially as it relates to the public education of minority and low-income children. One study found that the philosophical underpinnings for more conservative "banking education" agendas in the classroom were more likely to be supported by principals working in minority school settings as opposed to predominantly white settings (Hlebowitsh, 1993). Some researchers have openly stated the need for the instruction of disadvantaged youth to be less supportive of dialogue, to be less pupil-initiated, and to be more concerned with low-level questions (Medley, 1979; Rosenshine, 1979). As discussed earlier, low-level curriculum tracking experiences, which affect disproportionately high numbers of minority and low-income children, can themselves be interpreted as a form of banking education. Moreover, NCLB regulations, whose sanctions affect only Title 1 schools, often result in curriculum experiences for mostly low-income children that are immersed in the development of basic skills in reading and math.

THE LANGUAGE OF SCHOOLING

The function of language in the classroom seems, on the surface, to be a simple matter. Teachers usually teach using verbal language, and students are typically asked or required to respond verbally or in writing. The choice of language in the classroom seems simple as well. Because English is the most commonly spoken language in the United States, the classroom, in almost all settings, will be conducted in English. Language, however, has broader functions as well. Cazden (1988) has studied the nature of language in the classroom and has pointed out three distinct features of classroom language use. The first is obvious: language in the classroom does what we all expect it to do—it communicates manifest messages. The second feature of language in the classroom, however, speaks to the effects of the manifest messages and how they establish and maintain social relationships. The third is associated with the process by which individuals gain their self-identity. Cazden contends that this last feature of language is the least recognizable but perhaps the most important. We are all defined in large measure by the specific language we use. Our language clearly contributes to who we are, how others see us, and inevitably, how we see ourselves.

If we acknowledge that language carries at least three basic purposes (the communication of information, the establishment and maintenance of relationships with others, and the expression of one's identity), we have to admit that what we say, how we say it, what others say, and how we react to it all relate prominently to not only the function of communication, but also to the construction of social relations and self-identities. Language in this sense is more than communicating; language communicates something that will influence the social environment.

How, then, do we respond to the clear need to teach youth standard English in the school? If students use a different style of English (for instance, Black English), what should be the teacher's response? If teachers correct it, are they doing damage to the student's self-identity and to their social relations with the student? If they privilege it, are they contributing to the marginalization of the youths' language skills in a society where advancement depends on the use of standard English? The question should not necessarily be framed in binary terms—it is not a question of either teaching standard English or teaching nonstandard English, either teaching English or a foreign language. Rather the question should be: How we can teach children standard English and all the other forms of language beneficial to the life experiences of youth?

Bilingual Education

Bilingual education is perhaps the most misunderstood feature of modern schooling. Many citizens perceive that tax dollars are being spent to teach American children a foreign language instead of English. Such sentiments have been expressed by various politicians, especially conservatives who often speak of the dangers of bilingualism, of the linguistic schisms that it is likely to create in the nation, of the centrality of English to economic opportunity in the society, and of the historic decision to teach immigrant children in English.

Such views are commonly linked to an assimilationist position that embraces monolingual English instruction in public education. The American schools, the argument might follow, have historically aimed to ignore the native language of immigrant children in the interests of furthering the integration of such children into the society. Although there were some accommodations made in some schools toward dual language instruction in earlier times, especially during the late decades of the nineteenth century among German immigrants living in the Midwest, such instances were eventually reversed by the prevailing assimilationist impulses of the early twentieth century. The commitment to assimilation, in fact, caused some states to actually draft laws prohibiting the teaching of a foreign language in private and public schools alike—laws that were eventually struck down as unconstitutional (Ravitch, 1985). Many point to the vast assimilation project of twentieth-century America and argue that today's children should be treated no differently.

Given the linguistic diversity of the nation, the debate between advocates of English immersion and advocates of dual language instruction is still very much part of the political landscape of schooling. English is obviously the national language of the nation, but many people in America do not speak it or do not speak it very well. According to the U.S Census Bureau, seventeen percent of all Americans over the age of five, which is close to 45 million Americans, speak a language other than English in their homes. In 2000, 7 percent of all public school children were documented as English Language Learners (ELL)—that is, students whose native language is not English and whose difficulties with speaking, reading, and writing English were sufficient to deny them the opportunity to be successful in an English-only classroom. This ever-increasing level of linguistic variety in the nation, however, has not necessarily translated into a national call for dual language instruction; in fact, some of the evidence indicates quite the opposite. National polling data demonstrate that most Americans take an immersion view toward English language education in the school, believing that non-English speaking children should learn mostly in English. As depicted in Figure 13–3, this includes Hispanic parents and

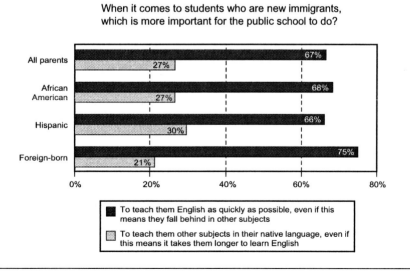

When it comes to students who are new immigrants, which is more important for the public school to do?

FIGURE 13–3 Learning to speak English as quickly as possible is seen as the cornerstone of assimilation, both as a practical necessity and as a symbol that a person intends to become an American. Parents fully reject the theory of bilingual education; parents who immigrated to the U.S. are even more opposed to it. Public Agenda 9/98.

foreign-born parents, who are often among the strongest supporters of English-only programs. Such polls, however, have been criticized for placing bilingual instruction in opposition to immersion, conveying to parents the false impression that bilingual instruction will not cultivate proficiency in English (Crawford, 1997). Krashen (1999), for instance, has asked parents to respond to views inherent in bilingual instruction, such as "developing literacy in the first language facilitates literacy development in English" and has found strong support for such views among them.

Federal legislation enacting bilingual education in America was passed in 1968. Federal monies for bilingual education were first authorized through Title VII of the Elementary and Secondary School Act of 1968, which is also known as the Bilingual Education Act. The bilingual programs emerging from this legislation were compensatory in nature, serving poor students born to families in which English was not the dominant language. The intention was to assist low-income children who were believed to be at an instructional disadvantage due to their limited English. The design of the program was not intended to further develop or strengthen the native cultural and linguistic background of the language minority student but to compensate for it. Part of the rationale for bilingual education also appealed to the view that non-English speaking children were suffering from low self-esteem that was brought about by the absence of their native language in the classroom.

Despite the presence of Title VII funds, the legal responsibility of school districts to offer bilingual programs was not formally resolved until 1974, in the Supreme Court ruling of *Lau vs. Nichols*. This case originated in 1970 as a class action suit that was brought by Chinese public school students against the San Francisco Unified School District. The essential complaint was that the school district had failed to provide bilingual education to Chinese pupils and that such a neglect represented a violation of the students' right to an equal educational opportunity. How could the Chinese students have an equal opportunity to learn, asserted the complainants, when the language used in the school was completely foreign to them? The school district openly admitted that only half of close to 3,000 students with limited English proficiency were receiving second language assistance, but that the right to an equal educational opportunity was not violated because all students were receiving the same curriculum, although some in a language foreign to them. All students, it was argued, come to school with advantages and disadvantages, including linguistic ones, and the school cannot be legally bound to provide special programs due to such differences.

The Supreme Court disagreed with this line of reasoning, believing that the Chinese students who were without bilingual assistance were effectively shut off from meaningful education due to their lack of English-speaking skills. Basing part of its decision on the Civil Rights Act of 1964, which bars discrimination because of race, color, or national origin in any program sponsored by the federal government, the Supreme Court stated that there is no equality of treatment merely by providing students with the same facilities, textbooks, teachers, and curriculum. The lesson of the ruling was straightforward: If a student arrives at school speaking a language other than English, it makes little sense to teach them to read and write in a language that they do not yet know or understand.

Lau v. Nichols mandated that schools had to get serious about helping students who were not yet proficient in English, but it did not mandate how it should be done. In elementary education, the clear implication of the ruling was that instruction in the child's first or native language for the initial years of education provided a foundation for learning to read and write in a second language. This would become the rationale for a national movement in bilingual education. Schools could also explore other educationally sound ways to deal with the English language deficits of their students, including (depending on the district's desires) programs that were heavy in their reliance on English or programs more in the direction of dual language or bilingual instruction (Ravitch, 1985).

Types of Bilingual Education

The dual language instructional model became especially prevalent in elementary schools and in regions of the country where large groups of students from one particular native language tradition (usually Spanish-speaking) were congregated. The most popular is known as transitional bilingual education, where students are subjected to dual language instruction and grade-appropriate materials prior to being mainstreamed into English-speaking classrooms. The intention here is to start with native language instruction in almost all the core subject areas and to slowly add English instruction until full mainstreaming into the regular classroom has been achieved. Usually transitional programs are divided into two types: early exit transitions and late exit transitions. The early exit program limits the exposure to bilingual instruction to about two years, while the late exit programs allows bilingual instruction to continue up until sixth grade (Baker, 1996). In America, the bilingual classroom is most often applied to Spanish-speaking children whose frequency in the school population allows entire classrooms to be designed with bilingual materials and activities. Contrary to popular opinion, the transitional model of bilingual education aims at assimilationist goals—it seeks to use the student's native language to teach English and to eventually make English the dominant language. In other words, transitional bilingual education uses bilingual means to carry out a monolingual result. Although some bilingual programs are now interested in teaching the continued maintenance or the advancement of the native language, transitional bilingual education offers what its name implies—a bilingual educational process designed to provide a transition from first language usage to English usage.

Another popular instructional approach used with students who have limited English proficiency is the English-as-a-Second Language (ESL) model. ESL is used mostly in settings where non-native speakers are from a wide range of linguistic backgrounds and where no one particular linguistic tradition has enough students to justify a transitional bilingual program. In an ESL model, English language learner (ELL) students are pulled out of their mainstream settings for a special instruction in English for part of the school day. This instruction takes on what is known as a "Sheltered English" approach. The ESL teacher carefully manages the vocabulary and language used to help teach the regular curriculum to the ELL students. Thus, the students use the resources of the ESL classroom to work on assignments related to the math, science, social studies, and language arts curriculum in the regular mainstreamed classroom. In this way, ESL typically operates in an English-only context that offers limited supplemental experiences in sheltered English, and as the case may be, sheltered math and sheltered science. Although it is officially a minority language program, ESL is clearly an approach favored by those who argue for English immersion. In fact, ESL is sometimes known as "structured immersion," because ESL students will usually spend a greater part of the day with their English speaking peers in a mainstream setting than in the ESL classroom. Figure 13–4 illustrates the difference in the amount of English used in a structured immersion program, such as ESL, and early as well as late exit bilingual education programs. The higher frequency of English utterances found in early-exit over late-exit programs is probably the result of the compression that the teachers in early-exit programs might feel to move the student along more quickly in English.

We should remember that the aim of both transitional bilingual education and ESL education is to take a student who is, in most cases, monolingual in a foreign language and to replace it with a proficiency in English. In this sense, both transitional bilingual and ESL programs are known as "subtractive" approaches because they see the native language as a bridge to English proficiency, and are not concerned with maintaining the native language once the student becomes an English speaker. The Department of Education (Ramirez, Yuen, & Ramsey, 1991) examined each of the three different "subtractive" approaches and found that there were no differences in the measured performances of the students on tests of English language proficiency, reading, and mathematics. The Department of

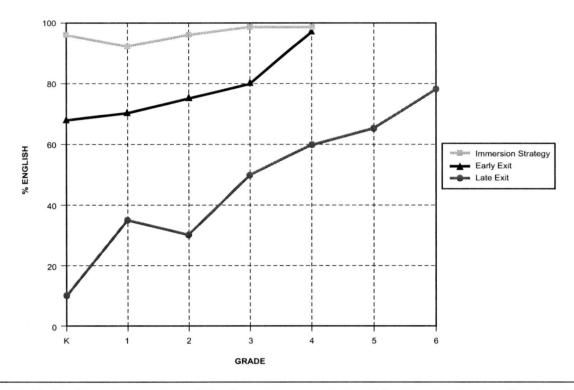

FIGURE 13–4 **Mean Proportion of Teacher Utterances in English.** SOURCE: Cazden, Courtney B. (1992). Language minority education in the United States: Implications of the Ramirez Report (http://www.ncela.gwu.edu/pubs/ncrcdsll/epr3/).

Education chose to interpret the finding of the report as an affirmation of its policy to encourage a variety of language minority language education programs. The fact that there were no differences between the programs testified to the fact that each could be viewed as equally effective and that school districts should decide how to configure their own language minority programs.

Schools can and often do combine bilingual and ESL resources (Krashen, 1999). A school might adopt a policy that uses a late-exit transitional program to teach all the core subjects to ELL students, combined with an ESL program as a supplement, and full mainstreaming in art, music, and physical education. After a year or so, math and science could move into a sheltered ESL setting, and then one year later into a mainstreamed setting. At the same time, everything else also moves either into a sheltered ESL approach or the mainstreamed classroom. Eventually full mainstreaming is achieved. Several have argued that once full mainstreaming is reached, the bilingual program should then turn its attention toward the further development of the student's first language or heritage language.

Interestingly, in 1998, voters in the State of California overwhelmingly passed a law, known as Proposition 227, which mandated that all ELL students be instructed in a sheltered ESL-style program. This meant the demise of most transitional bilingual education programs in California. Proposition 227 also mandated that ELL students should be enrolled in a sheltered English program, in most cases, for no longer than a year. The law, however, allowed for some waivers. Parents could ask for a waiver if they believed that their child (who has to be at least 10 years old) could learn English more effectively in an alternative program, or if their child, at any age, had special needs that could be better served in an alternative program. This has allowed some bilingual education programs to remain

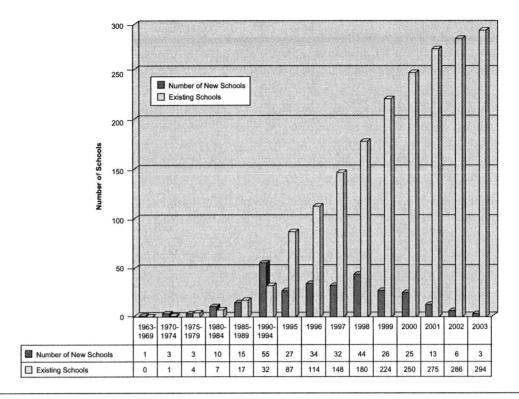

	1963-1969	1970-1974	1975-1979	1980-1984	1985-1989	1990-1994	1995	1996	1997	1998	1999	2000	2001	2002	2003
Number of New Schools	1	3	3	10	15	55	27	34	32	44	26	25	13	6	3
Existing Schools	0	1	4	7	17	32	87	114	148	180	224	250	275	286	294

FIGURE 13–5   The Rise of Dual Language Schools in the United States. Taken from Baker, C. (2006). *Foundations of bilingual education and bilingualism. Philadelphia: Multilingual Matters, Ltd*, p. 236.

vital in districts where there is parent support for them. But with close to 2 million ELL students, California's decision to embrace a program dedicated to structured immersion is notable. Some legal scholars see the California law as a violation of the Supreme Court decision of *Lau v. Nichols*, but because the law mandates sheltered English, it has thus far been upheld by a circuit court as constitutional.

Other less popular approaches to bilingual education take an "additive" approach, by aiming to teach students proficiency in two languages. Such programs teach everything in two languages, making them appropriate for both language minority and language majority youth. One additive approach, known as "two-way" bilingual education, teaches both the majority and minority languages to both language majority and language minority children. For instance, a two-way program in Spanish and English might teach in each language on alternate days or alternate instructional periods to all of the children in the school. Here the objective is for both language majority and language minority students to "add" a language to their communicative repertoire. Of course, such a program requires completely fluent bilingual teachers and dual language sets of curriculum materials. In states like Texas, California, Florida, and New York, where Spanish may be spoken widely in numerous communities and where one can encounter the language in various contexts, including in the popular culture, "two-way" bilingual education makes quite a bit of sense. Because they may not appeal to all parents, two-way bilingual schools are often designed as magnet schools or charter schools. As shown in Figure 13–5, two-way bilingual education has grown in popularity over the years and is typically done in a Spanish/English setting.

Continued Resistance

If the reasoning behind bilingual education seems sound, why does there continue to be so much resistance to it? Part of the problem turns on an argument that returns us to our "melting pot" versus "salad bowl" metaphors. The assimilationist nature of the "melting pot" position calls for an immersion approach that asks teachers to teach youth mostly, if not exclusively, in English, as has been done historically with a wide range of immigrant populations (where the loss of the mother tongue has been the norm). "Salad bowl" advocates, on the other hand, claim that initial instruction in a native language will not only assist in the eventual development of English, but will also grant student skills in another language that can be used in other social and cultural contexts. Although the research on the effects of bilingual education is conflicting, there is an overall belief, supported by the federal government and the courts, that children should be initially instructed in their native languages as a way to assist their development in English. Advocates of bilingual education are certain that it carries social and cognitive advantages for students and obvious nationalistic advantages for the society, especially in relation to international economic markets where multilingual competence is important. Much of the debate revolving around the effects of bilingual education is complicated by the need to control income, parent education, and immigration factors, and by the penchant to limit the judgment of bilingual education to achievement in the English language, ignoring important data on self-esteem, moral development, social adjustment, and employability.

SUMMARY

Public schooling in America has always had to find some way to build a common nation out of multiple ethnic, religious, and racial perspectives. Finding a common culture, with a common language, common knowledge base, and common value system has not been an easy project for American education. The assimilationist project of the twentieth century embraced a "melting pot" approach, a process by which all Americans were melded from many forms into a uniform one. In recent decades, increasing attention has been directed at finding a way to better balance a common culture with the culture and ethnic heritage of the student. The design of multicultural education approaches has resulted in "particularistic" forms of multicultural thinking, which lean in the direction of ethnocentrism, to "multiple-perspective" forms, which lean in the direction of fully integrated diversity. A similar situation has prevailed in bilingual education. The Supreme Court has ruled that ELL students must be given some language assistance, but the extent of this support is widely debated. The lines are still drawn between advocates of structured immersion, also known as "sheltered English," and advocates of extended dual-language education.

REFERENCES

Addams, J. (1908). Immigrants and their children. In Ellen C. Lagemann (Ed.), *Jane Addams on Education.* New York: Teachers College Press, 1985.

Apple, M. (1990). *Ideology and Curriculum.* London: Routledge and Kegan Paul.

Asante, M. K. (2000). The Afro-centric idea in education. In Eduardo Duarte and Stacey Smith, (Eds.), *Foundational perspectives in multicultural education.* New York: Longman.

Baker, C. (2006). *Foundations of bilingual education and bilingualism.* Philadelphia: Multilingual Matters Ltd.

Banks, J. A. and McGee-Banks, C. A. (2006). Multicultural Education: Issues and Perspectives. New York: Wiley.

Bowles, S., & Gintis, H. (1976). *Schooling in capitalist America.* New York: Basic Books.

Cazden, C. (1988). *Classroom discourse.* Portsmouth, NH: Heinemann.

Crawford, J. (1997). *Best evidence: Research foundations of the Bilingual Education Act.* Washington, DC: National Clearinghouse for Bilingual Education.

Dewey, J. (1916). *Democracy and education.* New York: The Free Press.

Freire, P. (1982). *The pedagogy of the oppressed.* New York: The Continuum Publishing Co.

Geortz, C. (1973). *The interpretation of cultures.* New York: Basic Books.

Gibson, R. (1986). *Critical theory and education.* London: Hodder and Stoughton.

Giroux, H. (1983). *Theory and resistance: A pedagogy for the opposition.* New York: Bergin Garvey.

Gutmann, A. (2000). Challenges of multiculturalism in democratic education. In Eduardo Duarte and Stacey Smith (Eds.), *Foundational perspectives in multicultural education.* New York: Longman.

Hlebowitsh, P. S. (1993). Philosophical orientations on the school curriculum. *NASSP Bulletin* 77(557):92–104.

Howe, H. (1993). *Thinking about our kids.* New York: Free Press.

Krashen, S. (1999). *Bilingual education: Arguments for and (bogus) arguments against.* www.ourworld.compuserve.com.

Lau v. Nichols 414 U.S. 563 (1974).

McLaren, P. (1994). *Life in schools.* New York: Longman.

McLaren, P. (2000). White terror and oppositional agency: Toward a critical multiculturalism. In Eduardo Duarte and Stacey Smith (Eds.), *Foundational perspectives in multicultural education.* New York: Longman.

Medley, D. (1979). The effectiveness of teaching. In P. L. Petersen and H. J. Walberg, *Research on Teaching.* Berkeley, CA: McCutchan.

National Center for Education Statistics. (1999). *NAEP civics: Report card for the nation.* Washington, DC: U.S. Department of Education.

National Center for Education Statistics. (2002). *The nation's report card: U.S history, 2001.* Washington, DC: U.S. Department of Education.

Patrick, J. (2000). Multicultural education and the civic mission of schools. In William G. Wraga and Peter S. Hlebowitsh (Eds.), *Research review for school leaders.* Mahwah, NJ: Lawrence Erlbaum Associates.

Public Agenda. (1998). *A lot to be thankful for: What parents want children to learn about America.* New York: Public Agenda.

Ramirez, J. D., Yuen, S. D., & Ramsey, D. R. (1991). *Longitudinal study of structured immersion strategy, early-exit and late-exit transitional bilingual education programs for language minority children.* San Mateo: Aguirre International.

Ravitch, D. (1985). Politicalization and the schools: The case of bilingual education. In J. W. Noll, *Taking sides.* Guilford, CT: Dushkin Publishing Group.

Ravitch, D. (1990). Multiculturalism: E pluribus plures. In K. Ryan and J. M. Cooper, (Eds.), *Kaleidoscope: Readings in education.* Boston: Houghton-Mifflin Co.

Rosenshine, B. (1979). Content, Time and Direct Instruction. In *Research on teaching: concepts, findings and implications,* P. L. Peterson and H. J. Walberg (eds.). Berkeley, CA: McCutchan Publishing Company.

Schlesinger, A. (1991). *The disuniting of America.* New York: Norton.

Schmidt, P. (25 March, 1992). New survey discerns deep divisions among U.S. youths on race relations. *Education Week.*

Schnaiberg, L. (22 January, 1997). Oakland Board revises 'ebonies' resolution. *Education Week.*

Stotsky, S. (1999). *Losing our language: How multicultural classroom instruction is undermining our children's ability to read, write and reason.* New York: The Free Press.

KEY QUESTIONS

1. What are the curricular consequences of a "melting pot" outlook on common learning?
2. How might you deal with the need to deal with common issues in a diverse classroom environment?
3. Explain how assimilating and diversifying processes exist in a kind of partnership.
4. Explain how a multiple perspective approach to multicultural education might be used in a high school history class or in the teaching of mathematics in the elementary school.
5. An African-American scholar recently wrote that "naturally, the person of African descent should be centered in his or her historical experiences as an African," (Asante, 2000). Do you agree with this assertion? If so, does the same principle apply to students from ethnic backgrounds, such as Irish Americans, Chinese Americans, or Italian Americans?
6. McLaren (2000) has referred to the effort to merge diversity with assimilationist goals as "conservative multiculturalism." Naming Schlesinger and Ravitch as conservative multiculturalists, McLaren states that such a position "uses the term diversity to cover up the ideology of assimilation. . . . In this view, ethnic groups are reduced to 'add-ons' to the dominant culture. Before you can be added on to the dominant culture, you must first adopt a consensual view of culture and learn to accept the essentially Euro-American patriarchal norms of the 'host' country" (p. 217). How would you respond to McLaren's analysis?
7. How can banking education result in the oppression of youth?
8. What are the essential assumptions of critical theory?
9. Why might a critical theorist criticize the dominance of Shakespearean readings in a high school English class?
10. What do you think of the view supported by critical theorists that equates schooling with preparation for a preordained place in the socio-economic status quo?
11. In your view, how should the school handle the education of language minority children?
12. What is the difference between an additive and a subtractive approach to bilingual education?
13. What are the potential advantages and disadvantages of a two-way bilingual program?
14. Explain the issues involved in the *Lau. v. Nichols* case.
15. What are your views on the decision of the California voters to pass Proposition 227?

RESEARCH EXERCISES

1. In *Losing Our Language*, Stotsky (1999) analyzed the 'ethnic' content of popular basal reading books used in elementary schools and found that non-European content represented, in some cases, as much as 100 percent of all the total foreign content in the readers. Conduct a similar content analysis of a reading program in a local school.

2. Analyze the ethno/mathematics or ethno/science curriculum materials available for use in school districts against your perception of what it means to respond to diversity concerns in the curriculum.

3. Observe a classroom and analyze its treatment of multiculturalism against the views discussed in the chapter (particularistic multicultural, contributions approach, ethnic/additive approach, transformative approach).

4. Research the manner in which bilingual education is handled in a school or school district, and examine it against its theoretical design.

5. Conduct a case study analysis of a two-way dual language program.

6. Use Freire's idea of banking education to analyze classrooms from fundamentally different class-based backgrounds.

7. Observe an ESL classroom and a transitional bilingual classroom and conduct a frequency count of the number of English utterances heard in each setting. What do the results tell you about the design of each program?

8. Here are the results of a national survey done with school age parents on the topic of multiculturalism. Conduct a similar survey in a school or school district.

Parents do not view lessons that emphasize the history of different groups as a problem, but parents from all groups recoil at hypothetical examples of lessons that seem to encourage dicisiveness among Americans. African Americans are most likely to believe the schools still do not give sufficent attention to minorities.

Are the schools paying too much attention to the harm done to African Americans in U.S. history, not enough attention, or are things about right?

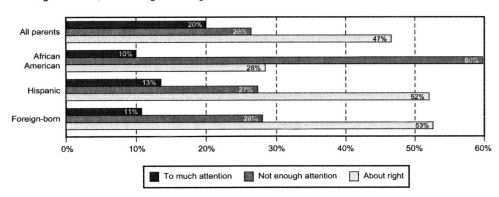

SOURCE: Public Agenda 9/98

How close does the following statement come to your own view:

In the past, the schools unfairly overlooked the contributions that minorities made to U.S. history.

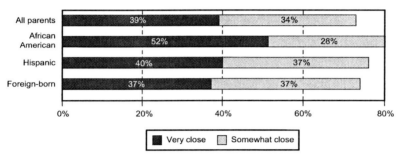

SOURCE: Public Agenda 9/98

Imagine a teacher who is teaching American history to an all-black class of students. If the lessons focused almost completely on the African American experience and struggle, do you think the students would benefit, that they would suffer, or would it make little difference?

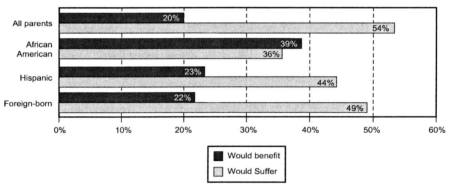

SOURCE: Public Agenda 9/98

If a teacher taught that America is a fundamentally racist country, would this upset you, would you be somewhat concerned, or would you not take it too seriously?

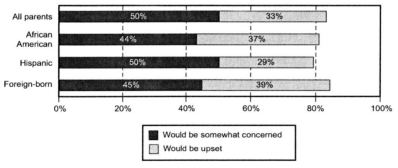

SOURCE: Public Agenda 9/98

CHAPTER 14

School Reform and the Shifting Sociopolitical Context Since Mid-Century

Since at least mid-century, the American schools have been beset by changes that some scholars have characterized as swings on a reform pendulum (Tanner, 1986; Goodlad, 1966). Each successive reform period has been influenced by shifting sociopolitical moods that have produced short-lived flurries of school reform, many of which would be later contradicted in ensuing periods of reform. When school reform is moved by prevailing sociopolitical conditions, it runs the risk of embracing a logic tied to narrow nationalistic causes, as opposed to broadly conceived professional ones. This often leaves the school vulnerable to new fashions that follow from new sociopolitical imperatives. The effect is that one extreme is undone by a counterextreme, which is itself undone (in time) by yet another counterextreme. The leading school reform ideas associated with the early Cold War period in the United States, for instance, were fundamentally different from, if not at odds with, the leading school reform ideas that were generated during the tumultuous period of social strive that marked the mid- and late-1960s.

The nature of school reform in America has clearly followed general sociopolitical trends. This was most obvious during the post-Sputnik era, but it has occurred with consistency well into the 1990s. When discussing school reform, we refer to national movements that have led to practical changes in the ways that teachers dealt with their students in classrooms. All of the major trends discussed in this chapter received quite a bit of support from external agencies (the government or private foundation), and/or received headline treatment in the news media. In almost all cases, the reforms were practical movements that had a constituency in the school and a lively presence in the professional literature. They are described here by decade, but the movements were fluid and often overlapped between the decades.

EDUCATION DURING THE COLD WAR AND SPACE RACE CRISIS: THE 1950s

In the early 1950s, curriculum reform was shaped by a "back-to-basics" retrenchment that surfaced mainly from conservative forces that gained strength during the early stages of the Cold War. Although there were many influential thinkers at the time, the work of Professor Arthur Bestor (1953; 1956) and Admiral Hyman Rickover (1959) was especially instrumental in getting the schools to accept this reductionist plan. Bestor was a professor of history who took an interest in arguing for the restoration of a strict academic curriculum in the public school, and Rickover was a practicing admiral in the United States Navy who wrote extensively of the failing of American education and who showed considerable fondness for the bipartite model of schooling used in Europe.

Buoyed by a nationalistic fervor to compete with the Soviets in all realms of global domination, Bestor and Rickover submitted what they viewed as a no-nonsense reform directive for the schools. The approach they advocated was practical and straightforward: focus the schools' program on the singular goal of disciplined intellectual training; reduce the course work in the high school to the core academic disciplines; relegate the role of vocational studies, art, music, and physical education in the unified school setting to an inferior status; and focus the early years of schooling on the inculcation of basic skills.

Bestor and Rickover represented a strong conservative reaction against the progressivism of the earlier decade. During the 1940s, the public schools had embraced a wide range of progressive initiatives, including a commitment to curriculum experimentation and a regard for life activities in teaching and learning. Bestor and Rickover were dismayed by these events and believed that the time had come for the school to recover its subject-centered core, to fulfill its overtly academic function and to cease its practice of attempting to build learning experiences around student's needs and interests. They were convinced that the schools were advancing an anti-intellectualism that would leave the country vulnerable to the exploits of its enemies. Because of the misguided progressivism of an earlier period, they claimed, America's status as a world power was showing signs of erosion. Their solution was to restore rigorous intellectual training in the school. In Rickover's (1959) words, "The educational process must be one of collecting factual knowledge to the limit of the [learner's] capacity. . . . Nothing can really make it fun" (p. 61). This was clearly a movement that aimed to revitalize the role of disciplinary knowledge in the curriculum. The stakes were high because Bestor and Rickover did their best to remind everyone that the very livelihood of the nation was dependent on the serious turn toward academic education that their views represented.

Rickover and Bestor had no trouble finding receptive audiences for their views. Stunned by the Soviets' advancements in space and their successful launch of the first satellite (Sputnik I), legislators aimed to support an unprecedented curriculum revision effort in the national security related areas of mathematics and science education. A general "get tough" attitude pervaded the emerging reform direction. The major changes included the strengthening of graduation and curriculum standards, the provision of special services for the gifted and talented, and the elevation of the doctrine of curriculum disciplinary as the centerpiece of school reform.

Clearly the changes wrought in the schools during the post-Sputnik era period were partly shaped by the demands that Bestor and Rickover raised during the early 1950s. The nature of the new reform, for instance, was palpably discipline-centered. Congress authorized a massive amount of money to the National Science Foundation (NSF), encouraging its involvement in the development of several national curriculum programs in the areas of science and math. Given the Soviet achievements in space, the American schools were faced with a national mandate to improve mathematics and science education and to sharpen the emphasis on the education of the nation's most gifted children. This gave the NSF an entry into educational reform. The NSF, for instance, not only sponsored the development of actual curricula in high school biology, chemistry, physics, and math, but it also financed a nation-wide network of teacher training institutes used to immerse teachers into the methodology of teaching these new curricula.

The NSF-sponsored programs and the wider effort to move the school toward subject-centered traditions took their conceptual lead from Jerome Bruner's *The Process of Education*, a report partly funded by the NSF (Tanner & Tanner, 1995). Bruner's work espoused a new manifesto for curriculum reform, an idea known as the "structure of a discipline" doctrine. To Bruner (1960), the term "structure" was representative of all the fundamental ideas and generalizations that comprised subject matter. "To learn structure," he contended, "is to learn how things are related" (p. 7). But the "structure" to which Bruner referred was discipline-specific; it was all about finding the structure within disciplinary lines rather than across them. Bruner also promoted something even more provocative. He asserted that each discipline was comprised of a concentration of ideas that could be taught in some intellectually honest way to any age group. In the words of Bruner (1960), "Intellectual activity is anywhere the same, whether at the frontier of knowledge or in a third-grade classroom" (p. 14).

This kind of thinking, coming from one of America's most distinguished psychologists, helped to widen the path of access to the high school curriculum for scientists and other scholar-specialists. Because the "structure of a discipline" put a great premium on discipline-specific skills and reconstructed the nature of the learner in the image of the scholar-specialist, the high school curriculum found itself under unprecedented levels of involvement from scholar specialists. The result was an aggrandizement of the abstract, the disciplinary, and the technical in the curriculum, as well as the demotion of learning tied to life experiences.

Another development central to the curriculum initiatives of the post-Sputnik climate was the passage of the National Defense Education Act of 1958. The purpose of the legislation was to "ensure trained manpower of sufficient quality and quality to meet the national defense needs of the United States." During the first four years of its operations, the NDEA authorized over 1 billion dollars worth of aid to the schools, funneling it through ten different title grants. Title 3 (a financial assistance program for science, mathematics, and foreign language instruction) received the lion's share of the appropriations. The bulk of this money went toward the purchase of large amounts of equipment and materials for mathematics and science instruction, as well as toward the purchase of the new teaching technology in foreign language instruction. No money went toward the funding of education in the arts or the humanities, as these areas simply did not fit into the war preparedness mode that characterized the NDEA's mission.

Another significant statement on the reform of the school was authored by one of the most influential educational statespersons of the time, James B. Conant. Conant, who had achieved national visibility as the president of Harvard University and the U.S. Ambassador to Germany, had a long history of involvement in education. After leaving his post as Ambassador, Conant was commissioned by the Carnegie Corporation to oversee a study of the American high school. The fruit of his labor was the *American High School Today* (1960), a work that outlined several basic recommendations for the reform of the public high school. Essentially, his report was friendly to the American comprehensive high school design. Although there were considerable pressures at the time to adopt the dual model of schooling used in Europe, which separated academic students from vocational students at preadolescence, Conant (1960) stood by the American model of education and maintained that a unified school could provide all youth with a general academic education, an individualized elective program, accelerated academic training for the college bound, and a first-rate vocational education program for the non-college bound. In this sense, one could argue that Conant saved the American school from falling prey to the dual system used in Europe, a change that was being promoted vigorously by H. G. Rickover and that even found its way to the floor of debate in Congress (Tanner & Tanner, 1995).

The success to Conant's proposal had to do with the manner in which he layered his thinking about the comprehensive high school with a concern for academics and the most academically inclined. He put a strong conservative edge on his proposal by recommending that the general education core of studies in the high school consist of traditional academic studies. There was no talk about interdisciplinary insight or socio-civic traditions in the core, although Conant did promote a senior-level course in Problems of Democracy. In regard to the academically inclined, Conant wanted to see advanced placement work available and more widespread use of ability groups on a subject-by-subject basis. In English class, for example, Conant advocated an XYZ arrangement of classes: one for the most able, another for the middle ground, and yet another for the so-called slowest learners. Besides endorsing ability groups, Conant recommended that aptitude tests be used more often, that class ranking of students and academic honors lists be kept, and that special counseling be provided for the most academically skilled.

Clearly the sociopolitical climate of the Cold War and space race affected the nature of school reform. It highlighted the need for the school to be attentive to the education of the academically able, to stress the importance of reform in the defense sensitive areas of math and science, and to maintain that the most empowering forms of learning were conducted in subject-centered contexts.

The nationalistic urges to use the school for the purposes of military and technological domination, however, eventually gave way to a new set of priorities, anchored in a new sociopolitical condition. Within a decade's time, a shift was witnessed away from the discipline-centered curricula of the Cold War period to the "humanizing" reforms of the late 1960s. The change was supported by a political climate that called attention to society's most pervasive problems (poverty, crime, civil rights, and drug abuse). These new conditions would call for new reforms in the schools.

HUMANIZING THE SCHOOLS IN A PERIOD OF SOCIAL PROTEST: THE 1960S

As the international crisis that surrounded the Sputnik spectacle began to abate, public interest took little time turning to the domestic front. Among the items at the top of the agenda was the question of racial separatism in the schools and its association with lost educational opportunity for minority groups. The federal government inaugurated a "War on Poverty" that marshaled an array of legislative and financial strategies designed to break the back of poverty and racial isolation in the society. The main tool for the government's plan was the public school. Thus, the emphasis in the school was no longer placed on the academically talented. The new educational gospel being preached spoke to the needs of the educationally disadvantaged. Moreover, the threat to the nation was no longer seen as coming from the outside, in the form of Soviet imperialism, but from the inside, in the form of civil strife, urban violence, abject poverty, and student protest. The school could not reasonably stand on a belief in the subject-centered curriculum. The times were calling for new levels of sensitivity to learner's needs and interests, and new child-centered approaches toward school reform were gaining ground.

This new period of reform had its share of unconventional views. Radical critics of education, whose proposals ranged from abolishing compulsory education to framing a more humanistic pedagogy, garnered an impressive readership in the popular press and in the popular bookseller markets. Many of these thinkers abided by a romantic-naturalist view of the world, taking their lead from the work of Rousseau and espousing the need for the classroom and school to be more sensitive to the felt needs and interests of the individual child. In 1970, the passions of this romantic fire were fanned with the publication of Charles Silberman's *Crisis in the Classroom* (1970). Receiving headline treatment in major newspapers and journals, Silberman's study portrayed the American schools as mindless, joyless, and oppressive, and his solution, not surprisingly, was to make schooling more interesting, joyful, and humane.

The appearance of a new radical/romantic confederacy in American education was very clearly a sign of the times. The abstract discipline-centered initiatives that grew out of the space race left a lingering foul taste on the American educational palate. A counterreform was now in order—one that was marked by the assertion of humanity, openness, social purpose, and individual relevance in the school.

The major figures emerging from the romantic left in American education included A. S. Neill (in England), John Holt, George Dennison, Herbert Kohl, Paul Goodman, Edgar Friedenberg, and Ivan Illich. Originating from literary circles, this radical/romantic group built its message with bitter tomes of social protest. There were essentially two main themes that provided the common ground. One theme maintained a deep hostility toward what was viewed as a profligate society and grim educational establishment. The other major theme expressed a romantic faith in the self-educating forces of a free and unhampered childhood and adolescence. Because the school, in the language of this genre, crippled the process of learning, destroyed the dignity of students, and mutilated the natural instincts for curiosity, a "do your own thing" ideology emerged.

The titles of the books and articles published by the radical/romantic element emphasized the dehumanizing and iniquitous nature of the educational establishment. Consider the following: Jonathan Kozol's *Death at an Early Age: The Destruction of the Hearts and Minds of Negro Children in the Boston Public Schools* (1967), Paul Goodman's *Compulsory Mis-education* (1964), and Nat Hentoff's *Our Children Are Dying* (1966). Charles Silberman (1970a; 1970b) published several critical essays of schooling in the *Atlantic Monthly* under the titles, "Murder in the Classroom" and "How the Public Schools Kill and Mutilate Minds." These writings were mostly about how the American school system had lost its humanizing soul.

As far as the school was concerned, the humanizing backlash of the 1960s manifested mainly as emotional protest. Unlike the Sputnik period, there was no systematically developed curriculum reform program. In fact, it was not until 1967 that the first signs of practical action began to make its way into the humanizing movement. These ideas were imported from England, drawn from the British Plowden Committee's report, *Children and their Primary Schools* (Central Advisory Council for Education, 1967), and came to be known as open education.

In its application, open education clearly meant different things to different people. It did not have well-articulated goals and never commanded the kind of foundational and governmental support that characterized many of the reform initiatives ten years earlier. In attempting to define the open education phenomenon, Charles Silberman (1973) maintained that it was not a model or set of techniques to be slavishly imitated or followed, but an approach to instruction that encompassed a "set of attitudes and convictions about the nature and purposes of teaching and learning . . ." (p. xix). Others were willing to try to outline the principles central to the operation of open education: "First, the room . . . is decentralized. Second, the children are free. . . . Third, the environment is rich in learning resources. . . . Fourth, the teacher and his aides work most of the time with individual children (Gross & Gross, 1970, p. 71).

Such a characterization described some of the more common manifestations of open education, but it failed to point to specific curriculum goals and procedures. Not surprisingly, the open classroom came to be considered "open" according to any number of criteria. A school could promote its commitment to openness by abolishing ability groups, by encouraging children to move about the classroom at will, by knocking down classroom walls to foster more physical freedom, by designing self-initiated learning units in a departmentalized classroom, by reorganizing the curriculum into more integrated units, or any combination of the above. The open classroom sadly had little more to offer than the idea of openness; this made it vulnerable to some of the laissez-faire romanticism that was expressed at the time. The overall practical effect in the classroom during this period was a recognition of the child in the teaching/learning equation and a proliferation of child-centered views that supported the place of unplanned experiences in the school. At the secondary school and university levels, this same mentality led to a multiplicity of electives in the curriculum, justified as relevant to the student's interests.

Clearly, the late 1960s represented an effort to bring the learner back into the discourse on the school curriculum. Years of neglect during the Cold War period, which glorified the subject matter and framed the learner as the passive recipient of the knowledge inherent in the subject matter, made such a movement virtually inevitable. Similarly, the earlier stress placed on math and science led to later concerns over the humanities, while the earlier emphasis on the academically inclined led to new concerns about the disadvantaged. In other words, the excesses of the earlier period of reform set the conditions for a subsequent correction. Unfortunately, this correction generated its own set of new excesses. Thus, it would only be a matter of time before the child-centered themes of the late 1960s would themselves be undone by a new counterreform. On the horizon was a new wave of reform designed to bring the school "back to basics," back to the familiar ground of the subject-centered curriculum; open classrooms, open schools, and alternative education would soon become anachronisms.

BACK-TO-BASICS AND THE EDUCATIONAL RETRENCHMENT: THE 1970S

The problems that beset the American economy during the 1970s created a conservative financial climate that threatened the fiscal budgets of several social institutions, including the public schools. Encumbered with a growing inflation and unemployment rate, the United States economy showed few optimistic signs. The taxpaying public responded to these circumstances by displaying an increasing reluctance to invest in comprehensive educational programs. This air of economic conservatism inevitably led to the promotion of cost-saving measures in public education. Efficiency values and productivity models were embraced as appropriate responses to the challenges of classroom instruction.

It was in this climate that the "back to basics" movement was unveiled. The renewed effort to devote the school curriculum to a strict basic skills education was accompanied by a new regard for accountability, performance assessment, and competency-based instruction. Back-to-basics also meant that the curriculum would be reduced to its least common denominator, that fundamental literacy and mathematics would take priority in the curriculum and that other aspects of the curriculum, notably the arts, writing, and more interdisciplinary approaches to learning, would take a back seat. "Back to basics" also valued whatever was most easily measured. It set its sights on minimum standards and advanced a skill-drill instructional mentality to achieve these standards.

Basic skill achievement was, in effect, a cost-saving idea. The schools would have to worry less about providing a comprehensive and resourceful education and focus instead on the fundamental processes. Competency-based strategies toward instruction seemed ideally suited for this because they could itemize exactly what needed to be taught and evaluate each component of the curriculum for mastery. A competency-based reading program, for instance, created a highly specific set of competencies, sequenced the competencies according to grade levels, directed the teacher to teach directly to each competency, and regulated each student's movement through the curriculum with mastery tests for each competency. The result was a highly skill-based school experience marked by low-level activities. What could not be effectively measured was not taught. Skills in oral communication, in writing, in argumentation, in problem solving, in cross-disciplinary insight, and in research skills, to name just a few, simply were not part of the instructional picture.

This period of reform also did not do much to advance the professional development of educators. Given the prevalence of competency-based systems of teaching, teachers had little room to exercise their intelligence and creativity. The most important judgments were already made for them; all they had to do was follow directions and issue the worksheets and skill-based activities already developed for them. It was in this climate, in fact, that "teacher proof" materials came into favor. These materials consisted of programmed learning workbooks, some varieties of computer assisted instruction, and highly prescriptive learning packages that scripted what teachers should say and do. Their orientation was to find a way to protect the curriculum from the teacher; hence, the term "teacher-proof."

Much of this retrenchment mentality was also fueled by nationally-visible studies that looked at the limits rather than to the possibilities of schooling. Christopher Jencks' *Inequality* (1972) was perhaps the most widely read. The focus of his report was to question whether school significantly affected economic differences and cognitive differences among school children. The central finding was that schools did not help to equalize the incomes of children, and that any effort to use the school for this end would be wasted. Jencks' further maintained that family background characteristics of the students were far more important in the development of cognitive skill than anything that the school did. This last proposition led to the popular conclusion that schools made no difference, which itself turned out to be a virtual command for educational divestiture. Because the public school was believed to be marginal to the economic and cognitive lives of children, alternative school options and earlier work opportunities were given more consideration and weight.

Many of the alternative school ideas were discussed and promoted in a series of federally-sponsored commissions' reports, including the report of the National Commission on the Reform of Secondary Education (1973), the report of the President's Science Advisory Committee (1974), and the report of the National Panel on High School and Adolescent Education (1976). Each work sought to narrow the responsibilities of the high school by advocating the workplace and other non-school settings as viable alternatives for education. To the panels and commissions of the 1970s, the reform emphasis was on reduction. An earlier compulsory school-leaving age, a shortened school day and year, a narrowed curriculum offering, and a commitment to sundry alternative schooling arrangements were among the salient recommendations coming from the national reports.

Like the basic-skills education initiative that was pushed during the early 1950s, the retrenchment period of the 1970s eventually evolved into a pursuit of academic excellence and an effort to structure the goals of schooling according to the wishes and demands of the military-industrial complex. In 1983, influenced by the *A Nation at Risk* report, public education was once again subjected to a spate of changes that resembled many of the conditions witnessed during the post-Sputnik period. As a strongly-worded report with considerable political backing, *A Nation at Risk* had a commanding presence and eventually lit the fuse for an explosion of another round of reform ideas.

ACADEMIC EXCELLENCE IN A PERIOD OF TECHNOLOGICAL AND ECONOMIC MOBILIZATION: THE 1980S

The 1980s brought the schools full circle, back to the subject-centered traditions that were popular during the 1950s. Generally speaking, the times called for a "get tough" approach to the curriculum that was modeled along familiar Cold War themes. The school, for instance, was asked to take on tougher graduate standards, to reaffirm the importance of the traditional academic curriculum, to renew its concern for the so-called gifted and talented, to examine itself in relation to schooling in other advanced nations, to stress the importance of mathematics and science education, and in direct contrast to what was valued only one decade earlier, to emphasize the importance of a longer school day and longer school year. All of these concerns were unfurled to the American people under the banner of "academic excellence," a Cold War era term. Replace past fears over the military prowess of the Soviet Union with new fears over the technological and economic prowess of the Japanese and the parallel was virtually complete.

The report of the National Commission on Excellence in Education (NCEE), otherwise known as *A Nation At Risk*, was undoubtedly the most influential document of the 1980s. Appointed by President Reagan, the NCEE engaged in a year-long study of the American school that culminated in the writing of its report. A significant portion of the report was dedicated to dramatizing the school's alleged low state, often with the use of strident war-related metaphors. "If an unfriendly foreign power had attempted to impose on America the mediocre educational performance that exists today, we might well have viewed it as an act of war. As it stands, we have allowed this to happen to ourselves. . . . We have, in effect, been committing an act of unthinking, unilateral educational disarmament" (p. 5).

By describing a nationwide educational calamity and influencing various media outlets to promulgate its message, the NCEE had set the stage for it own reform recommendations. The nature of these recommendations embraced the time-worn discipline-centered curriculum. It promoted the importance of the "basics" and the resolidification of the subject curriculum, aimed to increase and strengthen graduation requirements, placed a new emphasis on the importance of math and science education, and advanced the idea of tying evaluation standards to exit and promotion decisions. The NCEE report also called for new alternative ways to educate teachers, aiming to make it easier for someone with a college degree to teach in the schools without necessarily going through teacher preparation courses. Lastly, it supported merit pay for teachers and recommended increased course loads for students.

The onus for all of these so-called reforms fell squarely on the shoulders of state government. President Reagan repeatedly used the NCEE report as evidence that reform could be accomplished without any increase in federal monies and federal presence in education. It was not long after the release of *A Nation at Risk* that all 50 states established task forces that followed the reforms suggested by the NCEE. Within ten months of the report's introduction to the public, 44 states claimed to have raised their graduation requirements, 20 were considering a longer school day, and 42 were reexamining the way they certified and prepared teachers, especially in the areas of math and science (Uniteds States Department of Education, 1984).

The NCEE report, however, was not alone. During the 1980s, a raft of education reform reports focused on the reformulation of the school curriculum. Included in the reform discussion were proposals that advanced a conservative, one-track academic curriculum (Adler, 1982; Sizer, 1984), proposals that called for a reconceived commitment to general education (minus the placement of vocation education) in a comprehensive school program (Boyer, 1983; Goodlad, 1984), and proposals that recast the educational mission of the school in language that was responsive to techno-industrial goals (National Commission on Excellence in Education, 1983; National Science Board Commission, 1983; Task Force on Education for Economic Growth, 1983).

The effects of the academic excellence movement embodied in the *A Nation at Risk* report were absolutely felt in the redrafting of more stringent graduation requirements at the state levels and in the refocused concern for the disciplinary core of the high school academic curriculum. Most of the changes were institutional in nature—longer school days, more course time for academic subjects, and so forth. But these changes had ripple effects, especially in the manner in which the high school curriculum was configured, as interdisciplinary offerings lost their appeal, moving down into the middle school, and specialized courses in math, science, and foreign language study (as well as other traditional academic offerings) gained renewed popularity. This turned out to be an effective way to respond to achievement concerns, as the curriculum, across all the states, could now be better standardized and gauged to what students were expected to know in the traditional academic disciplines.

EXTENDING ACADEMIC EXCELLENCE THROUGH NATIONAL EDUCATION GOALS AND STANDARDS: THE 1990s

As the school moved toward a new decade, much of the reform thinking began to take on a new rhetoric that highlighted the need for variety and choice in the school curriculum, a theme once popular in the 1960s. New opportunities for parents to choose a school for their own children opened up. The establishment of charter schools and various interdistrict as well as intradistrict school choice options helped bring school choice into the vocabulary of school reform. Rather than working to influence a particular type of school reform, proponents called for the opening up of new school alternatives and choices as a way to improve public education. We will discuss the details of this still-formative movement in Chapter 15.

At the same time, school reform discussions in the 1990s never quite let go of the nationalizing features that the *A Nation at Risk* report highlighted. In fact, serious talk began to surface on the topic of national education goals and standards during the early 1990s. In a period associated with school choice, this might seem like an unusual, if not a paradoxical, occurrence. National goals or standards, especially if they manifest as national curricula or national tests, seem to contradict the rationale for school choice, which is to encourage schools to proliferate in multiple varieties as they respond to parental desires. The national standards movement, in fact, was criticized by those who wanted schools to operate in a free market atmosphere and by those who wanted to keep the federal government out of school policy. Other commentators, however, saw a symbiotic relation between standards and choice. Believing that unregulated school choice is a practical impossibility, advocates of standards saw a need for school choice to be circumscribed by and accountable to a core set of standards that was applicable to all schools, irrespective of their pedagogical style and curriculum emphasis.

The effort to simultaneously embrace school choice and national standards started with the *America 2000* report (U.S. Department of Education, 1990), which encouraged the adoption of school choice mechanisms, while also advancing national education goals, some of which implied the need for national curriculum standards. The report grew out of a 1989 meeting of the National Governors' Association. President Bush asked the governors of the nations (who are, in a manner of speaking, the chief operating officers of the nation's schools) to try to set some national goals for education. They settled on six goals. The goals were broad statements about increasing academic achievement, assisting with school readiness issues, increasing the holding power of the school, and ensuring the safety and learning integrity of the school environment.

In 1994, President Clinton, who attended the 1989 meeting of the National Governors Association as the Governor of Arkansas, signed legislation, known as *Goals 2000*, which not only embraced the original six goals of *America 2000*, but also introduced the idea of national standards as a way to ensure that national academic achievement goals were being met. One of the academic achievement goals, for instance, read "American students will leave grades four, eight and twelve having demonstrated competency in challenging subject matter, including English, mathematics, science, history and geography" (U.S Department of Education, 1990). To realize such a goal, the *Goals 2000* program tried to encourage the development of some consensus between the states over generally accepted subject area standards.

We should remember that in a decentralized system, national standards can only exist by voluntary state compliance. Some states have resisted the notion of standards, but most others, with varying degrees of success, have embraced them. It is clear that the emphasis on standards development was an extension of the academic excellence movement of the 1980s. If the states could together embrace the idea of curriculum standards, the American schools could take an important step toward emphasizing the academic tradition of schooling. As observed by Ravitch (1995),

> Much of the movement for standards aimed to reestablish priorities by clarifying that the schools were responsible, first and foremost, for developing the intelligence of their students. This was not meant to eliminate or disparage the numerous other social functions that had been assigned to the schools, but to emphasize that instruction in skills and knowledge was the sine quo non of the school responsibilities. (p. 5)

As a result of the influence of *Goals 2000*, curriculum standards were developed for several academic subject areas, from elementary to high school. Professional educational organizations led the way, providing states with content standards for their subject area. The National Council of Teachers of Mathematics, the National Council of Teachers of English, the National Council for the Social Studies, the National Council for History Education, and the National Council for Geographic Education all delivered drafts on standards. These were typically content standards, which are usually straightforward descriptions of the actual skills and knowledge specific to a content area.

Supporters claimed that curriculum standards were empowering to students, parents, and teachers. Students gained because standards set the groundwork for equal opportunity. They ensured that certain courses of study and certain learning expectations were accorded to all. They also framed the school experience in a decidedly coherent, if not predictable, form and allowed educators to assess, in clear and unambiguous terms, how well their students were performing.

The idea of national standards did not have uncritical support. Many political conservatives do not like them because they represented a quasi-federal government intrusion in the school and made it less likely that local decision-making would prevail. Others worried about the politicization of standards, especially in cultural hotbeds such as the teaching of American history or American literature. In 1994, a national controversy erupted over the release of Department of Education-sponsored history standards. Critics of the standards, mostly political conservatives, accused the standards of being politically correct, tainted by an overwhelming negative view toward the West, America, and white males. The controversy led to a formal condemnation of the standards by the U.S Senate. Some saw the battle fought over the history standards as emblematic of the difficulty of forging any national standards that could win broad-based support from the public (Ravitch, 1996).

Several critics also pointed to the possibility that standards could result in boxing in the school experience, in giving classroom sanction only to content standards that are easily described and tested. Thus, aspects of the school experience not easily captured by a standard, such as the development of a value system marked by honesty and patience, love of learning and ethical behavior, could get forgotten in the zeal for setting lessons to standards. Others argued that, far from empowering teachers, standards tended to chain them down with test-driven instruction geared to the standards and with formulaic textbooks.

National standards since have been developed in almost all subject areas of the school curriculum. It is up to the states to decide what to do with them. They could ignore them, adapt them to their own needs or embrace them as a national centralized system of schooling might. Few could have anticipated, however, how standards would play into the next round of school reforms.

THE NEW CENTURY: NO CHILD LEFT BEHIND AND THE DRIVE FOR ACCOUNTABILITY

The ratification of the federal No Child Left Behind legislation in 2002 represented yet another approach to school reform that highlighted a public accountability system for the learning outcomes of schooling. Led by a bipartisan initiative in Congress, No Child Left Behind (NCLB) was a modern-day recasting of the historic Elementary and Secondary School Act of 1964, and its flagship Title 1 program, which brings considerable resources to the cause of compensatory education for low-income children.

After years of neglect during the 1990s, the disadvantaged learner had once again reemerged as the main focal point for school reform. Faced with dramatic evidence of an achievement gap between the races and between income levels, federal legislators attempted to find a way to compel achievement in the school by installing a rigorous accountability system for the education of children in reading, math, and science. Noting that reading was a "civil right," Congress passed a law that, by title and design, would leave no child behind in the quest to bring literacy and numeracy to all American youth.

NCLB was a comprehensive reform bill that featured various initiatives. Through NCLB, for instance, only "highly-qualified teachers" could be hired in the public schools and federally-sponsored research aiming to identify scientifically-based teaching practices could be brought to the classrooms. NCLB's most public profile in the schools, however, revolved around an accountability system that encourages states to advance widespread proficiency in reading, math, and science education.

Testing for Proficiency

NCLB puts all states under the requirement of designing and implementing a statewide testing program intended to help schools certify the proficiency of students in reading, math, and science. The federal law explicitly states that each state shall adopt a testing program aligned to "challenging student academic achievement standards" and that such standards shall, among other things, include some specification of what "children are expected to know and be able to do" (Public Law 107-110; 20 USC 6311. Sec 1111 (b-1-a and b-1-c)). The role of standards, in this context, is meant to ensure that all children in the state have an equal opportunity to learn what they will be tested against on statewide examinations.

Each state is required to identify a proficiency cut score for each of the grade levels and tested domains on its state exams. The proficiency cut score is the minimal raw scale score one needs to be certified as proficient. The chosen cut score for each exam then becomes a baseline for measuring the annual yearly progress (AYP) of proficiency. States are free to not only design their own exams but to also set their own cut scores, with only modest direction from the federal authorities on what represents a valid or reasonable cut score. NCLB says, at a minimum, that the cut score cannot be lower than the average score of the state's lowest achieving subgroup (economically disadvantaged, major racial and ethnic groups, student with disabilities, LEP students) or the 20th percentile score on the state's tests. Once the cut score is set, the state must then determine the percentage of students it expects each school in the state to hit the cut score. A state can decide that, say, in 2004, 30 percent of the student population in each school must reach the cut score. It can go for a higher or a lower percentage, but once it sets the percentage, it is locked into a schedule that requires the state to increase the baseline percentage in equal increments of 1, 2, or 3 years, so that by 2012 all children (100 percent) are proficient. Table 14–1 depicts a possible schedule of percentages in relation to the states' cut score.

All schools in the states are then held accountable to the AYP cut score/percentage formula, meaning that each school is required to have a certain percentage of its children at or above the cut score. Because the public intention is to leave no child behind, NCLB also insists that not only the aggregate population meet the cut score, but all the subgroups as well (including subgroups categorized by income, race, ethnicity, students with disabilities, and students with limited English proficiency). That means that if one subgroup (say, students with disabilities), does not achieve the percentage expected on the cut score, the school will be considered out of compliance and put on a school improvement program—even if all the other scores are spectacular. To be put on the needs improvement list carries clear consequences, but only for schools receiving Title 1 monies, which would be schools with a relatively large population of children living in low-income families.

Title 1 federal funding is based on a formula that counts the number of students living in poverty, using Census data. The states then get money from the federal government and distribute it to districts "in need," usually based on numbers of students receiving free or reduced lunch in the district. For a school to qualify as a Title 1 school, it has to have about 40 percent of its student population living at or below the federal poverty line. Thus, Title 1 is often a good proxy for a high-poverty school. About 47 percent of all public school children attend schools that are eligible for Title 1 monies. The

Table 14–1 Two Examples of a AYP Schedule.

	School A	School B
	% that meets cut score for proficiency	% that meets cut score for proficiency
Y2004	30% meet the cut score	40% meet the cut score
2005	40%	40%
2006	50%	60%
2007	50%	60%
2008	60%	60%
2009	70%	80%
2010	80%	80%
2011	90%	80%
2012	100%	100%

point to remember is that the support services and the penalties that flow from NCLB apply only to Title 1 schools. This, however, does not mean that non-Title 1 schools are off the hook. Any public school could be labeled as failing, which could potentially harm enrollment and attendance-based state funding. Private schools are exempt from No Child Left Behind.

What are the consequences that derive from NCLB for Title 1 schools failing to meet the cut score/ percentage AYP formula? The law states that after two consecutive years of failing to meet AYP, a school receives technical assistance from the federal government so it can target key areas of improvement. Thus, if a school fails AYP because of low reading test scores, it might decide to reform the reading education program in the school by investing in new books, or extending remedial instructional opportunities, or even purchasing comprehensive in-service training for educators who teach reading, all in the interest of bringing up the test scores. If a school failed AYP because of one low-achieving subgroup in mathematics, it might decide to give more attention and more resources to the mathematics education of that particular group. The other main consequence of failing to achieve the cut score/percentage formula for proficiency for two consecutive years is a provision that allows the children in the school to voluntarily enroll in a public school of their choice that is not on the "needs improvement" list. The rationale behind this policy is to give choices to parents whose children might otherwise be trapped in low-performing schools. States are generally free to set the criteria for eligibility as a receiving school, weighing factors such as capacity, and whether preexisting choice programs, such as magnet schools, can be included in the list of eligible schools. If the students on failing school should opt to go to another school, the school district would be obligated to pay for the cost of transportation with federal NCLB money that must be set aside for such a purpose.

Studies done on the transfer policies sponsored by NCLB demonstrate low participation rates. In New York, only about 10 percent of eligible students actually opted for a transfer school in 2003; in Los Angeles the percentage was less than 1 percent. This low participation could be explained in any number of ways. It could be that despite finding itself on a "needs improvement" list, some neighborhood schools continue to retain the faith and trust of its parents. If a school found its way to the list because of a small subgroup discrepancy, parents and others are not likely to conclude that the school is suffering from some systemic or school-wide failure. NCLB, it should be said, draws a hard line between schools that meet and schools that fail to meet AYP, without acknowledging the difference between a school that might be on the list with a small subgroup shortfall, as opposed to a school that is comprehensively and chronically failing to meet AYP. Other parents might support their school even in the face of NCLB sanctions because they believe that much of what their school does well is simply not being picked up on the state measurement, or because they have otherwise had a satisfying experience with the school. Parents might also be hesitant to remove their children from their peer group, especially if the peer group has established friendships. Obviously, convenience factors and the availability of better choices also could also come into play. On this latter point, Sunderman and others (2005) found that the actual transfer schools that the students were selecting and enrolling were often only marginally better than the schools they were leaving (when measured by the percentage of students who actually met AYP in each school). The lack of available high-achieving school options for transfer is sometimes a function of a district's reluctance to include specialized magnet schools (with selective admissions requirements) on their list of eligible transfer schools.

If a school or school district is found to be below AYP requirements for three consecutive years, the first two conditions described continue to hold (programmatic improvements together with transfer policies), with a third layer added: the provision of supplemental educational experiences for children living at or below the poverty. Hence, NCLB monies are directed to families of disadvantaged youth for the purposes of purchasing supplemental tutorial services from a provider of their choice. School districts are expected to vet all the potential providers, notify parents of the availability of such services, process the applications, and ultimately monitor the experience against accountability standards and actual attendance. This means that the brochures, databases, application procedures, transportation plans, and other concerns needed to implement the supplemental services program all fall on the shoulders of the school.

NCLB defines the supplemental education service as "additional academic instruction designed to increase the academic achievement of students in low performing schools." This means that the service must be provided beyond the regular school day, with either the district taking it on itself or any number of private providers taking on a share of the work. Again, studies done on the supplement educational program demonstrate very low participation rates. In New York, only 12 percent of the eligible pool of students took advantage of the supplemental services program; in Chicago and Los Angeles it was 8 percent and 7 percent, respectively (Sunderman & others, 2005, p. 64). These low participation rates are more difficult to explain than the transfer usage rates. They might have something to do with finding enough qualified vendors to meet the demand or with a failure to notify parents of supplemental education options. Of course, parental apathy could also be a contributing factor.

If a school or school district continues to not meet the AYP regulations over four consecutive years, the sanctions begin to take on a more punitive and invasive character. Program improvements, transfer policies, and supplemental services remain in place, but the school is now allowed to engage other corrective actions, including the replacement of the staff viewed as most responsible for the school's failure to meet AYP, the implementation of an entirely new curriculum, the appointment of an outside expert to advise the school, the extension of the school year or school day, or the wholesale restructuring of the school's organization. Critics fear that teachers whose students fail to measure up to the AYP imperative will be viewed as less than desirable and terminated. The idea of equating good teaching with student test scores is, as indicated earlier, fundamentally problematic.

Finally, after five consecutive years of failing to meet the AYP standard, the school could be, in effect, dissolved, which means that it could be either taken over by the state for restructuring, handed over to a private management company, or recast as a charter school. In every case, most (if not all) of the existing staff will likely be terminated.

Because NCLB puts regulatory conditions on the states, a few other important regulatory details need to be remembered. The first is that the proficiency tests conducted by the states are not considered valid at the school building level unless at least 95 percent of the enrolled population takes the exam. In other words, schools are given a 5 percent leeway with their score reporting. Second, all subgroup data are only valid if they are of a sufficient size (in most cases, at least 30 students). Thus, any school with a subgroup smaller than 30 or so will not have the subgroup result count against the school. Students with disabilities severe enough to require special individualized educational programs (IEP) are allowed to take an alternative exam built around their IEP, but NCLB only allows 1 percent of the school population to exercise this alternative option. Students who transfer from other schools will have their test scores count only after being in a school for at least one year, and students with limited English proficiencies are given only one year before they are required to take the proficiency exams in English. Finally, a school that demonstrates at least 10 percent progress on the main indices of achievement while still failing to meet the AYP cut scores demands, is given what is called safe harbor, which means that it is viewed as neither in compliance nor in need of improvement. It goes into a holding pattern until subsequent year test results.

The Construct of Proficiency

Because NCLB expects the schools to produce proficient readers who are also numerate and scientifically literate, it has to also be certain that the schools can definitively demonstrate the attainment of such skills. Hence, NCLB dedicates considerable resources into the use of state exams designed to certify the proficiency levels of students. The construct of proficiency as it relates to reading, math, or science is a complex measurement enterprise that calls for careful testing routines. When we say that *x* students are proficient readers, we should expect that such a conclusion will be fundamentally valid and reliable.

From the perspective of NCLB, however, we can begin to see problems with the way that the construct of proficiency is defined and certified across the states. Because states are free to design their own tests, set their own cut scores, and encourage their own particular way to respond to testing demands in the curriculum, we find wildly different rates of proficiency being reported between the states. For instance, Massachusetts, Colorado, and Mississippi each claim that about 90 percent of their fourth graders are proficiency readers, based on their own state exam results, while California and South Carolina report proficiency rates closer to 30 percent. Are children really that much better at reading in Mississippi than in California? To make sense of these differences, it is useful to compare them to a stable metric of measured reading achievement. Because proficiency in reading has been measured at the state level since the early 1970s on the NAEP exam, we have a fairly good historical sense of the proficiency percentages in each state. Clearly, the NAEP is tougher than most state exams because all the states report a proficiency rate on the NAEP that is lower (sometimes astoundingly lower) than the rate reported on the state exams. These discrepancies underscore the complexity of making a construct claim for proficiency. The problems here go beyond differences in difficulty levels. The evidence, in fact, begins to go straight to the issue of construct validity. For example, Mississippi claims that 87 percent of its fourth graders are proficient readers on its state exams but the NAEP puts the number at about 18 percent—an astonishing difference. Using its state exams, Mississippi claims the second highest percentage of proficient fourth grade readers in the nation. But on the NAEP, Mississippi is ranked 50th—dead last among states. How can anyone take the claim of proficiency seriously when such wide differences exist in the tested rates? Obviously, such differences likely speak to some corruption in the design or the implementation of the either the state tests or the NAEP. Given its three-decade presence as the main testing gauge for reading proficiency, the NAEP is not the likely suspect. Table 14–2 depicts the extent of the discrepancy.

Table 14–2   Distribution of States by Percentage of 4th-Grade Students Scoring at the "Proficient" Level and Above on the State Reading Assessments and National Assessment of Educational Progress 2003 Reading Assessment.

Range (percentage points)	NAEP "Proficient" and Above	State "Proficient" and Above
	Number of States	
10–19	3	0
20–29	7	1
30–39	17	2
40–49	2	2
50–59	0	3
60–69	0	7
70–79	0	7
80+	0	7

McCombs, J. S., Kirby, S. N., Barney, H., Darilek, H., & Magee, S. (2005). *Achieving state and national literacy goals, a long uphill road.* http://www.rand.org/pubs/technical_reports/2005/RAND_TR180-1.pdf.

What might be at work at the state level to create such dramatic differences in the proficiency ratings between state level and NAEP results? As indicated, one possibility is simply a matter of where the state sets its proficiency cut score. A lower cut score obviously increases the pool of proficient students, which raises the very real possibility that score x on a given test could make one a proficient reader in state x but not in state y. As indicated, the difficulty index of the state exams is higher than NAEP, meaning that a higher score is easier to attain. Yet another factor might be the way that the schools are responding to the state level exams, meaning that much more direct teaching-to-the-test instruction could be going on in states with especially high state-level test scores than in states with lower state-level scores. All this, of course, raises the issue of construct validity—that is, whether we can be confident that the state exams reporting on proficiency are psychometrically sound and meaningfully representative of the construct of proficiency.

Consequences for the Classroom and the School

What are the consequences of NCLB in the classroom and in the general operation of the school? One clear effect is the specter NCLB raises for the rise of high stakes testing in the school. For instance, imagine the high stakes nature of the NCLB state exams in a school that is in its fourth year of sanctions and facing possible dissolution, or in a school where teachers have been told that they might face termination if they fail to lift their students' exam results significantly.

Naturally, a high stakes climate means that the curriculum will take a hard turn in the direction of what needs to be done to lift the test scores. Reading and math instruction are usually the main beneficiaries of this shift, as the school focuses its resources on what counts toward AYP. The effect may result in raising scores enough to put the school over the AYP guideline, but it could also result in a general impoverishment of the school experience—where art, music, and skills sets, such as critical thinking, creativity, cooperative behavior, and other matters that have no place on the state tests, are relegated as unimportant. The fact that such an impoverishment of the school experience would occur mostly in schools that disproportionately enroll children from low-income families raises obvious equity concerns. Survey data of teachers demonstrate support for the idea of accountability, but also show that NCLB sanctions could cause teachers to leave schools that are identified as needing improvement because of the consequences that result from failing to lift achievement above the state AYP line. This, of course, could prove to be counterproductive if it makes it more difficult to attract and ultimately retain good teachers in Title 1 schools.

Other fears associated with NCLB include the possibility that a school under NCLB pressures will not only put its focus on what is tested, but on who counts as most important for the school's continued survival through NCLB sanctions. That, of course, would be the students who are just above and below the proficiency cut score, or what Robert Brennan (2004) calls the "bubble students." Under these conditions, the school might put most of its resources into the education of the students who are most likely to save it from NCLB sanctions, and away from the students who are clearly and comfortably above the cut score line. This could result in a general neglect of higher achieving students. Of course, it could also prove to be an advantage for the higher achievers, as they would be free from the delimiting constraints associated with teaching-to-the-tests. Others worry that NCLB sanctions might come at the cost of viable neighborhood schools. By subjecting neighborhood schools to what many view as impossibly difficult standards of achievement, the conditions could be set for the dissolution of the neighborhood system, replaced by a more choice-based system that begins to border on privatization.

SUMMARY

The nature of school reform has always been influenced by sociopolitical context. During the Cold War period, hysteria over the conquering ambitions of the Soviet empire shaped the curriculum in very direct ways. Congress authorized federal money to be used in the development of a national network of curriculum programs, mostly in the area of math and science, designed to produce scientists and engineers needed for the defense of the nation. In the ensuing period, the socio-political temper was marked by domestic strife. The growth of the civil rights movement and the student protest movement, and concerns over urban decay helped to turn the school in the direction of humanizing initiatives, stressing the need for relevance, life experience, and choice. The subject-centered tradition of the Cold War was a distant memory. However, socio-political conditions would shift yet again, this time in the direction of retrenchment, efficiency, and cost-cutting measures. During the 1970s, the school found itself in the midst of a back-to-basics movement that featured competency-based learning. The popularity of efficient and low-cost instructional programs kept the school experience gauged at a low conceptual mark. As the 1980s approached, the Cold War themes of academic excellence experienced a renewal, this time in the context of global competition for technological and economic dominance. The school curriculum, once again, experienced a disciplined-centered turn. States helped to lock this shift into place by making graduation and course requirements more stringent. The logic of the academic excellence movement continued to play out during the 1990s, especially in the national call for the development of national curriculum standards for all academic subject area. The embrace of national standards, however, was tempered by a popular movement for school choice. At the turn of the new century, however, federal legislation, embodied in the tellingly titled No Child Left Behind legislation, put renewed focus on the low achiever, and enacted a system of accountability that has compelled schools to dedicate their instructional resources to the cause of lifting test scores in the domains of reading, math, and science. The nature of the support and sanctions flowing from the accountability mechanism has set the conditions for a retrenchment, if not impoverishment, of the school experience for children attending schools most affected by NCLB.

REFERENCES

Adler, M. J. (1982). *The paideia proposal.* New York: Macmillan Publishing.

Bestor, A. E. (1953). *Educational wastelands.* Urbana, IL: University of Illinois Press.

Bestor, A. E. (1956). *The restoration of learning.* New York: Alfred A. Knopf.

Boyer, E. (1983). *High school.* New York: Harper and Row.

Brennan, R. (2004). *Revolutions and evolutions in current educational testing.* Occasional Research Paper #7 Iowa Academy of Education, http://www.finefoundation.org/IAE/iae-z-op-brennan-1.pdf.

Bruner, J. S. (1960). *The process of education.* Cambridge: Harvard University Press.

Central Advisory Council for Education. (1967). *Children and their primary schools.* London: Her Majesty's Stationary Office.

Conant, J. B. (1960). *The American high school today.* New York: McGraw-Hill Book Co.

Finn, C. E., Petrille, M. J., & Vanourek, G. (1998). The state of the state standards, *Fordham Report,* 2(5), www.edexcellence.net.

Goodlad, J. I. (1966). *The changing school curriculum.* New York: Fund for the Advancement of Education.

Goodlad, J. I. (1984). *A place called school.* New York: McGraw-Hill.

Goodman, P. (1964). *Compulsory mis-education.* New York: Horizon Press.

Gross, R., & Gross, B. (16 May, 1970). A little bit of chaos. *Saturday Review.*

Hentoff, N. (1966). *Our children are dying.* New York: Viking Press.

Jencks, C. (1972a). *Inequality.* New York: Basic Books Inc.

Kozol, J. (1967). *Death at an early age.* Boston: Houghton Mifflin Co.

McCombs, J. S., Kirby, S. N., Barney, H., Darilek, H., Magee, S. (2005). *Achieving state and national literacy goals, a long uphill road,* http://www.rand.org/pubs/technical_reports/2005/RAND_TR180-1.pdf.

National Commission on Excellence in Education. (1983). *A nation at risk.* Washington, DC: U.S. Department of Education.

National Commission on the Reform of Secondary Education. (1973). *The reform of secondary education.* New York: McGraw-Hill Book Co.

National Panel on High School and Adolescent Education. (1976). *The education of adolescents.* Washington, DC: U.S. Government Printing Office.

National Science Board Commission. (1983). *Educating Americans for the twenty-first century.* Washington, DC: National Science Foundation.

President's Science Advisory Committee. (1974). *Youth: Transition to adulthood.* Chicago: The University of Chicago Press.

Public Law 107-110, *the No Child Left Behind Act of 2001,* from http://www.ed.gov/policy

Ravitch, D. (1995). *National standards in American education.* Washington, DC: Brookings Institute.

Ravitch, D. (1996). 50 states, 50 standards, *The Brookings Review* 14(3):6–9.

Rickover, H. G. (1959). *Education and freedom.* New York: E. P. Dutton and Co., Inc.

Silberman, C. E. (1970). *Crisis in the classroom.* New York: Random House.

Silberman, C. E. (1970a, June). How the public schools kill dreams and mutilate minds. *The Atlantic Monthly.*

Silberman, C. E. (1970b, July/August). Murder in the schoolroom. *The Atlantic Monthly.*

Silberman, C. E. (1973). *The open classroom reader.* New York: Random House.

Sizer, T. R. (1984). *Horace's compromise.* Boston: Houghton Mifflin Co.

Sunderman, G. L., Kim, J. S., & Orfield, G. (2005). *NCLB Meets School Realities.* Thousand Oaks, CA: Corwin Press.

Tanner, D. (1986). Are reforms like swinging pendulums? In H. J. Walberg and J. W. Keefe, *Rethinking reform: The principal's dilemma.* Reston, Virginia: National Association of Secondary School Principals.

Tanner, D., & Tanner, L. (1995). *Curriculum development.* New York: Macmillan Co.

Task Force on Education for Economic Growth. (1983). *Action for excellence.* Washington, DC: Education Commission of the States.

United States Department of Education. (1984). *A nation responds.* Washington, DC: U.S. Department of Education.

United States Department of Education. (1990). *America 2000.* Washington, DC: U.S. Department of Education.

KEY QUESTIONS

1. Describe the pendulum-like nature of school reform since mid-century.
2. Why are reactionary changes likely when schools respond to narrow nationalistic pressures?
3. What was the fundamental reform message offered by Arthur Bestor and Admiral Rickover during the 1950s?
4. What were some of the things that occurred in the school curriculum as a result of the forces unleashed by the Soviet launching of Sputnik?
5. What was Bruner's essential contribution to the nature of school reform during the post-Sputnik period?
6. What was the main message emerging from the Romantic-Left during the 1960s?
7. How did open education lead to a laissez-faire attitude in the curriculum?
8. What was competency-based instruction and why was it an attractive idea during the 1970s?
9. Explain how the idea of "teacher proof" materials fit into the context of back-to-basic and educational retrenchment.
10. Compare the nature of reform in the 1980s to the reforms undertaken during the post-Sputnik period.
11. Discuss the issue of construct validity in relation to proficiency. Try to explain why state rates of proficiency are usually higher than the NAEP rates.
12. Detail some of the classroom consequences, good and bad, of NCLB in a Title 1 school.

RESEARCH EXERCISES

1. Examine some of the major school reform documents published during the mid-1980s: Goodlad (1984); Boyer (1983); Sizer (1983); Adler (1982); National Science Board Commission (1983); and National Commission on Excellence in Education (1983). Analyze the work from the standpoint of their responsiveness to the nature of the learner and the values and aims of democracy.

2. Look in the annual editions of the *Education Index* for the number of articles appearing under the topic *crisis in education,* or *open education, teacher proof materials,* or any phrase that had temporary cache. Conduct a citation analysis all the way back to mid-century to frame out when the movement or idea came in and out of fashion and to expose what it had to say.

3. Survey teachers working in Title 1 schools on the topic of how NCLB regulations have affected their teaching. Are they committing less instructional time to non-tested areas than they did previous to NCLB reforms? Are they feeling a need to spend more time with lower achieving students and less time with higher achieving students? Is there any sense of wanting to leave the school because of expected sanctions?

4. Conduct a study on how effectively the transfer and supplemental education policies affiliated with NCLB are working in a school district with which you are familiar.

CHAPTER 15

The Idea of School Choice

Today most children in the United States are educated in a public school assigned to their residential community. Neighborhood schools, as they are known, are convenient to attend and are central to the functioning of the communities they serve. Because neighborhood schools are charged with the responsibility of educating the neighborhood's children, they often become centers for community involvement and shared community undertakings. Community bonds are created this way, as the life of the school (its homework assignments, athletic events, extracurricular activities) is shared in the homes of the neighborhood, and the life of the community (its common problems and concerns) is shared in the experience of the school. This is what happens when children who live together go to school together. This was the very principle embraced by the early Puritans in their efforts to keep the school close to the hands of the local population.

In recent years, however, the viability of a neighborhood school arrangement has been questioned by reformers who believe that there is a need to broaden the menu of school choices available to parents. They argue that parents should not be restricted to only the neighborhood school for the education of their children. What if, for instance, such a school was fundamentally inadequate? What if parents truly felt that their neighborhood school was unresponsive to their child's needs, or was otherwise an unhealthy or unsafe place? In such a case, should not parents have the option of choosing another school without being forced to resort to private schooling?

Today there is growing public acceptance of the right for parents to be able to exercise greater choice in selecting where their children go to school. The question that remains is determining how far these liberties of choice should go—specifically whether they should extend themselves to the public funding of private schools.

PUBLIC SCHOOL CHOICE PROGRAMS

Many parents have always had the option of exercising choice over their children's education. Parents who can afford private schooling can typically select any number of schools for their children, including those that abide by different philosophies or even different religious points of view. Advocates of school choice often cite this fact in their favor, arguing that school choice exists only for the wealthy and is denied to the very group of people who need it most—poor families stuck in poor neighborhoods with poor schools.

School choice options have come a long way and the term "choice" is now part of virtually every parent's vocabulary. The new reality is that parents enjoy a range and a frequency of school options that simply were not imaginable only, say, twenty years ago. State governments and public school districts have taken notice of the appeal that choice holds for many parents and have worked hard to bring a bounty of new possibilities to the school lives of children.

Intradistrict and Interdistrict Choice

Many school districts have, at a minimum, adopted an open-enrollment policy that gives parents the option of enrolling their children in any number of schools available within district boundaries. These choices could include neighborhood schools, as well as special theme magnet schools and even, as will be explained, charter schools. Such limited choice programs are known as intradistrict choice programs—school options made available to parents within the boundaries of a school district. Open enrollment, of course, had its origins in the school desegregation movement, but it is now very much part of a district's effort to offer a variety of school options to parents.

Some states also allow what is known as interdistrict choice, which entitles parents to select a school outside of their residential school district. The policy of interdistrict choice programs allows most of the money allocated for the student's education to follow the student to the receiving school district. However, in most cases, parents have to provide their own transportation, although exemptions are often given to disabled and low-income students. The receiving district, of course, can deny a transfer if it is at capacity or if the enrollment options result in creating racial imbalances. Some states have fashioned regulations that dissuade schools from using interdistrict transfers as a means to recruit athletes for sports competition purposes. Interdistrict choice, especially in more densely populated settings where districts are in reasonable proximity to each other, provides real choices to parents and allows parents to exploit the resources in an outside district if they prove to be especially needful for their own children.

Intradistrict and interdistrict choice programs have experienced considerable growth over the past two decades. One increasingly finds that the states are requiring districts to engage in some programmatic form of public school choice. In 2005, for instance, 24 states required their school districts to develop an open enrollment (intradistrict) school choice policy and 19 states required their school districts to participate in interdistrict choice programs (Education Commission of the States, 2005). The result of such active state support is that school choice programs have made significant inroads in the overall school enrollment. As noted in Figure 15-1, approximately 15 percent of the school-age population attends public-chosen schools (including schools chosen through open enrollment, and varieties of magnet and charter schools). The remaining 10 percent or so attend private schools, with approximately 80 percent of the private school population attending church-related schooling (NCES, 2006). The neighborhood school is still alive and well, representing 75 percent of the school enrollment, but choice programs are clearly taking on a visible profile.

Interestingly, parents from low-income settings seem to be taking advantage of public choice programs, as represented by their disproportionately high involvement in public chosen schools (see Figure 15-2). Intradistrict choice programs seem to be having some effect at reaching out to parents whose children might be trapped in high poverty/low performing schools. These parents report high levels of contentment with their public chosen school. Parents who sent their children to public chosen schools, for instance, were significantly more satisfied with the teachers, the academic standards, and the order and discipline of their schools than were parents who sent their children to neighborhood schools (NCES, 2006a).

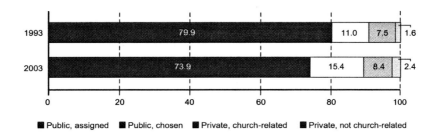

Type of school	1993	2003	Percentage point difference	Percent change
Public, assigned	79.9	73.9	−6.0	−7.5
Public, chosen	11.0	15.4	4.4	40.0
Private, church-related	7.5	8.4	0.9	12.0
Private, not church-related	1.6	2.4	0.8	50.0

NOTE: U.S. Department of Education, National Center for Education Statistics, School Readiness Survey of the 1993 National Household Education Surveys Program (NHES), School Safety and Discipline Survey of the 1993 NHES, and Parent and Family Involvement in Education Survey of the 2003 NHES, previously unpublished tabulations (May 2004).

FIGURE 15-1   Differences in Parental Choice: Percentage Distribution of Students in Grades 1-12, by Type of School: 1993 and 2003.

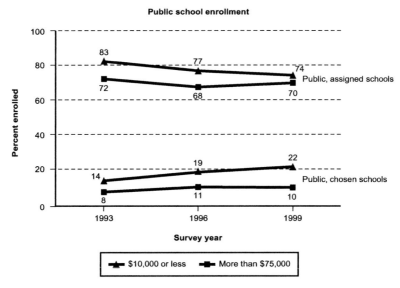

NOTE: Includes homeschooled students enrolled in public or private schools for 9 or more hours per week. The categories for household income are in current dollars, which have not been adjusted for inflation. Hence, they do not reflect the same purchasing power for the three years.
SOURCE: U.S. Department of Education, National Center for Education Statistics, School Readiness Survey of the National Household Education Surveys Program (NHES), 1993, School Safety and Discipline Survey of the NHES, 1993, Parent & Family Involvement Survey of the NHES, 1996, and the Parent Survey of the NHES, 1999.

FIGURE 15-2   Percentage of Students Enrolled in Grades 1-12 in Public, Assigned and Public, Chosen Schools by Lowest and Highest Household Income Groups ($10,000 or Less and More than $75,000): 1993, 1996, and 1999.

Charter Schools

The new public school choice option on the minds of many educators and parents today is the charter school. Charter schools are publicly-supported schools created and managed by any individual or group that fits within a state's eligibility requirements for charter school participation. Among the states with charter school laws, we can find schools operated by parents, teachers, community leaders, public organizations, and for-profit businesses.

Charter schools are intended to be innovative schools that would probably not exist in the normal policy environment of a school district. Charter school laws clear the way for various groups to ask the state (or depending on the state, the local school board) to approve the authorization of public money for the design and operation of a unique approach to schooling. Once approved, the charter school is free to operate without administrative control from either the state or the local district in which it resides. There are, of course, a few general rules that apply to all charter schools. They cannot charge tuition, they must be nonsectarian, they are subject to federal and state laws prohibiting discrimination, and they must comply with all health and safety standards. Beyond these basic requirements, charter schools are free to flex their creative muscles and to try ideas that might otherwise be viewed as too risky or unusual in a more traditional school setting. The idea is to allow a school to perform as it might in a free market, by essentially leaving it alone and allowing it to grow out of the local desires of teachers, parents, and community, as well as business leaders.

Although charter schools are free to operate as they wish, they are nevertheless held accountable to local district and/or state performance standards. Thus, the state can intervene to monitor and assess the performance of charter schools according to its own expectations. In fact, if a charter school cannot demonstrate adequate progress on state or district outcome measures, it can eventually be shut down by the state. In most cases, states hold charter schools to the same statewide assessment system used for all other public schools.

As of 2005, 41 states passed charter school legislation. The nature of charter school legislation varies across the states (Center for Education Reform, 2006). Twenty of the 41 states put no limit on the number of charters granted in the state. The remaining 21 states put some limit on the number, but a considerable margin separates the upper and lower frequency limits, as 850 schools are annually allowed in California to only 10 total schools in Iowa. Across the 41 charter school states, the duration of the charter granted to a school could range from a 3-year term to a 15-year term. In some states, private schools are not eligible, while in others, home schools and for-profit companies can apply for charters. Some states require the use of licensed teachers in charter schools; others will approve schools without licensed teachers; while yet others demand that a certain minimal percentage of teachers meet certification standards. Charter school enrollment still represents less than 1 percent of the total school enrollment population (NCES, 2005). However, in some states the percentages are significantly higher. Arizona, for instance, leads the country with approximately 4 percent of its student population attending charter schools.

Because they use public monies, charter schools, as indicated, must be nonsectarian, nondiscriminatory, and tuition-free. Advocates claim that these conditions allow charter schools to maintain the common school ideal (Bierlien & Molholland, 1994). Critics, however, wonder how any common school ideal can be served by allowing a school to operate around virtually any odd gathering of ideas (Engel, 2000). Most charter schools, for instance, are created to serve a special interest, usually for a special group of people seeking a unique and particular school experience. A charter school, for instance, could embrace a particularistic racial or ethnic identity. In California, as reported by Wells (1998), the central focus of some schools included "an emphasis on the ethnic culture, heritage and identity of the students.

Teachers at these schools presented history and culture from the point of view of the people in their communities, not from the perspective of mainstream public school textbooks, and curriculum" (p. 22). Is this an acceptable way of conceiving the common public school experience and the demand to secure a normative learning agenda, or it is more in the line of special interest and uncommon identity?

Interestingly, some evidence suggests that charter schools are contributing to the racial and ethnic isolation of their students. The National Center for Education Statistics (2000) found that close to one-third of all charter schools were racially distinct from the districts in which they were located. In other words, about one-third of charter schools, when compared to district-wide enrollment figures, could be considered either disproportionately white or disproportionately non-white. Charter schools reach out to LEP students at about the same rate as the non-chartered public schools, but are significantly less successful in reaching out to students with disabilities (NCES, 2000).

NAEP data comparing the performance of charter schools to their neighborhood school counterparts show that they perform no better in reading achievement and significantly worse in math achievement (NCES, 2003). Because charter schools tend to reach out to and attract low performing students (see Figure 15–3), NAEP researchers adjusted for student characteristics and still found that the mean scores

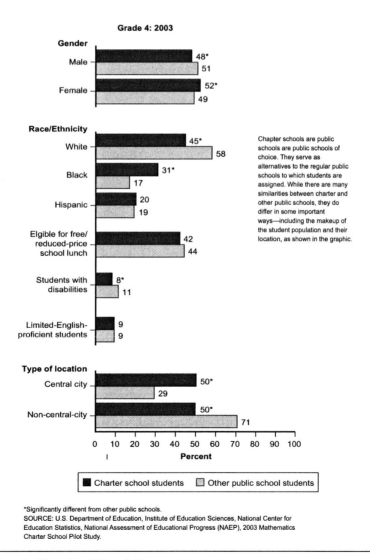

*Significantly different from other public schools.
SOURCE: U.S. Department of Education, Institute of Education Sciences, National Center for Education Statistics, National Assessment of Educational Progress (NAEP), 2003 Mathematics Charter School Pilot Study.

Figure 15–3   Who Attends Charter Schools?

in reading and math were lower than the noncharter public schools (NCES, 2006b). Charter school parents, however, report more satisfaction with the education that their children receive than parents from traditional neighborhood school settings, even after correcting for self-selection bias (Buckley & Schneider, 2006). The most current Gallup poll data show that about 50 percent of the American public favors the idea of charter school, although a robust 41 percent still oppose it (Rose & Gallup, 2006).

Magnet Schools

As indicated earlier, magnet schools were originally conceived in the policy context of a school district's desegregation strategy. The idea was to create and operate specially-designed schools, often dedicated to a particular theme or area of interest that would attract students from all the population sectors of the district. To ensure that the magnet schools were attractive enough to pull students from their neighborhoods, school districts often invested heavily in them, making them the leading schools in the district (Moore & Davenport, 1989).

Today magnet schools can be mostly found in urban and low socioeconomic districts, but they have become more than a desegregation method. Many districts have opened magnet schools for the sole purpose of offering school options to parents. At the high school level, magnet schools tend to highlight a particular subject area, such as mathematics, science, computers and technology, music and art, foreign language, and vocational or career education. They can also, especially at the elementary school level, highlight particular instructional methods. Unlike neighborhood schools, one-third of all magnet schools have a selective admissions policy. In states with large urban concentrations, the magnet school has a visible presence. In Illinois, for instance, 15 percent of all school children attend magnet schools; in California the percentage approaches 10 percent (NCES, 2003a). In Chicago, more than half of the entire student enrollment attends magnet schools (NCES, 2005a).

Even critics of magnet schools concede the role they have played in contributing to choice opportunities for parents and to the historic effort to desegregate the schools. They also claim that the magnet school has been a mixed blessing. Some evidence, for instance, points to the magnet school as a factor in the deterioration of neighborhood schools, especially in urban school districts. The problem is that good students living in bad neighborhoods will typically opt for a magnet school, thus leaving the neighborhood schools with a disproportionately large share of hard-to-educate students. Academically-motivated students coming from families supportive of education increasingly can no longer be found in neighborhood urban schools. This problem, known as creaming (as in creaming off the top), has resulted in a diminished school experience for those left behind in the neighborhood schools and in the dissolution of the community bonds to the neighborhood school. Of course, the trade-off is that good students can find good schools. Moreover, the affluent are less likely to exit the district and more overall opportunities exist for integrated experiences, at least within the district.

PRIVATIZATION, VOUCHERS, AND THE DEBATE OVER SCHOOL CHOICE

The debate over school choice programs becomes most fervent when the question turns to whether private school options should be included in the menu of school choice offerings. Those who support the full inclusion of private schools in school choice programs are, in effect, endorsing the privatization of schooling.

Privatization means that the operation of public schooling would allow for-profit corporations and any other interested parties to compete in the marketplace for clients (students), offering educational services paid for through a publicly-financed voucher. The voucher is, in essence, a government certificate that represents a designated amount of money to be used for the purchase of all or some part of a child's schooling. Under privatization, the government would likely issue a redeemable voucher or certificate to all parents with school-age children. Once in receipt of the voucher, parents would be free to enroll their children in a participating school of their choice. If they later found the school to be unsuitable, they could opt for another.

The idea of privatization is obviously a radical departure from the current system of financing and operating schools, which, in most cases, limits the expenditure of public money to public schools that are organized in local districts and under the regulation of state-imposed guidelines and rules. No states have embraced a state-wide voucher system yet, although a few small-scale experiments have been attempted, the most well-known being the Milwaukee Parental Choice Program.

The first systematic effort to articulate an educational voucher plan in the United States could be found in a book written by the economist Milton Friedman (1962), who believed that school improvement could be best realized by subjecting it to consumer choices. As a result, Friedman advanced the now-famous argument for "schools of choice." Schooling in the United States, he claimed, could be best improved by changing the financial and governance structure of public education in directions that encouraged schools to compete for students and that helped parents exercise consumer choice in deciding where their children should be educated. The idea was fairly simple: provide parents with redeemable vouchers (roughly equivalent to local per pupil expenditures) that could be spent on any school of their choice. Friedman saw no need to place any restrictions on the participating "voucher schools," stating that each school need only be monitored by the government much in the way, to use his analogy, that the government inspects restaurants to ensure minimum sanitary and safety standards.

The idea of using vouchers to buy schooling experiences can be difficult to understand in the abstract. Marked differences of opinion exist over the monetary size of vouchers, the eligibility requirements (if any) for the participating voucher schools and the general nature (and extent) of government regulations and restrictions placed on the participating schools. For instance, will admission requirements be allowed in the schools? Will the participating schools need to be accredited and follow some general curriculum framework of content standards? Will some schools be allowed to ask for more money over the cost of the voucher? Will religious-affiliated schools be allowed to participate? Or will the whole system generally be left to the winds of the marketplace, as Friedman recommends? These variations might make a difference in how one might react to vouchers.

Still, there are general keynotes to the idea that could help clarify whether or not education by voucher is appropriate in the United States. First, supporters for the general idea of vouchers claim that it will infuse the current system of schooling with a new assortment of schools. They assert that vouchers will break the back of an entrenched system of schooling marked by widespread curriculum uniformity and unresponsiveness to differences. The mechanism of market accountability is at the center of this belief because only the "best" schools will presumably survive in the competitive climate that vouchers will generate. Second, supporters of vouchers claim that the low-income parents will finally be empowered with some decision-making authority over the education of their children and have some options available to them that have long been available to parents with financial means. Backers of education-by-vouchers also claim that privatization will induce new openness in the area of school administration, build new circles of interaction among socioeconomic classes, and ultimately liberate the teacher from the tethers of an imposing school bureaucracy. All of these claims cut across specific voucher proposals. They are advanced for the general idea of vouchers.

Research conducted by Hoxby (2002) empirically supports the contention that public schools improve when placed in a voucher climate that requires them to compete for students. Using the Milwaukee voucher system for her experimental data, Hoxby followed the comparative achievement effects of fourth graders in schools that faced more competition (at least 2/3 of the students were eligible for vouchers), faced less competition (less than 2/3 of the students were eligible for vouchers), and a control group of schools that faced no competition. The consistent results, in all the tested academic core areas, showed that the schools facing more competition produced larger percentage gains in achievement than the control group and the group of schools facing less competition. As Hoxby (2002) phrased it, "it appears that public schools are induced to raise achievement when they are faced with competition" (p. 177).

Voucher proponents often cite evidence from national surveys that testify to the popularity of school options among parents. Few parents, in fact, are likely to deny an interest in exercising some choice or authority over their child's public education. When parents are asked if they should have the right to choose the school they want for the public education of their children, the response is solidly, and not surprisingly, in favor of choice (Public Agenda, 1999). The power to choose is, undeniably, not something taken lightly by parents. When the question of school choice is framed as a school reform strategy, parental views toward school choice take a different slant. The Carnegie Foundation for the Advancement of Teaching (1992) conducted a national survey on school choice that asked parents to state whether American education could be best improved by giving neighborhood schools the resources they need to achieve excellence or by letting schools compete for students with the understanding that good schools would flourish while weak ones would either improve or close. More than 80 percent of parents surveyed chose the neighborhood school response. Nevertheless, when asked if they would send their oldest children to a private or church-affiliated school if the tuition was paid for by the government, 46 percent of public school parents answered affirmatively (Rose & Gallup, 1999). NCES (2000a) data show higher levels of parental satisfaction in both public-chosen and private schools than in public-assigned schools. These higher ratings, however, should be weighed against the understanding that a family makes a financial investment in a private school, that most private schools have an affiliation with deeply-felt religious views, and that private schools (and some public-chosen schools) can deny certain students admission—all of which can prejudice satisfaction responses.

Despite being in favor of choice and vouchers, much of the public admits to knowing very little about them. A Public Agenda survey conducted in 1999 indicated that 63 percent of the general public claimed to know "very little or nothing" about school vouchers and that 80 percent of the general public believed that it needed "to learn more about vouchers" before offering an opinion. The lack of knowledge toward charter schools was even higher. But when the market rationale for school choice was explained, a large majority of parents believed that vouchers would indeed put pressure on the public school system to improve (Public Agenda, 1999).

Opponents believe that vouchers, in any form, will lead to a divided school system that fails to reaffirm the historical commitment to a common public school experience. They see the rise of an open school marketplace as a sign of abandonment of the public school ideal. They argue that public money should support a public mandate, not individualistic or familial mandates.

The call for vouchers obviously pins its faith on the belief that parents are the most suitable agents in determining how and where their children should be educated. In fact, a large part of the debate over vouchers revolves around the question of whether the main purpose of the school should be fashioned in the best interests of the family or the best interests of society. Some advocates of choice, like Coons and Sugarman (1978), contend that the school's main objective should be devoted to the family because maximizing the welfare of the family is the best way to maximize the welfare of the society. This view has been criticized by those who see the objective of schooling in broader and more collective terms. Antivoucher sentiment, in fact, sees family choice as basically selfish and antisocial, because it focuses on the wants of a single family rather than the needs of society. Public education, the reasoning might go, must be protected from the prevailing orthodoxies of parents and must be influenced instead by the general values and aims of democratic living. Wise and Darling-Hammond (1984) serve notice of the very thin line that voucher proponents walk. "If parents' choices of schools reinforce social class stratification and socialization," they state, "[then] we must accept the outcomes as justified by choice and as being in the child's best interests" (p. 43).

Moreover, critics of vouchers worry about the exercise of a for-profit mentality in a voucher setting which, far from acting in the best interests of children, puts its main sights on the bottom line and always defaults to what might be perceived to be best for business. As Darling-Hammond (1992) expressed it, for-profit schools have to decide if certain educational benefits can be skipped in order to ensure adequate profit margins, or if certain students should not be admitted because their needs are too expensive to teach. "Pursuing profits while pursuing the public's broader goals for children's education," she observes, "creates a clear and unavoidable conflict of interest." If, as Henry Ford once phrased it, "the business of business is business," what does it mean for the institution of schooling when it is practiced as a business? Certainly the business of public schooling is not business. Is there an unavoidable conflict of interest or uncomplimentarity between the institutions of business and public schooling? The corporate response, of course, is that most public schools operate wastefully and that, with sound planning, there is plenty of room for profit without any significant compromise on quality. If significant compromises on quality were the effect, they might add, the school would not likely be able to stay in business. In this way, the profit incentive is viewed as the best mechanism to induce or motivate innovative school change.

The Milwaukee Parental Choice Program (MPCP)

Initiated in 1990, the Milwaukee Parent Choice Program (MPCP) is the nation's longest and most far-reaching publicly-funded voucher program. The program was created through an unusual political alliance between Annette "Polly" Williams, a Democratic state representative who has openly championed African-American causes, and Republican Governor Tommy Thompson. Both wanted vouchers. Thompson embraced a more expansive free-market style of vouchers than did Williams, who believed that vouchers could be used to improve the particular problems of public education in predominantly poor African-American neighborhoods. William's version of vouchers proved to have more political traction and with Thompson's support, MPCP was born.

The intention of MPCP is to test whether children living in poor inner city families derive an educational benefit when their parents are given public money to purchase a private education. The original program was marked by several important restrictions. It offered vouchers to only low-income families living in the City of Milwaukee. To be eligible, students had to come from families with income of 1.75 times the poverty line or less. It excluded the participation of religious schools, capped the amount of the voucher at about $2,400, limited the number of children who could be given a voucher, and disallowed students who were already in private schools from participating. The participating private schools could not discriminate on the basis of race, religion, or gender, and had to select their students on a random basis. They also were expected to meet some very modest standards for school attendance, parental involvement, and student achievement (Witte, 2000).

The program, however, has since expanded and changed in orientation. The biggest change is that sectarian schools are now allowed to participate in the program. The maximum voucher allowance has doubled to about $5,800 and the number of student placements has expanded dramatically. Approximately 1,000 students participated in the program when it started in 1990. As of January 2005, there were almost 15,000 students in the program. Estimates indicate that about two-thirds of these are now served in religious schools. The rule against the participation of students already enrolled in private schools also changed. Now students in grades K-3 who were already in private schools, paying at their own expense, can be part of MPCP.

An evaluation of the first five years of the MPCP voucher program by John Witte (2000) showed no achievement differences between voucher students and comparable Milwaukee Public School students. Witte's conclusion was that MPCP was no miracle cure for the education of poor inner-city youth. He was not willing to assert that it has been a failure either, mostly because MPCP had provided new options to inner-city parents dissatisfied with their neighborhood schools and these parents did report increased satisfaction with their schools (with no appreciable loss in their children's' achievement). No achievement differences can be read to mean that the MPCP schools were no better than the regular public schools, but it can also be read to mean that they were no worse.

Witte's (2000) analysis also found that MPCP parents were more highly educated and more involved than parents in the comparison group, which led him to speculate that had these parents kept their children in their neighborhood schools, they could have become forces for change and improvement in those schools. This represents another variation on the creaming problem associated with magnet schools. Opponents of vouchers have argued that under privatization, the school can in fact lose the participation of key community members, mostly because dissatisfied parents are implicitly encouraged to walk away from their schools rather than have some hand in improving them. Hirschman (1970) observed that this phenomenon is an example of the economist's bias for exit over voice. The decision to voice a view in democratic community goes by the wayside when exit options are encouraged. Thus, rather than seeking improvements in the neighborhood schools, parents are instead persuaded to leave them—to shop around for another choice. As Raywid (1987) put it, "to assign parents full and unfettered responsibility for choosing their children's education in an open market is to telegraph the message that the matter is solely their affair and not the community's concern. . . . Thus, I fear that vouchers would bring in their wake a further downplaying of education on the public agenda and a further waning of public commitment to the enterprise" (p. 763).

Advocates of choice claim that there is no stronger voice than consumer voice, which speaks with the power of the purse. If neighborhood schools want to serve their communities, they better do it well enough to keep neighborhood families interested and willing to spend their voucher with them. What better way, they claim, to keep the school tuned into its public agenda. Some of the more recent evidence on MPCP gives these advocates a leg upon which to stand. For instance, Greene found that the students using vouchers in the Milwaukee program had significantly higher graduation rates than their low-income counterparts in the neighborhood schools. These are preliminary findings because a selection bias factor could be at work here, meaning that students whose families were motivated enough to apply for a voucher could be more likely (at least relative to students from nonvoucher families) to support and otherwise encourage their children to be successful in school.

HOME SCHOOLING

Not all children receive their schooling in a school. Some, in fact, are "schooled" at home, usually by their parents. The kind of education received by the child in the home is largely up to the family. Some home-school parents enroll their children in a school on a part-time basis, so they can take advantage of programs the family cannot provide, such as intramural sports, an advanced mathematics course, or laboratory courses in science. Others might draw from their community or even other families for activities. Several "home school/charter schools" have also opened up across the states, with the purpose of giving home-schooled children opportunities for group education and for general academic assistance or remedial education. In most cases, however, the education of the home-schooled child takes place in the home, under the direct guidance of a parent.

All states have compulsory education laws that validate the home as a school. In almost all states, home teachers do not need to be certified, but in many states, families are required to file a curriculum plan with the state and to subject their children to a testing program. States with especially low or limited regulatory requirements toward home schooling may have virtually no contact with the state, although all states do require parents to notify them of their intent to home school.

Home schooling gained early popularity during the child-centered period of the late 1960s. Many of the parents who joined the home schooling movement during the 1960s were seeking a more liberating and individualized experience for the children. They were convinced that the emotive climate of the home, together with the closeness of the family and the flexibility to pursue individual interests and desires, made it an ideal place for the schooling of children.

Today the decision to home school is more complex. Anxieties over the safety and security of the school and disappointment in the general academic quality of the school play a role. Many parents are flatly convinced that they could do a better job of educating their children than the public school, but their idea of what constitutes a good education is sometimes tied to a special interest agenda, often entangled with religious doctrine. Many parents believe that the best education is one that sanctions family-based viewpoints and values. The public school is, of course, at odds with such a position, not because it is against the family, but because its obligation is to the widest public good and to the task of providing an enlarging experience that transcends parochial or family-based prejudices. The school obviously cannot support or otherwise advocate for the religious views that many parents of home schooling see as requirements in the education of their children.

Home schooling is a steadily growing phenomenon. Estimates indicate that a little over a million American children were home schooled in 2003, a considerable increase from the 10,000 or so children who were believed to be home schooled during the late 1970s (NCES, 2006c). The home school enrollment is a difficult matter to accurately peg because many families fail to report to the state and students who drop out of home schools often go back to their neighborhood school (Lines, 1999). Still, the enrollment of home schoolers now hovers at around 2 percent of the total school age population. It is most popular with larger-sized (3 children or more) nuclear families in which only one parent is in the labor force. This makes obvious sense because of the significant time required on the site of the home to conduct a home school.

The research on home schools, like all choice programs, is controversial. The problem is fundamentally a sampling one. Home schoolers represent a unique demographic. In Rudner's (1999) study, home schooled children lived in mostly white nuclear families, with higher parent education levels and considerably more wealth than the average American family. It is difficult to say if Rudner's study captured the general characteristics of the home-schooling population. Whether it did or not, unless the children of home schoolers are compared with public school children representing a similar demographic, the odds are good that home-schooled children (coming from dual parent, high income, and educated families), will perform well on measures of achievement. In Rudner's study they did, scoring well above national averages across all grade levels and all subject areas. As Rudner himself stated, "I'm not saying it's the home schooling that's doing a good job. Take the same kids, similar family characteristics, and the same amount of parent involvement into the public schools and the kids would probably do just as well" (Schnaiberg, 1999). Still, the study was a clear affirmation that home-schooled children are academically able and academically prepared.

Detractors of home schooling, however, are less concerned about achievement scores and more concerned about educational outcomes not typically measured by the schools. First, they claim that there is no substitution for the group socialization that occurs in the context of the public school. Removed from students unlike themselves, home-schooled children are less likely than their public school counterparts to benefit from an interaction with a diversity of viewpoints, lifestyles, as well as political, religious, and sexual orientations. They are less likely to find face-to-face engagements across racial, economic, and ethnic lines. Some homeschoolers are, in fact, openly offended by the climate of diversity found in the public school. Critics also question how parents can conceivably be expected to properly manage the full comprehensive spectrum of the academic curriculum, especially when they typically have no training or experience in academic instruction or in the subject matter they are expected to teach. Finally, there is the problem of resources and the absence of the kind of equipment that might be needed to properly teach science, music, art, computer literacy, vocational education, and even physical education.

SUMMARY

Schooling is no longer a neighborhood affair. About one-fourth of all school-age children go to either private schools or public chosen ones. Public school districts are increasingly seeking ways to attend to the new regard for choice and have opened up options to parents both within and outside of district boundaries. Charter schools represent the newest arrival on the school choice scene. They are publicly funded schools designed to offer new variety on the menu of school choices available to parents. Other by-products of the choice movement include magnet schools, which were originally started as efforts to help with the causes of school desegregation and which now mainly exist for the purpose of offering choice to parents. Although they have undoubtedly helped to contribute to the desegregation of urban school districts, magnet schools also stand accused of contributing to the deterioration of neighborhood schools. The presence of the magnet schools has had the effect of siphoning away good students (who come from families supportive of education) from neighborhood schools.

The idea of having the opportunity to select a school, according to one's wishes, is the basic rationale behind the drive to privatize schooling. The privatization scheme creates a marketplace of school alternatives from which parents can select public or private/religious or not. Such choices could be empowered through a publicly-funded voucher system. Supporters believe that in the atmosphere of a free market, schools will improve because they will be accountable to the rigorous market demand of either competing or closing down. Detractors believe that under such a system the public school ideal is lost and a vast proliferation of alternative schools with alternative visions will spell disaster for the society. The Milwaukee Parental Choice Program (MPCP) is the nation's most visible experiment with parental vouchers. Although it is limited to low-income families and has a few other notable restrictions, it has become the main battleground for pro-voucher and anti-voucher voices. The data on achievement indicate that students participating in MPCP do no worse (or no better, if you prefer) than their non-voucher counterparts. Finally, the phenomenon of home schooling continues to grow in popularity and continues to yield impressive displays of academic achievement. Its critics, however, say that the point of public education is embodied in the interactions that school children have in the pluralistic setting of the school and that this is precisely what is most missing in the education of home-schooled children.

REFERENCES

Bierlien, L., & Molholland, L. A. (1994). *Comparing charter school laws: The issue of autonomy.* Tempe, AR: Morrison Institute of Public Policy.

Buckley, J., & Schneider, M. (2006). Are charter schools parents more satisfied with schools? *Peabody Journal of Education,* 811:57–78.

Carnegie Foundation for the Advancement of Teaching. (1992). *School choice: A special report.* Princeton, NJ: Carnegie Foundation for the Advancement of Teaching.

Center for Education Reform. (2006). *Charter schools laws across the states.* Washington, DC: Center for Education Reform.

Coon, J. E., & Sugarman, S. D. (1978). *Education and choice.* Berkeley, CA: University of Caledonia Press.

Darling-Hammond, L. (7 October, 1992). For-profit schooling: Where is the public good? *Education Week.*

Education Commission of the States. (2005). *State notes: Open enrollment: 50-state report.* Denver, CO.

Engel, M. (2000). *The struggle for control of public education: Market ideologies, democratic values.* Philadelphia, PA: Temple University Press.

Friedman, M. (1962). *Capitalism and freedom.* Chicago: University of Chicago Press.

Hirschman, A. (1970). *Exit, voice and loyalty.* Cambridge: Harvard University Press.

Hoxby, C. (2002). How school choice affects the achievement of public school students. In Paul Hill (Ed.), *Choice and Equity.* Stanford, CA: Hoover Institution Press.

Lines, P. M. (1999). *Homeschoolers: Estimating numbers and growth.* Washington, DC: U.S. Department of Education.

Moore, D., & Davenport, S. (1989). *The new improved sorting machine.* Chicago: Designs for Change.

National Center for Education Statistics. (2000). *The state of charter schools 2000: Fourth-year report.* Washington, DC: U.S. Department of Education.

National Center for Education Statistics. (2000a). *The condition of education.* Washington, DC: U.S. Department of Education.

National Center for Education Statistics. (2003). *America's charter schools: Results from the NAEP pilot study.* Washington, DC: U.S. Department of Education.

National Center for Education Statistics. (2003a). *Overview of public elementary and secondary schools and districts.* Washington, DC: U.S. Department of Education.

National Center for Education Statistics. (2005). *Digest of education statistics.* Washington, DC: U.S. Department of Education.

National Center for Education Statistics. (2005a). *Characteristics of the 100 largest public elementary and secondary schools and districts.* Washington, DC: U.S. Department of Education.

National Center for Education Statistics. (2006). *The condition of education.* Washington, DC: U.S. Department of Education.

National Center for Education Statistics. (2006a). *Trends in the use of school choice.* Washington, DC: U.S. Department of Education.

National Center for Education Statistics. (2006b). *A closer look at charter schools using hierarchical linear modeling.* Washington, DC: U.S. Department of Education.

National Center for Education Statistics. (2006c). *Home schooling in the United States: A statistical analysis.* Washington, DC: U.S. Department of Education.

Public Agenda. (1999). *On thin ice: How advocates and opponents could misread the public's views on vouchers and charter schools.* New York: Public Agenda.

Raywid, M. A. (1987). *Public choice, yes; vouchers, no!* Phi Delta Kappan 68(100):762–69.

Rose and Gallup. (2006). The 37th annual Phi Delta Kappa/Gallup Poll of the public's attitudes toward the public schools. *PDK.*

Rose and Gallup. (1999). The 31st Annual Phi Delta Kappa/Gallup Poll of the Public's Attitudes Toward the Public Schools. *PDK* 81(1):41–56.

Rudner, L. M. (1999). Scholastic achievement and demographic characteristics of home school students. *1998 Education Policy Analysis Archives* 7(8).

Schnaiberg, L. (31 March, 1999). Study finds home schoolers are top achievers on tests. *Education Week.*

Smrekar, C., & Goldring, E. (1999). *School choice in urban America: Magnet schools and the pursuit of equity.* New York: Teachers College Press.

Wells, A. S. (1998). *Charter school reform in California: Does it meet expectations?* Los Angeles, CA: UCLA Charter School Study.

Wise, A. E., & Darling-Hammond, L. (1984). Education by voucher: Private choice and the public interest. *Educational Theory* 24(1):29–53.

Witte, J. (2000). *The market approach to education: An analysis of America's first voucher program.* Princeton, NJ: Princeton University Press.

KEY QUESTIONS

1. As one parent stated it, "My experience of growing up and going to a neighborhood school was as you walked, you picked up the whole neighborhood. . . . Once you start busing and everybody is going all over the place, you don't have a community anymore. You don't have the parents going together to the PTO meetings, sports, extracurricular activities (Smrekar & Goldring, 1999, p. 74). What is your reaction to this parent?

2. Collect impressions from your friends and colleagues that testify to the unique characteristics of neighborhood schools.

3. What is the difference between a magnet school and a charter school?

4. Interdistrict choice programs typically have a few restrictions attached to them. What are they and why do you think they exist?

5. Explore the charter schools that have opened in your state or a state near you. Analyze them against your conception of public education.

6. How can someone support both the policy of school choice and the policy of national standards? How do you reconcile these policies?

7. What is the main contradiction between arguing for the importance of a common curriculum while also supporting school choice?

8. Explain the problem of creaming and its association with magnet schools.

9. Explain how a school vouchers system might work.

10. What are the basic arguments supporting school vouchers?

11. What are the basic arguments against school vouchers?

12. Do you argue with those who believe that market conditions will improve the operation of public schools? Why or why not?

13. How would you respond to someone who says: "It is a free society. If we are free to choose our own doctors and plumbers, why should we not also be free to choose our own child's school?"

14. Raywid (1987, p. 764) observed that a voucher plan "is a plan for financing schools, not improving them." What does she mean by this? Do you agree or disagree with her point?

15. Schools that operate in the marketplace are interested in one purpose, which is capturing the investment of a consumer. Schools for the athletically gifted, schools stressing a particular ethnic or cultural tradition, "Great Books" schools, foreign language immersion schools, technology schools, back-to-basics schools, open education schools, quasi-military schools, and schools stressing the virtues of capitalism could emerge in such an arrangement. Parents would have more choice and the interests of school variety would be served, but are the interests of society advanced under such an arrangement?

16. What are your feelings about home schooling? Should parents who home school be closely monitored by the state? Under what circumstances, if any, might you consider home schooling as an option for your own children?

RESEARCH EXERCISES

1. Examine the open enrollment policy of a school district. Detail the guidelines of participation in the policy and collect data on who uses the choice options, targeting subgroups by race/ethnicity and SES. Also focus on which schools gain or lose students through the choice policy, while trying to determine how such gains/loses affect the school.

2. Write a case study history of a local magnet school, tracing its founding and examining its development in the context of both desegregation and parental choice.

3. Using a survey, examine the reasons why parents choose to participate in a school choice program. What percentage of the reasons can be explained as school-related?

4. Examine the mission statement and the overall curriculum framework of a local charter school. Evaluate the extent to which such a school helps to advance what you see as the normative agenda of public schooling.

5. Survey the views of a group of principals working in urban neighborhood schools, specifically asking them to explain whether creaming (the loss of the top students in the neighborhood to magnet schools) is a problem that concerns them.

6. Examine the educational voucher programs used in other advanced nations, particularly in Scandinavian nations, and determine whether there are lessons to be learned for the United States.

7. Survey parental views of school vouchers against such variables as political party affiliation, ethnicity/race, income, and gender. Take some of the questions asked from the 37th Annual Phi Delta Kappa/Gallup Poll of the Public's Attitudes Toward the Public Schools and ask them to local parents, comparing your results to the national data reported in the PDK/Gallup poll.

Index

A

Ability-based classrooms, 294
Ability-based interclass grouping, 223
Ability-based reading group, 294
Ability-grouped settings, 224
Ability grouping, 293–295
Abington v. Schempp, 240, 241
Absolute poverty levels, 319
Academic excellence banner, 362
Academic freedom of teachers, 131–133
Academic-intellectual growth. *See* Intellectual-
    academic growth.
Academies, 221
Academy school, beginning of American-style, 158
Achievement, defined, 258
Achievement differences by income, 264
Achievement tests, 63
ACT, 258, 260
Activity analysis, 110
Addams, Jane, 202, 203–204, 334
Additive approach to bilingual education, 349
Adler, Mortimer, 100
Advanced placement, self-selected, 299
Advanced placement courses, 295
AFL. *See* American Federation of Labor.
AFT. *See* American Federation of Teaching.
Agostini v. Felton, 247
Aguilar v. Felton, 247
Aims
    defined, 53
    formation of, 54
    use in curriculum, 53
Alexander v. Holmes County, 303
Alternative licensure programs, 83
Alternative schools, 109
American 2000 report, 363
American Association of University Women
    (AAUW), 311
American Federation of Labor (AFL), 91
American Federation of Teaching (AFT), 84, 91
American Herbartians, 189
American Herbartianism in normal schools, 185
American Normal School Association, 89
American Revolution and schooling, 157
American society, common values of, 337
American Spelling Book, 162

Analogical thinking, 65
Ancillary services, 284
Anglicans, 156
Annual yearly progress (AYP) of proficiency, 366
Anti-sexist legislation, 311
Apartheid schools, 308
Apprentice education, 155
Aptitude, defined, 258
Armstrong, General Samuel, 200
    criticism of views by William Torrey Harris, 200
Assimilation, 335
Assimilationist goals, 347
Assimilationist position, 345
Attendance zone, redrawing of, 305
Authority of teachers, 79

B

Back to basics, 360–361
Back-to-basics retrenchment, 355
Bagley, William, 103
Banking education, 343, 344
Barre Normal School, 167
Basic skill achievement as cost-saving idea, 360
Basic skill tests, 258
Basic skills, 19
Basic skills education and perennialist, 101
Behavior modification, 45
Behaviorism, 44, 45
Behaviorist psychology, 112
Bell-curve distribution of scores, 260
Bennett, William J., 101
Berliner and Biddle's Student Achievement Law,
    259, 270
Bernard, Henry, 89
Bestor, Professor Arthur, 355, 356
Bethal School District v. Fraser, 134, 136
Between-class ability grouping
    in high school, 294
    in middle school, 294
Between-class grouping, 299
Between-class tracking, 299
Bible clubs in public schools, 236
Bilingual education, 344–349
    continued resistance to, 350
    national movement in, 346
    types of, 347–350

Bilingual Education Act, 346
Biological determinism, Montessori's argument against, 187
Black American struggle for schooling, 199–203
Black children, factors in reading underperformance of, 263–264
Black slaves, forbidding teaching of, 156
Black teachers, 72
Bloom's taxonomies, 36
Blow, Susan, 209, 210, 212
Board of Education of Oklahoma City Public Schools v. Dowell, 306, 307
Board of Education v. Allen, 247
Boarding schools, 156
Bobbitt, John Franklin, 110–112
Bode, Boyd, 112, 190
Book of Virtues, 102
Bridgewater Normal School, 167
Brown, Linda, 301
Brown II, 302
Brown v. the Board of Education of Topeka, 300, 301, 302, 306, 308
Bruner, Jerome, 356, 357
Bubble students, 370
Bureau of Refugees, Freedmen and Abandoned Lands, 199
Business taxes for public school funding, 231
Busing for desegregation, 305

C

Calvinists, 181
Capitalism, needs of, 343
Cardinal Principles Report of 1918, 89, 208, 209
seven objectives of, 208
Career-based growth, goals for, 12
Carnegie, Andrew, 201
Carnegie Foundation for the Advancement of Teaching, 384
Carnegie units, 9
Carter, James, 165, 167
Casa dei Bambini, 186
Catechism lessons, 154
Categorical aid programs, 234
Censorship, 132–133
Charity schools, 156, 161
for educating black and Indian children, 157
Charter school legislation, 380
Charter schools, 9, 363, 378, 380–382
performance of, 381
Chicago Teacher Federation, 92
Chief officer of education, responsibilities of state, 225
Child-benefit doctrine, 247
Child-centered movement, 107
Child-centered progressives, 108
Child centeredness, progressive criticism of, 190

Child study movement, 188–189
Children's House, 186
Choice programs, 367
public school, 377–382
Christmas, observing, 242
Church and state, 236–249
separation in U.S. Constitution, 159
union between, 149
Church/state entanglements, 248
Citizenship, 4
Citizenship education, 17
Civil Rights Act of 1964, 304, 346
Civil rights movement, 237, 304
Class, tracking, 295
Class distribution of teachers, 72
Classism in schools, 114
Classroom games, 59
Classroom performance, levels of, 32–34
Classroom practice, early European influences on, 182–187
Classroom simulations, 59
Cleveland City School District voucher program, 248, 249
Clinton, Governor Bill, 364
Clothing
gang-affiliated, 137
regulating student, 136
Coercion test, 238
Cognitive dissonance, 60
Cold War, 104
education during, 355–358
period, 103
themes, 362
Coleman report, 303, 304
Collateral learning, 64
Colonial New England, 149
Colonial school life, 152–155
Colonial schooling, 150–157
differences in, 155–157
Colonial schools, skill-drill exercises in, 153
Colonial south, literacy education in, 156
Colonies, illiteracy rates for women in, 152
Commission on the Reorganization of Secondary Education, 208
Committee for Public Education and Religious Liberty v. Nyquist, 248
Committee of Fifteen, 89, 102, 180, 181
Committee of Fifteen report, 208
Committee of Ten, 89, 102, 180, 181
Hall's criticism of, 188–189
identification of curriculum by, 177–181
Committee of Ten report, 208
Common culture, 336, 337
sources of, 335–337
Common history, 336
Common knowledge, shared, 337

Common values of American society, 337
Commonality, foundation of, 335
Comparative negligence, 131
Competency-based instruction, 109, 112, 360
Competency-based strategies, 112
    of instruction, 361
Competitive task structure, 59
Comprehensive curriculum, 299
Comprehensive high school, 7
Comprehensive institutions, secondary school as, 224
Comprehensive school, 209
    design of, 299
Comprehensive system, teaching in, 15–22
Compulsory public education, origins of, 160
Compulsory schooling, 4
Computer assisted instruction, 361
Computers
    home access to, 285
    in classroom, 285
Conant, James B., 357, 358
    endorsement of ability groups, 358
Concentrations, 184
    Herbart and, 184
Conditioned response, 44
Conduct unbecoming, 123–125
Conservative tradition, teaching in, 100–104
Consolidation of schools, 305
Constructed-response questions, 266
Content standards, 55
    statewide, 12
Continuing education of teachers, 79
Contracts, teacher, 138
Contributions approach to multicultural education, 340
Control in classrooms, 43–46
    external, 43, 44
    motivation for, 44
Controlling classrooms, 29
Cooperative learning, 59–60
"Core Knowledge Foundation," 104
Core values, 336
Corporate ideology, 117
Corporate tax for public school funding, 228
Correlations, 184
    Herbart and, 184
Cotton, John, 154
Counts, George, 113, 114, 115
Creaming, 386
Creation science, 245
Creationism, teaching of, 244–246
Creationism Act, 245
Creationism taught as religious view, 246
Credentialing, 80, 81
Criminal convictions, dismissal for, 124
Criterion-referenced exam, 260

Critical theory
    culture and 341–344
    of education, 115
Cross-national test outcomes, 272–276
Cultural commonality, 333–335
Cultural diversity, 333–335
Cultural-epoch theory, 184
Cultural hegemony, 341, 342
Cultural literacy, 38, 103 and essentialism, 104
Cultural relativity, 334
Cultural theorists and standardized exams, 343
Cultural unity, 335
Cultural vocabulary, 337
Culture and critical theory, 341–344
    epochs theory, 189
    of schooling, 335–339
    sources of common, 335–337
Curriculum
    as blueprint for school operations, 52
    as design, 52
    as subject matter, 52
    defining, 51–52
    design, 52
    development, 52
    differentiation, 189
    explicit, 53–63
    hidden, 116
    identification by Committee of Ten, 177–181
    latent, 63–64, 116
    null, 65
    streams, 7
    subject-centered philosophical position, 100
    tracks, 7
Curriculum standards, 54–56, 364
    setting of, 54
Curriculum tracking, 223, 276, 293–299
    criticism of, 298
    responses to criticism, 298
Cut score, proficiency. See Proficiency cut score.

D

Dame schools, 156, 159
    Puritan, 155
Dartmouth, founding of, 160
Decentralized governance, 8
Decision-making, sources for professional, 34–38
Decision-making skills, 59
Decisions, planned and emergent, 30–32
DeGarmo, Charles, 185
DeGarmo, Frank, 185
Democracy
    and experimentalism, 105
    essentialism and, 102–103
    perennialism and, 100
    philosophy of, 106
Demonstration, 57

Dennison, George, 359
Department of Defense, 227
Department of Education, 227
    federal, 12
Department of Justice, 227
Department of Labor, 227
Department of the Interior, 227
Departmentalization, 223
    in elementary schools, 224
Deregulating teaching profession, 84
De-schooling society, 109
Desegregation
    busing for, 305
    effects of, 308–310
    school, 300–310
Determination of reasonableness, 141
Dewey, John, 3, 4, 27, 28, 44, 54, 56, 64, 105, 106,
    114, 190, 202, 204, 211
    and educative process, 197–198
    and Hull House, 203
    laboratory school of, 198
Dewey laboratory school, 205 , 207
Dictionary of the English Language, 163
Didactic apparatus, Montessori's use of, 186
Direct instruction, 57
    guided practice in, 57
    teacher presentation in, 57
Discipline-centered curriculum, 362
Discipline-centered instruction, 58
Discussion-based instruction, 58
Dismissal of teacher, 138–140
    for financial exigency, 139
    for incompetence, 139
    for insubordination, 139
Districts, development of school, 159
Doctrine of mental discipline, 20, 103, 177
Doctrine of original goodness, 181–182
Doctrine of original sin, 181
Dover School District in Pennsylvania, 246
Dropout counting procedures, 278
Dropout rates
    by ethnicity and race, 280
    by gender, 280
    by income levels, 281
Dropouts, reasons for, 282, 283
Drug sniffing dogs, 142
Drunk driving by teacher, 124
Du Bois, W.E.B., 202
Dual language instruction, 345
    model, 347
Due process procedure, 138, 139, 140
    for tenured teacher, 139
Duty of care by teacher, 129–130

E

Early exit transitions, 347
Economic Opportunity Act, 304
Education
    critical theory of, 115
    in radical tradition, 113–118
    of girls in South, 156
    publicly-funded, 160
Education-by-vouchers, 383
Education of teachers, 82–86
    essential steps in programs, 84–85
Educational judgment, exclusion by, 132
Educational progress, national assessment of,
    259–271
Educative process, John Dewey and, 197–198
Edwards v. Aguillard, 245
Electives, 299
Electrical Club, 203
Elementary and Secondary Act of 1965, 227, 304
Elementary and Secondary School Act of 1964, 365
Elementary and Secondary School Act of 1968, Title
    VII of, 346
Elementary schools
    departmentalization in, 224
    of New England, 152
Eliot, Charles, 177
ELL students, 348
Emergent teacher decisions, 30–32
Endorsement test, 238
Engel v. Vitale, 240
English-as-a-Second Language (ESL) model, 347,
    348
English immersion, 345
Enrollment rates, historical record on, 5–6
Entanglements, 237, 247
Environmental factors and success, 198
Environmentalism, Lester Ward's, 203
Episcopal faith, Blacks, Indians, and poor whites in,
    156
Epperson v. Arkansas, 244
Equal treatment, 238
ESL. *See* English-as-a-Second Language.
Essentialism, 102–104
    connection to democracy of, 103, 104
    cultural literacy and, 104
Establishment Clause, 237, 238, 240, 241, 242, 243,
    245
    issues, 236
    violations, 241
Establishment violation, 239
Ethical issues within classroom, 125–129
Ethics, professional, 123–129
Ethnic-additive approach to multicultural
    education, 341

Ethnic-based schools, 340
Ethnic identity, 339
Ethnocentric instruction, 340
European culture, bias favoring, 339
Evaluating school experience, 62–63
Evaluation, 62
    as component of curriculum development, 62
    instrumentation used in, 63
Event dropout measure, 280
Everson v. Board of Education, 236
Evolution, theory of, 244
Excise tax for public school funding, 228, 231
Exclusion by educational judgment, 132
Existentialist nature of postmodernism, 117
Experimentalism, 105–107
    democracy and, 105
    pragmatism in, 106
Explicit curriculum, 53–63
Exploratory learning in middle schools, 224
Expression
    freedoms of, 131–137
    student, 134–135
    written, 135–136
Expressive goals, 30, 32
Expressive outcomes, 30
External classroom controls, 43, 44
Extracurricular activities, girls and, 316

F

Facilitative teaching, 108
Faculty psychology, 175–176
    Pestalozzi and, 182
Family and consumer science, 21
Family risk index, 326
Federal government, 226–227
    implementing legislation by, 226
    school governance by, 224
Federally-sponsored religion, ban on, 160
Felonies, dismissal for, 124
Female values, 310
Fighting words, 134
Financial exigency, dismissal for, 139
Financing of schools, state, 9
Finishing schools, 156
First Amendment right, 133, 134, 135
First Amendment to the Constitution, 236
Fiscal neutrality, 232
Flat grant programs, 232
Florida's voucher program, 249
Fordham Foundation, 84
Fordham institute, rating by, 56
Formative evaluation, 63
Foundation program, 232
Fourteenth Amendment to the Constitution, 138,
    199, 231, 236

Fourth Amendment, 140
Franklin, Benjamin, 158
Free Exercise challenge, 239
Free Exercise Clause, 236, 238, 242
Free Exercise exemptions, 239
Free schools, 109
Freedmen Bureau, 199
Freedom, teachers' academic, 131–133
Freedom of choice plan, 302, 303
Freedom of Press laws, 135
Freedoms of expression, 131–137
Freeman v. Pitts, 306, 307
Freshmen graduation rate, 278
Friedenberg, Edgar, 359
Friedman, Milton, 383
Friere, Paulo, 343
Froebel, Friedrich, 182, 185
Froebel's kindergarten, 185, 209
    occupations in, 211
Funding inequities between states, 235
Funding public education, 227

G

Gallaudet, Thomas, 167
Games, classroom, 59
Gary School Plan, 205
GED. See General Education Development certificate.
Gender and schooling, 310–318
Gender-based stereotypes, 312
Gender bias, 310–313
    debate, 311
Gender discrimination, 312
Gender distribution of teachers, 71–72
Gender-linked toys, 313
Gender-segregated classes, 313
Gender-segregated classrooms, 313
Gender stereotypes, 311
General Education Development certificate (GED) ,
    274, 278
General labor preparation, 21
Generative-creative level (III) of classroom
    performance, 32
GI Bills, 227
Gifts
    by Froebel, 211
    manipulating, 210
    Patty Smith Hill's changes to, 213
    symbolism of, 211
Girls, education in South, 156
Goals
    defined, 53
    for U.S. schooling, 12, 13–15
    use in curriculum, 53
Goals 2000, 364
Goodman, Paul, 359

Governance structure of school system, 8
Governors' authority in state education, 224–225
Grade-level orientations, 221–224
Grade retention policies, 42
Grammatical Institute of the English Language, 162
Great books, 102–103, 117, 176
Great books curriculum, 101
Great Depression, 114
Green factors, 303
Green standards, 303, 306, 308
Green v. County School Board of New Kent, 303
Gross receipt tax for public school funding, 228
Guided practice, in direct instruction, 57

H

Haley, Margaret, 92
Hall, G. Stanley, 188, 198, 212
Hampton Institute, 200
Hampton Normal and Industrial Institute, 200
Handiwork activities, 210
Harris, William Torrey, 102, 181, 184, 188, 200
    advocacy for public kindergarten, 209
    traditionalist viewpoint of, 180
Harvard College
    college for Native Americans, 155
    entrance requirements for, 153
    founding of, 150
Hazelwood v. Kuhlmeier, 132, 135, 136, 137
Head Start, 304
Health concerns
    poverty and, 324
    race/ethnicity, 324
Hentoff, Nat, 359
Herbart, Johann, 182, 183–185
    correlations and concentrations by, 184
    role of social studies and, 184
    teaching methodology and, 185
Heroes and holidays approach to multicultural
        education, 340
Hidden curriculum, 116
High, objective, uniform, state standard of
        evaluation. *See* HOUSSE.
High school, public beginning of, 168–169
High school education as societal requirement, 277
High stakes test, 41, 42
High stakes testing, 62
    rise of, 370
Higher education, female presence in, 318
Highly qualified teacher, criteria for, 86
Hill, Patty Smith, 212
    changes to gifts by, 213
    importance in kindergarten movement, 212
Hirsch, E.D., 103
Hispanic status dropout rate, 281
Hispanic teachers, 72
Historical knowledge, 337

Holt, John, 359
Home-reading conditions and reading achievement,
        265
Home school/charter schools, 387
Home-schooled children, 9
Home Schooling, 387–388
    detractors of, 388
    increase in, 387
Honors, 295
Honors courses, 299
Hornbook, 154
House, 224
HOUSSE (High, objective, uniform, state standard
        of evaluation), 86
Howard, General O. O., 199
Hull House, 203, 204
    John Dewey and, 203
Hunter approach, 39–40

I

Illich, Ivan, 359
Imitative-maintenance level (I) of classroom
        performance, 32, 33
Immoral conduct with student, 125
Implicit teaching, 30
Income, achievement differences by, 264
Incompetence, dismissal for, 139
Independent instruction, 61
Independent work, 61
Individual-personal growth
    goals for, 12
    instructional concerns of, 16
    teaching for, 15–17
Individualization in classroom, 15, 16
Individualization in instruction, 61
Individualization in school experience, 189
Induction, 81
Industrial age, public education in, 163
Infant schools, 162
Inquiry-based instruction, 60–61
Inquiry-based learning, 106, 205
In-service programs, 81
In-service training, 78, 79
Instruction
    defined, 30
    methods of, 56–61
Instructional decision, 31
Instructional methods, 56–61
Instructional objectives, 53
Insubordination, dismissal for, 139
Intellectual-academic growth
    goals for, 12
    teaching for, 19–21
Intelligent design, 246
Interclass grouping, 223
Interdisciplinary construction of subject matter, 204

Interdisciplinary visions, 223
Interdistrict choice, 9, 378
Interest inventory, 35
International comparisons of test scores, 272–276
Internet access in schools, 285
Intradistrict choice, 9, 378
Intrinsic motivation, 44
Investigative strategies, 35
Iowa Test of Basic Skills (ITBS), 258, 260
IQ tests, 258
ITBS. *See* Iowa Test of Basic Skills.
Itinerant schoolmaster, 158

J

Jackson v. Benson, 248
James Madison High School, 102
Jane Club, 203
Jefferson, Thomas, 3, 160
Jim Crow laws, 199
Jim Crow system, 300
Job analysis, 112
Job Corps, 304

K

Kansas City, Missouri School District (KCMSD), 306, 307
Kansas State Board of Education and evolution, 245
Keefe v. Geanakos, 128
Kilpatrick, William, 211
    Project Method, 206
Kindergarten
    American, 209–213
    as child-saving agency, 210
    first, 185
    Froebel's, 209
    St. Louis as center, 210
    training programs, 212
Kindergarten method, criticism of, 211
Kindergarten movement, Patty Smith Hill's
    importance in, 212
King, Martin Luther, 304
Kirpans, 243
Kohl, Herbert, 359
Kozol, Jonathan, 359

L

Laboratory school of John Dewey, 198
Lancaster, Joseph, 161
Lancaster method, 161
Land grant universities, 169
Land grants, 161
Land Ordinance of 1785, 161, 221
Language
    as commonality, 335
    of schooling, 344
    three basic purposes of, 344

Late-exit transitional program, 348
Late exit transitions, 347
Latent curriculum, 63–64, 116
Latin Grammar schools, 221
    Puritan, 155
Latin school, graduates of, 153
Lau vs. Nichols, 346, 349
Law of 1789, 164
Learner
    introduction into teaching/learning equation, 162
    nature of, 35–36
    responsiveness to, 36
Learning by doing, 108, 206
Lecture, teaching by, 57
Lee v. Weisman, 241
Legal and legislative influences in desegregation, 300–308
Legal ethics, 123–125
Legislative support by state legislatures, 225
Leisure time reading, 265–266
Lemon test, 237, 238, 242, 245, 246, 247, 248
    separation from, 249
Lemon v. Kurtzman, 237
Level I: imitative-maintenance classroom, 32, 33
Level II: meditative classroom, 33–34
Level III: creative-generative classroom, 34
Levy taxes, state, 227
Lexington Normal School, 167
Liability of teacher, 129–131
Liberal arts, ascendancy of traditional, 175–181
Liberal arts tradition, teachers in, 176
Licensing examinations for teachers, 81
Licensure examinations, 85
Licensure of teachers, 82–86
    alternative programs, 83
    provisional, 83
Licensure standards, 82
Literacy education in colonial south, 156
Literacy skills, differences in basic, 319
Local property taxes, 227
Local school board
    responsibilities of, 226
    school governance by, 224
Local school districts, 226
Logical features of subject matter, 206
Longitudinal tests, 261
Low-birthweight babies, developmental problems in, 324

M

Magnet schools, 304, 305, 367, 382
    and desegregation, 382
    special theme, 378
Majority to minority transfer, 304
Male values, 310

Manipulatives, Montessori's use of, 186
Mann, Horace, 3, 89, 165
    and state authority, 165–166
    effort toward teacher education, 166–168
    Fourth Annual Report, 165
    Second Annual Report, 165
    Seventh Annual Report, 166
Marshall, Justice Thurgood, 306
Maslow's hierarchy, 36
Massachusetts Bay Colony, 149
Massachusetts Law of 1642 for compulsory
        education, 150
Massachusetts Law of 1647, 151, 159
Massachusetts Law of 1789, 159, 165
Master's degree in teaching, 74
Mastery learning, 112
    instruction, 109
    programs, 61
Math achievement, international data on, 314
Mathematics report card, 266–271
McLean v. Arkansas Board of Education, 245
McMurray, Charles, 185
Mediative level (II) of classroom performance, 32
Melting pot society, 339, 350
Men and Women's club, 203
Mental discipline, doctrine of, 20, 103, 175–177,
        177
Mentor teachers, course load for, 78
Mentoring beginning teacher, 77, 78
Merit pay for teachers, 362
Metal detectors, 142
Middle colonies marginal role in educating youth,
        156
Middle schools, exploratory learning in, 224
Milliken II, 306
Milliken v. Bradley, 305, 306
Milwaukee Parental Choice Program (MPCP), 248,
        383, 385–386
Minimal provision philosophy, 232
Minority children, factors in reading
        underperformance of, 263–264
Minority teachers as role models, 73
Mission statement of school, 53
Missouri v. Jenkins, 306, 307
Modernist view, 116
Moments of Silence, 241
Monitorial instruction, 161–162
Monolingual English instruction, 345
Montessori, Maria, 182, 185
Morrill Act of 1862, 169, 227
Motivation in classroom control, 44
    intrinsic, 44
Moving school, 158
Mozert v. Hawkins County, 239

Multicultural education, 339–341
    contributions approach to, 340
    ethnic-additive approach to, 341
    heroes and holidays approach to, 340
    hierarchy of approaches to, 340–341
    transformative approach to, 341
Multiculturalism
    ethnocentric views on, 340
    particularistic, 340
Multiple intelligences, 36

N

NAEP. *See also* National Assessment of Educational
        Progress.
NAEP exam, 369
NAEP math assessment
    achievement gaps in, 266, 269
    content areas in, 266
    criterion levels for, 266
    gender difference on, 269
NAEP reading exam, 260
    criterion levels in, 261
Nation at Risk, 361, 362, 363
National Assessment of Educational Progress
        (NAEP), 227, 260, 337
    as criterion-referenced exam, 260
    See also NAEP.
National Association for the Advancement of
        colored People (NAACP), 202
National Association of School Superintendents, 89
National Center for Education Statistics (NCES),
        259–260, 276, 278, 283, 381
National Commission on Excellence in Education
        (NCEE), 362
National Commission on the Reform of Secondary
        Education, 361
National Council of Teachers of English, 20
National Defense Education Act of 1958, 227, 357
National dropout data, 283
National Education Association (NEA), 88–91, 177
    criticism of, 90
    political action group. *See also* NEA-PAC.
    preamble to constitution, 89
National education goals and standards, academic
        excellence through, 363–365
National Governors' Association, 363
National identity, 339
National Merit Scholarship program, 227
National Negro Business League, 202
National Panel on High School and Adolescent
        Education, 361
National School Lunch Act, 36
National Science Foundation (NSF) , 20, 227, 356
National Science Teachers Association, 20, 298

National standards, 364, 365
National standards movement, 363
National Teachers' Association (NTA), 88
Nationalism, 4
Nationalizing influences in schools, 11–12
Native American children, schools for, 155
Nature of learner, 35–36
NCEE. *See* National Commission on Excellence in Education.
NCLB. *See* No Child Left Behind Act.
NEA. *See* National Education Association.
NEA-PAC (National Education Association political action group), 90
Negligence
    comparative, 131
    determining, 130–131
Negotiated salary schedules, 75–76
Neighborhood schools, 377, 378
Neill, A.S., 359
Networking in classroom, 285
New England Primer, 154, 155, 162
New England town schools, 152
New Jersey v. TLO, 141
Niagara movement, 202
1950s, education during, 355–358
1960s, education during, 358–360
1970s, education during, 360–361
1980s, education during, 362–363
1990s, education during, 363–365
No Child Left Behind Act (NCLB), 11, 40, 41, 56, 65, 86
    and accountability, 365–370
    consequences in classroom and school, 370
    private school exemption from, 367
Nonpreferentialism, 238
Norm-referenced exams, 260
Normal schools, 71–72, 165, 167, 185
    as part of universities, 168
    curriculum, 168
Normative environment, school as, 3–6
Northern abolitionist societies, 156
Northwest Ordinance of 1785, 221
NSF. *See* National Science Foundation.
NTA. *See* National Teachers Association.
Nuclear family, traditional, 323
Null curriculum, 65, 343

O

Oakland Unified School District, 336
Objectives
    defined, 53
    use in curriculum, 53
Observational data, 63
Occupational preparation, 21

Occupations, 210
OECD. *See* Organization for Economic Cooperation and Development.
Office of Economic Opportunity, 304
Office of Educational Research and Improvement, 227
Oklahoma City Public Schools declared unitary, 306
Old Deluder Act, 151
Omission training, 46
On-time graduation rate, 278
One way busing, 305
Ongoing evaluation, 63
Ontogeny, 189
Open classroom, 360
Open education, 359
Open-ended experiences, 108
Open enrollment, 378
    system of, 302
Opportunity to learn (OTL), 259, 270, 276
Opportunity to learn factors, 259
    poverty and, 325
Oppositional thought in school experience, 116
Organization for Economic Cooperation and Development (OECD), 273
    Program for International Student Assessment (PISA), 273
Original goodness, doctrine of, 181
Original sin, doctrine of, 181
Oswego Normal School, Pestalozzian methods at, 187–188
Otherness, 117
OTL. *See also* Opportunity to learn.
Out-of-field teachers, 80, 81
Outcomes, 41

P

Parducci v. Rutland, 133
Parochial schools, Title 1 in, 247
    See also Religious schools.
Particularistic multiculturalism, 340
Patriotism among parents, 337
Pauper schools
    public financing of, 161
    public schools as, 161
Pavlov, 44
Pedagogical judgments, 31
Pedagogy, defined, 30
Pentagram, 244
People for the American Way, 336
Perennialism, 100–102
    basic skills education and, 101
    democracy and, 100
    skill-drill strategies and, 101
    vocational education and, 100

Performance assessment, 360
Performance standards, 55
Permanent studies, 100
Personal income tax for public school funding, 228
Personal views of teachers, 133
Per-weighted pupil funding levels, 234
Pestalozzi, Johann, 182–183
    Americanization of, 187–188
    faculty psychology and, 182
    sense perception and, 183
Pestalozzian methods, 187–188
    teachings in, 188
Philanthropic school movement, 161–162
Philosophy of democracy, 106
Phylogeny, 189
Physical pat down, 141
Piaget's developmental processes, 36
Pickering v. Board of Education, 133
PISA. *See* Program for International Student
    Assessment.
Planned instruction, 30–32
Plato, 3
Plessy, Homer, 300
Plessy v. Ferguson, 199, 300
Political character of teachers, 74
Political views, teacher support of, 126
Politically correct standards, 364
Positive reinforcement, 46
Post-elementary education, girls admitted to, 1158
Postmodernism, 116–118
    existentialist nature of, 117
Poverty
    and race, 319
    and school readiness skills, 319
    in home, 319–326
    threshold, 319
Poverty levels
    absolute, 319
    relative, 319
Pragmatism in experimentalism, 106
Prayer at school ceremonies, 241
Preschool years, poverty during, 319
Prescriptive learning packages, 361
President's Science Advisory Committee, 361
Private schools, 156
Private tuition schools, 159
Privatization of schooling, 382–386
Probable cause, 140, 141
Problem-based instruction, 60
Problem-driven instruction, 60
Problem-focused curriculum, 205
Professional decision-making, sources for, 34–38
Professional development
    activities, 78
    options, 79
Professional ethics, 123–129

Professional teacher organizations, 88–92
Proficiency
    construct of, 369–370
    standards, 55
    testing for, 365–368
Proficiency cut score, 366
    failure to meet, 367–368
Program for International Student Assessment
    (PISA), 274.
Programmed instruction, 112
Programmed learning workbooks, 361
Progressive criticism of child centeredness, 190
Progressive movement, 190, 199
Progressive tradition, teaching in, 105–113
Progressivism, 204
    and cause of social reform, 197–199
Project-based learning, 61
Project Method, William Kirkpatrick's, 206
"Property right" status, 138
Property taxes, local, 227
Proposition 227, 348
Protest
    philosophy of, 115
    theory of, 115
Provisional teaching license, 83
Psychological features of subject matter, 206
Public choice programs, 378
Public education
compulsory, 160
    funding of, 227
    in industrial age, 163
    origins of, 160
Public high schools, spread of, 169
Public school, Lester Ward's support of, 198–199
Public schools as pauper schools, 161
Publicly-funded education, 160
Publicly-funded schooling, opposition to, 164
Pullout programs, 15
Punishment
    effects of, 45
    use for behavior control, 44, 45
Puritans, 150
    and public system of schooling, 151
    state-sponsored schooling by, 149

Q

Quakers, 156
    literacy education to both sexes, poor, and
        minorities, 157

R

Race
    distribution of teachers by, 72
    poverty and, 319
Radical/romantic confederacy in education, 359
Radical tradition, education in, 113–118

Rate bills, 164
Reading achievement
    by gender, international data on, 314
    gender difference in scores, 264
    importance of, 261
Reading groups, 294
Reading report card, 260–266
Reasonable cause, 140
Reasonableness, determination of, 141
Reconstruction of experience, 106
Relative poverty levels, 319
Religion courses in public schools, 236
Religious apparel in school, 243
Religious character of teachers, 74
Religious doctrine, teacher support of, 126
Religious holidays, 242–244
Religious schools, state aid to, 247–249
    See also Parochial schools.
Religious symbols, 242–244
Republic, 3
Rickover, Admiral Hyman, 355, 356, 357
Role models, teachers as, 29, 123
Role playing activities, 58–59
Romantic idealism, 185, 209
Romantic naturalism, 107–**109**
Romantic-naturalist view of world, 358
Rousseau, Jean Jacques, 107, 181–182, 358
Rousseauian form, 190
Rousseauian line, 189

S

Salad bowl metaphor, 339, 350
Salaries, teacher, 75–76, 81
    negotiated schedules of, 75–76
Sales receipt tax for public school funding, 228
San Antonio Independent School District v. Rodriguez,
    231, 232
Santa Fe Independent District v. Doe, 242
SAT scores, 258, 260
Satellite assignments, 305
SBR. *See* Scientifically-based research.
School achievement, understanding, 258–259
School-based differences by gender, 314–318
School board, responsibilities of local, 226
School choice options, 363
School choice programs, 382–386
    advocates of, 386
School desegregation, 300–310
School District of the City of Grand Rapids v. Ball, 247
School districts, development of, 159
School dropouts, 277–284
School experience, oppositional thought in, 116
School governance, 224–227
School pairings, 305
School prayer, 240–242

School readiness skills, poverty and, 319
School tax, 164
Schooling
    culture of, 335–339
    language of, 344
    technology and, 285–286
School-level orientations, 221–224
Schurz, Mary, 209
Science-Technology and Society (STS), 20
Scientific management, 109
    of curriculum, 110
Scientific method, intelligence in, 105
Scientifically-based programs, 40
Scientifically-based research (SBR), 40
Scopes Monkey trial of 1925, 244
Search and seizure, 140–142
Secondary school
    as comprehensive institution, 224
    as specialized high school, 224
Secretary of Education, 227
    federal, 12
    in Massachusetts, first state, 165
Self-contained classroom, 223
Self-directed learning, 61, 108
Self-initiation, 61
Sense perception and Pestalozzi, 183
Separate but equal, 300, 308
    doctrine, 301
Serrano v. Priest, 231, 232
Settlement House Movement, 203–204
Settlement houses for indigent, 203
Sexual orientation of teacher, 124
Shared common knowledge, 337
Sheldon, E.A., 187
Sheltered English approach, 347
Sikh faith, 243
Silberman, Charles, 359
Silent meditation, 241
Simulations, classroom, 59
Single-parent families, rise of, 323
Single-sex classes, 313
Situational context of teaching, 28
Skill-based objectives, 58
Skill-drill exercises in colonial schools, 153
Skill-drill strategies and perennialist, 101
Skinner, B. F., 45
Smith-Hughes Act of 1917, 227
Social Darwinism, 198
Social efficiency, 109–113
Social powers of individual, 183
Social protest, humanizing schools during, 358–360
Social reconstructionism, 113–115
Social reform, progressivism and cause of, 197–199
Socialist doctrine in social reconstructionism, 114
Socialization, 336

Societal requirement, high school education as, 277
Societal values and aims, 37
Society for the Propagation of the Gospel in Foreign Parts (SPG), 156
Socio-civic growth
    goals for, 12
    teaching for, 17–19
Socio-economic status, 326
Socio-personal learning opportunities, 224
Socratic questioning method, 58
Software applications in classroom, 285
South, education of girls in, 156
Southern Leadership Christian Conference, 237
Soviets in space, 356
Space race crisis, education during, 355–358
Special education categories, boys in, 311
Special education programs, supplemental funding, 234
Specialized courses, 19–20
Specialized magnet schools, 224
Specialized teachers, 224
Spiritual Milk for American Babes Drawn out of the Breasts of Both Testaments for Their Souls' Nourishment, 154
Sputnik I, 356
Standardized exams, cultural theorists and, 343
Standardized tests, 41
State aid to religious schools, 247–249
State authority, Horace Mann and rise of, 165–166
State Board of Education
    attempts to abolish, 166
    duties of, 225
State course requirements, 10–11
State curriculum requirements, 38
State-funded public school, 160
State funding of school districts, 234
State government, school governance by, 224
State legislatures, legislative support by, 225
State levy taxes, 227
State lotteries to fund education, 228
State regulation of schools, 8–9
State superintendent, responsibilities of, 225
State tax revenue for public school funding, 228
Statewide examinations, 366
Statewide testing program, 365
Status dropout measure, 280
Stimulus-response bond in learning, 44–45
Strip search, 141
Structure of discipline doctrine, 357
Structured immersion, 347
STS. See Science-Technology and Society.
Student discovery, 58
Student expression, 134–135

Subject matter
    curriculum as, 52
    judgment concerning, 37–38
    logical features of, 206
    psychological features of, 206
    tracking, 295
Subject matter as activity, conception of, 204–208
Subtractive approaches to English instruction, 347
Summative evaluations, 63
Sumner, Charles, 300
Superintendent
    advisory capacity of, 226
    responsibilities of, 226
    responsibilities of state, 225
Swann v. Charlotte Mecklenburg Board of Education, 305
Symbolic speech, 134, 136–137

T

T-shirts, regulating student, 136
Taylor, Frederick, 109
Teacher authority, 79, 81
Teacher-directed instruction, 57
Teacher dismissal, 138–140
Teacher education, Mann's effort toward, 166–168
Teacher education schools, 167
Teacher effectiveness, 39–41
Teacher effects research, 39, 40
Teacher facilitation, 58
Teacher induction, 77–78
Teacher-initiated instruction, 57
Teacher liability, 129–131
Teacher presentation
    in direct instruction, 57
Teacher proof materials, 113, 361
Teacher qualifications in tracked classes, 297–298
Teacher tenure, 138–140
Teacher's salaries, 75–76
Teachers, prime role of, 176
Teachers' academic freedom, 131–133
Teachers' personal views, 133
Teaching
    approaches, 28
    in conservative tradition, 100–104
    in progressive tradition, 105–113
    methodology, 185
Teaching/learning equation, introduction of learner into, 162
Teaching profession
    characteristics of, 75
    status of, 75–81
Teaching-to-the-test, 41–43
Technical schools, 21

Technological and economic mobilization, period of, 362–363
Technologies in classroom, 285
Technology and schooling, 285–286
Tenth Amendment to Constitution, 160, 221
Tenure, teacher, 138–140
Tenure contracts, 138
Term contracts, 138
Test scores, international comparisons of, 272–276
Testing for proficiency, 365–368
Thinking skills, 19
Thompson, Tommy, 385
Time on task principle, 39
Time out, 46
Tinker v. Des Moines Independent School District, 134, 136
Title 1 federal funding, 366
Title 1 services in parochial schools, 247
Title IX legislation, 311
Town schools of New England, 152
Tracked children, teacher expectations for, 296–297
Tracking, 293–295
    alternatives to, 299
    by subject matter, 295
    entire class, 295
    forms of, 295
    inequities in, 296–298
    reasons for, 295–296
Traditional humanists, 177
Traditional nuclear family, 323
Traditionalist viewpoint of William Torrey Harris, 180
Transformative approach to multicultural education, 341
Transitional bilingual education, 347
Tuskegee Institute, 200, 201
TV watching and reading achievement, 265
Two-way bilingual education, 349
Two-way busing, 305

U

U.S. Constitution, separation of church and state in, 159
Unified school setting, 7
Unified system, teaching in, 15–22
Uniserve, 91
Unit, 224
Unitary, Oklahoma City Public Schools declared, 306
Unitary status of school, 303
Unreasonable search, 140
Unwed mothers, dismissal of, 125
Upward Bound, 304

V

Verbal praise, 46
Vernonia District v. Acton, 142
Vertical equity, 234
Vocational education, 21
    and perennialist, 100
    economic effects of, 22
Vocational growth
    goals for, 12
    teaching for, 21–22
Vocational subject matter as activity, 207, 208
Volunteer service organizations, 18
Voucher program, Florida's, 249
Voucher programs, religious schools in, 248
Voucher schools, 383
Vouchers, 382–386
    critics of, 385
    opponents to, 384

W

Wald, Lillian, 203
Wallace v. Jaffree, 241
War on Poverty, 358
Ward, Lester, 3, 198–199
    support for public school, 198
Washington, Booker T., 200
    as advisor to presidents, 201
Watson, John, 44
Webster, Daniel, 164
Webster, Noah, 162
Westminster Catechism, 154
Whipping posts, 153
White, middle-class teachers, 72
Wiccan religion, 244
Williams, Annette "Polly," 385
Wirt, William, 205
Wisconsin Model of Academic Standards, 55
Within-class ability grouping, 298
Women in teaching, 71
Working People Social Science Club, 203
Written expression, 135–136

X

XYZ approach, 294

Y

Yale, founding of, 160
Young, Ella Flagg, 89

Z

Zelman v. Simmons-Harris, 248